1945 to 1953
O.H.V. & S.V. SINGLES

Models: 16H, Big 4, 18, ES2, 19 & 50
Rigid Frame - Girder Forks
Spring Frame - Road-holder Forks
Featherbed Frame - Swingarm

WORKSHOP MANUALS
AND
ILLUSTRATED PARTS LISTS

A Floyd Clymer Publication by www.VelocePress.com 2023

INTRODUCTION

Welcome to the world of digital publishing ~ the book you now hold in your hand was printed using the latest state of the art digital technology. The advent of print-on-demand has forever changed the publishing process, never has information been so accessible and it is our hope that this book serves your informational needs for years to come. If this is your first exposure to digital publishing, we hope that you are pleased with the results. Many more titles of interest to the classic automobile and motorcycle enthusiast, collector and restorer are available via our website at www.VelocePress.com. We hope that you find this title as interesting as we do.

NOTE FROM THE PUBLISHER

The information presented is true and complete to the best of our knowledge. All recommendations are made without any guarantees on the part of the author or the publisher, who also disclaim all liability incurred with the use of this information.

TRADEMARKS

We recognize that some words, model names and designations, for example, mentioned herein are the property of the trademark holder. We use them for identification purposes only. This is not an official publication.

INFORMATION ON THE USE OF THIS PUBLICATION

This manual is an invaluable resource for those interested in performing their own maintenance. However, in today's information age we are constantly subject to changes in common practice, new technology, availability of improved materials and increased awareness of chemical toxicity. As such, it is advised that the user consult with an experienced professional prior to undertaking any procedure described herein. While every care has been taken to ensure correctness of information, it is obviously not possible to guarantee complete freedom from errors or omissions or to accept liability arising from such errors or omissions. Therefore, any individual that uses the information contained within, or elects to perform or participate in do-it-yourself repairs or modifications acknowledges that there is a risk factor involved and that the publisher or its associates cannot be held responsible for personal injury or property damage resulting from the use of the information or the outcome of such procedures.

WARNING!

One final word of advice, this publication is intended to be used as a reference guide, and when in doubt the reader should consult with a qualified technician.

IMPORTANT NOTE ON PAGE NUMBERING IN THIS MANUAL

Each of the publications reproduced in this manual are individually numbered to the bottom center of each page. If the publication has an index those page numbers will correspond to that index.

The page numbers to the right and left-hand upper corner of each page are the cumulative page numbers in the book. These are the page numbers used in the 'contents' list below.

CONTENTS - WORKSHOP MANUALS

SECTION 1: 1945-1946 Girder Forks Maintenance & Repair data extracted from the workshop manual for the Norton WD16H. .... page 1

SECTION 2: 1947-1954 Workshop Manual for both S.V. & O.H.V. Rigid & Spring Frame 'Road-holder' forks 16H, Big 4, 18 & ES2. .... page 7

APPENDIX: 1950 and later data extracted from 1956 workshop manual for 16H, Big 4, 18, & ES2 models with 'Laydown' gearbox. .... page 53

SECTION 3: 1953-1958 Workshop Manual exclusive to the O.H.V. 'Swing-arm' 19S, 50 & ES2 models. .... page 61

SECTION 4: 1958-1963 Maintenance & Repair data for the 'Featherbed' models 50 & ES2 extracted from the P106/P workshop manual published in 1970. .... page 103

CONTENTS - ILLUSTRATED PARTS LISTS

SECTION 5: 1948-1949 Illustrated Parts List for the S.V. & O.H.V. Rigid & Spring Frame, 'Road-holder' forks 16H, Big 4, 18 & ES2. .... page 153

SECTION 6: 1956 Illustrated Parts List for the O.H.V. 'Swing-arm' Model 19S, 50 & ES2 and the rigid frame model 19. .... page 229

SECTION 7: 1959 Illustrated Parts List for the 'Featherbed' frame Models 50 & ES2 fitted with Alternator & Coil electrics. .... page 261

IMPORTANT INFORMATION RELATING TO THE CONTENTS OF THIS MANUAL

1945-1946: The first section of this manual includes a copy of the appropriate repair and maintenance data for the girder forks as fitted to the WD16H model. This information is included as the 1945-1946 post-war civilian 16H and 18 models were also fitted with girder forks. However, based on our research, overhaul information for girder forks was never included in any of the factory workshop manuals for the post-war civilian models.

1947-1954: The second section includes a copy of a 1947 factory workshop manual for both the S.V. and O.H.V. rigid frame and spring frame (plunger) 16H, Big4, 18 and ES2 models that were fitted with 'Road-holder' forks. It also includes additional information extracted from the 1956 publication of this same workshop manual relating to the changes that took place during the 1947 to 1954 model run, including the change from an 'Upright' to a Laydown' gearbox and lighting equipment. This additional information is appended at the end of the section and any data that is identical and included in the 1947 publication has been omitted. Consequently, this manual would be applicable to all four models from 1947 to 1954 at which time the 16H, Big4 and 18 were discontinued and the ES2 had received swing-arm rear suspension.

1953-1958: The third section includes a copy of a 1956 factory workshop manual exclusive to the O.H.V. swing-arm 19S, ES2 and 50 models. As the ES2 received swing-arm rear suspension in 1953, this manual would be applicable to all three models from 1953 to 1958, at which time the 19S was discontinued.

1958-1963: The pages in the fourth section of this manual were extracted from the P106/P Norton factory publication 'Maintenance Manual and Instruction Book' dated 1970 for the Model 50, ES2, 88, 99, 650 and 750 models. As the 19S was discontinued in 1958 and is no longer included in the model list, this extracted data would be applicable to the 1958 to 1963 Model 50 and ES2 (see below).

EVOLUTION OF THE COMBINATION MANUALS: The publication of these 'combination' manuals began in 1960 with the P101 manual followed by the P106 and finally the P106/P manual of 1970. While these 'combination' manuals made publication less expensive than those for individual models the information for multiple different motorcycles is often merged together. Consequently, separating out the appropriate data for a specific model, or series of motorcycles can be a time consuming and confusing exercise.

Even more unfortunately, the P106/P manual makes no reference to the model years that are covered. However, as it only includes the model 50 and ES2 and knowing that the 19S was discontinued in 1958 it is reasonable to assume that it is intended to cover these two models from 1958 through 1963, at which point Norton discontinued manufacturing their single-cylinder machines. Therefore, we have extracted the information that is exclusive to the Model 50 and ES2 from the P106/P manual. However, this means that the paragraphs and illustrations in the P106/P section may no longer be sequentially numbered and we request you overlook this minor issue as it does not affect the correctness of the data in any way.

IMPORTANT: Please note that repair information for the AMC MKII versions of the models 50 and ES2 is not included in this publication.

NORTON GIRDER FRONT FORKS

MAINTENANCE & REPAIR FOR MODEL WD16H

Para. 79 - Removal

Para. 80 - Refitting

Para. 81 - Dismantling

Para, 82 - Reconditioning

Para. 83 - Reassembly

Section 1 - Pages Extracted From WD16H Manual

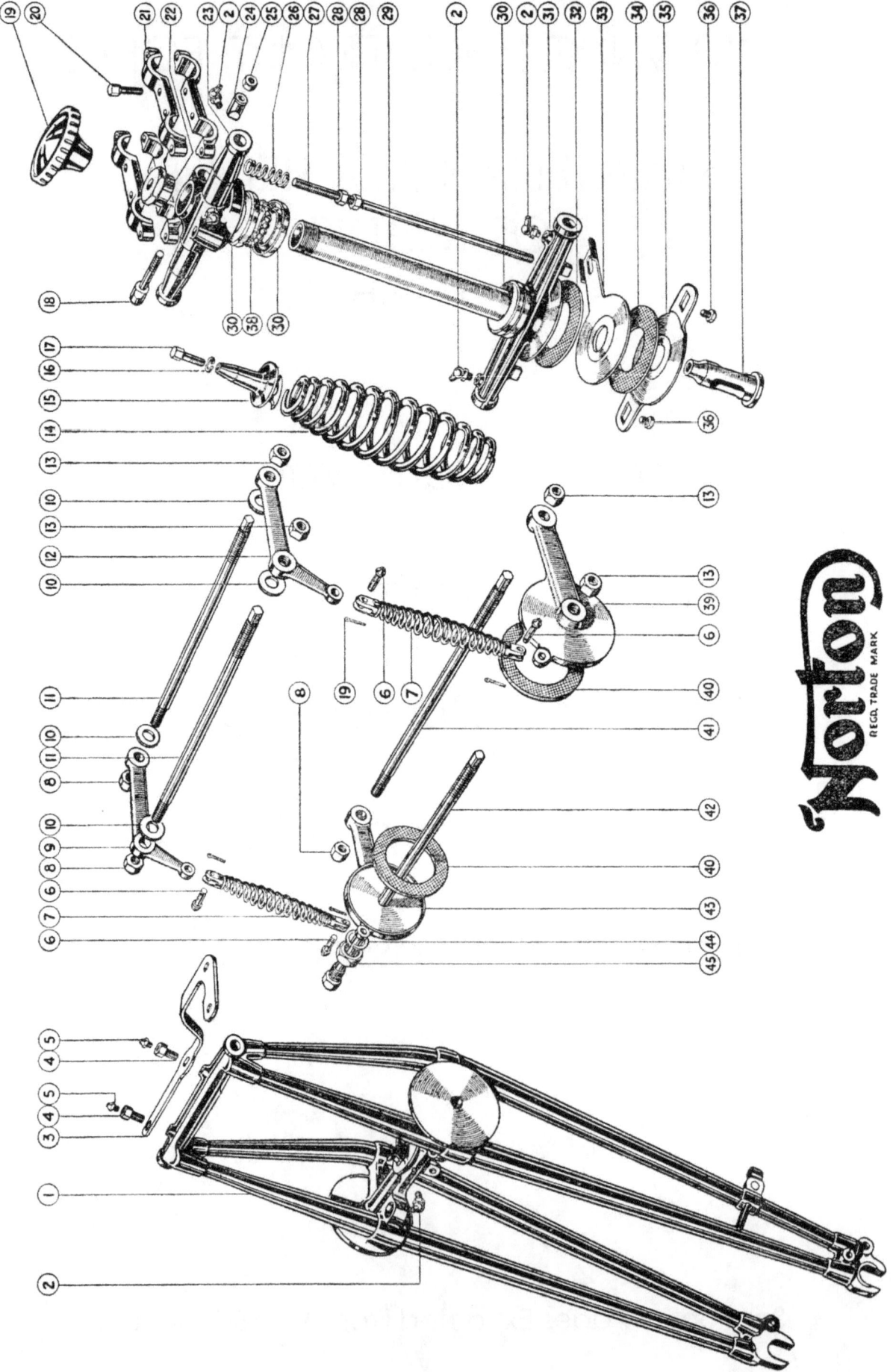

FRONT FORKS

1. Fork Girder.
2. Fork Angle Grease Nipple.
3. Speedometer Fork Attachment Bracket.
4. Speedometer Fork Attachment Bracket Bolt and Grease Nipple Adaptor.
5. Grease Nipple.
6. Fork Rebound Spring Jaw Joint Pin.
7. Fork Rebound Spring.
8. Fork Offside Spindle Nut.
9. Fork Offside Link.
10. Fork Spindle Knurled Adjusting Washer.
11. Fork Top Spindle.
12. Fork Nearside Link.
13. Fork Nearside Spindle Nut.
14. Fork Spring.
15. Fork Spring Lug.
16. Fork Spring Attachment Bolt Spring Washer.
17. Fork Spring Attachment Bolt.
18. Fork Top Clip Bolt.
19. Fork Steering Damper Knob.
20. Fork Handlebar Half-clip Bolt.
21. Fork Handlebar Half-clip.
22. Fork Steering Column Nut.
23. Fork Top Clip.
24. Fork Top Clip Bolt Sleeve.
25. Fork Top Clip Bolt.
26. Fork Steering Damper Adjuster Spring.
27. Fork Steering Damper Rod.
28. Fork Steering Damper Rod Nut.
29. Fork Steering Column.
30. Fork Ball Race.
31. Fork Crown.
32. Fork Steering Damper Friction Disc.
33. Fork Steering Damper Friction Plate.
34. Fork Steering Damper Friction Disc.
35. Fork Steering Damper Bottom Plate.
36. Fork Steering Damper Bottom Plate Fixing Bolt
37. Fork Steering Damper Bottom Lug.
38. Fork Ball Race Bearings.
39. Fork Nearside Bottom Link.
40. Fork Shock Absorber Friction Disc.
41. Fork Bottom Rear Spindle.
42. Fork Bottom Front Spindle.
43. Fork Offside Bottom Link.
44. Fork Shock Absorber Adjusting Nut Spring Washer.
45. Fork Shock Absorber Adjusting Nut.
46. Fork Rebound Spring Jaw Joint Pin Split Cotter.

FRONT FORKS

79. REMOVAL OF FRONT FORKS FROM FRAME.

Place a block of wood or jack under the engine of such a height that the front wheel is clear of the ground.

Remove front wheel.

Remove front mudguard, held by a bolt holding the guard to the fork and the four bolts holding the guard stays and front stand to the fork ends.

Remove the handlebars. The bars are held by two split clips with four bolts to each clip.

Remove the bolts and the bars are free from the head clips.

Remove speedometer cables, inner and outer, from the fork.

Remove steering damper knob from the fork by releasing the steering column nut.

Turn knob until the rod is released from the "T" piece at the bottom of the column, and the knob with the rod and the column nut will leave the fork as one assembly.

Remove the bolt holding the steering damper anchorage plate to the frame, below the head lug.

Remove switch lever from head lamp.

Remove switch panel from the back of the head lamp, held by three screws.

Remove the wires attached to the bulb holders, and the switch panel can be passed through the fork girders and rest on the tank.

Remove the head clip bolt and nut. This is composed of three parts, the bolt, the sleeve and the nut.

Remove the head clip from the fork column. The head clip must be forced over the end of the column to overcome the action of the fork spring.

Fork will now drop from the frame.

80. FITTING OF FORKS TO THE FRAME.

Examine the ball bearings and their races.

The races are all pressed into position and are easily removed and replaced.

The only one that may present any difficulty is the one in the head clip. A chisel type of tool is required to remove this race. The tool should be forced between the back of the race and the clip.

The clip should be removed from the fork for this operation.

If the head races have been removed from the frame, refit.

The race in the bottom of the frame head lug has oil hole drilled in it and the top is plain.

Fit the ball bearings to the top head race. (17 balls—5/16in. diameter.)

Grease the bottom head race with a thick grease.

Fit a set of ball bearings into a spare race, offer the bearings in the race, against the bottom race, press bearings home and carefully remove the spare race, and the grease will hold the bearings in position.

Fit fork column through the head lug until the end of the column is at the top of the lug.

Force the head clip into position on top of the lug.

Place a steel rod under the crown lug at the end of the column so that when the rod is lifted, the column is forced through the head lug.

Place a second rod on the top of the fork girder, resting on the head clip, so that when pressure is put on the rod, the clip is forced onto the top of the head lug.

Lift the bottom rod, press down the top one, and the end of the column is forced through the head clip.

Fit the assembly of the damper knob, rod and column nut.

Screw damper rod into the "T" piece at the bottom of the fork column and the nut to the column.

If the assembly of the damper knob, rod and column nut has been dismantled, the order of assembly is—fit the two nuts to the end of the rod with the longer threaded portion, screw the nuts to the end of the thread and lock together; fit spring and column nut; fit the damper knob to the rod and tighten down.

Fit the head clip bolt and nut. The bolt may be fitted from either side, but at the Works it is fitted from the " nearside."

Fit the bush first with the cut-away side against the column, then the bolt with the cut-away side against the column.

Fit the washer and nut. **Do not** tighten nut.
Check the forks for free movement on races.

The forks should have free movement with no end play.

Adjust by tightening or slackening the column nut.

Place the thumb of the left hand at the top of the steering column, resting on the column and the head clip, lift the forks and any play can be felt.

When the adjustment is correct, tighten the head clip bolt.

Fit the two wires to the lamp holders, the wire from the second switch terminal should be connected to main bulb holder. The other to the pilot bulb holder.

Fit panel to the back of the head lamp.

Fit handlebars, front wheel, brake and speedometer cables.

Fit the steering damper anchorage plate to the frame.

Do not strain plate. Any distortion will cause uneven action of the damper.

81. DISMANTLING OF FORKS.

Remove forks from the frame. (Para. 79.)

Hold the fork assembly in a vice. Use lead clamps on the jaws of the vice.

Place the column in the vice jaws, with the forks lying horizontal.

Remove the two rebound springs.

Remove the top offside fork link. The links on the offside of the forks have plain holes and the nearside tapped.

Remove the nuts holding the top offside link and the link can be tapped from the spindles.

Remove the knurled washers from the spindles.

Remove the nearside link complete with the spindles.

Remove the head clip from the centre spring, held by a taper lug.

Remove the bolt and the lug can be tapped from the clip.

The other end of the spring is attached to a lug on the bridge of the girder.

Do not remove this end of the spring unless the spring needs replacing.

To remove the spring, turn spring in a clockwise direction and it will screw off the lug.

Remove the bottom front spindle. Girder and the shock absorber discs are free.

Remove the bottom rear spindle.

Remove the steering damper bottom plate, held by two bolts, and the damper plates with the bottom lug are free.

82. RECONDITIONING OF FORK BEARINGS.

When the forks are dismantled and the parts examined it may be found that the forks, spindles and the bearings in the girder, head clip and the column, are worn, and oversized spindles may be necessary.

Oversize spindles are supplied with a diameter of 9/16in., i.e., 1/16in. oversize.

Before fitting the spindles, the bearings will have to be re-bored to 35/64in., leaving 1/64in. to be reamed.

When drilling care must be taken that the drill runs true and is fed at right angles to the girder. It is advisable to use a four-grooved core type of drill.

Clamp the girder to the face plate of a drilling machine, the bearing taken on the centre girder lug damper face, and drill the one side of the girder at the centre lug. Move the table, and with the girder held in the same manner, place packing piece under the bottom of the top girder lug and drill bearing. Reverse girder on face plate and drill the opposite side.

When drilling column and head clip, place lug on a spigot, entered on the opposite side of the bearing to the side to be drilled. The machine face of the lug should bear on a flat surface at right angles to the spindle. Drill one side of both lugs, change spigot for one with a diameter of 35/64in. and drill second sides.

A 9/16in. reamer ground with sufficient lead at the start should be used and passed straight through the lug to ensure that both sides of the bearing are in alignment.

The off-side bottom link will have to be opened to 9/16in. diameter hole to take the bolt type bottom front spindle.

Assembly Forks (para. 83.)

83. ASSEMBLY OF FORKS.

Fit drilled ballrace to the head clip and plain to the column.

Fit steering damper plates on to the damper lug—the bottom plate, friction disc, friction plate and friction disc.

Fit spring to girder.

Fit the fork shock absorber adjusting nut to the bottom front spindle.

Fit the fork shock absorber adjusting nut spring washer.

Fit the offside link to the spindle.

Fit the friction disc on link.

Fit the spindle into the girder.

Fit the bottom rear spindle into the nearside link.

Fit knurled washer to spindle.

Fit spindle into the fork column. When fitting the spindle to the column, hold the damper lug, with plates in position, in the column, and the spindle must pass through the lug.

Fit knurled washer to spindle.

Fit the offside bottom link, now attached to the girder, to the rear spindle (attached to the column) and fit the friction disc to the nearside link.

Fit rear spindle into offside link and front into nearside.

Fit the nuts to the bottom spindles. **DO NOT** tighten.

Fit top spindles into the nearside link. The end of the spindles should be 7/16in. through the link.

Fit knurled washers to the spindles.

Fit head clip loosely to the spring.

Fit the nearside link with the spindles to the top of the girder and the head clip.

Fit knurled washers to the spindles.

Fit offside link.

Fit nuts.

Fit the rebound springs to the top links.

Fit head clip over column.

Fit rebound springs to the bottom links.

Tighten fork spring bolt.

Adjust forks until the knurled washers can just be rotated by hand, with no side play.

Tighten all the nuts and re-check washers

MAINTENANCE MANUAL

AND

INSTRUCTION BOOK

FOR

THE UNAPPROACHABLE

MOTOR CYCLE

MODELS 16 H, BIG 4, 18 & ES 2

Publication Date 1947
includes an appendix that covers
later (through 1954) models in this series.

Telephone:
ASTon Cross 0776-7-8
(Private Branch Exchange)

NORTON MOTORS LIMITED
BRACEBRIDGE STREET
BIRMINGHAM, 6
ENGLAND.

Telegrams:
"Nortomo
Birmingham."

PRICE - 1/-.

IMPORTANT INFORMATION RELATING TO THE CONTENTS OF THIS MANUAL

1945-1946: The first section of this manual includes a copy of the appropriate repair and maintenance data for the girder forks as fitted to the WD16H model. This information is included as the 1945-1946 post-war civilian 16H and 18 models were also fitted with girder forks. However, based on our research, overhaul information for girder forks was never included in any of the factory workshop manuals for the post-war civilian models.

1947-1954: The second section includes a copy of a 1947 factory workshop manual for both the S.V. and O.H.V. rigid frame and spring frame (plunger) 16H, Big4, 18 and ES2 models that were fitted with 'Road-holder' forks. It also includes additional information extracted from the 1956 publication of this same workshop manual relating to the changes that took place during the 1947 to 1954 model run, including the change from an 'Upright' to a Laydown' gearbox and lighting equipment. This additional information is appended at the end of the section and any data that is identical and included in the 1947 publication has been omitted. Consequently, this manual would be applicable to all four models from 1947 to 1954 at which time the 16H, Big4 and 18 were discontinued and the ES2 had received swing-arm rear suspension.

1953-1958: The third section includes a copy of a 1956 factory workshop manual exclusive to the O.H.V. swing-arm 19S, ES2 and 50 models. As the ES2 received swing-arm rear suspension in 1953, this manual would be applicable to all three models from 1953 to 1958, at which time the 19S was discontinued.

1958-1963: The pages in the fourth section of this manual were extracted from the P106/P Norton factory publication 'Maintenance Manual and Instruction Book' dated 1970 for the Model 50, ES2, 88, 99, 650 and 750 models. As the 19S was discontinued in 1958 and is no longer included in the model list, this extracted data would be applicable to the 1958 to 1963 Model 50 and ES2 (see below).

EVOLUTION OF THE COMBINATION MANUALS: The publication of these 'combination' manuals began in 1960 with the P101 manual followed by the P106 and finally the P106/P manual of 1970. While these 'combination' manuals made publication less expensive than those for individual models the information for multiple different motorcycles is often merged together. Consequently, separating out the appropriate data for a specific model, or series of motorcycles can be a time consuming and confusing exercise.

Even more unfortunately, the P106/P manual makes no reference to the model years that are covered. However, as it only includes the model 50 and ES2 and knowing that the 19S was discontinued in 1958 it is reasonable to assume that it is intended to cover these two models from 1958 through 1963, at which point Norton discontinued manufacturing their single-cylinder machines. Therefore, we have extracted the information that is exclusive to the Model 50 and ES2 from the P106/P manual. However, this means that the paragraphs and illustrations in the P106/P section may no longer be sequentially numbered and we request you overlook this minor issue as it does not affect the correctness of the data in any way.

IMPORTANT: Please note that repair information for the AMC MKII versions of the models 50 and ES2 is not included in this publication.

INDEX.

	Paragraph
Ammeter	105
Battery, maintenance	106
Big End, examination	33
Brakes, dismantling	68
Brakes, assembling	69
Carbon, removal	10
Carburetter, adjustment	87
Carburetter, maintenance	88
Carburetter, dismantling	82
Carburetter, assembling	83
Carburetter, easy starting	85
Carburetter, float chamber	86
Carburetter, slow running	84
Carburetter, throttle stop	85
Contact Breaker, adjustment	96
Contact Breaker, cleaning	97
Clutch, dismantling	43
Clutch, examination	44
Clutch, assembly	45
Crankcase, dismantling	35
Crankcase, assembling	38
Cylinder Barrel, removal	11, 12
Cylinder Barrel, fitting	17, 18
Cylinder Head, removal	8, 12
Cylinder Head, fitting	9, 18
Dynamo Brushes	102
Dynamo, lubrication	103
Dynamo, removal	101
Dynamo, fitting	101
Electrical Cables	109
Electrical System, maintenance	94
Engine, removal	34
Engine, fitting in frame	39
Foot Change, dismantling	54
Foot Change, assembling	55
Front Forks, removal	72
Front Forks, dismantling	74
Front Forks, assembling	75
Front Forks, fitting	73
Front Forks, maintenance	70
Gearbox, removal	46
Gearbox, dismantling	48, 50, 51
Gearbox, assembling	49, 52, 53
Gearbox, fitting	47
Handlebar Levers	78, 79, 80, 81
Head Lamp	107
Head Lamp Switch	110
High Tension Lead	98
High Tension Pickup	99
Horn	111
Hubs, dismantling	62, 64, 66
Hubs, assembling	63, 65, 67

	Paragraph
Legshields	89
Legshields, fitting	90
Lubrication System	1
Magdyno, removal	32
Magdyno, fitting	32
Magneto, lubrication	95
Magneto, timing	27
Main Bearings, removal	36
Main Bearings, fitting	37
Oil Bath Chaincase, removal	41
Oil Bath Chaincase, fitting	42
Oil Circulation	5
Oil Control Valve	31
Oil Filter	2
Oil Level	4
Oil Pump	3, 30
Oil Pump, removal	28
Oil Pump, fitting	29
Petrol Tank, removal	6
Petrol Tank, fitting	7
Piston, removal	22
Piston, fitting	23
Piston Ring, removal	22
Rocker Box, removal	12
Rocker Box, dismantling	19
Rocker Box, fitting	18
Small End Bush, removal	24
Small End Bush, fitting	24
Sparking Plug, maintenance	100
Steering Head, adjustment	71
Spring Frame, dismantling	76
Spring Frame, assembling	77
Tail Lamp	108
Tappet Adjustment	20, 21
Timing Gears, removal	28
Timing Gears, fitting	29
Timing Gear Bushes	40
Timing Panel, removal	25
Timing Panel, fitting	26
Tyres, maintenance	91
Tyres, removal	92
Tyres, fitting	93
Valves, removal	13
Valves, grinding	14
Valves, fitting	15
Valve Guides, removal	16
Valve Guides, fitting	16
Voltage Control Unit	104
Wheels, removal	56, 58, 60
Wheels, fitting	57, 59, 61

DATA.

Model.	Big 4.	16 H.	18 & ES2
Cubic Capacity	596 c.c.	490 c.c.	490 c.c.
Bore	82 m/m	79 m/m	79 m/m
Stroke	113 m/m	100 m/m	100 m/m
Compression Ratio	4.5 - 1	4.9 - 1	6.6 - 1
Sparking Plug	K.L.G. FE.70	K.L.G. FE.70	K.L.G. F.70
Ignition Timing.			
Before top, fully advanced	$\frac{7}{16}''$	$\frac{7}{16}''$	$\frac{5}{8}''$
Magneto Points, gap	.012"	.012"	.012"
Plug Points, gap	.015"	.015"	.015"
Valve Timing.			
Inlet opens before top	$\frac{11}{32}''$	$\frac{9}{32}''$	$\frac{5}{16}''$
Exhaust closes after top	$\frac{11}{32}''$	$\frac{9}{32}''$	$\frac{5}{16}''$
Tappet Clearance Cold.	See para. 20 for	Engine Nos. followed	by letter Q.
Inlet	.002"	.002"	Both push rods to
Exhaust	.003"	.003"	be free to rotate.
Amal Carburetter.			
Type	276 A.T.	276 A.T.	276 A.U.
Main Jet	160	160	160
Throttle Valve	6/5	6/5	6/4
Needle Position	Middle	Middle	Middle
Piston Clearances.	.007"	.007"	.007"
Top of Skirt	.006"	.006"	.006"
Bottom of Skirt	.004"	.004"	.004"
	.003"	.003"	.003"
Engine Sprocket, Solo	19 tooth	19 tooth	20 tooth
Engine Sprocket, Sidecar	16 tooth	16 tooth	18 tooth
Gear Ratios, Solo	4.9, 5.93, 8.67, 14.6		4.66, 5.64, 8.24, 13.84
Gear Ratios, Sidecar	5.8, 7.02, 10.3, 17.2		5.16, 6.25, 9.14, 15.3
Petrol Tank Capacity	$2\frac{3}{4}$ galls. approx.		
Oil Tank Capacity	4 pints approximate		
Gearbox Capacity	$\frac{1}{2}$ pint approximate		
Chaincase Capacity	$\frac{1}{2}$ pint approximate		
Tyre Pressures	* Front 18lbs.	Rear 23lbs.	

* Later Manual Says 20lbs

INTRODUCTION.

In preparing these instructions the elementary details and preliminary information that may be necessary to the absolute novice has been omitted, on the assumption that the majority of NORTON owners are already acquainted with the elementary details of starting, driving and maintenance. In connection with the latter we would stress the advisability of cultivating the habit of routine cleaning, lubrication, examination and adjustment of your machine. By this means many minor annoyances will be avoided and major breakdowns averted, and you will acquire the pride of ownership which marks the true enthusiast.

Below is a plan view of the machine with all controls clearly indicated. A short study of this will familiarize you with the position and function of each control. Without wishing to become elementary a description of the best method of ensuring an easy start may not be inappropriate. With the petrol turned on, the air lever partly closed and the ignition lever in about its middle position, slightly flood the carburetter until petrol seeps (not drips) from the bottom of the carburetter mixing chamber and turn the easily starting screw (Fig. 20) in a clockwise direction. Depress the kickstarter until the resistance of compression is felt, raise the exhaust valve lifter and depress the kickstarter a further two or three inches. Release the exhaust valve lifter and allow the kickstarter to return to its normal position. Give a long swinging kick on the starter, carrying it as far round as possible. With the controls correctly set the engine should now start up.

When taking over a new machine it is only necessary to add petrol and oil to the respective tanks before use; the lubrication points having received the necessary greasing at the Works. It is advisable, however, to see that the steering damper is slackened off and adjusted to your particular requirements.

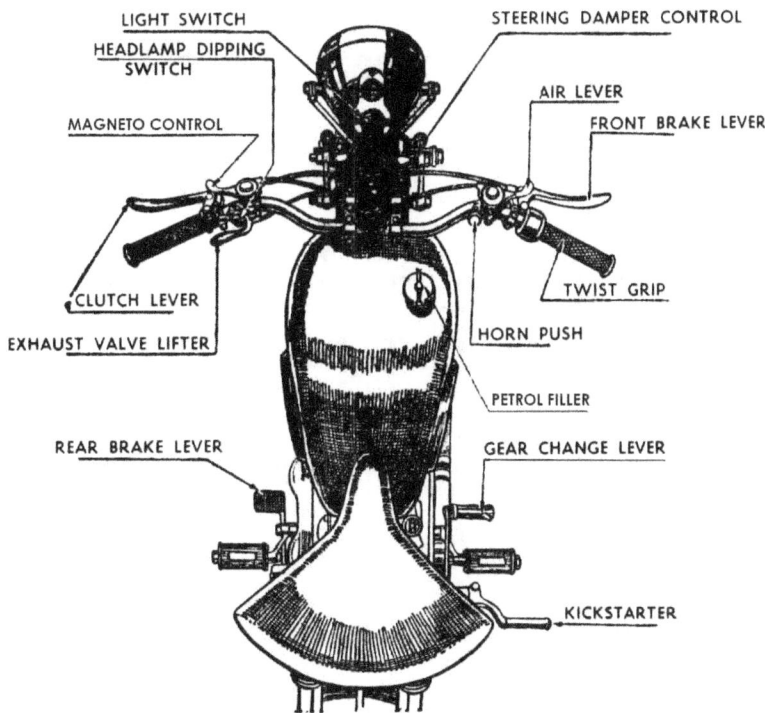

Fig. 1. Plan of machine showing controls

New machines should not be driven at more than 35 miles per hour for the first 500 miles in top gear or a correspondingly slower speed in the lower gears. Avoid "over revving" and slogging or labouring of the engine. It is advisable during the running in period not to open the throttle more than ¼ to ⅓. The use of running-in compound during the initial stages of the engine's life is strongly recommended. The compound, several brands of which are available and may be obtained from all NORTON agents, contains "colloidal graphite," which forms a graphoid surface on all working surfaces of the engine and greatly assists in preserving their high quality finish. The compound should be mixed with the lubricating oil in the proportion of one pint to each gallon during the running-in, but if its use is continued after this period only half the quantity should be used.

Under all usual circumstances when the machine is travelling at 25 miles per hour or over the air lever should be fully open and the ignition fully advanced, and only during starting or when the engine shows a tendency to pink should the ignition be retarded. Remember that these are high efficiency engines which give of their best when running at relatively high revolutions, and do not be afraid to change into a lower gear at the first signs of labouring. We would stress that the highest possible use should be made of the gearbox, which is quite capable of withstanding all the loads likely to be imposed on it by normal usage.

At the end of this book will be found a trouble tracing chart, reference to which will greatly facilitate the locating and rectifying of any but the most unusual troubles which may be likely to cause an involuntary stop.

LUBRICATION.

At the Works, Wakefield Castrol Oils have been used for many years exclusively with highly successful results; the correct grades for the models dealt with in this handbook being:—

WAKEFIELD CASTROL XXL, for Summer use.
WAKEFIELD CASTROL XL, for Winter use.

Other very suitable oils for NORTON machines are:—

PRICES' MOTORINE "B" DE LUXE or TRIPLE SHELL, for Summer use.
PRICES' MOTORINE "C" or DOUBLE SHELL, for Winter use.

These oils should be used in the engine and gearbox.

For oilbath chaincase use Wakefield's "Castrolite," Single Shell or Price's Motorine E.

All bearings not automatically lubricated are fitted with nipples for grease gun lubrication, and a good quality grease, such as Wakefield Castrolease Medium, Prices' Belmoline, or Shell Retinax, should be used at these points.

Below is a lubrication chart indicating the approximate periods at which the various lubrication points should receive attention. If this chart is adhered to, excessive wear will not occur on any of the moving parts, the life of the machine will be prolonged and its performance considerably enhanced.

NOTE.—On a new machine, drain and flush out oil tank after 500 miles. Remove crankcase drain plug and allow to drain. Gearbox is most readily filled by means of an oil gun; if oil is poured in, allow plenty of time and operate kickstarter occasionally. Beware of air-locks. Remove level indicator plug from oilbath chaincase and fill to this level.

LUBRICATION CHART.

Period	Location	Lubricant	Period	Location	Lubricant
Every 200 miles.	Oil tank, top up	Oil	Every 2,000 miles.	Brake pedal	Grease
Every 1,000 miles.	Spring Frame Fork Ends	Grease		Brake shoe cams (sparingly)	Grease
				Brake rod jaw joints	Oil
	Control cables	Oil		Speedometer driving box	Grease
	Control levers	Oil		Drain and refill oil tank	Oil
	Brake cable "U" clip	Oil		Steering head races	Grease
	Gearbox control rod pins	Oil		Saddle front pivot	Oil
	Wheel bearings	Grease	Every 5,000 miles.	Gearbox, drain and refill	Oil
	Rear chain	Grease			
	Gearbox, top up	Oil		Commutator end bracket	Oil
	Oil bath, top up	Oil		Telescopic Forks	See para 70
Every 2,000 miles.	Footchange lever	Grease	Every 10,000 miles.	Oilbath, drain and refill	Oil

THE ENGINE.

1. ENGINE. LUBRICATION SYSTEM.

This is of the dry sump type. The oil flows from the oil tank to the pump by gravity, assisted by suction from the feed side of the oil pump, through the gears, and is forced under pressure to various parts of the engine, drains to the lowest part of the crankcase—that is the sludge trap—and by suction from the return side of the pump is lifted back to the oil tank.

2. THE FILTER.

The only filter in the oil system is of the gauze type and is fitted on the feed side of the oil circuit, attached to the adaptor screwed into the oil tank, to which the feed pipe is connected.

Clean filter, when oil tank is drained, every 2,000 miles.

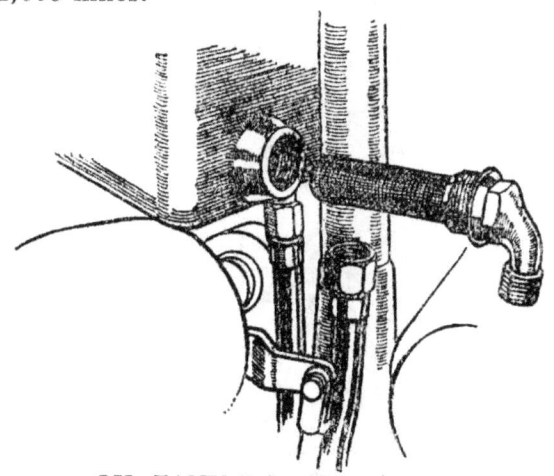

OIL TANK FILTER. (Fig 2.)

3. ENGINE OIL PUMP.

This is of the gear type. The pump contains two pairs of gears, one on the feed side and the other on the return side.

The gears on the return side are twice the width of those on the feed, having twice the pumping capacity. This ensures that the crankcase is free from oil when the engine is running.

To check the return of the oil to the tank, remove the oil filler cap. The oil return pipe can then be seen. After the engine has been running for a few minutes, the oil return flow will be spasmodic, due to the greater capacity of the return gears.

4. OIL LEVEL.

The oil level in the oil tank should not be above three-quarters and not below half.

If the level is above the three-quarter mark, when the engine is running, the pressure built up in the oil tank by the oil return side of the pump will force the surplus oil through the air release pipe on to the road.

Always run engine for a few minutes before checking oil level. It is posible when an engine has been idle for any length of time for the oil to syphon through the return gears to the sump.

When this happens, all the oil is returned to the tank in the first few minutes that the engine is running.

When the oil level is below the half full mark there is such a small quantity of oil that it tends to over-heat.

5. THE CIRCULATION OF THE OIL.

The oil is forced from the pump,

1. To the rear wall of the cylinder.
2. To the big-end bearing.
3. To the pressure control valve.

1. The oil passes through the timing panel to the mouth of the crankcase, through the base of the cylinder, up the cylinder wall and feeds the rear of the cylinder and piston.

2. The oil passes down the timing panel through the big end restriction jet, along the timing shaft, up the flywheel and is sprayed on to the roller big-end.

3. The oil pressure control valve is a spring-loaded ball, and acts as a safety valve, in the oil circuit. When the pressure of the oil lifts the ball from its seat, the oil passes the ball and is sprayed upon the timing gears. When the engine is assembled at the Works, the valve ball spring adjusting screw is screwed home and released 1½ threads. This is the only adjustment in the oiling system and it is not advisable to remove the ball from the valve unless it is suspected that the ball is sticking or not seating.

From the cylinder the oil drains down the sides of the crankcase and is picked up by ducts and carried to the main bearings and the timing gear bearings.

The oil collects in the timing case to such a level that the oil pump pinion is immersed, carrying oil to the half-time pinion and the timing gears.

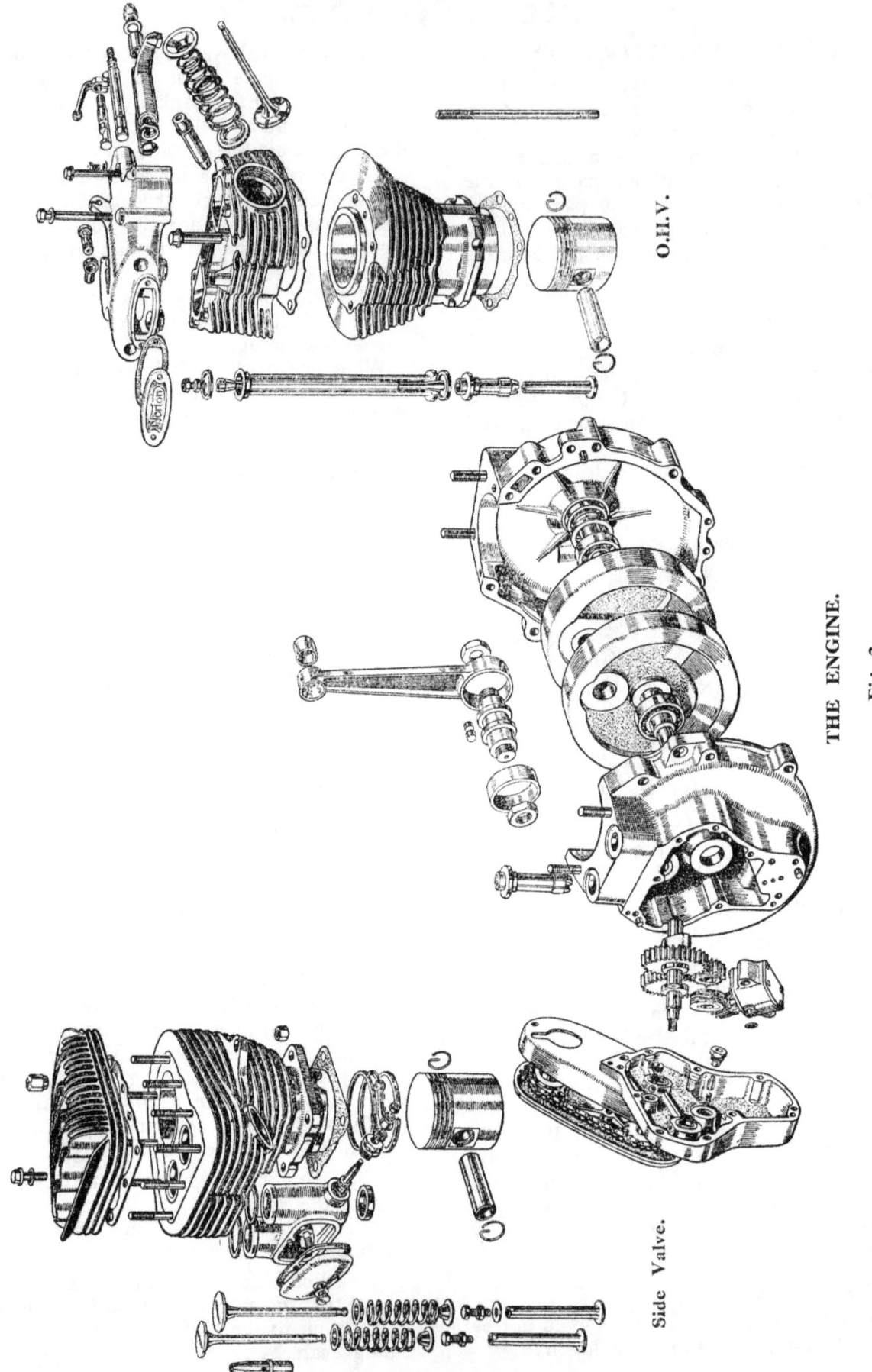

THE ENGINE.
Fig. 3.

O.H.V.

Side Valve.

On S.V. engines oil passes from the timing chest to the valve spring compartment via a longitudinal slot in the tappet guide; surplus oil being allowed to drain back into the crankcase.

On O.H.V. engines a lead is taken from the oil return pipe to a banjo fitting on the rocker box, feeding oil to the rocker shafts and ball ends. Surplus oil returns down the pushrod cover tubes to the crankcase. Excess oil from the O.H.V. valve spring chambers drains back through drilled holes in the cylinder head and barrel.

Oil is fed to the magdyno chain by passing through the inlet cam spindle bush into the chain case. Any excess of oil accumulated in the case, drains through the breather pipe.

Crankcase pressure is also released by a valve on the driving side of the crankcase and oil mist is fed to the rear chain.

All the oil drains to the base of the crankcase to the sludge-trap, is picked up by the suction of the return side of the pump and returned to the tank.

The oil-way from the sludge-trap is situated so that any foreign matter is left in the trap. This leaves the case when the crankcase drain plug is removed and the oil drained.

MAINTENANCE OF ENGINE.
DECARBONISING.

6. REMOVAL OF PETROL TANK.

It is not necessary to drain tank, but make sure that the petrol tap levers are in the "Off" position, that is, with the round end of the lever pressed in.

Disconnect petrol pipes from taps. Use two spanners, holding the union nut with one, and the tap union with the other.

Remove the four bolts and washers, and the tank is free from the frame.

Four shouldered rubber washers and steel washers should be on the tank brackets.

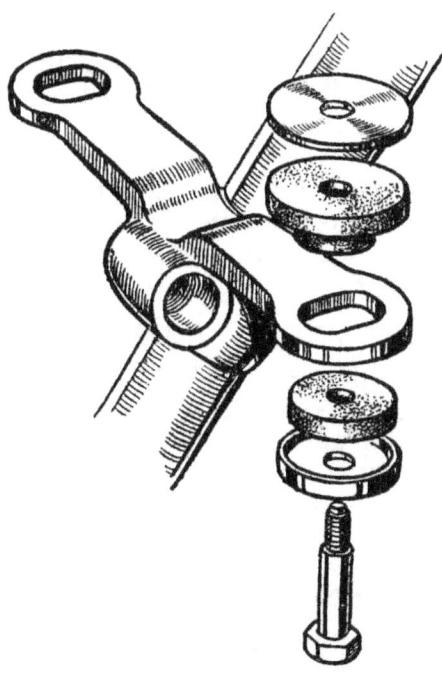

The order in which the washers for the tank mounting should be placed. (Fig. 4.)

7. FITTING OF TANK.

Place the four shouldered rubber washers on the frame tank brackets, with the steel washers above.

Place tank in position and fit cupped steel and rubber washers on to the tank bolts. (Fig. 4)

Fit bolts to tank and tighten down evenly.

Ensure that the tank is clear of the frame.

Fit petrol pipes, using the two spanners as when removing.

8. REMOVAL OF CYLINDER HEAD. 16H and BIG 4.

The cylinder head is held to the barrel by nine studs and nuts.

Remove sparking plug lead, spark-plug, and holding down stud nuts.

Remove cylinder head and joint washer.

9. FITTING OF CYLINDER HEAD. 16H and BIG 4.

Examine joint washer. If damaged or shows any signs of blowing, replace.

Fit cylinder head, cylinder head stud nuts, and tighten down evenly.

Fit sparking plug and lead.

10. REMOVAL OF CARBON.

Scrape carbon from top of piston and cylinder head.

Both are of the alloy type and care must be taken not to damage them.

Place an old piston ring at the top of the bore, and resting on top of piston. It will prevent the carbon being removed at the edge of the piston and end of the bore.

After an engine has been used for any considerable time, wear in the bore and the rings takes place, allowing a small amount of oil to pass.

The carbon on the piston edge and the top of the bore acts as an oil seal and if removed, engine may use a little more oil till carbon is re-formed.

The carbon deposit in the valve ports and valve spring compartment cannot be removed unless the valves are removed.

Valves need NOT be removed at every de-carbonization.

11. REMOVAL OF CYLINDER BARREL. 16H and BIG 4.

Remove petrol tank (see Para 6).

Cylinder barrel can be removed with or without the cylinder head in position.

Remove sparking plug and lead.

Remove carburetter, which is fitted to the induction stud by split ring and bolt.

Ease bolt and remove carburetter complete with pipes from the induction stub, when carburetter will hang on the control cables.

Remove valve cover and rotate engine till both valves are closed and piston at bottom of stroke.

Remove exhaust valve lifter control from arm by raising the arm and detaching inner cable.

This releases the return spring.

Screw out cable adjuster from cylinder barrel, and the cable is now free.

Remove exhaust valve lifter from valve chest by unscrewing the hexagon headed bush carrying the lifter spindle.

Remove cylinder base nuts and lift cylinder off crankcase supporting the valve chest which is a separate casting, with one hand. The top joint between the cylinder and valve chest is made oil tight with composition washers, the lower seals being of rubber.

A paper washer is fitted between barrel and crankcase.

With the cylinder removed the piston is exposed and the cylinder can be dealt with on the bench.

It is essential to cover the crankcase mouth with clean rag to prevent the ingress of any foreign matter.

12. REMOVAL OF ROCKER BOX, CYLINDER HEAD AND CYLINDER BARREL.
O.H.V. MODELS.

Remove carburetter attached to induction stub by split ring and bolt.

Remove exhaust pipe or complete exhaust system in one piece.

Disconnect the oil feed pipe from rocker box.

Rotate engine till both valves are seated and remove sparking plug.

Slacken the 9 rocker box securing bolts and remove those which are accessible. The three centre rear bolts must remain in the box until it is removed. Support the upper ends of the push rod cover tubes with one hand, lift the box about ¼" and withdraw from the cylinder head.

Remove the push rods and cover tubes together with the composition and rubber washers from either end of the cover tubes.

Keep the inlet and exhaust push rods separately for re-fitting in their original positions. Rocker box may be left suspended by exhaust valve lifter cable or completely removed.

Remove cylinder head nuts and cylinder head. If tight tap beneath inlet port with mallet or wooden block.

Revolve engine till piston is at bottom of stroke and remove cylinder barrel (this need not be done at every decarbonisation as piston top can be cleaned as S.V. models, para. 10.).

Cover crankcase mouth with rag to prevent ingress of dirt or foreign matter.

13. REMOVAL OF VALVES FROM CYLINDER OR HEAD.

Compress valve springs with a suitable type of valve compressor.

When springs are compressed the valve cotters will fall from the valve stems.

Remove valve compressor.

Remove valves.

Remove valve springs and collars from valve spring compartment.

Remove carbon from underside of valve heads.

DO NOT POLISH VALVE STEMS.

Check valve stems in guides; if free, do not touch guides, unless they are badly worn.

If guides and valves show no signs of excessive wear, re-grind valve seats.

Always grind the seats when new valves are fitted.

14. GRINDING OF VALVE SEATS.

Use as little grinding compound as possible.

Place valve in guide and grind lightly, using a screwdriver or hand vice.

Do not revolve valve a complete turn, but

oscillate, frequently raising valve from seat and placing in a different position.

Do not over-grind valve seats (a wide seat is not necessary).

When seat is ground sufficiently, that is, when the marks of the grinding make a complete ring on the seat and on the valve, remove all signs of grinding paste from seat, valve and valve pockets.

If the valves or the seats are badly burnt or pitted, it may be impossible to obtain a perfect seat by grinding. The seats will then have to be re-cut, and the valves re-faced.

15. FITTING OF VALVES.

Thoroughly clean valves, seats, and valve pockets. Fit valve springs and collars. Lubricate valve stems.

Fit valves into guides, compress valve springs, and fit cotters.

If the valve cotters are greased with a thick grease, the grease will hold the cotters in place until the springs are released.

16. REMOVING AND RE-FITTING OF VALVE GUIDES.

Valve guides are a driving fit in the cylinder barrel or head.

To remove, tap out with a double diameter drift.

Use the drift to replace or fit new ones.

Seats must be trued-up with cutter after refitting of guides, to ensure that the guides and seats are in alignment.

17. FITTING OF CYLINDER BARREL. S.V. ENGINES.

Position piston rings so that ring gaps are equally spaced.

Lubricate rings, barrel and piston.

Rotate engine until piston is near the top of its travel with the connecting rod leaning towards the front engine tube.

Fit paper washer to crankcase mouth, ensuring that cylinder feed oil hole is unobstructed.

Place rubber washers on tappet guides and composition washers on upper end of the valve spring chamber and place the latter in position on the crankcase.

Fit barrel over piston; it may be necessary to obtain assistance when entering rings into barrel and to support the valve spring chamber.

Having ensured that the valve spring chamber casting is correctly located, tighten the four cylinder base nuts evenly.

Fit exhaust valve lifter, making certain that the lifting portion is correctly positioned beneath the washer on the tappet.

Fit exhaust valve cable adjuster and return spring and attach cable to lifter lever. Adjust tappets (para. 20-21).

18. FITTING OF CYLINDER BARREL, CYLINDER HEAD AND ROCKER BOX. O.H.V. ENGINES.

Position piston rings so that gaps are equally spaced.

Lubricate rings, barrel and piston, and rotate engine till piston is near top of stroke.

Fit paper washer to crankcase mouth, ensuring that cylinder oil feed hole is unobstructed.

Fit barrel over piston and slide right home.

Clean cylinder head joint faces and fit aluminium gasket.

Fit cylinder head and tighten head nuts evenly.

Place the three rear centre bolts in position in the rocker box and position the box on the cylinder head, having smeared the joint faces with jointing compound.

Loosely fit the remaining bolts and place the push rods and cover tubes in the positions which they previously occupied with the composition washers at the upper end and the rubber washers at the bottom.

Evenly tighten the rocker box bolts. Re-fit the remaining components.

Remove rocker cover and check push rod adjustment (para. 20-21).

19. DISMANTLING AND RE-ASSEMBLY OF ROCKER BOX. O.H.V. ENGINES.

Whilst rocker box is removed it may be necessary to remove the rockers for examination or re-bushing. Remove the inspection cover and the rocker spindle nuts and washers, and with a soft punch against the threaded end, drift the spindles out of position.

The rockers with their washers and shims may be extracted from the box.

Remove the exhaust valve lifter by first removing the small securing screw, when the lifter may be withdrawn.

The rocker bushes are a press fit in the rockers and may be pressed or drawn out as shown in fig. 5.

Rocker ball ends and pads requiring renewing may be drifted out with a punch.

Press in new rocker ends, ensuring that the hole in the shank of the ball end is lined up with the oil hole in the rocker arm.

New rocker bushes may be pressed in or drawn into position by reversing the method of extraction illustrated.

New bushes should be reamed with $\frac{9}{16}''$ dia. reamer after fitting.

The re-assembly of the rockers in the box may require a little patience. Fig. 3 shows clearly the position of the various parts. Note that the steel shims on either side of the spring washer are identical, the thrust washer at the opposite end being much thicker.

Obtain a bar slightly smaller than the large spindle hole and having a lead on one end. Insert this into the hole far enough to allow the shims and spring washer to be placed over it. Carefully thread the rocker into position (it may be necessary to slightly withdraw the bar to get the rocker right home), centralise the washers as nearly as possible, remove bar and insert spindle, having previously smeared it with oil.

Using soft punch tap spindle part way through rocker.

Compress spring washer by means of screwdriver inserted into push rod hole and bearing on rocker arm and place thrust washer in position; the pressure of the spring washer will hold it until the spindle is knocked further home.

It is unlikely that the washer will be in true alignment with the spindle and will, therefore, be pinched between the rocker box and the shoulder on the spindle when the latter is tapped further into position. To release the washer tap the opposite end of the spindle once only.

Re-insert the screwdriver and again compress the spring washer. This will enable the thrust washer to be persuaded to drop over that part of the spindle on which it fits.

Insert tin strip or end of steel rule between rocker box and thrust washer, tap spindle fully home, remove tin strip, ensure that rocker is free to move, fit copper washer and dome nut and tighten.

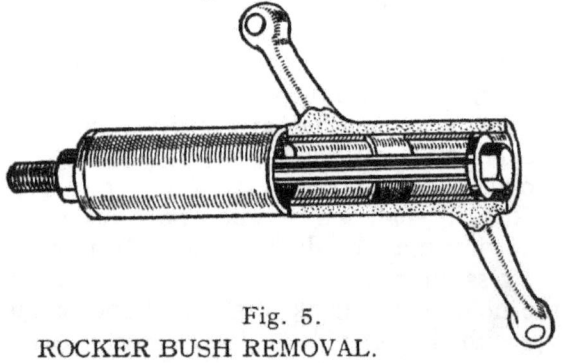

Fig. 5.
ROCKER BUSH REMOVAL.

20. TAPPET OR PUSH ROD ADJUSTMENT ON MACHINES WHERE ENGINE NO. IS FOLLOWED BY THE LETTER Q.

Engines having a number followed by the above suffix are fitted with a modified cam form which requires rather more careful positioning of the cam than previously.

For both O.H.V. and S.V. engines proceed as follows:—

To adjust inlet valve clearance rotate engine till exhaust valve is just lifting. Adjust inlet tappet or push rod (para. 21). To adjust exhaust valve clearance rotate engine till inlet valve has just closed. Adjust exhaust tappet or push rod.

On S.V. engines there should be .010" clearance between tappet head and valve on inlet and exhaust.

On O.H.V. engines both push rods should be free to rotate without any up and down movement.

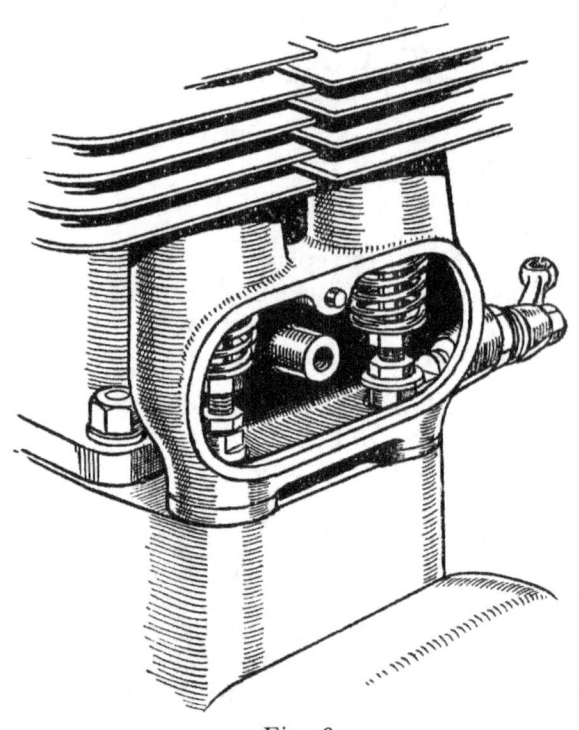

Fig. 6.
S.V. TAPPET ADJUSTMENT.

Set clearances with engine cold.

When timing engine with these cams there should be a .017" feeler inserted between cam and crankcase rocker pad.

Adjust afterwards to correct clearance.

21. TO ADJUST TAPPETS OR PUSH RODS.

Release the middle hexagon—locking the nut—by placing one spanner on the bottom hexagon—the tappet stem or push rod—and the second on the locking nut.

Turn the top hexagon—the tappet head or push rod adjuster—in the desired direction, and when the correct clearance is obtained, tighten locking nut.

Check clearance after tightening locking nut.

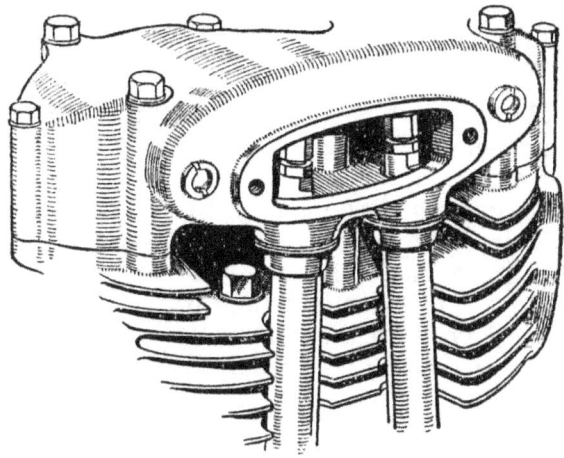

Fig. 7.
O.H.V. PUSH ROD ADJUSTMENT.

22. REMOVAL OF PISTON AND RINGS.

Remove cylinder barrel. (Para. 11-12.)
Remove one circlip and the gudgeon pin.
Gudgeon pin is a running fit in the piston and small end bush.
Mark piston to ensure it is fitted the same way when replacing.
Remove rings from piston.

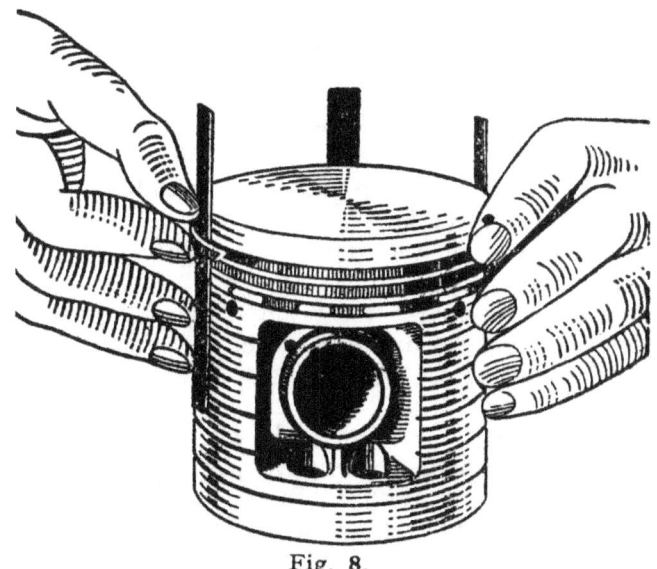

Fig. 8.

Place three thin metal strips approximately $\frac{1}{2}$" wide × 2" long, behind the rings equally spaced and the rings may be readily removed. (Fig. 8.)

If it is decided not to fit new rings, it is not advisable to remove the carbon from the back of the ring or the bottom of the ring groove.

If it is decided to fit new rings, the grooves in the piston should be thoroughly cleaned. A portion of a broken hack-saw blade is an ideal tool for the job.

When the grooves have been cleaned, check the new ring for size in the grooves.

There should be a side clearance of .002".

Check rings in the cylinder bore for the correct width of gap.

Place ring in bore, push ring down bore, using the piston as a guide.

The ring gap should be:

Compression ring .... .012"—.016".
Scraper .... .005".

Check gap with feeler gauge.

23. REFITTING PISTON.

Fit rings to piston.
Fit piston to connecting rod with the piston in the same position as before dismantling.
Fit circlip. It is advisable to always replace circlip and fit a new one.
Fit cylinder barrel. (Para. 17-18.)

24. REMOVING AND FITTING OF SMALL END BUSH.

If when the cylinder barrel and piston are removed it is found that the small end bush is worn it should be renewed.

Bush must be withdrawn from connecting rod.

Obtain a bolt at least twice the length of the bush, place a washer at the head of the bolt with an outside diameter less than the bush. Place bolt in bush.

Over the screwed end of the bolt place a piece of tubing longer than the bush, with an inside diameter slightly larger than the outside of the bush.

Fit nut to bolt and tighten. As nut is tightened, the bush will be drawn from the rod.

Care must be taken so that no strain is taken by the rod.

Fit new bush in the same manner.

Before fitting bush to rod, the inside diameter should be reamed to the size of the pin, as when fitted in the rod the bush will compress, leaving sufficient metal for true-ing with the reamer. If this is not done, too much metal will need to be taken away with the reamer.

Drill oil-holes in the bush before reaming to size.

The gudgeon pin should be a running fit in the small-end and the piston.

25. REMOVAL OF TIMING PANEL.

Remove magdyno chain cover held by three cheese headed screws.

Remove sprockets with chain in position. If difficulty is experienced a withdrawing tool should be obtained. The cam spindle sprocket is held by taper and key; the magdyno shaft is not keyed.

Remove panel screws and note that the top three are shorter than the bottom three. Two countersunk screws are inside the mag. chain case.

When withdrawing the panel see that the big end feed jet is not lost and that any shims fitted to the cam spindles remain in position.

Remove big end feed jet spring.

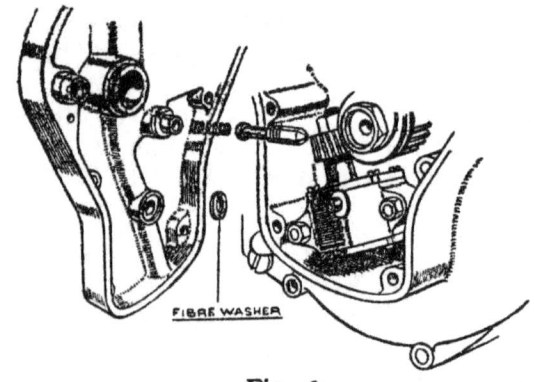

Fig. 9

26. FITTING TIMING PANEL.

Clean the edges of the timing chest and the panel.

Smear the edges with gold-size or jointing compound.

Check fibre washer on the oil pump nipple, connecting pump to panel.

Place panel in position and the washer should prevent the edges of the panel meeting the case by 1/32". This ensures that when the panel pins are tightened, the washer is compressed, making an oil-tight joint.

Fit spring and jet in jet holder.

Fit panel and panel screws and tighten down evenly.

27. IGNITION TIMING.

Place chain and sprocket in position and tighten cam wheel sprocket nut only.

Place gearbox change-speed lever in top gear position.

Advance ignition fully.

Rotate engine by turning the rear wheel, until both valves are closed and the piston is at the top of its stroke.

The position of the piston can be ascertained by placing a thin rod into the cylinder, via the compression or sparking plug hole.

Hold rule on the top of the piston and take the reading of the rule as it leaves the cylinder.

Turn the rear wheel backwards still holding the rule on top of the piston till the rule shows the correct figure. (See data sheet.)

Remove magdyno contact breaker cover.

Turn contact breaker in clockwise direction till the points open.

Insert thin feeler gauge or thin piece of paper, between the points.

Turn the contact breaker in an anti-clockwise direction till the points hold the feeler.

Turn contact breaker in a clockwise direction till the feeler is just free, that is when the points have just commenced to open.

Place a tube over the end of the shaft and sharply tap tube, forcing sprocket on to the taper of the shaft.

Tighten down nut carefully, so as not to turn the shaft.

When nut is tightened down, check timing

Fit contact breaker cover.

Fit magdyno chain cover.

Fit compression plug or sparking plug.

28. REMOVING TIMING GEARS, OIL PUMP, AND TAPPETS.

Remove timing panel (para. 25), timing gears and oil pump are now visible.

Remove oil pump nuts and withdraw oil pump from studs.

Remove oil pump worm, LEFT HAND thread.

Timing gears may now be removed ensuring that any shims fitted to either end of the spindles are not lost.

Withdraw pinion from timing shaft using, if necessary, a sprocket drawer.

Unless absolutely necessary the tappets should not be removed as it is necessary to remove the tappet guides before the tappets may be withdrawn. The tappet guides are pressed into the crankcase and may be extracted by means of a sprocket drawer.

The inlet and exhaust tappets should not be interchanged.

29. FITTING TAPPETS, TIMING GEAR AND OIL PUMP.

If new timing gears have been fitted then they will need checking and re-shiming for end float. When fully home in the case the side of the gear should be clear of the boss carrying the pressure release valve. Shims should be added until this condition is obtained.

Fit timing cover, pull and push on inlet cam spindle and shim up till end float is just perceptible.

End float on exhaust cam spindle can only be properly checked when crankcase halves are separated.

Tappets must be entered into tappet guides from inside timing chest before the guides are pressed into position.

This necessitates a tubular drift to finally force the guides home.

Tappet guides are located radially by a peg in top face of crankcase, which fits into a hole in tappet guide collar. Hole and peg should be as nearly in alignment as possible before pressing or tapping the guide into position.

Fit half-time pinion to mainshaft and rotate engine till crankpin is on T.D.C.

Fit cam gears, meshing the marked teeth with the appropriate markings on the pinion.

Fit and tighten oil pump worm, LEFT HAND thread, using punch or peg spanner.

Fit oil pump, ensuring that both faces are quite clean and using a minimum of jointing compound to avoid the oil holes becoming obstructed.

Check fibre washer on oil pump nipple and fit timing panel (para. 26).

Time magneto (para. 27).

30. OIL PUMP.

The oil pump is of the gear type. It is not advisable to dismantle it.

When pump is removed from timing chest, test for play in the spindle by pulling and pushing the worm wheel.

Revolve spindle and place fingers on the oil holes and the action of the gears should be felt if the pump is in good condition.

When revolving pump, any foreign matter obstructing the gears will be felt. Wash out with paraffin.

31. OIL CONTROL VALVE.

This is fitted in a boss on the inside of the timing panel. It is an assembly of a ball, spring and adjusting screw. The adjustment is set at the works and should not need any attention.

The control valve acts a safety valve in the oil circuit. When the oil is cold, the oil pressure in the circuit tends to become excessively high, but the excess of pressure lifts the ball from its seat, allowing the oil to spray on to the timing gears.

If for any reason this is dismantled, the order of assembly is—ball, spring and adjuster nut.

Tighten the nut home and then screw out one and a half turns and lock with centre punch.

32. REMOVAL AND FITTING OF MAGDYNO.

The removal of the magdyno is simplified if the timing panel is removed.

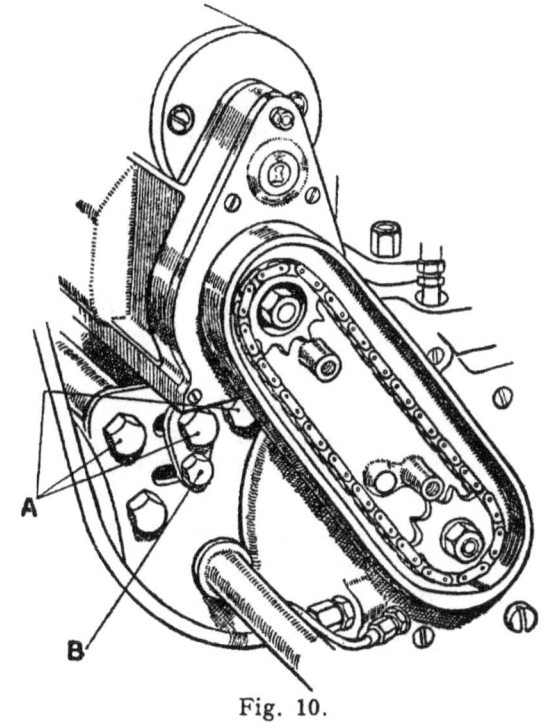

Fig. 10.

Remove timing panel. (Para. 25.)

Remove leads from dynamo (3.), and high tension lead from sparking plug.

Remove the locking bolt marked " B " in Fig. 10.

Remove the centre bolt of the three marked " A."

Ease the nuts off the outside bolts marked " A."

Magdyno can now be removed.

Replace in the reverse order.

Do not tighten the bolts until the panel is refitted and the chain adjusted.

With the bolts slack, the magdyno can be moved in the desired direction, to correct the chain adjustment.

33. EXAMINATION OF THE ROLLER BIG END.

With the cylinder removed, the big-end can be examined for wear.

Rotate the flywheels until the big-end is in the topmost position.

Hold connecting rod with both hands, pull and push, and any up and down play can be felt.

DO NOT USE SIDE PRESSURE.

Do not mistake side float for end play.

A small amount of rock is of no importance.

If any appreciable up and down movement is present a new crankpin bearing is necessary. The dismantling of the flywheels and fitting of crankpin is a skilled job requiring equipment not normally available to the average rider. The flywheel assembly should be returned to the works for this replacement.

34. REMOVING ENGINE FROM FRAME.

Remove the tank, (para. 6), magdyno (para. 32) and exhaust valve lifter cable.

Remove carburetter, which may be left suspended from cables, remove exhaust pipe and silencer, a 'C' spanner is supplied in tool kit to fit exhaust pipe locking ring on O.H.V. model.

Remove clip bolts and nuts, and silencer bolt, and the pipe and silencer can be removed as one unit.

Remove oil pipes from the crankcase. If the oil has not been drained from the oil tank, plug the end of the feed pipe.

Remove oil bath, engine sprocket, and clutch. (Para. 41.)

Remove front and rear engine plates completely. Remove engine cradle bolts and lift engine clear of frame.

35. PARTING OF THE CRANKCASE HALVES.

Remove crankcase drain plug and drain any oil that may be in the sump.

Remove cylinder barrel (para 11-12), piston (para. 22), timing gear and oil pump (para. 28).

Remove key from driving shaft.

Remove all the crankcase bolts and stud nuts, also the cheese headed screw from sump.

Crankcase halves can now be parted. Remove timing side first.

If leverage is necessary, revolve flywheels until the crankpin is at the mouth of the case, place a lever against the crankpin nut and lever outwards.

To remove the driving side of the case, lift the half of the case with the flywheels and lightly drop the end of the driving shaft on to a block of hard wood, then the case should leave the shaft.

36. REMOVAL OF BEARINGS FROM CRANKCASE.

It should be possible to remove the bearings from the case by tapping a shaft through the bearings, the shaft having a diameter slightly larger than the engine shaft, but small enough to pass through the bearing, should the bearing be tight in the case, without damage.

If the bearings are too tight in the housing to be removed by this method, the case should be heated round the bearing housings, when they should drop out.

Do not heat case sufficiently to destroy the temper of the bearings and do not use a concentrated flame.

37. FITTING OF BEARINGS TO CRANKCASE.

Test bearings, to be a sliding fit on shafts.

Press the ball bearing lightly in to the driving side of the case.

Fit the spacing washer next to the ball bearing.

Press the roller bearing lightly in to driving side of the case.

38. ASSEMBLY OF CRANKCASE.

Fit flywheels into case, and fit and tighten all bolts.

Test for side float in the flywheels, there should be .005".

If the float is excessive, remove wheels from case.

Fit pen steel washers to the engine and timing shafts to take up the excess of float.

Fit the same thickness of washers on each shaft, keeping the wheels central in the case.

Check side float.

If the side float is correct, check connecting rod for being central in case.

There is side float in the big-end.

Place fingers on the bottom of the connecting rod and push rod towards the timing side of the case.

Measure the distance from the end of the small-end bush to the side of the crankcase mouth on the timing side.

Push rod to driving side of case and take the same measurement, from the driving side.

The two measurements should be within 1/64" of each other.

Rod can be lined up by transferring the pen steel washers on the driving and timing shafts to whichever side needs them, to obtain the correct alignment.

When the correct alignment is obtained, remove wheels from case.

Lubricate main bearings and big-end.

Smear the two edges of the case with gold-size or jointing compound.

Fit wheels into the case and tighten all bolts and nuts.

Fit timing gears (para. 29), and panel (para. 26).

39. FITTING ENGINE TO FRAME.

Fitting of the engine to the frame should present no difficulty.

Lift engine into cradle and insert the two cradle bolts.

Starting at rear engine plates fit all bolts loosely, working finally to the front engine plate bolt.

Tighten all nuts.

Fit clutch, oil bath, etc.

Fit and time magdyno.

40. REMOVING AND FITTING OF TIMING GEAR BUSHES.

When engine is dismantled it may be found that the timing gear bushes require replacement. This is not a job to be undertaken by the average owner. The timing cover and half crankcase should be despatched to our service department.

THE TRANSMISSION.

41. REMOVAL OF OIL BATH.

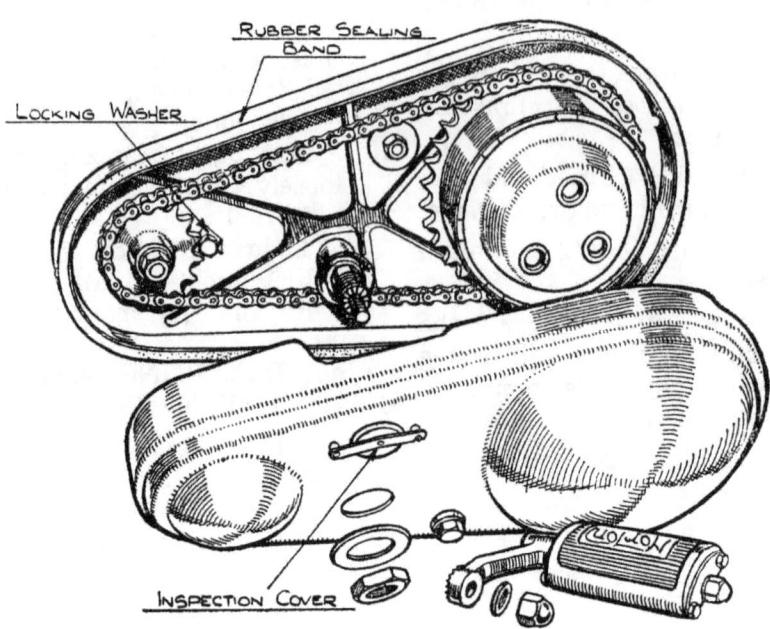

Fig. 11.

Remove the footrests, footrest rod, and brake pedal.

Remove the large nut holding the outer portion of the oil bath, and remove the outer portion.

Remove clutch spring screws, springs and cups (three of each), clutch outer plate, clutch thrust pin, and clutch retaining nut.

Engage low gear and obtain assistance to hold the rear wheel while the nut is being removed.

Remove clutch body.

A special tool may be obtained for this purpose if necessary.

Remove engine sprocket (a claw-type extractor will remove this), and engine sprocket, clutch and chain can be removed together.

Remove rear portion of oil bath, held to the crankcase by bolt, to the engine plate by a nut, to the rear chain guard by a bolt, and by a nut on the gear box pivot bolt.

42. FITTING OF OIL BATH.

Assemble in the reverse order.

Examine rubber washer fitted round the flange of the inner portion. This must be in a good condition to retain the oil in the case.

Fill oil bath with oil to the level of the plug near the bottom of the outer portion of the oil bath.

43. CLUTCH—TO DISMANTLE.

Remove outer portion of the oil bath, and clutch. (Para 41.)

A steel band is pressed round the clutch sprocket to prevent an excess of oil entering the clutch plates.

The plates can be removed with the band in position, but it must be removed to examine the driving slots in the sprocket.

Remove circlip holding clutch plates on to the body.

Remove plates.

There are six plain steel plates, and five steel plates with ferodo inserts.

Remove clutch sprocket.

Place an old gearbox main axle (if available) in a vice with the splined end above the jaws, and fit body to axle.

Remove the three screws holding the front cover plate.

Remove the cover plate, and the clutch shock absorber rubbers. (Fig. 12)

A large " C " spanner is needed to remove the rubbers. This is placed over the body and engaged in the splines, and the large rubbers compressed while the small ones are removed.

The handle of the spanner should be of such a length that the load can be taken by the users thigh, allowing both hands to be free to remove the rubbers.

A substitute for a " C " spanner can be made by fixing a handle to an old plain steel clutch plate.

Compress large rubbers and remove the small.

A small, sharp-pointed tool is necessary to remove the rubbers, as after use they adhere to the body.

Large rubbers are easily removed, after the small have been withdrawn.

Remove body from axle and replace in the reverse position.

Remove the three stud nuts on the back cover plate.

Back plate, roller race, back cover and body can be separated.

44. EXAMINATION OF CLUTCH PARTS.

Examine clutch inserts. They should be " proud " of the plate.

Fitting of separate inserts to a plate is not advisable, as the new insert would be " proud " of the remainder and take all the drive on the plate in which it had been fitted.

It is advisable, if possible, to replace plates with either new or reconditioned ones.

If all the new inserts are fitted to a plate, ensure that the inserts are level and flat and all contact the steel plates, taking their share of the drive.

Examine the drive on the plates for wear.

The plates with the inserts, drive on the outside diameter, and the plain steel, on the inside.

The splines on the body and the plain steel plates driven by the body rarely show any sign of wear.

The tongues on the plates with inserts, driving the sprocket, may show signs of wear and they may have " cut " in to the driven part of the sprocket.

This wear obstructs the free movement of the plates when the clutch is operated.

This can be rectified by filing or grinding the tongues on the plates square. Also the edge of the driven part of the sprocket.

The only effect this will have on the clutch is a slight amount of "back-lash" when the clutch is engaged or disengaged.

Examine plain steel plates for any roughness. The back plate sometimes develops this fault.

Examine the roller race, rollers and the cage.

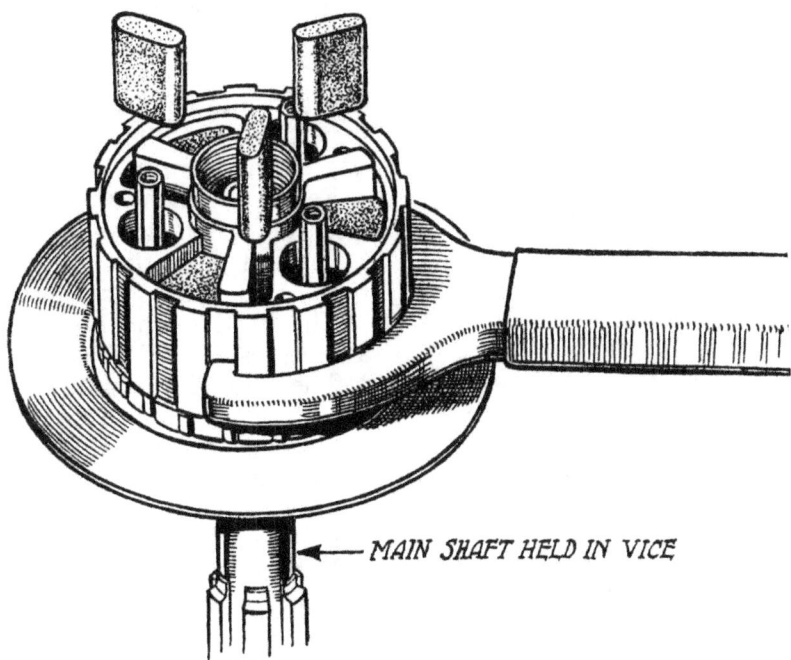

MAIN SHAFT HELD IN VICE

Fig. 12.

Examine the back cover plate face for wear by the clutch body centre.

Examine clutch shock absorber rubbers. They may have become soft or cracked.

45. ASSEMBLY OF CLUTCH.

Fit clutch body back cover plate to body, ensuring that the holes in the cover plate are in line with the holes in the body, and the spring studs an easy fit.

Fit clutch body centre and fit clutch large shock absorber rubbers in the position to take the drive.

Compress the rubbers in position and fit the small ones.

Fit body front cover and tighten screws.

Fit roller race on to the back cover plate. fit clutch back plate, and spring studs, fit stud nuts and tighten. Lock nuts with a centre punch.

Test roller race for freeness on its track.

Fit steel band on to the sprocket. This should not be tight enough to distort the sprocket.

Check all the clutch plates in the sprocket and on body for freeness.

Fit sprocket to body. Revolve sprocket on race to check free movement.

Fit plates to sprocket and body. Order of fitting is—plain steel, inserts, plain, etc.

It will be noticed on examination that the plates are slightly bevelled on the one edge. Fit the bevelled edge towards the sprocket.

Revolve sprocket, ensuring that the plates are free.

Fit circlip, retaining the plates, and fit clutch to Gearbox axle.

Fit clutch thrust pin, clutch outer plate, spring cups, springs, and spring pins. Tighten right home.

Fit oil bath outer portion. (Para. 42.)

THE GEARBOX.

46. REMOVAL OF GEARBOX FROM FRAME.

Remove kickstarter crank, gear indicator, and gear lever.

Remove gearbox outer cover and release clutch cable from clutch arm.

Remove cable adjuster from inner cover.

Remove oil bath outer portion, clutch and engine sprocket. (Para. 41.)

Remove rear portion of oil bath (para. 41), rear chain guard, held at the rear by a bolt and nut, and remove rear chain.

Remove rear wheel. (Para. 58 or 60.)

Remove toolbox held by three bolts, and rear mudguard, held by six bolts.

Remove large hexagon nut on the top gearbox bolt, also the two bolts holding the gearbox adjuster plate.

Unscrew the adjuster bolt from the gearbox bolt and withdraw the top gearbox bolt.

Remove the gearbox bottom bolt and nut, and lift gearbox from frame.

47. FITTING OF GEARBOX TO THE FRAME.

To refit the gearbox, reverse the order of the removal operations.

When fitting the top bolt, the tapped hole in the bolt must be in such a position as to allow the adjuster bolt to enter.

48. REMOVAL AND DISMANTLING OF GEARBOX END COVER.

Removal of end cover and gears may be readily carried out with the gearbox in position but for a complete overhaul it is best removed from the frame.

Remove split cotter and pin from the jaw joint on the control rod.

Remove the nuts holding the end-cover to the box, and remove end-cover complete.

Remove kick-starter axle return spring and cover from the bush, and the kick-starter pawl pin from axle, when the pawl, plunger, and spring are free.

Remove clutch worm lever from worm, also the clutch worm nut.

Pressed into the end-cover is the steel bush, that carries the kick-starter axle.

The head of the bush is recessed to take a compressed cork washer.

The end of the axle is bored out and a phosphor bronze bush is pressed in, to carry one end of the layshaft.

In the cover a ball journal bearing is pressed, to carry the end of the mainshaft (or axle).

Between this bearing and the kick-starter wheel, a dished steel washer is fitted, with the concave side next to the bearing.

The bearing can be pressed from the panel.

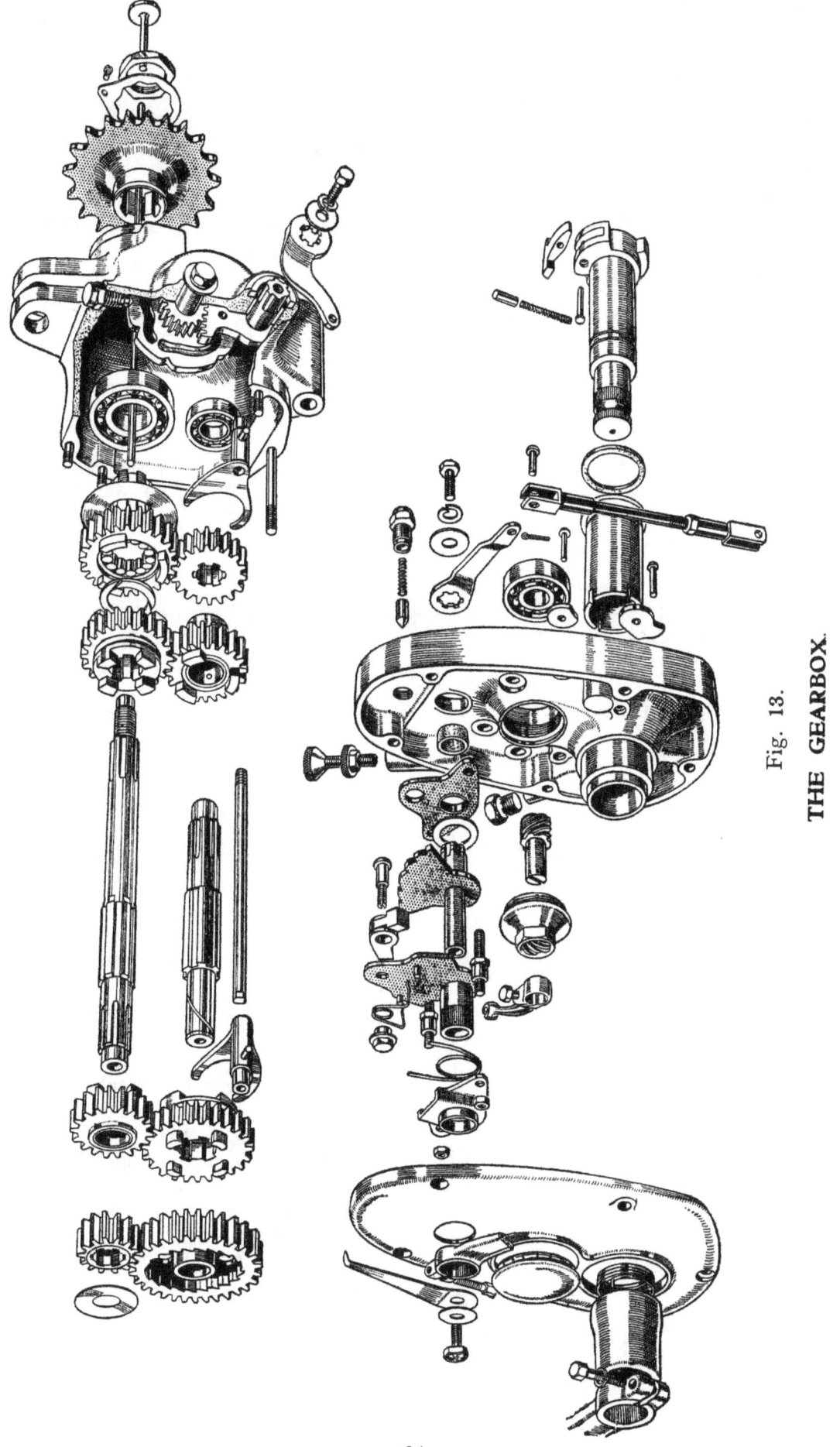

Fig. 13. THE GEARBOX.

49. ASSEMBLY OF GEARBOX END COVER. (INNER.)

Press the kick-starter axle steel bush into the cover, also the ball journal bearing into the cover.

Examine kick-starter pawl. The tip of the pawl that engages with the kick-starter and low gear wheel is the portion where the wear takes place. If worn, replace.

Fit pawl, plunger and spring to axle, by placing in position and inserting the pawl pin.

Fit clutch worm nut, clutch worm, and kick-starter axle.

Kick-starter crank, spring and cover and the clutch worm lever can be fitted before or after the cover is fitted to the box.

Fit dished steel washer to layshaft.

Fit cover to the box. A paper washer is fitted between the cover and the box.

Fit and tighten the seven nuts.

Fit clutch cable adjuster.

Fit clutch worm lever to worm.

Fit cultch cable to arm, adjust as necessary and tighten clip pin.

Fit outer cover, gear lever and gear indicator.

Fit kick-starter crank return spring; the end should be three slots round from its free position.

Fit kick-starter crank return spring cover.

Fit kick-starter crank to axle. The crank should not be upright. It should incline a little in the direction of its travel.

Fill gearbox with oil to the level of the filler-plug.

50. REMOVAL OF THE GEARS FROM THE GEARBOX.

Fit a length of steel tubing over the end of the gearbox main axle, from which the clutch has been removed, and retain by the clutch nut.

This will hold the axle in position while the gears are removed from the box.

Remove end cover. (Para. 48.)

Remove the low gear and kick-starter wheel—the large wheel on the layshaft. This has a phosphor bronze bush pressed into the centre.

Remove the small wheel on the main axle (or shaft), the main axle pinion.

Remove the second gear wheel from the main axle. This has a phosphor bronze bush, loose on the axle and in the wheel.

Remove the striker fork shaft, by screwing out of the box with a spanner on the machined flats at the end.

Remove the layshaft second gear and the striker fork.

Remove the main axle and third gear and the striker fork.

Remove the layshaft with its two remaining gears, exposing the roller race at the far end of the box.

The inner race with the rollers and cage will remain on the shaft, leaving the outer race in the box.

51. REMOVAL OF THE CAM PLATE FROM THE GEARBOX.

Remove the domed hexagon nut from the top of the gearbox. This contains the cam plate indexing plunger.

Remove the plunger and spring.

Remove the cam plate quadrant lever, held by a bolt and two washers, one plain and one spring.

Remove the cam plate quadrant, held by a bolt and two washers, one plain and one spring.

Remove the cam plate.

The cam plate quadrant works in a phosphor bronze bush. This can be pressed from the box.

The outside of the boss carrying the bush is recessed to take a pressed cork oil retaining washer.

The cam plate spindle also works in a phosphor bronze bush that can be pressed out.

Remove the temporary tubular distance piece, fitted on to the clutch end of the main axle.

Remove the main axle carefully. The phosphor bronze thrust washer will remain on the axle.

If the axle has been carefully removed, the rollers in the main gear wheel should remain in position.

Fit a tin or cardboard tube to replace the main axle in the main gear wheel to retain the rollers in position.

Remove the gearbox sprocket, held by a nut with a LEFT HAND THREAD. The nut is locked by a locking washer and screw.

If the gearbox is in the frame, obtain assistance to hold the rear wheel while the sprocket nut is removed.

If the gearbox is removed from the frame, the sprocket can be held by passing a length of old chain round the sprocket, holding the two ends in the vice. Obtain assistance to hold the box, and remove the nut.

When the sprocket is removed the main gear wheel can be removed from the box complete with rollers.

At the back of the main gear wheel a large pen-steel washer is fitted. This washer obstructs the oil flowing to the bearing in the box, allowing only sufficient to lubricate the bearing.

The bearing carrying the main axle can be pressed out of the box. At the back of the bearing a pen-steel washer is fitted between the bearing and the case.

The outer race of the layshaft bearing left in the case can be removed by carefully warming the case.

52. FITTING OF CAM PLATE.

If the bushes carrying the cam plate and quadrant spindles have been removed from the box, replace or re-new.

Fit the quadrant to the box but do not fit the retaining bolt.

Round the circumference of the cam plate five " V " grooves are machined. The indexing plunger engages in these grooves. Each groove corresponds with a gear position.

Three of the grooves are close together. They are in the following order—bottom (first), neutral (the shallow one), and second.

The other two are third and top (fourth).

The cam plate gear must be meshed with the quadrant in such a manner that when the quadrant is moved to its extreme position in either direction, the end grooves have passed the plunger by an equal distance.

Fit the cam plate, meshing the teeth on the spindle with the teeth on the quadrant.

Fit plunger, spring and domed nut. Do not screw the nut down tight. Allow the plunger to lightly touch the circumference of the cam plate.

Turn the quadrant to its extreme position in one direction, and check the distance the groove has passed the plunger.

Turn the quadrant to its other extreme and again check the distance the groove has passed the plunger.

When the gears are correctly meshed, fit the cam plate retaining bolt and two washers, the spring washer next to the bolt head.

Tighten down the plunger domed nut.

Fit the compressed cork washer to the quadrant spindle.

Fit the quadrant lever to the shaft, using the splines that allow the highest position for the lever with bottom gear engaged. If any attempt is made to fit the lever any higher, the lever will foul the boss carrying the quadrant spindle.

Fit bolt and nut, the spring washer next to the bolt head.

53. FITTING GEARS INTO GEARBOX.

Fit pen-steel washer to the boss before fitting main axle bearing.

Fit main axle bearing to box.

Fit layshaft bearing outer race to box.

Fit rollers into the main gear wheel, smearing the assembly with grease.

Fit the tin or cardboard tube used in dismantling to retain the rollers.

Fit large pen-steel washer to main gear wheel and fit main gear wheel to box.

Fit gearbox sprocket, tighten the nut, and fit the locking washer.

Remove carefully the tube holding the rollers in position in the main gear wheel.

Fit phosphor bronze thrust washer to the main axle so that the side with the oil grooves will be against the hardened steel washer in the main gear holding the rollers in position.

Place cam plate in second gear position.

Fit main axle to main gear wheel.

Fit the tubular distance piece used in dismantling, to the clutch end of the axle.

Fit third gear wheel (20 teeth) to the layshaft, followed by the top gear wheel (18 teeth).

Fit the inner race, with rollers and cage, to the end of the shaft.

Grease rollers, and fit shaft to box.

Fit striking fork to the main axle third gear (22 teeth) and fit third gear with the fork onto the axle.

Fit the second fork to the layshaft second gear (24 teeth) and fit the second gear with the fork to the layshaft.

The pegs on the striking forks fit in the cam plate slots.

With the gearbox in the frame, little trouble will be experienced in holding the first fork in position.

Fit the first fork in position and hold with a screw-driver or similar tool while the second is placed in position.

Fit striking fork shaft and screw it into the case.

Fit the remaining gears.

The chamfered side of the main axle pinion (13 teeth) is fitted first.

Fit end covers. (Para. 49.)

Check adjustment of the control rod.

The adjustment of the rod should allow the pins in the jaw points to be free when top or bottom gear is engaged.

Remove tubular distance piece from axle.

54. DISMANTLING OF POSITIVE FOOT CHANGE.

Remove outer end cover. (Para. 48.)

Remove return spring cover plate, held by two nuts.

Remove return spring.

Remove pawl carrier. This slides off the ratchet plate spindle, complete with the pawls and pawl spring.

Remove the ratchet lever, held to the back of the control box by a bolt with a spring and plain washer.

Remove the ratchet plate. At the back of the plate a plain steel washer is fitted.

At the back of the control box a plunger is fitted. The plunger engages in the back of the ratchet.

Remove the ratchet plunger by removing the dome nut at the back of the box, releasing the plunger and spring.

Remove the two nuts at the back of the box. These nuts lock the pawl carrier stops studs.

Remove the pawl carrier stop studs, screwed into the box.

Remove the cam plate.

Remove the pawls from the pawl carrier by removing the sleeved nut on the pawl pin. The end of the pawl pin with the screwdriver slot will have to be held while the nut is removed.

When the nut is removed, the pawls and the return spring are free.

55. ASSEMBLY OF POSITIVE FOOT CONTROL.

Fit the pawls and spring to the pawl carrier. When the nut is tight, the pawls must have free movement.

Place cam plate in position and fit the two carrier stops holding the cam plate.

Fit the carrier stop stud locknuts at the back of the box.

Fit the ratchet plate, the splined end of the spindle through bush in the cam plate, the steel washer between the ratchet and box.

Fit the felt washer onto the splined end of the shaft and into the boss on the back of the box.

Fit the ratchet lever, as high as possible with the bottom gears engaged.

Fit the remaining bolt and washers, the spring washer next to the bolt head.

Fit the plunger and spring.

Fit the pawl carrier complete with the pawls. The pawls can be sprung into position with a screwdriver.

Fit return spring cover and the two nuts and grease as necessary.

Fit outer cover, gear lever, and gear indicator. Fit kick-starter crank.

WHEELS AND HUBS.

56. FRONT WHEEL, REMOVAL.

Place machine on both stands. Detach brake cable from cam lever and cable adjuster from brake plate. Remove spindle nut from off-side of spindle. Slacken pinch bolt in near side fork end. Take the weight of the wheel in the left hand and withdraw the spindle by means of a Tommy Bar placed through the hole in the head of the spindle.

57. FRONT WHEEL, FITTING.

Re-assemble in the reverse order. Insert spindle from near side. Lock pinch bolt in near side fork end after tightening the spindle nut.

58. REAR WHEEL, REMOVAL RIGID FRAME.

Place machine on the rear stand. Roll back the rubber tube on the rear lamp lead, exposing the brass connection. Break the wire by parting the connector. Remove the tail piece of the mudguard by removing the two bolts holding it to the main portion and the two bolts at the bottom of the tail piece holding the stays.

Disconnect speedometer driving cable. Remove wheel spindle, distance piece and speedometer driving box.

Remove the hub stud nuts, draw the wheel clear of the three studs and the wheel will drop to the ground.

When the wheel has been removed by the

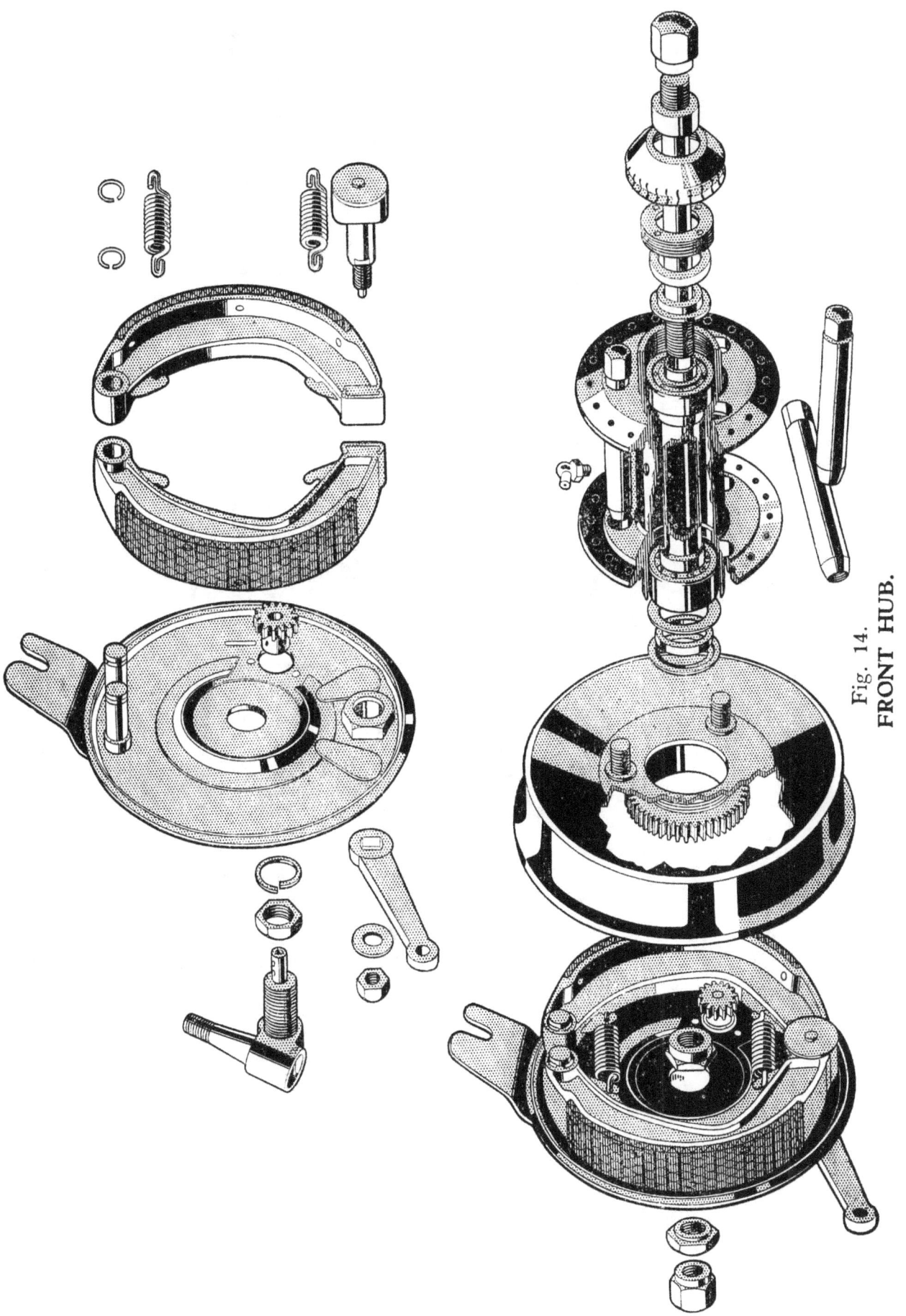

Fig. 14.
FRONT HUB.

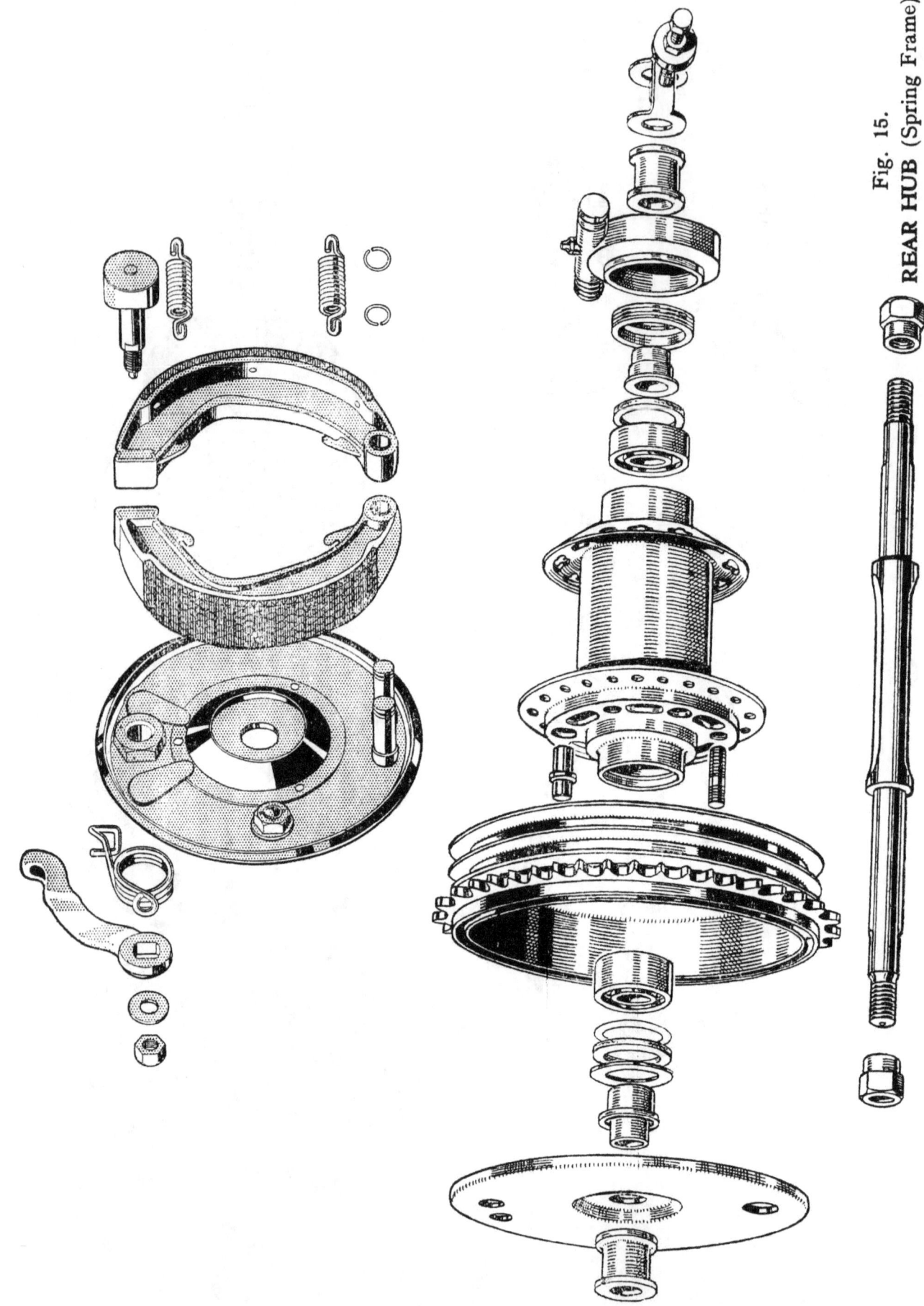

Fig. 15. **REAR HUB** (Spring Frame)

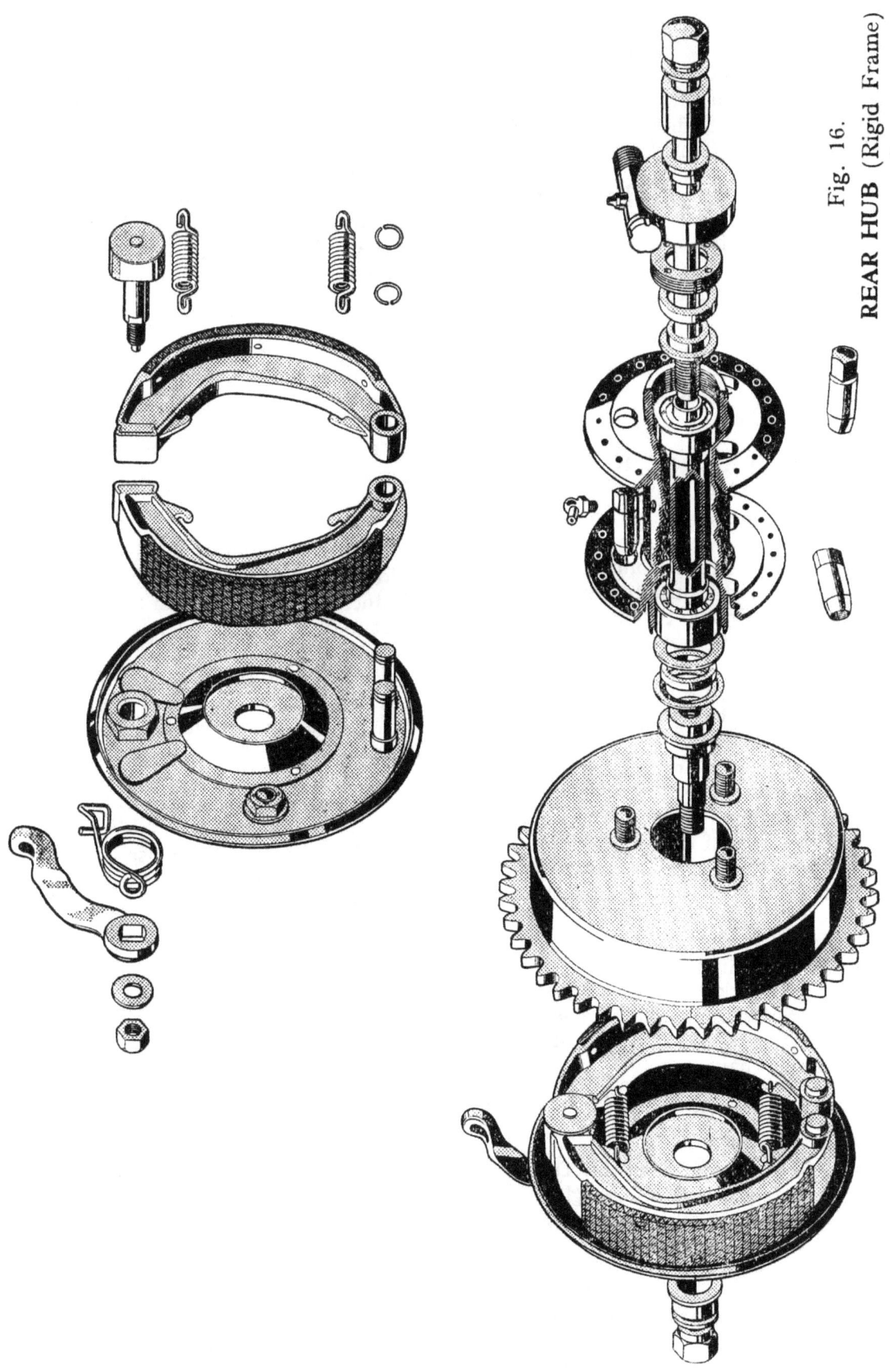

Fig. 16. **REAR HUB** (Rigid Frame)

above method, the brake drum is left in position.

To remove the wheel complete with brake drum, remove tail piece of mudguard, rear chain, anchorage bolt holding the brake anchorage arm to the frame and ease the spindle nuts, when the wheel can be removed from the fork ends of the frame.

59. REAR WHEEL, FITTING. RIGID FRAME.

When refitting the wheel, reverse the removal operations.

Ensure that the spindle is hard against the chain adjusters.

When refitting the chain spring link ensure that the closed end of the spring faces the direction of travel of the chain.

Check rear brake.

60. REAR WHEEL, REMOVAL. SPRING FRAME.

With machine on rear stand, remove rear chain and mudguard tail piece. Disconnect tail lamp lead at the brass connection.

Remove brake rod adjusting nut. Disconnect speedometer drive. Slacken rear wheel spindle nuts and withdraw the wheel from the fork ends.

61. REAR WHEEL, REFITTING. SPRING FRAME.

See that fork ends are lying reasonably parallel. Place wheel in position ensuring that the ears of the adjusting stirrup are lying flat against the sides of the fork end and that the cupped adjuster washer is located on the small shoulder at the open end of the fork end slot.

Make sure that the anchor pad on the brake plate is entering the slot on the inside of the near-side fork end.

Fit rear chain with the closed end of the spring connecting clip facing the direction of travel of the chain.

Track up the wheel and adjust until there is $\frac{3}{8}''$ to $\frac{1}{2}''$ up and down movement midway between the sprockets.

NOTE.—It is important that this condition is obtained with the weight of the machine on the rear wheel.

Adjust brake rod as necessary. Reconnect speedometer drive.

62. DISMANTLING SPRING FRAME REAR HUB.

Remove rear wheel complete. (Para. 60.) Remove spindle nuts, adjusting stirrups, brake plate, speedometer driving box and distance pieces.

Remove ball-race locking ring from plain side of hubshell.

Remove distance piece and felt washer Knock out the spindle and it will bring with it the single row bearing fitted to the plain side of the hub.

Drift out the remaining bearing together with the peened in washer, the felt and pen steel washers fitted into the brake drum side of the hubshell. Separate brake drum and hubshell if necessary.

63. RE-ASSEMBLING SPRING FRAME REAR HUB.

Re-assemble in reverse order.

Pack bearings with grease before assembly. Ensure that long end of spindle protrudes through the brake side of the hub.

64. REAR HUB, DISMANTLING. RIGID FRAME.

Remove rear wheel. (Para. 58.)

Remove locking ring, felt washer and distance piece from plain side of hub.

Drift out inner sleeve, it will bring with it the single row bearing.

Using a suitable punch knock out the bearing in the brake side of the hub, together with the peened in washer, felt washer and pen steel washer.

65. REAR HUB, RE-ASSEMBLY. RIGID FRAME.

Pack bearings with grease.

Fit single row bearing to screwed side of hub.

Fit inner sleeve, the long end into the single row bearing.

Fit distance piece, felt washer and locking ring and tighten.

Press double row bearing into position in opposite side of hub, followed by the pen steel washer, felt washer and the dished washer. Lightly rivet the dished washer into position.

66. FRONT HUB, DISMANTLING.

With machine on both stands remove front wheel. (Para. 56.)

Remove brake plate together with its inner and outer distance piece.

Remove locking ring, felt washer and distance piece from opposite side of hub.

With suitable punch knock the bearing in the brake side further into the hub, until the single row bearing drops clear.

Remove distance tube.

From this side of the hub, drift out the remaining bearing, together with the peened in washer, felt washer and pen steel washer.

67. FRONT HUB, RE-ASSEMBLING.

Pack bearings with grease.

Press single row bearing into position followed by the distance piece (with collar against the bearing) felt washer and locking ring which can be tightened up.

Insert distance tube through brake side of hub, ensuring that it is right home against the bearing just fitted.

Press double row bearing into position.

Fit pen steel washer and felt washer.

Lightly rivet remaining washer into its recess.

BRAKES.

68. DISMANTLING OF THE BRAKES.

Remove brake plate from the drum.

Remove brake lever return spring from the lever.

Remove nut and washer from the cam spindle.

Remove brake lever.

Remove cam and spindle from bush in the brake plate.

Tap the end of the spindle lightly until the cam is clear of the shoes.

Remove brake shoe return springs.

Remove the circlips retaining shoes to the pivot pins.

Remove the brake shoes.

Cam spindle bush can be removed from the plate after removing the nut holding bush to the plate.

69. ASSEMBLY OF BRAKES.

Fit cam spindle bush to plate.

Fit brake shoes. Smear a little oil on the pivot pins.

Fit ONE shoe to pivot pin.

Fit spring to the shoe fitted to the pin, near pin.

Hold second shoe near to the one fitted and fit the spring, stretch the spring and fit second shoe to pivot pin.

Fit second spring to both shoes.

Fit cam spindle to plate. Hold shoes apart with screwdriver or similar tool and allow cam to pass the ends of the shoes.

Fit NEW circlips to pivot pins.

This is simplified if a length of rod is obtained with the same diameter as the pivot pin.

Fit circlip to the rod.

Place a piece of tubing over the rod. Place rod at the end of the pivot pin. Tap end of tube and circlip is forced on to the pin and into the groove.

FRONT FORKS.

70. MAINTENANCE.

Replenish damping oil at approximately 5,000 mile intervals.

Remove hexagon headed filler plug from top of each fork leg. Remove drain plug from each fork end. Allow oil to drain out and operate the forks a time or two to eject the last drops.

Replace drain plugs.

Refill each leg with a measured ½ pint of Wakefield's Castrolite, Single Shell or Price's Motorine E. Work the forks a few times to remove any air-locks.

Replace filler plugs.

71. STEERING HEAD ADJUSTMENT.

Place a wooden block or box under the engine cradle of sufficient height to raise the front wheel clear of the ground. Place thumb of left hand on the joint between the steering head of the frame and the fork head clip.

Attempt to lift the forks with the right hand. Any movement at the head races will be readily felt.

To adjust, slacken the steering column locking nut and the pinch bolt clamping each leg into the fork crown.

Adjust by means of the nut situated on the steering column below the head clip, until all play is removed, but the forks are still free to rotate on the head races.

Re-tighten the steering column locking nut and the pinch bolts.

72. REMOVAL OF FRONT FORKS FROM FRAME.

This may be carried out either with or without the front wheel and mudguard in position.

Remove switch panel from headlamp.

Detach steering damper arm from frame.

Detach speedometer driving and lighting cables from speedometer head.

Remove all cables from the handlebar levers, remove handlebars.

Slacken off steering damper completely, remove steering column locking nut complete with damper knob and rod.

Remove oil filler plugs and speedometer panel.

Remove head clip and head race adjusting nut.

Withdraw forks carefully to avoid losing any head race balls.

Take care to avoid spilling any damping oil from the fork legs. If any oil is lost it will be necessary to replenish as instructed. (Para. 70.)

73. FITTING OF FORKS TO THE FRAME.

Examine head races and balls (17 per race).

Races are pressed into their housings and may readily be knocked out for renewal.

Note that the races fitted in the frame embody a small hole to allow the entry of grease.

Liberally grease the track in the race fitted to the bottom of the steering column and the top frame race. Place 17 balls in position in each and carefully insert the column through the frame.

Place the top race and dust cover in position and screw the adjusting nut down the column till the hexagon is finger tight against the top race.

Refit the head clip and speedometer panel, the column locking nut loosely and the filler plugs which should be tightened up.

Adjust the head races. (Para. 71.)

Refit all remaining parts and check that all bolts and nuts have been tightened.

74. FORK LEG, DISMANTLING.

This may be carried out with the forks in position, but before commencing the work it is advisable to obtain from our Service Department a "pull through" to facilitate removal and replacement of the main tube.

Remove front wheel. (Para. 56.)

Remove front mudguard.

Remove oil filler and drain plugs from top and bottom of fork leg and allow oil to drain off.

Slacken the pinch bolt in the crown lug.

Fork end, complete with bottom cover, springs and main tube may be withdrawn.

If difficulty is encountered the "pull-through" already mentioned should be screwed into the top of the main tube which can then be tapped out with a mallet.

Remove from the main tube the top leather washer (this may have stuck to the inside of the upper cover), the short buffer spring and main spring.

Remove the bottom cover, held to the fork end by two screws.

Remove leather washer.

Remove locking ring from top of fork end.

Withdraw fork end from main tube.

The remaining components may now be removed from the main tube.

75. FORK LEG, ASSEMBLY.

Thoroughly clean all components and obtain any renewals necessary.

Attach the bottom bush to the main tube by means of the securing nut.

Place fork end in position on the main tube.

Fit shouldered bush into fork end followed by the super oil seal, being very careful that the leather has its radiused side uppermost.

Screw home the locking ring and tighten sufficiently to be secure without distorting the case of the super oil seal.

Fit the smaller of the two leather washers over the locking ring followed by the main spring, the buffer spring and the remaining leather washer.

Fit bottom cover and securing screws.

Screw "pull-through" into top end of main tube and pass through crown lug and head clip.

Draw into position by means of Tommy Bar inserted across the "pull-through," and temporarily tighten the pinch bolt in the crown lug.

Remove "pull-through."

Fit filler plug to main tube and slacken pinch bolt. Lock main tube in position with filler plug. Re-tighten pinch bolt.

Fit drain plug to fork end.

Remove filler plug.

Replenish with oil. (Para. 70.)

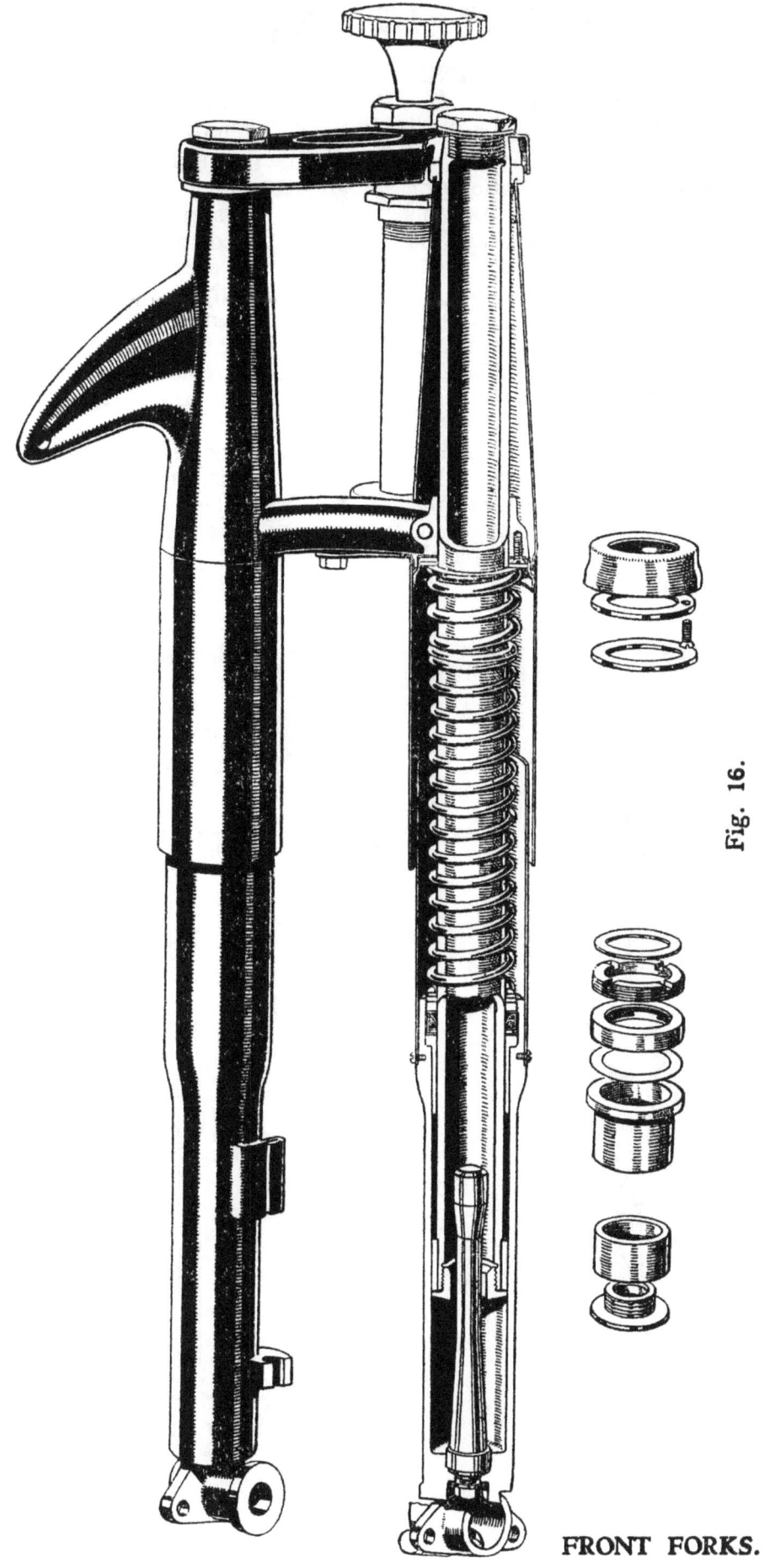

Fig. 16.

FRONT FORKS.

SPRING FRAME.

76. DISMANTLING REAR SPRINGING.

Remove rear wheel (Para. 60.)

Slacken the pinch bolt across the top of the rear frame member.

Unscrew the locking bolt at bottom of stationary bearer rod a few turns and tap the bolt head with a hammer to release the bearer rod from its taper.

Remove bottom bolt.

Withdraw bearer rod upwards.

Insert a tyre lever or large screw driver between the frame member and the side of the top and bottom spring covers.

Lever sideways until sufficient of the central hole is exposed beyond the edge of the rear member to insert a $\frac{1}{4}''$ or $5/16''$ diameter rod fitted with suitable washers and wing nuts into the hole to prevent the assembly flying apart when completely removed from the frame.

77. RE-ASSEMBLY OF REAR SPRINGING.

Thoroughly clean all components and smear the bearing surfaces with oil or grease.

Fit the springs and covers to the fork ends and compress the assembly by means of the rod used during dismantling, until it is sufficiently compressed to enter the jaw of the rear member.

Place the assembly as far as possible into the jaw, remove the rod and tap the assembly into an approximately central position.

Smear the bearer rod with oil and insert taper end first into the upper end of the rear frame member.

Push or tap the bearer rod right home.

Fit and tighten bottom bolt.

Tighten top pinch bolt.

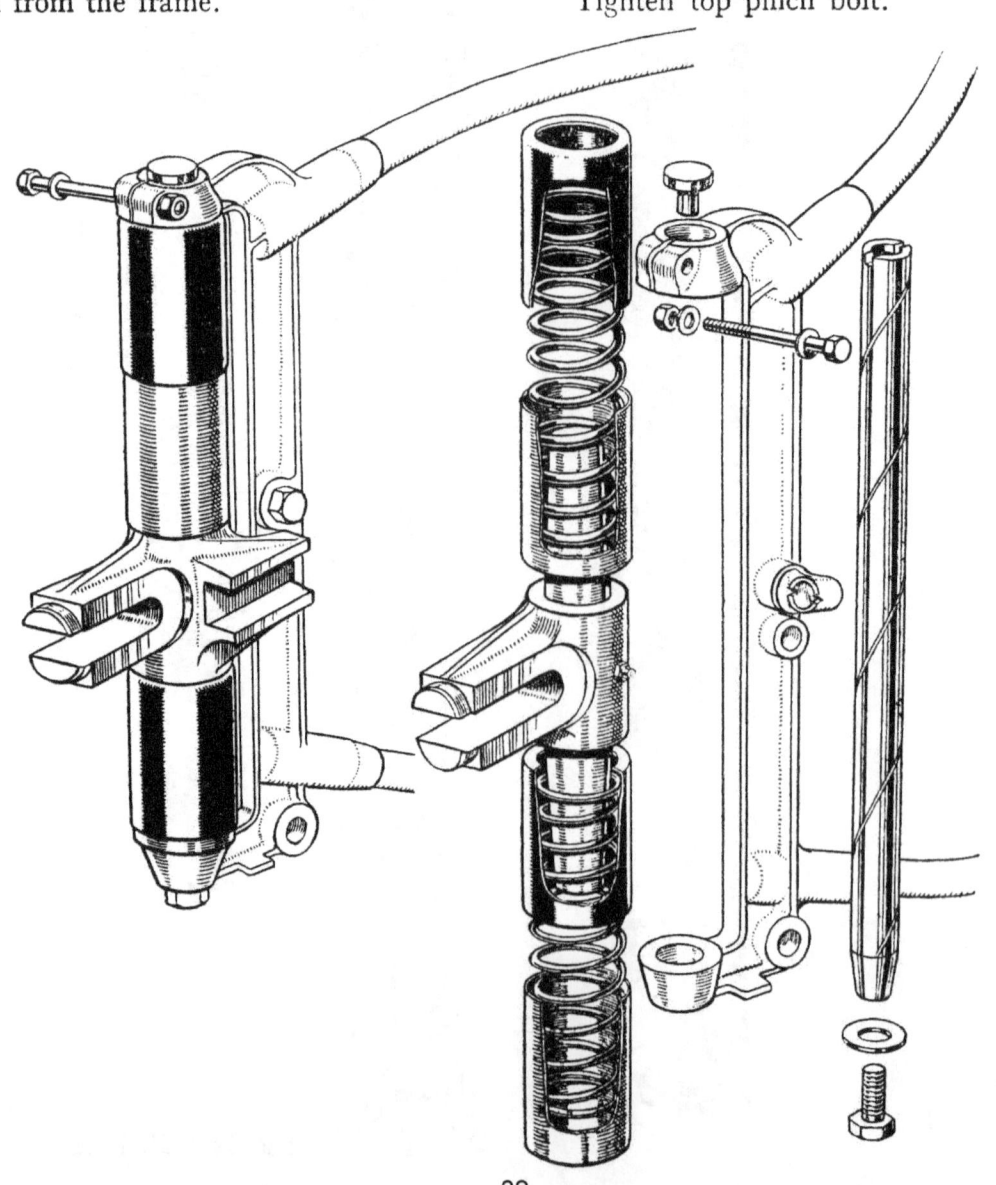

HANDLEBAR FITTINGS.

78. IGNITION AND AIR CONTROL LEVERS.

The ignition and air control levers are shown in Fig. 18 in the position in which they should be assembled, having first greased both sides of the lever.

After fitting the adjusting nut it should be tightened to give the required tension.

To remove the control cables from the lever, open the lever as far as possible, hold the outer cable, and as the lever is closed, pull the outer cable from the lever body.

Remove nipple from the lever.

To fit the cables, fit nipple into the lever, close the lever, pull the outer cable away from the lever and fit the cable to the lever body.

79. CLUTCH AND FRONT BRAKE CONTROL LEVERS.

The clutch and front brake controls are so simple as to require no instructions for their dismantling or assembly.

The pivot bolts have shoulders machined on them, allowing the nuts on the bolts to be tightened while allowing clearance for easy movement of the lever.

To remove the clutch cable from the lever, turn the clutch operating arm on the clutch worm by other means than the cable, and the nipple can be removed from the arm, and inner and outer cables can be removed from the lever.

To remove the brake cable from the lever, remove the split cotter and pin holding the " U " clip to the brake arm, and the inner and outer cables can be removed from the lever.

Re-assemble in the reverse order.

80. EXHAUST LIFTER LEVER.

The arrangement of the exhaust lifter lever is similar to the clutch and brake, only smaller.

To remove the cables from the lever, turn the operating arm on the exhaust lifter by other means than the cable and remove the inner cable from the arm. Remove the nipple on the other end of the cable from the lever and the nipple will pass through the large hole in the lever body.

When re-assembling, the cables must be fitted to the lever first.

Fig. 17.
TWIST GRIP.

Fig. 18.
IGNITION AND AIR CONTROL.

81. TWIST GRIP.

The twist grip assembly is shown in Fig. 17.

To assemble the twist grip, grease the portion of the handlebar where the grip works.

Fit the sleeve to the bar.

Grease the drum on the sleeve.

Fit spring and adjuster bolt and nut to the bottom half clip.

Thread the cable through the hole in the half clip.

Fit the nipple to the drum on the sleeve.

(Sufficient length of cable can be obtained by lifting the throttle slide and holding in position by piece of soft wood placed in the air intake.)

Fit the top half clip.

Adjust the tightness of the grip with the adjusting screw and lock in the desired position.

Dismantle in the reverse order.

AMAL CARBURETTER.

82. DISMANTLING OF THE CARBURETTER.

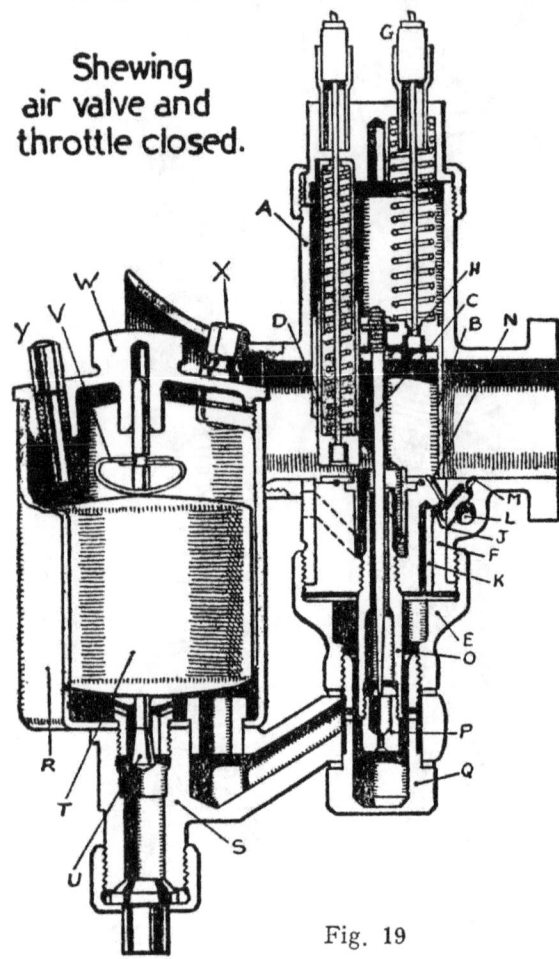

Shewing air valve and throttle closed.

Fig. 19

A. Mixture Chamber.
B. Throttle Valve.
C. Jet Needle and Clip.
D. Air Valve.
E. Mixing Chamber Union Nut.
F. Jet Block.
G. Cable Adjusters.
H. Jet Block Barrel.
J. Pilot Jet.
K. Passage to Pilot.
L. Pilot Air Passage.
M. Pilot Outlet.
N. Pilot By-pass.
O. Needle Jet.
P. Main Jet.
Q. Float Chamber Holding Bolt.
R. Float Chamber.
S. Needle Seating.
T. Float.
U. Float Needle.
V. Float Spring Clip.
W. Float Chamber Cover.
X. Float Chamber Lock Screw.
Y. Tickler.

Remove the carburetter.

Remove the slides and needle. The slides and needle can be examined without removing the cables.

The throttle slide is the one that is drum-shaped and has the jet needle attached to it.

To remove the throttle slide from the cable, compress the spring, allowing the nipple on the end of the cable to leave the hole in which it is fitted, and on releasing the spring allow the nipple to pass through the larger hole, and the slide is free from the cable.

To remove the air slide, compress spring as before and release nipple from the end of the slide, and the slide is free.

To remove the needle from the throttle slide, remove the spring clip at the top of the slide. The needle is normally fitted into the middle notch.

The lower the needle the weaker the mixture.

Remove the float chamber. It is held by a bolt at the base of the mixing chamber. There are two fibre washers on this bolt, one under the head and one between the float and mixing chambers.

To remove the float and needle.

Release the float chamber cap locking screw and remove the cap.

Compress the spring clip on the top of the float and lift float from the chamber.

Remove the bolt at the base of the float chamber, and the needle will fall out.

On the bolt at the base of the float chamber two fibre washers are fitted in the same order as on the bolt at the base of the mixing chamber.

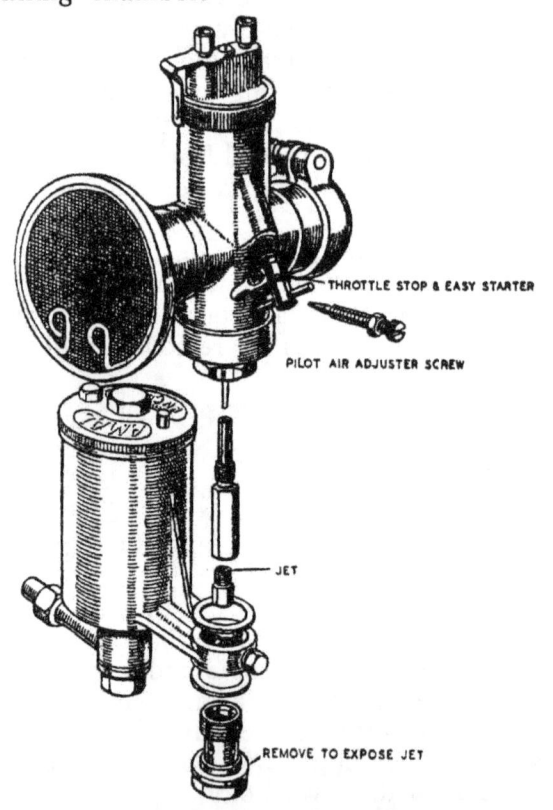

VIEW OF CARBURETTER.
Fig. 20.

Remove the jet. The main jet is now exposed and can be removed from the needle jet.

Remove the needle jet from the jet block.

Remove the jet block by removing the union nut at the base of the mixing chamber.

83. RE-ASSEMBLY OF THE CARBURETTER.

Fit needle jet to the jet block.

Fit main jet to needle jet.

Fit jet block to mixing chamber, located by groove and pin.

Fit mixing chamber union nut and fibre washer.

Fit float to the float chamber.

Fit float needle through the base of the chamber and the centre of the float, compress the spring clip on the top of the float and allow the needle to enter the clip.

Release the clip and the clip will drop into the groove in the needle.

Fit the chamber top and lock with the locking bolt.

Fit the chamber to the mixing chamber. (Two fibre washers.)

Fit the bolt holding the union to the base of the float chamber. (Two fibre washers.)

Fit needle to throttle slide in middle position.

Thread cables through the mixing chamber, the throttle cable to be nearer to the cylinder barrel. The throttle cable has the shorter length of inner cable protruding from the outer cable.

Fit return springs to cables, the larger to the throttle.

Fit slides to cables.

Fit air slide to throttle slide.

Fit slides to the mixing chamber, carefully entering the needle into the needle jet. DO NOT FORCE.

Fit mixing chamber top.

Fit carburetter upright on induction stub.

84. SLOW RUNNING ADJUSTMENT

Start engine and screw pilot air adjuster (Fig. 20) right home whilst carefully closing the throttle. The engine should now eight stroke and run heavily.

Gradually unscrew the pilot air screw; the engine speed will increase and the throttle will need further closing.

Repeat the process until by a combination of throttle and pilot air adjustment a regular even slow running is obtained.

85. THROTTLE STOP AND STARTING SETTING.

It is desirable to be able to close the twist grip completely without the engine stopping, for this purpose an adjustable throttle stop is provided (Fig. 20).

Slacken the small screwdriver headed locking pin and holding the shaped stop piece against the mixing chamber body with the left thumb, rotate the adjuster until a slight increase in engine revolutions is heard.

Turn the adjuster back until the engine resumes its original speed and re-tighten the screw.

For easy starting rotate the adjustment as far as possible in a clockwise direction. This will raise the throttle slide to the best starting position. Return the adjuster to its normal position after starting.

86. FLOAT CHAMBER.

The function of the float chamber is to control the petrol in the carburetter at the correct level and anything which upsets its correct working will cause constant flooding, heavy engine running and high petrol consumption.

Dirt on the needle seating, a bent needle, a punctured float, a badly worn needle, or a carburetter not fitted upright will all give the above symptoms.

87. MIXTURE ADJUSTMENT.

The pilot air adjuster controls the mixture of air and petrol up to $\frac{1}{8}$ throttle opening, from $\frac{1}{8}$ to $\frac{3}{4}$ throttle the mixture is controlled by the needle in the throttle valve. From $\frac{3}{4}$ to full throttle the main jet is the control. Weak mixture is indicated by spitting and blue flames from the carburetter, pinking, running hot and plug points showing indications of intense heat.

To cure, raise needle in throttle valve one notch.

Rich mixture is indicated by thumpy running, black exhaust and the engine does not respond readily to throttle opening.

To remedy lower the needle.

88. CARBURETTER MAINTENANCE.

Clean regularly by dismantling and washing in clean petrol.

Clean all holes with a fine bristle.

Renew any worn or damaged parts.

LEGSHIELDS.

89.

A standard set of these Legshield fittings comprises:—

- 2 Legshield Blades.
- 2 Legshield Blade Brackets.
- 2 Legshield Blade Brackets Back Plates.
- 4 ¼" pins and nuts for above.
- 1 Horn Bracket extension plate with ⅜" pin and nut.
- 1 7/16" dia. rod 24½" long with nuts.
- 1 7/16 dia. rod 23.7/16" long with nuts.
- 1 Distance tube 13⅛" long.
- 1 Distance tube 6⅞" long.
- 1 Distance tube 5⅞" long.
- 2 Distance tubes 1.7/16" long.
- 4 Distance tubes 3⅜" long.
- 2 Legshield Attachment brackets for tank platform.
- 2 Thin tank rubbers.

90. FITTING INSTRUCTIONS.

Remove the front petrol tank bolts and slacken the rear bolts.

Remove the front tank platform top rubbers and replace with the thin rubbers supplied.

Over the rubbers place the attachment brackets so that the arm with the 7/16" hole points downwards and is to the rear of the tank bolt. Place the plain steel washers from under the tank over the brackets and insert the front tank bolts through the middle of the three holes in the attachment brackets but do not tighten up.

Place the 13⅛" distance tube between the legs of the attachment brackets, insert the longer of the 7/16" dia. rods and in each end place a 1.7/16" distance tube.

Remove crankcase engine plate bolt carrying the horn and insert in its place the remaining 7/16" rod. Attach the extension bracket to the horn and place in position on the left hand end of the rod.

Fit the 5⅛" distance tube next to the horn and the 6⅞" tube on the opposite side.

Fit the legshield brackets loosely to the blades, place the 3⅜" distance tubes between the bracket arms and fit the legshield to the rods with the deep valance on the inside, nearest the engine.

Fit the securing rod nuts. Tighten all nuts and bolts.

TYRES.

91. MAINTENANCE.

Keep tyres at correct pressures. See data sheet.

Examine regularly and remove any flints, etc., which may have become embedded in the tread.

Replace valve cap as soon as possible should one become lost.

92. REMOVAL.

Deflate tube by removing valve inner.

Remove valve nut and push the bead of the cover into the well of the rim at a point opposite the valve, and proceed to remove cover, commencing at the valve.

Remove one side completely.

Remove tube and other side of cover.

93. FITTING.

Lubricate with french chalk the cover beads, inner tube, and inside of rim.

Fit one side of cover, fit inner tube and inflate slightly.

Ensure that valve is protruding squarely through the rim.

Fit remaining side of cover, commencing opposite the valve and forcing the cover into the well of the rim.

Inflate to recommended pressure.

ELECTRICAL SECTION.

94. ESSENTIAL MAINTENANCE.

Battery. Inspect the battery regularly and keep acid level to the top of the separators by adding distilled water.

UNLESS YOU DO THIS YOUR BATTERY WILL QUICKLY DETERIORATE.

Wiring. Keep all connections and terminals tight. See that the cables are clear of moving parts.

Dynamo. Keep brushes and commutator clean. (Para. 102.)

Magneto. Keep contact breaker clean. If necessary polish the contacts with fine carborundum stone or emery cloth and afterwards wipe with cloth moistened with petrol. (Para. 97.) Occasionally check contact breaker opening (using gauge on ignition spanner). (Para. 96.)

Replace high-tension cable if it becomes worn or perished.

Head Lamp. Focus head lamp after fitting new bulb. (Para. 107.)

IGNITION.

95. LUBRICATION.

The cam is lubricated by a wick, contained in the contact breaker base, which must be given a few drops of thin machine oil about every 2,500 miles.

To get at the wick, remove the spring arm carrying the moving contact and withdraw the screw carrying the wick. (Fig. 21.)

When replacing the contact breaker components see that the small backing spring is fitted immediately under the securing screw and spring washer, and that the bent portion faces outwards.

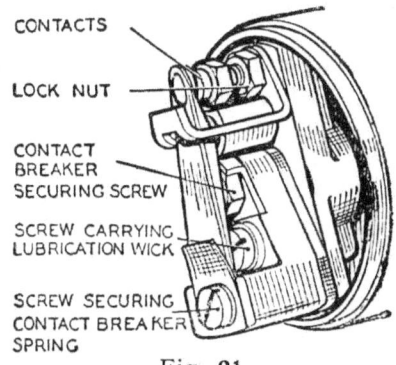

Fig. 21.

96. ADJUSTMENT.

After dismantling the contact breaker in order to lubricate, the contact setting should be checked.

Turn the engine until the contacts are fully opened and insert the gauge provided, .010 inch—.012 inch thickness, between the contacts.

The gauge should be a sliding fit.

If there is an appreciable variation from the gauge, slacken the lock nut and turn the contact screw by its hexagon head until the gap is set to the gauge.

Tighten the lock nut.

97. CONTACT BREAKER—CLEANING.

Remove the contact breaker cover and examine the contacts.

If they are dirty, they must be cleaned by polishing with a very fine carborundum stone or very fine emery cloth; afterwards wipe away any dirt or metal dust with a petrol-moistened cloth.

Cleaning of the contacts is made easier if the spring arm carrying the moving contact is removed as described in paragraph 95.

Examine the spring arm of the contact breaker and wipe away any rust.

Adjust as described in paragraph 96.

98. H.T. CABLE.

Should be 7 m/m. in diameter, rubber covered ignition cable.

The cable must be replaced if the rubber insulation has perished or shows cracks and becomes brittle.

To fit the new cable to the pick-up terminal, thread the knurled moulded nut over the lead, bare the cable for about ¼ inch, thread the wire through the metal washer

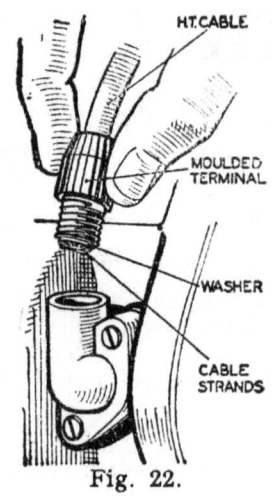

Fig. 22.

removed from the old cable and bend back the strands.

Finally, screw the nut into its terminal.

99. PICK-UP.

Examine the pick-up or high tension terminal (magneto end).

See that the carbon brush moves freely in its holder, being careful not to stretch the brush spring unduly.

While the pick-up is removed, clean the slip ring track and flanges by holding a soft cloth on the ring while the engine is slowly turned by hand.

100. SPARKING PLUG.

Clean periodically by dismantling and removing all carbon from the electrodes.

Scrape inside of plug body clean of carbon, re-assemble and set gap at .015"—.025".

LIGHTING AND ACCESSORIES.

101. DYNAMO—TO REMOVE AND REPLACE.

Take off the connections from the dynamo terminals.

Unscrew the hexagon headed nut from the driving end cover of the Magdyno.

Slacken the two screws securing the band clip, and draw the dynamo out of its mounting.

When replacing, slide the dynamo through the band clip so that fixing screw passes through its hole in the end cover and the gears mesh correctly.

Tighten the end nut and the band clip fixing screws and remake the connections to the dynamo terminals. Make certain that the dynamo is connected correctly, i.e., cable from cut-out and regulator terminal " D " to dynamo terminal " D " and cable from cut-out and regulator terminal " F " to dynamo terminal " F."

102. DYNAMO BRUSHES.

Test if brushes are sticking.

Clean with petrol, and if necessary ease the sides by lightly polishing on a smooth file.

Replace brushes in their original positions.

If the brushes are worn so that the flex is exposed on the running face, new brushes must be fitted.

Brushes are pre-formed so that bedding to the commutator is unnecessary.

A commutator in good condition will be smooth and free from pits or burned spots.

Clean the commutator with a petrol-moistened cloth.

If this is ineffective, carefully polish with a strip of very fine glass paper while rotating the armature.

103. LUBRICATION.

About every 4,000-5,000 miles add a few drops of good quality thin machine oil to the lubricator on the commutator end bracket. The bearing at the driving end is packed with grease which will last until it is necessary for the dynamo to undergo a complete overhaul.

104. CUT-OUT AND REGULATOR UNIT.

This unit (Fig. 24) which is housed beneath the saddle, consists of the cut-out

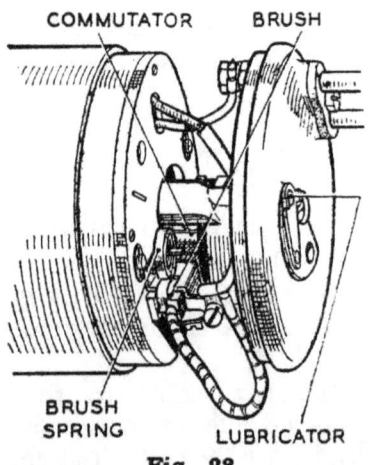

Fig. 23.

which is an automatic switch to prevent discharge of the battery when the dynamo is not charging, and the voltage regulator which controls the output of the dynamo. With a fully charged battery the dynamo is only permitted to pass a small charge to the battery, whilst with a fully discharged battery a heavy charge is passed in order to boost up the battery rapidly. Both components are accurately set and should not be tampered with or adjusted.

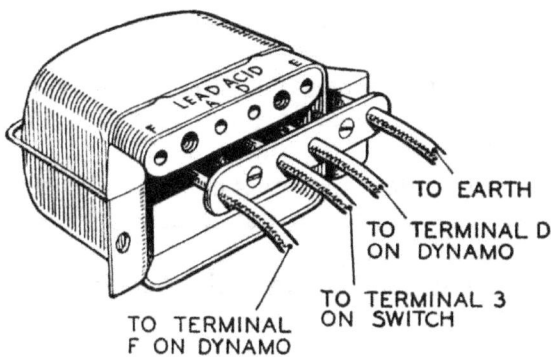

Fig. 24.

105. AMMETER.

Fitted in the switch panel of the headlamp, this instrument indicates when current is being taken from the battery in a greater quantity than is being fed to the battery (discharge).

It also shows when the dynamo is charging and hence by means of the regulator the state of charge of the battery.

106. BATTERY.

When examining a battery, do not hold naked lights near the vents as there is a danger of igniting the gas coming from the plates.

Remove the vent plugs and see that the ventilating holes in each are quite clear.

Remove any dirt by means of a bent wire.

A clogged vent plug will cause the pressure in the cell to increase, due to gases given off during charging, and this may cause damage.

Make sure that the rubber washer is fitted under each vent plug, otherwise the electrolyte may leak.

Battery—Topping-up.

About once a month, remove the battery lid, unscrew the filler caps and pour a small quantity of **distilled** water into each of the cells to bring the acid level with tops of the separators.

Acid must not be added to the battery unless some is accidentally spilled.

Should this happen, the loss must be made good with acid diluted to the same specific gravity as the acid in the cells.

This should be measured by means of a hydrometer.

Checking Battery condition.

The state of charge of the battery should be examined by taking hydrometer readings of the specific gravity of the acid in the cells.

The specific gravity readings and their indications are as follows:—

1.280—1.300. Battery fully charged.
About—1.210. Battery about half discharged.
Below—1.150. Battery fully discharged.

These figures are given assuming the temperature of the acid is about 60° F.

Each reading should be approximately the same.

If one cell gives a reading very different from the rest, it may be that the acid has been spilled or has leaked from this particular cell, or there may be a short circuit between the plates.

This will necessitate its return to a Repair Depot for rectification.

Wipe the top of the battery to remove all dirt or water.

Note.

Do not leave the battery in a discharged condition for any length of time.

If a motor cycle is to be out of use, the battery must first be fully charged, and afterwards given a refreshing charge about every two weeks.

Earthing Connections.

Check that the lead from the negative terminal is securely connected to the cycle frame or other suitable earth.

Charging.

If the previous tests indicate that the battery is merely discharged, and if the acid level is correct, the battery must be recharged from an external supply.

107. HEADLAMP.

Removing Lamp Front and Reflector. (Fig. 25.)

To remove the lamp front and reflector, release the fixing clip at the bottom of the lamp.

When replacing the front, locate the top of the rim first, then press on at the bottom and secure by means of the fixing clip.

To remove the bulb holder, press back the securing springs.

Setting and Focussing.

The lamp must be set to ensure that the main driving beam is projected parallel with the road surface.

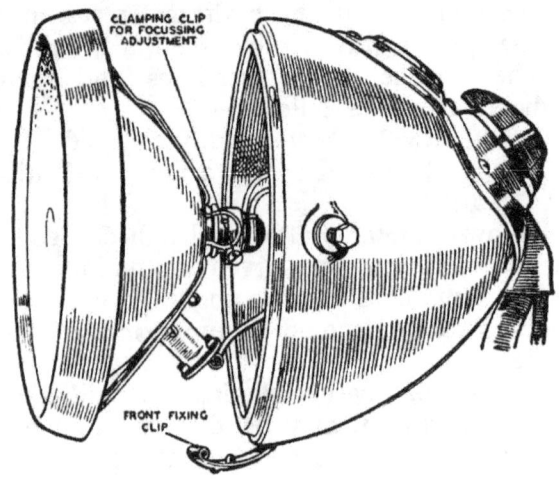

VIEW OF HEADLAMP.
Fig. 25.

To obtain the best driving light, the bulb should be correctly focussed in the reflector.

To adjust the position of the bulb, remove the front and reflector, and slacken the screw on the clamping clip at the back of the reflector.

Slide the bulb holder backwards or forwards until the best lighting is obtained and finally tighten the clamping screw.

Cleaning.

Care must be taken when handling the reflector to prevent it from becoming finger-marked.

It can, however, be cleaned by polishing with a fine chamois leather.

Metal polishes must **not** be used.

The bulbs should be a 6 volt, 24 watt double filament Lucas No. 70 (main), and a 6 volt, 3 watt S. B. C. (pilot), Lucas No. 200.

108. TAIL LAMP.

The rear portion of this lamp is removable for bulb replacement by giving it a half turn in an anti-clockwise direction, when it will become detached from its fixing.

The correct bulb is a 6 volt, 3 watt S.B.C. Lucas No. 200.

109. CABLES.

Before making any alterations to the wiring or removing the switch from the headlamp, disconnect the positive lead at the battery to avoid the danger of short circuits.

The lead, about 1 foot long, from the positive battery terminal, is connected to the lead from the switch by means of a brass connector.

The connector is insulated by a rubber sleeve, which must be pushed back to allow the connector to be unscrewed.

Do not allow the brass connector to touch any metal part of the engine as this will short circuit the battery.

When connecting up again, pull the rubber sleeve over the connector.

110. LIGHTING SWITCH.

All leads to the headlamp are taken direct to the switch, which, together with the ammeter, is incorporated in a small panel.

The panel can be removed when the three fixing screws are withdrawn.

The ends of all the cables are identified by means of coloured sleevings.

The colour scheme and the diagram of connections are shown in the wiring diagram.

111. HORN.

Electric horns are adjusted to give their best performance before leaving the works and will give a long period of service without any attention.

If the horn becomes uncertain in action, or does not vibrate, it has not necessarily broken down.

The trouble may be due to a discharged battery or a loose connection, or short circuit in the wiring of the horn.

The performance of the horn may be upset by the fixing bolt working loose, or by the vibration of some part adjacent to the horn.

To check this, remove the horn from its mounting, hold it firmly in the hand by its bracket, and press the push.

If the note is still unsatisfactory, the horn may require adjustment and should be taken to a Lucas Service Station.

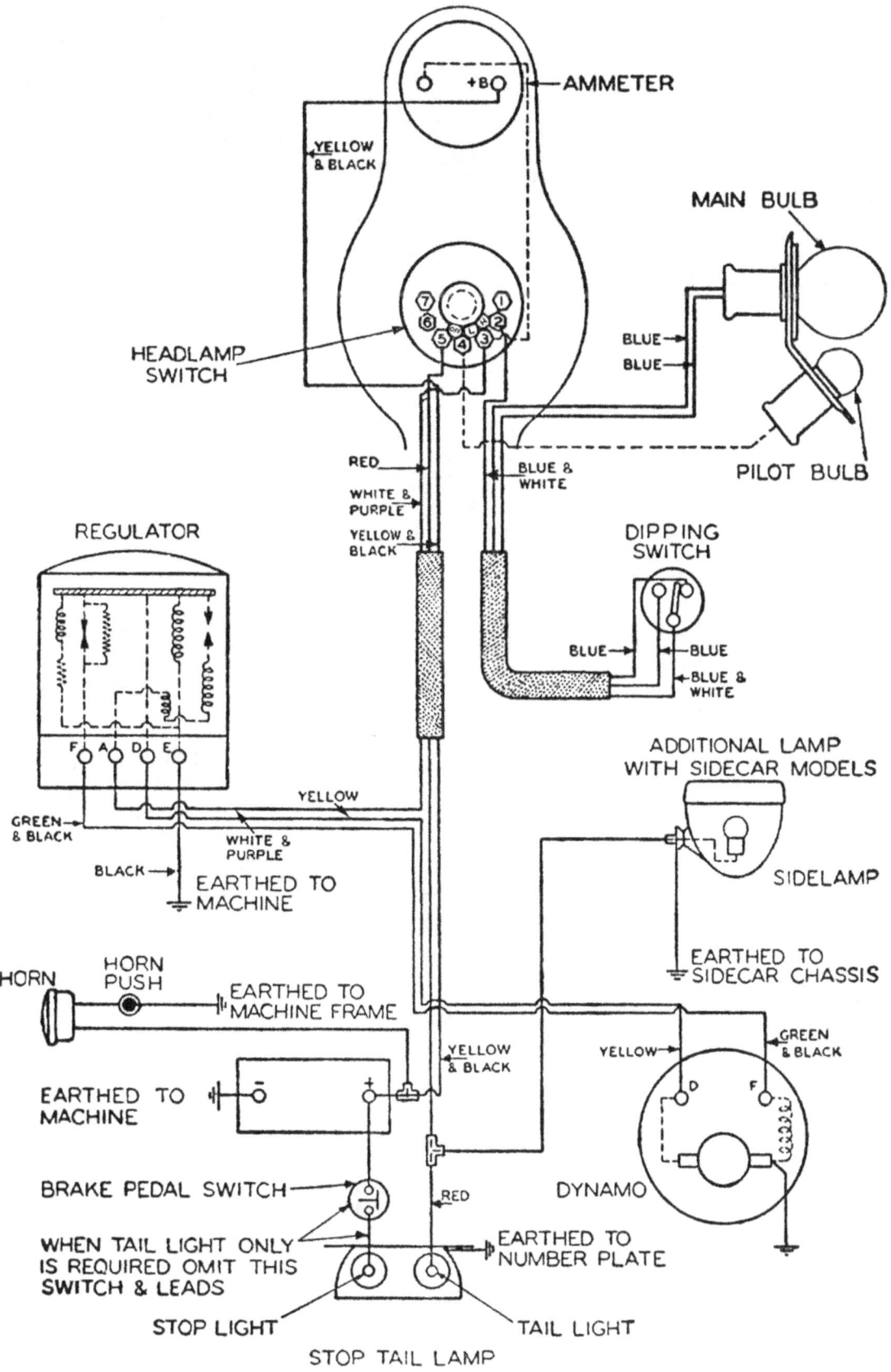

Wiring Diagram for 1937-47 Nortons with Lucas "Magdyno," DU Headlamp, and Compensated Voltage Control (no instrument panel)

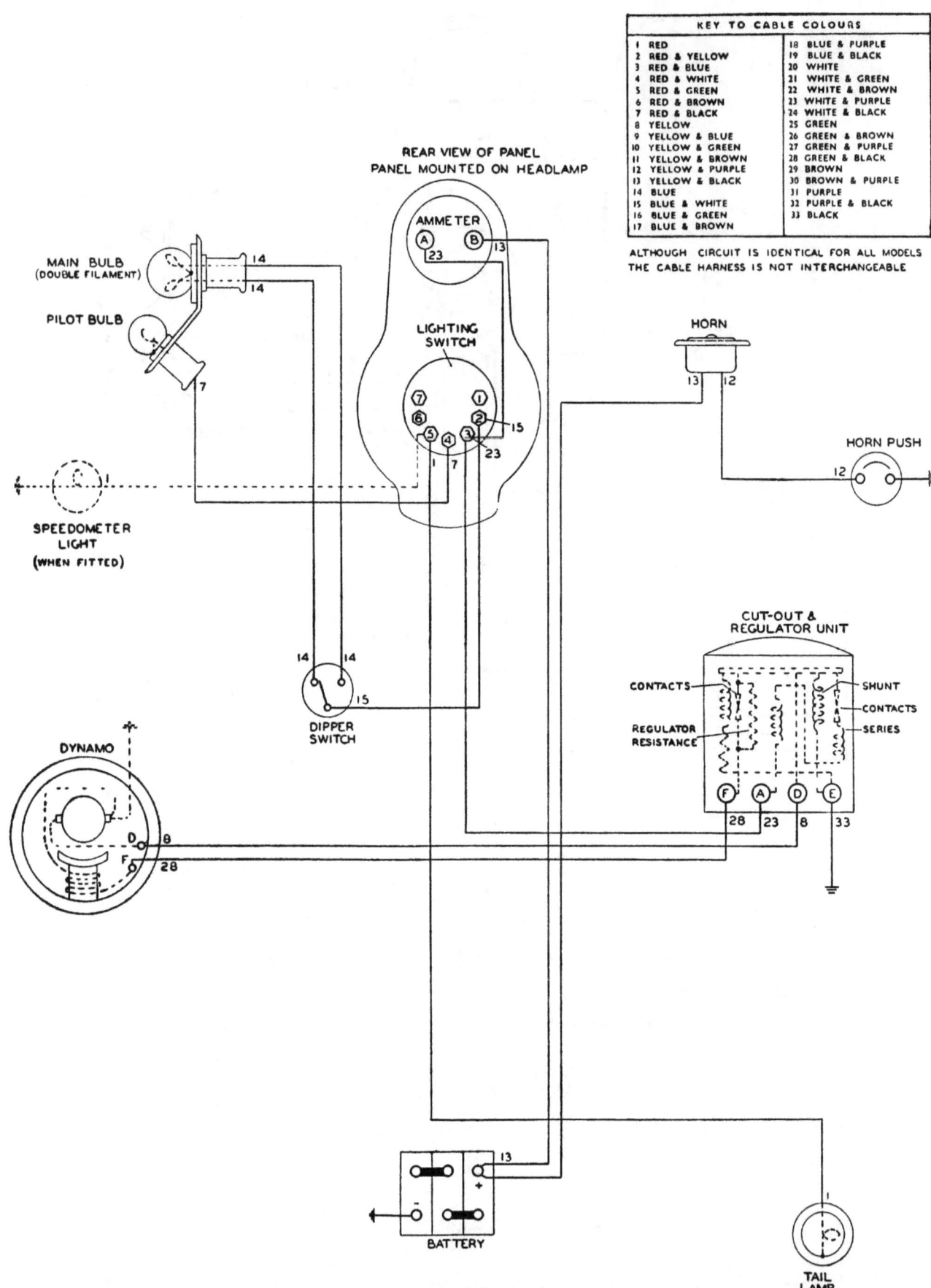

WIRING DIAGRAM FOR LUCAS MAGDYNO LIGHTING AND HORN EQUIPMENT.

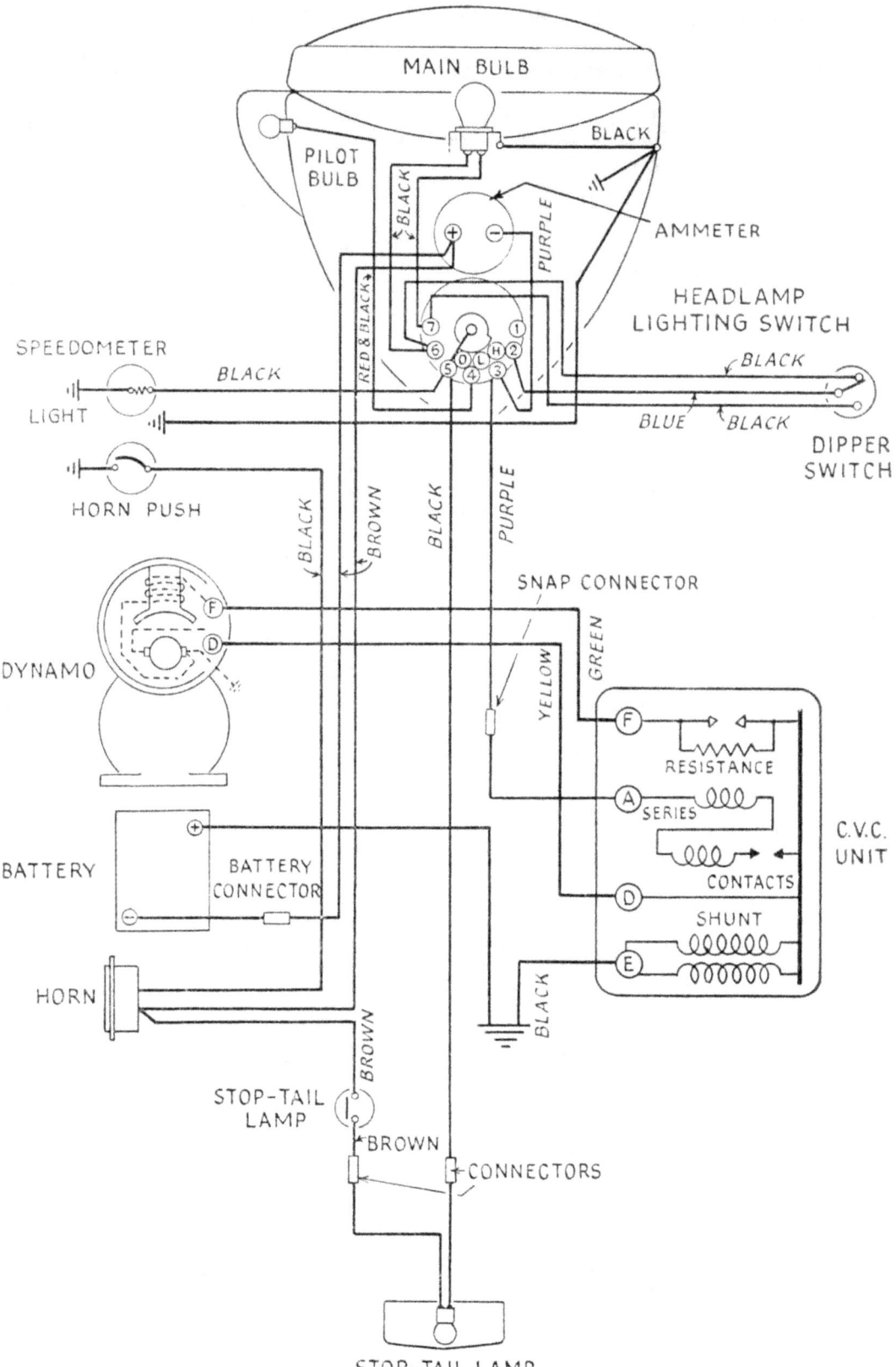

WIRING DIAGRAM FOR LUCAS "MAGDYNO" LIGHTING EQUIPMENT WITH SSU700P/1 HEADLAMP

This applies to 1953 to 1955 Nortons with compensated-voltage-control and a "positive earth" system of wiring. On 1955 models the lead to the stop-tail lamp is taken from the battery negative instead of from the horn. The battery positive lead has *black* sleeving.

LOCATING AND RECTIFYING POSSIBLE TROUBLES.

TROUBLE.	POSSIBLE CAUSES.	REMEDY.
Failure to Start.	Faulty plug. Faulty H.T. lead. Contact breaker points dirty or out of adjustment.	Remove plug, place plug body in contact with cylinder, revolve engine. If blue spark of fair intensity occurs, plug and ignition O.K.
	Pick-up brush worn or broken. Slip ring oily.	If no spark, change plug, and if still no spark, remove plug from H.T. lead, hold end of lead 1/8" from cylinder and revolve engine. In the event of there being still no spark, examine contact breaker points and check their gap. Examine pick-up brush and clean slip ring.
	Failure of petrol to reach mixing chamber.	Ensure that petrol is flowing down feed pipes. Clean carburetter.
	Broken throttle wire.	Ensure that throttle slide rises as twist grip is revolved.
Erratic Slow Running.	Pilot adjustment requires re-setting.	With throttle about 1/8" open and air closed, adjust pilot screw until good idling is obtained.
	Worn inlet valve guide.	Remove valve spring and test valve for side play in guide.
	Faulty valve seats.	Examine and re-grind as necessary.
Loss of Power.	No tappet clearance.	Check and re-set as required.
	Exhaust valve lifter holding valve off seat.	Ensure that there is some movement in cable before lever begins to lift valve.
	Front chain too tight.	Adjust.
	Loose carbon wedged on valve seat.	Can usually be removed by kicking engine over a few times.
	Broken piston rings.	Examine and replace as required.
Excessive Oil Consumption.	If accompanied by black smoke from exhaust, broken piston rings, worn rings or barrel.	Examine and make necessary replacements.
	Oil pump not returning.	With engine running an intermittent stream of oil should be seen upon opening oil tank filler cap.
	If unaccompanied by exhaust smoke, faulty oil pump timing cover connection.	Ensure that the necessary pressure is generated between timing cover and oil pump nipple fibre washers as instructed in para. 26.
Engine Runs Harshly.	Mag. chain too tight.	Adjust as in para. 32.
Engine Cuts Out at Large Throttle Openings.	Dirt in carburetter.	Clean and re-adjust.

LOCATING AND RECTIFYING POSSIBLE TROUBLES.

TROUBLE.	POSSIBLE CAUSES.	REMEDY.
Inefficient Brakes. (Front or Rear)	Grease on lining.	Examine and wash in petrol. Do not wash in paraffin.
	Tightness in mechanism.	Make sure that cam is free in its bearing and pedal not binding on spindle due to mud.
Slipping Clutch.	Cable adjusted too tightly.	Re-adjust cable until there is some movement on handle-bar lever before clutch operates.
	Inner cable too long. Clutch worm lever fouling gear box casing.	Shorten and re-adjust.
	Oil on plates (usually caused by overfilling oil bath).	Dismantle clutch plates and wash in petrol.
	Tightness in operating mechanism.	Examine, clean and free off as necessary.
Clutch Hard to Free.	Clutch cable adjuster screwed right out, clutch worm lever not at correct angle and therefore not having a straight pull.	Re-set clutch worm lever to give straight pull. Shorten inner cable and re-adjust.
Failure to Effect Gear-Changing.	Gearbox control rod out of adjustment. Over revving especially from 1st to 2nd.	Re-set as instructed in para. 53.
Gear-Changing Accompanied by Excessive Noise.	Slack rear chain.	Adjust as necessary.
Footchange Lever hard to Operate.	Footchange requires greasing.	Nipple on indicator retaining screw.
Failure of Footchange Lever to Return to Normal Position.	Broken hairpin return spring.	Remove positive mechanism cover and front plate. Examine spring, renew as required.
Steering Rolls or Wanders.	Loose head adjustment.	
Steering Poor on Corners with tendency for Machine to Lie over too much.	Loose fork adjustment.	
Whistling Noise from Front Wheel.	Speedo drive gear box requires greasing.	Use grease gun nipple on speedo gearbox.
Twist Grip Closes if Released.	Tension requires adjusting.	Screw in adjuster one or two turns.
Steering appears Tight on Corners.	Steering damper binding, caused by bent frame anchor bracket.	Remove anchor bracket and re-set to correct angle.

NOTES ON PARAGRAPH NUMBERING IN THE FOLLOWING APPENDIX

The appendix following this 1947 manual includes references to paragraph numbers. These references relate to paragraphs within the appendix, not the 1947 manual.

However, there is an exception regarding reference to paragraph 41 which is a duplication of that same paragraph in the 1947 manual. For the sake of convenience, it is reproduced below.

41. REMOVAL OF OIL BATH.

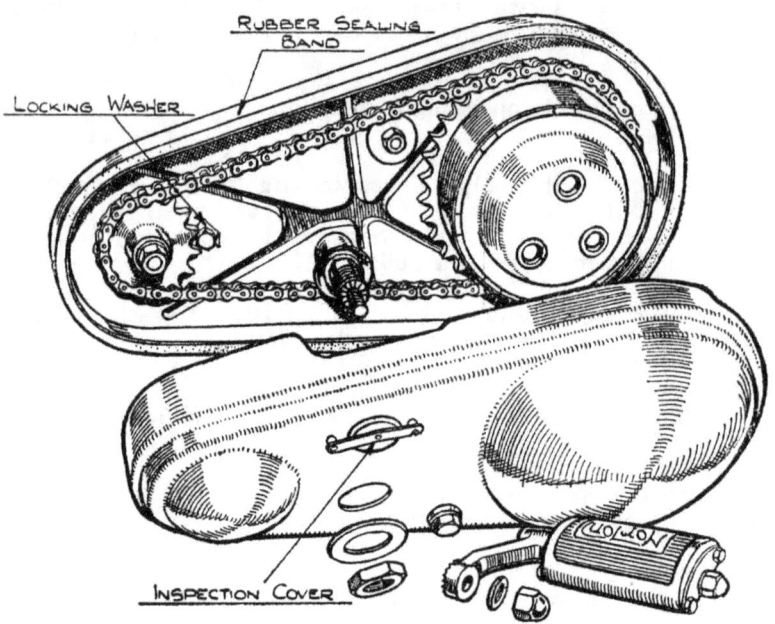

Fig. 11.

Remove the footrests, footrest rod, and brake pedal.

Remove the large nut holding the outer portion of the oil bath, and remove the outer portion.

Remove clutch spring screws, springs and cups (three of each), clutch outer plate, clutch thrust pin, and clutch retaining nut.

Engage low gear and obtain assistance to hold the rear wheel while the nut is being removed.

Remove clutch body.

A special tool may be obtained for this purpose if necessary.

Remove engine sprocket (a claw-type extractor will remove this), and engine sprocket, clutch and chain can be removed together.

Remove rear portion of oil bath, held to the crankcase by bolt, to the engine plate by a nut, to the rear chain guard by a bolt, and by a nut on the gear box pivot bolt.

APPENDIX TO THE 1947 WORKSHOP MANUAL

FOR

THE UNAPPROACHABLE

MOTOR CYCLE

MODELS 16 H, BIG 4, 18 & ES 2

Additional data extracted from the 1956 Workshop Manual for changes to these same models including 'Laydown' gearbox and lighting. This appendix should be used in conjunction with the 1947 Workshop Manual.

(See previous page)

THE GEARBOX

46. REMOVAL FROM FRAME.

Remove kick starter crank, gear indicator and gear lever.

Remove outer cover held by seven cheese head screws and release the clutch cable from the operating arm by rotating the worm with a large screwdriver.

Remove cable adjuster from inner cover.

Remove oil bath, clutch and engine sprocket. (Para. 41).

Remove rear portion of oil bath (para. 41), rear chain guard and rear chain.

Remove nut and adjuster bolt from the offside of the gear box top bolt and extract the bolt from the nearside.

Remove prop stand spring and nut from the offside of the gearbox bottom bolt, remove the nut and tap out the bolt.

The whole box may now be swung round in an anti-clockwise direction and lifted out of the frame on the offside.

47. FITTING TO FRAME.

Reverse the order of removal operations, leaving the top and bottom bolts slack until the primary chain has been correctly tensioned ($\frac{1}{4}/\frac{3}{8}$in. up and down movement) by means of the adjuster on the offside of the machine. Remember that any adjustment of the primary chain will affect the rear chain.

48. CLUTCH WORM LEVER, ADJUSTMENT.

When further adjustment of the clutch cable is impossible or brings the clutch worm lever into an unsuitable position, further adjustment may be obtained at the clutch worm lever accessible through the oval cover attached to the gearbox outer cover by two screws. This oval cover also forms an outrigger bearing for the clutch worm and is a good fit in the outer cover. Should it be difficult to remove after the screws have been withdrawn, it should be tapped round until the ends stand away from the outer cover and thus provide two lips beneath which suitable levers may be inserted, but care should be taken to avoid overstraining the small cover. After slackening the cable adjuster right down, the lever may be rotated on the shank of the worm by releasing the pinch bolt and holding the shank by means of the slot machined across its end, whilst rotating the lever in an anti-clockwise direction until it is about 45° below the horizontal. Re-adjust the cable as necessary and check that when the clutch is withdrawn the angle between the cable and the worm lever is approximately a right angle.

49. OUTER COVER, REMOVAL AND FITTING.

Remove the kick starter crank by releasing its pinch bolt and pulling off the crank.

Remove gear indicator by unscrewing the centre bolt from the positive spindle.

Remove the gear change lever by unscrewing the pinch bolt and pulling off the lever.

Remove the seven cheese headed screws holding the cover in position and withdraw the cover carefully in order to avoid tearing the paper washer fitted to this joint. If the joint is difficult to break, there is a point at either end which overhangs the inner cover to which careful punching may be applied.

No difficulty should be experienced when refitting, the coverscrews should all be just pinched down and finally tightened in opposite pairs.

Some oil will have been lost due to the cover removal and should be replenished through the clutch worm inspection hole until oil begins to drip from the level plug hole normally plugged by the square headed level plug situated to the rear of and on the same level as the kick starter crank.

50. POSITIVE FOOT CHANGE, DISMANTLING.

With the outer cover removed the positive foot change mechanism becomes accessible. To dismantle, remove the two nuts securing the U section outer plate and withdraw the plate followed by the lever return spring, pawl carrier and ratchet plate. Note that there is a spacing shim fitted behind the latter. It is unlikely that the cam plate secured behind the shoulders of the two studs which carry the assembly will ever need removal, but the procedure is obvious.

51. POSITIVE FOOTCHANGE, ASSEMBLY.

Examine all parts for wear likely to result in lost movement, particularly the spindle bushes in both covers, the ends of the pawls and the pawl pin; obtain any replacements necessary and re-assemble, checking first that the two studs are quite secure and placing the spacing shim on the short shaft of the ratchet plate. Remember to insert the knuckle pin visible through the aperture in the inner cover into the hole in the ratchet plate arm whilst the ratchet plate is being fitted. Spread the pawls to enter the ratchet teeth whilst pushing home the pawl carrier.

52. INNER COVER, REMOVAL.

Screw the clutch cable adjuster as far down as possible, and with a large screwdriver and movable spanner, rotate the clutch worm lever in a clockwise direction till the cable nipple is clear of the lever and withdraw the cable from its slot in the lever. Unscrew the adjuster and the cable is completely disconnected from the gearbox.

Remove the eight nuts securing the cover and withdraw it from the studs, being careful not to tear the paper washer fitted to the joint. The cover will bring with it the kick starter crank, clutch worm and fittings and the mainshaft bearing. para. 48.(previous page).

53. INNER COVER, FITTING.

Thoroughly clean the joint faces and apply a little jointing compound to each face, place the paper washer in position over the studs and against the gearbox face. Fit the cover into position. It will probably be necessary to press the kick starter pawl into its recess in the kick starter crank before the cover can be pushed right home. Fit the eight securing nuts and washers and just pinch each one, finally tightening the nuts in opposite pairs. Refit the clutch cable and adjust as described in para. 48

54. INNER COVER, DISMANTLING.

The dismantling of the footchange mechanism having already been dealt with, only the clutch operating mechanism and kick starter remain. The clutch worm may be completely unscrewed from its nut and with the nut removed from the cover, the main shaft bearing may be drifted out. The hardened roller in the end of the clutch worm which rubs on the clutch thrust rod may also be drifted out and a replacement fitted if necessary. Lever off the cupped pressing which covers the kick starter return spring and remove the spring, when the kick starter axle complete may be withdrawn from its bush. This will enable the pawl pin, pawl, plunger and spring to be removed. If the nose of the pawl is badly worn or chipped, it should be renewed.

It is unlikely that the kick starter bush will ever require renewal, but it may be drifted out if necessary.

55. INNER COVER, ASSEMBLING.

Examine the kick starter cam and stop pieces riveted into the cover. They should never need renewing, but may have worked loose and require re-riveting.

Press the kick starter axle bush and mainshaft bush into the cover and screw home the clutch worm nut. Fit kick starter pawl, plunger and spring to kick starter axle. Remaining parts may be fitted now or after the cover is fitted to the gearbox.

When fitting the kick starter return spring, its free end which locates in one of the slots in the bush should be forced round into the second or third slot beyond its free position.

56. REMOVAL OF GEARS.

If the clutch has been removed, it will be necessary to fit a short length of tubing over the end of the main axle and hold it in place with a clutch nut to retain the axle in position whilst the gears are being removed.

Remove end cover (paras. 49 and 52).

Remove the low gear and kick starter wheel – the large gear on the layshaft which has a bronze bush pressed into its centre.

Remove the small wheel from the end of the main axle.

Remove the mainshaft second gear; this is fitted with a fully floating bush. Unscrew the striker fork shaft by means of the two flats machined on its outer end and remove it together with the layshaft second gear and the striker fork.

Remove the tubular distance piece or clutch and withdraw the main axle together with the third gear and striker fork.

The bore of the main gear wheel, which still remains in position, carries 13 rollers which should be retained in position by inserting a roll of stiff paper in place of the main axle now removed. The axle will bring with it the bronze clutch thrust washer which should be examined, and if there are no grooves visible across the face which rubs on the main gear wheel, it should be renewed. Withdraw the layshaft and the two remaining gears, which will expose the outer race of the layshaft roller bearing in the far end of the box. The inner race with rollers and cage will most probably come away with the layshaft. The outer race may be removed by gently heating the case and dropping it – joint face downwards on the bench or a wooden block.

Remove axle sprocket nut which has a left hand thread and is held with a locking

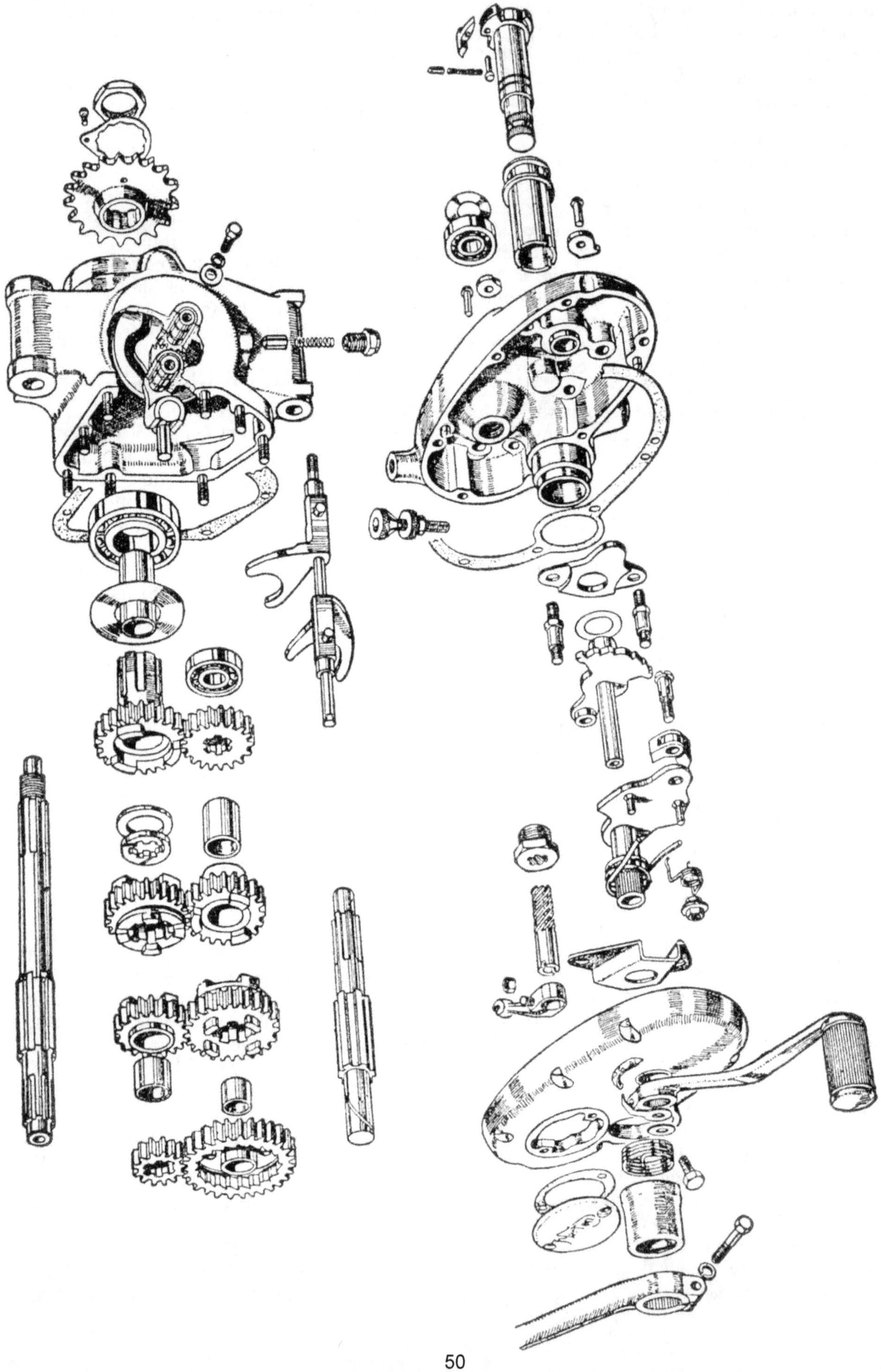

FIG. 13. NORTON GEARBOX 1950 ONWARDS

washer and screw, and withdraw the main gearwheel. If the gearbox is in the frame and the rear chain in position, obtain assistance to hold the rear wheel whilst the nut is being removed.

If the gearbox is removed from the frame, the sprocket may be held by passing a length of old chain around it and holding the ends in a vice.

Examine the steel roller retaining washer and if it is badly scored or worn down, it should be renewed. The main gear wheel bearing may be drifted from the shell. Remember that there is a pen steel washer fitted either side of this bearing.

57. REMOVAL OF CAM PLATE.

Remove the domed hexagon nut from beneath the forward side of the gearbox. This contains the cam plate indexing plunger which will drop out when the nut is removed.

Remove the two bolts fitted with spring and plain washers visible on the forward side of the gearbox shell. These secure the cam plate and cam plate quadrant, both of which may be pushed through into the box when the bolts are removed. Both cam plate and quadrant are carried in a bronze bush. It is unlikely that these bushes will ever require renewing, but they may be readily pressed or drifted out should the necessity arise.

58. FITTING CAM PLATE.

Place the quadrant in position and secure it with its bolt and washers. Place the cam plate in position so that one of the end grooves in its circumference is across the centre of the indexing plunger hole in the gearbox shell and meshing its gear with the last tooth but one on the quadrant, ensuring that the correct end of the quadrant rack is being used. Assemble the positive mechanism on to the inner cover (para. 51). Place cover in position and connect quadrant lever to ratchet by means of knuckle pin (para. 53).

Set positive footchange to top gear and check that the indexing plunger groove lies in the correct position to mesh with the indexing plunger when fitted. Withdraw cam plate and re-mesh as necessary until the correct position is obtained when the cam plate bolts and washers should be fitted and tightened. Fit indexing plunger, spring and plunger bush.

59. FITTING GEARS INTO GEARBOX.

Drop pen steel washer (the smaller of the two) into the bottom of the bearing housing before pressing in the bearing. Fit main gear wheel bearing and layshaft bearing outer race.

Fit rollers (13) to main gear wheel, smearing the assembly with grease, and insert the paper tube to retain the rollers.

Fit large pen steel washer over the shank of the main gear wheel, press the wheel home in its bearing, fit gearbox axle sprocket, tighten the nut, fit locking washer and pin.

Fit bronze clutch thrust washer to main axle so that the face having the three oil grooves will be against the main gear wheel. Carefully remove the paper tube from the main gear and insert main axle into position.

Fit distance tube in place of clutch and add clutch nut.

Fit third gear wheel (20 teeth) and top gear wheel (18 teeth) to layshaft and fit inner race with rollers and cage to end of the shaft. Grease the rollers and fit shaft into box.

Set the cam plate into the second gear position, i.e., with indexing plunger in the groove next to the shallow neutral groove.

Fit striking fork to mainshaft third gear (22 teeth) and fit gear to main axle, meshing it with the layshaft gear already in position.

Fit the second fork to the layshaft second gear (24 teeth) and fit the second gear with the fork to the layshaft. The pegs on the striking forks fit into the cam plate slots.

With the gearbox in the frame, little trouble will be experienced in holding the first fork in position. Fit the first fork in position and hold with a screw driver or similar tool whilst the second is placed in position.

Fit striking fork shaft and screw into the case.

Fit the remaining gears.

Fit end cover (paras. 55 and 53).

Remove tubular distance piece from clutch end of mainshaft. Remember to finally refill with oil to the level plug level (para. 49).

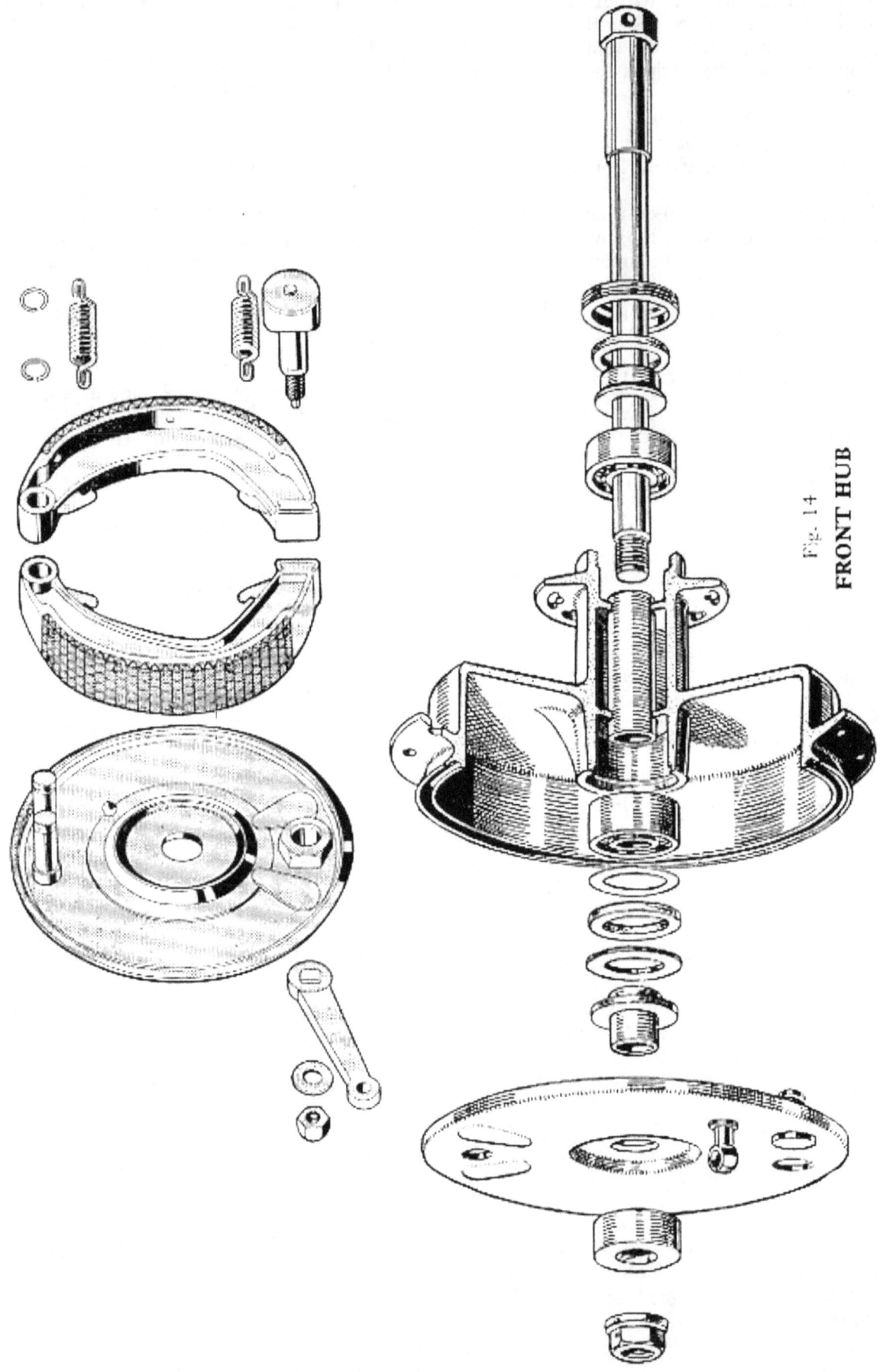

Fig. 14
FRONT HUB

Lighting and Accessories

105. DYNAMO—INSPECTION OF COMMUTATOR & BRUSHGEAR.

About once every six months remove the dynamo cover for inspection of commutator and brushes.

The brushes must make firm contact with the commutator. The brushes are held in boxes by means of springs; move the brush to see that it is free to slide in its holder. If it sticks remove it and clean with a cloth moistened with petrol. Care must be taken to replace the brushes in their original position, otherwise they will not bed properly on the commutator. If, after long service, the brushes have become worn to such an extent that they will not bear properly on the commutator, they must be replaced. Always use genuine Lucas brushes. Brushes should be fitted by a Service Agent.

Now examine the commutator. It should be free from any trace of oil or dirt and should have a highly polished appearance. Clean a dirty or blackened commutator by pressing a fine dry cloth against it while the engine is slowly turned over by hand. If the commutator is very dirty, moisten the cloth with petrol.

106. LUBRICATION.

The bearings in the dynamo are packed with grease during assembly and will last until it is necessary for the dynamo to undergo a complete overhaul.

107. CUT-OUT AND REGULATOR UNIT.

This unit (Fig. 24) which is housed inside the tool box, consists of the cut-out which is an automatic switch to prevent discharge of the battery when the dynamo is not charging, and the voltage regulator which controls the output of the dynamo. With a fully charged battery the dynamo is only permitted to pass a small charge to the battery, whilst with a fully discharged battery a heavy charge is passed in order to boost up the battery rapidly. Both components are accurately set and should not be tampered with or adjusted.

110. HEADLAMP.

To remove the headlamp front, slacken the securing screw at the top of the lamp. It will then be possible to detach the front rim complete with Light Unit assembly.

To replace, locate the metal tongue in the slot at the bottom of the lamp, press on the front and secure in position by tightening the screw.

Setting and focussing.

Stand the motorcycle in front of a light-coloured wall at a distance of about 25 ft. With the main driving light switched on, the height of the beam centre from the ground should be the same as the height of the centre of the headlamp from the ground. If necessary slacken the bolts securing the headlamp and move the lamp until the beam is projected straight ahead and parallel with the ground. The headlamp must be focussed so that the main driving light gives a uniform beam without any dark centre. If the bulb needs adjusting, remove the lamp front and reflector, as described above, and slacken the bulb holder clamping clip at the back of the reflector. Move the bulb holder backwards and forwards until the correct position is obtained, and then tighten the clamping clip.

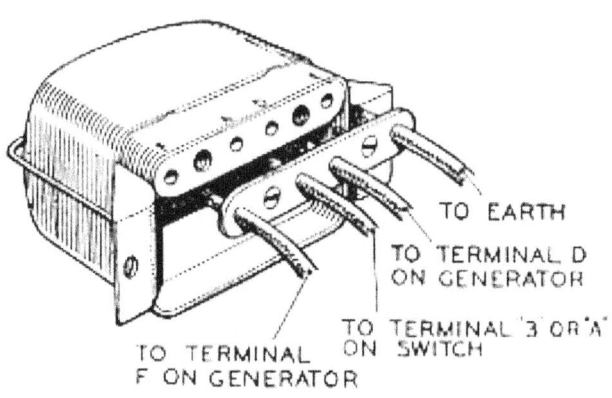

Fig. 24

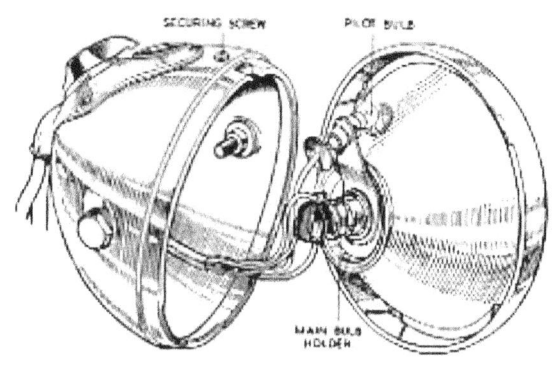

Fig. 25

Replacement of Bulbs.

To gain access to the bulbs, remove the front rim and light unit assembly as already described and detach the bulb holder which is held in position by two spring loaded pegs. When replacement of a bulb is necessary, it is important not only that the same size bulb is fitted, but also that it has a high efficiency and will focus in the reflector. Cheap and inferior bulbs may have a filament of such a shape that it is impossible to focus correctly. Only Lucas genuine spare bulbs should be used and care should be taken when fitting the main bulb to insert it the correct way, i.e., with the dipped beam filament above the centre filament. To assist in this operation bulbs are marked TOP on the metal cap. Correct replacement bulbs are:—

Headlamp (main): Lucas No. 169.
6 volt, 30/30 watt.
Headlamp (pilot): Lucas No. 988.
6 volt, 3 watt.

111. TAIL LAMP.

The tail lamp is fitted with a 6 volt 3 watt single contact bulb (Lucas No. 200). The portion of the lamp carrying the red glass can be removed by pushing in and turning to the left. When refitting, engage the bayonet fixing, push in and turn to the right to secure the body in position.

Maintenance Manual and Instruction Book

FOR

THE UNAPPROACHABLE

MOTOR CYCLE

Models No. 19, ES2 and 50

Publication date 1956

NORTON MOTORS LIMITED

BRACEBRIDGE STREET, BIRMINGHAM, 6, ENGLAND

Telephone:
ASTon Cross 3711 (P.B.X.)

Telegrams:
"Nortomo, Birmingham."

IMPORTANT INFORMATION RELATING TO THE CONTENTS OF THIS MANUAL

1945-1946: The first section of this manual includes a copy of the appropriate repair and maintenance data for the girder forks as fitted to the WD16H model. This information is included as the 1945-1946 post-war civilian 16H and 18 models were also fitted with girder forks. However, based on our research, overhaul information for girder forks was never included in any of the factory workshop manuals for the post-war civilian models.

1947-1954: The second section includes a copy of a 1947 factory workshop manual for both the S.V. and O.H.V. rigid frame and spring frame (plunger) 16H, Big4, 18 and ES2 models that were fitted with 'Road-holder' forks. It also includes additional information extracted from the 1956 publication of this same workshop manual relating to the changes that took place during the 1947 to 1954 model run, including the change from an 'Upright' to a Laydown' gearbox and lighting equipment. This additional information is appended at the end of the section and any data that is identical and included in the 1947 publication has been omitted. Consequently, this manual would be applicable to all four models from 1947 to 1954 at which time the 16H, Big4 and 18 were discontinued and the ES2 had received swing-arm rear suspension.

1953-1958: The third section includes a copy of a 1956 factory workshop manual exclusive to the O.H.V. swing-arm 19S, ES2 and 50 models. As the ES2 received swing-arm rear suspension in 1953, this manual would be applicable to all three models from 1953 to 1958, at which time the 19S was discontinued.

1958-1963: The pages in the fourth section of this manual were extracted from the P106/P Norton factory publication 'Maintenance Manual and Instruction Book' dated 1970 for the Model 50, ES2, 88, 99, 650 and 750 models. As the 19S was discontinued in 1958 and is no longer included in the model list, this extracted data would be applicable to the 1958 to 1963 Model 50 and ES2 (see below).

EVOLUTION OF THE COMBINATION MANUALS: The publication of these 'combination' manuals began in 1960 with the P101 manual followed by the P106 and finally the P106/P manual of 1970. While these 'combination' manuals made publication less expensive than those for individual models the information for multiple different motorcycles is often merged together. Consequently, separating out the appropriate data for a specific model, or series of motorcycles can be a time consuming and confusing exercise.

Even more unfortunately, the P106/P manual makes no reference to the model years that are covered. However, as it only includes the model 50 and ES2 and knowing that the 19S was discontinued in 1958 it is reasonable to assume that it is intended to cover these two models from 1958 through 1963, at which point Norton discontinued manufacturing their single-cylinder machines. Therefore, we have extracted the information that is exclusive to the Model 50 and ES2 from the P106/P manual. However, this means that the paragraphs and illustrations in the P106/P section may no longer be sequentially numbered and we request you overlook this minor issue as it does not affect the correctness of the data in any way.

IMPORTANT: Please note that repair information for the AMC MKII versions of the models 50 and ES2 is not included in this publication.

INDEX

	Paragraph
Ammeter	99
Battery, maintenance	100
Big End, examination	28
Brakes, adjustment	63
Brakes, dismantling and assembly	64
Carbon, removal	9
Carburetter, tuning	80
Carburetter, rich mixture	82
Carburetter, weak mixture	83
Carburetter, maintenance	81
Carburetter, dismantling	78
Carburetter, assembling	79
Contact Breaker, adjustment	91
Contact Breaker, cleaning	92
Clutch, adjustment	36
Clutch, dismantling	38
Clutch, examination	39
Clutch, assembly	40
Crankcase, dismantling	30
Crankcase, assembling	33
Cylinder Barrel, fitting	14
Cylinder Head, removal	8
Cylinder Head, fitting	14
Dynamo Brushes	96
Dynamo, lubrication	97
Electrical Cables	102
Electrical System, maintenance	89
Engine, removal	29
Engine, fitting in frame	34
Foot Change, dismantling	45
Foot Change, assembling	46
Front Forks, removal	67
Front Forks, dismantling	69
Front Forks, assembling	70
Front Forks, fitting	68
Front Forks, maintenance	65
Gearbox, removal	41
Gearbox, dismantling	43, 47, 49, 51
Gearbox, assembling	44, 48, 50, 53, 54
Gearbox, fitting	42
Handlebar Levers	74, 75, 76, 77
Head Lamp	101
Head Lamp Switch	103
High Tension Lead	93
High Tension Pick-up	94
Horn	104
Hubs, dismantling	59, 61
Hubs, assembling	60, 62
Legshields	84

	Paragraph
Legshields, fitting	85
Lubrication System	1
Magdyno, removal	27
Magdyno, fitting	27
Magneto, timing	22
Main Bearings, removal	31
Main Bearings, fitting	32
Oil Bath Chaincase, removal	37
Oil Bath Chaincase, fitting	37
Oil Circulation	5
Oil Control Valve	26
Oil Filter	2
Oil Level	4
Oil Pump	3, 25
Oil Pump, removal	23
Oil Pump, fitting	24
Petrol Tank, removal	6
Petrol Tank, fitting	7
Piston, removal	17
Piston, fitting	18
Piston Ring, removal	17
Rocker Box, removal	8
Rocker Box, dismantling	15
Rocker Box, fitting	14
Small End Bush, removal	19
Small End Bush, fitting	19
Sparking Plug, maintenance	95
Steering Head, adjustment	66
Swing arm, dismantling	71
Swing arm, assembling	72
Swing arm and Rear Suspension Units	73
Tail, Stop and Number Plate Lamp	105
Timing Gears, removal	23
Timing Gears, fitting	24
Timing Gear Bushes	35
Timing Panel, removal	20
Timing Panel, fitting	21
Tyres, maintenance	86
Tyres, removal	87
Tyres, fitting	88
Valves, removal	10
Valves, grinding	11
Valves, fitting	12
Valve Guides, removal	13
Valve Guides, fitting	13
Voltage Control Unit	98
Wheels, removal	55, 57
Wheels, fitting	56, 58

DATA

Identification Marks

Engine No. and prefix letters stamped on driving side of crankcase below cylinder base. Quote fully if writing or ordering parts. Frame No. stamped on tubular part of front tank lug should be identical to engine number.

	19S	ES2	50
Cubic Capacity	596cc. (36.363 cu in.)	490cc. (29.896 cu in.)	348cc. (21.232 cu in.)
Bore	82mm. (3.228ins.)	79mm. (3.110ins.)	71mm. (2.795ins.)
Stroke	113mm. (4.449ins.)	100mm. (3.937ins.)	88mm. (3.465ins.)
Compression Ratio	6.4	7.1	7.3
Sparking Plug		KLG FE80 Three Point	
	Lodge 2HLN		Champion NA8

Ignition Timing

Before TDC			
fully advanced	11/16" (17.46mm.)	$\frac{5}{8}$" (15.875mm.)	11/16" (17.46mm.)
Magneto points gap	.012" (.305mm.)	.012" (.305mm.)	.012" (.305mm.)
Plug points gap	.020"-.022" (.55mm.)	.020"-.022" (.55mm.)	.020"-.022" (.55mm.)

Valve Timing

Cam gears and half time pinion marked for ease of setting. Proceed as directed in Para. 24.

Tappet Clearance cold

Inlet … PUSH RODS FREE TO ROTATE WITHOUT
Exhaust … UP AND DOWN MOVEMENT

Amal Carburetter

Type	Monobloc 376	Monobloc 376	Monobloc 376
Main Jet	270	270	210
Throttle Valve	376/4	376/4	376/3½
Needle Position	3	3	2
Pilot Jet	30	30	30
Choke Size	1.1/16" (26.98mm.)	1.1/16" (26.98mm.)	1" (25.4mm.)

Engine Sprocket

Solo	21	20	18
Sidecar	19		

Gear Ratios

Solo	4.53, 6.04, 8.03, 12.2,	4.75, 6.55, 8.4, 12.7	5.28, 7.02, 9.34, 14.1
Sidecar	5, 6.65, 8.85, 13.35		

Chains

Primary Chain:
Pitch	½"	½"	½"
Width	.305"	.305"	.305"
Length	76 links	76 links	75 links

Rear Chain:
Pitch	$\frac{5}{8}$"	$\frac{5}{8}$"	$\frac{5}{8}$"
Width	¼"	¼"	¼"
Length	90 links	90 links	90 links

Magdyno Chain:
Pitch	$\frac{3}{8}$"	$\frac{3}{8}$"	$\frac{3}{8}$"
Width	.155"	.155"	.155"
Length	44 links	44 links	44 links

Petrol Tank capacity	3¼ galls. approx. (14.27 litres)		
Oil Tank capacity	4 pints approx. (2.27 litres)		
Tyre size—front	3.25 × 19		
Tyre size—rear	3.25 × 19		
Tyre pressure—rear	25 (1755gms/sq/cm)	23 (1618gms/sq/cm)	23 (1618gms/sq/cm)
Tyre pressure—front	22 s/car (1548gms/sq/cm)	20 (1410gms/sq/cm)	20 (1410gms/sq/cm)
Weight—empty	390lbs (176 kilos)	385lbs (173.6 kilos)	380lbs (171 kilos)

INTRODUCTION

In preparing these instructions the elementary details and preliminary information that may be necessary to the absolute novice have been omitted, on the assumption that the majority of NORTON owners are already acquainted with the elementary details of starting, driving and maintenance. In connection with the latter we would stress the advisability of cultivating the habit of routine cleaning, lubrication, examination and adjustment of your machine. By this means many minor annoyances will be avoided and major breakdowns averted, and you will acquire the pride of ownership which marks the true enthusiast.

Below is a plan view of the machine with all controls clearly indicated. A short study of this will familiarize you with the position and function of each control. Without wishing to become elementary a description of the best method of ensuring an easy start may not be inappropriate. With the petrol turned on, the air lever partly closed and the ignition lever in about its middle position, slightly flood the carburetter until petrol seeps (not drips) from the bottom of the carburetter mixing chamber and very slightly open the throttle. Depress the kickstarter until the resistance of compression is felt, raise the exhaust valve lifter and depress the kickstarter a further two or three inches. Release the exhaust valve lifter and allow the kickstarter to return to its normal position. Give a long swinging kick on the starter, carrying it as far round as possible. With the controls correctly set the engine should now start up.

When taking over a new machine it is only necessary to add petrol and oil to the respective tanks before use; the lubrication points having received the necessary greasing at the Works. It is advisable, however, to see that the steering damper is slackened off and adjusted to your particular requirements.

New machines should not be driven at more than 35 miles per hour for the first 500 miles in top gear or a corresponding slower speed in the lower gears. Avoid "over-revving" and slogging or labouring of the engine. It is advisable during the running in period not to open the throttle more than $\frac{1}{4}$ to $\frac{1}{3}$. The use of running-in compound during the initial stages

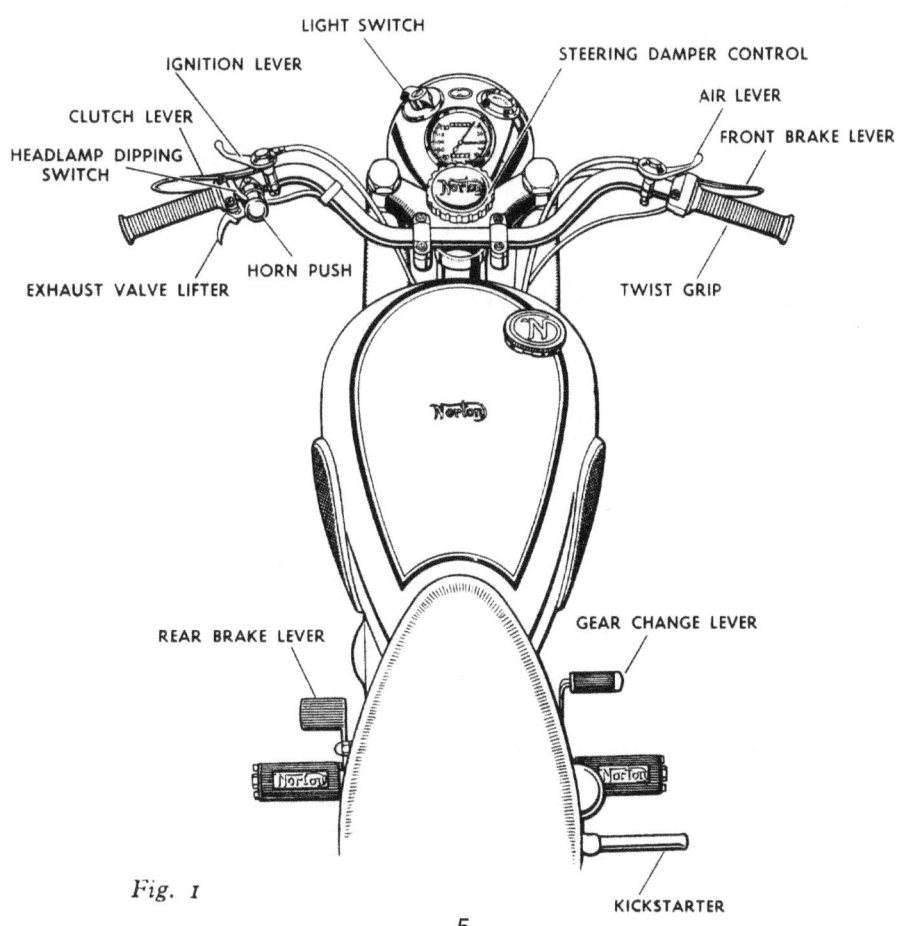

Fig. 1

of the engine's life is strongly recommended. The compound, several brands of which are available may be obtained from all NORTON agents, contains " colloidal graphite," which forms a graphoid surface on all working surfaces of the engine and greatly assists in preserving their high quality finish. The compound should be mixed with the lubricating oil in the proportion of one pint to each gallon during the running-in, but if its use is continued after this period only half the quantity should be used.

Under all usual circumstances when the machine is travelling at 25 miles per hour or over the air lever should be fully open and the ignition fully advanced, and only during starting or when the engine shows a tendency to pink should the ignition be retarded. Remember that these are high efficiency engines which give of their best when running at relatively high revolutions, and do not be afraid to change into a lower gear at the first signs of labouring. We would stress that the highest possible use should be made of the gearbox, which is quite capable of withstanding all the loads likely to be imposed on it by normal usage.

At the end of this book will be found a trouble tracing chart, reference to which will greatly facilitate the locating and rectifying of any but the most unusual troubles which may be likely to cause an involuntary stop.

CLEANING

Before attempting to polish the enamel on any part of the machine, all traces of grit adhering to the various components should be washed off, preferably with a reasonably high pressure hose. Polish the enamel periodically with a good quality wax polish. Note that chromium plating is not impervious to rust and should be wiped down when possible, after being in the rain. Wash off any road grit and clean with one of the chromium polishes available from any garage. Do NOT use ordinary metal polish.

LUBRICATION

At the Works, Wakefield Castrol Oils have been used for many years exclusively with highly successful results; the correct grades for the models dealt with in this book being:—

WAKEFIELD CASTROL XXL, for Summer use.
WAKEFIELD CASTROL XL, for Winter use.

Other very suitable oils for NORTON machines are:—

SHELL X-100-40 or B.P. ENERGOL S.A.E. 40 for Summer use.
SHELL X-100-30 or B.P. ENERGOL S.A.E. 30 for Winter use.
MOBILOIL " BB " for Summer use.
MOBILOIL " A " for Winter use.

These oils should be used in the engine and gearbox.

For oilbath chaincase use Wakefield's "Castrolite," Shell X-100-20, Price's Energol S.A.E. 20, or Mobiloil Arctic.

All bearings not automatically lubricated are fitted with nipples for grease gun lubrication, and a good quality grease, such as Wakefield Castrolease Heavy, B.P. Energrease C3, Shell Retinax or Mobiloil Hub Grease should be used at these points.

Below is a lubrication chart indicating the approximate periods at which the various lubrication points should receive attention. If the chart is adhered to, excessive wear will not occur at any of the moving parts, the life of the machine will be prolonged and its performance considerably enhanced.

NOTE.—On a new machine, drain and flush out oil tank after 500 miles. Remove crankcase drain plug and allow to drain. Remove level indicator plug from oilbath chaincase and fill to this level.

LUBRICATION CHART

Period	Location	Lubricant	Period	Location	Lubricant
Every 200 miles.	Oil tank, top up	Oil.	Every 2,000 miles.	Brake pedal	Grease.
				Brake shoe cams ... ... (sparingly)	Grease.
Every 1,000 miles.	Control cables	Oil.		Brake rod jaw joints ...	Oil.
	Control levers	Oil.		Speedometer driving box	Grease.
	Brake cable "U" clip ...	Oil.		Drain and refill oil tank	Oil.
	Rear chain	Grease.		Steering head races ...	Grease.
	Gearbox, top up	Oil.	Every 5,000 miles.	Gearbox, drain and refill	Oil.
	Oil bath, top up	Oil.		Commutator end bracket	Oil.
				Telescopic forks	See para. 70
			Every 10,000 miles.	Oil bath, drain and refill	Oil.

CONTROLS

Throttle Twist Grip. On right handlebar. Twist inwards to open. When shut, warm engine should continue to tick over by adjustment of cable and throttle stop on carburetter. Twist grip may be adjusted to close when released or to remain open as preferred.

Air Lever. On right handlebar. Close when starting from cold, open as soon as engine will run properly with full air. Should remain open for normal running.

Ignition Lever. On left handlebar. Fully advanced when closed fully, retarded when cable in tension. Retard about one third for starting.

Exhaust Valve Lifter. On left handlebar. Enables engines to be readily rotated. Used also for stopping engine.

Front Brake Lever. On right handlebar. Careful operation required. Should be used in conjunction with rear brake pedal.

Clutch Lever. On left handlebar. Allows engine to run with gear engaged without forward movement of machine. Release very gently to obtain forward motion.

Rear Brake Pedal. Pad adjacent to L.H. footrest. Press gently to bring vehicle to rest.

Gear Change Lever. Pad adjacent to R.H. footrest. Engages the various gears (4) and neutral or free engine position. Move upward for 1st gear and down for each other gear. Use deliberate pressure—a jabbing action is incorrect.

Kickstarter. Lever behind R.H. footrest. Depress to rotate engine.

Steering Damper Control. Plastic knob in centre, forward of handlebar. Rotate clockwise to stiffen handlebar movement (where fitted).

Light Switch. Left hand top of lamp. Rotating 3 positional switch 1-off: 2-low: 3-high.

Headlamp Dipping Switch. Trigger on left handlebar. Dips main headlamp beam.

Horn Push. On top of dipper switch body on left handlebar.

THE ENGINE

1. ENGINE, LUBRICATION SYSTEM.

This is of the dry sump type. The oil flows from the oil tank to the pump by gravity, assisted by suction from the feed side of the oil pump, through the gears, and is forced under pressure to various parts of the engine, drains to the lowest part of the crankcase—that is the sludge trap—and by suction from the return side of the pump is lifted back to the oil tank.

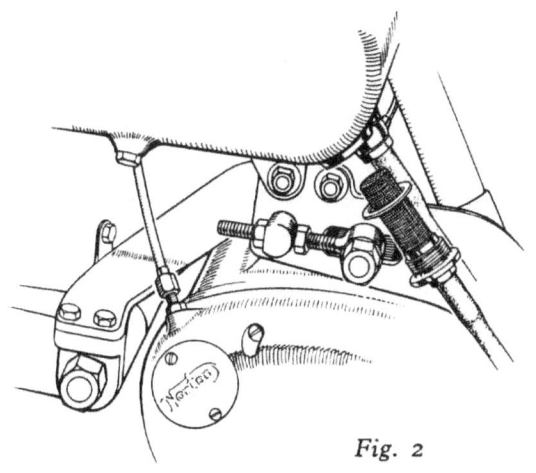

Fig. 2

2. THE FILTER.

The only filter in the oil system is of the gauze type and is fitted to the feed side of the oil circuit, attached to the adaptor screwed into the oil tank, to which the feed pipe is connected.

Clean filter, when oil tank is drained, every 2,000 miles.

3. ENGINE OIL PUMP.

This is of the gear type. The pump contains two pairs of gears, one on the feed side and the other on the return side.

The gears on the return side are twice the width of those on the feed, having twice the pumping capacity. This ensures that the crankcase is free from oil when the engine is running.

To check the return of the oil to the tank, remove the oil filler cap. The oil return pipe can then be seen. After the engine has been running for a few minutes, the oil return flow will be spasmodic, due to the greater capacity of the return gears.

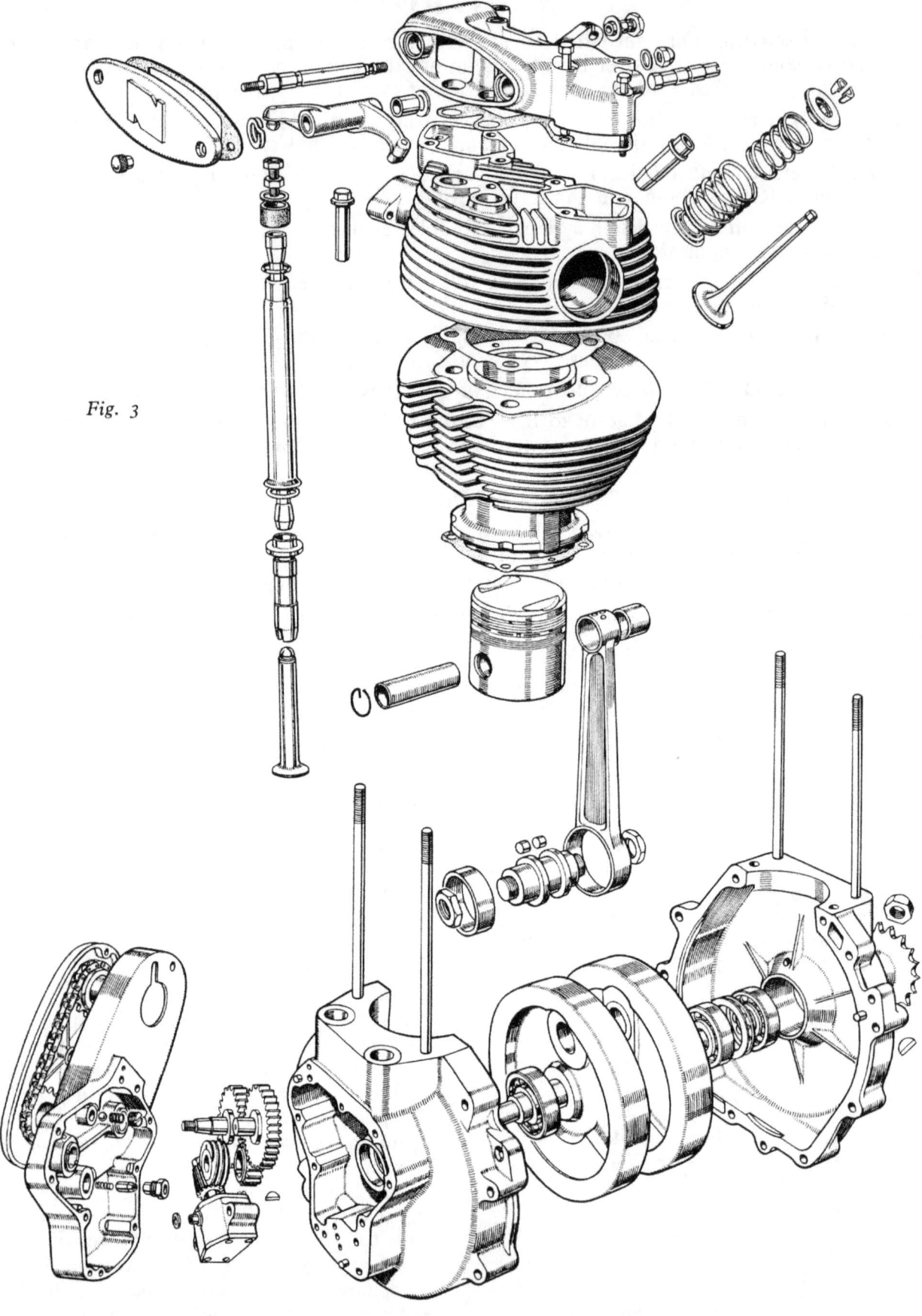

Fig. 3

4. OIL LEVEL.

The oil level in the oil tank should not be above three-quarters and not below half.

If the level is above the three-quarter mark when the engine is running, the pressure built up in the oil tank by the oil return side of the pump will force the surplus oil through the air release pipe on to the road.

Always run engine for a few minutes before checking oil level. It is possible when an engine has been idle for any length of time for the oil to syphon through the return gears to the sump.

When this happens, all the oil is returned to the tank in the first few minutes that the engine is running.

When the oil level is below the half full mark there is such a small quantity of oil that it tends to over-heat.

5. THE CIRCULATION OF THE OIL.

The oil is forced from the pump,

1. To the rear wall of the cylinder.
2. To the big-end bearing.
3. To the pressure control valve.

1. The oil passes through the timing panel to the mouth of the crankcase, through the base of the cylinder, up the cylinder wall and feeds the rear of the cylinder and piston.

2. The oil passes down the timing panel through the big end restriction jet, along the timing shaft, up the flywheel and is sprayed on to the roller big-end.

3. The oil pressure control valve is a spring-loaded ball, and acts as a safety valve, in the oil circuit. When the pressure of the oil lifts the ball from its seat, the oil passes the ball and is sprayed upon the timing gears. When the engine is assembled at the Works, the valve ball spring adjusting screw is screwed home and released 1½ threads. This is the only adjustment in the oiling system and it is not advisable to remove the ball from the valve unless it is suspected that the ball is sticking or not seating.

From the cylinder the oil drains down the sides of the crankcase and is picked up by ducts and carried to the main bearings and the timing gear bearings.

The oil collects in the timing case to such a level that the oil pump pinion is immersed, carrying oil to the half-time pinion and the timing gears.

A further timed breather is incorporated in the driving side mainshaft and releases pressure through a small hole in the underside of the mainshaft bearing boss.

A lead is taken from the oil return pipe to a banjo fitting on the rocker box, feeding oil to the rocker shafts and ball ends. Surplus oil returns down the pushrod cover tubes to the crankcase. Excess oil from the O.H.V. valve spring chambers drains back through drilled holes in the cylinder head and barrel.

Oil is fed to the magdyno chain by passing through the inlet cam spindle bush into the chain case. Any excess of oil accumulated in the case, drains through the breather pipe.

Crankcase pressure is released by a valve on the driving side of the crankcase and oil mist is fed to the rear chain.

All the oil drains to the base of the crankcase to the sludge-trap, is picked up by the suction of the return side of the pump and returned to the tank.

The oil-way from the sludge-trap is situated so that any foreign matter is left in the trap This leaves the case when the crankcase drain plug is removed and the oil drained.

MAINTENANCE OF ENGINE
DECARBONISING

6. REMOVAL OF PETROL TANK.

It is not necessary to drain tank, but make sure that the petrol tap levers are in the " Off " position, that is, with the round end of the lever pressed in.

Disconnect petrol pipes from taps.

Remove the four bolts and washers, and the tank is free from the frame.

Four shouldered rubber washers and steel washers should be on the tank brackets.

7. FITTING OF TANK.

Place the four shouldered rubber washers on the frame tank brackets, with the steel washers above.

Place tank in position and fit cupped steel

and rubber washers on to the tank bolts. (Fig. 4).

Fit bolts to tank and tighten down evenly.
Ensure that the tank is clear of the frame.
Fit petrol pipes, using the two spanners as when removing.

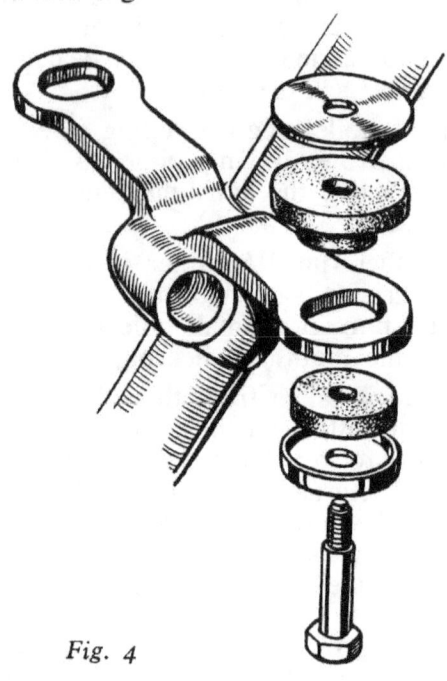

Fig. 4

8. REMOVAL OF ROCKER BOX CYLINDER HEAD and CYLINDER BARREL.

Unscrew the rocker oil feed pipe top connection from the centre of the nearside of the box, taking care not to lose the fibre washer from either side of the banjo. Disconnect exhaust valve lifter cable from lever and completely release the nine bolts holding the box to cylinder head. All but the rearmost bolt can be completely withdrawn whilst the box is in position. If necessary break joint by tapping box with mallet or light block of wood. A thin composition washer is fitted between head and box, do not tear this during removal.

Lift out pushrods now protruding from head.

To remove the cylinder head, remove the exhaust system complete, slacken the air filter hose clip on the carburetter air intake, and push the hose into the air filter sufficient to enable the carburetter to be withdrawn when the two flange nuts and petrol feed pipe have been removed.

Disconnect high tension lead from sparking plug. Slacken each of the four cylinder head nuts and completely remove.

NOTE! A plain steel washer is fitted beneath each cylinder head nut.

Tap beneath inlet port with light block or mallet to break joint if necessary. The head should be lifted off from the timing side of the engine as it will bring with it the pushrod cover tubes held in position by rubber sleeves. Ensure that neither of the rubber rings forming the cover tube bottom seal is lost during this process.

Revolve engine till piston is around bottom dead centre position and lift off cylinder barrel; avoid tearing paper washer.

The barrel need not be removed for decarbonisation as the piston top can be readily cleaned with barrel in position and piston on top dead centre.

Immediately barrel is removed, cover crankcase mouth with clean rag to prevent ingress of dirt or foreign matter.

9. REMOVAL OF CARBON.

Scrape carbon from top of piston and cylinder head.

Both are of the alloy type and care must be taken not to damage them.

Place an old piston ring at the top of the bore, and resting on top of piston. It will prevent the carbon being removed at the edge of the piston and end of the bore.

After an engine has been used for any considerable time, wear in the bore and the rings takes place, allowing a small amount of oil to pass.

The carbon on the piston edge and the top of the bore acts as an oil seal and if removed, engine may use a little more oil until carbon is re-formed.

The carbon deposit in the valve ports and valve spring compartment cannot be removed unless the valves are removed.

Valves need NOT be removed at every de-carbonisation.

10. REMOVAL OF VALVES FROM CYLINDER HEAD.

Compress valve springs with a suitable type of valve compressor.

When springs are compressed the valve cotters will fall from the valve stems.

Remove valve compressor.
Remove valves.
Remove valve springs and collars from valve spring compartment.
Remove carbon from underside of valve heads.

DO NOT POLISH VALVE STEMS.

Check valve stems in guides; if free, do not touch guides, unless they are badly worn.

If guides and valves show no signs of excessive wear, re-grind valve seats.

Always grind the seats when new valves are fitted.

11. GRINDING OF VALVE SEATS.

Use as little grinding compound as possible.

Place valve in guide and grind lightly, using a screwdriver or hand vice.

Do not revolve valve a complete turn, but oscillate, frequently raising valve from seat and placing in a different position.

Do not over-grind valve seats (a wide seat is not necessary).

When seat is ground sufficiently, that is, when the marks of the grinding make a complete ring on the seat and on the valve, remove all signs of grinding paste from seat, valve and valve pockets.

If the valves or the seats are badly burnt or pitted, it may be impossible to obtain a perfect seat by grinding. The seat will then have to be re-cut, and the valves re-faced, or new valves fitted.

12. FITTING OF VALVES.

Thoroughly clean valves, seats, and valve pockets. Fit valve springs and collars. Lubricate valve stems.

Fit valves into guides, compress valve springs, and fit cotters.

If the valve cotters are greased with a thick grease, the grease will hold the cotters in place until the springs are released.

13. REMOVING AND RE-FITTING OF VALVE GUIDES.

Valve guides are a driving fit in the cylinder barrel or head.

To remove, warm head and tap out with a double diameter drift.

Use the drift to replace or fit new ones.

Seats must be trued-up with cutter after refitting of guides, to ensure that the guides and seats are in alignment.

Oversize valve guides are usually available if required.

14. FITTING OF CYLINDER BARREL, CYLINDER HEAD AND ROCKER BOX.

Position piston rings so that gaps are equally spaced.

Lubricate rings, barrel and piston, and rotate engine till piston is near top of stroke.

Fit paper washer to crankcase mouth, ensuring that cylinder oil feed hole is unobstructed.

Fit barrel over piston and slide right home.

Clean cylinder head joint face on both head and barrel, and place aluminium gasket on top of barrel in position it previously occupied.

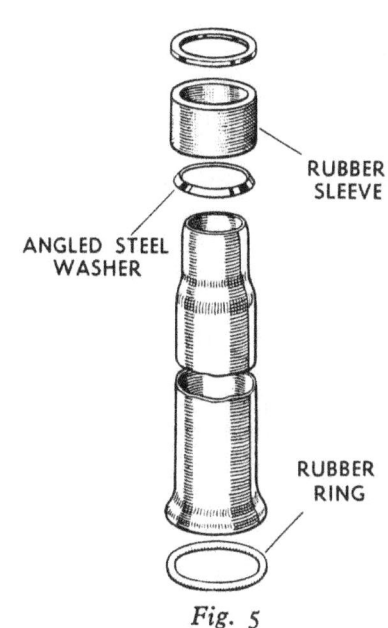

Fig. 5

Fit head ensuring that the lower ends of the push rod cover tubes are seating correctly between the tappet guide collar and the flange on the bottom of the push rod cover tubes.

If the cover tubes have been withdrawn from the head, ensure that they are replaced as shown in Fig. 5. The flat steel washer being placed in the bottom of the enlarged push rod tunnel and held in position by the rubber sleeve. The angled washer being placed over the reduced end of the cover tube before pushing the tube home into the head. Smear with oil to assist re-assembly.

Fit cylinder head nuts and lightly pinch each one. Finally, tighten in diagonal pairs. Replace push rods in position.

Clean rocker box and cylinder head joint faces and fit paper washer, smearing head with oil to hold washer in place.

Insert bolt in rearmost rocker box hole and place box in position.

Fit and pinch up all nine bolts finally tightening down evenly.

Fit remaining components, remove inspection cover and check push rod adjustment—no clearance but push rods free to rotate.

15. DISMANTLING & RE-ASSEMBLY OF ROCKER BOX.

Whilst rocker box is removed it may be necessary to remove the rockers for examination or re-bushing. Remove the inspection cover and the rocker spindle nuts and washers, and with a soft punch against the larger threaded end, drift the spindles out of position.

The rockers with their washers and shims may be extracted from the box.

Remove the exhaust valve lifter by first removing the small securing screw, when the lifter may be withdrawn.

The rocker bushes are a press fit in the rockers and may be pressed or drawn out as shown in Fig. 7.

Rocker ball ends and pads requiring renewing may be drifted out with a punch.

Press in new rocker ends, ensuring that the hole in the shank of the ball end is lined up with the oil hole in the rocker arm.

New rocker bushes may be pressed in or drawn into position by reversing the method of extraction illustrated.

New bushes should be reamed with 9/16" dia. reamer after fitting.

The re-assembly of the rockers in the box may require a little patience. Fig. 6 shows clearly the position of the various parts. Note that the steeel shims on either side of the spring washers are identical, the thrust washer at the opposite end being much thicker.

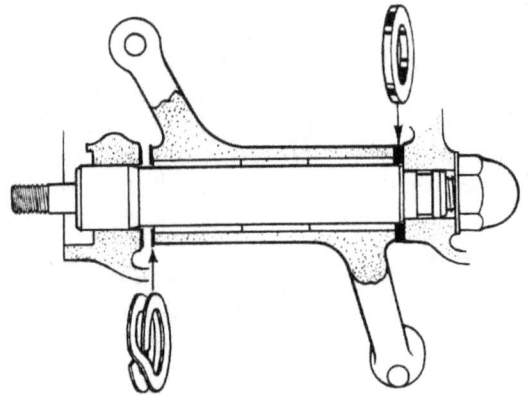

Fig. 6

Obtain a bar slightly smaller than the large spindle hole and having a lead on one end. Insert this into the hole far enough to allow the shims and spring washer to be placed over it. Carefully thread the rocker into position (it may be necessary to slightly withdraw the bar to get the rocker right home), centralise the washers as near as possible, remove bar and insert spindle, having previously smeared it with oil.

Using soft punch tap spindle part way through rocker.

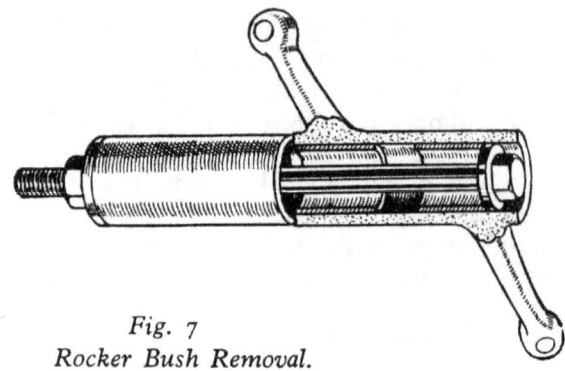

Fig. 7
Rocker Bush Removal.

Compress spring washer by means of screwdriver inserted into push rod hole and bearing on rocker arm and place thrust washer in position; the pressure of the spring washer will hold it until the spindle is knocked further home.

It is unlikely that the washer will be in true alignment with the spindle and will, therefore, be pinched between the rocker box and the shoulder on the spindle when the latter is tapped further into position. To release the washer tap the opposite end of the spindle once only.

Re-insert the screwdriver and again compress the spring washer. This will enable the thrust washer to be persuaded to drop over that part of the spindle on which it fits.

Insert tin strip or end of steel rule between rocker box and thrust washer, tap spindle fully home, remove tin strip, ensure that rocker is free to move, fit copper washer and dome nut and tighten.

16. TO ADJUST PUSH RODS.

Release the middle hexagon—the locking nut—by placing one spanner on the bottom hexagon—the tappet stem or push rod—and the second on the locking nut.

Turn the top hexagon—the tappet head or push rod adjuster—in the desired direction, and when the correct clearance is obtained, tighten locking nut.

Check clearance after tightening locking nut.

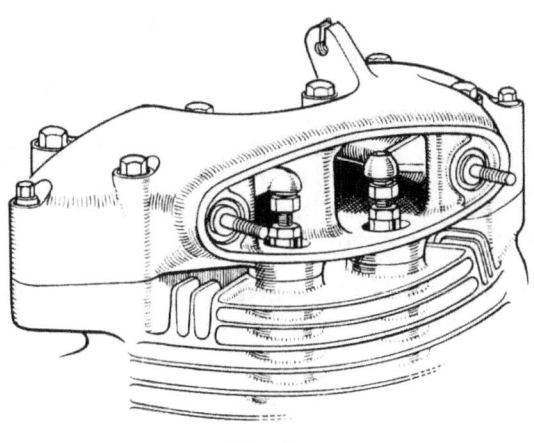

Fig. 8

17. REMOVAL OF PISTON & RINGS.

Remove cylinder barrel (Para. 8).

Remove one circlip and the gudgeon pin.

Gudgeon pin is a running fit in the piston and small end bush.

Mark piston to ensure it is fitted the same way when replacing.

Remove piston rings. These may be readily "peeled" out of their grooves with the aid of a narrow bladed pen knife.

If it is decided not to fit new rings, it is not advisable to remove the carbon from the back of the ring or the bottom of the ring groove.

If it is decided to fit new rings, the grooves in the piston should be thoroughly cleaned. A portion of a broken hack-saw blade is an ideal tool for the job.

When the grooves have been cleaned, check the new ring for size in the grooves.

There should be a side clearance of .002".

Check rings in the cylinder bore for the correct width of gap.

Place ring in bore, push ring down bore, using the piston as a guide.

The ring gap should be:

Compression ring ... .012"—.016"

Scraper ... ... .005"

Check gap with feeler gauge.

18. REFITTING PISTON.

Fit rings to piston.

Fit piston to connecting rod with the piston in the same position as before dismantling.

Fit circlip. It is advisable to always replace circlip and fit a new one.

Fit cylinder barrel (Para. 14).

19. REMOVING AND FITTING OF SMALL END BUSH.

If when the cylinder barrel and piston are removed it is found that the small end bush is worn it should be renewed.

Bush must be withdrawn from connecting rod.

Obtain a bolt at least twice the length of the bush, place a washer at the head of the bolt with an outside diameter less than the bush. Place bolt in bush.

Over the screwed end of the bolt place a piece of tubing longer than the bush, with an inside diameter slightly larger than the outside of the bush.

Fit nut to bolt and tighten. As nut is tightened, the bush will be drawn from the rod.

Care must be taken so that no strain is taken by the rod.

Fit new bush in the same manner.

Before fitting bush to rod, the inside diameter should be reamed to the size of the pin, as when fitted in the rod the bush will compress, leaving sufficient metal for true-ing with the reamer. If this is not done, too much metal will need to be taken away with the reamer.

Drill oil-holes in the bush before reaming to size.

The gudgeon pin should be a running fit in the small-end and the piston.

20. REMOVAL OF TIMING PANEL.

Remove magdyno chain cover held by three cheese headed screws.

Remove sprockets with chain in position. If difficulty is experienced a withdrawing tool should be obtained. The cam spindle sprocket is held by taper and key; the magdyno shaft is not keyed.

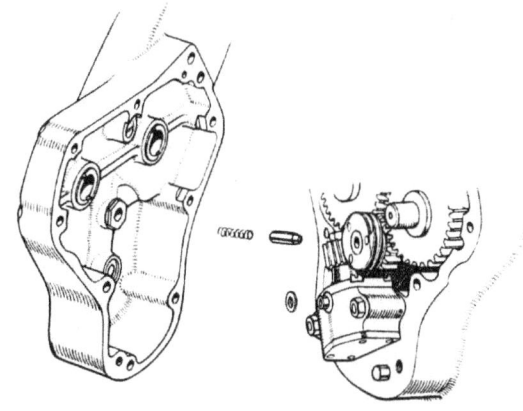

Fig. 9

Remove panel screws and note that the top three are shorter than the bottom three. Two countersunk screws are inside the mag. chain case.

When withdrawing the panel see that the big end feed jet is not lost and that any shims fitted to the cam spindles remain in position.

Remove big end feed jet spring.

21. FITTING TIMING PANEL.

Clean the edges of the timing chest and the panel.

Smear the edges with gold-size or jointing compound.

Check fibre washer on the oil pump nipple, connecting pump to panel.

Place panel in position and the washer should prevent the edges of the panel meeting the case by 1/32". This ensures that when the panel pins are tightened, the washer is compressed, making an oil-tight joint.

Fit spring and jet in jet holder.

Fit panel and panel screws and tighten down evenly.

22. IGNITION TIMING.

Place chain and sprocket in position and tighten cam wheel sprocket nut only.

Place gearbox change-speed lever in top gear position.

Advance ignition fully.

Rotate engine by turning the rear wheel, until both valves are closed and the piston is at the top of its stroke.

The position of the piston can be ascertained by placing a thin rod into the cylinder, via the sparking plug hole.

Hold rule on the top of the piston and take the reading of the rule as it leaves the cylinder.

Turn the rear wheel backwards still holding the rule on top of the piston till the rule shows the correct figure. (See data sheet).

Remove magdyno contact breaker cover.

Turn contact breaker in clockwise direction till the points open.

Insert thin feeler gauge or thin piece of paper, between the points.

Turn the contact breaker in an anti-clockwise direction till the points hold the feeler.

Turn contact breaker in a clockwise direction till the feeler is just free, that is when the points have just commenced to open.

Place a tube over the end of the shaft and sharply tap tube, forcing sprocket on to the taper of the shaft.

Tighten down nut carefully, so as not to turn the shaft.

When nut is tightened down, check timing.
Fit contact breaker cover.
Fit magdyno chain cover.
Fit sparking plug.

23. REMOVING TIMING GEARS, OIL PUMP, AND TAPPETS.

Remove timing panel (Para. 20), timing gears and oil pump are now visible.

Remove oil pump nuts and withdraw oil pump from studs.

Remove oil pump worm, LEFT HAND thread.

Timing gears may now be removed ensuring that any shims fitted to either end of the spindles are not lost.

Withdraw pinion from timing shaft using, if necessary, a sprocket drawer.

Unless absolutely necessary the tappets should not be removed as it is necessary to remove the tappet guides before the tappets may be withdrawn. The tappet guides are pressed into the crankcase and may be extracted by means of a sprocket drawer.

The inlet and exhaust tappets should not be interchanged.

24. FITTING TAPPETS, TIMING GEAR AND OIL PUMP.

If new timing gears have been fitted then they will need checking and re-shimming for end float. When fully home in the case the side of the gear should be clear of the boss carrying the pressure release valve. Shims should be added until this condition is obtained.

Fit timing cover, pull and push on inlet cam spindle and shim up till end float is just perceptible.

End float on exhaust cam spindle can only be properly checked when crankcase halves are separated.

Tappets must be entered into tappet guides from inside timing chest before the guides are pressed into position.

This necessitates a tubular drift to finally force the guides home.

Tappet guides are located radially by a peg in top of crankcase, which fits into a hole in tappet guide collar. Hole and peg should be as nearly in alignment as possible before pressing or tapping the guide into position.

Fit half-time pinion to mainshaft and rotate engine till crankpin is on T.D.C.

Fit cam gears, meshing the marked teeth with the appropriate markings on the pinion.

Fit and tighten oil pump worm, LEFT HAND thread, using punch or peg spanner.

Fit oil pump, ensuring that both faces are quite clean and using a minimum of jointing compound to avoid the oil holes becoming obstructed.

Check fibre washer on oil pump nipple and fit timing panel (Para. 21).

Time magneto (Para. 22).

25. OIL PUMP.

The oil pump is of the gear type. It is not advisable to dismantle it.

When pump is removed from timing chest, test for play in the spindle by pulling and pushing the worm wheel.

Revolve spindle and place fingers on the oil holes and the action of the gears should be felt if the pump is in good condition.

When revolving pump, any foreign matter obstructing the gears will be felt. Wash out with paraffin.

26. OIL CONTROL VALVE.

This is fitted in a boss on the inside of the timing panel. It is an assembly of a ball, spring and adjusting screw. The adjustment is set at the works and should not need any attention.

The control valve acts as a safety valve in the oil circuit. When the oil is cold, the oil pressure in the circuit tends to become excessively high, but the excess of pressure lifts the ball from its seat, allowing the oil to spray on to the timing gears.

If for any reason this is dismantled, the order of assembly is—ball, spring and adjuster nut.

Tighten the nut home and then screw out one and a half turns and lock with centre punch.

27. REMOVAL AND FITTING OF MAGDYNO.

The removal of the magdyno is simplified if the timing panel is removed.

Remove timing panel (Para. 20).

Remove leads from dynamo (3), and high tension lead from sparking plug.

Remove the locking bolt marked " B " in Fig. 10.

Remove the centre bolt of the three marked "A."

Ease the nuts off the outside bolts marked "A."

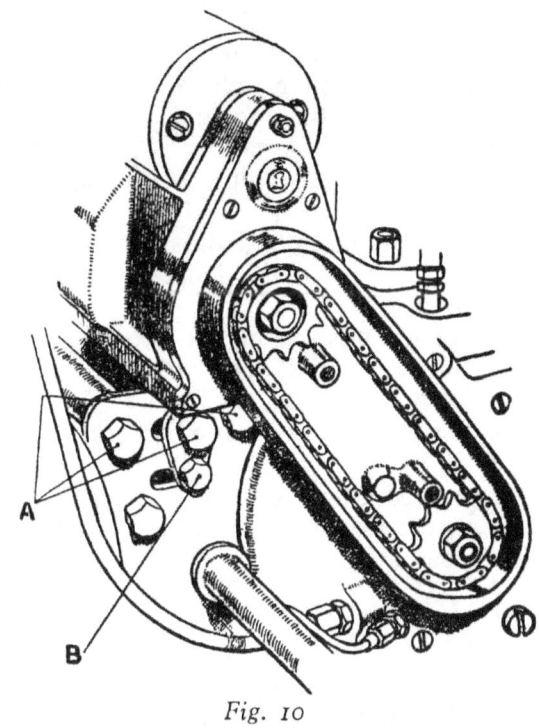

Fig. 10

Magdyno can now be removed.

Replace in the reverse order.

Do not tighten the bolts until the panel is refitted and the chain adjusted.

With the bolts slack, the magdyno can be moved in the desired direction, to correct the chain adjustment.

28. EXAMINATION OF THE ROLLER BIG END.

With the cylinder removed, the big-end can be examined for wear.

Rotate the flywheels until the big-end is in the topmost position.

Hold connecting rod with both hands, pull and push, and any up and down play can be felt.

DO NOT USE SIDE PRESSURE.

Do not mistake side float for end play.

A small amount of rock is of no importance.

If any appreciable up and down movement is present a new crankpin bearing is necessary. The dismantling of the flywheels and fitting of crankpin is a skilled job requiring equipment not normally available to the average rider. The flywheel assembly should be returned to the works for this replacement.

29. REMOVING ENGINE FROM FRAME.

Remove the tank (Para. 6), magdyno (Para. 27) and exhaust valve lifter cable.

Remove carburetter, which may be left suspended from cables, remove exhaust pipe and silencer, a " C " spanner is supplied in tool kit to fit exhaust pipe locking ring on O.H.V. models.

Remove clip bolts and nuts, and silencer bolt, and the pipe and silencer can be removed as one unit.

Remove oil pipes from the crankcase. If the oil has not been drained from the oil tank, plug the end of the feed pipe.

Remove oil bath, engine sprocket, and clutch. (Para. 37).

Remove front and rear engine plates completely. Remove engine cradle bolts and lift engine clear of frame.

30. PARTING OF THE CRANKCASE HALVES.

Remove crankcase drain plug and drain any oil that may be in the sump.

Remove cylinder barrel (Para. 8), piston (Para. 17), timing gear and oil pump (Para. 23).

Remove key from driving shaft.

Remove all the crankcase bolts and stud nuts, also the cheese headed screws from sump.

Crankcase halves can now be parted. Remove timing side first.

If leverage is necessary, revolve flywheels until the crankpin is at the mouth of the case, place a lever against the crankpin nut and lever outwards.

To remove the driving side of the case, lift the half of the case with the flywheels and lightly drop the end of the driving shaft on to a block of hard wood, when the case should leave the shaft.

31. REMOVAL OF BEARINGS FROM CRANKCASE.

It should be possible to remove the bearings from the case by tapping a shaft through the bearings, the shaft having a diameter slightly larger than the engine shaft, but small enough to pass through the bearing, should the bearing be tight in the case, without damage.

If the bearings are too tight in the housing to be removed by this method, the case should be heated round the bearing housings, when they should drop out.

Do not heat case sufficiently to destroy the temper of the bearings and do not use a concentrated flame.

32. FITTING OF BEARINGS TO CRANKCASE.

Test bearings, to be a sliding fit on shafts.

Press the ball bearing lightly in to the driving side of the case.

Fit the spacing washer next to the ball bearing.

Press the roller bearing lightly in to driving side of the case.

33. ASSEMBLY OF CRANKCASE.

Fit flywheels into case, and fit and tighten all bolts.

Test for side float in the flywheels there should be .005".

If the float is excessive, remove wheels from case.

Fit pen steel washers to the engine and timing shafts to take up the excess of float.

Fit the same thickness of washers on each shaft, keeping the wheels central in the case.

Check side float.

If the side float is correct, check connecting rod for being central in case.

There is side float in the big-end.

Place fingers on the bottom of the connecting rod and push rod towards the timing side of the case.

Measure the distance from the end of the small-end bush to the side of the crankcase mouth on the timing side.

Push rod to driving side of case and take the same measurement, from the driving side.

The two measurements should be within 1/64" of each other.

Rod can be lined up by transferring the pen steel washers on the driving and timing shafts to whichever side needs them, to obtain the correct alignment.

When the correct alignment is obtained, remove wheels from case.

Lubricate main bearings and big-end.

Smear the two edges of the case with gold-size or jointing compound.

Fit wheels into the case and tighten all bolts and nuts.

Fit timing gears (Para. 24), and panel (Para. 21).

34. FITTING ENGINE TO FRAME.

Fitting of the engine to the frame should present no difficulty.

Lift engine into cradle and insert the two cradle bolts.

Starting at rear engine plates fit all bolts loosely, working finally to the front engine plate bolt.

Tighten all nuts.

Fit clutch, oil bath, etc.

Fit and time magdyno.

35. REMOVING AND FITTING OF TIMING GEAR BUSHES.

When engine is dismantled it may be found that the timing gear bushes require replacement. This is not a job to be undertaken by the average owner. The timing cover and half crankcase should be despatched to our service department.

THE TRANSMISSION

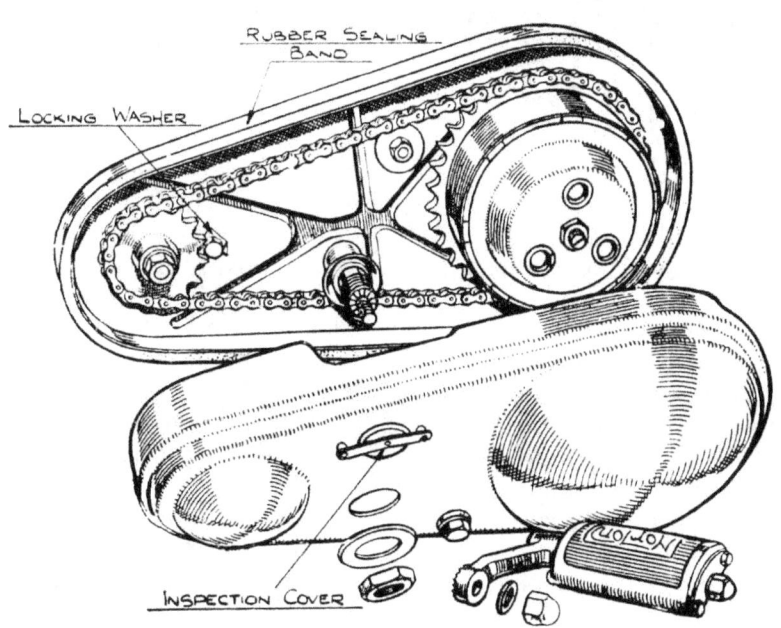

Fig. 11

36. CLUTCH ADJUSTMENT.

In order to obtain quick, clean gear-changing and freedom from clutch drag, correct clutch adjustment is vital.

Screw down cable adjuster as far as possible.

Remove oil bath outer portion (Para. 37) release nut locking the adjuster stud in the centre of the aluminium clutch pressure plate and screw in the stud, until contact with the push rod can be felt.

Screw back exactly half a turn and re-lock nut.

Re-adjust cable adjuster until there is $\frac{1}{8}''$-3/16" idle movement before tension occurs in the cable.

Correct clutch spring adjustment is obtained when the adjusting screws are flush with ends of the spring boxes and when individual adjustment has been made to ensure clutch pressure plate withdraws squarely as seen when the oil bath cover is removed and the clutch lever operated.

37. REMOVAL AND RE-FITTING OF OIL BATH.

Remove the footrests, footrest rod and brake pedal.

Remove the large nut holding the outer portion of the oil bath, and remove the outer portion.

Remove clutch spring screws, springs and cups (three of each), clutch outer plate, clutch thrust rod and clutch retaining nut.

Engage low gear and obtain assistance to hold the rear wheel while the nut is being removed.

Remove clutch body.

A special tool may be obtained for this purpose if necessary.

Remove engine sprocket (a claw-type extractor will remove this), and engine sprocket clutch and chain can be removed together.

Remove rear portion of oil bath, held to

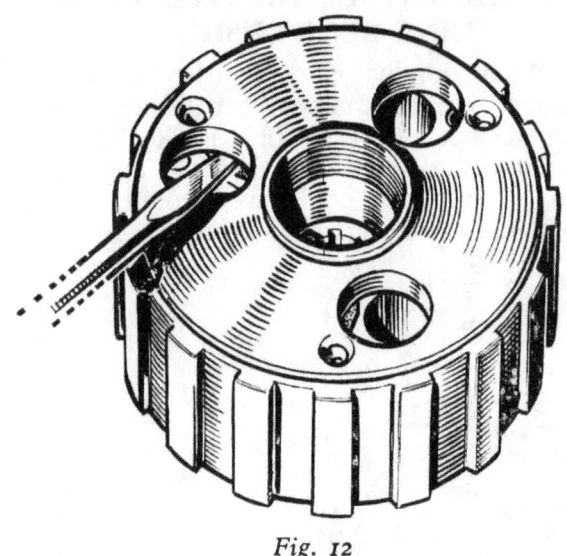

Fig. 12

the crankcase by bolt, to the engine plate by a nut, to the rear chain guard by a bolt, and by a nut on the gear box pivot bolt.

Re-assemble in the reverse order.

Examine rubber washer fitted round the flange of the inner portion. This must be in a good condition to retain oil in the case. If band has stretched, it is permissible to cut out the necessary amount, providing that the joined ends are placed on the top run of the chaincase.

Fill oil bath with oil to the level of the plug near the bottom of the outer portion of the oil bath.

38. CLUTCH—TO DISMANTLE.

Remove outer portion of the oil bath, and clutch (Para. 37).

Remove clutch plates—4 with inserts and 5 plain steel plates spaced alternately.

Remove clutch sprocket.

Place an old gearbox main axle (if available) in a vice with the splined end above the jaws, and fit body to axle.

Remove the three screws holding the front cover plate and tap the plate round until a screwdriver can be used to prise it off. Fig. 12.

A large "C" spanner is needed to remove the rubbers. This is placed over the body and engaged in the splines, and the large rubbers compressed while the small ones are removed.

The handle of the spanner should be of such a length that the load can be taken by the user's thigh, allowing both hands to be free to remove the rubbers.

A substitute for a "C" spanner can be made by fixing a handle to an old plain steel clutch plate.

Compress large rubbers and remove the small.

A small sharp-pointed tool is necessary to remove the rubbers, as after use they adhere to the body.

Large rubbers are easily removed after the small have been withdrawn.

Remove body from axle and replace in the reverse position.

Remove the three studs on the back cover plate.

Back plate, roller race, back cover and body can be separated.

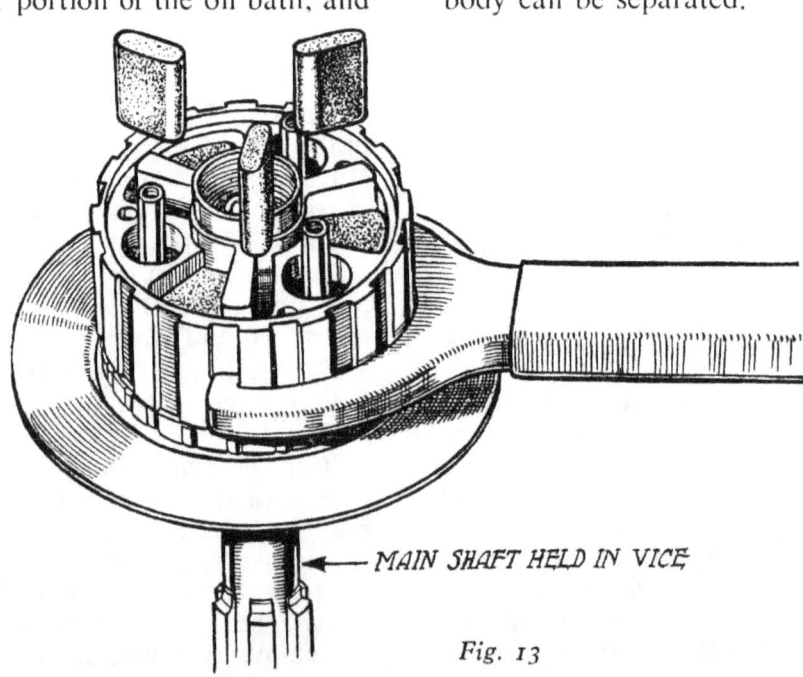

← MAIN SHAFT HELD IN VICE

Fig. 13

39. EXAMINATION OF CLUTCH PARTS.

Examine clutch inserts. They should be "proud" of the plate.

Fitting of separate inserts to a plate is not advisable, as the new inserts would be "proud" of the remainder and take all the drive on the plate in which it had been fitted.

It is advisable, if possible, to replace plates with either new or reconditioned ones.

If all the new inserts are fitted to a plate, ensure that the inserts are level and flat and all contact the steel plates, taking their share of the drive.

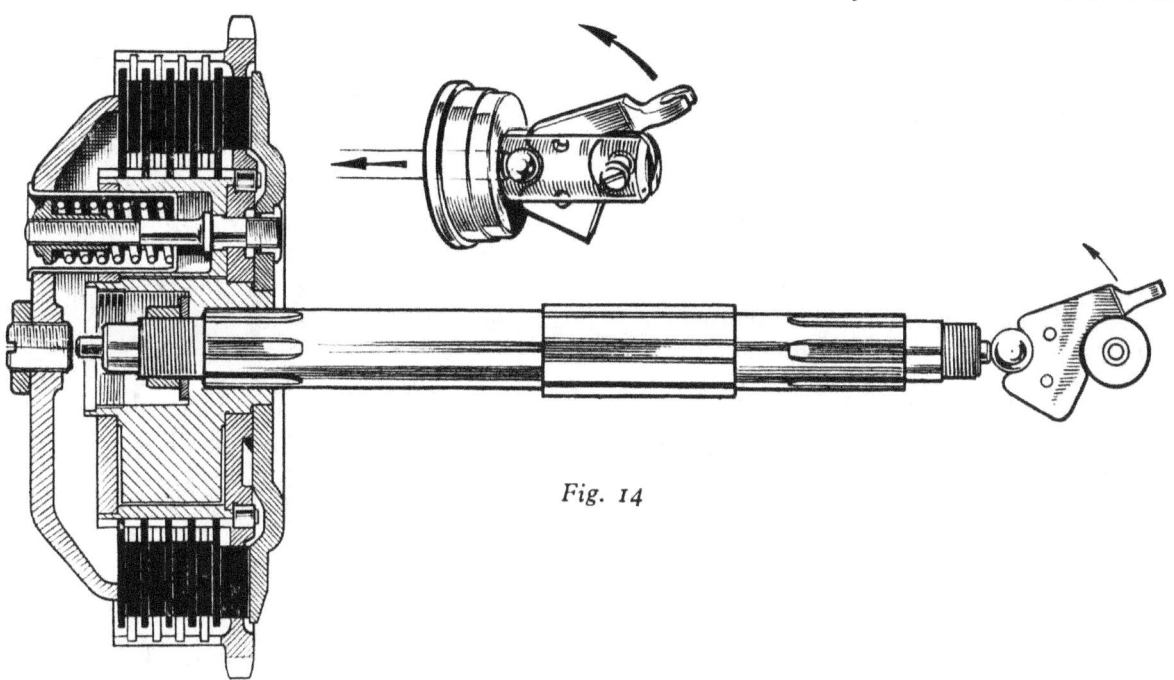

Fig. 14

Examine the drive on the plates for wear.

The plates with the inserts, drive on the outside diameter, and the plain steel, on the inside.

The splines on the body and the plain steel plates driven by the body rarely show any signs of wear.

The tongues on the plates with inserts, driving the sprocket, may show signs of wear and they may have "cut" in to the driven part of the sprocket.

This wear obstructs the free movement of the plates when the clutch is operated.

This can be rectified by filing or grinding the tongues on the plates square. Also the edge of the driven part of the sprocket.

The only effect this will have on the clutch is a slight amount of "back-lash" when the clutch is engaged or disengaged.

Examine plain steel plates for any roughness. The back plate sometimes develops this fault.

Examine the roller race, rollers and the cage.

Examine the back cover plate face for wear by the clutch body centre.

Examine clutch shock absorber rubbers. They may have become soft or cracked.

40. ASSEMBLY OF CLUTCH.

Fit clutch body back cover plate to body, ensuring that the holes in the cover plate are in line with the holes in the body, and the spring studs an easy fit.

Fit clutch body centre and fit clutch large shock absorber rubbers in position to take the drive.

Compress the rubbers in position and fit the small ones.

Fit body front cover and tighten screws.

Fit roller race on to the back cover plate, fit clutch plate back, and spring studs, fit stud nut and tighten. Lock nuts with a centre punch.

Test roller race for freeness on its track, and apply a little anti-centrifuge grease.

Check all the clutch plates in the sprocket and on the body for freeness.

Fit sprocket to body. Revolve sprocket on race to check free movement.

Fit plates to sprocket and body. Order of fitting is—plain steel, inserts, plain, etc.

Revolve sprocket, ensuring that the plates are free.

Fit clutch to Gearbox axle.

Fit clutch thrust rod, clutch outer plate spring cups, springs, and spring pins. Tighten right home.

Fit oil bath outer portion. (Para. 37).

GEARBOX

41. REMOVAL FROM FRAME.

The oil bath chaincase and clutch, having been removed, remove kickstarter crank, gear indicator and gear lever, also clutch lever inspection and oil filler cover.

Disconnect clutch inner wire from operating lever, unscrew cable adjuster and remove.

Remove top and bottom gearbox bolt. Swing gearbox round until fixing points lie approximately horizontal and manoeuvre the box out through the offside of the frame.

42. FITTING TO FRAME.

Reverse the order of removal operations, leaving the top and bottom bolts slack until the primary chain has been correctly tensioned ($\frac{1}{4}/\frac{3}{8}''$ up and down movement) by means of the adjuster on the offside of the machine. Remember that any adjustment of the primary chain will affect the rear chain.

43. OUTER COVER, REMOVAL.

Remove the kick starter crank by releasing its pinch bolt and pulling off the crank.

Remove gear indicator by unscrewing the centre bolt from the positive spindle.

Remove oil filler and inspection plate, and disconnect clutch inner wire from operating lever.

Do not remove foot change pedal.

Remove five screws holding cover in position, and carefully pull the cover away by means of the footchange pedal. Take care not to tear paper washer.

44. OUTER COVER, FITTING.

Ensure paper washer is undamaged or carefully scrape off old washer and fit new.

Ensure also foot change pawl spring not dislodged and lying correctly with its straight leg uppermost, each leg resting on the rocking pawl (Fig. 16) before fitting cover. Replace remaining parts.

Some oil will have been lost due to cover removal and should be replenished through the filler hole after the level plug: i.e., the small hexagon headed pin to the rear of the kickstarter axle, has been removed. Engine oil should be slowly poured in until it commences to drip from this screw hole.

45. POSITIVE FOOT CHANGE, DISMANTLING.

Removal of the outer cover will bring with it the positive footchange mechanism.

To dismantle, remove gear indicator and withdraw ratchet plate and spindle.

Remove pawl spring.

Remove operating lever, disengage return spring legs from pawl pin and withdraw pawl carrier.

New return spring cannot be fitted without removing spring stop plate.

46. POSITIVE FOOT CHANGE, ASSEMBLY.

Obtain any necessary replacements and ensure all parts clean.

Smear oil on moving parts.

Place return spring in position and fit plate.

Place washer on pawl carrier spindle, insert into bush and push home whilst manoeuvering spring legs into position in groove in pawl pin.

Refit pawl spring with cranked leg to ground.

Fit ratchet and spindle.

Refit operating lever and gear indicator before fitting cover.

Use indicator to move ratchet plate into position to pilot operating pin into selector fork roller whilst fitting cover. Probably necessary to remove indicator, finally, to adjust lever to individual requirements.

47. INNER COVER, REMOVAL.

With outer cover already removed, remove ratchet plate with spindle.

Remove locking ring securing clutch operating lever body and withdraw body, ensuring that $\frac{1}{2}''$ steel ball does not become lost. Remove mainshaft nut now exposed.

Remove the seven nuts holding the cover to the shell and withdraw the cover from the studs, tapping behind the front end to loosen if necessary. Avoid damaging paper washer.

48. INNER COVER, FITTING.

Ensure paper washer undamaged and faces clean.

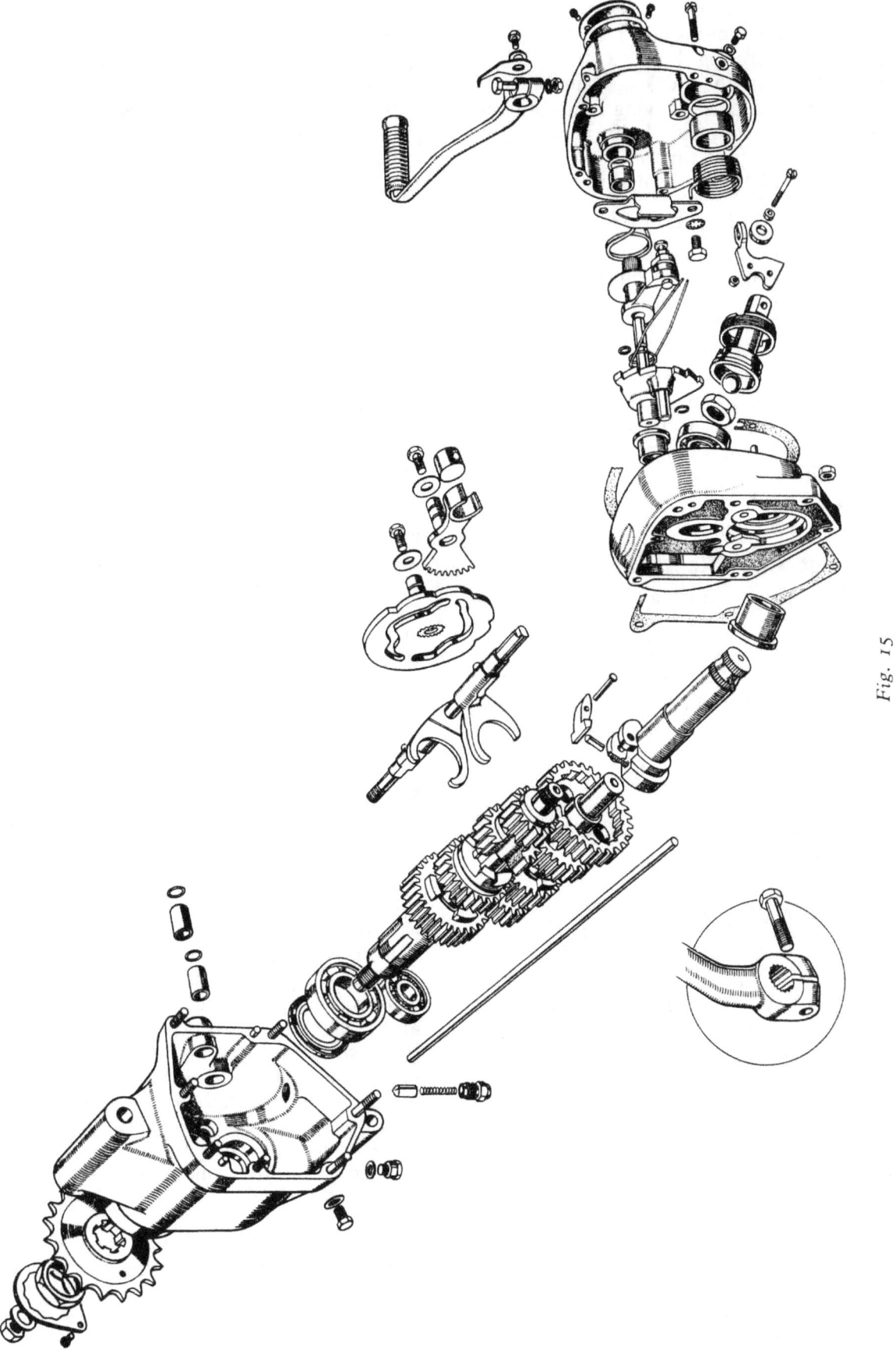

Fig. 15

Fit cover and its seven securing nuts, just pinching all down and finally tightening opposite nuts in pairs.

Fit and tighten mainshaft nut.

Fit clutch operating body with ball but before tightening the locking ring ensure that the operating lever is lying in alignment with clutch cable adjuster hole, in order to obtain a straight pull on the cable.

Fit ratchet plate and spindle.

49. INNER COVER, DISMANTLING.

The footchange mechanism having been already dealt with, and the clutch operating parts having been removed in order to enable inner cover to be withdrawn, only the kickstarter mechanism remains.

Lever out return spring end from hole in kickstarter axle when the axle can be withdrawn from its bush. Removal of the pawl pin results in pawl, plunger, spring falling out of position.

If the nose of the pawl is worn or chipped, it should be renewed.

50. INNER COVER, ASSEMBLING.

Examine pawl cam and stop pieces rivetted to cover, if loose re-rivet.

Fit pawl spring, plunger, pawl and pin.

Insert axle into bush, fit return spring.

NOTE that clutch operating mechanism cannot be re-assembled until cover is fitted to box.

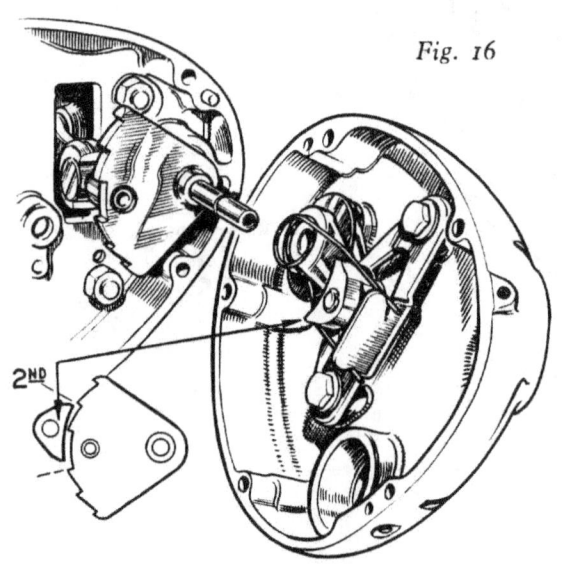

Fig. 16

51. REMOVAL OF GEARS.

If the clutch has been removed, it will be necessary to fit a short length of tubing over the end of the main axle and hold it in place with a clutch nut to retain the axle in position whilst the gears are being removed.

Remove end cover. (Paras. 43 and 47).

Remove the low gear and kickstarter wheel the large gear on the layshaft which has a bronze bush pressed into its centre.

Remove the small wheel from the end of the main axle.

Remove the mainshaft second gear; this is fitted with a fully floating bush. Unscrew the striker fork shaft by means of the two flats machined on its outer end and remove it together with the layshaft second gear and the striker fork.

Remove the tubular distance piece or clutch and withdraw the main axle together with the third gear and striker fork.

Withdraw the layshaft and the two remaining gears.

Gently warming the box and dropping it face downwards on a wooden block will withdraw the layshaft bearing.

Remove axle sprocket nut which has a left hand thread and is held with a locking washer and screw, and withdraw the main gearwheel. If the gearbox is in the frame and the rear chain in position, obtain assistance to hold the rear wheel whilst the nut is being removed.

If the gearbox is removed from the frame, the sprocket may be held by passing a length of old chain around it and holding the ends in a vice.

52. REMOVAL OF CAM PLATE.

Remove the domed hexagon nut from beneath the forward side of the gearbox. This contains the cam plate indexing plunger which will drop out when the nut is removed.

Remove the two bolts fitted with plain washers visible on the forward side of the gearbox shell. These secure the cam plate and cam plate quadrant, both of which may be pushed through into the box when the bolts are removed. Both cam plate and quadrant are carried in a bronze bush. It is unlikely that these bushes will ever require renewing, but they may be readily pressed or drifted out should the necessity arise.

53. FITTING CAM PLATE.

Place the quadrant in position and secure it with its bolt and washers. Place the cam plate in position so that one of the end grooves in its circumference is across the centre of the indexing plunger hole in the gearbox shell and meshing its gear with the last tooth but one on the quadrant, ensuring that the correct end of the quadrant rack is being used. Assemble the positive mechanism onto the inner cover. Place cover in position and connect quadrant lever to ratchet by means of knuckle pin (Para. 46).

Set positive footchange to top gear and check that the indexing plunger groove lies in the correct position to mesh with the indexing plunger when fitted. Withdraw cam plate and re-mesh as necessary until the correct position is obtained when the cam plate bolts and washers should be fitted and tightened. Fit indexing plunger, spring and plunger bush.

54. FITTING GEARS INTO GEAR BOX.

Fit the main gear wheel, press the wheel home in its bearing, fit gearbox axle sprocket, tighten the nut, fit locking washer and pin.

Fit distance tube in place of clutch and add clutch nut.

Fit third gear wheel (20 teeth) and top gear wheel (18 teeth) to layshaft and fit inner race with rollers and cage to the end of the shaft. Grease the rollers and fit shaft into box.

Set the cam plate into the second gear position, i.e., with indexing plunger in the groove next to the shallow neutral groove.

Fit striking fork to mainshaft third gear (22 teeth) and fit gear to main axle, meshing it with the layshaft gear already in position.

Fit the second fork to the layshaft second gear (24 teeth) and fit the second gear with the fork to the layshaft. The pegs on the striking forks fit into the cam plate slots.

With the gearbox in the frame, little trouble will be experienced in holding the first fork in position. Fit the first fork in position and hold with a screw driver or similar tool whilst the second is placed in position.

Fit striking fork shaft and screw into the case.

Fit the remaining gears.

Fit end cover (Para. 44).

Remove tubular distance piece from clutch end of mainshaft. Remember to finally refill with oil to the level plug. (Para. 44).

WHEELS AND HUBS

55. FRONT WHEEL, REMOVAL.

Place machine on centre stand. Detach brake cable from cam lever and cable adjuster from brake plate. Remove spindle nut from off-side of spindle. Slacken pinch bolt in near side fork end. Take the weight of the wheel in the left hand and withdraw the spindle by means of a tommy bar placed through the hole in the head of the spindle.

56. FRONT WHEEL, FITTING.

Re-assemble in the reverse order. Insert spindle from near side. Lock pinch bolt in near side fork end after tightening the spindle nut.

57. REAR WHEEL, REMOVAL.

With machine on centre stand, disconnect tail and stop lamp leads by pulling the cable either side of the rubber covered snap connection behind the number plate. Slacken off by two or three turns the lifting handle end bolts and the central bolt above the tail piece joint. This will enable the tail portion of the mudguard to be removed.

Disconnect speedometer driving cable.

Remove the three rubber plugs from the end of the hub and with suitable box spanner, unscrew the sleeve nuts then exposed.

Remove wheel spindle and distance piece and draw wheel off its studs.

This method of wheel removal leaves the chain and brake drum in position.

To remove wheel complete with brake drum, disconnect rear chain and remove chainguard. Remove brake rod adjusting nut, disconnect brake torque arm from frame and disconnect speedometer drive. Release wheel spindle and nut from near side stub axle, enabling wheel to be slid along the adjusting slots and removed.

58. REAR WHEEL, REFITTING.

Reverse dismantling operations. Fit spring link to chain with closed end of spring facing direction of travel, ensure chain adjuster plates correctly seated and when all is tightened, check rear chain for correct tension. There should be $\frac{3}{4}''$ slack midway

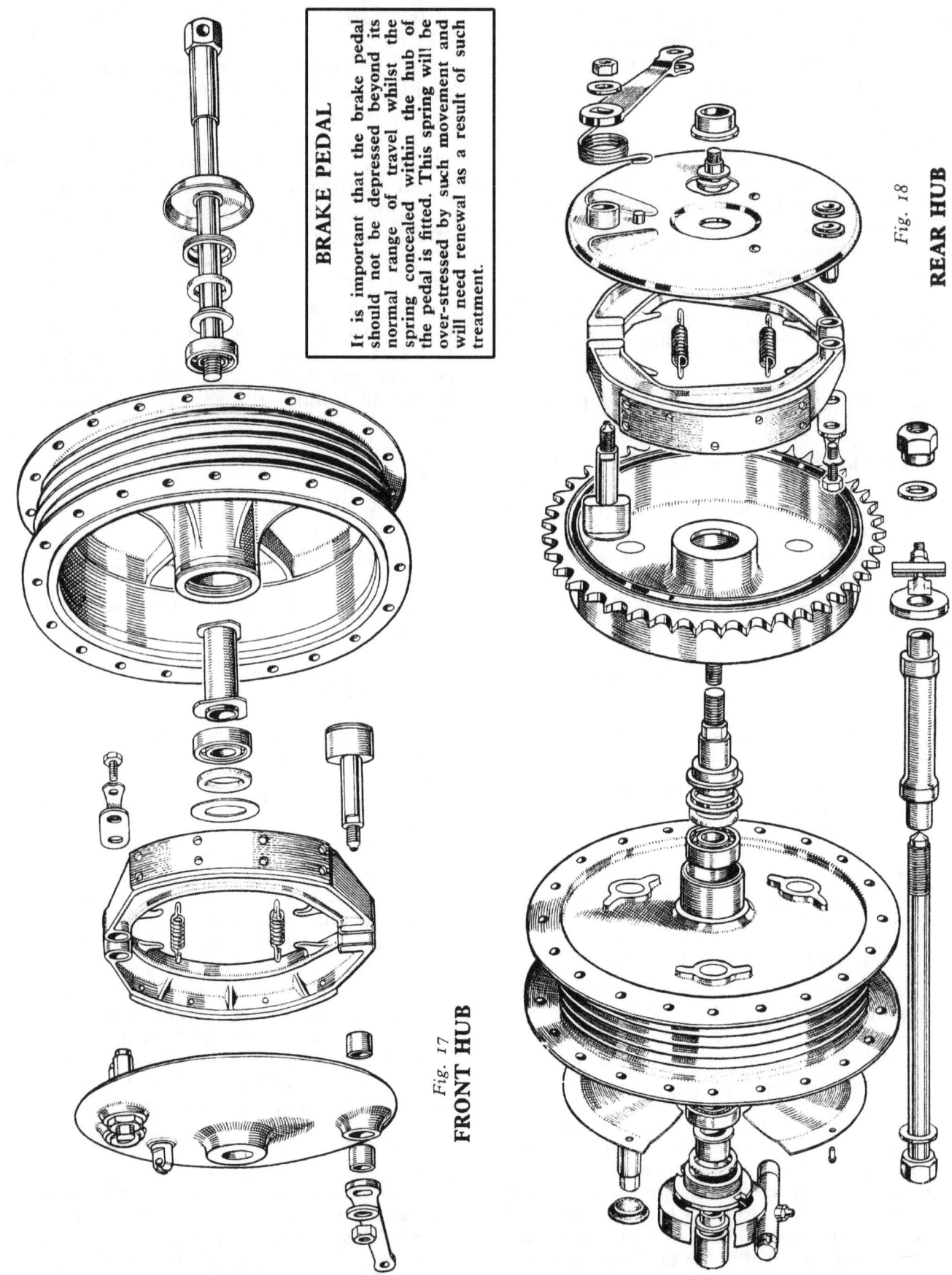

BRAKE PEDAL

It is important that the brake pedal should not be depressed beyond its normal range of travel whilst the spring concealed within the hub of the pedal is fitted. This spring will be over-stressed by such movement and will need renewal as a result of such treatment.

Fig. 17
FRONT HUB

Fig. 18
REAR HUB

between the sprockets with the weight of the machine on the wheels. Adjust rear brake as necessary.

59. REAR HUB, DISMANTLING.

Remove rear wheel (Para. 57). Remove locking ring, felt washer and distance piece from plain side of hub.

Drift out inner sleeve, it will bring with it the single row bearing.

Using a suitable punch, knock out the bearing in the brake side of the hub, together with the peened in washer, felt washer and pen steel washer.

60. REAR HUB, RE-ASSEMBLING.

Pack bearing with grease, wiping off surplus.

Fit single row bearing to screwed side of hub, fit inner sleeve with the long end into the single row bearing.

Fit distance piece, felt washer and locking ring and tighten.

Press double row bearing into position on opposite side of hub, followed by the pen steel washer and dished washer. Lightly rivet the dished washer into position.

61. FRONT HUB, DISMANTLING.

Remove front wheel (Para. 55).
Remove brake plate.
Remove locking ring, felt washer and distance piece from opposite side of hub.
With suitable punch knock the bearing in the brake side further into the hub until the single row bearing drops clear.
Remove distance tube.
From this side of the hub drift out the remaining bearing, together with the peened in washer, felt washer and pen steel washer.

62. FRONT HUB, RE-ASSEMBLING.

Pack bearings with grease.
Press single row bearing into position followed by the distance piece (with collar against the bearing), felt washer and locking ring which can be tightened up.
Insert distance tube through brake side of hub, ensuring that it is right home against the bearing just fitted.
Press double row bearing into position.
Fit pen steel washer and felt washer.
Lightly rivet the remaining washer into its recess.

BRAKES

63. BRAKES, ADJUSTMENT, FRONT.

The cable adjuster situated at the lower end of the operating cable may be screwed outwards as necessary to maintain minimum clearance between brake linings and drum, until such time as operation of the handlebar lever results in the cam lever moving beyond its best position, i.e., right angle between cable and lever.

At this stage the cable " U " clip should be disconnected and the cam lever removed and re-fitted so that the side which was originally outside is now inside. This will restore the position of the lever to something like that which it originally occupied and provide a new lease of life.

REAR:

The adjusting nut on the rear end of the brake rod is the only form of adjustment available.

Remember that adjustment of the rear chain will necessitate adjustment also at this point.

64. DISMANTLING AND ASSEMBLY.

Remove brake plate from the drum.

Remove brake lever return spring from the lever.
Remove nut and washer from the cam spindle.
Remove brake lever.
Remove cam and spindle from bush in the brake plate.
Tap the end of the spindle lightly until the cam is clear of the shoes.
Remove brake shoe return springs.
Remove the small pin from the end of each pivot pin and lift off the pivot pin tie plate.
Remove the brake shoes.
Cam spindle bush can be removed from the plate after removing the nut holding bush to the plate.

TO RE-ASSEMBLE:

Fit cam spindle bush to plate.
Fit brake shoes. Smear a little oil on the pivot pins.
Fit ONE shoe to pivot pin.
Fit spring to the shoe fitted to the pin near pin.
Hold second shoe near to the one fitted and fit the spring, stretch the spring and fit second shoe to pivot pin.

Fit second spring to both shoes.

Fit cam spindle to plate. Hold shoes apart with screwdriver or similar tool and allow cam to pass the ends of the shoes.

Fit tie plate over shoulders on pivot pins, fit and tighten both pins.

FRONT FORKS

65. MAINTENANCE.

Replenish damping oil at approximately 5,000 mile intervals.

Remove hexagon headed filler plug from top of each fork leg. Remove drain plug from each fork end. Allow oil to drain out and operate the forks a time or two to eject the last drops.

Replace drain plugs.

Re-fill each leg with a measured ¼ pint of Wakefield's Castrolite, Shell X-100-20, B.P. Energol S.A.E. 20 or Mobiloil Arctic.

Work the forks a few times to remove any air-locks.

Replace filler plugs.

66. STEERING HEAD ADJUSTMENT.

Place a wooden block or box under the engine cradle of sufficient height to raise the

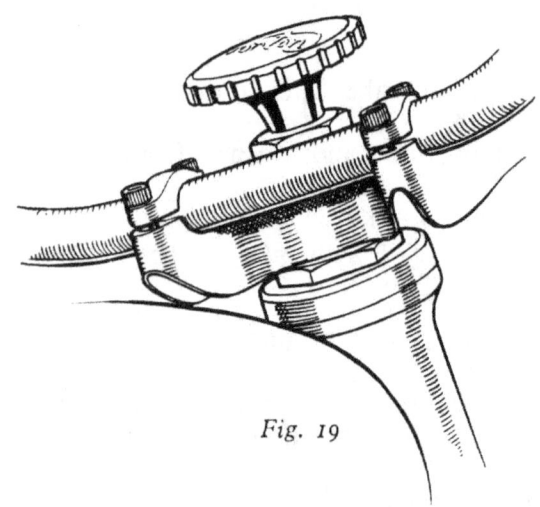

Fig. 19

front wheel clear of the ground. Place thumb of left hand on the joint between the steering head of the frame and the fork head clip.

Attempt to lift the forks with the right hand. Any movement at the head races will be readily felt.

To adjust, slacken the steering column locking nut AND THE PINCH BOLT NUT clamping each leg into the fork crown.

Adjust by means of the nut situated on the steering column below the head clip, until all play is removed, but the forks are still free to rotate on the head races.

Re-tighten the steering column locking nut and the pinch bolts.

67. REMOVAL OF FRONT FORKS FROM FRAME.

This may be carried out either with or without the front wheel and mudguard in position.

Disconnect wiring from headlamp (Para. 101).

Detach steering damper arm from frame.

Detach speedometer driving and lighting cables from speedometer head.

Remove all cables from the handlebar levers, remove handlebars.

Slacken off steering damper completely, remove steering column locking nut complete with damper knob and rod.

Remove oil filler plugs and speedometer panel.

Remove head clip and head race adjusting nut.

Withdraw forks carefully to avoid losing any head race balls.

Take care to avoid spilling any damping oil from the fork legs. If any oil is lost it will be necessary to replenish as instructed. (Para. 65).

68. FITTING OF FORKS TO THE FRAME.

Examine head races and balls (17 per race).

Races are pressed into their housings and may readily be knocked out for renewal.

Note that the races fitted in the frame embody a small hole to allow the entry of grease.

Liberally grease the track in the race fitted to the bottom of the steering column and the top frame race. Place 17 balls in position in each and carefully insert the column through the frame.

Place the top race and dust cover in position and screw the adjusting nut down the column until the hexagon is finger tight against the top race.

Refit the head clip and speedometer panel, the column locking nut loosely and the filler

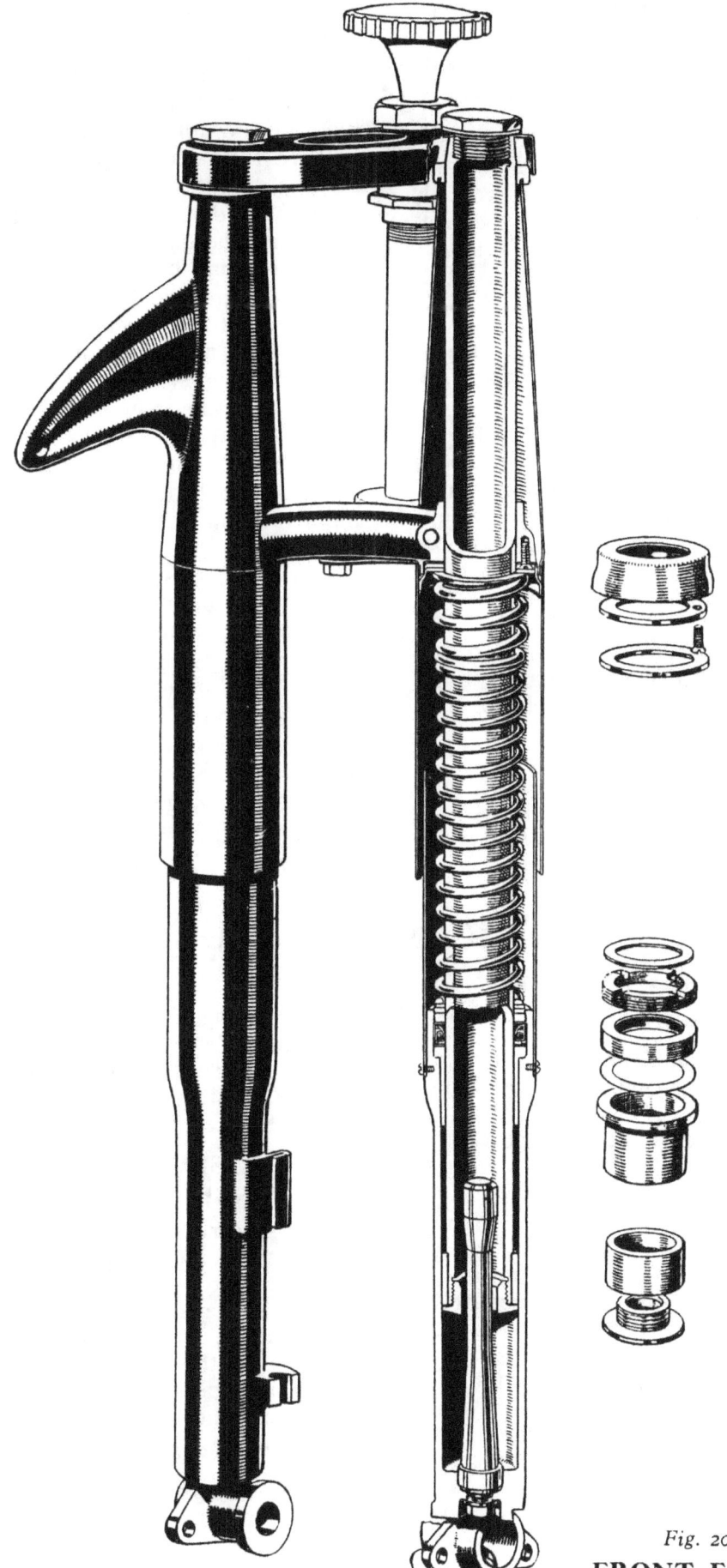

Fig. 20
FRONT FORKS

plugs which should be tightened up.

Adjust the head races. (Para. 66).

Refit all remaining parts and check that all bolts and nuts have been tightened.

69. FORK LEG, DISMANTLING.

This may be carried out with the forks in position, but before commencing the work it is advisable to obtain from our Service Department a "pull through" to facilitate removal and replacement of the main tube.

Remove front wheel. (Para. 55).

Remove front mudguard.

Remove oil filler and drain plugs from top and bottom of fork leg and allow oil to drain off.

Slacken the pinch bolt in the crown lug.

Fork end, complete with bottom cover, springs and main tube may be withdrawn.

If difficulty is encountered the "pull through" already mentioned should be screwed into the top of the main tube which can then be tapped out with a mallet.

Remove from the main tube the top leather washer (this may have stuck to the inside of the upper cover) and main spring.

Remove the bottom cover, held to the fork end by two screws.

Remove leather washer.

Remove locking ring from top of fork end. Withdraw fork end from main tube.

The remaining components may now be removed from the main tube.

70. FORK LEG, ASSEMBLY.

Thoroughly clean all components and obtain any necessary renewals.

Attach the bottom bush to the main tube by means of the securing nut.

Place fork end in position on the main tube.

Fit shouldered bush into fork end followed by the super oil seal, the side with exposed spring being uppermost.

Screw home the locking ring and tighten sufficiently to be secure without distorting the case of the super oil seal.

Fit the smaller of the two leather washers over the locking ring followed by the main spring and the remaining leather washer.

Fit bottom cover and securing screws.

Screw "pull through" into top end of main tube and pass through crown lug and head clip.

Draw into position by means of tommy bar inserted across the "pull through" and temporarily tighten the pinch bolt in the crown lug.

Remove "pull through."

Fit filler plug to main tube and slacken pinch bolt. Lock main tube in position with filler plug. Re-tighten pinch bolt.

Fit drain plug to fork end.

Remove filler plug.

Replenish with oil. (Para. 65).

REAR SPRINGING

71. SWINGING ARM REMOVAL AND DISMANTLING.

As there is neither adjustment nor lubrication necessary to the swinging arm pivot, no periodic maintenance is necessary, but the time may arrive when it becomes necessary to dismantle the assembly, possibly to renew the silentbloc bushes.

Remove rear wheel (Para. 57). Remove shock absorber units by removing the bolts securing the top and bottom members to the frame and swinging arm respectively. Remove the pivot bolt by first removing the oil bath chaincase outer portion and the clutch (Paras. 37 and 38), removing the nut at the offside end of the pivot bolt and drifting the bolt right out of position, enabling the swinging arm to be withdrawn.

The silentbloc bushes are pressed into the cross tube of the swinging arm and may be knocked out of position, preferably using a drift only slightly smaller than the bore of the cross tube but longer than the hole in the outer sleeve of the silentbloc. Soaking in release oil may assist in the removal of over-tight bearings.

72. RE-ASSEMBLY AND RE-FITTING SWINGING ARM.

Press or drift one new bush into swinging arm until its outer sleeve is flush with the end of the cross tube. Insert distance piece from opposite side and press home the other bush. Place swinging arm in position, ensuring that the brackets for attaching the shock absorber are on the top side, re-fit pivot bolt and nut and tighten.

73. REAR SUSPENSION UNITS.

These fittings embody quite complicated oil damping arrangements which are carefully set to provide the correct suspension characteristics for your machine. They are sealed and are virtually leakproof and should NOT BE INTERFERED WITH. In the unlikely event of any attention being necessary, their removal is quite simple and straightforward and they should be taken to your usual Norton dealer or to the nearest Norton distributor.

No attempt whatever should be made by the normal rider to dismantle, drain or refill these units.

HANDLEBAR FITTINGS

74. IGNITION AND AIR CONTROL LEVERS.

The ignition and air control levers are shown in Fig. 22 in the position which they should be assembled, having first greased both sides of the lever.

After fitting the adjusting nut it should be tightened to give the required tension.

To remove the control cables from the lever, open the lever as far as possible, hold the outer cable, and as the lever is closed, pull the outer cable from the lever body.

Remove nipple from the lever.

To fit the cables, fit nipple into the lever, close the lever, pull the outer cable away from the lever and fit the cable to the lever body.

75. CLUTCH AND FRONT BRAKE CONTROL LEVERS.

The clutch and front brake controls are so simple as to require no instructions for their dismantling or assembly.

The pivot bolts have shoulders machined on them, allowing the nuts on the bolts to be tightened while allowing clearance for easy movement of the lever.

To remove the clutch cable from the lever, turn the clutch operating arm on the clutch worm by other means than the cable, and the nipple can be removed from the arm, and inner and outer cables can be removed from the lever.

To remove the brake cable from the lever, remove the split cotter and pin holding the "U" clip to the brake arm, and the inner and outer cables can be removed from the lever.

Re-assemble in the reverse order.

76. EXHAUST LIFTER LEVER.

The arrangement of the exhaust lifter lever is similar to the clutch and brake, only smaller.

To remove the cables from the lever, turn the operating arm on the exhaust lifter by other means than the cable and remove the inner cable from the arm. Remove the nipple on the other end of the cable from the lever and the nipple will pass through the large hole in the lever body.

When re-assembling, the cables must be fitted to the lever first.

77. TWIST GRIP.

The twist grip assembly is shown in Fig. 21.

To assemble the twist grip, grease the portion of the handlebar where the grip works.

Fit the sleeve to the bar.

Grease the drum on the sleeve.

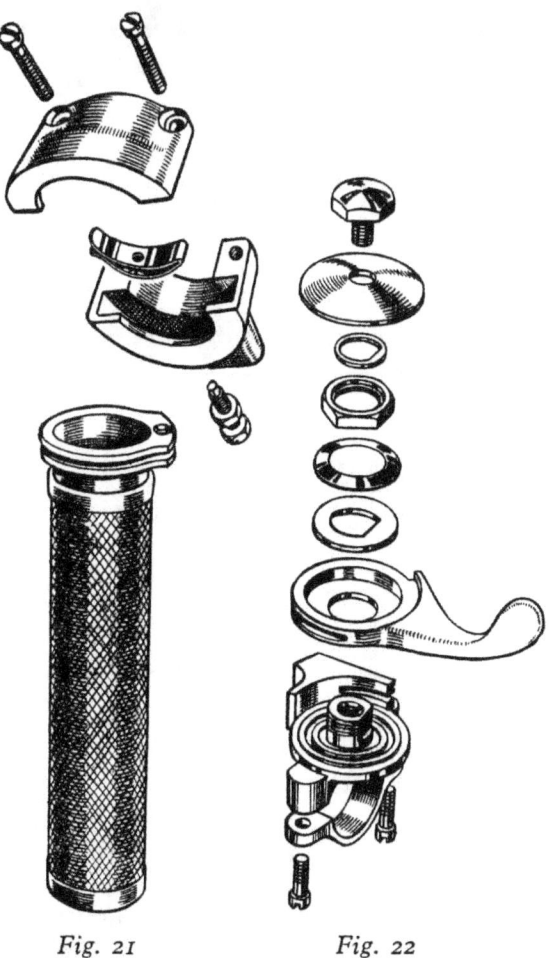

Fig. 21
Twist grip

Fig. 22
Ignition and Air Control

Fit spring and adjuster bolt and nut to the bottom half clip.

Thread the cable through the hole in the half clip.

Fit the nipple to the drum on the sleeve.

(Sufficient length of cable can be obtained by lifting the throttle side and holding in position by a piece of soft wood placed in the air intake).

Fit the top half clip.

Adjust the tightness of the grip with the adjusting screw and lock in the desired position.

Dismantle in the reverse order.

AMAL CARBURETTER

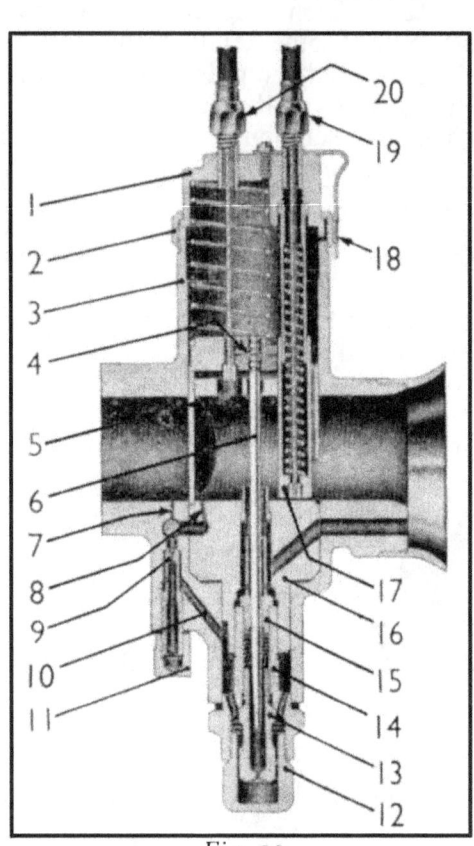

Fig. 23

Diagrammatic section through Mixing Chamber

1—Mixing Chamber Top.
2—Mixing Chamber Cap.
3—Carburetter Body.
4—Jet Needle Clip.
5—Throttle Valve.
6—Jet Needle.
7—Pilot Outlet.
8—Pilot by-pass.
9—Pilot Jet.
10—Petrol feed to pilot jet.
11—Pilot Jet Cover Nut.
12—Main Jet Cover.
13—Main Jet.
14—Jet Holder.
15—Needle Jet.
16—Jet Block.
17—Air Valve.
18—Mixing Chamber Cap Spring.
19—Cable Adjuster (Air).
20—Cable Adjuster (Throttle).
21—Tickler.
23—Banjo.
29—Pilot Air Adjusting Screw.
30—Throttle Adjusting Screw.

78. DISMANTLING OF CARBURETTER.

The easiest way to remove the carburetter is to turn both petrol taps off and disconnect feed pipe from carburetter, remove the two nuts securing carburetter flange and unscrew the knurled ring immediately below where the control cables enter the top of the mixing chamber body so that the slides may be withdrawn, either before or after the carburetter is removed. The air and throttle valves may be left on the cables unless it is desired to change or renew the cables or valves.

The throttle valve needle may be removed or adjusted for position by removal of the spring clip at the top of the slide.

Remove the float chamber cover by removing the three screws securing it, and withdraw the hinged float, this will enable the nylon needle which controls the flow of fuel to be withdrawn and cleaned.

Removal of the nut at the base of mixing chamber gives access to the main jet which may be unscrewed from the jet holder which also carries the needle jet, accessible by removal of jet holder. Removal of these parts enables the jet block to be pushed or tapped out through the large end of the mixing

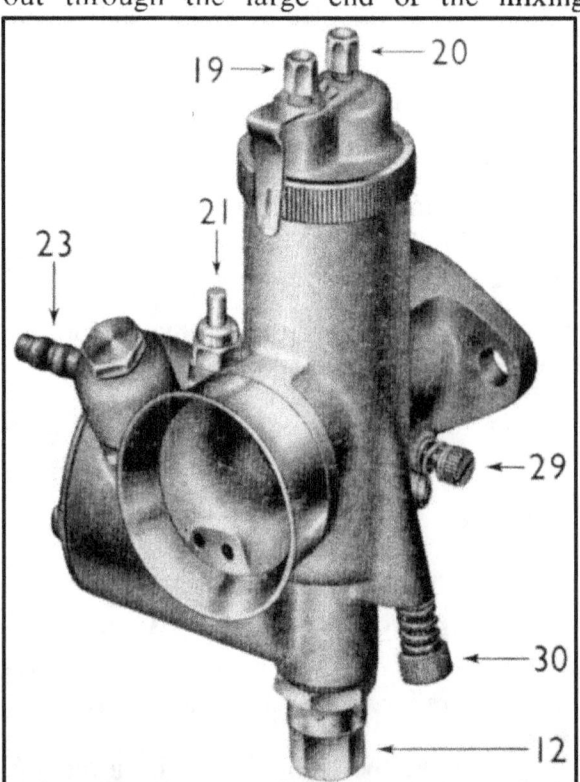

Fig. 24
General view of Carburetter

chamber body when the jet block locating screw has been removed. This screw lies to the left of and slightly below the pilot air adjuster which is the horizontal milled headed screw equipped with restricting spring.

79. RE-ASSEMBLY of CARBURETTER.

Re-assembly should present no difficulty but the following points should be watched. The washer fitted to the stub of the jet block should be in good condition, also the one fitted to the needle jet holder. When fitting throttle valve ensure that taper needle really enters the centre hole in the jet block, and that throttle works freely when mixing chamber top cap be fitted and secured. Fit float with narrow side of hinge uppermost and ensure that side cover washer and body are clean and undamaged to obtain a petrol tight joint.

80. CARBURETTER TUNING.

There are four distinct phases of tuning and each must be handled separately to obtain best results for any particular set of conditions. For all these positions the air valve should be fully open, the engine should be at its normal working temperature, and the machine should be driven on a slight up gradient to ensure engine pulling whole time.

1st MAIN JET.

This jet controls the fuel supply when the throttle is more than $\frac{3}{4}$ open. With the throttle fully open and the engine pulling hard, slightly close the air lever when there should be a slight falling off of speed indicating a reasonably correct mixture. If maximum speed is obtained before the throttle is fully open, then a larger main jet is required; similarly if there is an increase in speed with the air lever slightly closed.

2nd SLOW RUNNING.

Having fixed the main jet, set the throttle adjusting screw to provide a fairly fast idling with the twist grip in the fully closed position and the ignition (where manually controlled) set for best slow running. Screw out the throttle adjusting screw until the engine begins to falter; now adjust the pilot air screw in or out as necessary to make the engine run evenly and faster. Lower the throttle adjusting screw further to reduce engine speed until a position of the pilot air screw is found at which the engine runs evenly and steadily on the smallest throttle opening.

3rd THROTTLE VALVE CUTAWAY.

With the throttle valve about a $\frac{1}{4}$ open (marking the twist grip if necessary in order to readily find this position whilst riding) note whether there is any spitting (indicating weakness) or jerky running under load (indicating richness). In the former event try screwing in the pilot air screw slightly and if this is ineffective, a throttle valve having less cutaway, i.e., stamped with a lower number and the reverse for jerky running.

4th THROTTLE VALVE NEEDLE.

With the throttle about $\frac{3}{4}$ open and the needle in a low position try the machine for acceleration. If results are poor and partially closing the lever provides improved conditions, raise the needle a notch or two until the best position is found.

5th RE-CHECK IDLING.

To ensure that subsequent adjustments have not upset the condition.

81. MAINTENANCE.

Clean periodically by dismantling and washing in clean petrol, cleaning out all holes by blowing. Whilst dismantled examine throttle valve needle and float needle for wear, and all fibre washers, renewing as necessary. Check that throttle valve is not unduly worn in the mixing chamber body.

82. RICH MIXTURE.

Indicated by black exhaust smoke, exces-

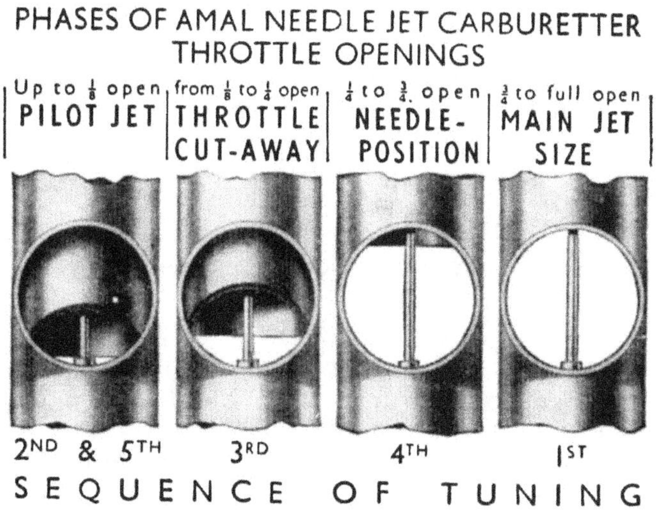

PHASES OF AMAL NEEDLE JET CARBURETTER THROTTLE OPENINGS

Up to $\frac{1}{8}$ open	from $\frac{1}{8}$ to $\frac{1}{4}$ open	$\frac{1}{4}$ to $\frac{3}{4}$ open	$\frac{3}{4}$ to full open
PILOT JET	THROTTLE CUT-AWAY	NEEDLE-POSITION	MAIN JET SIZE
2ND & 5TH	3RD	4TH	1ST

SEQUENCE OF TUNING

Fig. 25

sive soot on plug, lumpy running, petrol blown back from air intake.

Assuming that carburation has previously been satisfactory, suspect:—flooding due to punctured float, dirt on float needle seating or worn needle or seat. Worn throttle valve needle or needle jet, air cleaner choked.

83. WEAK MIXTURE.

Indicated by spitting back, poor acceleration, overheating, erratic slow running or improved performance with air lever partly shut.

Again assuming carburetter has been correctly set, suspect:—fuel blockage, either main supply or within carburetter. Worn inlet valve guide, air leaks at engine carburetter connection, worn throttle valve, loose jets.

LEGSHIELDS

84.

A standard set of these Legshield fittings comprises:—
- 2 Legshield Blades.
- 2 Legshield Blade Brackets.
- 2 Legshield Blade Brackets Back Plates.
- 4 $\frac{1}{4}''$ pins and nuts for above.
- 1 Horn Bracket extension plate with $\frac{3}{8}''$ pin and nut.
- 1 7/16" dia. rod $24\frac{1}{2}''$ long with nuts.
- 1 7/16" dia. rod 23.7/16" long with nuts.
- 1 Distance tube $13\frac{1}{8}''$ long.
- 1 Distance tube $6\frac{7}{8}''$ long.
- 1 Distance tube $5\frac{7}{8}''$ long.
- 2 Distance tubes 1.7/16" long.
- 4 Distance tubes $3\frac{3}{8}''$ long.
- 2 Legshield Attachment brackets for tank platform.
- 2 Thin tank rubbers.

85. FITTING INSTRUCTIONS.

Remove the front petrol tank bolts and slacken the rear bolts.

Remove the front tank platform top rubbers and replace with the thin rubbers supplied.

Over the rubbers place the attachment brackets so that the arm with the 7/16" hole points downwards and is to the rear of the tank bolt. Place the plain steel washers from under the tank over the brackets and insert the front tank bolts through the middle of the three holes in the attachment brackets but do not tighten up.

Place the $13\frac{1}{8}''$ distance tube between the legs of the attachment brackets, insert the longer of the 7/16" dia. rods and in each end place a 1.7/16" distance tube.

Remove crankcase engine plate bolt carrying the horn and insert in its place the remaining 7/16" rod. Attach the extension bracket to the horn and place in position on the left hand side of the rod.

Fit the $5\frac{1}{8}''$ distance tube next to the horn and the $6\frac{7}{8}''$ tube on the opposite side.

Fit the legshield brackets loosely to the rods with the deep valance on the inside, nearest the engine.

Fit the securing rod nuts. Tighten all nuts and bolts.

TYRES

86. MAINTENANCE.

Always keep tyres at the correct pressures (see data page at front of book). Remove any stones which may be embedded in the tread. Replace valve dust cap if lost.

87. REMOVAL.

Deflate tube by removing valve cap and core. Remove rim nut and security bolt nut if security bolt fitted. Push the beads of the cover down into the well of the rim at a point opposite to the valve. Insert a small tyre lever between the bead and the rim near to the valve. Ease the bead off the rim using a second lever inserted a short distance away. Repeat until one bead is free of the rim.

Remove security bolt and tube, and remove the second bead in a similar manner.

88. FITTING.

Fit rim band. Dust tube, beads and rim with French chalk. Slightly inflate tube and place within cover on top of wheel with valve in line with hole in rim. Fit the underneath bead by hand, completing the operation with levers. Thread valve and stem of security bolt through appropriate holes. Fit second bead starting opposite valve. See that security bolt and tube are not being pinched between cover and rim. Inflate. Fit rim nut and security bolt nut. Adjust pressures to manufacturers' recommendation and fit dust cap.

ELECTRICAL SECTION

89. ESSENTIAL MAINTENANCE.

Battery. Inspect the battery regularly and keep acid level to the top of the separators by adding distilled water.

UNLESS YOU DO THIS YOUR BATTERY WILL QUICKLY DETERIORATE.

Wiring. Keep all connections and terminals tight. See that the cables are clear of moving part.

Dynamo. Keep brushes and commutator clean. (Para. 96).

Magneto. Keep contact breaker clean. If necessary polish the contacts with fine carborundum stone or emery cloth and afterwards wipe with cloth moistened with petrol (Para. 92). Occasionally check contact breaker opening (using gauge on ignition spanner) (Para. 91).

Replace high-tension cable if it becomes worn or perished.

Ignition

90. TIMING CONTROL.

The ignition control is cable operated from a handlebar lever; adjustment of the cable may be made by sliding the rubber cover up the cable outer casing and adjusting the hexagon screw thus exposed. Renewal may be carried out by unscrewing the control barrel (Fig. 26), drawing cable and plunger upwards as far as possible and sliding the nipple sideways out of the hole in the plunger. Thread replacement cable through casing and solder nipple to end. Insert through appropriate parts, slide nipple into plunger, screw home control barrel, adjust and replace rubber shroud.

91. CONTACT BREAKER LUBRICATION AND ADJUSTMENT.

The cam is lubricated by a wick, contained in the contact breaker base, which must be given a few drops of thin machine oil about every 2,500 miles.

To get at the wick, remove the spring arm carrying the moving contact, and withdraw the screw carrying the wick. (Fig. 26).

When replacing the contact breaker components see that the small backing spring is fitted immediately under the securing screw and spring washer, and that the bent portion faces outwards.

After dismantling the contact breaker in order to lubricate, the contact setting should be checked.

Turn the engine until the contacts are fully opened and insert the gauge provided, .010 inch—.012 inch thickness, between the contacts.

The gauge should be a sliding fit.

If there is an appreciable variation from the gauge, slacken the lock nut and turn the contact screw by its hexagon head until the gap is set to the gauge.

Tighten the lock nut.

92. CONTACT BREAKER—CLEANING.

Remove the contact breaker cover and examine the contacts.

If they are dirty, they must be cleaned by polishing with a very fine carborundum stone or very fine emery cloth; afterwards wipe away any dirt or metal dust with a petrol-moistened cloth.

Cleaning of the contacts is made easier if the spring arm carrying the moving contact is removed as described in paragraph 91.

Examine the spring arm of the contact breaker and wipe away any rust.

Adjust as described in paragraph 91.

93. H.T. CABLE.

Should be 7 m/m. in diameter, P.V.C. or keoprene covered ignition cable.

The cable must be replaced if the rubber insulation has perished or shows cracks and becomes brittle.

To fit the new cable to the pick-up ter-

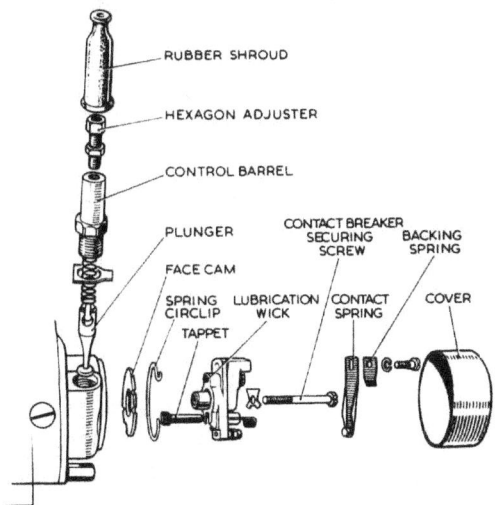

Fig. 26

minal, thread the knurled moulded nut over the lead, bare the cable for about ¼ inch, thread the wire through the metal washer removed from the old cable and bend back the strands.

Finally, screw the nut into its terminal.

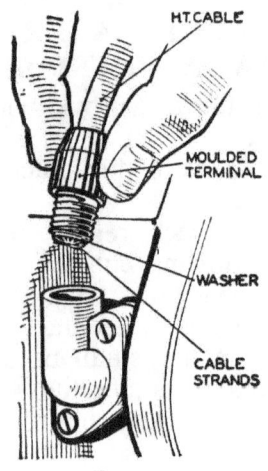

Fig. 27

94. PICK-UP.

Examine the pick-up or high tension terminal (magneto end).

See that the carbon brush moves freely in its holder, being careful not to stretch the brush spring unduly.

While the pick-up is removed, clean the slip ring track and flanges by holding a soft cloth on the ring while the engine is slowly turned by hand.

95. SPARKING PLUG.

Clean periodically by dismantling and removing all the carbon from the electrodes.

Scrape inside of plug body clean of carbon, re-assemble and set gap at .020"—.022".

Lighting and Accessories

96. DYNAMO—INSPECTION OF COMMUTATOR & BRUSHGEAR.

About once every six months remove the dynamo cover for inspection of commutator and brushes.

The brushes must make firm contact with the commutator. The brushes are held in boxes by means of springs; move the brush to see that it is free to slide in its holder. If it sticks remove it and clean with a cloth moistened with petrol. Care must be taken to replace the brushes in their original position, otherwise they will not bed properly on the commutator. If, after long service, the brushes have become worn to such an extent that they will not bear properly on the commutator, they must be replaced. Always use genuine Lucas brushes. Brushes should be fitted by a Service Agent.

Now examine the commutator. It should be free from any trace of oil or dirt and should have a highly polished appearance. Clean a dirty or blackened commutator by pressing a fine dry cloth against it while the engine is slowly turned over by hand. If the commutator is very dirty, moisten the cloth with petrol.

97. LUBRICATION.

The bearings in the dynamo are packed with grease during assembly and will last until it is necessary for the dynamo to undergo a complete overhaul.

98. CUT-OUT AND REGULATOR UNIT.

This unit (Fig. 28) which is housed inside the tool box, consists of the cut-out, which is an automatic switch to prevent discharge of the battery when the dynamo is not charging, and the voltage regulator, which controls the output of the dynamo. With a fully charged battery the dynamo is only permitted to pass a small charge to the battery, whilst with a fully discharged bat-

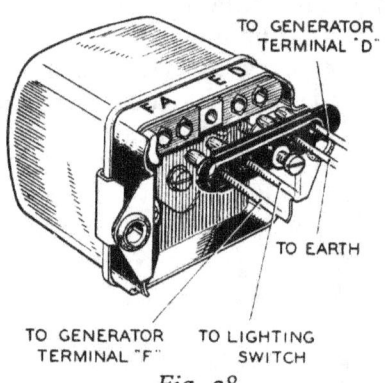

Fig. 28

tery a heavy charge is passed in order to boost up the battery rapidly. Both components are accurately set and should not be tampered with or adjusted.

99. AMMETER.

Fitted in the switch panel of the head lamp, this instrument indicates when the current is being taken from the battery in a greater quantity than is being fed to the battery (discharge).

It also shows when the dynamo is charging, and hence by means of the regulator the state of charge of the battery.

100. BATTERY.

When examining a battery, do not hold naked lights near the vents as there is a danger of igniting the gas coming from the plates.

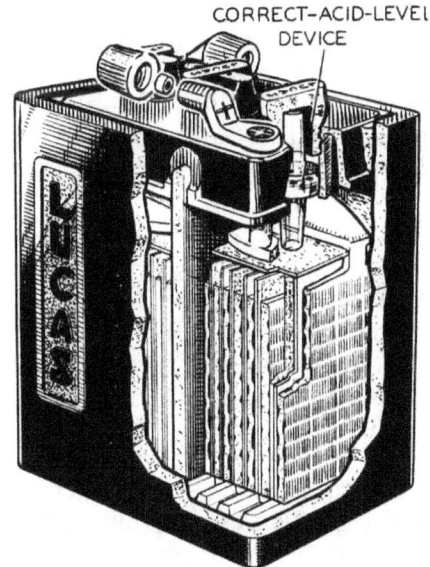

Fig. 29

Remove the vent plugs and see that the ventilating holes in each are quite clear.

Remove any dirt by means of a bent wire.

A clogged vent plug will cause the pressure in the cell to increase, due to the gases given off during charging, and this may cause damage.

Make sure that the rubber washer is fitted under each vent plug, otherwise the electrolyte may leak.

Battery—Topping-up.

About once a fortnight or more often in warm climates check the level of the electrolyte in the battery cells and add distilled water as necessary. The battery is fitted with a device which indicates when the level is correct (Fig. 29). Pour distilled water round the flange of the tube (exposed when the plug is removed) until no more drains through into the cell. Lift the tube slightly to clear the water from the flange and the level will be correct.

Wipe dirt and moisture from the battery top.

Checking Battery Condition.

The state of charge of the battery should be examined by taking hydrometer readings of the specific gravity of the acid in the cells.

The specific gravity reading and their indications are as follows:—
 1.280—1.300. Battery fully charged.
 About—1.210. Battery about half-charged.
 Below—1.150. Battery fully discharged.

These figures are given assuming the temperature of the acid is about 60° F.

Each reading should be approximately the same.

If one cell gives a reading very different from the rest, it may be that the acid has been spilled or has leaked from this particular cell, or there may be a short circuit between the plates.

This will necessitate its return to a Repair Depot for rectification.

Wipe the top of the battery to remove all dirt and water.

Note.

Do not leave the battery in a discharged condition for any length of time.

If a motor cycle is to be out of use, the battery must first be fully charged, and afterwards given a refreshing charge about every two weeks.

Earthing Connections.

Before disconnecting the battery, note which terminal is connected to the machine and re-connect accordingly.

Charging.

If the previous tests indicate that the battery is merely discharged, and if the acid level is correct, the battery must be recharged from an external supply.

101. HEADLAMP.

The headlamp switch, which carries also the switch, ammeter and speedometer, incorporates a Lucas Light Unit, which embodies a "pre-focus" bulb ensuring a correct beam without any necessity for focussing.

A group of snap connectors within the headlamp, and accessible when the light unit

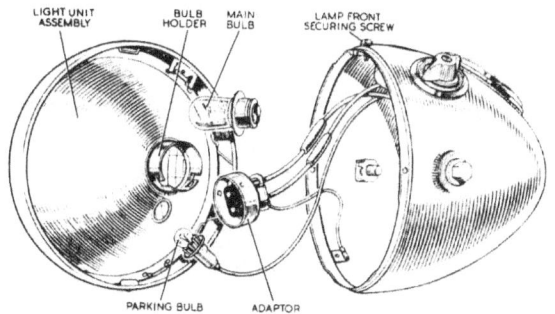

Fig. 30

has been removed, greatly facilitates headlamp removal.

Setting.

Check the setting of the lamp. Stand the machine about 25ft. from a light coloured wall and adjust the headlamp position until the main driving beam is projected straight ahead and parallel to the ground, the centre of the beam being the same height as the headlamp centre.

Bulb Replacement.

To remove the headlamp front, slacken the screw at the top of the lamp and lift off the front rim complete with light unit assembly. The pilot bulb is carried in a small metal plate in the base of the lamp body. The plate must be slid out in order to replace the bulb. To replace " pre-focus " bulbs, twist the back shell in the centre of the reflector, back in an anti-clockwise direction and pull off. The bulb may now be removed from the rear of the reflector. Place the correct bulb in the holder, engage the projectors on the inside of the back shell with the slots in the bulb holder, press home and twist in a clockwise direction. To replace headlamp front, locate the bottom of the light unit assembly in the lamp body, press into position and tighten locking screw.

Note.

It is important that only genuine Lucas bulbs should be used as replacements in order to ensure accuracy and correct focussing.

Main bulb Lucas No. 373 6 volt 30/24 watt. Pre-Focus Cap.

Pilot bulb Lucas No. 988 6 volt 3 watt. Miniature Bayonet Cap.

102. CABLES.

To connect cables to battery unscrew knurled plastic nut and withdraw the collett. Bare about one inch of cable and thread through knurled nut and collett. Bend cable strands back over small end of collett. Draw back into nut and tighten nut on terminal.

Snap connectors, i.e. rubber-covered push/pull connections, are used liberally throughout the electrical circuit, and appear when connected as a small rubber sleeve or bunch of sleeves when grouped. Disconnect by pulling apart and re-connect by holding cable in pliers the metal nipple soldered to cable end. Hold rubber covered portion in fingers and press cable home with pliers. Ensure rubber sleeves always covering metal portion of connectors when in use.

103. LIGHTING SWITCH.

The switch, together with ammeter and speedometer, is carried in headlamp shell, and connections are accessible when headlamp front and light unit assembly is removed. The various cables will be readily recognisable by their coloured sleeving.

104. HORN.

Electric horns are adjusted to give their best performance before leaving the works, and will give a long period of service without any attention.

If the horn becomes uncertain in action, or does not vibrate, it has not necessarily broken down.

The trouble may be due to a discharged battery or a loose connection, or short circuit in the wiring of the horn.

The performance of the horn may be upset by the fixing bolt working loose, or by the vibration of some part adjacent to the horn.

To check this, remove the horn from its mounting, hold it firmly in the hand by its bracket, and press the push.

If the note is still unsatisfactory, the horn may require adjustment and should be taken to a Lucas Service Station.

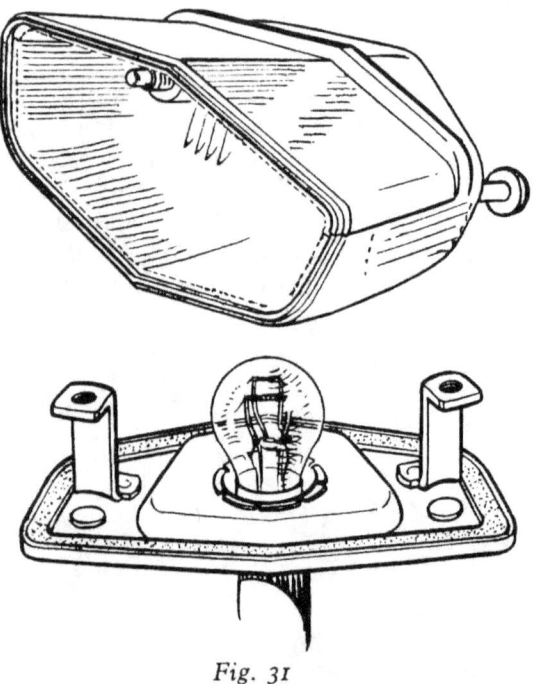

Fig. 31

105. TAIL, STOP AND NUMBER PLATE LAMP.

This lamp is equipped with a double filament bulb; one 3 watt filament to provide rear light and number plate illumination, and an 18 watt filament controlled by the action of the rear brake.

To obtain access to the bulb, remove the two screws securing the plastic cover and lift off the cover. The bulb holder has staggered slots to ensure correct fitting. The correct bulb is Lucas No. 384 6 volt 6/18 watt.

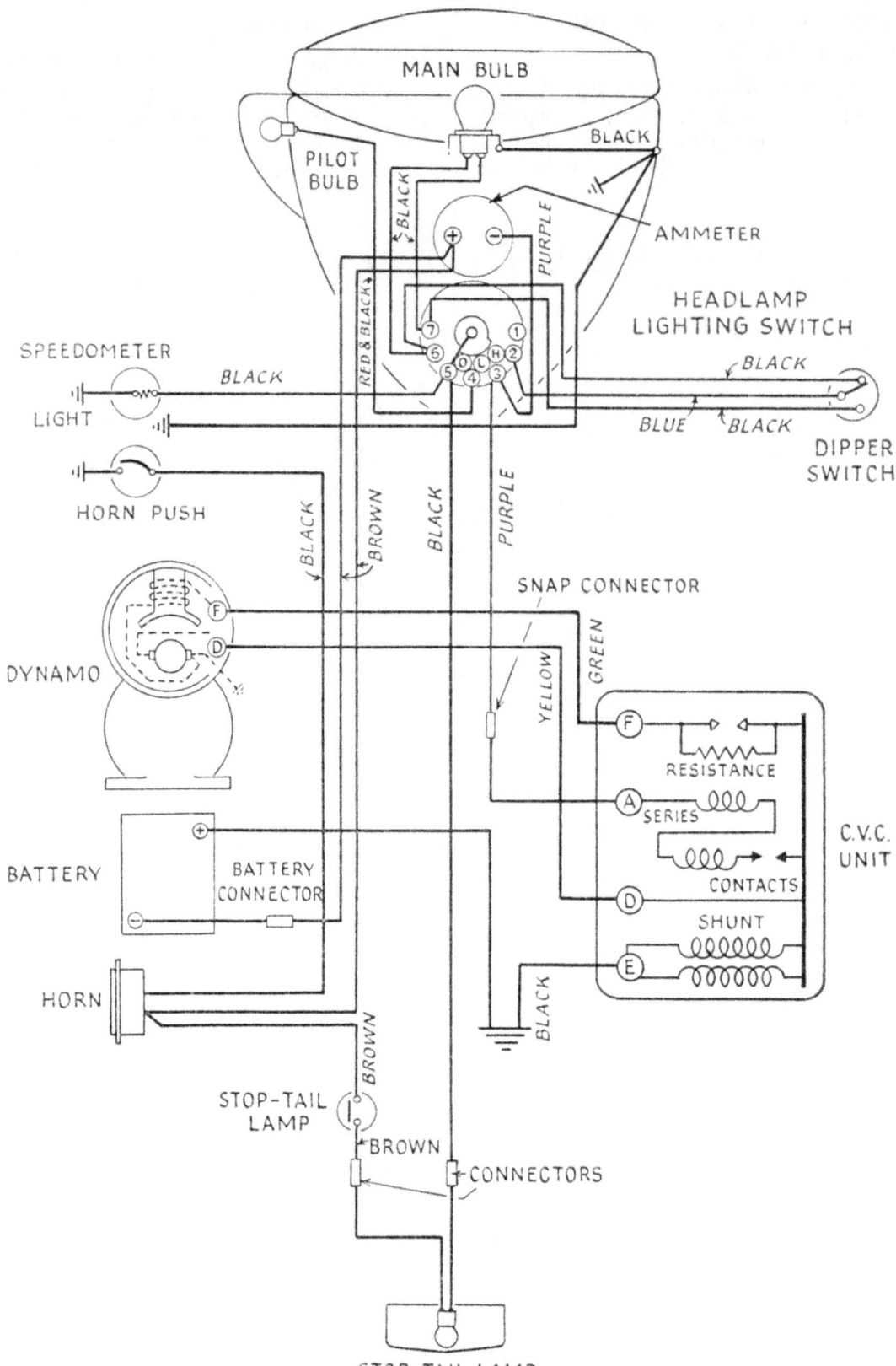

WIRING DIAGRAM FOR LUCAS "MAGDYNO" LIGHTING EQUIPMENT WITH SSU700P/1 HEADLAMP

This applies to 1953 to 1955 Nortons with compensated-voltage-control and a "positive earth" system of wiring. On 1955 models the lead to the stop-tail lamp is taken from the battery negative instead of from the horn. The battery positive lead has *black* sleeving.

38

WIRING DIAGRAM FOR ELECTRICAL EQUIPMENT

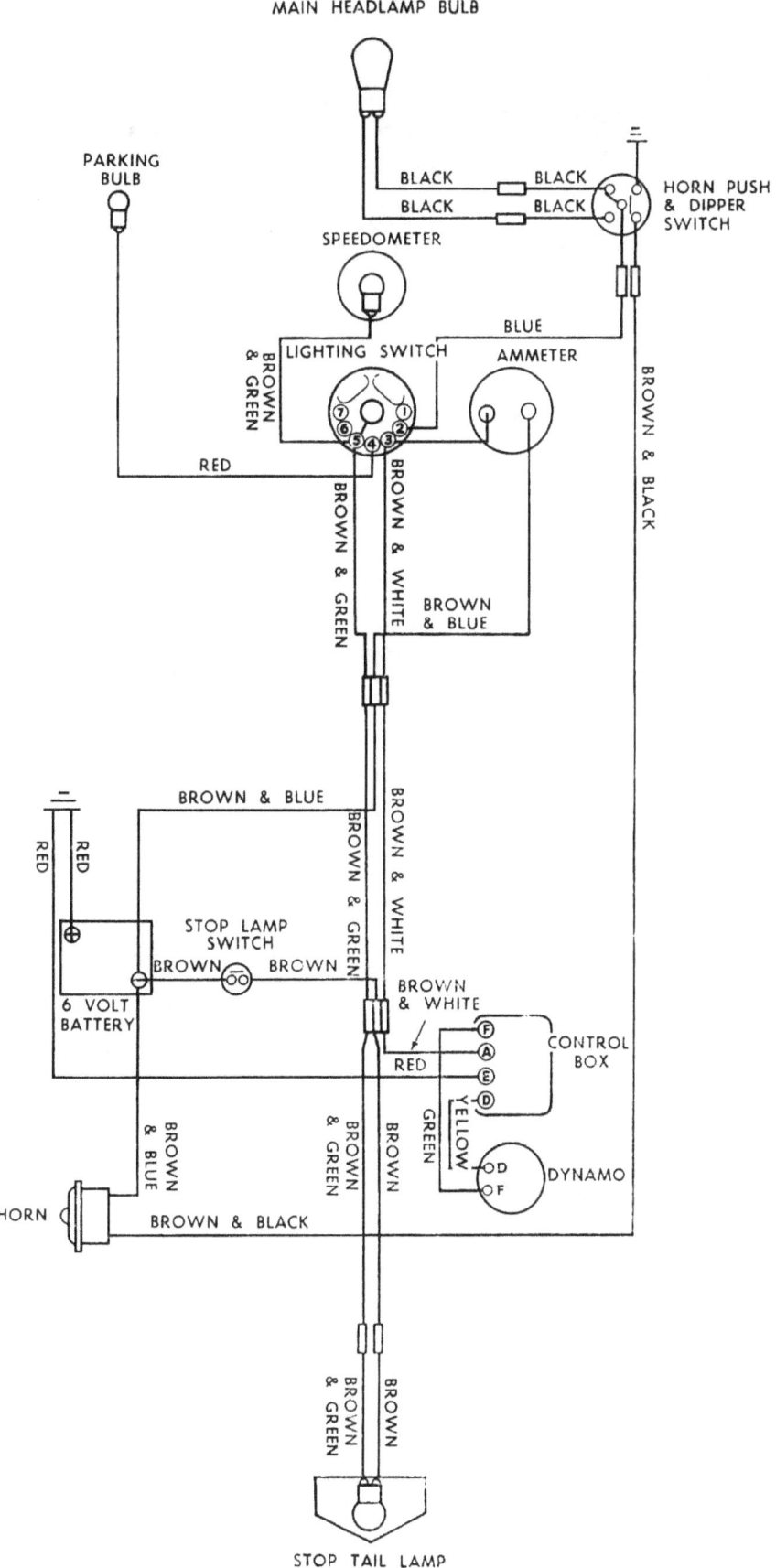

(1956-1958 'Magdyno' Models 19, ES2 & 50 with MCH58 Headlamp)

LOCATING AND RECTIFYING POSSIBLE TROUBLES

TROUBLE	POSSIBLE CAUSES	REMEDY
Failure to Start.	Faulty plug. Faulty H.T. lead. Contact breaker points dirty or out of adjustment.	Remove plug, place plug body in contact with cylinder, revolve engine. If blue spark of fair intensity occurs, plug and ignition O.K.
	Pick-up brush worn or broken. Slip ring oily.	If no spark, change plug, and if still no spark, remove plug from H.T. lead, hold end of lead 1/8" from cylinder and revolve engine. In the event of there being still no spark, examine contact breaker points and check their gap. Examine pick-up brush and clean slip ring.
	Failure of petrol to reach mixing chamber.	Ensure that petrol is flowing down feed pipes. Clean carburetter.
	Broken throttle wire.	Ensure that throttle slide rises as twist grip is revolved.
Erratic Slow Running.	Pilot adjustment requires re-setting.	With throttle about 1/8" open and air closed, adjust pilot screw until good idling is obtained.
	Worn inlet valve guide.	Remove valve spring and test valve for side play in guide.
	Faulty valve seats.	Examine and re-grind as necessary.
Loss of Power.	No tappet clearance.	Check and re-set as required.
	Exhaust valve lifter holding valve off seat.	Ensure that there is some movement in cable before lever begins to lift valve.
	Front chain too tight.	Adjust.
	Loose carbon wedged on valve seat.	Can usually be removed by kicking engine over a few times.
	Broken piston rings.	Examine and replace as required.
Excessive Oil Consumption.	If accompanied by black smoke from exhaust, broken piston rings, worn rings or barrel.	Examine and make necessary replacements.
	Oil pump not returning.	With engine running an intermittent stream of oil should be seen upon opening oil tank filler cap.
	If unaccompanied by exhaust smoke, faulty oil pump timing cover connection.	Ensure that the necessary pressure is generated between timing cover and oil pump nipple fibre washers as instructed in para. 21.

LOCATING AND RECTIFYING POSSIBLE TROUBLES

TROUBLE	POSSIBLE CAUSES	REMEDY
Engine Runs Harshly.	Mag. chain too tight.	Adjust as in Para. 27.
Engine Cuts Out at Large Throttle Openings.	Dirt in carburetter.	Clean and re-adjust.
Inefficient Brakes (Front or Rear).	Grease on lining.	Examine and wash in petrol. Do not wash in paraffin.
	Tightness in mechanism.	Make sure that cam is free in its bearing and pedal not binding on spindle due to mud.
Slipping Clutch.	Cable adjusted too tightly.	Re-adjust cable until there is some movement on handle-bar lever before clutch operates.
	Inner cable too long. Clutch worm lever fouling gear box casing.	Shorten and re-adjust.
	Oil on plates (usually caused by overfilling oil bath).	Dismantle clutch plates and wash in petrol.
	Tightness in operating mechanism.	Examine, clean and free off as necessary.
Clutch Hard to Free.	Clutch cable adjuster screwed right out, clutch worm lever not at correct angle, and therefore not having a straight pull.	Re-set clutch worm lever to give straight pull. Shorten inner cable and re-adjust.
Failure to Effect Gear-Changing.	Over revving, especially from 1st to 2nd.	
Gear Changing Accompanied by Excessive Noise.	Slack rear chain.	Adjust as necessary.
Failure of Footchange Lever to Return to Normal Position.	Broken hairpin return spring.	Remove positive mechanism cover and front plate. Examine spring, renew as required.
Steering Rolls or Wanders.	Loose head adjustment.	
Twist Grip Closes if Released.	Tension requires adjusting.	Screw in adjuster one or two turns.
Steering appears Tight on Corners.	Steering damper binding, caused by bent frame anchor bracket.	Remove anchor bracket and re-set to correct angle.

NOTES

Maintenance Manual and Instruction Book

FOR

The Unapproachable

REGD. TRADE MARK

MOTOR CYCLE

Models No. 50 and ES2

(Pages extracted from the 1970 factory P106/P manual)

NORTON VILLIERS LIMITED

NORTON MATCHLESS DIVISION

PLUMSTEAD ROAD, WOOLWICH
LONDON, S.E.18, ENGLAND

Telephone: WOOlwich 1223

IMPORTANT INFORMATION RELATING TO THE CONTENTS OF THIS MANUAL

1945-1946: The first section of this manual includes a copy of the appropriate repair and maintenance data for the girder forks as fitted to the WD16H model. This information is included as the 1945-1946 post-war civilian 16H and 18 models were also fitted with girder forks. However, based on our research, overhaul information for girder forks was never included in any of the factory workshop manuals for the post-war civilian models.

1947-1954: The second section includes a copy of a 1947 factory workshop manual for both the S.V. and O.H.V. rigid frame and spring frame (plunger) 16H, Big4, 18 and ES2 models that were fitted with 'Road-holder' forks. It also includes additional information extracted from the 1956 publication of this same workshop manual relating to the changes that took place during the 1947 to 1954 model run, including the change from an 'Upright' to a Laydown' gearbox and lighting equipment. This additional information is appended at the end of the section and any data that is identical and included in the 1947 publication has been omitted. Consequently, this manual would be applicable to all four models from 1947 to 1954 at which time the 16H, Big4 and 18 were discontinued and the ES2 had received swing-arm rear suspension.

1953-1958: The third section includes a copy of a 1956 factory workshop manual exclusive to the O.H.V. swing-arm 19S, ES2 and 50 models. As the ES2 received swing-arm rear suspension in 1953, this manual would be applicable to all three models from 1953 to 1958, at which time the 19S was discontinued.

1958-1963: The pages in the fourth section of this manual were extracted from the P106/P Norton factory publication 'Maintenance Manual and Instruction Book' dated 1970 for the Model 50, ES2, 88, 99, 650 and 750 models. As the 19S was discontinued in 1958 and is no longer included in the model list, this extracted data would be applicable to the 1958 to 1963 Model 50 and ES2 (see below).

EVOLUTION OF THE COMBINATION MANUALS: The publication of these 'combination' manuals began in 1960 with the P101 manual followed by the P106 and finally the P106/P manual of 1970. While these 'combination' manuals made publication less expensive than those for individual models the information for multiple different motorcycles is often merged together. Consequently, separating out the appropriate data for a specific model, or series of motorcycles can be a time consuming and confusing exercise.

Even more unfortunately, the P106/P manual makes no reference to the model years that are covered. However, as it only includes the model 50 and ES2 and knowing that the 19S was discontinued in 1958 it is reasonable to assume that it is intended to cover these two models from 1958 through 1963, at which point Norton discontinued manufacturing their single-cylinder machines. Therefore, we have extracted the information that is exclusive to the Model 50 and ES2 from the P106/P manual. However, this means that the paragraphs and illustrations in the P106/P section may no longer be sequentially numbered and we request you overlook this minor issue as it does not affect the correctness of the data in any way.

IMPORTANT: Please note that repair information for the AMC MKII versions of the models 50 and ES2 is not included in this publication.

Index

	Page
Amal Carburetter	36
Cleaning	7
Controls	8
Data	4
Electrical Section	39
Engine—Models ES2 and 50	11
Front Forks	31
Gearbox	24
Handlebar Fittings	35
Introduction	6
Locating and Rectifying possible troubles	49
Lubrication	7
Maintenance of Engine-Decarbonising	12
Notes	46
Rear Springing	34
Running-in	7
Transmission	19
Tyres	38
Wheels, Hubs and Brakes	28

	Paragraph
Alternator	122
Battery	129
Brakes	98, 99
Big End, examination	64
Carbon removal	46
Carburetter, dismantling	111
Carburetter, assembly	112
Carburetter, maintenance	114
Carburetter, rich mixture	115
Carburetter, tuning	113
Carburetter, weak mixture	116
Chain adjustment	71
Clutch, adjustment	72
Clutch, assembly	76
Clutch, dismantling	74
Clutch, examination of parts	75
Crankcase	66, 67, 68, 69
Cylinder Head, removal	45
Cylinder Head, fitting	51
Electrical Section	120 to 135
Electrical Wiring Diagrams	Page 48
Engine, removal from frame	65
Foot Change, dismantling and assembly	80, 81
Forks, Front, maintenance	100
Forks, Front, removal	102
Forks, Front, refitting	103
Forks, Front, dismantling	104
Forks, Front, assembly	105
Forks, Rear, pivotted removal and assembly	106
Gearbox	77 to 89
Handlebar fittings	108, 109, 110
Headlamp	130
Hubs, dismantling	94, 96
Hubs, assembly	95, 97
Ignition	121
Ignition Timing, coil ignition models	59
Lubrication System	40
Oil Bath, removal and fitting	73
Oil Circulation	44
Oil Filters	41
Oil Level	43
Oil Pump	42, 62
Petrol Tank, removal and fitting	70A
Pistons, fitting	55
Pistons, removal	54
Piston Rings, removal	54
Plug, Sparking	135
Rocker (Tappet), adjustment	53
Rocker, removal and fitting	52
Small End Bush, removal and fitting	56
Steering Head, adjustment	101
Suspension, rear	107
Tappets, removal and fitting	60, 61
Timing Gear Bushes, removal and fitting	70
Timing Panel, removal and fitting	57, 58
Tyres, maintenance	117
Tyres, removal	118
Tyres, fitting	119
Valves, grinding	48
Valves, removal	47
Valve Guides, removal and fitting	50
Valve Pressure Relief, removal and fitting	63
Wheels, removal	90, 92
Wheels, fitting	91, 93

Data

IDENTIFICATION MARKS. Engine No. and Prefix numbers stamped on driving side of crankcase below cylinder base flange. Frame No. stamped on left hand frame gusset below battery box. Should be the same as the Engine No. Quote fully when writing or ordering spares.

	Model 50	Model ES2
Bore	71 mm. (2.795")	79 mm. (3.110")
Stroke	88 mm. (3.465")	100 mm. (3.937")
Capacity	348 cc. (21.232 cu. in.)	490 cc. (29.896 cu. in.)
Compression Ratio	7.3 to 1	7.1 to 1
Sparking Plug	KLG. FE75 or FE80	KLG. FE75 or FE80
	Lodge 2HLN.	Lodge 2HLN.
	Champion N5.	Champion N5.

IGNITION TIMING
B.T.D.C. fully advanced — 38° $\tfrac{15}{32}$" 11.88 mm. | 38° $\tfrac{17}{32}$" 13.5 mm.

VALVE TIMING
Tappet clearance cold
Inlet
Exhaust

Marked on all engines. Mesh gears and sprockets as instructed. Push rods to be free to rotate without up and down movement with piston on compression stroke.

AMAL CARBURETTER

	Model 50	Model ES2
Type	Monobloc 376	Monobloc 376
Main Jet	210	270
Throttle Valves	3½	4
Needle Jet	106	106
Needle position	2	3
Pilot Jet	30	30
Choke Size	1"	1$\tfrac{1}{16}$"

ENGINE SPROCKET

	Model 50	Model ES2
Solo	17T	20T
Sidecar	16T and 17T gearbox	18T

GEAR RATIOS

	Model 50	Model ES2
Solo	5.59, 6.8, 9.5 and 14.28, to 1	4.75, 5.8, 8.08 and 12.16, to 1
Sidecar	6.64, 8.07, 11.3 and 16.97, to 1	5.28, 6.45, 8.97 and 13.45, to 1

CHAINS

	Model 50	Model ES2
Primary	½" × .305" × 74 rollers	½" × .305" × 76 rollers
Rear	⅝" × ¼" × 97 rollers	⅝" × ¼" × 98 rollers
Distributor/Magneto	⅜" × $\tfrac{5}{32}$" × 44 rollers	⅜" × $\tfrac{5}{32}$" × 44 rollers
Camshaft	—	
Petrol Tank Capacity	3⅝ gallons, approx. 16 litres.	
Oil Tank Working Capacity	4½ pints or 2.3 litres.	
Tyre size front	3.00" × 19"	3.00" × 19"
Tyre size rear	3.50" × 19"	3.50" × 19"
Tyre pressure front solo	25 lbs. p.s.i.	25 lbs. p.s.i.
Tyre pressure rear solo	22 lbs. p.s.i.	22 lbs. p.s.i.
Weight dry	380 lbs. approx.	385 lbs. approx.

NOTES

Introduction

In preparing these instructions the elementary details and preliminary information that may be necessary to the absolute novice have been omitted, on the assumption that the majority of NORTON owners are already acquainted with the elementary details of starting, driving and maintenance. In connection with the latter we would stress the advisability of cultivating the habit of routine cleaning, lubrication, examination and adjustment of your machine. By this means many minor annoyances will be avoided and major breakdowns averted, and you will acquire the pride of ownership which marks the true enthusiast.

Below is a plan view of the machine with all controls clearly indicated. A short study of this will familiarise you with the position and function of each control.

To start the engine from cold, turn on the petrol and very slightly flood the carburetter, until petrol seeps from the top of the float chamber.

On coil ignition models, turn the ignition key in the top of the headlamp switch in a clockwise direction to 'IGN'. In cold conditions, close or partly close the air lever, this should however, be fully opened as soon as possible after the engine has started.

On single cylinder models only, rotate the engine with the kickstarter until the resistance of compression is felt, raise the exhaust valve lifter and depress the kickstarter a further 2" only. Release the lifter and allow the starter pedal to return to its normal position. A good swinging kick on the starter should set the engine going.

Machines with magneto ignition have a cut-out button for stopping the engine, this is similar to a horn button and is fitted on the handlebar.

With coil ignition machines, always remember to TURN OFF THE IGNITION AND REMOVE THE KEY when leaving the machine.

Should the battery become run down the engine can be started, either by turning the key to 'EMG' position, when a far more 'hefty' kick is required than when starting normally, or by push starting in say 2nd gear with the switch in the normal ignition position.

When an engine with Lucas equipment has been started in 'EMG' switch position, it must be immediately switched over to normal 'IGN', otherwise damage to contact points and condenser will result.

A flat battery can be recharged at an increased rate by the procedure outlined under the heading of Increased Charging in the electrical section.

All models provide for a reserve fuel supply. The single petrol tap is of the two positional type, the knurled circular knob being pulled out for normal running and turned and pulled a further amount when the reserve is required. The reserve should supply fuel for about 5 to 8 miles dependant upon how the machine is driven.

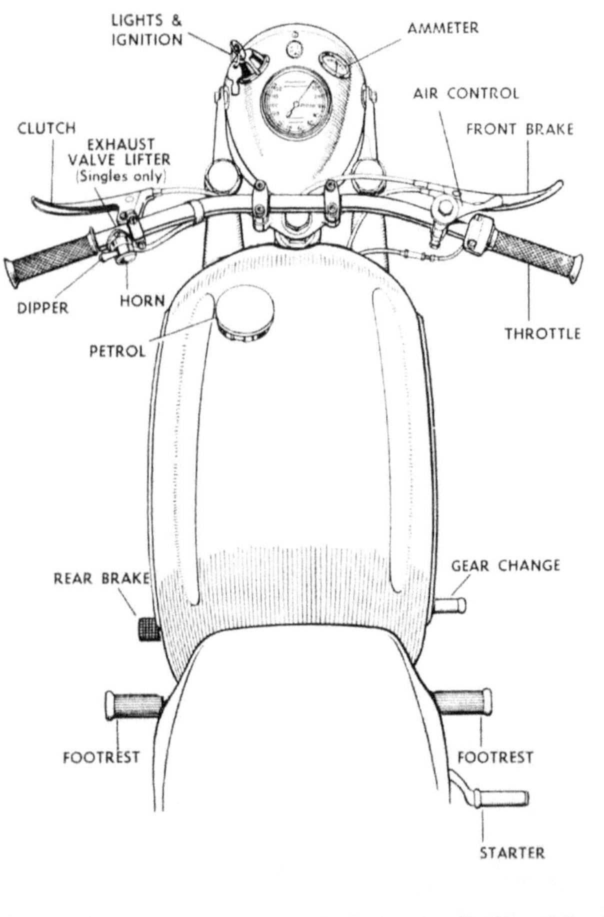

Fig 1

Running-In

Although the machine will have been greased up and all points requiring oil will have been dealt with at the works, prior to the road test, it is always a safe policy to ensure that there is adequate oil in the oil tank, gearbox and oilbath chaincase. Remember to remove the level plug from the chaincase before topping up.

Immediately the engine has been started, remove the oil tank filler cap and check that the oil is circulating. If the machine has been standing, oil should be returning in a constant stream and should be visible on looking in the filler orifice. After a few moments, when the return pump has scavenged the sump clear of oil having collected there during standing, the stream will become intermittent.

The first 1000 miles in the life of a new machine are of the utmost importance and the advisability of careful running-in cannot be overstressed. At no time during the first 500 miles, should the throttle be more than $\frac{1}{4}$ to $\frac{1}{3}$ open and care should be taken to avoid labouring of the engine by 'hanging on' to too high a gear when conditions warrant a change down.

This does not mean that road speeds should be strictly limited to 30 m.p.h.—a model 50 or ES2 could be run under level conditions at 40—45 m.p.h.

A high road speed is not detrimental if it is obtained without opening the throttle wide: for example, when going down hill. Speed can be varied quite appreciably, but the engine must always run lightly loaded.

When the 500 mile figure has been reached, short bursts of higher speed may be indulged in but allow the engine to reach these easily and progressively. When 1200 to 1500 miles have been covered, it should be possible to use the the machines full capabilities with safety.

Over-revving in the lower gears and violent acceleration should be avoided even when the machine is fully run-in—it merely reflects bad riding causing excessive noise and overloading of chains, clutch, gearbox, etc.

The use of running-in compound during the initial stages of the engine's life is strongly recommended. The compound, several brands of which are available and may be obtained from all Norton dealers, contains "colloidal graphite" which forms a graphoid surface on all working faces and greatly assists in preserving their high quality finish. The compound should be mixed with the lubricating oil in the proportion of one pint to one gallon of oil during running-in, but if its use is continued after this period, only half the quantity should be used. Remember that these are high efficiency engines which give of their best when running at relatively high revolutions and a change should be made to a lower gear immediately there are any signs of labouring. To obtain the best possible performance from your machine, full use should be made of the gearbox, which is quite capable of withstanding all the loads likely to be imposed upon it by normal use.

At the end of this book will be found a trouble tracing chart, reference to which will greatly facilitate the location and rectifying of any but the most unusual troubles which may be likely to cause an involuntary stop.

Cleaning

Before attempting to polish the enamel on any part of the machine, all traces of grit adhering to the various components should be washed off, preferably with a reasonably high pressure hose. Polish the enamel periodically with a good quality wax polish. Note that chromium plating is not impervious to rust and should be wiped down when possible, after being in the rain. Wash off any road grit and clean with one of the chromium polishes available from any garage. Do NOT use ordinary metal polish.

Lubrication

LUBRICANTS TO USE. Efficient lubrication is of vital importance and it is false economy to use cheap oils and grease. We recommend the following lubricants to use in machines of our make.

RECOMMENDED LUBRICANTS

Efficient lubrication is of vital importance and it is false economy to use cheap grades of oil. When buying oils or grease, it is advisable to specify the brand as well as the grade and, as an additional precaution, to buy from sealed containers.

ENGINE

Ambient temperature above 32° F use S.A.E. 20/50 or straight S.A.E. 30 oil.

Ambient temperature below 32° F use S.A.E. 10/30 or S.A.E. 20 oil.

The following brands are recommended:

Mobiloil, Castrol, Energol, Essolube, Shell, Regent Advanced Havoline.

GEARBOX

Ambient temperature above 32° F: S.A.E. 50 or GX90

Ambient temperature below 32° F: S.A.E. 30

HUB AND FRAME PARTS

Mobilgrease MP, Castrolease Heavy, Energrease C3, Regent Marfax, Shell Retinax A. or C.D.

TELEDRAULIC FRONT FORKS

Mobiloil Arctic (S.A.E. 20), Castrolite (S.A.E. 10W-30), Energol (S.A.E. 20), Essolube 20 (S.A.E. 20) Shell X-100 Motor Oil 20/20 W (S.A.E. 20)

REAR CHAINS

Mobilgrease MP, Esso Fluid Grease, Energrease A.O., Castrolease Grease Graphited

LUBRICATION CHART

Period	Location	Lubricant	Period	Location	Lubricant
Every 200 miles.	Oil tank, top up	Oil	Every 2000 miles.	Contact break spindle ES2 and 50	Oil
Every 1000 miles.	Control cables	Oil	Every 3000 miles.	Magneto C.B. rocker arm and cam ring	Oil
	Control levers	Oil	Every 5000 miles.	Gearbox, drain and refill	Oil
	Brake cable 'U' clip	Oil		Brake cams, cam spindles and shoe pivot pins	Grease
	Gearbox, top up	Oil			
	Oilbath, top up	Oil			
Every 2000 miles.	Brake pedal	Grease	Every 10,000 miles.	Front forks	See para. 100
	Brake rod jaw joints	Oil		Oilbath, drain and refill	Oil
	Speedo gearbox	Grease		Hub bearings, repack	Grease
	Drain and refill oil tank	Oil			

Controls

Throttle Twist Grip. On right handlebar. When shut, warm engine should continue to tick over by adjustment of cable and throttle stop on carburetter. Twist grip may be adjusted to close or remain open when released, as preferred.

Air Lever. On right handlebar. Close or partly close when starting from cold. Open as soon as engine will run properly with full air. Should remain open for normal running.

Gear Change Lever. Adjacent to right footrest. Engages the various gears (4) and neutral or free engine position between bottom and second gear. Move upward for first or bottom gear and downwards for all other gears. Use deliberate pressure—do not jab.

Kickstarter. Lever behind right footrest. Depress to rotate engine.

Steering Damper (when fitted). Knob or wing nut behind handlebar centre. Rotate clockwise to stiffen handlebar movement.

Exhaust Valve Lifter. (Single cylinder models only). Beneath left handlebar. Enables engine to be readily rotated by releasing compression. It is important that it is not 'over adjusted' and it should only just lift the valve from its seat.

Front Brake Lever. On right handlebar. This is, perhaps, the most important control on the machine and its proper use should be mastered at the earliest opportunity. Because, when the brakes are applied, weight of rider and machine is transferred forward, more braking power can be applied to the front wheel before it will lock than to the rear. On a firm, dry surface, therefore, it will be found that the brake can be applied very hard without risk of locking the wheel. The rear brake should, of course, be applied at the same time, but in the case of an emergency stop you should not withdraw the clutch until the last moment before coming to rest, as otherwise the rear wheel may be locked causing the machine to skid.

The front brake should be adjusted so that the lever comes almost parallel with the handlebar when the brake is hard on and in this way with practice, it will be found that with the brake applied with the fingers, the twist grip can be operated with the inside of the thumb to make downward gear changes.

Different road conditions of course, call for modified braking technique and on a road away from the traffic, the rider should find out for himself how hard the brakes can be applied without locking either wheel. On a very wet road when grease and mud films have been washed away, it will be found that the front brake can be used hard without risk of a skid provided the machine is kept in a straight line. In damp greasy conditions, the brakes should only be 'caressed' and the machine slowed by use of the gearbox. On ice and snow the brakes should not be used at all and the machine should be allowed to roll to rest in a low gear.

When riding in traffic queues with many pedestrians about, you should ride with the front brake lever 'in your hand', you can then apply it as you think instead of having to 'find it' and consequently grab it.

Always remember that you cannot match the stopping power of a modern four wheeled vehicle if you do not use both brakes properly.

Clutch Lever. On left handlebar. Allows engine to run with gear engaged without forward movement of machine. Release gently to obtain forward motion.

Rear Brake Pedal. Adjacent to left footrest. It is important that this control should be properly adjusted so that when the brake is quickly applied the wheel is not suddenly locked. The pedal stop should be set so that with the rider normally seated with insteps on the footrests and left foot in a 'normal rotational' position on its rest, the pad is just below the ball of the foot. To apply the brake, it is then merely necessary to 'rotate' the foot to make contact with the pad. If the pedal pad is set too high, it becomes necessary to step on it which is dangerous apart from the rider having to ride 'splayed footed' since his boot must then be alongside the pedal pad instead of above it.

Lighting and Ignition Switch. Left hand top of headlamp body. Three positional rotating light switch—off, low and high. Central removable ignition key—OFF straight in line. Ignition ON, turn clockwise. Emergency starting, turn anti-clockwise.

Models with Magneto Ignition have a lighting switch giving similar positions but without the ignition switch in the centre.

Headlamp Dipping Switch and Horn Push. Combined fitting on inside of left handlebar. It is desirable that when the dipper switch lever is in the 'UP' position, the main filament should be on, then when the switch lever is 'flipped down' the dipped beam is obtained. Remember that this is a very important control when riding at night and a light 'flicked' the wrong way at a critical moment of dazzle may cause an accident.

If the dip switch becomes non-positive in action, dismantle it and apply a spot of oil to the lever pivot and change over toggle.

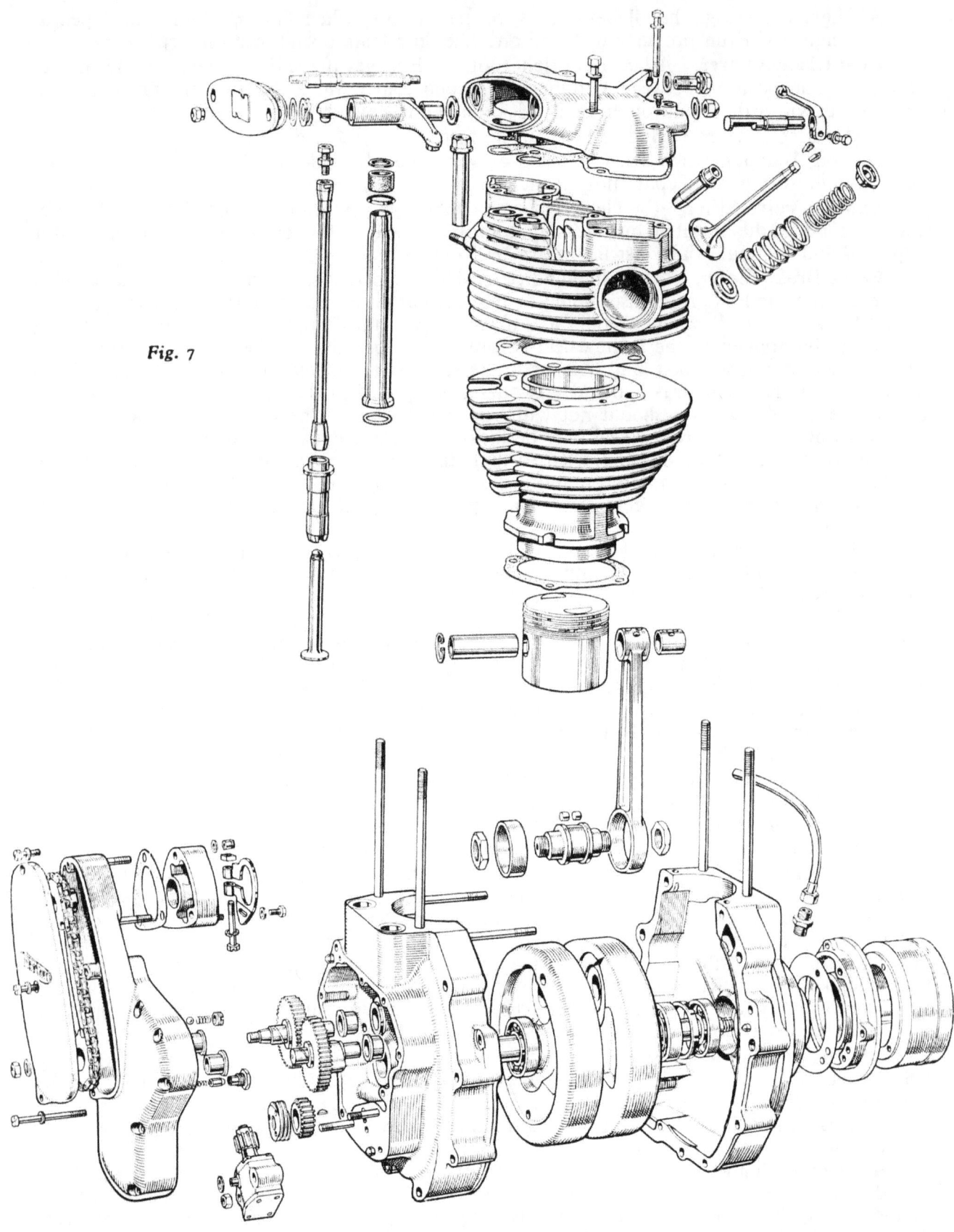

Fig. 7

THE ENGINE Models ES2 & 50

40. ENGINE LUBRICATION SYSTEM

This is of the dry sump type. The oil flows from the oil tank to the pump by gravity, assisted by the suction from the feed side of the oil pump, round the gears, and is forced under pressure to the big end bearings with a by-pass to the rear cylinder wall.

Oil by-passing a relief valve in the timing cover adequately lubricates the timing gear before returning to the sump.

The sump is then scavenged by the larger capacity return side of the pump and the oil is returned to the tank. A connection in the return pipe between pump and tank feeds the overhead valve gear.

41. THE FILTER

The purpose of the tank filter is to ensure that the feed to the engine is never blocked by a large foreign body. It is of coarse mesh and large dimensions so as not to restrict the flow of cold oil. It need not be removed when the oil is changed, it is better on all models to remove the tank complete from the machine and wash it out thoroughly with paraffin or petrol at say every 2nd or 3rd oil change. The filter is then automatically cleaned without removal and does not have its joint disturbed. Should it be necessary to remove it, the rubber or plastic pipe should be removed and a ring spanner employed. It should be noted that the filter occupies a higher position in the tank than does the drain plug and therefore small particles of foreign matter are trapped in the bottom of the tank until such time as the drain plug is removed.

42. ENGINE OIL PUMP

This is of the gear type. The pump contains two pairs of gears, one on the feed side and the other on the return side.

The gears on the return side are twice the width of those on the feed, having twice the pumping capacity. This ensures that the crankcase is free from oil when the engine is running.

To check the return of the oil to the tank, remove the oil filler cap. The oil return pipe can then be seen. After the engine has been running for a few minutes, the oil return flow will be spasmodic, due to the greater capacity of the return gears.

43. OIL LEVEL

Maintain at or near the 'Recommended Oil Level' usually indicated by a transfer on the outside of the tank.

If the level is maintained higher than this, the excess may be discharged via the oil tank breather pipe, especially at high speeds and cause over oiling of the rear chain and oil to be deposited on the rear tyre.

Conversely, if the machine is used mainly about town without much high speed work, then the rear chain may not receive sufficient oil. Under these conditions, a higher level should be maintained. See also under 'Chain Maintenance'.

Always run the engine for a few minutes before checking oil level. It is possible when an engine has been idle for any length of time for the oil to drain through the pump into the sump.

When this happens, all the oil is returned to the tank in the first few minutes that the engine is running. In some cases after very long standing, there may be so much oil in the sump, that some will be discharged via the crankcase breather before the return pump has fully scavenged the sump.

If the oil level in the tank is allowed to become too low, then there is risk of overheating due to the relatively small quantity which is in circulation.

44. CIRCULATION OF THE OIL

The oil is forced from the pump.

1. To the big end bearing.
2. To the pressure control valve.

1. The oil passes down the timing panel through the big-end restriction jet, along the timing shaft, up the flywheel and is sprayed on to the roller big-end.

2. The oil pressure control valve is a spring-loaded ball, and acts as a safety valve, in the oil circuit. When the pressure of the oil lifts the ball from its seat, the oil passes the ball and is sprayed upon the timing gears. When the engine is assembled at the Works, the valve ball spring adjusting screw is screwed home and released 1½ threads. This is the only adjustment in the oiling system and it is not advisable to remove the ball from the valve unless it is suspected that the ball is sticking or not seating.

From the cylinder the oil drains down the sides of the crankcase and is picked up by the ducts and carried to the main bearings and the timing gear bearings.

The oil collects in the timing case to such a level that the oil pump pinion is immersed, carrying oil to the half-time pinion and the timing gears.

A timed breather is incorporated in the driving side mainshaft and releases pressure through a small hole in the underside of the mainshaft bearing boss.

A lead is taken from the oil return pipe to a banjo fitting on the rocker box, feeding oil to the rocker shafts and ball ends. Surplus oil returns down the pushrod cover tubes to the crankcase. Excess oil from the O.H.V. spring chambers drains back through drilled holes in the cylinder head and barrel.

Oil is fed to the contact breaker chain by passing through the inlet cam spindle bush into the chain case. Any excess of oil accumulated in the case, drains through the breather pipe.

Crankcase pressure is released by a valve on the driving side of the crankcase and oil mist is fed to the rear chain.

All the oil drains to the base of the crankcase to the sludge trap, is picked up by the suction of the return side of the pump and returned to the tank

The oil-way from the sludge-trap is situated so that any foreign matter is left in the trap. This leaves the case when the crankcase drain plug is removed and the oil drained.

Maintenance of Engine

45. REMOVAL OF ROCKER BOX, CYLINDER HEAD and BARREL

Remove petrol tank (para.70A) and unscrew the rocker oil feed pipe top connection from the centre of the near side of the rocker box, taking care not to lose the fibre or copper washer from either side of the banjo. Disconnect exhaust valve lifter cable from lever and completely release the 9 bolts holding the box to cylinder head. If necessary break joint by tapping box with mallet or light block of wood. A thin composition washer is fitted between head and box, do not tear this during removal.

Lift out push rods now protruding from head. To remove the cylinder head, remove the exhaust system complete, slacken the air filter clip (when fitted) on the carburetter air intake, and remove the two nuts securing the carburetter flange. Remove the air filter, followed by the carburetter. Disconnect H.T. lead from sparking plug. Slacken each of the four cylinder head nuts and completely remove.

NOTE—A plain steel washer is fitted beneath the cylinder head nuts.

Tap beneath the inlet port with wooden block or mallet to break joint if necessary. The head should be lifted off from the timing side of the engine as it will bring with it the pushrod cover tubes held in position by rubber sleeves. Ensure that neither of the rubber rings forming the cover tube bottom seal is lost during this process.

The barrel need not be removed for de-carbonisation, as the piston crown can be readily cleaned with the barrel in position and piston on top dead centre. Should it be decided to take off the barrel, rotate engine until piston is around bottom centre position and lift off the barrel; avoid tearing paper washer if possible. Immediately the barrel is removed, cover crankcase mouth with clean rag to prevent the ingress of dirt.

46. REMOVAL OF CARBON

Scrape carbon from top of piston and cylinder head.

Both are of the alloy type and care must be taken not to damage them.

Place an old piston ring at the top of the bore, and resting on top of piston. It will prevent the carbon being removed at the edge of the piston and end of the bore.

After an engine has been used for any considerable time, wear in the bore and the rings takes place, allowing a small amount of oil to pass.

The carbon on the piston edge and the top of the bore acts as an oil seal and if removed, engine may use a little more oil until carbon is reformed.

The carbon deposit in the valve ports and valve spring compartment cannot be removed unless the valves are removed.

Valves need NOT be removed at every de-carbonisation.

47. REMOVAL OF VALVES

Compress valve springs with a suitable type of valve compressor.

When springs are compressed the valve cotters will fall from the valve stems.

Remove valve compressor.

Remove valves.

Remove valve springs and collars from valve spring compartment.

Remove carbon from underside of valve heads.

Check valve stems and guides; if free, do not touch guides, unless they are badly worn.

If guides and valves show no sign of excessive wear, re-grind valve seats.

Always grind the seats when new valves are fitted.

48. GRINDING OF VALVE SEATS

Use as little grinding compound as possible and use fine only if the seats are not pitted.

Place valve in guide and rotate to and fro with either a rubber sucker on the head of the valve or a valve grinding tool on the stem. Lift the valve off the seat frequently whilst grinding to redistribute the compound.

Do not overgrind valve seats (a wide seat is not necessary but the exhaust can be wider than the inlet to give a better heat path). When the seat is ground sufficiently, that is when the valve and seat show 100% contact, remove all traces of grinding paste from seat, valve and port. Use a small piece of rag for this purpose and place in a waste bin immediately so that there is no risk of some other engine part being wiped with it afterwards.

If the valves or the seats are badly burnt or pitted, it may be impossible to obtain a perfect seat by grinding. The seat will then have to be re-cut, and the valves re-faced or new valves fitted.

49. FITTING OF VALVES

Thoroughly clean valves, seats, and valve pockets. Fit valve springs and collars. Lubricate valve stems.

Fit valves into guides, compress valve springs, and fit cotters.

If the valve cotters are greased with a thick grease the grease will hold the cotters in place until the springs are released.

50. REMOVING AND REFITTING OF VALVE GUIDES

Valve guides are a driving fit in the cylinder head.

To remove, warm head and tap out with a double diameter drift.

Use the drift to replace or fit new ones.

Seats must be trued-up with cutter after refitting of guides, to ensure that the guides and seats are in alignment.

Oversize valve guides are usually available if required.

51. FITTING OF CYLINDER BARREL, CYLINDER HEAD AND ROCKER BOX

Position piston rings so that gaps are equally spaced.

Lubricate rings, barrel and piston, and rotate engine till piston is near top of stroke.

Fit paper washer to crankcase mouth, ensuring that cylinder oil feed and drain holes are not obstructed.

Fit barrel over piston and slide right home.

Clean cylinder head joint face on both head and barrel, and place aluminium gasket on top of barrel in position it previously occupied.

Fit head ensuring that the lower ends of the pushrod cover tubes are seating correctly between the tappet guide collar and the

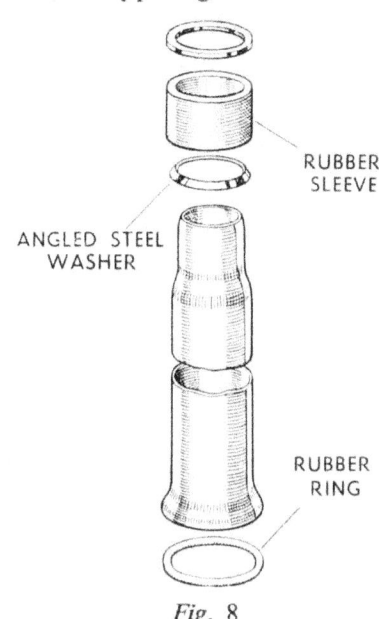

Fig. 8

flange on the bottom of the push rod cover tubes.

If the cover tubes have been withdrawn from the head, ensure that they are replaced as shown in Fig. 8. The flat steel washer being placed in the bottom of the enlarged push rod tunnel and held in position by the rubber sleeve. The angled washer being placed over the reduced end of the cover tube before pushing the tube home into the head. Smear with oil to assist re-assembly.

Fit cylinder head nuts and lightly pinch each one. Finally, tighten diagonal pairs. Replace push rods in position.

Clean rocker box and cylinder head joint faces and fit paper washer, smearing head with oil to hold washer in place.

Place box in position.

Fit and pinch up all nine bolts finally tightening down evenly.

Fit remaining components, remove inspection cover and check push rod adjustment—no clearance but push rods free to rotate.

52. DISMANTLING and RE-ASSEMBLY OF ROCKER BOX

Whilst rocker box is removed, it may be necessary to remove the rockers for examination or re-bushing. Remove the inspection cover and the rocker spindle nuts and washers, and with a soft punch against the larger threaded end, drift the spindles out of position.

The rockers with their washers and shims

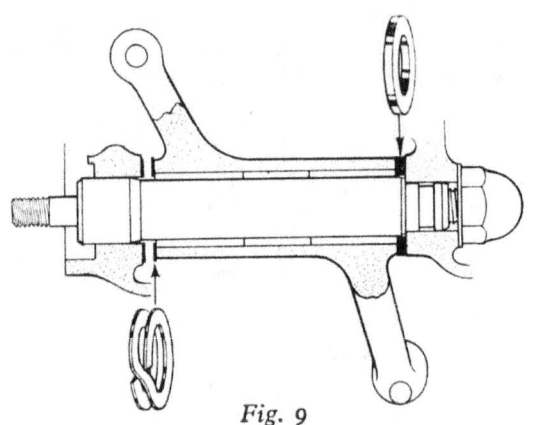

Fig. 9

may be extracted from the box.

Remove the exhaust valve lifter by first removing the small securing screw, when the lifter may be withdrawn.

The rocker bushes are a press fit in the rockers and may be pressed or drawn out as shown in Fig. 10.

Rocker ball ends and pads requiring renewing may be drifted out with a punch.

Press in new rocker ends, ensuring that the hole in the shank of the ball end is lined up with the oil hole in the rocker arm.

New rocker bushes may be pressed in or drawn into position by reversing the method of extraction illustrated.

New bushes should be reamed with $\frac{9}{16}$ in. diameter reamer after fitting.

The re-assembly of the rockers in the box may require a little patience. Fig. 9 shows clearly the position of the various parts.

Note that a steel shim fits between the double spring washer and the aluminium spindle boss in the box at the push rod side and the much thicker thrust washer fits at the valve side.

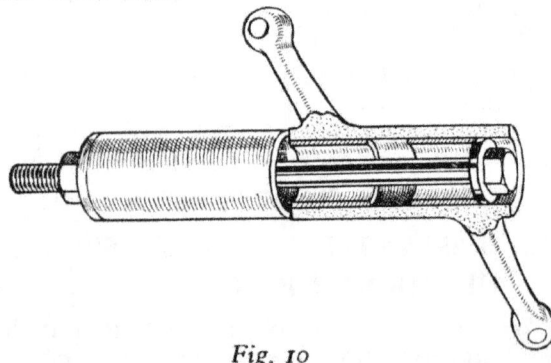

Fig. 10

Obtain a bar or tube smaller than the large spindle hole—push rod side. Insert this far enough into the hole to allow the shim and spring washer to be placed over it.

Carefully position rocker over the end of the bar and push it approximately into position, centralise washers as near as possible. Remove bar, smear spindle with oil and insert from push rod side. Using soft punch tap spindle part way through rocker.

Push rocker over by hand to compress spring washer and place thrust washer in position; the pressure of the spring washer will hold it until the spindle is knocked further home.

It is unlikely that the washer will be in true alignment with the spindle and will, therefore, be pinched between the rocker box and the shoulder on the spindle when the latter is tapped further into position.

With hand pressure on rocker, again compress spring washer. This will enable the thrust washer to be positioned on the full diameter of the spindle which can now be tapped fully home. Ensure that the rocker is free to move, fit copper washer and dome nut and tighten.

53. TO ADJUST TAPPETS

Release the middle hexagon—the locking nut—by placing one spanner on the flats on push rod end—and the second on the locking nut ($\frac{1}{4}$" Whit.).

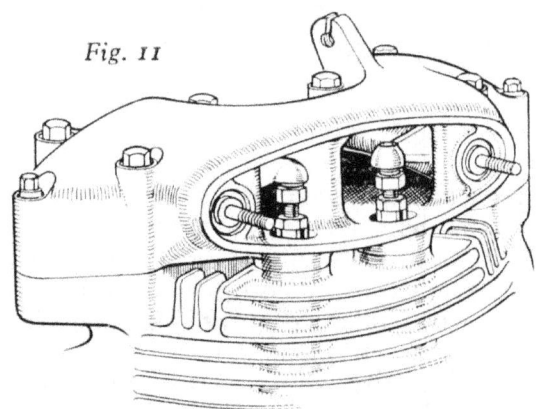

Fig. 11

Turn the top hexagon—the tappet head or push rod adjuster—in the desired direction, and when the correct clearance is obtained, tighten locking nut.

Check clearance after tightening locking nut.

When replacing inspection cover, great care should be exercised to avoid over-tightening as this would result in distortion of the cover, with possible breakage or oil leakage.

When adjusting the exhaust tappet, set on the slack, rather than on the tight side. Check tappets immediately there is any sign of loss of compression.

54. REMOVAL OF PISTON and RINGS

Remove cylinder barrel (para. 45).

Remove one circlip and the gudgeon pin.

Gudgeon pin is a running fit in the piston and small end bush.

Mark piston to ensure it is fitted the same way when replacing.

Remove piston rings. These may be readily "peeled" out of their grooves with the aid of a narrow bladed pen knife.

If it is decided not to fit new rings, it is not advisable to remove the carbon from the back of the ring or the bottom of the ring groove.

If it is decided to fit new rings, the grooves in the piston should be thoroughly cleaned. A portion of a broken hack-saw blade is an ideal tool for the job.

When the grooves have been cleaned, check the new ring for size in the grooves.

There should be a side clearance of .002".

Check rings in the cylinder bore for the correct width of gap.

Place ring in bore, push ring down bore, using the piston as a guide.

The ring gap should be:

Compression ring ... .010"—.012"
Scraper ... ... .010"—.012"

Check gap with feeler gauge.

55. REFITTING PISTON

Fit rings to piston.

Fit piston to connecting rod with the piston in the same position as before dismantling.

Fit circlip. It is advisable to always replace circlip and fit a new one.

Fit cylinder barrel (para. 51).

56. REMOVING AND FITTING OF SMALL END BUSH

If when the cylinder barrel and piston are removed, it is found that the small end bush is worn or has worked loose in the eye of the connecting rod, it should be replaced.

By far the best way of doing this is to return the connecting rod to the Service Department for the bush to be renewed and reamed square with the big end eye of the rod. Of course, this necessitates dismantling the bottom half of the engine and splitting the flywheels, but if the small end bush is badly worn, then it would be a good thing to examine the big end bearing at the same time.

Should it be necessary to replace the bush without splitting the flywheels, it can be done but great care is necessary to ensure that it is fitted and reamed as square as possible. To withdraw the bush from the connecting rod, obtain a bolt at least twice the length of the bush, place a washer at the head of the bolt with an outside diameter less than the bush. Place bolt in bush.

Over the threaded end of the bolt, place a piece of tubing longer than the bush, with an inside diameter slightly larger than the outside of the bush. Fit nut to bolt and tighten. As nut is tightened, the bush will be drawn from the rod.

Care must be taken that no strain is taken by the rod. Fit new bush in the same manner, taking particular care that it starts square. Drill the oil holes. Use an expanding reamer and ream in stages to size. Work from both sides and support rod whilst reaming. Gudgeon pin should be a running fit in the small end and the piston. Size of bore of bush fitted —.8745" to .8750".

57. REMOVAL OF TIMING PANEL

Remove chain cover held by 3 cheese headed screws. Remove sprockets with chain in position. If difficulty is experienced, a withdrawal tool should be obtained. The cam spindle sprocket is held by taper and key; the contact breaker shaft is not keyed. Re-

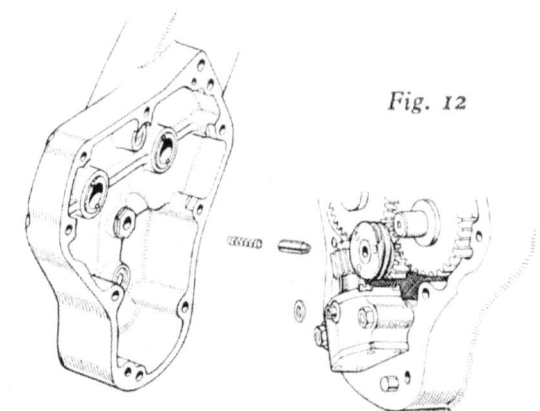

Fig. 12

move the contact breaker assembly by removing the set pin holding the clamping plate to the contact breaker housing, disconnecting the coil lead and withdrawing the contact breaker or merely disconnect the coil lead and remove the timing cover with the breaker still in position.

Remove panel screws and note that the top three are shorter than the bottom three. Two hexagon headed screws are inside the contact breaker chain case.

When withdrawing the panel see that the big end feed jet is not lost and that any shims fitted to the cam spindles remain in position.

Remove big end feed jet and spring.

58. FITTING TIMING PANEL

Clean the edges of the timing chest and the panel.

Smear the edges with gold-size or jointing compound.

Check fibre washer on the oil pump nipple, connecting pump to panel.

Place panel in position and the washer should prevent the edges of the panel meeting the case by 1/64". This ensures that when the panel pins are tightened, the washer is compressed, making an oil-tight joint.

Fit spring and jet in jet holder.

Fit panel and panel screws and tighten down evenly.

59. IGNITION TIMING (see also para. 121)

The contact breaker in which is incorporated the automatic advance mechanism, is chain driven from the inlet cam spindle, the sprocket being located on the tapered shaft and held with a central screw. Before attempting to check or time the ignition, ensure that the driving chain is correctly adjusted. Remove the chain cover, and slacken the two 'Allen' nuts and the hexagon nut

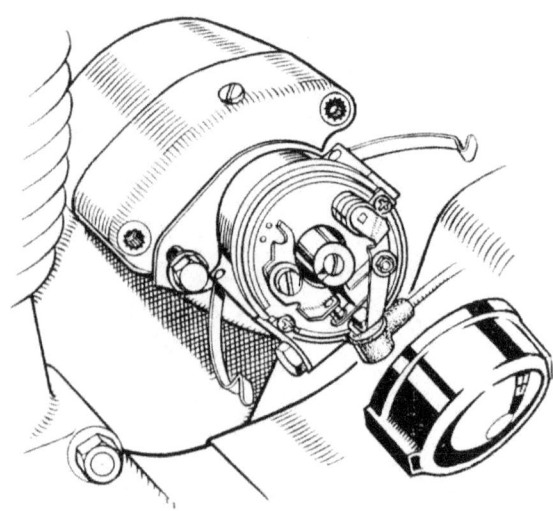

Fig. 13

holding the distributor housing to the timing cover extension and move the housing on its studs until there is about $\frac{3}{16}$" whip in the chain. Tighten the three nuts.

Set the contact breaker points to .015" when wide open. Set the piston on T.D.C. both valves closed. Slacken the contact breaker sprocket screw and release the sprocket from its taper, levering gently behind the sprocket or using a suitable withdrawal tool if necessary. The contact breaker body should be located from its housing so that the coil wire terminal is at the 6 o'clock position which will bring the oil hole in the spigot in line with the plug in the top of the housing at the same time the elongated hole in the clamping plate should be locked centrally about the set pin in the housing. Slacken the clamping bolt and rotate as necessary to obtain these conditions. DO NOT ATTEMPT TO ROTATE THE SQUARE NUT ON THE CLAMPING BOLT.

Rotate engine backwards until piston is 38° before top dead centre. With a small screwdriver in the slot in the cam end (not in central screw head) rotate the cam clockwise until points just break using either cigarette paper or the electrical method to ensure the accuracy necessary for satisfactory operation.

60. REMOVING TIMING GEARS, OIL PUMP AND TAPPETS

Remove timing panel (para. 57), timing gears and oil pump are now visible.

Remove oil pump nuts and withdraw oil pump from studs.

Remove oil pump worm, LEFT HAND THREAD. If a suitable peg spanner is not available, it can be unscrewed with a hammer and blunt-ended punch.

Timing gears may now be removed ensuring that any shims fitted to either end of the spindles are not lost.

Withdraw pinion from timing side mainshaft using, if necessary, a sprocket drawer.

Unless absolutely necessary the tappets should not be removed as it is necessary to remove the tappet guides before the tappets may be withdrawn.

The tappet guides are pressed into the crankcase and should be extracted by heating the case using a soft flame or immersing in boiling water.

Now with a soft drift or hide hammer, drive on the tappet feet to start the guides moving out. As soon as there is sufficient room, lever out by means of the flange on top of the guide.

The inlet and exhaust tappets should not be interchanged.

61. FITTING TAPPETS, TIMING GEAR AND OIL PUMP

If new timing gears have been fitted then they will need checking and re-shimming for end float. When fully home in the case, the side of the gear should be clear of the boss carrying the pressure release valve. Shims should be added until this condition is obtained.

Fit timing cover, pull and push on inlet cam spindle and shim up till end float is just perceptible.

End float on exhaust cam spindle can only be properly checked when crankcase halves are separated.

Tappets must be entered into tappet guides from inside timing chest before the guides are pressed into position.

This necessitates a tubular drift to finally force the guides home.

Tappet guides are located radially by a peg in top of crankcase, which fits into a hole in tappet guide collar. Hole and peg should be as nearly in alignment as possible before pressing or tapping the guide into position.

Fit half-time pinion to mainshaft and rotate engine till crankpin is on T.D.C.

Fit cam gears, meshing the marked teeth with the appropriate markings on the pinion.

Fit and tighten oil pump worm, LEFT HAND thread, using punch or peg spanner.

Fit oil pump, ensuring that both faces are quite clean.

Check fibre washer on oil pump nipple and fit timing panel (para. 58).

Time ignition (para. 59).

62. OIL PUMP

The oil pump is of the gear type. It is not advisable to dismantle it.

When pump is removed from timing chest, test for play in the spindle by pulling and pushing the worm wheel.

Revolve spindle and place fingers on the oil holes and the action of the gears should be felt if the pump is in good condition.

When revolving pump, any foreign matter obstructing the gears will be felt. Wash out with paraffin.

63. OIL CONTROL VALVE

This is fitted in a boss on the inside of the timing panel. It is an assembly of a **ball**, spring and adjusting screw. The adjustment is set at the works and should not need any attention.

The control valve acts as a safety valve in the oil circuit. When the oil is cold, the oil pressure in the circuit tends to become excessively high, but the excess of pressure lifts the ball from its seat, allowing the oil to spray on to the timing gears.

If for any reason this is dismantled, the order of assembly is—ball, spring and adjuster nut.

Tighten the nut home and then screw out one and a half turns and lock with centre punch.

64. EXAMINATION OF THE ROLLER BIG END

With the cylinder removed, the big-end can be examined for wear.

Rotate the flywheels until the big-end is in the topmost position.

Hold connecting rod with both hands, pull and push, and any up and down play can be felt.

DO NOT USE SIDE PRESSURE.

Do not mistake side float for end play.

A small amount of rock is of no importance.

If any appreciable up and down movement is present a new crankpin bearing is necessary. The dismantling of the flywheels and fitting of crankpin is a skilled job requiring equipment not normally available to the average rider. The flywheel assembly should be returned to the works for this replacement.

65. REMOVING ENGINE FROM FRAME

The engine and gearbox assembly is intended to be removed from the frame as a unit, and for this purpose it is advisable to support the frame on a block or box to provide rather more stability than is available from a central stand. Remove the petrol tank, oil bath chaincase, the oil tank and battery, together with their platform. Remove also the engine steady stay and disconnect all cables and electric wiring likely to prevent the engine/gearbox assembly being removed when all attachments are released.

Remove the remaining bolts holding the engine/gearbox assembly to the frame and lift the assembly clear of the frame. It will probably be necessary to obtain assistance to hold the cycle steady whilst removing the unit. No difficulty should be experienced in disconnecting the engine from the gearbox or vice versa.

66. PARTING OF THE CRANKCASE HALVES

Remove crankcase drain plug and drain any oil that may be in the sump.

Remove cylinder barrel (para. 45), piston (para. 54), timing gear and oil pump (para. 60).

Remove key from driving shaft.

Remove all the crankcase bolts and stud nuts. also the cheese headed screws from sump.

Crankcase halves can now be parted. Remove timing side first.

If leverage is necessary, revolve flywheels until the crankpin is at the mouth of the case. place a lever against the crankpin nut and lever outwards.

To remove the driving side of the case, lift the half of the case with the flywheels and lightly drop the end of the driving shaft on to a block of hard wood, when the case should leave the shaft.

67. REMOVAL OF BEARINGS FROM CRANKCASE

Deal with one half of the crankcase at a time and heat up with a soft flame taking care not to concentrate great heat in one area. Knock the case, joint face downwards on a flat wooden surface, when the bearings should fall out.

68. FITTING OF BEARINGS TO CRANKCASE

The bearings should be a 'light driving fit' on the shafts and should be checked before assembly. If they are over tight, ease the shaft down carefully with emery tape.

Heat the halves of the crankcase as for removal and press the ball bearing lightly into the driving side of the case. Fit the spacer ring next to the ball bearing. Press the outer race of the roller bearing up against the spacer with its flange towards the spacer.

To the timing side case fit the outer race of its roller bearing again flanged side first.

69. ASSEMBLY OF CRANKCASE

Fit flywheels into case, and fit and tighten all bolts.

Test for side float in the flywheels; there should be .005".

If the float is excessive, remove wheels from case.

Fit pen steel washers to the driving and timing shafts to take up the excess of float.

Fit the same thickness of washers on each shaft, keeping the wheels central in the case.

Check side float.

If the side float is correct, check connecting rod for being central in case.

There is side float in the big-end.

Place fingers on the bottom of the connecting rod and push rod towards the timing side of the case.

Measure the distance from the end of the small-end bush to the side of the crankcase mouth on the timing side.

Push rod to driving side of case and take the same measurement, from the driving side.

The two measurements should be within 1/64" of each other.

Rod can be relined up by transferring the pen steel washers on the driving and timing shafts to whichever side needs them, to obtain the correct alignment.

When the correct alignment is obtained, remove wheels from case.

Lubricate main bearings and big-end.

Smear the two edges of the case with gold-size or jointing compound.

Fit the wheels into the case and tighten all bolts and nuts.

Fit timing gears (para. 61), and panel (para. 58).

70. REMOVING AND FITTING OF TIMING GEAR BUSHES

When engine is dismantled it may be found that the timing gear bushes require replacement. This is not a job to be undertaken by the average owner. The timing cover and half crankcase should be despatched to our Service Department.

70A. PETROL TANK—REMOVAL

Ensure that the petrol tap is in the off position. Disconnect the petrol pipe using two spanners if necessary, holding the tap with one whilst releasing the union nut with the other.

Remove the dualseat by releasing the single Dzus fastener at the back, then lift the seat and withdraw rearwards from the two pegs on the frame at the front. These carry the seat by means of rubber bushes secured to its underside.

Release the single rubber band which secures the tank at the rear and unscrew the two inverted bolts at the front.

These have rubber washers above and below the lugs on the frame, the lower ones being in steel cups and the upper ones having a plain steel washer between them and the tank itself.

The bolts are shouldered so that when fully tightened the rubber washers are not over compressed.

The tank can now be lifted clear.

THE TRANSMISSION

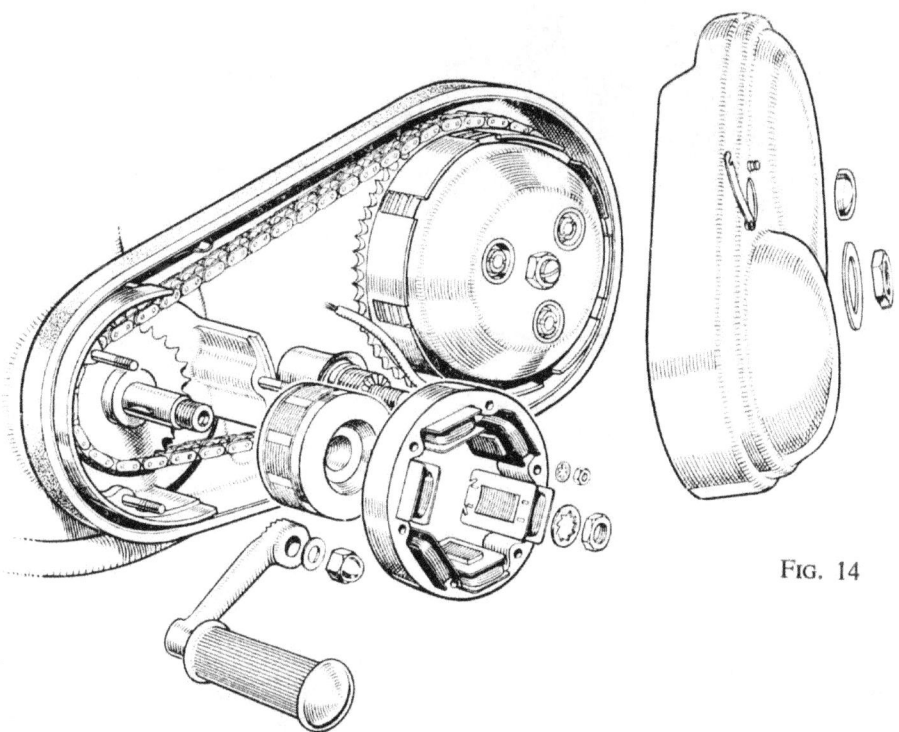

Fig. 14

71. CHAIN ADJUSTMENT

If maximum chain life and minimum power loss is to be obtained, chains must be run in correct adjustment and be properly lubricated.

The gearbox pivots on its lower mounting bolt and there are elongated holes in the mounting plates for the top bolt so that the box can be moved back and forward to adjust primary chain tension.

A drawbolt fitted to the gearbox top bolt has a $\frac{3}{16}''$ Whit. hexagon nut on either side of a stop rivetted to the offside mounting plate.

Primary Chain. To tighten the primary chain therefore, remove the chaincase inspection cap, slacken forward drawbolt nut and run it back with the fingers one or two threads. Slacken top gearbox bolt ($\frac{7}{16}''$ Whit. hex.) and slacken only slightly, bottom bolt ($\frac{3}{8}''$ Whit. hex.). With a spanner on rearward drawbolt nut, pull gearbox back until the chain is tight. Now slacken rearward nut a few turns and tighten the forward nut so that it pushes the gearbox forward until there is $\frac{1}{2}''$ to $\frac{3}{4}''$ up and down movement in the run of the chain midway between the sprockets. Tighten top and bottom gearbox bolts and operate kickstarter to check for tightest point of chain tension. There should be $\frac{1}{2}''$ up and down movement minimum. Set on the slack rather than the tight side with the primary chain. Tighten the forward drawbolt

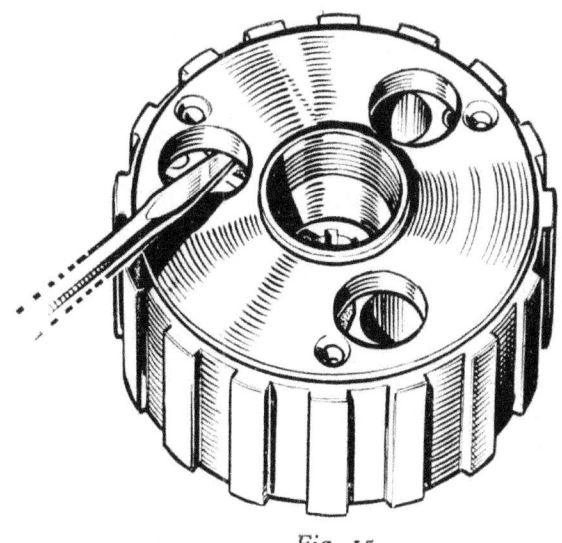

Fig. 15

nut against the stop so that it tends to push the gearbox forward all the time and tighten the rearward nut just sufficiently to prevent it becoming lost. In this way backlash in the

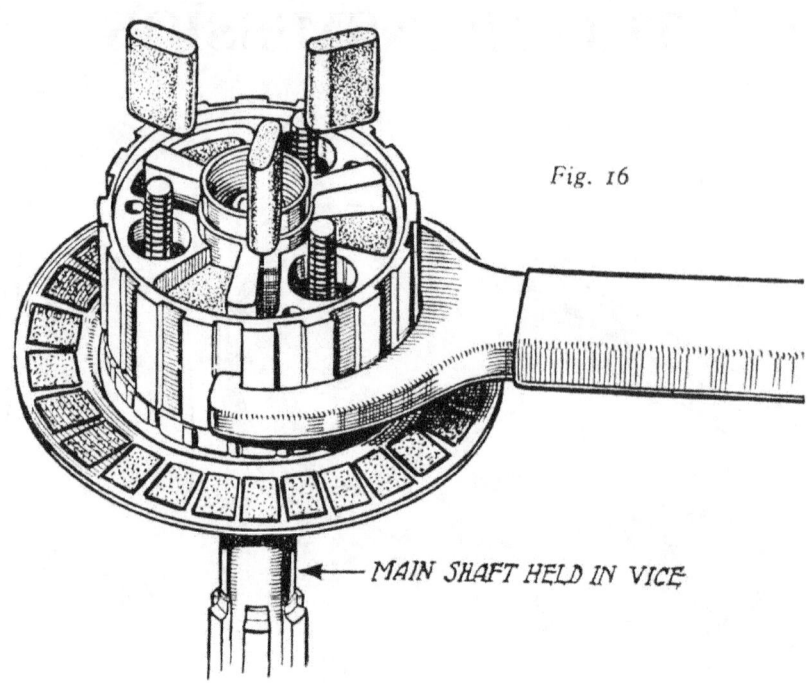

Fig. 16

← MAIN SHAFT HELD IN VICE

adjusting mechanism will be all taken up so as to hold the gearbox forward against the greater pull of the rear chain.

The pull of the rear chain, always greater than that of the primary, can move the gearbox back after say, a jerky start, or a very quick gearchange up or down, or when rider and passenger sit on the machine, if the rear chain tension has been set too tight with the weight of the machine only on the wheels.

The important point to remember in view of this is that any final adjusting movement should always be in a forward direction.

Rear Chain. Before adjusting the rear chain make certain that the front is adjusted as described above.

Check that the ends of the rear wheel adjuster screws are hard up against the collars on the rear wheel spindle nuts and then slacken the spindle nuts ($\frac{1}{2}$" Whit. hex). Do not slacken fully but about half a turn so that the spindle will not move about too easily in the fork ends.

Slacken the adjuster screw locknuts ($\frac{3}{16}$" Whit. hex.) and count the number of flats you unscrew each adjuster ($\frac{1}{8}$" Whit. hex) so that you move the spindle back the same amount each side, and thus maintain wheel alignment.

WITH THE REAR SHOCK ABSORBERS COMPRESSED TO MID-STROKE there should be $\frac{3}{4}$" to 1" up and down movement in the run of the chain mid-way between the sprockets. At this point the chain is at its tightest.

Obtain assistance if necessary to hold the shock absorbers down—it will help if it is done single handed—to set the shock absorbers to the softest position and sit astride the rear number plate cuff (taking care not to break the tail lamp), with the machine off the stand, of course. The tension of the chain can now be checked with the left hand. Check for the tightest point as described for primary. Tighten wheel spindle nuts and adjuster locknuts, holding the adjusters themselves with a second spanner if necessary to prevent them screwing in and thus away from the wheel spindle, as the locknuts are tightened.

After adjustment of rear chain, check rear brake adjustment as, of course, this is altered by movement of rear wheel spindle.

Check wheel alignment, preferably with a straight edge, and note that because the rear tyre has a greater cross section than has the front, when the wheels are in line, a straight edge placed squarely on the side of the rear tyre at two points, should pass the front tyre leaving a small gap (usually about $\frac{1}{8}$" to $\frac{3}{16}$") at two points, and when the straight edge is transferred to the opposite side of the machine, these gaps should be the same.

Should this not be so, note whether chain requires to be tightened or slackened, slacken wheel spindle nut on appropriate side and by means of adjuster, move wheel in required direction.

Tighten all nuts and check again.

If the chain has been slackened off, and to ensure that the rear spindle is hard up against the adjusters, place a hammer shaft, or piece of wood between rear tyre and offside pivoted fork tube (swinging arm). 'Lever' wheel over towards nearside and tighten offside nut.

Pull wheel forward on nearside by 'squeezing' lower run of chain against pivoted fork tube with left hand whilst tightening spindle nut with right. (If the machine has a full chaincase, it is possible to apply some weight to the top run of the chain through the inspection orifice and obtain the same effect).

Rear Chain Lubrication. This is by oil vapour fed to it by the oil tank vent pipe which is connected to the forward end of the chainguard or chaincase. The amount of oil the chain receives will vary according to the way the machine itself is used. For example, with a normal oil level in the tank, and using the machine for a ride to work or short trips about town, the chain may not receive much oil, but if long fast runs are undertaken, it will certainly receive more which may become too much if a long full-bore run is made on say, a motorway. It will help to use a higher oil level in the tank for short journeys and a lower one for very fast ones, remembering that with a very low level there may be overheating at very high speeds due to the smaller amount in circulation.

Chain Hints. CHAINS SHOULD NEVER BE RUN OVERTIGHT. It is better to run them on the slack side provided they are not so slack that they make contact with the inside of their cases or guards.

If the primary chain is run too slack an intermittent metallic tap will be heard as the lower run 'flips' upwards and strikes the underside of the tube in the chaincase which surrounds the footrest hanger. When this happens, of course, the chain should be adjusted up.

There should always be sufficient oil in the front chaincase for the lower run of the chain to 'dip' as if the chain is run for only a short distance with insufficient oil, it will overheat and wear rapidly and oleate of rust formed in its bearings will give the remaining oil a 'cocoa like' appearance.

Most riders are aware that when the springclip is fitted to the connecting link, its blind end should be fitted pointing in the direction in which the chain travels. Many do not seem to know however, that the spring is not flat, but has a concave and convex side. It should be fitted blind end forward and convex side out so that it holds the side plate snugly up against the bushes of the inner links.

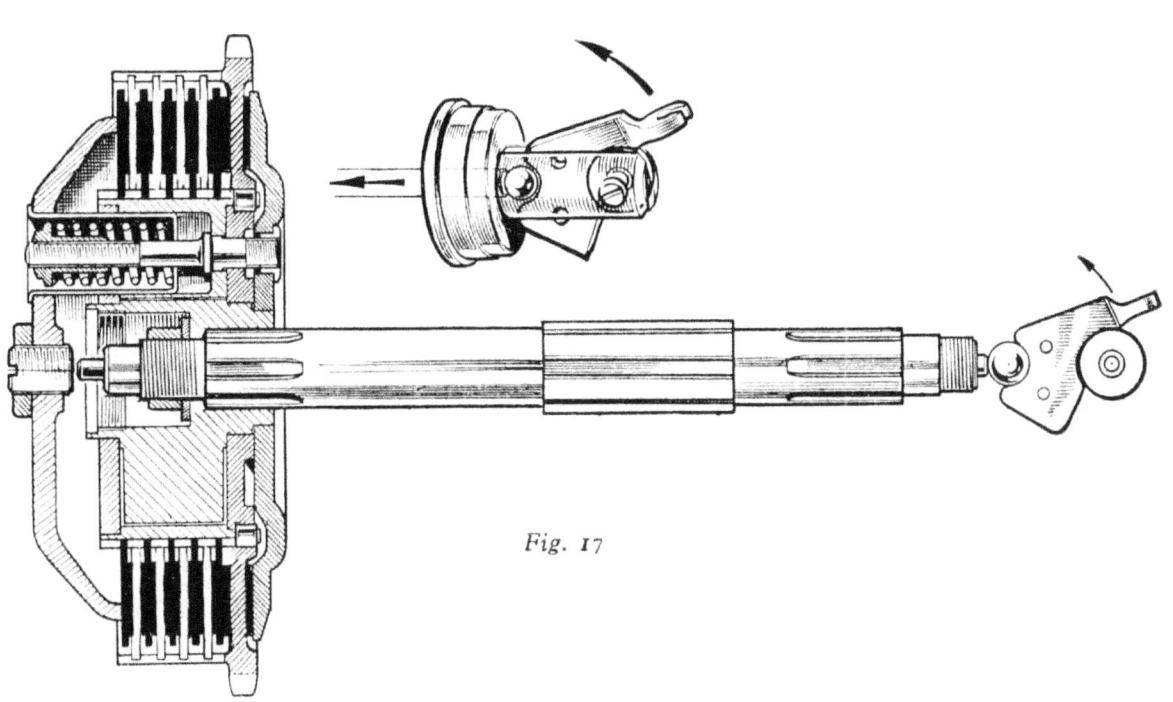

Fig. 17

Rear chain life can be increased by removing the chain, say every 1000 miles (for this purpose keep an old chain to join on to the present one and run it round the sprockets whilst the chain is removed). This will greatly facilitate removal and refitting.

Wash the chain thoroughly in paraffin and after allowing the paraffin to dry off, immerse the chain in lubricant which has been heated in a container until liquid. After about 10 minutes immersion during which the chain is moved about with a stick to 'work' the joints and ensure penetration of the lubricant, the latter is allowed to cool with the chain still in it. After cooling the chain is removed and the surplus grease wiped off. The chain can then be refitted to the machine after cleaning the chain wheels.

It should be noted that not all greases are suitable for heating to thinness without deterioration, and when purchasing the purpose for which the lubricant is required should be stated, as special ones are marketed for the job.

It is useful to know the extent of chain wear, and wear up to $\frac{1}{4}''$ per foot of chain length is accommodated by the depth of hardening of the bearing surfaces, and when this limit is reached, the chain should be replaced.

The test should be made carefully to ensure an accurate result. The chain is first washed in paraffin to ensure all joints are free and laid unlubricated on a flat board. If it is anchored at one end by a nail, the necessary tension to pull it out to its fullest extent can be applied with one hand, whilst measuring between the centres of the bearing pins.

72. CLUTCH ADJUSTMENT

The clutches of all these machines have bonded on friction material and it is bonded to the driven plates instead of inserts in the driving plates and chainwheel as on earlier models.

In order to obtain quick clean gear changing and freedom from clutch drag, correct adjustment is vital.

With the control cable adjuster slackened off, there should be about $\frac{1}{8}''$ free movement in the small operating lever in the kickstarter case. This is illustrated on the extreme right of Fig. 17. If there is more or less than this, the primary chaincase outer half should be removed (para. 73).

Now release the locknut ($\frac{7}{16}''$ Whit. hex.) on the adjuster screw in the centre of the aluminium pressure plate and set the screw as necessary. If it is first screwed in until it is hard on the pushrod and then slackened back half a turn this should give about the right amount of free movement in the lever as described.

Tighten the locknut and adjust the cable so that there is about $\frac{1}{8}''$ free movement at the handlebar lever. The clutch pressure plate should now come off squarely and rotate true laterally when the kickstarter is operated with the clutch withdrawn. If it does not do so, adjust individual springs to obtain this result.

If the clutch is dismantled for any reason such as cleaning of the plates, check that the nut securing the clutch centre to the gearbox mainshaft is tight before refitting the pressure plate and springs, etc.

If a replacement handlebar lever is fitted at any time, make certain that it has the correct centres for cable nipple and fulcrum pin these should be $\frac{7}{8}''$.

73. REMOVAL AND REFITTING OF OIL BATH

Remove the brake pedal by withdrawing the jaw joint pin and unscrewing the grease nipple from the pedal boss. Take care whilst doing so not to push the pedal down farther than it normally travels as otherwise the pedal return spring housed in the pedal boss will be strained and require to be replaced.

Remove the left hand footrest and the large nut screwed on to the footrest tube ($1\frac{1}{8}''$ Whit. hex.). This will enable the outer cover to be withdrawn exposing the driving chain clutch and generator. Remove the three nuts holding the stator and withdraw it from its studs drawing the cable carefully through the grommet in the inner chaincase until the stator can safely be rested on the rear engine plates. Remove mainshaft nut and rotor from mainshaft.

Remove primary chain and withdraw engine sprocket using sprocket puller. Remove the three clutch spring nuts, springs and cups and clutch pressure plate.

Engage top gear and obtain assistance to hold the rear wheel while the clutch retaining nut is being slackened. The rear brake can be held on with a ring spanner on the cam spindle nut.

With the clutch centre nut removed, the clutch itself can be withdrawn, it is on a parallel spline but if tight, a special withdrawal tool can be obtained from the Service Department.

Remove the three countersunk 'Allen' screws securing the stator housing to the crankcase. The inner chaincase is now held by three screws at the front end, by the nut on the nearside gearbox bottom bolt and by the nut on a hexagon spacer stud on the nearside engine/gearbox plate.

Note the paper washer fitted between crankcase and chaincase.

Re-assemble in the reverse order watching that the slots in the stator housing are correctly positioned to pass the chain and fitting the spring on the chain connecting link with its closed end pointing in the direction of travel of the chain and with its convex side out. Do not fit outer portion until clutch has been adjusted (para. 72). Note that the rubber sealing band has a thin lip on one edge only. This should be on the outer diameter of the band and towards the outer cover. If the band has stretched it is permissible to cut a piece out and join with wire provided the joint is positioned on the top side of the case.

Fit stator with the edge from which the leads are taken innermost and drawing surplus cable through to behind the inner portion. Fit outer cover, giving the rim a few blows with the ball of the hand or a rubber mallet whilst tightening the nut. Do not overtighten or the case may be distorted. Usually one or two threads only should protrude through the nut.

74. CLUTCH—TO DISMANTLE

Remove the outer portion of the oil bath (para. 73). Remove clutch spring adjuster nuts with divided screwdriver, or use a small screwdriver on one side only. There is a locking 'pip' under the head of these screws and considerable torque may be necessary to get over it during the first one or two revolutions.

Pressure plate will now come away, remove clutch plates, and note that the first driven plate has bonded friction material on one side only and must therefore always be the end plate.

Disconnect primary chain and remove clutch chainwheel. Engage top gear and unscrew clutch centre nut. R.H. thread, $\frac{7}{8}''$ Whit. hexagon box spanner required. Remove nut and single spring washer. Clutch centre can now be withdrawn from splined gearbox mainshaft.

To dismantle the clutch centre and examine the shock absorber rubbers, remove the three screws holding the front cover plate and tap the plate round until a screwdriver can be used to prise it off (Fig. 15).

At the works, the rubbers are removed by mounting the clutch centre on an old mainshaft held in a vice and with a special 'C' spanner on the splines of the centre the large rubbers are compressed whilst the small ones are removed first.

A small sharp pointed tool is necessary to remove the rubbers, as after use they adhere to the body. Large rubbers are easily removed after the small ones have been withdrawn.

The body is then removed from the mainshaft, the 'spider' or shock absorber centre is taken out and the body turned upside down on the bench.

The three nuts on the spring studs should then be removed when the backplate, roller race, race plate and body can be separated.

If a spare mainshaft and special 'C' spanner are not available, the rubbers can be removed from the shock absorber with the clutch centre on the mainshaft of the machine.

A spare 'driven' clutch plate is necessary on which should be welded a piece of steel tube for a handle about 24" long. (This is a useful tool to have in the workshop in any case as it provides a good means of holding the clutch centre whilst the centre nut is tightened or slackened).

Top gear should be engaged and the rear wheel stopped with the brake, or a rod passed through the spokes of the wheel which must be held on a spoke nipple hard up against the rim and then allowed to come up against the tubes of the pivoted fork (swinging arm) —remove rear chaincase or guard as necessary.

Now using the tool as described turn the clutch centre to compress the large rubbers and 'pick' out the small ones. The large ones will now come out easily and the body dismantled as described above.

75. EXAMINATION OF CLUTCH PARTS

Examine the driven plates with their bonded on strips of friction material and ensure that none are missing. Clean them thoroughly with petrol and a stiff brush. Place the plain driving plates together and check that they are flat. These should be of the 'pin point planished' type—that is they should have small 'pop' marks all over. Plates so treated will stand high temperatures without buckling.

The splines on the body and the bonded plates which drive the body rarely show any signs of wear, but the tongues on the plain driving plates may be worn and may have cut slots in the chainwheel. This wear obstructs the free movement of the plates when the clutch is operated, this can be rectified by carefully filing or grinding the tongues on the plates square also the driving edge of the slots in the chainwheel.

The only effect this will have on the clutch is a slight amount of backlash, when the clutch is engaged or disengaged.

Examine roller race, rollers and cage, examine the race plate, face and bore for wear by the clutch body centre or 'spider'. Examine the shock absorber rubbers, they may have become soft or cracked. Examine the 'spider' itself for wear on race plate and cover plate diameters also the internal splines for any fractures.

76. ASSEMBLY OF CLUTCH

Fit race plate to clutch body, ensuring that the holes in the plate are in line with the holes in the body, and the spring studs an easy fit. Fit roller cage, rollers and back plate. Fit shock absorber centre or 'spider' in body and lock up nuts on studs. Fit large rubbers followed by small ones. Fit cover plate and three screws (these may be countersunk or have cheese heads). See illustration for correct position of large and small rubbers. Test roller race for freeness on its track, and apply a little medium grease or anti-centrifuge grease.

Check all the clutch plates on the body and in the sprocket (clutch case) for freeness.

Fit sprocket to body, revolve sprocket on race to check free movement, fit plates as follows:

First a double sided bonded driven plate followed by a plain driving plate and so on in alternate order until the last bonded plate which is single sided is fitted. This, of course, should present its plain steel side to the pressure plate.

Fit clutch to gearbox mainshaft, fit spring washer and nut, engage top gear and tighten nut.

Fit clutch push rod, clutch pressure plate, spring cups, springs and spring adjuster nuts. Screw up nuts until studs come up just flush with end of nuts, and adjust as necessary to ensure square withdrawal of pressure plate.

Gearbox

77. REMOVAL FROM FRAME

With this frame it is not possible to remove the gearbox as a separate unit and if, therefore, it becomes necessary to remove the gearbox shell, then it is essential to lift the engine/gearbox assembly from the frame as described in para. 65 and to remove the gearbox as a subsequent operation.

78. OUTER COVER, REMOVAL

Remove the kickstarter crank by unscrewing the pinch bolt taking it right out and pulling off the crank. Remove gear indicator by unscrewing the centre bolt from the positive spindle. Remove oil filler and inspection plate and disconnect clutch inner wire from operating lever.

Do not remove foot change pedal.

Remove five screws holding cover in position and carefully pull the cover away by means of the footchange pedal. Take care not to tear paper washer.

79. OUTER COVER, FITTING

Ensure paper washer is undamaged or carefully scrape off old washer and fit new.

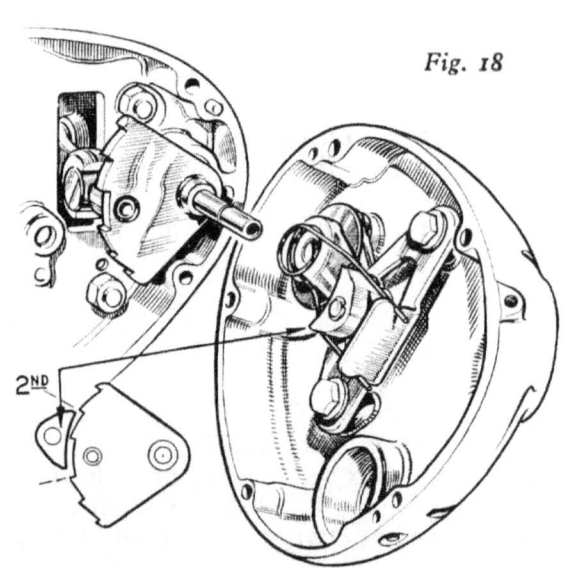

Fig. 18

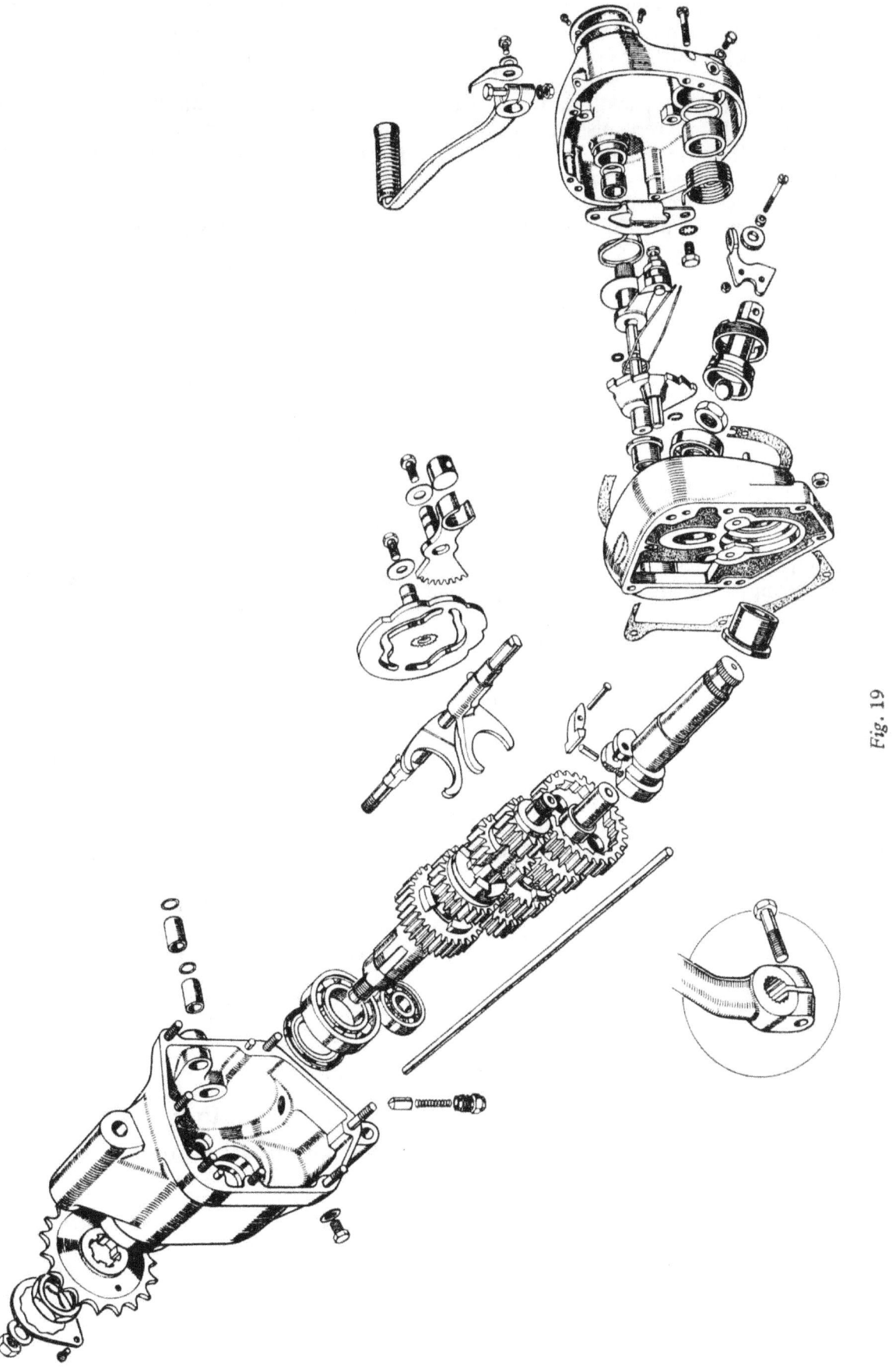

Fig. 19

Ensure also foot change pawl spring not dislodged and lying correctly with its straight leg uppermost, each leg resting on the rocking pawl (Fig. 18) before fitting cover. Replace remaining parts.

Some oil will have been lost due to cover removal and should be replenished through the filler hole after the level plug: i.e. the small hexagon headed pin to the rear of the kickstarter axle, has been removed. Engine oil should be **slowly** poured in until it commences to drip through this screw hole.

80. POSITIVE FOOT CHANGE DISMANTLING

Removal of the outer cover will bring with it the positive footchange mechanism.

To dismantle, remove gear indicator and withdraw ratchet plate and spindle.

Remove pawl spring.

Remove operating lever, disengage return spring legs from pawl pin and withdraw pawl carrier.

New return spring cannot be fitted without removing spring stop plate.

81. POSITIVE FOOT CHANGE ASSEMBLY

Obtain any necessary replacements and ensure all parts clean.

Smear oil on all moving parts.

Place return spring in position and fit plate.

Place washer on pawl carrier spindle, insert into bush and push home whilst manoeuvring springlegs into position in groove in pawl pin.

Refit pawl spring with straight leg uppermost.

Fit ratchet and spindle.

Refit operating lever and gear indicator before fitting cover.

Use indicator to move ratchet plate into position to pilot operating pin into selector fork roller whilst fitting cover. Probably necessary to remove indicator, finally, to adjust lever to individual requirements.

82. INNER COVER, REMOVAL

With outer cover already removed, remove ratchet plate with spindle. Before unscrewing locking ring securing clutch withdrawal device, mark rotational position of lever slot on end cover just outside lock ring. Otherwise it is unlikely that operating lever will be at correct angle for cable entry when outer cover is fitted.

Unscrew lock ring (R.H. thread) and remove operating lever body ensuring that $\frac{1}{2}''$ steel ball does not become lost. Unscrew mainshaft nut now exposed (R.H. thread).

Remove the seven nuts holding the cover to the shell and withdraw the cover from the studs, tapping behind the front end to loosen if necessary. Avoid damaging the paper washer.

83. INNER COVER, FITTING

Ensure paper washer undamaged and faces clean.

Fit cover and its seven securing nuts, just pinching all down and finally tightening opposite nuts in pairs.

Fit and tighten mainshaft nut.

Fit clutch operating body with ball but before tightening the locking ring ensure that the operating lever is lying in alignment with clutch cable adjuster hole, in order to obtain a straight pull on the cable.

Fit ratchet plate and spindle.

84. INNER COVER, DISMANTLING

The footchange mechanism having been already dealt with, and the clutch operating parts having been removed in order to enable inner cover to be withdrawn, only the kickstarter mechanism remains.

Lever out return spring end from hole in kickstarter axle when the axle can be withdrawn from its bush. Removal of the pawl pin results in pawl, plunger and spring falling out of position.

If the nose of the pawl is worn or chipped, it should be renewed.

If kickstarter crank has been positioned on its splines in a too near vertical position, a large wadered foot may have inadvertently held the crank far enough back whilst riding for the pawl to run continually in mesh with the ratchet annulus in the 1st gear wheel. Both these parts should therefore, be examined for wear.

85. INNER COVER, ASSEMBLING

Examine pawl cam and stop pieces rivetted to cover, if loose re-rivet.

Fit pawl spring, plunger, pawl and pin.

Insert axle into bush, fit return spring.

NOTE that the clutch operating mechanism cannot be re-assembled until cover is fitted to box.

86. REMOVAL OF GEARS

If the clutch has been removed, it will be

helpful to fit a short length of tubing over the end of the main axle and hold it in place with a clutch nut to retain the axle in position whilst the gears are being removed.

Remove end cover (paras. 78 and 82).

Remove the low gear and kickstarter wheel the large gear on the layshaft which has a bronze bush pressed into its centre.

Remove the small wheel from the end of the main axle.

Remove the mainshaft second gear; this is fitted with a fully floating bush. Unscrew the striker fork shaft by means of the two flats machined on its outer end and remove it together with the layshaft second gear and the striker fork.

Remove the tubular distance piece on clutch and withdraw the main axle together with the third gear and striker fork.

Withdraw the layshaft and the two remaining gears.

Gently warming the box and dropping it face downwards on a wooden block will withdraw the layshaft bearing.

Remove axle sprocket nut which has a left hand thread and is held with a locking washer and screw, and withdraw the main gearwheel. If the gearbox is in the frame and the rear chain in position, obtain assistance to hold rear wheel whilst the nut is being removed.

If the gearbox is removed from the frame, the sprocket may be held by passing a length of old chain around it and holding the ends in a vice.

87. REMOVAL OF CAM PLATE

Remove the domed hexagon nut from beneath the forward side of the gearbox shell. This serves as a bush for the camplate indexing plunger and spring which will come away with it when the nut is unscrewed.

Remove the two hexagon set pins, with washers, from the forward side of the gear box. The cam plate also cam plate quadrant, can now be extracted from inside the gear box shell. Wear on the two bushes for the cam plate and quadrant can cause the gears to disengage due to bad indexing.

Renew the "O" rings on both shafts if oil leakage occurs.

Should these bushes require replacement, they can be pressed or drifted out, preferably heating the shell first.

88. FITTING CAM PLATE

Insert the quadrant through the gear box, secure it with its set pin and washer. Raise the lever portion, until the top radius is in line with the top right hand stud for the case cover (top gear position).

Fit the cam plate to engage with the quadrant so that only the first two teeth are visible through the slot in the cam plate.

Secure the cam plate with its set pin and washer. Put back the plunger, spring, and domed nut.

89. FITTING GEARS INTO GEARBOX

Fit the main gearwheel, make sure spacer which bears on oil seal is in position as the sleeve of the gear passes through the bearing in the wheel. Fit the axle sprocket, tighten the nut *left hand thread*, fit locking washer and set screw.

Check the fit of the layshaft in the ballrace in gearbox shell—it should be a hand push fit. If it is tight, ease the end of the shaft down with emery tape.

Fit third gear wheel (free pinion) 20T to layshaft followed by fixed pinion 18T. This must be fitted with its flat side to the free pinion and its slightly raised centre to the ballrace. Fit layshaft in gearbox. Oil mainshaft on plain portion and fit in sleeve gear.

Set the cam plate in neutral position, i.e. with indexing plunger in the shallow groove. Fit the selector fork to mainshaft third gear (21T) and fit to mainshaft, meshing it with the layshaft gear already in position. Fit the other selector fork to the layshaft second gear (24T). Fit this to layshaft, engage pegs on selector forks with slots in cam plate, fit selector fork spindle and screw home. It is not difficult to fit this spindle, even with the gearbox in the frame, use a screwdriver if necessary to 'lift' the inner selector fork into position whilst the spindle carrying the outer fork is passed through it.

The selector forks are identical and can, therefore, be interchanged but it is advisable to replace them in their original positions.

Fit mainshaft free pinion, mainshaft fixed pinion and low gear wheel to layshaft. There are no shims.

Fit end cover taking care that joint washer is undamaged and properly positioned.

Fit remainder of parts as described in para. 85 inner cover assembling, and para. 83 inner cover fitting.

Finally, remember to refill the gearbox with oil to correct level.

Wheels, Hubs and Brakes

90. FRONT WHEEL REMOVAL

Place machine on centre stand, remove split pin from brake control clevis pin and withdraw pin. Unscrew cable adjuster from brake plate. Unscrew wheel spindle nut (R.H. thread) and release pinch stud nut in L.H. fork end.

Take the weight of the wheel in left hand and withdraw spindle by means of a tommy bar placed through the hole in the head of the spindle. Withdraw spindle and as wheel is removed, take great care not to allow the brake plate to fall from the drum (its bevelled edge can be badly damaged if it is allowed to fall). Place spindle and dust cover in a clean place to avoid contamination with grit.

91. FRONT WHEEL—FITTING

Re-assemble in reverse order, grease spindle lightly. Fit brake plate into drum and as wheel is lifted into forks, position dust cover on L.H. side and make certain that torque stop on brake plate engages slot in R.H. fork leg. Pass spindle through with right hand. Fit and tighten spindle nut. Deflect forks a few times to 'centre' nearside leg on spindle. DO NOT overtighten pinch stud nut on L.H. side. The lug on the leg can be broken if this is overtightened. Re-connect and adjust brake cable.

92. REAR WHEEL—REMOVAL

Place machine on centre stand, on de Luxe models only remove rear number plate.

Remove the three rubber plugs from offside rear hub and with box or socket spanner remove three sleeve nuts then exposed.

Unscrew right hand portion of wheel spindle and withdraw. Remove spacer and speedometer drive gearbox and allow the latter to hang on its cable.

Withdraw wheel from brake drum by pulling to offside when it should come clear of brake drum which is left in position.

The standard models do not now have a detachable rear mudguard portion and one should therefore stand on the nearside and incline the machine slightly towards one on the stand, when the wheel can be withdrawn with the right hand from the offside.

On de Luxe models, if the tyre is deflated the wheel can be withdrawn rearwards through the space left by the removal of the number plate. With the tyre inflated, it may be necessary to incline the machine as for standard models to get the wheel clear.

If it is necessary to remove the wheel complete with brake, remove chaincase or chainguard and disconnect the chain, remove brake rod adjusting nut but **do not** push the brake pedal down to withdraw rod from roller. Disconnect the 'dead' lead from stoplamp switch. Disconnect speedometer drive cable, and slacken both sides of the wheel spindle. The wheel should now slide out of the fork ends and be removed as described above but it may be necessary to remove the offside silencer due to greater width caused by the offside portion of the wheel spindle remaining in the hub.

93. REAR WHEEL—REFITTING

Reverse dismantling operations and if fitting with brake complete make certain torque stop on brake plate properly engages with slot in left hand fork end. Engage brake rod in cam lever roller and push wheel spindle up against adjuster screws. Position speedometer gearbox for correct cable take-off angle and tighten both sides of spindle. Connect speedometer drive cable—do not overtighten gland nut.

Fit rear chain taking care to fit clip to connecting link as described in para. 71—**Chain Hints**. Check rear chain tension.

Fit chaincase or chainguard. Adjust rear brake. Re-connect stop switch 'dead' lead. On de Luxe models refit number plate.

When fitting rear wheel only with brake drum already in situ, incline machine as necessary to position wheel under mudguard or tail fairing. Turn brake drum by hand so

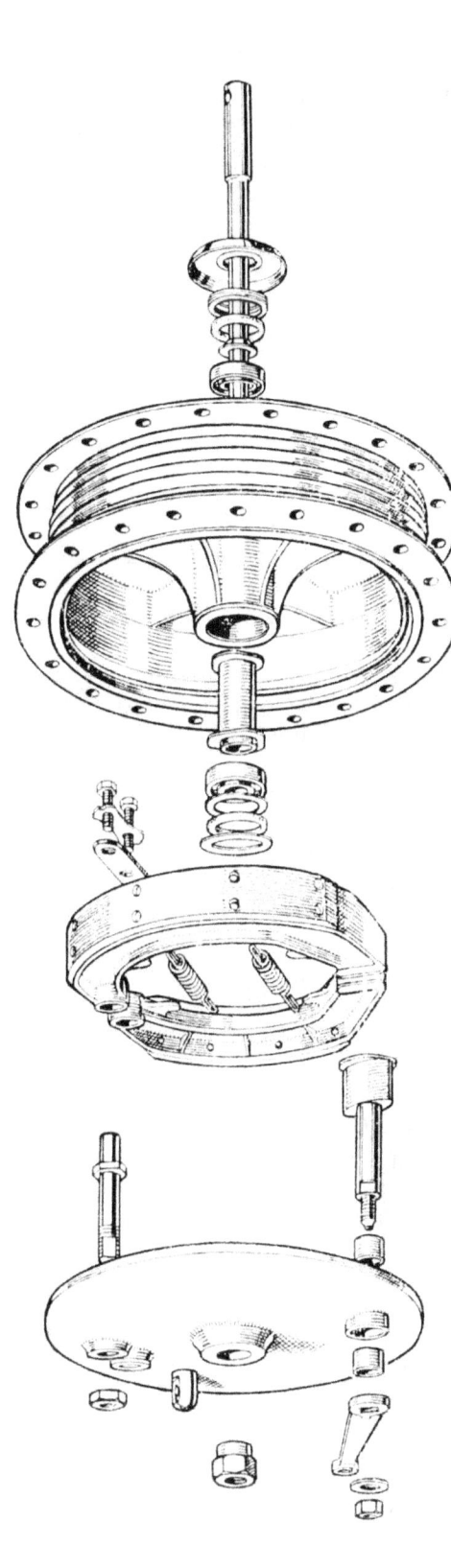

Fig. 20 **FRONT HUB**   Fig. 21 **REAR HUB**

that one of the three studs is approximately in line with tubes of pivotted fork (swinging arm). This facilitates getting the bearing boss on the hub past the other two studs and fitting the hub to the brake drum. Fit and tighten three sleeve nuts and replace rubber plugs. Fit speedometer drive gearbox taking great care that its driving dogs properly engage with the slots in the hub bearing lock ring. Position spacer and fit R.H. part of divided spindle. Take care that the washer on this passes the end of the adjuster screw in the fork end and that as the spindle is screwed home its head does not catch on the adjuster screw and bend it.

Tighten spindle and on de Luxe models re-fit number plate.

94. REAR HUB—DISMANTLING

Remove rear wheel (para. 92). Unscrew very carefully the left hand threaded locking ring which drives the speedometer gearbox. Take out distance piece and felt washer.

Now take the rear wheel spindle, leave on it the thick washer and thread over it the dull plated spacer which fits between speedometer gearbox and fork end.

Insert this assembly through the double row ball race at the opposite side of the hub —the brake drum side. Drive on the end of the spindle with a hide hammer or mallet carefully until a stop is felt. This should have commenced to move the single row bearing out of the lock ring side of the hub. It cannot be moved any further with the spindle and spacer because the double row bearing will have come up against a shoulder in the hub.

Remove spindle and spacer and using front wheel spindle, insert threaded end in double row bearing on brake drum side. Hold square and tap gently with mallet when bearing spacer should be driven from inner race of bearing taking with it the single row bearing from the opposite side.

Now insert rear spindle with dull plated spacer through shouldered bearing spacer and pass into hub from lock ring side.

Carefully centre in double row bearing, hold square and carefully drive out. As this bearing comes out it will bring with it steel cup washer, felt washer and pen steel washer.

95. REAR HUB—RE-ASSEMBLING

Pack bearings with grease (see table of lubricants) with care not to overfill.

Fit the single row bearing into threaded side of hub, fit shouldered bearing spacer with long end into single row bearing. Fit shouldered distance piece, felt washer and locking ring and tighten. (L.H. thread. Do not damage slots which drive speedometer gearbox).

Press double row bearing into position on opposite side of hub. It can be driven home square by using rear spindle and dull plated spacer, as described for removal.

Fit pen steel washer, felt washer and steel cup or dished washer. Lightly rivet the latter washer into position.

96. FRONT HUB—DISMANTLING

Remove front wheel (see para. 90). Remove brake plate. Unscrew lock ring (R.H. thread) using a peg spanner or if not available, a hammer and pin punch. If the ring does not move easily, try tapping from different holes and heat the hub with a soft flame such as a gas ring with a low light.

Remove felt washer and distance washer. Now insert front wheel spindle from brake side and drive with hide hammer or mallet. This will move the double row bearing further into the hub and at the same time drive the single row bearing out.

Drive carefully until this bearing just drops clear, if you drive harder the spacer which fits between the bearings will be damaged. Now withdraw the front wheel spindle, pass it through the bearing spacer still in the hub and holding it central, drive the double row bearing out. This will take with it the large steel washer, felt washer and pen steel washer.

97. FRONT HUB—RE-ASSEMBLING

Pack bearings with grease as for rear hub. Press single row bearing into position, followed by distance washer with flat side to bearing, felt washer and locking ring, which can be tightened up. Insert distance tube small end first into hub, ensuring that it is right home against the bearing just fitted.

Enter double row bearing squarely into hub, pass front wheel spindle through until it enters opposite bearing. Drive on end of spindle until double row bearing comes up against the distance tube and stops. Fit pen steel washer, this is the small one, felt washer and large steel washer and lightly rivet the latter into position.

98. BRAKES, ADJUSTMENT, Front

Clearance between the brake shoes and

drum can be reduced by unscrewing the adjuster on the cable. Continual adjustment causes the expander lever to occupy a position with lost leverage. To restore leverage, take off the cable and reverse the expander lever.

To improve brake efficiency, release the spindle nut a few turns, hold the brake hard on, retighten the spindle nut at the same time. The brake shoes will then centralize. On models before 1964 enlargen spindle hole in brake plate by $\frac{1}{32}''$ to centralize.

Rear

If the rear brake pedal is depressed in excess of its normal travel, the return spring (in the pedal) will stretch and become ineffective. The pedal position can be adjusted, within limits, by releasing the pedal spindle and setting the stop to the desired position. If the brake has been disturbed, centralize the brake shoes, by releasing the left hand spindle nut and press hard on the pedal and tighten the spindle nut at the same time. On machines made before 1964 enlargen spindle hole in brake plate by $\frac{1}{32}''$.

99. BRAKES, DISMANTLING AND ASSEMBLY

Remove brake plate from drum. Remove nut and washer from cam spindle. Remove cam lever.

Remove springs from shoes. This is best done with a screwdriver placed against one of the spring hooks and held in position with one hand, now knock the screwdriver with the palm of the other hand to push the spring off the lug on the shoe. The spring may fly off so care should be taken that it is not lost.

Turn back the tabwasher and unscrew the two hexagon headed set screws which secure the shoes to the pivot pins. Lift off the pivot pin tie plate and remove the brake shoes.

The cam can now be withdrawn. It may be tight in its bush if the cam lever nut has been overtight as this causes the end of the spindle to become swelled. When this happens the end immediately behind the flats should be eased down with emery tape.

If the cam will pass through the bush but is tight, it can be eased down more easily after removal.

On the rear brake plate only, the cam spindle bush can be removed after unscrewing its locknut from the inside.

TO RE-ASSEMBLE

Remove all traces of rust and dirt from the expander cam and pivot pins, apply a slight smear of grease. For ease in working the brake plate can be held in a smooth jaw vice, clamping it by the torque stop. Fit the brake shoes, tie plate and tab washer and set screws. If the tab washer has been used on more than one occasion discard it and use a new one. Fit the shoe springs, by anchoring the end farthest away from the operator, use a length of stout string in the free end of the spring, stretch the spring with one hand and guide the spring onto its anchorage with the other hand. Alternatively use a narrow blade screwdriver. Finally fit the expander lever with its nut and washer. The washer on the rear brake expander, together with the rim on the brake plate, prevents the rear brake shoes being removed from the pivot pins, unless the linings are badly worn. Removing the expander cam will allow the shoes to be detached from the plate.

Front Forks

100. MAINTENANCE

The oil from both fork tubes, which may be contaminated by swarf, should be drained and refilled with fresh oil at the first 1,000 miles and again at 10,000 miles. Use one of the grades shown in the table of lubricants.

Each fork leg has a small cheese headed set screw as a drain plug and with a suitable receptacle placed on the ground, these screws should be removed one at a time, taking care not to lose the small fibre or aluminium washer which makes the seal.

Now hold the front brake on and move the forks up and down to expel the oil. Allow a few minutes for draining and repeat on the other side.

Next refit the drain plugs with their washers and place the machine on the centre stand.

Unscrew the large filler plug on top of each fork leg and 'pull up' the front wheel to expose the springs. Place a block of wood or similar under the wheel to hold the springs clear. Using two spanners, unscrew the filler plug nuts from top of the damper rods.

Remove the block and allow the forks to move to full extension. Pour in a measured 5 fluid ozs. (142 c.c's.) of 20 grade oil in each leg.

Because these forks have springs inside the main tubes the oil is slow to run down and patience is therefore necessary when re-filling.

Before refitting the filler plugs to the damper rods, make certain that their locknuts are screwed down to the end of the thread on the rod. Lock the two together and screw in, and tighten filler plugs.

101. STEERING HEAD ADJUSTMENT

With the machine on its centre stand, and the front wheel clear of the ground, check the steering head bearing for adjustment by:—

Place the fingers of the left hand, round the space between the rear of the handlebar lug and the frame, with the right hand grasp the end of the front mudguard and try to raise and lower the fork assembly. Any movement or slack in the bearing will be apparent. To adjust release the two pinch stud nuts clamping the fork tubes (see fig. 22). Release the domed nut for the fork column which has a $\frac{11}{16}$" Whitworth hexagon. To take up movement use an opened spanner to screw down and turn the nuts on the column below the handlebar lug, retighten the dome nut and recheck. The bearing should be devoid of movement and free from friction. Retighten the fork tube pinch stud nuts.

The steering head bearings for the 1964 models are of the cup and cone type, with 18 loose $\frac{1}{4}$" dia ball bearings in each bearing. The cup portion is a press fit into the head lug. To remove the cups use a piece of steel tubing through the head lug to drive out the cups, shifting the tubing from one side of the cup to the other to eject it square with the lug. Use an old screwdriver, or taper wedge to take off the cone on the fork column.

Thief-proof Lock. A lock is incorporated in the handlebar lug, two keys are supplied with each new machine.

102. REMOVAL OF FRONT FORKS

Place machine on centre stand or on a stout wooden box under engine. Release brake and clutch cables from handlebar levers. Remove handlebar clips and allow bar to rest on tank.

Unscrew both filler plugs on top of fork legs and pull forks and wheel up, placing a block of wood or similar under the tyre to hold the wheel up whilst the filler plugs are unscrewed from the top of the damper rods. A thin $\frac{5}{16}$" Whit. open ended spanner is necessary for this along with the filler plug spanner.

Remove filler plugs and their washers. Remove headlamp and allow to hang by the cables. Disconnect front brake cable from brake plate and remove front wheel.

Remove top column nut and give headclip a sharp jar upwards with hide hammer or mallet to free it from tapers on main tubes. Remove headclip followed by top covers with lamp brackets and their rubber washers. (On some 1960 and 1961 machines it is necessary to remove the steering lock stop plate before the steering column can be withdrawn and this applies to 1962 machines if they are fitted with steering dampers either solo or sidecar). This is secured with a single $\frac{5}{16}$" × 26T bolt with washers, spacer and nut to the trouser plate on the frame immediately below the headlug.

Remove steering column nut and dust cover and carefully withdraw forks.

To remove the steering head bearings (see para 101 for 1964 models) without damage, use a piece of steel strip $1\frac{3}{4}$" long x .9" wide about $\frac{1}{2}$" thick, with a radius on both ends to lay flat across both the inner and outer member of the bearing, when inserted endwise through the bearing. A central hole in the strip for a pilot drift will facilitate removal.

103. REFITTING FRONT FORKS

Apply some heavy grease to the top cone portion of the bearing, fill 18 balls, fit the cone to the cup part.

Load the ball track on the column race by the same method. Introduce the column through the frame, with care not to dislodge the bearings. Fit top shim washer, dust cover, screw down column nut.

Fit lamp brackets, their top rubber washers and headclip. Release nuts on pinch studs in fork crown. Adjust head bearings and tighten top column nut and check that tightening of this does not alter bearing setting.

Pull up forks to expose springs and damper rods. Fit filler plugs and washers to damper rods, first ensuring that the locknuts are already screwed down to the end of the thread on the rod.

Tighten filler plugs to pull main tubes into their tapers in headclip and tighten pinch stud nuts on crown.

It is assumed that the oil in the fork legs has not been drained if the forks were removed complete with mudguard and stays in position. Refit headlamp, handlebars and front wheel and re-connect control cables. Check headlamp for correct height and lateral position of beam.

104. FORK LEG, DISMANTLING

The individual legs may be dismantled either with the forks in position in the frame or otherwise.

Having drained the oil, unscrew the filler plug from the top of the leg and lift it sufficiently for an open ended spanner to be used to slacken the nut which locks the damper rod into the filler plug.

Release the pinch stud nut on the fork crown and pull jerkily on the fork end when the leg should be withdrawn complete.

If necessary partly replace the filler plug without its washer, screwing it down a few threads and tap it smartly with a mallet or hide hammer to release the leg from the taper in the headclip.

The upper ends of the main tubes may be rusty where they pass inside the top covers (lamp brackets) and this may make them difficult to withdraw. It will help to remove the headclip complete and the covers and clean off the rust with emery tape and smear with oil. Additionally, the slot in the crown where the pinch stud passes through can be expanded slightly with an old screwdriver.

Now with the leg removed, the damper unit and spring complete can be withdrawn by unscrewing the $\frac{3}{16}''$ Whit. hex. set screw in the bottom end of each fork leg.

Remove the plated bottom cover which is screwed into the fork end and when this is removed, the fork end can be pulled off leaving the flanged top bush and oil seal

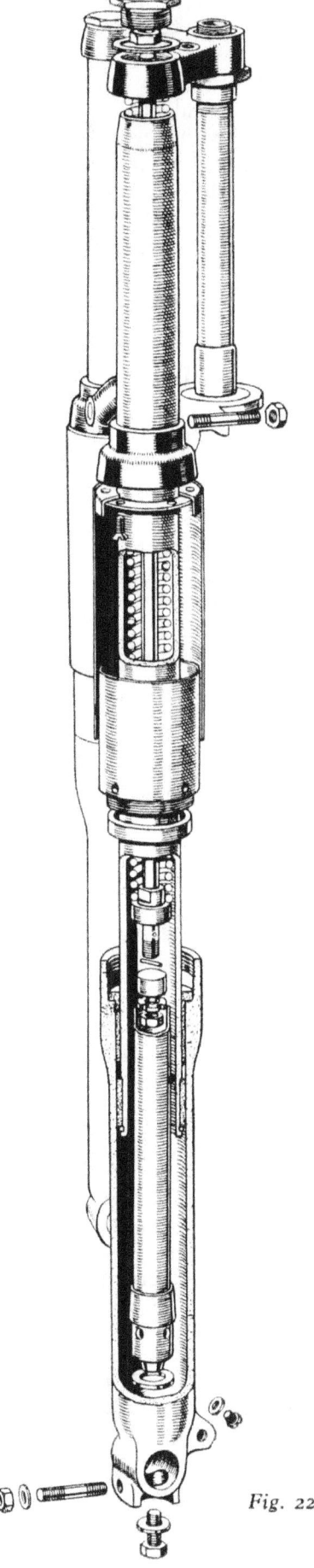

Fig. 22

on the main tube. The steel bush on the bottom end of the tube is attached by a circlip.

If it is desirable to dismantle the damper unit, the top gland nut should be unscrewed and the rod withdrawn from the cylinder, after which removal of the nut from the bottom of the rod will enable the cup, slotted washer and cross pin to be removed.

No difficulty should be experienced in fitting new bushes either to the top of the fork end or the bottom of the main tube.

105. FORK LEG, ASSEMBLY

Thoroughly clean all components and lightly smear each one with oil before placing into position.

Fit crosspin, cup and slotted washer to short screwed end of damper rod. Fit and tighten securing nut.

Insert this assembly into the damper cylinder and screw home the top gland nut. Hold the cylinder whilst this is done with a good fitting tommy bar through the holes in the base.

The cylinder can easily be damaged if it is held in a vice. Place fibre washer over extension on damper cylinder and insert in fork end and secure with set screw and thick washer. Fit fork spring over damper rod followed by aluminium centraliser and screw on filler plug locknut, bevelled edge first, right up to end of thread.

Fit steel bush to bottom end of main tube making certain that circlip is properly fitted and not distorted. Fit bronze bush, paper washer and oil seal to main tube. Oil seal should have its spring towards paper washer and flange of bronze bush. Pass damper rod and spring through main tube from bottom end, carefully entering bush and oil seal into fork leg. Using screwed plated cover, push oil seal in square and screw cover home. Do not overtighten this but it can be tightened best after the wheel spindle has been fitted when the leg cannot turn. Lightly grease upper part of main tube and pass through fork crown. A pull through is available if necessary—part No. 13685, price 10/- Lightly clamp pinch stud nuts to prevent legs dropping out if necessary. Pour 5 fluid ozs. of 20 grade oil in each leg (142 c.c.).

Push up fork leg to expose damper rod and spring, fit filler plug washer and screw filler plug up to locknut already on damper rod.

Screw up filler plug nuts to pull main tubes hard up into taper in head clip, make certain head bearing adjustment is correct, tighten nuts on pinch studs in crown.

Rear Springing

106. PIVOTTED FORK—REMOVAL AND ASSEMBLY (Swinging arm)

Remove chaincase or chainguard.
Remove rear wheel complete with brake. Remove bottom shock absorber attachment bolts, nuts and washers, and swing the shock absorbers clear. Slacken top bolts if necessary

Remove nut and washer from one end of pivotted fork bolt on frame gusset plate and withdraw bolt from opposite side. Fork or arm should now be pushed forward to clear gusset plates, turned and withdrawn.

If the 'Clayflex' bearings require to be replaced, the fork should be returned to the works for the old bearings to be removed and new ones fitted.

To re-assemble reverse this procedure, fit and tighten the bottom shock absorber bolts before tightening the fork (arm) pivot bolt on the frame. This will ensure that the 'Clayflex' bearings are clamped in approximately the correct rotational position.

107. REAR SUSPENSION UNITS

These fittings embody quite complicated oil damping arrangements which are carefully set to provide the correct suspension characteristics for your machine. They are sealed and are virtually leak proof and should **not be interfered with.** In the unlikely event of any attention being necessary, their removal is quite simple and straightforward and they should be taken to your usual Norton dealer or the nearest Norton distributor.

It is quite permissible to remove the covers in order to grease the spring to promote silent operation.

These units are adjustable to three positions by means of the 'C' spanner provided. The soft or normal solo position is in use when the abutments spot welded to the damper body are in engagement with the topmost positions on the bottom spring collar which has a scroll or face cam, or when this part is rotated as far as possible in an anti-clockwise direction when viewed from above. Rotation in a clockwise direction (by means of the key) will result in the stronger positions being engaged. It is important that both units are adjusted to the same position.

No attempt whatever should be made by the normal rider to dismantle, drain or refill these units.

When these units are fitted to the machine it is important that they should be primed first as they will lose their prime if they have been laid horizontally for only a short time.

To prime mount vertically in a vice by the lower mounting lug, set to the soft position, pull down on top cover and remove split collet. Remove covers and spring and now operate damper rod over its full range until smooth even resistance is felt on extension but none at all on compression. If you cannot get this result the damper is faulty.

Refit covers and spring and collets and refit to machine keeping vertical.

Handlebar Fittings

108. AIR CONTROL LEVER

To remove the control cable from the lever, open the lever as far as possible, hold the outer cable, and as the lever is closed, pull the outer cable from the lever body.

Remove nipple from the lever.

To fit the cable, fit nipple into the lever, close the lever, pull the outer cable away from the lever and fit the cable to the lever body.

109. CLUTCH AND FRONT BRAKE CONTROL LEVERS

The clutch and front brake controls are so simple as to require no instructions for their dismantling or assembly.

The screws on which the levers pivot can be adjusted to reduce side clearance between lever and fulcrum part of clip as the lower side of each lever is threaded and a self locking nut fitted.

To remove the clutch cable from the lever, take off the inspection cap from gearbox end and with a screwdriver, lift up the small operating lever. At the same time pull the outer cable clear of the handlebar lever.

It should be noted that if replacement levers are at any time obtained, the one for clutch operation with an A.M.C. gearbox should have $\frac{7}{8}''$ centres between cable nipple and fulcrum screw.

This is not the same on earlier machines with Norton/Burman gearboxes and these require levers having $1\frac{1}{16}''$ centres.

Now unscrew the cable adjuster from the brake plate and the cable will come clear. Re-assemble in reverse order.

110. TWIST GRIP

The twist grip assembly is shown in Fig. 23.

To assemble the twist grip, grease the portion of the handlebar where grip works.

Fit sleeve to the bar.

Grease the drum on the sleeve.

Fit spring and adjuster bolt and nut to the bottom half clip.

Thread the cable through the hole in the half clip.

Fit the nipple to the drum on the sleeve.

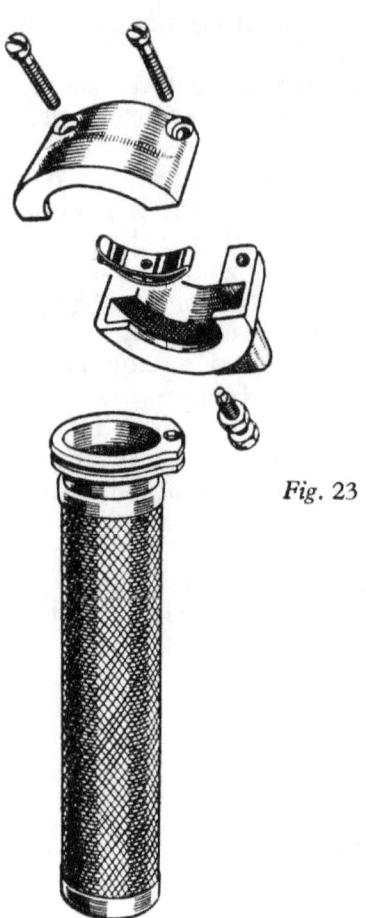

Fig. 23

Amal Carburetter

111. DISMANTLING OF THE CARBURETTER

The easiest way to remove the carburetter is to turn the petrol tap off and disconnect feed pipe from carburetter, remove the two nuts securing carburetter flange and unscrew the knurled ring immediately below where the control cables enter the top of the mixing chamber body so that the slides may be withdrawn, either before or after the carburetter is removed. The air and throttle valves may be left on the cables unless it is desired to change or renew the cables or valves.

The throttle valve needle may be removed or adjusted for position by removal of the spring clip at the top of the slide.

Remove the float chamber cover by removing the three screws securing it, and withdraw the hinged float and spacer, this will enable the nylon needle which controls the flow of fuel to be withdrawn and cleaned.

Removal of the nut at the base of the mixing chamber gives access to the main jet which may be unscrewed from the jet holder which also carries the needle jet, accessible by removal of jet holder. Removal of these parts enables the jet block to be pushed or tapped out through the large end of the mixing chamber body when the jet block locating screw has been removed. This screw lies to the left of and slightly below the pilot air adjuster which is the horizontal milled headed screw equipped with restricting spring.

112. RE-ASSEMBLY OF CARBURETTER

Re-assembly should present no difficulty but the following points should be watched. The washer fitted to the stub of the jet block should be in good condition, also the one fitted to the needle jet holder. When fitting throttle valve ensure that taper needle really enters the centre hole in the jet block, and throttle works freely when mixing chamber top cap is fitted and secured. Fit float with narrow side of hinge uppermost, replace spacer, and ensure that side cover washer and body are clean and undamaged to obtain a petrol tight joint.

(Sufficient length of cable can be obtained by lifting the throttle slide and holding in position by piece of soft wood placed in the air intake).

Fit the top half clip.

Adjust the tightness of the grip with the adjusting screw and lock in the desired position.

Dismantle in the reverse order.

113. CARBURETTER TUNING

There are four distinct phases of tuning and each must be handled separately to obtain best results for any particular set of conditions. For all these positions the air valve should be fully open, the engine should be at its normal working temperature, and the machine should be driven on a slight up gradient to ensure engine pulling the whole time.

1st MAIN JET.

This jet controls the fuel supply when the throttle is more than ¾ open. With the throttle fully open and the engine pulling hard, slightly close the air lever when there should be a slight falling off of speed indicating a reasonably correct mixture. If maximum speed is obtained before the throttle is fully open, then a larger main jet is required; similarly if there is an increase in speed with the air lever slightly closed.

2nd SLOW RUNNING.

Having fixed the main jet, set the throttle

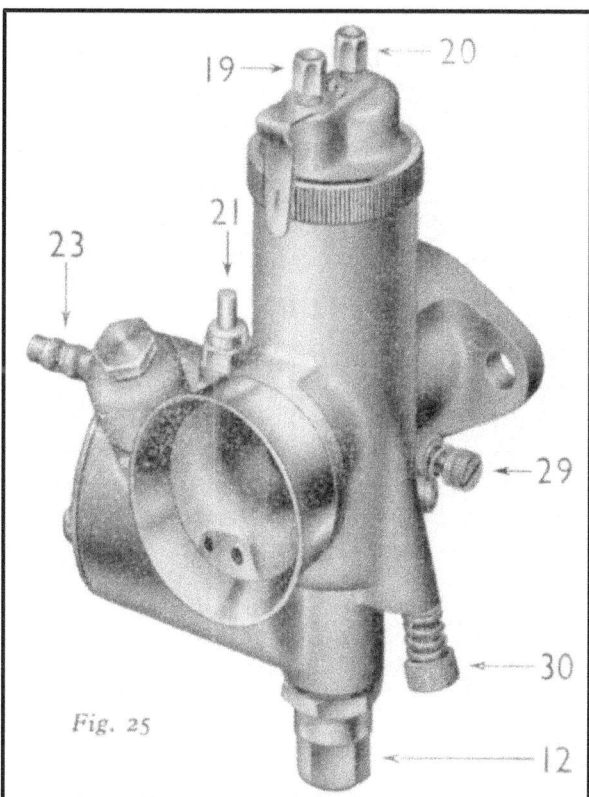

Fig. 25

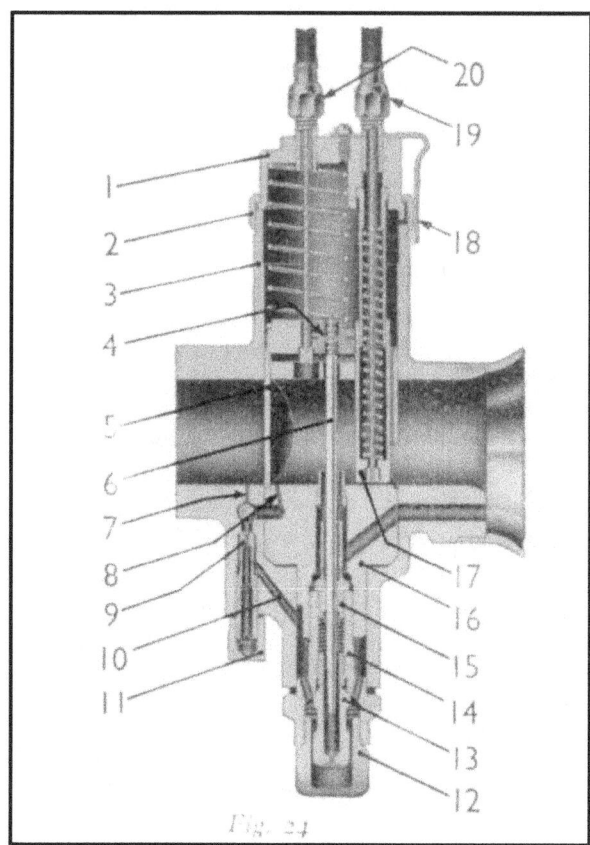

1—Mixing Chamber Top	14—Jet Holder
2—Mixing Chamber Cap	15—Needle Jet
3—Carburetter Body	16—Jet Block
4—Jet Needle Clip	17—Air Valve
5—Throttle Valve	18—Mixing Chamber Cap Spring
6—Jet Needle	
7—Pilot Outlet	19—Cable Adjuster (Air)
8—Pilot by-pass	20—Cable Adjuster (Throttle)
9—Pilot Jet	21—Tickler
10—Petrol feed to pilot jet	23—Banjo
11—Pilot Jet Cover Nut	29—Pilot Air Adjusting Screw
12—Main Jet Cover	30—Throttle Adjusting Screw
13—Main Jet	

adjusting screw to provide fairly fast idling with the twist grip in the fully closed position and the ignition (where manually controlled) set for best slow running. Screw out the throttle adjusting screw until engine begins to falter; now adjust the pilot air screw in or out as necessary to make the engine run evenly and faster. Lower the throttle adjusting screw further to reduce engine speed until a position of the pilot air screw is found at which the engine runs evenly and steadily on the smallest throttle opening.

3rd THROTTLE VALVE CUTAWAY.

With the throttle valve about ¼ open (marking the twist grip if necessary in order to readily find this position whilst riding) note whether there is any spitting (indicating weakness) or jerky running under load (indicating richness). In the former event try screwing in the pilot air screw slightly and if this is ineffective, a throttle valve having less cutaway, i.e., stamped with a lower number and the reverse for jerky running.

4th THROTTLE VALVE NEEDLE.

With the throttle about ¾ open and the needle in a low position try the machine for acceleration. If the results are poor and partially closing the lever provides improved conditions, raise the needle a notch or two until the best position is found.

5th RE-CHECK IDLING.

To ensure that subsequent adjustments have not upset the condition.

114. MAINTENANCE

Clean periodically by dismantling and washing in clean petrol, cleaning out all holes by blowing. Whilst dismantled examine throttle valve needle and float needle for wear and all fibre washers, renewing as necessary. Check that throttle valve is not unduly worn in the mixing chamber body.

115. RICH MIXTURE

Indicated by black exhaust smoke, excessive soot on plug, lumpy running, petrol blown back from air intake.

Assuming that carburation has previously been satisfactory, suspect:—flooding due to punctured float, dirt on float needle seating or worn needle or seat. Worn throttle valve needle or needle jet, air cleaner choked.

116. WEAK MIXTURE

Indicated by spitting back, poor acceleration, overheating, erratic slow running or improved performance with air lever partly shut.

Again assuming carburetter has been correctly set, suspect:— fuel blockage, either main supply or within carburetter. Worn inlet valve guide, air leaks at engine carburetter connection, worn throttle valve, loose jets.

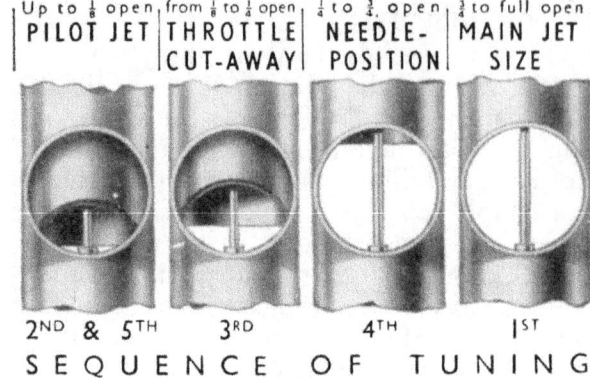

Fig. 26

Tyres

117. MAINTENANCE

Always keep tyres at the correct pressures, (see data page at front of book). Remove any stones which may be embedded in the tread. Replace valve dust cap if lost.

118. REMOVAL

Deflate tube by removing valve cap and core. Remove rim nut and security bolt nut if security bolt fitted. Push the beads of the cover down into the well of the rim at a point opposite to the valve. Insert a small tyre lever between the bead and the rim near to the valve. Ease the bead off the rim using a second lever inserted a short distance away. Repeat until one bead is free of the rim.

Remove security bolt and tube, and remove the second bead in a similar manner.

119. FITTING

Fit rim band. Dust tube, beads and rim with French chalk. Slightly inflate tube and place within cover on top of wheel with valve in line with hole in rim. Fit the underneath bead by hand, completing the operation with levers. Thread valve and stem of security bolt through appropriate holes. Fit second bead starting opposite valve. See that security bolt and tube are not being pinched between cover and rim. Inflate. Fit rim nut and security bolt nut. Adjust pressure to manufacturer's recommendation and fit dust cap.

Electrical Section

All the machines covered by this book have A.C. generators, and all have coil ignition.

The essentials of this form of lighting and ignition consist of the following units.

Alternator. For the generation of Alternating Current.

Rectifier. For conversion of A.C. to Direct Current to enable battery to be charged.

Battery. For current storage.

Coil. For conversion of low tension voltage to high tension.

Switch. For control of ignition and lighting.

120. ESSENTIAL MAINTENANCE

Battery. Inspect regularly and frequently and maintain acid level to top of separators by addition of distilled water. The level check should be made after the machine has been standing and not immediately after a run when the electrolyte will be gassing and showing a higher level.

On Lucas PUZ7E batteries, after standing, the acid level should be just to the top of the plates, that is just visible when the filler plugs are removed. On Exide 3EV11 and 3EV9 batteries, again after standing, the level should be to but not above the lower of the two lines marked on the case.

If the levels on either battery are in any way on the high side, there will be risk of overspilling and resultant acid damage to plated and enamelled parts of the machine.

Battery terminals should be kept clean and greased and a periodic check should be made to ensure that the wires themselves are not corroding. On Lucas batteries, clean up the end of the terminal with a smooth file if there is any doubt about the screw on terminal making firm contact. The Exide batteries employ a tag terminal secured with a screw and this must make clean contact with the battery terminal post.

It is well worth while paying attention to these connections as if for any reason, the battery becomes out of circuit, the light bulbs will burn out, even with quite low engine revolutions. ALL BATTERIES TO HAVE POSITIVE TERMINAL CONNECTED TO 'EARTH'.

Wiring. Keep all connections and terminals tight and ensure cables are clear of moving parts. Examine carefully stop and tail lamp leads for being properly positioned in the aluminium clip on the left hand side number plate mounting stud. The clip must hold the connectors themselves, and the longer lead which passes round the inside of the mudguard must also be in the clips and not foul the tyre at the front end of the guard where it passes through the grommet.

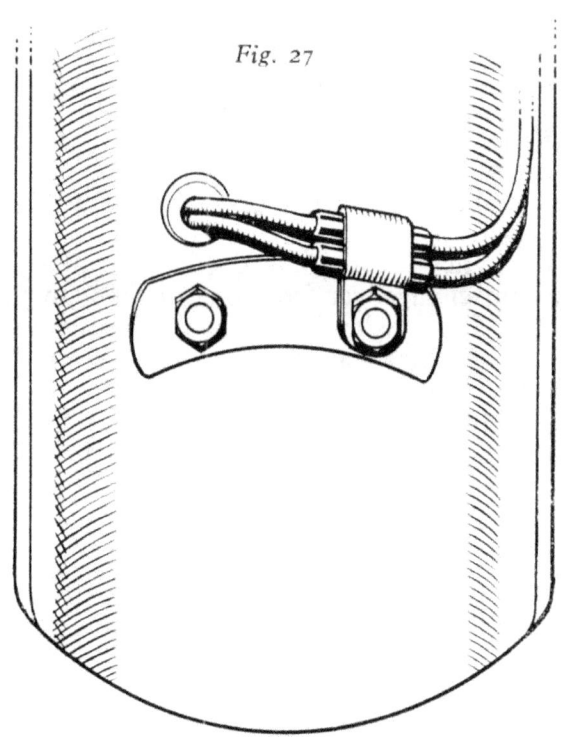

Fig. 27

EARLY MODELS ONLY

Any surplus wire on the lamp side of the snap connectors should be 'fed back' through the grommet into the space between the number plate and outside of mudguard.

These remarks regarding stop/tail lamp leads apply to all Standard models. De luxe machines are slightly different and on these it is important that the leads are clipped or taped to the tubular stay which supports the tail portion of the rear fairing.

Contact Breaker

Check points for correct gap and cleanliness. Gap should be set to .015" plus or minus .001".

To lubricate the A.T.D., it is necessary to remove the cover and then the two Phillips head screws which secure the base plate.

The timing will not be lost by removing this plate, but the points gap setting should be checked on refitting. Models 50 and ES2 having non-positive lubrication of the driving chain, have a small screw on top of the contact breaker housing. This should be removed and a few drops of engine oil put in every 2000 miles.

Headlamp. Set the beam so that with the main filament 'on', it is just below horizontal, with the machine loaded as for the larger proportion of night riding. For example, if most of your night riding is done with a passenger, set the beam with the weight of two people up. The main beam should never be set above horizontal. Do not employ bulbs of greater wattage than those normally fitted, as the generator will then not maintain the battery charge state.

Oil the dipper switch pivot and toggle lever periodically, it can be very dangerous, if this switch sticks and does not make an instant changeover from one filament to the other. It is desirable that the switch is connected so that when its lever is lowered, the dipped beam is in use. Keep the glass of the light unit clean, a thin mud covering very much reduces the light. Check that the light unit is properly 'keyed' in the lamp rim ensuring its correct rotational position for angle of dipped beam.

121. IGNITION

In the "OFF" position when key in top of switch in headlamp lies in line with machine. Turn key in clockwise direction for normal "ON" position. Turn key in anti-clockwise direction for emergency starting, i.e., **starting with flat battery. Return key to normal "ON"** position when engine running.

Ignition timing must be very carefully set if best conditions are to be obtained: the correct figures are:—
Models ES2 and 50 — 38° Fully advanced; 8° Fully retarded, before T.D.C. It should be noted that the auto advance unit on the single cylinder models has 15° range (30 crankshaft degrees).

See para. 59 for timing procedure.

122. ALTERNATOR. Lucas RM15

Since the alternator has no commutator, brush mechanism bearings or oil seals, it requires no maintenance apart from occasionally checking that its leads are intact and its connectors clean and tight. Examine the grommet in the rear half of the chaincase as if this becomes perished, the leads may chafe on the relatively sharp edge of the hole.

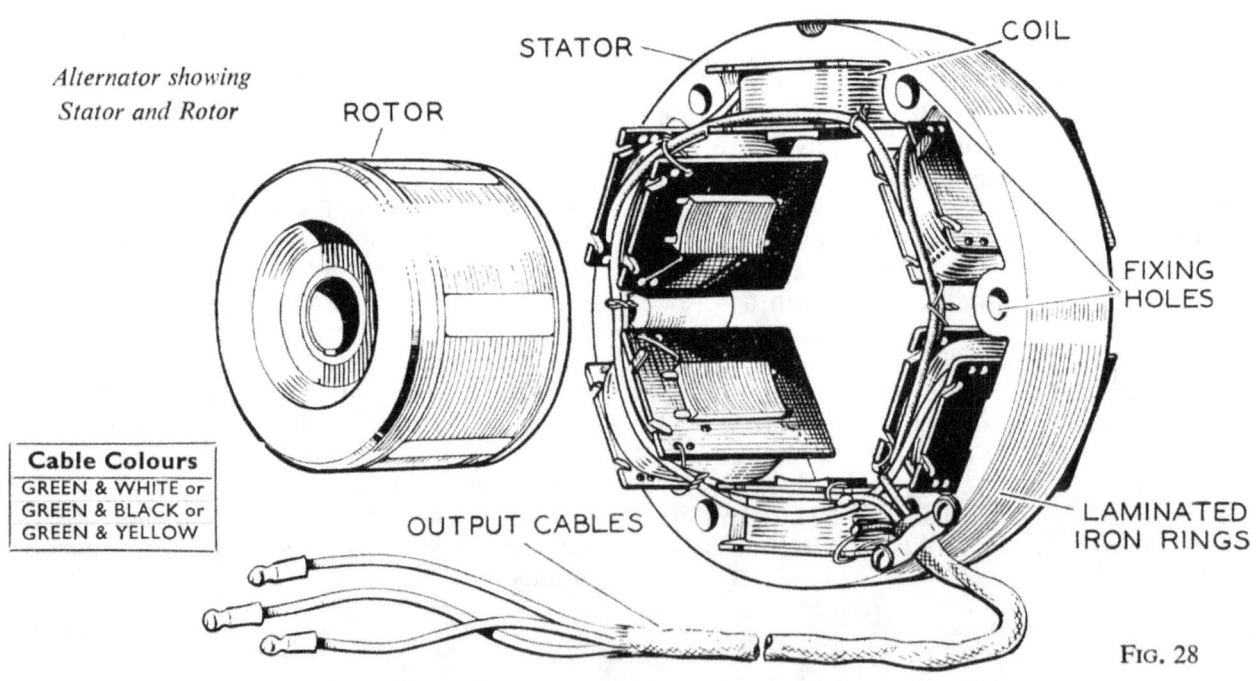

Alternator showing Stator and Rotor

Cable Colours
GREEN & WHITE or
GREEN & BLACK or
GREEN & YELLOW

FIG. 28

There should always be at least .005" clearance between the rotor and the pole pieces on the stator and this clearance should be checked whenever the stator is refitted.

Note that the stator should be fitted with the lead taken off side towards the outer primary chaincase and not towards the inner portion of the chaincase.

The rotor is secured to the mainshaft by nut and key and may be withdrawn when the nut is removed. It may be necessary to remove the stator (secured by three nuts and fan disc washers) if the rotor is tight on the shaft but the shaft is parallel.

There is no necessity to fit keepers to the rotor poles when the rotor is removed. Wipe off any metal swarf which may have collected on the pole tips and place the rotor in a clean place.

As mentioned above, the stator is capable of being fitted into the spigot recess either way round, but it will only operate satisfactorily in one position.

123. SWITCH

The switch together with the ammeter and speedometer is carried on the headlamp shell and connections are accessible when headlamp front and light unit assembly are removed. The various cables will be readily recognisable by their coloured sleeving.

Normal Running. Under normal running conditions (i.e. ignition switch in IGN position) electrical energy in the form of rectified alternating current passes to the battery from the alternator — the rate of output depending on the position of the lighting switch. When no lights are in use, the alternator output supplies the ignition coil and trickle charges the battery. When the lighting switch is turned, the output is automatically increased to meet the additional load of parking lights and again when the main bulb is in use.

Emergency Starting (coil ignition models)

An emergency starting position is provided on the ignition switch for use if the battery has become discharged.

Under these conditions, the alternator is connected direct to the ignition coil, allowing the engine to be started independently of the battery.

When kickstarting with the switch in the EMG position, a considerably 'heftier' kick may be necessary than is the case when making a normal start. If the ignition timing is, for any reason, only slightly out, it may not be possible to obtain an EMG start with the kickstarter.

A push start should then be tried, in 2nd gear with the switch in normal IGN position.

A further point which should be noted is that, if the alternator leads have been changed over to obtain the increased charge rate, it may not be possible to obtain a start in the EMG position. In this case the leads should be temporarily changed back or a push start tried as described above.

124. INCREASED CHARGING RATE

Should the battery become run down due to prolonged slow riding in traffic, or during running-in or due to parking with lights on for long periods and whenever a sidecar is fitted an increased charge rate can be obtained by a simple wiring alteration.

The alternator leads after emerging from the primary chaincase, join the main harness by means of a 3-way snap connector. On models 50 and ES2 this is rather out of the way and it may be necessary to remove the battery and battery box in order to gain access to it. On twin cylinder models, it may be clipped to the H.T. leads where they leave the distributor or higher up near the top of the battery box.

The colours are:—Light green or green and white. Dark green or green and black and green and yellow.

Disconnect the dark green or green and black and the green and yellow and reverse these two connectors.

That is connect the green and black alternator cable to the green and yellow harness cable. Connect the green and black harness cable to the green and yellow alternator cable.

With the light switch in the off position, the ammeter should show approx. twice the previous output. When the lights are switched on to either 'pilot' or 'head' however, the output remains as before.

WHENEVER A SIDECAR IS PERMANENTLY ATTACHED TO ONE OF THESE MACHINES this alteration should be carried out as otherwise the added consumption of the sidecar lamp or lamps will not be compensated for and the battery will slowly run down.

On a solo machine on a long daylight run using the increased output, the battery may become overcharged which can result in damage to the battery and damage to plated and enamelled parts of the machine due to acid spillage.

125. RECTIFIER

The rectifier is a device to allow current to flow in one direction only. It is connected to provide full-wave rectification of the alternator output current.

The Rectifier requires no maintenance beyond checking that the connections are clean and tight.

The nuts clamping the rectifier plates together must not UNDER ANY CIRCUMSTANCES be slackened as the presseure has been carefully set during manufacture to give correct rectifier performance. A separate nut is used to secure the rectifier to the machine and it is important to check periodically that the rectifier is firmly attached to its mounting point. It should make firm metal to metal contact to ensure a good electrical connection.

126. COIL

An ignition coil of orthodox type is attached to a suitable position on the frame by a bolt and clip. Like the rectifier, the coil should only require occasional checking for cleanliness and tightness of mounting and terminals.

128. CONTACT BREAKER

Chain driven from the inlet cam spindle, the sprocket is fitted on a taper and held with a central set screw and washer.

Removal of the sprocket and the single screw holding the clamping flange to the housing allows the complete contact breaker assembly to be withdrawn provided that the coil wire has been disconnected from the terminal on the base plate. Normal routine maintenance can be carried out without removing the contact breaker.

Contact Breaker setting. Check the contact breaker after the first 500 miles running and subsequently every 6000 miles.

To check the gap, remove the sparking plug, and rotate the engine slowly until the lobe of the cam is directly under the heel of the breaker points. In this position the points are wide open and a .015" feeler should be a sliding fit. Take care to enter the feeler square without side influence or an accurate result will not be obtained. The gap should be from .014" to .016"

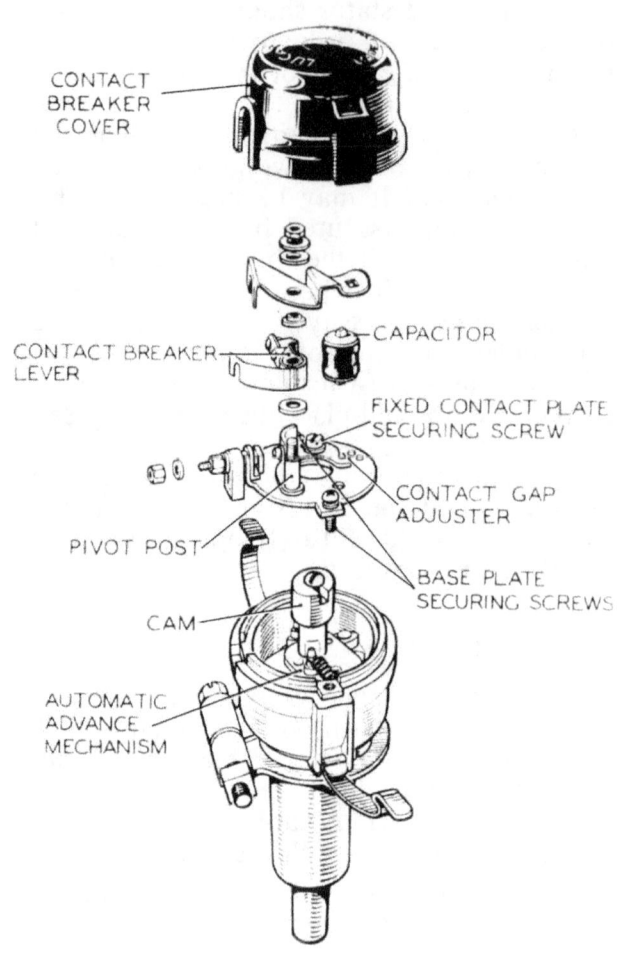

Fig. 30

To adjust the gap, keep the engine in the position giving maximum contact opening and slacken the screw securing the fixed contact plate. Insert a screwdriver between the two studs or pips on the base plate and the notch in the fixed contact plate, and adjust the position of the plate until the correct gap is obtained. Tighten the securing screw and re-check the gap.

Lubrication and cleaning. To be carried out every 6000 miles. Remove and clean the distributor cover and unscrew the two screws securing the contact breaker base plate.

Remove the base plate and lubricate the automatic advance mechanism with clean engine oil, paying particular attention to the pivots. Re-fit the base plate.

Examine the contact breaker. The contacts must be free from grease or oil. If they are burned or blackened, clean with fine carborundum stone or very fine emery cloth, afterwards wiping away any trace of dirt or metal dust with a clean petrol-moistened cloth.

Contact cleaning is made easier if the contact breaker lever carrying the moving contact is removed. Before re-fitting the contact breaker lever, lightly smear the cam and pivot post with clean engine oil.

No grease or oil must be allowed to get on or near the contacts.

After cleaning, check the contact breaker setting.

Important note. In comparison to the twin cylinder machines, the driving chain does not obtain the same degree of lubrication on these engines, therefore, there is an additional lubricating point.

Removal of the small screw in the top of the housing carrying the contact breaker discloses an oilway into which a few drops of engine oil should be injected every 2000 miles.

Renewing High Tension Cables. Replace the high tension cables when these show signs of perishing or cracking, using 7 mm. p.v.c. or neoprene-covered rubber ignition cable. It is advisable to fit new H.T. cable connectors when renewing the ignition cables.

129. BATTERY—Lucas PUZ7E/11

When examining a battery, do not hold naked lights near the vents as there is a danger of igniting the gas coming from the plates.

Remove the vent plugs and see that the ventilating holes in each are quite clear.

Remove any dirt by means of a bent wire.

A clogged vent plug will cause the pressure in the cell to increase, due to gases given off, during charging, and this may cause damage.

Make sure that the rubber washer is fitted under each vent plug, otherwise the electrolyte may leak.

Battery — Exide 3EV9. This battery is fitted on de Luxe models and requires similar maintenance to the Lucas one.

All these machines should have the battery positive terminal connected to the frame of the machine, i.e., Positive earth.

See para. 120—Essential Maintenance.

Battery—Topping-up. About once a fortnight or more often in warm climates check the level of the electrolyte in the battery cells and add distilled water as indicated in para. 120.

Wipe dirt and moisture from battery top.

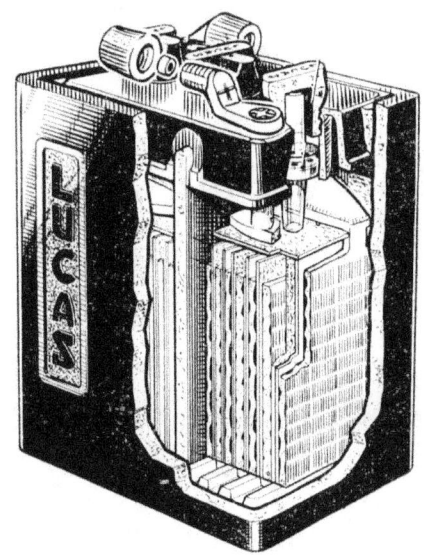

Fig. 31

Checking Battery Condition. The state of charge of the battery should be examined by taking hydrometer readings of the specific gravity of the acid in the cells.

The specific gravity readings and their indications are as follows:

1.280—1.300. Battery fully charged.
About — 1.210. Battery about half discharged.
Below—1.150. Battery fully discharged.

These figures are given assuming the temperature of the acid is about 60°F.

Each reading should be appoximately the same.

If one cell gives a reading very different from the rest, it may be that the acid has been spilled or leaked from this particular cell, or there may be a short circuit between the plates.

This will necessitate its return to a Repair Depot for rectification.

Wipe the top of the battery to remove all dirt or water.

Note. Do not leave the battery in a discharged condition for any length of time.

If a motor cycle is to be out of use, the

battery must first be fully charged, and afterwards given a refreshing charge about every two weeks.

Earthing Connections. The positive terminal must be connected to the frame or earth terminal. The Rectifier will be damaged if a battery is only momentarily connected wrong way round.

Charging. If the previous tests indicate that the battery is merely discharged, and if the acid level is correct, the battery must be recharged from an external supply.

130. HEADLAMP

The headlamp which carries also the switch, ammeter, and speedometer, incorporates a Lucas light unit.

Setting headlamp beam. See para. 120.

Bulb Replacement. To remove the headlamp front, slacken the screw at the top of the lamp and pull off the front rim complete with light unit assembly.

The pilot bulb holder is a 'spring' fit in the reflector itself and has a 'cushioning' rubber washer which should not be misplaced or lost when the holder is pulled out of the reflector.

To gain access to the headlamp bulb, push on the adaptor and twist in an anti-clockwise direction to take it off. The bulb can now be removed from the rear of the reflector.

Place the correct replacement bulb in the holder, engage the projections on the inside of the adaptor, noting that they will only engage in one position, press on and secure by twisting to the right (turn clockwise).

Lucas replacement bulbs should always be used, the pilot bulb is No. 988—6v. 3w. with miniature bayonet cap. Main bulb No. 373—6v. 30/24w. with pre-focus cap. Stop/Tail bulb Lucas No. 384—6v. 6/18w.

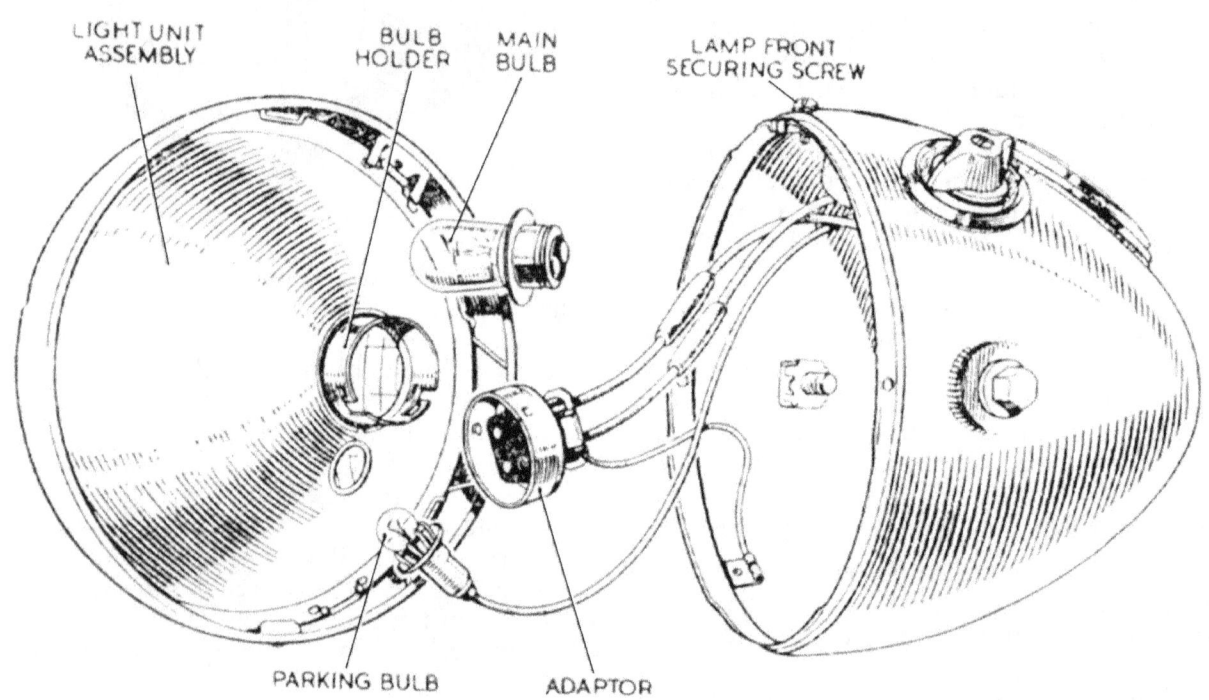

Fig. 32 Light Unit—bulb removal

131. TAIL, STOP AND NUMBER PLATE LAMP

This is Lucas No. 564 which incorporates twin 'Reflex' reflectors, thus eliminating the necessity of fitting a separate reflector.

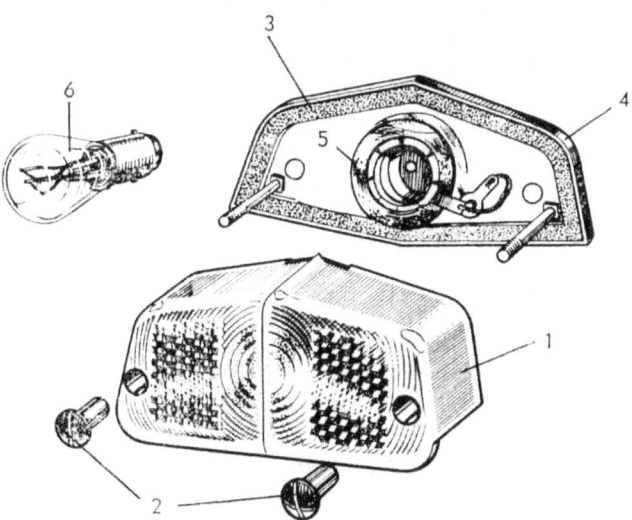

1. Lens and Window
2. Nut
3. Gasket
4. Base Assembly
5. Grommet
6. Bulb

Fig. 33 Tail, Stop and Number Plate Lamp

This lamp is fitted with a double filament bulb having a 6 watt filament for the normal rear and number plate light and an 18 watt controlled by the rear brake.

To obtain access to the bulb, remove the two securing screws and the plastic lens complete. The bulb has unequally positioned bayonet pins so that it cannot be incorrectly fitted into the holder.

132. CABLES

To connect leads to a Lucas battery, unscrew knurled plastic terminal nut and withdraw collet (small thick washer).

Bare the end of the cable (about ½") and thread the bared end through the knurled nut and collet. Coil up the surplus wire against the end of the collet, feed back collet and wire into knurled terminal nut and screw on to terminal post firmly. Do not overtighten or the nut may burst.

To connect the leads to an Exide battery, the leads on the machine have soldered on tag terminals. The battery terminals incorporate set screws which should be removed, the tags threaded on and the screws firmly replaced.

Snap connectors, i.e. rubber covered push-pull connections are used at many points in the wiring system.

They appear when connected as a small rubber sleeve, or bunch of sleeves when grouped. Disconnect by pulling apart and reconnect by holding in cable pliers, the metal nipple soldered to cable end. Hold rubber covered portion in fingers and press nipple home with pliers. Ensure rubber sleeves are always covering metal portions of connectors when in use.

Special pliers are available from some accessory houses for assembling these fittings and they are so constructed that both nipples can be pressed into the sleeve at the same time.

133. LIGHTING AND IGNITION SWITCH

The switch is carried in the headlamp shell and connections are accessible when headlamp front and light unit assembly is removed. The cables are identified by various colours.

The switch on coil ignition machines—Lucas PRS8—is complicated and should, on no account be dismantled.

With magneto ignition, fewer connections are involved and a switch similar to those employed on earlier D.C. systems is used.

134. HORN

Electric horns are adjusted to give their best performance before leaving the works and will give a long period of service without any attention.

If the horn becomes uncertain in action, or does not vibrate, it has not necessarily broken down.

The trouble may be due to a discharged battery or a loose connection, or short circuit in the wiring of the horn.

The performance of the horn may be upset by the fixing bolt working loose, or by the vibration of some part adjacent to the horn.

To check this, remove the horn from its mounting, hold it firmly in the hand by its bracket, and press the push.

If the note is still unsatisfactory, the horn may require adjustment and should be taken to a Lucas Service Station.

135. SPARKING PLUG

Clean periodically, say every 3000 miles, and if of detachable type, dismantle and clean thoroughly. Never unscrew the gland nut with other than a ring or box spanner and do not hold the plug in a vice by the gland nut. The plug body itself, may be held in a vice whilst the gland nut is unscrewed with a ring spanner. Clean the electrode insulator with glass paper—not emery cloth and clean the inside of the body with emery tape wrapped round a screwdriver or on an arbor in a drilling machine. Clean the earth points on the body with a wire brush and re-assemble making certain that the gas sealing washer is in position on the insulator and that the central electrode is properly centralised when the gland nut is tightened. Reset gap or gaps as necessary—.015" to .020" for magneto ignition. Gaps can usually be a little larger with coil equipment.

Non-detachable plugs should be cleaned with a wire brush and if they are oiled, flushed out with a small quantity of petrol.

Notes

GEAR RATIOS

All machines with A.M.C. gearboxes up to and including 1959, had a rather large drop in ratio from top to third gear.

To bring these gearboxes into line with 1960 and later machines, it is necessary to replace the main sleeve gear, the layshaft free pinion (3rd gear) and the engine sprocket. The net result of this being chiefly, to lower top gear and allow the twin cylinder engines in particular, to more nearly reach maximum r.p.m. in that gear.

FITTING SIDECARS TO 'FEATHERBED' FRAMES

We emphasise that if sidecars are fitted to these models without reducing the trail, they will not handle well.

For this reason a special fork crown and column and head clip are available which, because of different dimensions also require new top fork covers with lamp brackets. These parts reduce the trail and with an outfit properly aligned and set up, give very good steering.

This crown and column employs a steering damper with two friction discs which centre on a large diameter boss on the underside of the crown. These parts will not fit the solo crown.

There is also a steering damper for the solo crown which employs a single friction disc of different dimensions and it is therefore important to state for which crown a damper is required when ordering.

Stronger fork springs and rear shock absorber springs are also available, and should be fitted.

Because of the added electrical consumption of a sidecar lamp or lamps, an A.C. generator may not maintain the battery state unless an increased output is obtained as described in para. 124.

FITTING A FOG OR SPOT LAMP

The correct method is to connect an additional dip switch (i.e. a single pole, two-way switch) in series with the existing dip switch in order to be able to select for operation either the headlamp or the fog/spot lamp, when the main lighting switch is turned on position 'H'. To do this:

1. Disconnect the feed cable (normally blue) from the centre main terminal of the existing dipswitch.

2. Connect this cable to the centre main terminal of the new switch.

3. Connect one of the two remaining terminals of the new switch to the centre main terminal of the existing switch.

4. Connect the 3rd terminal of the new switch to one of the fog or spot lamp terminals.

5. Connect the other terminal of the foglamp to 'earth'—frame of machine.

The advantage of this method of connection is that electrical overloading due to the simultaneous use of headlamp and foglamp is prevented, and, further, the correct distribution of light to suit differing driving conditions is assured.

FITTING RACING FOOTRESTS— REAR SET

Manx type racing footrests, either folding or fixed can be fitted to Standard featherbed frames. To do so it is necessary to drill a $\frac{7}{16}$" hole in the gusset plate of the frame on each side.

Its position is $1\frac{1}{4}$" below and $\frac{3}{8}$" forward of the centre of the pivoted fork (swinging arm) attachment bolt. It is not correct to drill a hole on the offside to match the standard brake pedal mounting hole on the nearside.

VALVE GEAR LUBRICATION

On all the machines covered by this book, an oil feed to the valve gear is taken from the return oil pipe between oil pump and tank.

Because the valve gear is at a higher level than the end of the return pipe in the tank, it is necessary to have a restriction in the end of this pipe to create a pressure to force the oil to this higher level.

This restriction may vary slightly in individual tanks and if for this or any other reason, the valves or rockers of a particular engine appear to obtain insufficient lubrication, an oil tank return union adaptor as is fitted to 250 c.c. twins can be interchanged with the existing one. This has a restriction built into its outlet at the tank end and may thus give an increased supply to the valve gear. The part No. is 22148.

VIBRATION

In cases where vibration seems excessive on single and twin cylinder models, in addition to checking the tightness of all engine/frame attachment bolts, etc., particular attention should be paid to the cylinder head steady attachments.

Due to heat, the enamel may 'give' slightly under the pressure of nuts and washers and lockwashers of the spring or 'fan disc' type also tend to settle down. The nuts and bolts concerned, therefore, should be checked for tightness, especially at the first 500 mile service.

DIFFICULT STARTING—De Luxe Models

This can be brought about by failure of the extended lever on the carburetter float 'tickler' to actually depress the float when moving within the limit of travel imposed by the slot in the side panel. The remedy is to 'set' the lever slightly at the point where it makes contact with the plunger.

SET SCREWS SECURING BRACKETS TO SILENCERS

Due to the enamel on the brackets 'giving' slightly under heat from the silencer pommels, the screws tend to slacken during initial mileage. If they are not well tightened by the time 500 miles have been covered, they may be lost. Check with good fitting ring spanner after say, 200 miles, and again at 500.

STOP/TAIL LAMP LEADS

Reference is made to the Electrical Section of this book under Essential Maintenance—Wiring.

Stop/Tail lamps are not fitted to the number plates when the machines leave the works because of risk of breakage in transit. It therefore falls upon the dealer to fit and connect the lamp. It should be connected and the wires positioned as shown in the diagram. The snap connectors themselves must be in the aluminium clip provided and should be positioned horizontally above the left hand number plate stud. Surplus wire on the lamp side should be fed back through the grommet in the guard and then if the long lead is also positioned in the clips in the mudguard no trouble will be experienced due to the rear tyre chafing the wires (see Fig. 27).

OWNERS SHOULD CHECK THIS WIRING ON TAKING DELIVERY as if it is not properly carried out there is risk of a short circuit which can cause failure of the lights and also ignition in the case of a coil ignition model.

150

ELECTRICAL WIRING DIAGRAM for models ES2 and 50

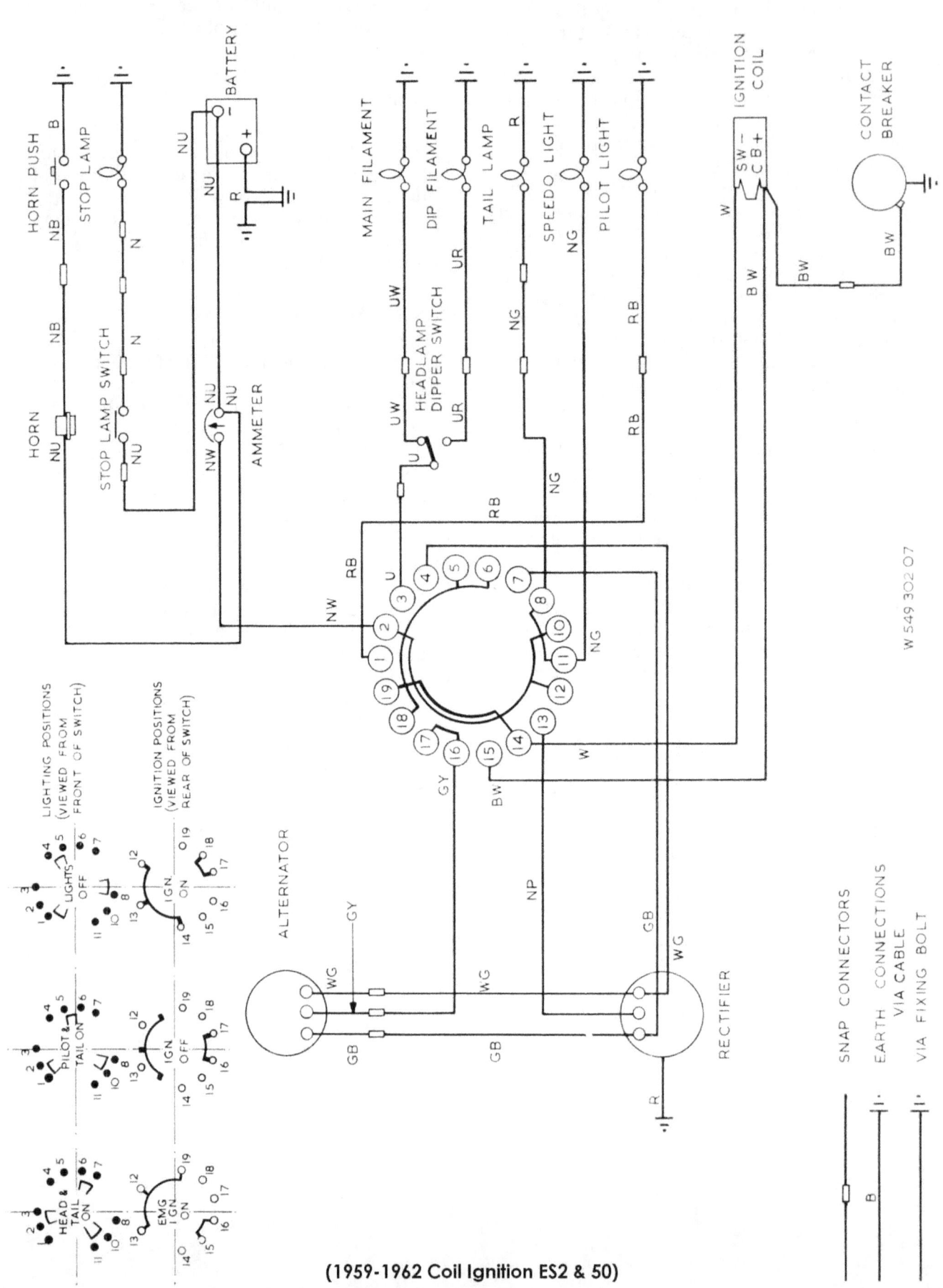

(1959-1962 Coil Ignition ES2 & 50)

LOCATING AND RECTIFYING POSSIBLE TROUBLES

TROUBLE	POSSIBLE CAUSE	REMEDY
Failure to start.	Over flooding.	Open twist grip and kick vigorously a few times.
	Weak mixture due to failure to close air lever (if cold).	Ensure that air slide falls as lever is shut.
	Broken throttle cable.	Ensure that throttle slide rises as twist grip is rotated.
	Lack of fuel.	Check that there is petrol in tank.
	Failure of fuel to reach mixing chamber.	Check that petrol taps, or tap, is in the "on" position and that petrol is flowing through.
		Clean Carburetter.
	Contact breaker points dirty or out of adjustment	Remove high tension lead from the plug and hold end about ⅛ in. from cylinder whilst revolving engine. If no spark, examine contact breaker points, clean, check gap. Check lights.
	Battery flat.	
Miss-Firing.	Faulty plug.	Change plug.
	Faulty high tension lead.	Examine high tension lead, renew if necessary.
	Water on plug.	
Erratic slow running.	Uneven mixture distribution.	Check and clean carburetter.
	Pilot air screw requires resetting.	Adjust as in para. 113.
	Air leaks from carburetter joint or sparking plug.	Check joint washer and nuts for tightness. Check plug for tightness.
	Faulty valve seats.	Examine and regrind as necessary.
	Worn inlet valve or guides.	Dismantle, check and renew as necessary.
Loss of power.	No tappet clearance.	Check and reset as necessary.
	Broken piston rings.	Examine and replace.
	Tight front chain.	Adjust.
Excessive oil consumption.	Broken piston rings. Worn cylinder block.	Examine and replace as necessary.
	Oil not returning to tank, due to:— Stoppage in oil way; pump drive failed; pump gears fouled by foreign matter.	Examine and make necessary replacements. Trace through and clean out or take any other action necessary.
Engine runs harshly.	Tight chains.	Check and adjust.
Engine cuts out at large throttle openings.	Dirt in carburetter. Dirt in filters.	Dismantle and clean.
	Dirt in petrol tap.	Remove petrol taps and clean.
	Condenser broken down.	Change condenser, clean contacts.
Loss of oil pressure.	Oil overheated or unsuitable.	Drain and refill with fresh oil of correct grade.
	Oil pump nipple washer failed.	Examine and renew.
	Timing side oil seal worn or collapsed.	Examine and renew.
	Pressure release valve plunger stuck.	Examine, clean and free off.
	Pump failed.	Examine for foreign matter.

LOCATING AND RECTIFYING POSSIBLE TROUBLES

TROUBLE	POSSIBLE CAUSE	REMEDY
Inefficient brakes. (Front and Rear)	Grease on lining.	Examine and wash in petrol. Do not wash in paraffin.
	Tightness in mechanism.	Make sure that cam is free in its own bearing and pedal is not binding on spindle due to mud.
Slipping clutch.	Cable adjusted too tightly.	Re-adjust cable until there is some movement on handle bar lever before clutch operates.
	Clutch push rod adjusted 'hard on'.	Re-adjust, para. **72**.
	Oil on plates (usually caused by over-filling oil bath).	Dismantle clutch plates and wash in petrol.
	Tightness in operating mechanism.	Examine, clean and free off as necessary.
Clutch hard to free.	Water in cable.	Lubricate.
Gear changing accompanied by excessive noise.	Slack rear chain.	Adjust as necessary.
Failure of footchange lever to return to normal position.	Broken hairpin return spring.	Remove gearbox cover. Examine spring, renew as required.
Steering rolls or wanders.	Loose head adjustment.	Adjust as necessary.
Twist grip closes if released.	Tension requires adjusting.	Screw in adjuster one or two turns.
Steering appears tight on corners.	Steering damper binding, caused by bent frame anchor bracket.	Remove anchor bracket and re-set to correct angle.

SPARE PARTS LIST

Models 1, 16H, 18 and ES2 for 1948 and 1949

Models 30, 40, 30M and 40M for 1946 to 1949 inclusive

Price - One Shilling

NORTON MOTORS LIMITED

Bracebridge Street, Birmingham 6, England

Phone Aston Cross 0776-7-8 (Private Branch Exchange)

Grams "Nortomo, Birmingham."

IMPORTANT INFORMATION RELATING TO THE PARTS LISTS INCLUDED IN THIS MANUAL

It should be noted that the early parts lists also include the 30, 40, 30M & 40M and the later parts lists include the 88 & 99 twins.#

The first parts list included is a reproduction of the 1948 and 1949 factory parts list for the S.V. and O.H.V. spring frame (plunger) Big 4, 16H, 18 and ES2 models fitted with 'Road-holder' forks and 'upright' gearbox (it also includes the 1946 to 1949 model 30, 40, 30M and 40M).

The second parts list is a reproduction of the 1956 factory parts list for the O.H.V. swing-arm, 'laydown' gearbox ES2, 19S and 50 models and the rigid frame model 19.

The third parts list is a reproduction of the 1959 PS206 factory parts list for the ES2 and 50 'featherbed' frame models fitted with alternator & coil electrics (it also includes the 88 and 99 twins).

When the four workshop manuals in this publication are used in conjunction with these three illustrated parts lists, they provide a comprehensive maintenance and repair manual exclusive to the 1945 to 1963 Norton 16H, Big4, 18, 19S, 19, 50 and ES2 series.

INDEX.

	Page
Air control cable	38
Amal carburetters	25
Battery carrier and fittings	70
B.T.H. magneto and fittings	71
Carburetter (Amal)	25
Carburetter (remote needle type)	29
Carburetter (type 10 T.T.)	28
Chains (front and rear)	57
Clutch control cable	38
Clutch group	48
Connecting rods	24
Control cable adjusters and nipples	37
Crankcase, engine plate bolts, studs, etc. (O.H.C. models)	11
Crankcase, engine plate bolts, studs, etc. (S.V. and O.H.V. models)	12
Crankcase and fittings	5
Cylinder barrel and head	23
Dry sump oil pump and drive parts (O.H.C. models)	22
Dry sump oil pump and drive parts (S.V. and O.H.V. models)	22
Electric horn and fittings	73
Engine plates (front and rear)	62
Engine sprocket	57
Exhaust control cable	39
Exhaust lifter control lever	37
Exhaust lifter and fittings—for crankcase and rocker box (S.V. and O.H.V. models)	14
Exhaust lifter and fittings—for O.H.C. rocker box	15
Exhaust pipes and fittings	30
Float chamber	27
Flywheels, assemblies and big end bearings	8
Footrests and fittings	60
Forks and steering damper (Norton Road holder)	32
Frame	62
Frame rear springing	62
Front brake control cable	38
Front brake and clutch control levers	36
Front chaincase and fittings	57
Front chainguard and fittings	59
Front hubs and fittings	55
Front mudguard, stays and fittings	64
Gear control rod and fittings	51
Gearbox axle sprocket	48
Gearbox fixing bolts	44
Gearbox—foot change parts	49
Gearbox front chain adjuster	44
Gearbox pinions, shafts and bearings	44
Gearbox shell	44
Handlebar and fittings	34
Headlamp and parts	72
Hub brake shoes and linings	55
Hubs (parts common to both front and rear)	56
Kickstarter parts	48
Legshields and fittings	74

	Page
Magdyno parts (Lucas)	72
Magneto and air control levers	34
Magneto control cable	38
Magneto or Magdyno driving parts and fittings	21
Magneto and fittings (B.T.H.)	71
Main bearings	10
Mattress and fittings (Manx models)	70
Number plates and fittings (front and rear)	66
O.H.C. vertical shaft drive and rocker box, etc.	17
Oil tank and fittings	41
Overhead rockers	17
Petrol tanks and fittings	39
Pillion footrests and fittings	71
Pillion seat and fittings	70
Pistons and rings	24
Positive foot change parts	49
Prop stand	64
Push rods and fittings (for O.H.V. models)	15
Racing number plates and stone guard	66
Rear brake pedal and fittings	60
Rear brake rod and fittings	60
Rear carrier	70
Rear chain adjusters	57
Rear chainguard and fittings	59
Rear hubs and fittings	53
Rear lamp and fittings	73
Rear mudguard, stays and fittings	68
Remote needle type carburetter (Models 30 and 40 Manx)	29
Revolution counter	71
Rocker box and fittings (for O.H.V. models)	15
Rubber cable clips	75
Saddle and fittings	69
Sidecar chassis and fittings	75
Silencer, megaphone and fittings	30
Speedometer and fittings	70
Stand and fittings (front)	69
Stand and fittings (rear)	69
Stone guard (Manx models)	66
Tappets	14
Throttle control cable	38
Timing gear	14
Tool box and fittings	69
Tools	74
Transfers	75
Twist grip	37
Type 10 T.T. carburetter (Models 30 and 40 International)	28
Tyre security bolts	56
Valve cover and fittings (S.V. models)	15
Valves, guides, springs and fittings	24
Voltage regulator and fittings	73
Wheel—complete assemblies (front and rear)	51
Wheel rims and spokes	53
Wheel with hub shell only (front and rear)	51

INSTRUCTIONS FOR ORDERING SPARE PARTS.

This Spare Parts List deals with replacement parts for Models 1, 16H, 18 and ES2 of 1948, 1949 manufacture, and for Models 30, 30M, 40 and 40M of 1945, 1946, 1947, 1948 and 1949 manufacture.

It is most essential that the Engine and Frame Number of the machine is stated. The Engine Number is to be found on the transmission side of the Crankcase, and the Frame Number is stamped on the Head Lug of the Frame, below the steering damper anchor plate. It is always advisable to order parts on a separate sheet, and not to include on the same sheet other matter of a different nature; this facilitates prompt despatch.

It is found in a number of instances that money orders and postal orders are sent in parcels containing patterns; this is inadvisable. We strongly recommend parts as patterns being despatched separately, and a covering letter sent containing the remittance for replacement parts.

RETURNING MACHINES FOR OVERHAULING.

When returning machines or parts for repair or overhaul, these should be sent carriage paid, and with the sender's name and address in full **securely** attached. It is also advisable to state on the tally that a letter has been sent respecting the parts, and giving the date. All easily detached fittings should be removed, such as Lamps, Horns, Tool Bags, Speedometers, etc.; these are liable to be lost or damaged in transit, and the Company cannot accept any responsibility for them.

ESTIMATES FOR REPAIRING MACHINES.

We are always prepared to give approximate estimates for the cost of repairs; it is quite impossible to give a firm quotation. Additional parts may be found necessary during the process of repair, unforeseen when preparing an estimate. Should our estimate for repair not be accepted, a charge may be made in accordance with work entailed in dismantling and re-assembling. When we give an estimate for the cost of repairs, and this is curtailed by the owner, we cannot accept any responsibility for the performance of the machine; it is always preferable to accept our estimate in full.

TERMS OF BUSINESS.

Our terms are strictly nett cash with order or cash against prepayment invoice. The exact amount, plus 5% to cover postage or carriage and packing (subject to a minimum of 6d.), packing cases or crates to be extra, must be remitted, or when the cost of the parts required is unknown, a sum likely to cover the cost should be enclosed; if the amount remitted is more than the cost of the parts that are ordered, the balance will be returned. Cheques and postal orders should be made payable to " Norton Motors, Ltd.," and crossed Barclays Bank, Ltd. Prices quoted in this list do not include the cost of carriage or fitting. We reserve the right to alter prices or specification of any parts at any time without notice. Where parts are urgently required, remittance may be sent by Telegraphic Money Order, **but it is absolutely essential that the sender fill in his name and address in the space provided on the Post Office Money Order Form.** Unless this is done, the Post Office do not give us the information in the telegram. It is necessary that all orders given by wire or 'phone should be confirmed by letter at the earliest opportunity.

DEPOSIT ACCOUNT.

We strongly recommend riders of our machines to open a deposit account; this can be done by depositing with us not less than £10. This will ensure goods to that value being despatched with the least possible delay. When ordering by 'phone, wire or post, this often avoids great inconvenience, and for the benefit of the depositor, a monthly statement of account is rendered, showing credit balance. Under no circumstances whatever can parts be despatched without remittance covering same has been sent, unless a deposit account is opened. Should the machine be disposed of at a later date, we are always prepared to remit any amount that may be remaining.

PARTS BY C.O.D. SYSTEM.

Unless remittance is received with order, parts are despatched by C.O.D. System or against proforma invoice at our discretion.

PART No.	PLATE No.	DESCRIPTION.	QTY.	USED. ON.	PRICE EACH. £ s. d.

CRANKCASE AND FITTINGS.

PART No.	PLATE No.	DESCRIPTION.	QTY.	USED. ON.	PRICE EACH. £ s. d.
C2/1	...	Crankcase with timing cover, magneto chain cover and bushes (Less studs and tappet guides)	1	18, ES2 1, 16H,	12 12 0
A11/1	...	Crankcase with bevel cover, magneto chain cover and bushes	1	30	17 0 0
A10/1	...	Crankcase with bevel cover, magneto chain cover and bushes	1	40	17 0 0
A11M/1	...	Crankcase with bevel cover, magneto chain cover and bushes	1	30M	22 0 0
A10M/1	...	Crankcase with bevel cover, magneto chain cover and bushes	1	40M (1946/7)	22 0 0
C10M/1	...	Crankcase with bevel cover, magneto chain cover and bushes	1	40M (1948/9)	22 0 0
A2/703	A.38	Driving side half crankcase	1	1, 16H, 18, ES2	4 0 0
A11/703	...	Driving side half crankcase	1	30	4 10 0
A10/703	...	Driving side half crankcase	1	40	4 10 0
A11M/703	...	Driving side half crankcase	1	30M	7 0 0
A10M/703	...	Driving side half crankcase	1	40M (1946/7)	7 0 0
C10M/703	...	Driving side half crankcase	1	40M (1948/9)	7 0 0
C2/704	A.44	Timing side half crankcase	1	1, 16H, 18, ES2	5 6 0
A11/704	...	Timing side half crankcase	1	30	9 4 0
A10/704	...	Timing side half crankcase	1	40	9 4 0
A11M/704	...	Timing side half crankcase	1	30M	11 0 0
A10M/704	...	Timing side half crankcase	1	40M (1946/7)	11 0 0
C10M/704	...	Timing side half crankcase	1	40M (1948/9)	11 0 0

(Halves of crankcases cannot be supplied separately. Therefore, it is necessary to return the sound half also timing or bevel covers for matching in the works).

PART No.	PLATE No.	DESCRIPTION.	QTY.	USED. ON.	PRICE EACH. £ s. d.
A2/2	A.8	Crankcase cylinder stud	4	1, 16H	1 0
A3/2	A.15	Crankcase cylinder stud	4	18, ES2	1 0
A11/2	B.31	Crankcase cylinder stud	4	30, 30M	1 6
A10/2	B.31	Crankcase cylinder stud	4	40, 40M	1 6
A2/3	C.39	Crankcase cylinder stud nut	3	1, 16H	1 8
C2/686	C.38	Crankcase cylinder stud nut (long)	1	1, 16H	1 8
C2/6	A.20	Crankcase timing cover with bushes	1	16, 16H, 18, ES2	2 10 0
A11/7	B.15	Crankcase bevel cover with bush	1	30	2 5 0
A11M/7	B.15	Crankcase bevel cover with bush	1	30M,(40M 1948/9)	2 7 6
A10/7	B.15	Crankcase bevel cover with bush	1	40	2 5 0
A10M/7	B.15	Crankcase bevel cover with bush	1	40M (1946/7)	2 7 6
A11/38	B.14	Crankcase bevel cover bush	1	30, 30M, 40, 40M	6 0
A11/44	B.31	Crankcase bevel cover paper washer	1	30, 30M, 40, 40M	10
A11/45	B.67	Oil filter for crankcase bevel chamber	1	30, 30M, 40, 40M	5 0
E5264	B.66	Oil filter washers	1	30, 30M, 40, 40M	3
A11/36	...	Crankcase sump screw	1	30, 30M, 40, 40M	6
A3/93	A.16	Timing cover screw cheese head (top)	3	1, 16H, 18, ES2	5
C2/96	A.17	Timing cover screw cheese head (bottom)	3	1, 16H, 18, ES2	5
C2/37	A.18	Timing cover screw, countersunk	2	1, 16H, 18, ES2	5
A11/687	...	Crankcase bevel cover screw	5	30, 30M, 40, 40M	5

158

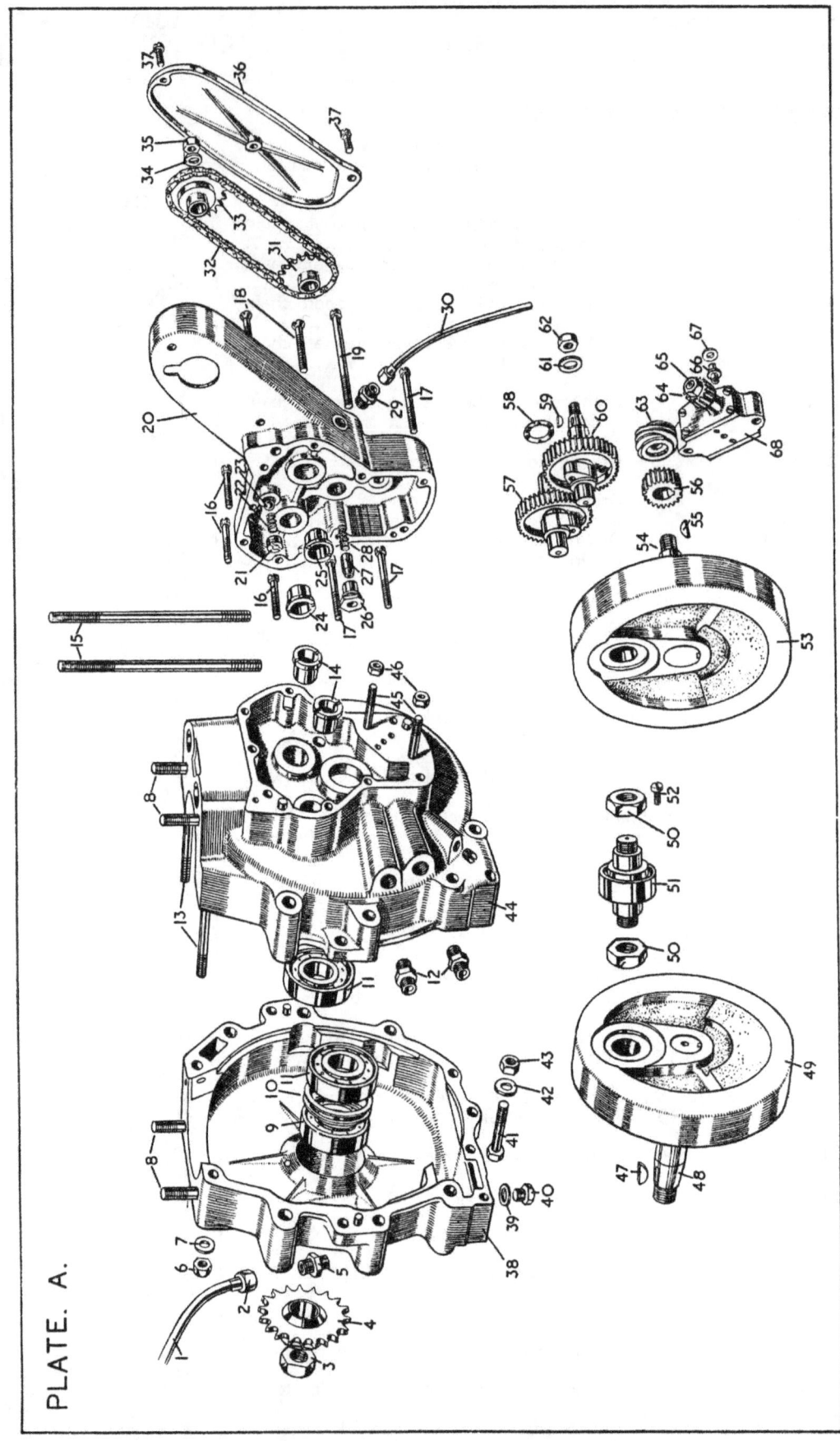

PLATE. A.

PART No.	PLATE No.	DESCRIPTION.	QTY.	USED ON.	PRICE EACH. £ s. d.
CRANKCASE AND FITTINGS—cont.					
A2/9	A.36	Magneto chain cover	1	1, 16H, 18, ES2	16 0
A11M/9	B.3	Magneto chain cover	1	30M, 40M	17 6
A11/9	B.51	Magneto chain cover	1	30, 40	16 0
C2/687	A.37	Magneto chain cover screw (short)	2	1, 16H, 18, ES2	5
A11/688	B.2	Magneto chain cover screw (long)	1	30, 40, 30M, 40M	9
C2/688	A.19	Magneto chain cover screw (long)	1	1, 16H, 18, ES2	9
A11/687	B.1	Magneto chain cover screw (short)	1	30, 40, 30M, 40M	5
A2/722		Fibre washers for cheese head screws	9	1, 16H, 18, ES2	1
A2/10	A.30	Magneto chain cover pipe with nut	1	1, 16H, 18, ES2	3 0
A2/11	A.29	Magneto chain cover pipe union	1	1, 16H, 18, ES2	1 6
A11/717	B.23	Crankcase bottom bevel chamber pressure release pipe	1	30, 30M, 40, 40M	3 0
A2/718	B.24	Crankcase bottom bevel chamber pressure release pipe nut	1	30, 30M, 40, 40M	3
A11/719	B.25	Crankcase bottom bevel chamber pressure release pipe union	1	30, 30M, 40, 40M	2 6
C2/12	A.27	Timing cover and mainshaft oil connection jet	1	1, 16H, 18, ES2	4 0
A11/12	B.12	Bevel cover and mainshaft oil connection jet	1	30, 30M, 40, 40M	4 0
C2/13	A.26	Timing cover and mainshaft oil connection jet holder	1	1, 16H, 18, ES2	5 0
A11/13	B.13	Bevel cover and mainshaft oil connection jet holder	1	30, 30M, 40, 40M	5 0
A2/14	A.28	Mainshaft oil connection jet spring	1	1, 16H, 18, ES2	3
A11/14	B.11	Mainshaft oil connection jet spring	1	30, 30M, 40, 40M	3
A11/716	B.10	Mainshaft oil connection jet holder nut	1	30, 30M, 40, 40M	1 0
A2/15	A.23	Pressure release ball $\frac{1}{8}$in.	1	1, 16H, 18, ES2	3
A2/16	A.22	Pressure release ball spring	1	1, 16H, 18, ES2	2
C2/17	A.21	Pressure release ball screw	1	1, 16H, 18, ES2	8
A11/42	B.18	Pressure release adjusting screw	1	30, 30M, 40, 40M	2 0
A11/43	B.19	Pressure release adjusting screw locknut	1	30, 30M, 40, 40M	4
A11/15	B.21	Pressure release ball $\frac{7}{32}$in.	1	30, 30M, 40, 40M	3
A11/16	B.20	Pressure release ball spring	1	30, 30M, 40, 40M	3
C2/18	A.14	Camshaft bush crankcase (inlet or exhaust)	2	1, 16H, 18, ES2	5 0
C2/19	A.25	Camshaft bush (timing cover) inlet	1	1, 16H, 18, ES2	5 0
A2/20	A.24	Camshaft bush (timing cover) exhaust	1	1, 16H, 18, ES2	5 0
13765	A.40	Crankcase drain plug	1	1, 16H, 18, ES2	1 0
13881	A.39	Crankcase drain plug washer	1	1, 16H, 18, ES2	3

PART No.	PLATE No.	DESCRIPTION.	QTY.	USED ON.	PRICE EACH. £ s. d.
CRANKCASE AND FITTINGS—cont.					
E3336	B.32	Crankcase drain plug	1	30, 30M, 40, 40M	1 0
E5264	B.33	Crankcase drain plug washer	1	30, 30M, 40, 40M	3
A2/476	...	Crankcase breather with pipe (driving side)	1	1, 16H, 18, ES2	3 6
A2/707	A.5	Crankcase breather	1	1, 16H, 18, ES2	2 0
A2/708	A.1	Crankcase breather pipe	1	1, 16H, 18, ES2	1 3
A2/718	A.2	Crankcase breather pipe nut	1	1, 16H, 18, ES2	3
A11/476	...	Crankcase breather with pipe (driving side)	1	30, 30M, 40, 40M	5 6
A2/707	B.45	Crankcase breather (driving side)	1	30, 30M, 40, 40M	2 0
A11/708	B.47	Crankcase breather pipe (driving side)	1	30, 30M, 40, 40M	3 6
A2/718	B.46	Crankcase breather pipe nut (driving side)	1	30, 30M, 40, 40M	3
A11M/720	B.48	Crankcase pressure release pipe (front)	1	30M, 40M	4 0
A2/718	B.49	Crankcase pressure release pipe nut	1	30M, 40M	3
A11/719	B.50	Crankcase pressure release pipe union (front)	1	30M, 40M	2 6
A2/721	A.12	Crankcase oil delivery or return pipe union	1	1, 16H, 18, ES2	2 6
A11/721	B.22	Crankcase oil delivery or return pipe union	1	30, 30M, 40, 40M	3 0
A11/719	B.27	Crankcase to rocker box oil pipe union	1	30, 30M, 40, 40M	2 6
A11/8	B.26	Oil pump tell tale	1	30, 40	12 0
A11/39	B.70	Cylinder feed lubrication crankcase bolt	1	30, 30M, 40, 40M	7 0
A11/878	B.69	Cylinder feed lubrication bolt nut	1	30, 30M, 40, 40M	1 0
A11/879	B.71	Cylinder feed lubrication bolt washer	1	30, 30M, 40, 40M	3
A11/40	B.67	Cylinder feed lubrication adjuster screw	1	30, 30M, 40, 40M	2 0
A11/41	B.68	Cylinder feed lubrication adjuster screw nut	1	30, 30M, 40, 40M	4
FLYWHEELS, ASSEMBLIES AND BIG END BEARINGS.					
C7/24	...	Flywheels complete with shafts, crankpin bearing and con rod	1	1	11 3 0
C3/24	...	Flywheel complete with shafts, crankpin bearing and con rod	1	18, ES2	11 3 0
C2/24	...	Flywheels complete with shafts, crankpin bearing and con rod	1	16H	11 3 0
A11/24	...	Flywheels complete with shafts, crankpin bearing and con rod	1	30	13 0 0
A11M/24	...	Flywheels complete with shafts, crankpin bearing and con rod	1	30M	18 0 0
A10/24	...	Flywheels complete with shafts, crankpin bearing and con rod	1	40	13 0 0
A10M/24	...	Flywheels complete with shafts, crankpin bearing and con rod	1	40M (1946/7)	18 0 0
C10M/24	...	Flywheels complete with shafts, crankpin bearing and con rod	1	40M (1948/9)	18 0 0
C7/25	A.53	Flywheel timing side with shaft	1	1	3 8 0
C2/25	A.53	Flywheel timing side with shaft	1	16H, 18, ES2	3 8 0
A11/25	B.60	Flywheel timing side with shaft	1	30	3 15 0
A11M/25	B.60	Flywheel timing side with shaft	1	30M	5 0 0
A10/25	B.60	Flywheel timing side with shaft	1	40	3 15 0
A10M/25	B.60	Flywheel timing side with shaft	1	40M (1946/7)	5 0 0

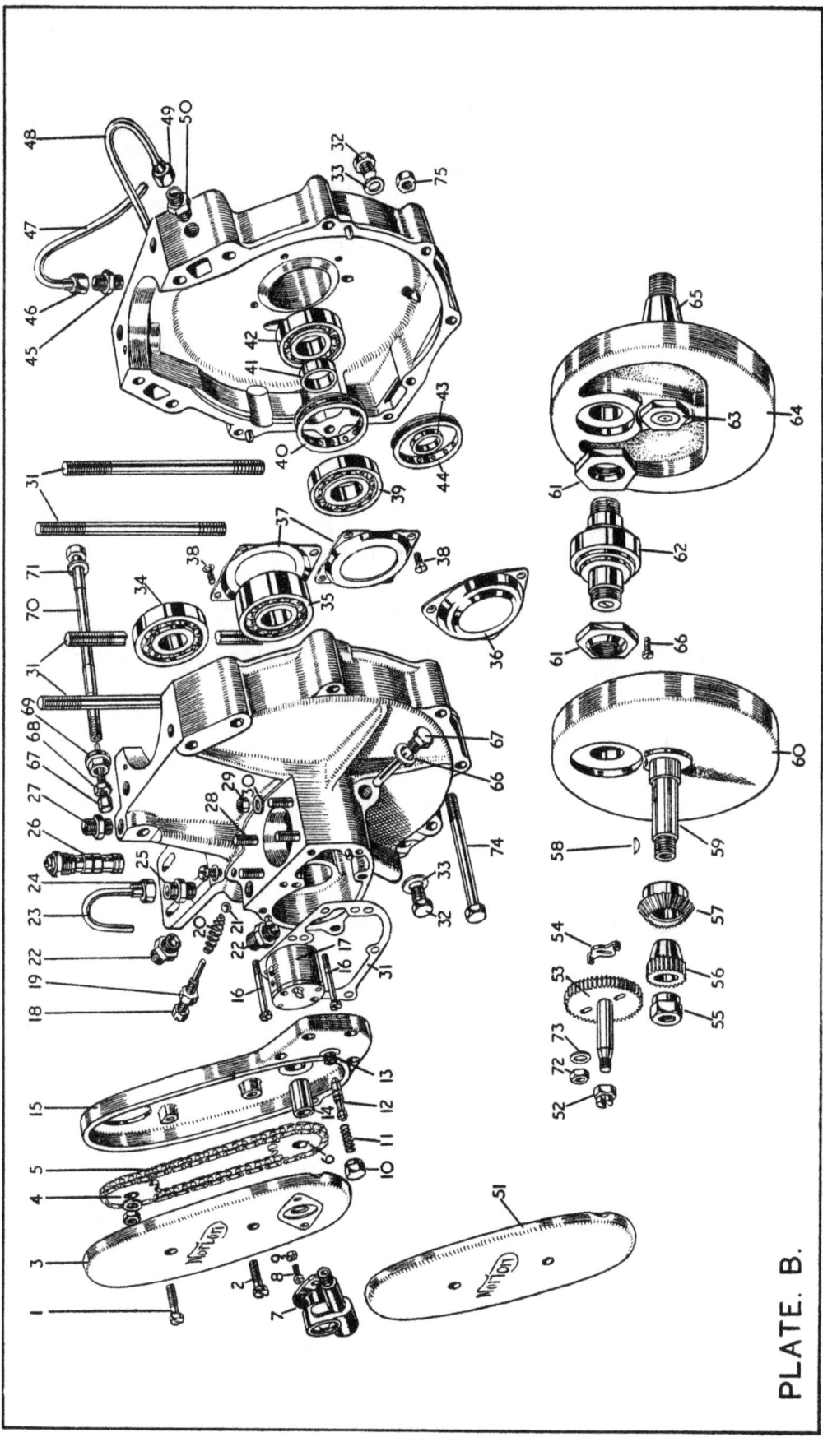

PLATE. B.

PART No	PLATE No.	DESCRIPTION.	QTY.	USED ON.	PRICE EACH. £ s. d.
FLYWHEELS, ASSEMBLIES AND BIG END BEARINGS—cont.					
C10M/25	B.60	Flywheel timing side with shaft	1	40M (1948/9)	5 0 0
C7/26	A.49	Flywheel driving side with shaft	1	1	3 8 0
C2/26	A.49	Flywheel driving side with shaft	1	16H, 18, ES2	3 8 0
A11/26	B.64	Flywheel driving side with shaft	1	30	3 10 0
A11M/26	B.64	Flywheel driving side with shaft	1	30M	4 17 6
A10/26	B.64	Flywheel driving side with shaft	1	40	3 10 0
A10M/26	B.64	Flywheel driving side with shaft	1	40M (1946/7)	4 17 6
C10M/26	B.64	Flywheel driving side with shaft	1	40M (1948/9)	4 17 6
C2/705	A.54	Timing side flywheel shaft	1	1, 16H, 18, ES2	1 5 0
A11/705	B.59	Timing side flywheel shaft	1	30, 30M, 40, 40M	1 15 0
A2/706	A.48	Driving side flywheel shaft	1	1, 16H, 18, ES2	1 7 6
A11/706	B.65	Driving side flywheel shaft	1	30, 30M, 40, 40M	2 0 0
E3682		Key for flywheel shaft	1	All Models	4
A11/723	B.63	Timing or driving side flywheel shaft securing nut	1	30, 30M, 40, 40M	2 6
A11/724		Timing side flywheel shaft plug	1	30, 30M, 40, 40M	1 0

NOTE:—We recommend Flywheels be returned to the works for the fitting of Shafts.

PART No	PLATE No.	DESCRIPTION.	QTY.	USED ON.	PRICE EACH. £ s. d.
A2/27	A.51	Crankpin bearing with nuts	1	1, 16H, 18, ES2	2 16 0
A11/27	B.62	Crankpin bearing with nuts	1	30	3 16 0
A11M/27	B.62	Crankpin bearing less nuts	1	30M, 40M	4 10 0
A10/27	B.62	Crankpin bearing with nuts	1	40	3 16 0

NOTE:—Crankpin bearing for Manx models is supplied less nuts, unless ordered additionally.

PART No	PLATE No.	DESCRIPTION.	QTY.	USED ON.	PRICE EACH. £ s. d.
A2/28	A.50	Crankpin bearing nut	2	1, 16H, 18, ES2	1 4
A11/28	B.61	Crankpin bearing nut	2	30	4 0
A11M/28	B.61	Crankpin bearing nut	2	30M	4 0
A10/28	B.61	Crankpin bearing nut	2	40	4 0
A10M/28	B.61	Crankpin bearing nut	2	40M	4 0
A2/29	A.52/B.66	Crankpin bearing nut locking screw	2	All Models	3

NOTE:—Crankpin Spare Parts cannot be supplied separately, each Outer Race has its individual Pin.

MAIN BEARINGS.

PART No	PLATE No.	DESCRIPTION.	QTY.	USED ON.	PRICE EACH. £ s. d.
A2/30	A.9	Mainshaft ball bearing driving side	1	1, 16H, 18, ES2	1 2 0
A2/32	A.11	Mainshaft roller bearings	2	1, 16H, 18, ES2	1 10 4
A11/31	B.34	Mainshaft ball bearing timing side	1	30, 40	1 5 6
A11M/31	B.35	Mainshaft ball bearing timing side	1	30M, 40M	1 15 0
A11/32	B.39	Mainshaft bearing driving side roller	1	30, 30M, 40, 40M	1 19 0
A11/30	B.42	Mainshaft bearing driving side ball	1	30, 30M, 40, 40M	1 3 6
A2/33	A.10	Mainshaft bearing driving side oil spacing ring	1	1, 16H, 18, ES2	2 0
A11/33	B.40	Mainshaft bearing driving side oil spacing ring	1	30, 40	2 0
A10/33	B.44	Mainshaft bearing driving side oil spacing ring	1	30M, 40M	2 0
A11/834	B.41	Mainshaft bearing distance piece driving side	1	30, 40	9
A11M/835	B.43	Mainshaft bearing distance piece driving side	1	30M, 40M	9

PART No.	PLATE No.	DESCRIPTION.	QTY.	USED ON.	PRICE EACH. £ s. d.
MAIN BEARINGS—cont.					
A11/34	B.36	Mainshaft bearing securing plate	2	30, 40	3 6
A11M/34	B.37	Mainshaft bearing securing plate	2	30M, 40M	3 6
A11/35	B.38	Mainshaft bearing securing plate screw	3	30, 40	3
			4	30M, 40M	3
A2/46	...	Mainshaft packing washer	1	1, 16H, 18, ES2	4
A11/46	...	Mainshaft packing washer between mainshaft bearing and flywheel driving side	1	30, 30M, 40, 40M	4

CRANKCASE, ENGINE PLATE BOLTS, STUDS, ETC., O.H.C. MODELS.

PART No.	PLATE No.	DESCRIPTION.	QTY.	USED ON.	PRICE EACH. £ s. d.
12747	W.20	Front engine plate and horn attachment bolt	1	30, 40	2 6
E3238	W.18	Front engine plate and horn attachment bolt nut	1	30, 40	5
E5375	W.19	Front engine plate and horn attachment washer	2	30, 40	3
E3224	W.21	Horn fixing bolt nut	1	30, 40	4
E4256	W.14	Front and rear engine plate crankcase bolt	4	30, 40	2 6
E3238	W.22	Front and rear engine plate crankcase bolt nut	4	30, 40	5
E5375	W.15	Front and rear engine plate crankcase bolt washer	8	30, 40	3
E4268	W.23	Rear engine plate frame attachment bolt, ⅞in. x 7/16in.	2	30, 40	1 6
E4261	W.26	Crankcase and rear engine plate stud bottom	1	30, 40	1 6
E3223	W.27	Crankcase and rear engine plate stud nut	2	30, 40	4
E4262	B.74/W.28	Crankcase frame cradle bolt	2	30, 30M, 40, 40M	2 6
E3223	B.75/W.29	Crankcase frame cradle bolt nut	2	30, 30M, 40, 40M	4
13289	X.31	Front engine plate and frame bolt (drilled)	1	30M, 40M	7 6
E3227	X.33	Front engine plate and frame bolt nut	1	30M, 40M	5
11809	X.32	Front engine plate and frame bolt washer	2	30M, 40M	3
10410	X.28	Crankcase and front engine plate bolt, bottom	1	30M.(40M) 1948/9	1 6
E3238	X.30	Crankcase and front engine plate bolt nut	1	30M.(40M) 1948/9	5
E5375	X.29	Crankcase and front engine plate bolt washer	2	30M, (40M 1948/9	3
13294	X.25	Crankcase and front engine plate bolt, top	1	30M, (40M 1948/9	2 6
E3224	X.27	Crankcase and front engine plate bolt nut	1	30M, (40M 1948/9	4
E5376	X.26	Crankcase and front engine plate bolt washer	2	30M, (40M 1948/9	3
13293	...	Crankcase bolt front (centre)	1	30M, (40M 1948/9	5 0
E3238	...	Crankcase bolt front nut	1	30M, (40M 1948/9	5
E5375	...	Crankcase bolt front washer	2	30M, (40M 1948/9	3
E4251	...	Crankcase and front chainguard attachment bolt	1	30M, (40M 1948/9	2 6
E3224	...	Crankcase and front chainguard attachment bolt nut	2	30M, (40M 1948/9	4
E5376	...	Crankcase and front chaincase attachment bolt washer	2	30M, (40M 1948/9	3
E4268	X.2	Rear engine plate frame attachment bolt	2	30M, 40M	1 6
10432	X.1	Crankcase and rear engine plate bolt	2	30M, (40M 1948/9	2 6

PART No	PLATE No.	DESCRIPTION.	QTY.	USED ON.	PRICE EACH. £ s. d.
CRANKCASE, ENGINE PLATE BOLTS, STUDS, ETC., O.H.C. MODELS—cont.					
E3238	... X.6	Crankcase and rear engine plate bolt nut .	2	30M, (40M 1948/9)	5
E5375	... X.5	Crankcase and rear engine plate bolt nut washer	4	30M, (40M 1948/9)	3
E4261	... X.7	Crankcase and rear engine plate stud bottom	1	30M, (40M 1948/9)	1 6
E3223	... X.9	Crankcase and rear engine plate bolt nut .	2	30M, (40M 1948/9)	4
E5456	... X.8	Crankcase and rear engine bolt washer ...	2	30M, (40M 1948)	3
13294	...	Crankcase and front engine plate bolt ...	2	40M (1945/6/7)	2 6
E3224	...	Crankcase and front engine plate bolt nut	2	40M (1945/6/7)	4
E5376	...	Crankcase and front engine plate bolt washer	2	40M (1945/6/7)	3
E4251	...	Bottom crankcase and front chainguard attachment bolt	1	40M (1945/6/7)	2 6
E3224	...	Bottom crankcase and front chainguard attachment bolt nut	2	40M (1945/6/7)	4
E4260	...	Crankcase bolt top (front)	1	40M (1945/6/7)	1 6
E3224	...	Crankcase bolt top nut	1	40M (1945/6/7)	4
E5376	...	Crankcase bolt top washer	2	40M (1945/6/7)	3
E4251	...	Crankcase and rear engine plate bolt	3	40M (1945/6/7)	2 6
E3224	...	Crankcase and rear engine plate bolt nut	3	40M (1945/6/7)	4
E5376	...	Crankcase and rear engine plate bolt washer	6	40M (1945/6/7)	3
13870	... A.41	Crankcase bolt, short	3	30, 30M, 40, 40M	1 0
E3223	... A.43	Crankcase bolt nut	3	30, 30M, 40, 40M	4
E5456	... A.42	Crankcase bolt washer	3	30, 30M, 40, 40M	4
CRANKCASE, ENGINE PLATE BOLTS, STUDS, ETC., SIDE AND O.H.V. MODELS.					
E4256	... Y.1	Mag. platform bolt, $\frac{7}{16}$in. diameter	1	1, 16H, 18, ES2	2 6
E3238	... Y.9	Mag. platform nut, $\frac{7}{16}$in. diameter	1	1, 16H, 18, ES2	5
E5377	... Y.2	Mag. platform nut washer	2	1, 16H, 18, ES2	3
E3209	... A.13	Top crankcase stud, $\frac{5}{16}$in. diameter	2	1, 16H, 18, ES2	2 6
E3223	... A.6	Top crankcase stud nuts, $\frac{5}{16}$in. diameter ..	2	1, 16H, 18, ES2	4
E5456	... A.7	Top crankcase stud nut washer	2	1, 16H, 18, ES2	4
E3166	... Y.33	Front engine plate crankcase bolt, $\frac{7}{16}$in. dia.	2	1, 16H, 18, ES2	2 6
E3238	... Y.35	Front engine plate bolt nut	2	1, 16H, 18, ES2	5
E5375	... Y.34	Front engine plate bolt nut washer	2	1, 16H, 18, ES2	3
E4256	...	Rear engine plate bolt, $\frac{7}{16}$in. diameter ...	2	1, 16H, 18, ES2	2 6

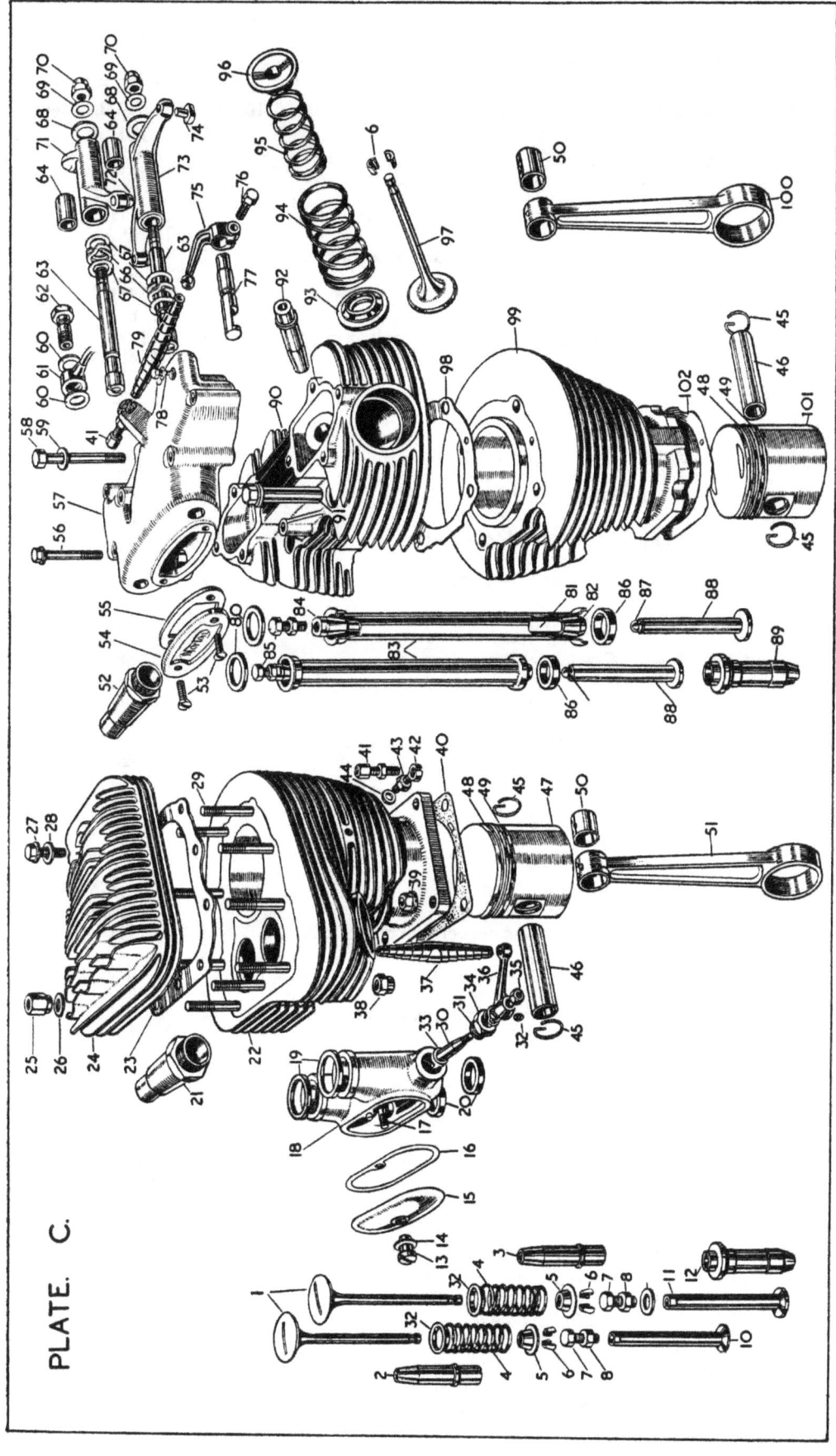

PLATE. C.

PART No.	PLATE No.	DESCRIPTION.	QTY.	USED ON.	PRICE EACH. £ s. d.

CRANKCASE, ENGINE PLATE BOLTS, STUDS, ETC., SIDE AND O.H.V. MODELS—cont.

PART No.	PLATE No.	DESCRIPTION.	QTY.	USED ON.	£ s. d.
E3238	...	Rear engine plate bolt nut	2	1, 16H, 18, ES2	5
E5375	...	Rear engine plate bolt washer	2	1, 16H, 18, ES2	3
E4268	... Y.3	Rear engine plate bolt, 7/16in. diameter	2	1, 16H, 18, ES2	1 6
11779	...	Bottom front crankcase stud, 3/8in. diameter	1	1, 16H, 18, ES2	2 6
E3224	...	Bottom front crankcase stud nut	1	1, 16H, 18, ES2	4
E4259	...	Rear bottom crankcase bolt, 3/8in. diameter	1	1, 16H, 18, ES2	2 6
E3224	...	Rear crankcase bolt nut	1	1, 16H, 18, ES2	4
E5376	...	Rear crankcase bolt washer	1	1, 16H, 18, ES2	3
E4262	... X.11	Engine cradle bolt, 5/16in. diameter	1	1, 16H, 18, ES2	2 6
E3223	... X.10	Engine cradle bolt nut	1	1, 16H, 18, ES2	4
13040	... Y.38	Front engine plate stud, 1/2in. diameter	1	1, 16H, 18, ES2	2 6
E3227	... Y.36	Front engine plate stud nut	2	1, 16H, 18, ES2	5
11809	... Y.37	Front engine plate stud nut washer	2	1, 16H, 18, ES2	3
13870	... A.41	Crankcase bolt, short	3	1, 16H, 18, ES2	1 0
E3223	... A.43	Crankcase bolt nut	3	1, 16H, 18, ES2	4
E5456	... A.42	Crankcase bolt washer	3	1, 16H, 18, ES2	4

TIMING GEAR.

PART No.	PLATE No.	DESCRIPTION.	QTY.	USED ON.	£ s. d.
C2/58	... A.56	Half time pinion	1	1, 16H, 18, ES2	10 0
A2/59	... A.55	Half time pinion key	1	1, 16H, 18, ES2	3
C2/60	... A.57	Exhaust cam wheel complete	1	1, 16H	2 7 0
C3/60	... A.57	Exhaust cam wheel complete	1	18, ES2	2 7 0
C2/61	... A.60	Inlet cam wheel complete	1	1, 16H	2 10 0
C3/61	... A.60	Inlet cam wheel complete	1	18, ES2	2 10 0
C2/694	... A.58	Cam wheel packing washer	2	1, 16H, 18, ES2	2

TAPPETS.

PART No.	PLATE No.	DESCRIPTION.	QTY.	USED ON.	£ s. d.
C2/63	... C.12	Tappet guide	2	1, 16H	12 6
C3/63	... C.89	Tappet guide	2	18, ES2	12 6
C2/689	...	Tappet guide location peg	2	1, 16H, 18, ES2	3
C2/75	...	Tappet adjustable inlet, complete	1	1, 16H	12 6
C2/76	...	Tappet adjustable exhaust, complete	1	1, 16H	12 6
C3/75	... C.88	Tappet complete	2	18, ES2	12 6
C2/691 (In)	... C.10	Tappet only, inlet	1	1, 16H	10 0
C2/691 (Ex)	... C.11	Tappet only, exhaust	1	1, 16H	10 0
C2/692	... C.9	Tappet washer (exhaust)	1	1, 16H	6
C2/77	... C.7	Tappet adjuster	2	1, 16H	2 0
A2/78	... C.8	Tappet adjuster nut	2	1, 16H	6
C3/693	... C.87	Tappet ball end	2	18, ES2	3 6

EXHAUST LIFTER AND FITTINGS.
For Crankcase and Rocker Box. (Side and O.H.V. Models).

PART No.	PLATE No.	DESCRIPTION.	QTY.	USED ON.	£ s. d.
C2/64	... C.30	Exhaust valve lifter	1	1, 16H	5 0
C3/64	... C.77	Exhaust valve lifter	1	18, ES2	7 0

PART No.	PLATE No.	DESCRIPTION.	QTY.	USED. ON.	PRICE EACH. £ s. d.

EXHAUST LIFTER AND FITTINGS—cont.
For Crankcase and Rocker Box. (Side and O.H.V. Models.)

PART No.	PLATE No.	DESCRIPTION.	QTY.	USED ON.	PRICE £ s. d.
A3/66	C.78	Exhaust valve lifter securing pin	1	18, ES2	5
C2/67	C.36	Exhaust valve lifter lever	1	1, 16H	9 8
A2/67	C.75	Exhaust valve lifter lever	1	18, ES2	9 8
A2/68	C.76	Exhaust valve lifter lever securing bolt	1	18, ES2	6
E3229	C.35	Exhaust valve lifter lever securing nut	1	1, 16H	4
10771	C.32	Exhaust valve lifter lever securing nut washer	1	1, 16H	3
A2/69	C.37	Exhaust valve lifter return spring	1	1, 16H	2 8
A3/69	C.79	Exhaust valve lifter return spring	1	18, ES2	2 8
C2/65	C.34	Exhaust valve lifter copper washer	1	1, 16H	3
C2/690	C.33	Exhaust valve lifter rubber sealing washer	1	1, 16H, 18, ES2	6
C2/695	C.31	Exhaust valve lifter bush	1	1, 16H	2 3
C2/728	C.42	Exhaust valve lifter cable adjuster stop	1	1, 16H	2 3
13933	C.43	Exhaust valve lifter cable adjuster stop nut	1	1, 16H	3
13834	C.44	Exhaust valve lifter cable adjuster stop spring washer	1	1, 16H	3

EXHAUST LIFTER FITTINGS (For O.H.C. Rocker Box).

PART No.	PLATE No.	DESCRIPTION.	QTY.	USED ON.	PRICE £ s. d.
A11/64	F.39	Exhaust lifter cam	1	30, 40	3 6
A11/67	F.37	Exhaust lifter cam lever	1	30, 40	9 6
A2/68	F.36	Exhaust lifter lever bolt	1	30, 40	6
A3/69	F.35	Exhaust lifter cam return spring	1	30, 40	2 8
A11/728	F.34	Exhaust lifter cable stop (for panel cover)	1	30, 40	2 3
E3231	F.32	Exhaust lifter cable stop nut	1	30, 40	4
11796	F.33	Exhaust lifter cable stop washer	1	30, 40	3
A11/695	F.38	Exhaust lifter cam bush (for panel cover)	1	30, 40	2 3

VALVE COVER AND FITTINGS (Side Valve Models).

PART No.	PLATE No.	DESCRIPTION.	QTY.	USED ON.	PRICE £ s. d.
C2/696	C.18	Valve chest (alum)	1	1, 16H	1 5 0
C2/70	C.15	Valve chest cover	1	1, 16H	12 6
C2/71	C.16	Valve chest cover washer	1	1, 16H	3
C2/72	C.17	Valve chest cover securing stud	1	1, 16H	8
C2/73	C.13	Valve chest cover securing stud nut	1	1, 16H	3 6
C2/74	C.14	Valve chest cover stud nut fibre washer	1	1, 16H	4
C2/697	C.19	Valve chest sealing washer, top	2	1, 16H	6
C3/88	C.20	Valve chest sealing washer, bottom	2	1, 16H	6

PUSH RODS AND FITTINGS (For O.H.V. Models).

PART No.	PLATE No.	DESCRIPTION.	QTY.	USED ON.	PRICE £ s. d.
C3/82	C.81	Push rod, complete	2	18, ES2	15 0
C3/83	C.82	Push rod, bottom	2	18, ES2	5 6
C3/86	C.84	Push rod, top	2	18, ES2	5 0
C3/87	C.85	Push rod adjuster and locknut	2	18, ES2	6 0
C3/84	C.83	Push rod cover	2	18, ES2	7 0
C3/88	C.86	Push rod cover, bottom, sealing washer	2	18, ES2	6
C3/89	C.80	Push rod cover, top, sealing washer	2	18, ES2	6

ROCKER BOX AND FITTINGS (O.H.V. Models).

PART No.	PLATE No.	DESCRIPTION.	QTY.	USED ON.	PRICE £ s. d.
C3/90	C.57	Rocker box with cover	1	18, ES2	4 15 0
C3/92	C.54	Rocker box inspection cover	1	18, ES2	3 0
C3/94	C.53	Rocker box inspection cover screw	2	18, ES2	6
C3/95	C.55	Rocker box inspection cover washer	1	18, ES2	1 0
C3/108	C.58	Rocker box securing bolt, long	7	18, ES2	1 3
C3/110	C.56	Rocker box securing bolt, short	2	18, ES2	9
A3/109	C.59	Rocker box securing bolt washer	7	18, ES2	3
C3/699	M.42/C.61	Rocker box lubrication pipe with banjo connection	1	18, ES2	5 0
C3/700	C.62	Rocker box lubrication pipe connection bolt	1	18, ES2	2 6
C3/701	C.60	Rocker box lubrication pipe connection bolt washer	2	18, ES2	4

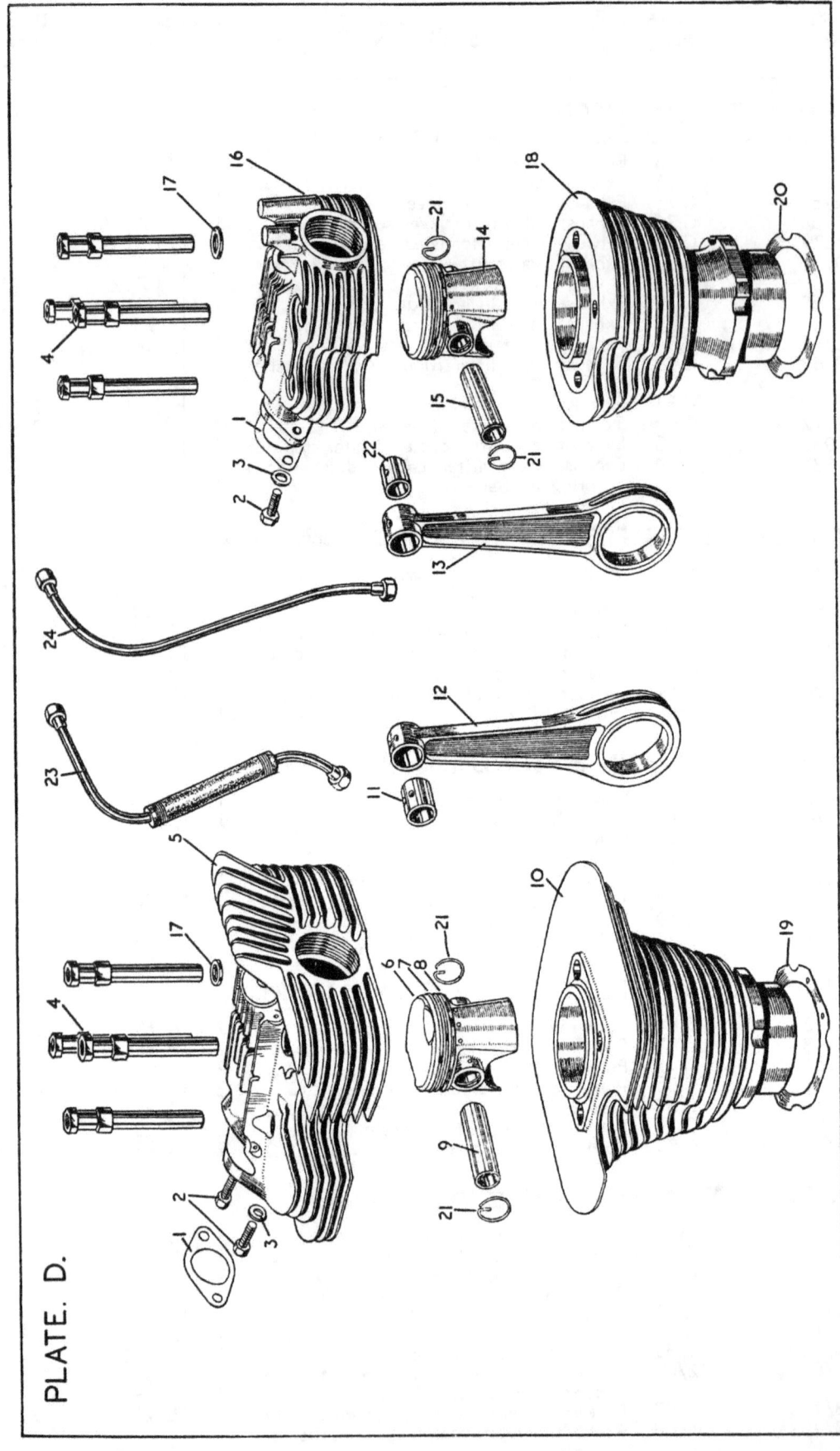

PLATE. D.

PART No.	PLATE No.	DESCRIPTION.	QTY.	USED ON.	PRICE EACH. £ s. d.

OVERHEAD ROCKERS.

PART No.	PLATE No.	DESCRIPTION.	QTY.	USED ON.	£	s.	d.
C3/96	C.64	Rocker bush	4	18, ES2		5	0
C3/97	C.63	Rocker shaft	2	18, ES2		19	6
C3/98	C.67	Rocker shaft shim washer (as necessary)		18, ES2			3
C3/102	C.70	Rocker shaft nut	2	18, ES2			6
13802	C.69	Rocker shaft nut copper washer	2	18, ES2			3
13794	C.68	Rocker shaft washer, large	2	18, ES2			6
13818	C.66	Rocker shaft thrust spring washer	2	18, ES2			4
C3/99	C.71	Rocker arm, inlet	1	18, ES2	1	11	6
C3/100	C.73	Rocker arm, exhaust	1	18, ES2	1	11	6
C3/104	C.72	Rocker arm ball end	2	18, ES2		3	6
C3/105	C.74	Rocker arm pad	2	18, ES2		5	0

O.H.C. VERTICAL SHAFT DRIVE AND ROCKER BOX, ETC.

PART No.	PLATE No.	DESCRIPTION.	QTY.	USED ON.	£	s.	d.
A11/748	B.57	Mainshaft bevel	1	30, 40 ...	3	0	0
A11M/748	B.57	Mainshaft bevel	1	30M, 40M	3	0	0
A11/749	B.58	Mainshaft bevel key	1	30, 30M, 40, 40M			4
A11/750		Mainshaft bevel washer	1	30, 30M, 40, 40M			4
A11/751	E.20	Vertical shaft bottom bevel	1	30, 30M, 40, 40M	5	0	0
A11/752	E.17	Vertical shaft bottom bevel housing with bush	1	30, 30M, 40, 40M	2	15	0
A11/753	E.19	Vertical shaft bottom bevel bush	1	30, 30M, 40, 40M		13	0
A11/754	E.7	Vertical shaft top or bottom bevel collar	1	30, 30M, 40, 40M			6
A11/755	E.5	Vertical shaft top or bottom bearing	2	30, 30M, 40, 40M		16	6
A11/756	E.16	Vertical shaft bottom bearing dished washer	1	30, 30M, 40, 40M		1	0
A11/757	E.6	Vertical shaft top rubber ring, steel cup	1	30, 30M, 40, 40M		2	6
A11/758	E.10	Vertical shaft top rubber ring	1	30, 30M, 40, 40M		1	6
A11/759	E.15	Vertical shaft bottom rubber ring, steel cup	1	30, 30M, 40, 40M		2	6
A11/760	E.13	Vertical shaft bottom rubber ring	1	30, 30M, 40, 40M		1	6
A11/761	E.12	Vertical shaft tube top or bottom union nut	2	30, 30M, 40, 40M		7	0
A11/762	E.11	Vertical shaft tube top or bottom union nut washer	2	30, 30M, 40, 40M			6
A11/763	E.14	Vertical shaft	1	30	3	10	0
A11M/763	E.14	Vertical shaft	1	30M	3	10	0
A10/763	E.14	Vertical shaft	1	40	3	10	0
A10M/763	E.14	Vertical shaft	1	40M (1946/7)	3	10	0
C10M/763	E.14	Vertical shaft	1	40M (1948/9)	3	10	0
A11/764	E.8	Vertical shaft top or bottom coupling	2	30, 30M, 40, 40M		12	6
A11/764P		Vertical shaft top or bottom coupling (thick) (for Pool petrol)	1	30, 30M, 40, 40M		12	6
A11/765	E.9	Vertical shaft tube	1	30, 30M, 40, 40M		7	0
A11/766	E.18	Vertical shaft bottom bearing housing packing washer	1	30, 30M, 40, 40M			6
A11/767	E.1	Vertical shaft top bevel	1	30, 30M, 40, 40M	4	0	0
A11/768	E.4	Vertical shaft top bevel housing with bush	1	30, 40 ...	2	15	0
A11M/768	E.4	Vertical shaft top bevel housing with bush	1	30M, 40M	2	15	0

170

PLATE. E.

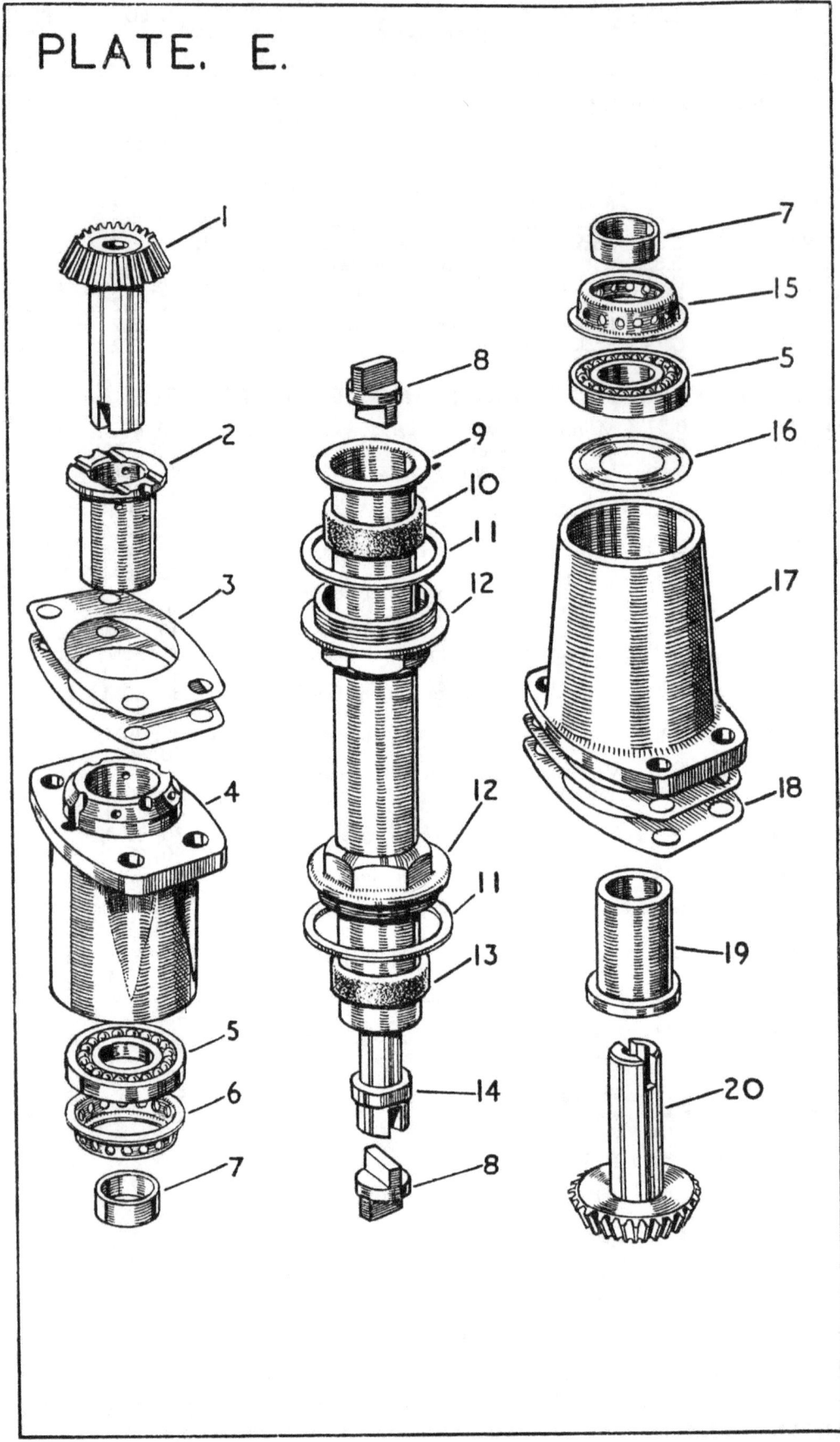

18

PART No.	PLATE No.	DESCRIPTION.	QTY.	USED ON.	PRICE EACH. £ s. d.

O.H.C. VERTICAL SHAFT DRIVE AND ROCKER BOX, ETC.—cont.

PART No.	PLATE No.	DESCRIPTION.	QTY.	USED ON.	£	s.	d.
A11/769	E.2	Vertical shaft top bevel bush	1	30, 40		13	0
A11M/769	E.2	Vertical shaft top bevel bush	1	30M, 40M		13	0
A11/770	E.3	Vertical shaft top bevel housing washer	1	30, 30M, 40, 40M			6
A11/771	F.10	Camshaft bevel	1	30, 30M, 40, 40M	3	10	0
A11/772	F.9	Camshaft bevel securing nut	1	30, 30M, 40, 40M			4
A11/773	F.11	Camshaft bevel locating peg	1	30, 30M, 40, 40M			2
A11/774	...	Camshaft bevel packing washer	1	30, 30M, 40, 40M			8
A11/775	F.17	Distance piece between mainshaft and ballrace	1	30, 30M, 40, 40M			9
A11/776	F.19	Rocker box with cover	1	30, 40	8	0	0
A11M/776	F.19	Rocker box with cover	1	30M, 40M	10	0	0
A11/777	F.30	Rocker box panel cover	1	30, 40	2	5	0
A11M/777	F.30	Rocker box panel cover	1	30M, 40M	2	7	6
A11/778	F.64	Valve guide lubrication pipe	1	30, 30M, 40, 40M		1	6
A11/779	F.65	Valve guide lubrication pipe nut	1	30, 30M, 40, 40M			3
A11/780	F.66	Valve guide lubrication pipe union	1	30, 30M, 40, 40M		2	0
A11/781	F.12	Rocker box inspection cover	1	30, 40		5	0
A11M/781	F.2	Rocker box inspection cover	1	30M, 40M		12	6
A11/782	F.3	Rocker box inspection cover washer	1	30, 40			8
A11M/782	F.3	Rocker box inspection cover washer	1	30M, 40M			8
A11/719	F.16	Rocker box or crankcase oil feed pipe union	1	30, 30M, 40, 40M		2	6
A11/783	B.28/F.71	Vertical shaft top or bottom bevel housing studs	8	30, 30M, 40, 40M			6
E3231	B.29/F.73	Vertical shaft top or bottom bevel housing stud nut	8	30, 30M, 40, 40M			4
11796	B.30/F.72	Vertical shaft top or bottom bevel housing stud washer	8	30, 30M, 40, 40M			3
A11/784	F.1	Rocker box inspection cover screw	1	30, 30M, 40, 40M			4
A11/687	F.311	Rocker box panel cover screw or crankcase bevel cover screw	1	30, 30M, 40, 40M			5
A11/785	F.18	Camshaft bearing (rocker box) (ball)	1	30, 30M, 40, 40M		19	0
A11/786	F.28	Camshaft bearing (panel cover) (roller)	1	30, 40	1	12	0
A11M/786	F.28	Camshaft bearing (panel cover) (roller)	1	30M, 40M	1	12	0
A11/787	F.15	Camshaft bearing rocker box retaining washer	1	30, 30M, 40, 40M		3	6
A11/35	F.14	Camshaft bearing rocker box retaining washer screws	1	30, 30M, 40, 40M			3
A11/788	F.27	Distance piece between cams and roller bearing	1	30, 30M, 40, 40M			9
A11/789	D.24	Rocker box oil feed pipe	1	30, 40		7	6
A11M/789	D.23	Rocker box oil feed pipe	1	30M, 40M		10	6
A11/790	F.13	Camshaft	1	30, 40		17	0
A11M/790	F.13	Camshaft	1	30M, 40M	1	0	0
A11M/791	...	Plug for camshaft	1	30M, 40M			9
A11M/792	F.8	Camshaft oil feed jet	1	30M, 40M		4	0
A2/13	F.7	Camshaft oil feed jet holder	1	30M, 40M		5	0
A2/14	F.6	Camshaft oil feed jet spring	1	30M, 40M			3
A11M/793	F.4	Camshaft oil feed jet holder nut	1	30M, 40M		1	0
A11/794	F.25	Cam inlet (No. 6212)	1	30	1	10	0
A10/794	F.25	Cam inlet (No. 6466)	1	40, 40M	1	10	0

19

PLATE. F.

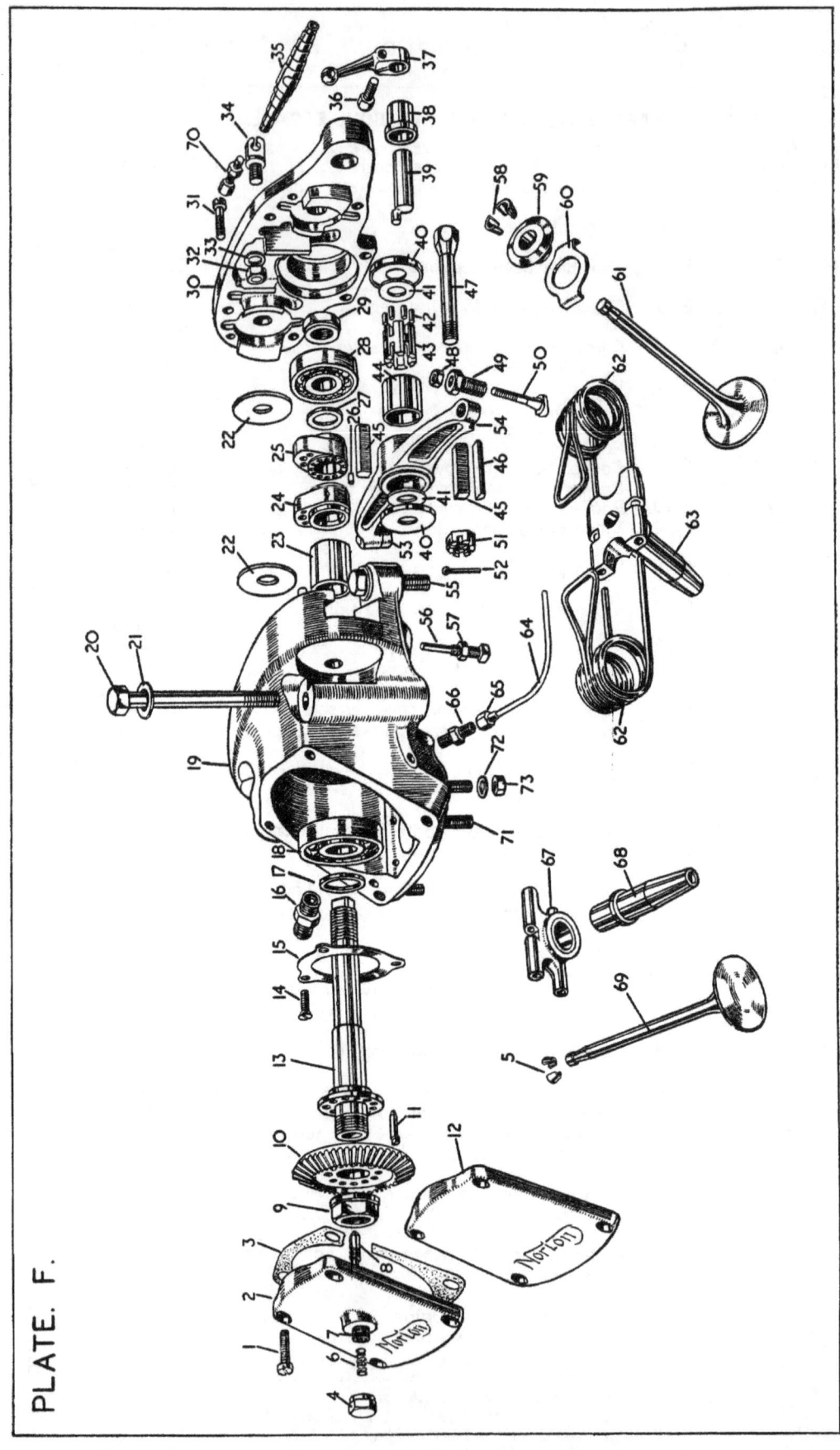

PART No.	PLATE No.	DESCRIPTION.	QTY.	USED. ON.	PRICE EACH. £ s. d
O.H.C. VERTICAL SHAFT DRIVE AND ROCKER BOX, ETC.—cont.					
A11M/794	F.25	Cam inlet (No. 11587)	1	30M	1 10 0
A11/795	F.24	Cam exhaust (No. 6213)	1	30	1 10 0
A10/795	F.24	Cam exhaust (No. 6389)	1	40, 40M	1 10 0
A11M/795	F.24	Cam exhaust (No. 11588)	1	30M	1 10 0
A11/796	F.26	Cam securing roller	1	30, 30M, 40, 40M	4
A11/797		Cam key	1	30, 30M, 40, 40M	4
A11/798	F.23	Camshaft slotted bush	1	30, 30M, 40, 40M	3 6
A11/799	F.29	Camshaft nut (left-hand thread) panel cover end	1	30, 30M, 40, 40M	8
A11/800		Camshaft packing washer	1	30, 30M, 40, 40M	2
A11/801	F.54	Cam rocker (inlet or exhaust)	2	30, 30M, 40, 40M	1 17 0
A11/802	F.53	Cam rocker pad (inlet or exhaust)	2	30, 30M, 40, 40M	5 0
A11/803	F.50	Rocker adjusting screw	2	30, 30M, 40, 40M	4 6
A11/804	F.49	Rocker adjusting screw sleeve	2	30, 30M, 40, 40M	3 6
A11/805	F.48	Rocker adjusting screw nut	2	30, 30M, 40, 40M	6
A11/806	F.44	Cam rocker bush	2	30, 30M, 40, 40M	5 0
A11/807	F.43	Cam rocker roller cage	2	30, 30M, 40, 40M	17 0
A11/808	F.42	Cam rocker rollers (per rocker)	1	30, 30M, 40, 40M	5 0
A11/809	F.41	Cam rocker roller retaining washers	4	30, 30M, 40, 40M	2
A11/810	F.47	Cam rocker pivot bolt	2	30, 30M, 40, 40M	7 0
A11/811	F.51	Cam rocker pivot bolt nut	2	30, 30M, 40, 40M	8
A11/812	F.52	Cam rocker pivot bolt cotter pin	2	30, 30M, 40, 40M	2
A11/813	F.22	Cam rocker cork washer	4	30, 30M, 40, 40M	4
A11/814	F.40	Cam rocker cork washer steel cup	4	30, 30M, 40, 40M	6
A11/815	F.45	Cam rocker box rubber pad	4	30, 30M, 40, 40M	8
A11/816	F.46	Cam rocker box rubber pad roller	2	30, 30M, 40, 40M	6
A11/817	F.56	Rocker box rubber pad bottom adjusting screw	2	30, 30M, 40, 40M	4
A11/818	F.57	Rocker box rubber pad bottom adjusting screw nut	2	30, 30M, 40, 40M	2
A11/108(L)	F.20	Rocker box bolt, long	2	30, 30M, 40, 40M	1 6
A11/108(S)	F.55	Rocker box bolt, short	2	30, 30M, 40, 40M	1 0
E5455	F.21	Rocker box bolt washer	4	30, 30M, 40, 40M	3

MAGNETO OR MAGDYNO DRIVING PARTS AND FITTINGS.

PART No.	PLATE No.	DESCRIPTION	QTY.	USED ON.	PRICE £ s. d
C2/79	A.31	Magneto sprocket (engine)	1	1, 16H, 18, ES2	8 6
A2/79	B.6	Magneto sprocket (engine)	1	30, 30M, 40, 40M	8 6
A2/80	A.62/B.72	Magneto sprocket securing nut	1	30, 40, 1, 16H, 18, ES2	8

PART No.	PLATE No.	DESCRIPTION.	QTY.	USED ON.	PRICE EACH. £ s. d.
MAGNETO OR MAGDYNO DRIVING PARTS AND FITTINGS—cont.					
E5376	A.61/B.73	Magneto sprocket securing nut washer	1	30, 40, 1, 16H, 18, ES2	3
A2/81	... A.59	Magneto sprocket key	1	All Models	3
A11M/80	... B.52	Magneto sprocket and rev. counter drive nut	1	30M, 40M	2 6
C2/112	... A.33	Magdyno sprocket	1	1, 16H, 18, ES2	8 6
A11/112	... B.4	Magneto (B.T.H.) or magdyno sprocket	1	30, 30M, 40, 40M	8 6
A2/115	... A.35	Magdyno sprocket securing nut	1	All Models	8
A2/116	... A.34	Magdyno sprocket securing nut washer	1	All Models	3
E6270	... H.28	Base stud for B.T.H. magneto	3	30M, 40M	9
E4267	... H.30	Base stud for Lucas magdyno	3	30, 40	6
E3837	... H.31	Long nut securing magneto or magdyno to platform	1	30, 30M, 40, 40M	3 0
E3224	... H.29	Short nut securing magneto or magdyno to platform	2	30, 30M, 40, 40M	4
E5455	...	Washer for magneto base stud	3	30, 30M, 40, 40M	3
C2/117	... Y.4	Magdyno platform	1	1, 16H, 18, ES2	6 0
E3831	... Y.6	Magdyno platform countersunk screw	4	1, 16H, 18, ES2	5
1518A	... Y.5	Magdyno platform countersunk screw shake proof washer	4	1, 16H, 18, ES2	4
A2/118	... Y.7	Magdyno platform locking plate	1	1, 16H, 18, ES2	2 0
E3798	... Y.8	Magdyno platform locking plate pin	1	1, 16H, 18, ES2	4
C2/113	... A.32	Magdyno chain (44 link)	1	1, 16H, 18, ES2	11 8
A11/113	... B.5	Magdyno chain (46 link)	1	30, 30M	11 8
A10/113	... B.5	Magdyno chain (45 link)	1	40, 40M	11 8
DRY SUMP OIL PUMP AND DRIVE PARTS. **Side and O.H.V. Models.**					
A2/128	... A.68	Dry sump gear pump, complete	1	1, 16H, 18, ES2	3 0 0
A2/129	... A.65	Dry sump gear pump spindle nut	1	1, 16H, 18, ES2	5
A2/130	... A.64	Dry sump gear pump spindle worm gear wheel	1	1, 16H, 18, ES2	6 6
A2/131	...	Dry sump gear pump spindle worm gear wheel key	1	1, 16H, 18, ES2	3
A2/132	... A.66	Dry sump gear pump body and timing cover connection bush	1	1, 16H, 18, ES2	8
A2/133	... A.67	Dry sump gear pump body and timing cover connection fibre washer	1	1, 16H, 18, ES2	3
C2/134	... A.63	Engine mainshaft pump driving worm	1	1, 16H, 18, ES2	7 6
E4440	... A.45	Dry sump gear pump crankcase stud	2	1, 16H, 18, ES2	9
E3231	... A.46	Dry sump gear pump crankcase stud nut	2	1, 16H, 18, ES2	4
DRY SUMP OIL PUMP AND DRIVE PARTS. **O.H.C. Models.**					
A11/128	... B.17	Dry sump gear pump, complete	1	30, 30M, 40, 40M	3 5 0

PART No	PLATE No.	DESCRIPTION.	QTY.	USED ON.	PRICE EACH. £ s. d.

DRY SUMP OIL PUMP AND DRIVE PARTS. O.H.C. Models—cont.

A11/729	B.54	Dry sump gear pump spindle driving plate	1	30, 30M, 40, 40M	1 6
A11/134	B.56	Engine mainshaft pump driving pinion	1	30, 30M, 40, 40M	11 0
A11/730	B.55	Engine mainshaft pump driving pinion nut	1	30, 30M, 40, 40M	2 0
A11/731	B.53	Pump and magneto drive gear wheel	1	30, 30M, 40, 40M	1 5 0
A11/732	B.16	Oil pump securing screw	2	30, 30M, 40, 40M	6

NOTE.—Dry sump pump parts cannot be supplied separately. It is necessary to return the complete pump to the works for attention.

CYLINDER BARREL AND HEAD.

C7/135	C.22	Cylinder barrel with valve guides	1	16H	7 0 0
C2/135	C.22	Cylinder barrel with valve guides	1	1	7 5 0
C3/135	C.99	Cylinder barrel	1	18, ES2	5 0 0
A11/135	D.18	Cylinder barrel	1	30	6 5 0
A11/135AL		Cylinder barrel (aluminium)	1	30	9 10 0
A11M/135	D.10	Cylinder barrel	1	30M	10 0 0
A10/135	D.18	Cylinder barrel	1	40	6 0 0
A10/135AL		Cylinder barrel (aluminium)	1	40	9 10 0
A10M/135	D.10	Cylinder barrel	1	40M (1946/7)	10 0 0
C10M/135	D.10	Cylinder barrel	1	40M (1948/9)	10 0 0
C7/136	C.24	Cylinder head	1	1	3 0 0
C7/136	C.24	Cylinder head	1	16H	3 0 0
C3/136	C.90	Cylinder head with valve guides	1	18, ES2	7 0 0
C7/137	C.23	Cylinder head joint washer	1	1	7 0
C2/137	C.23	Cylinder head joint washer	1	16H	5 0
C3/137	C.98	Cylinder head joint washer	1	18, ES2	2 0
A11/136	D.16	Cylinder head with valve guides (cast iron)	1	30	7 16 0
A11/136AL		Cylinder head with valve guides (aluminium)	1	30	16 15 0
A11M/136	D.5	Cylinder head with valve guides	1	30M	17 10 0
A10/136	D.16	Cylinder head with valve guides (cast iron)	1	40	7 16 0
A10/136AL		Cylinder head with valve guides (aluminium)	1	40	16 15 0
A10M/136	D.5	Cylinder head with valve guides	1	40M	17 10 0
C2/152	C.27	Compression plug	1	1, 16H	5 6
C3/153	C.28	Compression plug copper abestos washer	1	1, 16H	5
A2/154	C.21	Carburetter adaptor	1	1, 16H	9 6
A3/154	C.52	Carburetter adaptor	1	18, ES2	9 6
C2/155	C.29	Cylinder head holding down stud	9	1, 16H	1 0
A3/156	C.91	Cylinder head holding down stud nut	4	18, ES2	2 0
A2/156	C.25	Cylinder head holding down stud nut	9	1, 16H	1 8
E5455	C.26	Cylinder head holding down stud nut washer	9	1, 16H	3
A11/156	D.4	Cylinder head holding down sleeve nut	4	30, 30M	7 6
A10/156	D.4	Cylinder head holding down sleeve nut	4	40, (40M 1946/7)	7 6
C10/156	D.4	Cylinder head holding down sleeve nut	4	40M (1948/9)	7 6
E6662	D.17	Cylinder head sleeve nut washer	4	30, 30M, 40, 40M	3
C3/157	C.102	Cylinder base paper washer	1	18, ES2	5
C2/157	C.40	Cylinder base paper washer	1	1, 16H	5
A11/157	D.20	Cylinder base paper washer	1	30	5
A10/157	D.20	Cylinder base paper washer	1	40	5
A11/726	D.19	Compression plate, ½ m/m to 2 m/m	1	30, 30M	2 0
A10/726	D.19	Compression plate, ½ m/m to 2 m/m	1	40, 40M	2 0
A11/727	D.1	Carburetter flange washer	1	30, 30M, 40, 40M	3
E3798	D.2	Carburetter flange bolt	2	30, 30M, 40, 40M	4
11796	D.3	Carburetter flange bolt washer	2	30, 30M, 40, 40M	3

PART No	PLATE No.	DESCRIPTION.	QTY.	USED ON.	PRICE EACH. £ s. d.

VALVES, GUIDES, SPRINGS AND FITTINGS.

PART No	PLATE No.	DESCRIPTION.	QTY.	USED ON.	£ s. d.
A2/141	C.1	Valve only (inlet or exhaust)	2	16H	12 0
C7/141	C.1	Valve only (inlet or exhaust)	2	1	12 0
A3/142	C.97	Valve only (inlet or exhaust)	2	18, ES2	12 0
A11/142	F.69	Valve inlet	1	30	19 6
A11M/142	F.69	Valve inlet	1	30M	19 6
A10/142	F.69	Valve inlet	1	40	19 6
A10M/142	F.69	Valve inlet	1	40M	19 6
A11/143	F.61	Valve exhaust	1	30, 30M	19 6
A10/143	F.61	Valve exhaust	1	40	19 6
A10M/143	F.61	Valve exhaust	1	40M	19 6
A2/138	C.2	Valve guide inlet	1	1, 16H	6 6
A2/139	C.3	Valve guide exhaust	1	1, 16H	6 6
A3/140	C.92	Valve guide (inlet or exhaust)	2	18, ES2	6 6
A11/138	F.68	Valve guide inlet	1	30, 30M, 40, 40M	8 0
A11/139	F.63	Valve guide exhaust	1	30, 30M, 40, 40M	18 6
A11/148	F.67	Inlet valve guide bottom collar	1	30, 30M, 40, 40M	9 0
A2/144	C.4	Valve spring (inlet or exhaust)	2	1, 16H	1 0
A3/145	C.95	Valve spring small inner (inlet or exhaust)	2	18, ES2	1 0
A3/146	C.94	Valve spring outer (inlet or exhaust)	2	18, ES2	2 0
A11/144	F.62	Hairpin valve spring	4	30, 30M, 40, 40M	6 0
C2/147	C.32	Valve spring cup top	2	1, 16H	1 0
A2/148	C.5	Valve spring cup bottom	2	1, 16H	2 0
A3/147	C.96	Valve spring cup top	2	18, ES2	5 6
A3/148	C.93	Valve spring bottom collar	2	18, ES2	1 0
A11/147	F.59	Hairpin valve spring top cup	2	30, 30M, 40, 40M	6 0
A11/725	F.60	Hairpin valve spring top cup plate	2	30, 30M, 40, 40M	1 0
A2/149	C.6	Valve split cotter (2 pairs per valve)	2	1, 16H, 18, ES2	1 0
A11/150	F.5	Valve cotter inlet (2 halves)	2	30, 30M, 40, 40M	1 0
A11/151	F.58	Valve cotter exhaust (2 halves)	2	30, 30M, 40, 40M	1 0

CONNECTING RODS.

PART No	PLATE No.	DESCRIPTION.	QTY.	USED ON.	£ s. d.
A2/158	C.51	Connecting rod with small end bush	1	1, 16H	2 4 0
A3/158	C.100	Connecting rod with small end bush	1	18, ES2	2 4 0
A11/158	D.13	Connecting rod with small end bush	1	30	2 4 0
A11M/158	D.12	Connecting rod with small end bush	1	30M, (40M 1946/7)	3 5 0
C10M/158	D.12	Connecting rod with small end bush	1	40M (1948/9)	3 5 0
A10/158	D.13	Connecting rod with small end bush	1	40	2 4 0
A2/159	C.50/D.22	Small end bush	1	1, 16H, 18, ES2, 30	7 0
A11M/159	D.11	Small end bush	1	30M, 40, 40M	7 0

PISTONS AND RINGS.

PART No	PLATE No.	DESCRIPTION.	QTY.	USED ON.	£ s. d.
C7/160	C.47	Piston only	1	1	2 9 6
C2/160	C.47	Piston only	1	16H	2 5 3
C3/160	C.101	Piston only	1	18, ES2	2 5 3
A11/160	D.14	Piston only	1	30	2 5 3
A11M/160	D.6	Piston only	1	30M	3 10 0
A10/160	D.14	Piston only	1	40	2 5 3
A10M/160	D.6	Piston only	1	40M (1946/7)	3 10 0
C10M/160	D.6	Piston only	1	40M (1948/9)	3 10 0
A11/160		Piston only, high compression (for use with alcohol fuel)	1	30	2 13 8

PART No.	PLATE No.	DESCRIPTION.	QTY.	USED ON.	PRICE EACH. £ s. d.
PISTONS AND RINGS—cont.					
A11M/160(HC)		Piston only, high compression (for use with alcohol fuel)	1	30M	3 10 0
A10/160(HC)		Piston only, high compression (for use with alcohol fuel)	1	40, (40M 1946/7)	3 10 0
C10/160(HC)		Piston only, high compression (for use with alcohol fuel)	1	40M (1948/9)	3 10 0
C7/702	...	Piston complete with rings, gudgeon pin and circlips	1	1	3 5 9
C2/702	...	Piston complete with rings, gudgeon pin and circlips	1	16H	3 2 9
C3/702	...	Piston complete with rings, gudgeon pin and circlips	1	18, ES2	3 2 9
A11/702	...	Piston complete with rings, gudgeon pin and circlips	1	30	3 2 9
A11M/702	...	Piston complete with rings, gudgeon pin and circlips	1	30M	4 11 7
A10/702	...	Piston complete with rings, gudgeon pin and circlips	1	40	3 2 9
A10M/702	...	Piston complete with rings, gudgeon pin and circlips	1	40M (1946/7)	4 11 7
C10M/702	...	Piston complete with rings, gudgeon pin and circlips	1	40M (1948/9)	4 11 7
C7/161	... C.48	Piston ring	2	1	3 4
A2/161	... C.48	Piston ring	2	16H, 18, ES2, 30	3 0
A11M/161	... D.7	Piston ring	2	30M	3 0
A10/161	... D.7	Piston ring	2	40, 40M	3 0
C7/162	... C.49	Scraper piston ring	1	1	4 0
A2/162	... C.49	Scraper piston ring	1	16H, 18, ES2, 30	4 0
A11M/162	... D.8	Scraper piston ring	1	30M	4 0
A10/162	... D.8	Scraper piston ring	1	40, (40M 1946/7)	4 0
C10/162	... D.8	Scraper piston ring	1	40M (1948/9)	4 0
A2/163	... C.46	Gudgeon pin	1	1, 16H, 18, ES2, 30	10 0
A11M/163	... D.9	Gudgeon pin	1	30M	12 6
A10/163	... D.15	Gudgeon pin	1	40	10 0
A10M/163	... D.9	Gudgeon pin	1	40M	12 6
A2/164	C.45/D.21	Gudgeon pin circlip	2	All Models	6

Pistons and rings can be supplied in the following oversizes: .010, .020, .030, .040. State size when ordering.

AMAL CARBURETTERS.

PART No.	PLATE No.	DESCRIPTION.	QTY.	USED ON.	PRICE EACH. £ s. d.
276/AT	...	Amal-Norton carburetter complete	1	1, 16H	3 6 0
276/AU	...	Amal-Norton carburetter complete	1	18, ES2	3 10 3
276/408	... G.13	Mixing chamber	1	1, 16H	14 0
276/407	... G.13	Mixing chamber	1	18, ES2	14 0
6/031	... G.4	Mixing chamber cap	1	1, 16H, 18, ES2	2 6
6/032B	... G.5	Mixing chamber top	1	1, 16H, 18, ES2	2 6
6/033	... G.30	Mixing chamber union nut	1	1, 16H, 18, ES2	2 3
4/035	... G.1	Cable adjusters	1	1, 16H, 18, ES2	6
4/263	... G.11	Throttle valve spring	1	1, 16H, 18, ES2	4
6/040	... G.29	Washer for jet block	1	1, 16H, 18, ES2	2
4/230	... G.6	Spring clip for needle	1	1, 16H, 18, ES2	6

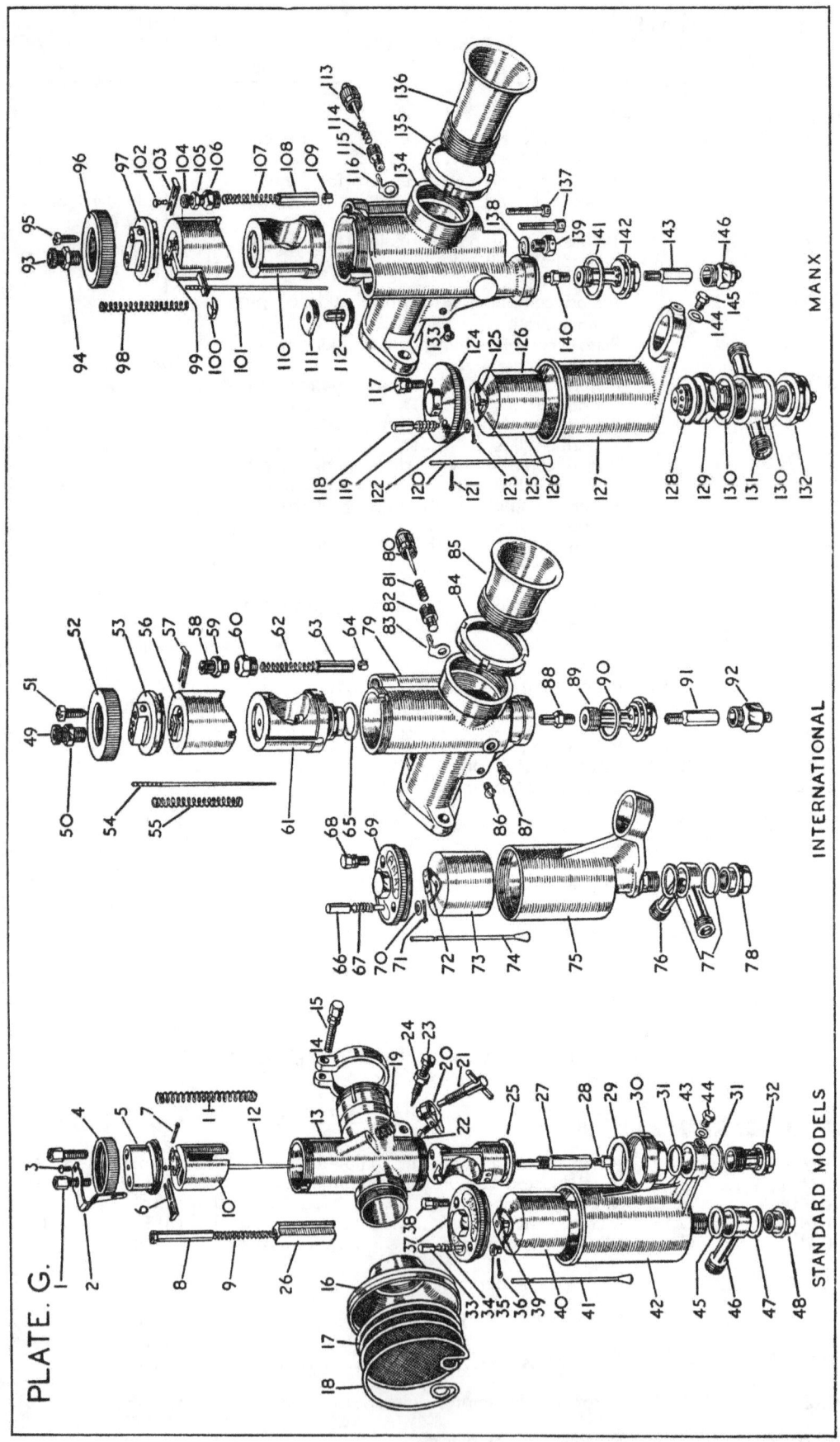

PART No.	PLATE No.	DESCRIPTION.	QTY.	USED ON.	PRICE EACH. £ s. d.
AMAL CARBURETTERS—cont.					
4/042	... G.28	Jet No. 160	1	1, 16H, 18, ES2	8
4/043	... G.32	Holding bolt	1	1, 16H, 18, ES2	3 0
6/045	... G.26	Air valve	1	1, 16H, 18, ES2	3 9
4/046	... G.9	Air valve spring	1	1, 16H, 18, ES2	4
6/047	... G.8	Air valve guide	1	1, 16H, 18, ES2	1 0
6/042	... G.10	Throttle valve 6/5	1	1, 16H, 18, ES2	6 0
6/052	... G.10	Throttle valve 6/4	1	18, ES2	6 0
4/053	... G.31	Holding bolt washer	1	1, 16H, 18, ES2	2
206/058	... G.25	Jet block and barrel complete	1	1, 16H	7 6
206/059	... G.25	Jet block and barrel complete	1	18, ES2	7 6
4/060	... G.7	Split cotter for throttle valve	1	1, 16H, 18, ES2	1
4/061	... G.27	Needle jet	1	1, 16H, 18, ES2	2 6
6/065	... G.12	Needle	1	1, 16H, 18, ES2	2 0
13/129	... G.23	Air adjusting screw	1	1, 16H, 18, ES2	9
16/010	... G.24	Air adjusting screw locknut	1	1, 16H, 18, ES2	2
4/235	... G.2	Spring clip for top	1	1, 16H, 18, ES2	9
4/241	... G.3	Screw for spring clip	1	1, 16H, 18, ES2	2
15/2546	... G.21	Throttle stop screw	1	1, 16H, 18, ES2	1 2
15/1860	... G.20	Throttle stop body	1	1, 16H, 18, ES2	1 2
13/203	... G.19	Spring	1	1, 16H, 18, ES2	4
15/1988	... G.22	Screw	1	1, 16H, 18, ES2	1
30/109	... G.16	Air intake body	1	1, 16H, 18, ES2	3 5
30/080	... G.18	Air intake gauze spring clip	1	1, 16H, 18, ES2	1 2
6/201	... G.14	Outlet clip	1	1, 16H, 18, ES2	2 6
4/048	... G.15	Outlet clip pin	1	1, 16H, 18, ES2	6
30/110	... G.17	Air intake gauze complete	2	1, 16H, 18, ES2	1 6
FLOAT CHAMBER.					
64/156B	... G.42	Float chamber body	1	1, 16H, 18, ES2	14 0
14/208B	... G.37	Float chamber cover	1	1, 16H, 18, ES2	3 9
14/014R	... G.39	Bow spring for float	1	1, 16H, 18, ES2	4
14/015	... G.40	Float	1	1, 16H, 18, ES2	3 9
14/021	... G.38	Cover locking screw	1	1, 16H, 18, ES2	4
14/024	... G.41	Needle complete	1	1, 16H, 18, ES2	1 6
14/209	... G.33	Tickler	1	1, 16H, 18, ES2	10
14/210	... G.35	Tickler stop	1	1, 16H, 18, ES2	9

PART No.	PLATE No.	DESCRIPTION.	QTY.	USED ON.	PRICE EACH. £ s. d.
FLOAT CHAMBER—cont.					
14/032	G.34	Tickler spring	1	1, 16H, 18, ES2	2
14/289	G.36	Tickler cotter	1	1, 16H, 18, ES2	1
13/153	G.44	Plug screw	1	1, 16H, 18, ES2	3
14/039	G.43	Plug screw washer	1	1, 16H, 18, ES2	1
14/175	G.45	Needle seating washer	1	1, 16H, 18, ES2	2
14/035	G.46	Banjo	1	1, 16H, 18, ES2	3 0
14/036	G.48	Banjo nut	1	1, 16H, 18, ES2	9
14/037	G.47	Banjo nut washer	1	1, 16H, 18, ES2	2
1BE	...	Float chamber complete	1	1, 16H, 18, ES2	1 7 0

TYPE 10 T.T. CARBURETTER. Models 30 and 40 International.

PART No.	PLATE No.	DESCRIPTION.	QTY.	USED ON.	PRICE EACH. £ s. d.
10TT/30	...	Carburetter complete	1	30	7 3 0
10TT/40	...	Carburetter complete	1	40	7 3 0
175/043	G.79	Mixing chamber body	1	30	2 5 0
175/060	G.79	Mixing chamber body	1	40	2 5 0
TT/3334	G.53	Mixing chamber top	1	30, 40	3 3
TT/3338	G.52	Mixing chamber cap	1	30, 40	3 3
TT/2626	G.58	Air cable adjuster	1	30, 40	6
TT/2627	G.59	Air cable adjuster locknut	1	30, 40	2
TT/3360	G.49	Throttle cable adjuster	1	30, 40	6
TT/3369	G.50	Throttle cable adjuster locknut	1	30, 40	2
TT/3367	G.51	Adjusting screw for lock plunger	1	30, 40	2
TT/2507	G.60	Air barrel top	1	30, 40	10
175/108	G.61	Choke adaptor 1⅛in. bore	Machined in position with mixing chamber body, which should be sent to Amal Ltd.	1	30, 40	15 0
175/101	G.61	Choke adaptor 1 3/16 in. bore		1	30, 40	15 0
TT/3326	G.88	Main jet	1	30, 40	1 6
TT/3970	G.91	Needle jet	1	30, 40	2 6
TT/3971	G.54	Jet needle	1	30, 40	2 0
4/230	G.57	Jet needle clip	1	30, 40	6
134/104	G.56	Throttle valve (please state no. of cut-way)	1	30, 40	6 6
TT/2558	G.55	Throttle valve spring	1	30, 40	4
TT/2502	G.63	Air valve	1	30, 40	1 6
TT/2558	G.62	Air valve spring	1	30, 40	4
15/625	G.89	Jet holder	1	30, 40	3 9
TT/3348	G.92	Jet holder plug screw	1	30, 40	9
134/107	G.65	Adaptor washer	1	30, 40	2
36/006	G.90	Float chamber arm washer	1	30, 40	2
TT/2981	G.80	Pilot needle	1	30, 40	1 6
TT/2966	G.82	Pilot needle insert	1	30, 40	1 6
TT/2980	G.81	Pilot needle spring	1	30, 40	3
TT/2982	G.83	Pilot needle spring catch	1	30, 40	2
TT/2503	G.64	Nipple holder for air valve	1	30, 40	2
TT/2403	G.86	Small plug screw	1	30, 40	3
134/105	G.87	Adaptor location peg	1	30, 40	4
175/118	G.85	Air intake tube 1⅛in. bore	Machined in position with mixing chamber body, which should be sent to Amal Ltd.	1	30, 40	7 6
185/121	G.85	Air intake tube 1 5/32 in. bore		1	30, 40	7 6
175/117	G.85	Air intake tube 1 3/16 in. bore		1	30, 40	7 6
175/119	G.84	Lock ring for air intake tube	1	30, 40	3 0
14/314	G.75	Float chamber body only	1	30, 40	1 10 0
14/138	G.69	Cover complete	1	30, 40	3 9
14/021	G.68	Cover lock screw	1	30, 40	4
14/031	G.66	Tickler	1	30, 40	10
14/032	G.67	Tickler spring	1	30, 40	2

PART No.	PLATE No.	DESCRIPTION.	QTY.	USED ON.	PRICE EACH. £ s. d.

TYPE 10 T.T. CARBURETTER. Models 30 and 40 International—cont.

PART No.	PLATE No.	DESCRIPTION.	QTY.	USED ON.	£	s.	d.
14/033	G.71	Tickler cotter pin	1	30, 40			1
14/189	G.70	Tickler washer	1	30, 40			1
14/0245	G.74	Float needle	1	30, 40		1	6
14/017	G.73	Float	1	30, 40		3	9
14/279	G.72	Float bow spring	1	30, 40			4
14/173	G.76	Banjo	1	30, 40		3	0
14/037	G.77	Washer for banjo	2	30, 40			2
14/036	G.78	Banjo nut	1	30, 40			9

REMOTE NEEDLE TYPE CARBURETTER. Models 30 and 40 Manx.

PART No.	PLATE No.	DESCRIPTION.	QTY.	USED ON.	£	s.	d.
RN/30M		Carburetter complete	1	30M	8	4	0
RN/40M		Carburetter complete	1	40M	8	4	0
185/060	G.134	Mixing chamber body	1	40M	2	15	0
185/281	G.134	Mixing chamber body	1	30M	2	15	0
TT/3334	G.97	Mixing chamber top	1	30M, 40M		3	3
185/108	G.96	Mixing chamber cap	1	30M, 40M		3	3
TT/2626	G.104	Air cable adjuster	1	30M, 40M			6
TT/2627	G.105	Air cable adjuster locknut	1	30M, 40M			2
TT/3360	G.93	Throttle cable adjuster	1	30M, 40M			6
TT/3369	G.94	Throttle cable adjuster locknut	1	30M, 40M			2
TT/3367	G.95	Adjusting screw for mixing chamber top	1	30M, 40M			2
185/107	G.110	Choke adaptor 1⅛in. bore	1	30M, 40M		15	0
185/294	G.110	Choke adaptor 1$\frac{5}{32}$in. bore	1	30M, 40M		15	0
185/295	G.110	Choke adaptor 1$\frac{3}{16}$in. bore	1	30M, 40M		15	0
TT/3326	G.143	Main jet	1	30M, 40M		1	6
185/109	G.140	Needle jet	1	30M, 40M		2	6
185/119	G.101	Jet needle	1	30M, 40M		2	0
185/150	G.100	Jet needle clip	1	30M, 40M			2
134/107	G.99	Throttle valve complete w/Needle Carrier (please state cut-away no.)	1	30M, 40M		8	0
TT/2558	G.98	Throttle valve spring	1	30M, 40M			4
15/625	G.142	Jet holder	1	30M, 40M		3	9
TT/3348	G.146	Jet holder plug	1	30M, 40M			9
185/137	G.139	Mixing chamber base plug	1	30M, 40M			9
59/027	G.138	Mixing chamber base plug washer	1	30M, 40M			2
185/110		Primary choke	1	30M, 40M		2	0
185/138	G.137	Choke adaptor screw	1	30M, 40M			6
TT/2502	G.108	Air valve	1	30M, 40M		1	6
TT/2558	G.107	Air valve spring	1	30M, 40M			4
TT/2507	G.106	Air barrel top	1	30M, 40M			10
TT/2403	G.133	Small plug screw	1	30M, 40M			3
TT/2503	G.109	Air valve nipple holder	1	30M, 40M			2
185/106	G.112	Needle chamber top cap	1	30M, 40M		1	6
185/120	G.111	Needle chamber top cap spring	1	30M, 40M			9
185/105	G.102	Cable stop peg	1	30M, 40M			3
185/141	G.103	Needle clip for cable stop peg	1	30M, 40M			6
TT/2981	G.113	Pilot adjuster needle	1	30M, 40M		1	6
TT/2966	G.115	Pilot adjuster needle inserts	1	30M, 40M		1	6
TT/2980	G.114	Pilot adjuster spring	1	30M, 40M			3
TT/2982	G.116	Pilot adjuster catch	1	30M, 40M			2
175/108	G.136	Air intake tube 1⅛in. bore	1	30M, 40M		7	6
185/121	G.136	Air intake tube 1$\frac{5}{32}$in. bore	1	30M, 40M		7	6
175/101	G.136	Air intake tube 1$\frac{3}{16}$in. bore	1	30M, 40M		7	6
175/119	G.135	Air intake tube lock ring	1	30M, 40M		3	0
36/006	G.141	Washer for float chamber	2	30M, 40M			2
14/532		Float chamber complete	1	30M, 40M	2	7	6
14/225R	G.127	Float chamber body only	1	30M, 40M	1	7	0
14/138	G.124	Cover complete	1	30M, 40M		3	9
14/021	G.117	Cover lock screw	1	30M, 40M			4
14/031	G.118	Tickler	1	30M, 40M			10
14/032	G.119	Tickler spring	1	30M, 40M			2
14/033	G.123	Tickler cotter pin	1	30M, 40M			1

Note: Choke adaptors and Air intake tubes are "Machined in position with mixing chamber body, which should be sent to Amal Ltd."

PART No.	PLATE No.	DESCRIPTION.	QTY.	USED ON.	PRICE EACH. £ s. d.

REMOTE NEEDLE TYPE CARBURETTER. Models 30 and 40 Manx—cont.

Part No.	Plate No.	Description	Qty	Used On	£ s. d.
14/189	G.122	Tickler washer	1	30M, 40M	1
14/245	G.120	Float needle	1	30M, 40M	1 6
14/304	G.126	Float	1	30M, 40M	3 9
14/279	G.125	Float bow spring	1	30M, 40M	4
193/084	G.121	Float securing cotter pin	1	30M, 40M	1
14/253	G.129	Needle valve seating	1	30M, 40M	5 0
14/252	G.128	Needle valve seating washer	1	30M, 40M	2
14/232	G.145	Body base plug screw	1	30M, 40M	6
14/241	G.144	Washer for body base plug screw	1	30M, 40M	1
14/251	G.131	Banjo	1	30M, 40M	7 6
14/275	G.130	Washer for banjo	2	30M, 40M	2
14/255	G.132	Banjo nut	1	30M, 40M	1 6

EXHAUST PIPES AND FITTINGS.

Part No.	Plate No.	Description	Qty	Used On	£ s. d.
C7/165	H.38	Exhaust pipe	1	1	1 5 0
C2/165	H.38	Exhaust pipe only	1	16H	1 5 0
C3/165	H.41	Exhaust pipe only	1	18, ES2	1 5 0
A11/165	H.41	Exhaust pipe only	1	30, 40	1 5 0
A11M/165	H.41	Exhaust pipe only	1	30M, 40M	1 15 0
A3/166	H.39	Exhaust pipe flange washer (cylinder head)	1	18, ES2, 30, 30M, 40, 40M	6
A3/167	H.40	Exhaust pipe flange locking nut (cylinder head)	1	18, ES2, 30, 40	8 0
A11M/167	H.40	Exhaust pipe flange locking nut (cylinder head)	1	30M, 40M	8 0
A2/168	H.45	Exhaust pipe clip	1	1, 16H	2 6
12343	H.47	Exhaust pipe clip bolt	1	1, 16H	8
E3229	H.46	Exhaust pipe clip bolt nut	1	1, 16H	4
10245	H.48	Exhaust pipe attachment bolt	1	1, 16H	3 4
E3238	H.50	Exhaust pipe attachment bolt nut	1	1, 16H	5
E5375	H.49	Exhaust pipe attachment bolt washer	1	1, 16H	3
A11M/168	H.51	Exhaust pipe clip	1	30M, 40M	5 0
E3798	H.52	Exhaust pipe clip bolt	1	30M, 40M	8
E3223	H.53	Exhaust pipe clip bolt nut	1	30M, 40M	4
E5456	H.54	Exhaust pipe clip bolt washer	2	30M, 40M	4
E4010	H.55	Exhaust pipe clip engine plate attachment bolt	1	30M, 40M	1 0
E3224	H.57	Exhaust pipe clip engine plate attachment bolt nut	1	30M, 40M	4
E5376	H.56	Exhaust pipe clip engine plate attachment bolt washer	2	30M, 40M	3

SILENCER MEGAPHONE AND FITTINGS.

Part No.	Plate No.	Description	Qty	Used On	£ s. d.
A2/169	H.42	Silencer	1	1, 16H, 18	3 10 0
B4/169	H.42	Silencer	1	ES2, 30, 40	3 10 0
13037		Silencer support stud	1	1, 16H, 18	2 8
E3224		Silencer support stud nut	1	1, 16H, 18	4
E4010	H.43	Silencer sleeve bolt	1	1, 16H, 18, ES2, 30, 40	1 0
E5376	H.44	Silencer sleeve bolt washer	1	1, 16H, 18, ES2, 30, 40	3
E3801	H.58	Silencer clip bolt	1	1, 16H, 18, ES2, 30, 40	5
E3231	H.59	Silencer clip bolt nut	1	1, 16H, 18, ES2, 30, 40	4
11796		Silencer clip bolt nut washer	1	1, 16H, 18, ES2, 30, 40	3
A11M/167	H.35	Megaphone	1	30M	1 15 0
A10M/167	H.35	Megaphone	1	40M	1 15 0
11307	H.34	Megaphone frame support stud	1	30M, 40M	3 6
E4010	H.32	Megaphone frame support stud bolt	1	30M, 40M	1 0

PLATE. H.

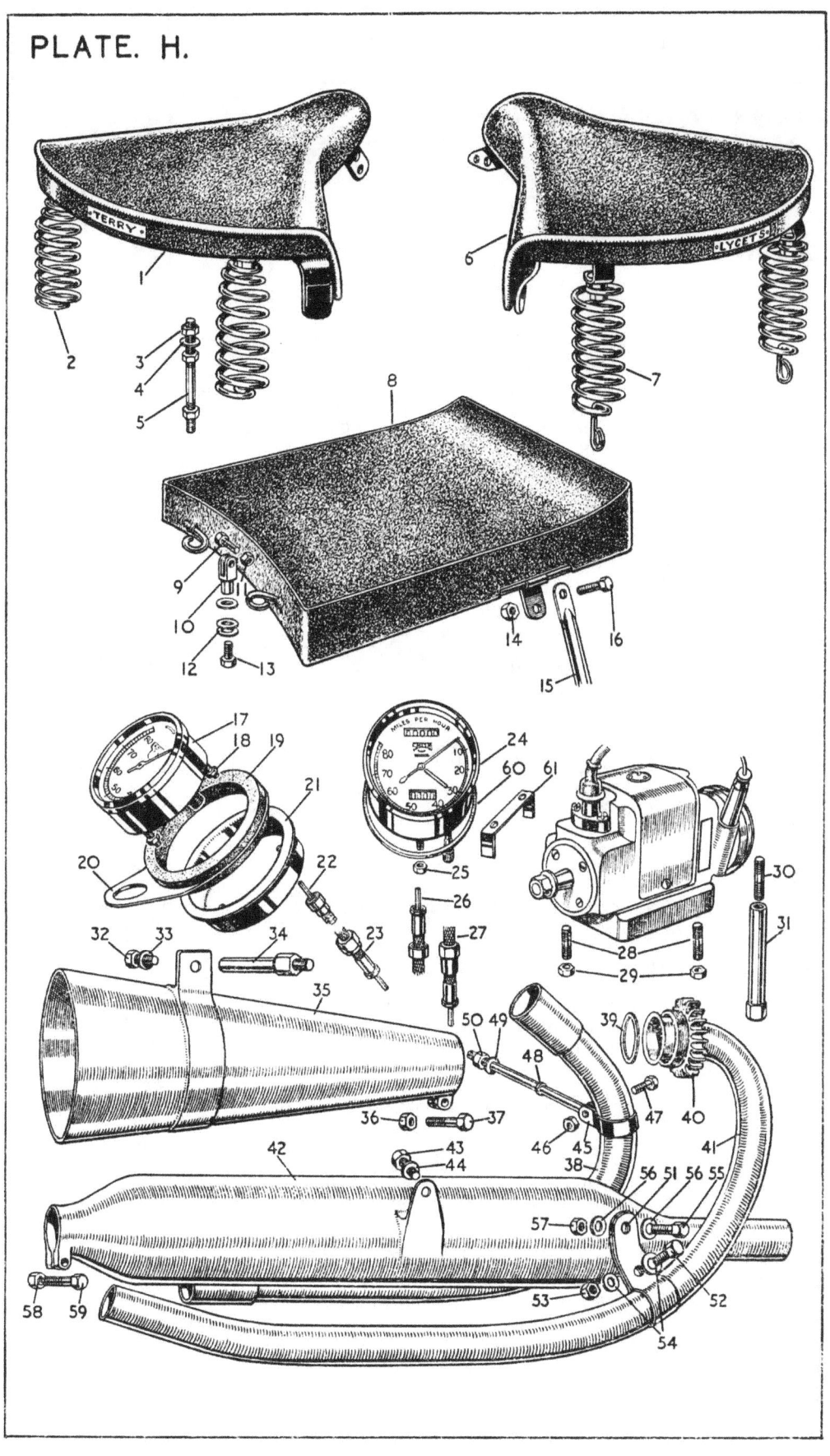

PART No	PLATE No.	DESCRIPTION.	QTY.	USED ON.	PRICE EACH. £ s. d.

SILENCER MEGAPHONE AND FITTINGS—cont.

PART No	PLATE No.	DESCRIPTION.	QTY.	USED ON.	£	s.	d.
E5376	H.33	Megaphone frame support stud bolt washer	1	30M, 40M			3
E3801	H.37	Megaphone clip bolt	1	30M, 40M			5
E3231	H.36	Megaphone clip bolt nut	1	30M, 40M			4
11796		Megaphone clip bolt washer	1	30M, 40M			3

NORTON ROAD-HOLDER FORKS AND STEERING DAMPER.

PART No	PLATE No.	DESCRIPTION.	QTY.	USED ON.	£	s.	d.
B11M/170		Road-holder fork complete	1	30M, 40M	25	0	0
B2/170		Road-holder fork complete	1	30, 40, 1, 16H, 18, ES2	25	0	0
B2/605	J.7	Main tube	2	All Models		2	0
B2/606	J.29	Main tube bottom bush	2	All Models		6	6
B2/607	J.31	Main tube bottom bush locking nut	2	All Models		3	9
B2/608	J.30	Main tube bottom bush locking nut washer	2	All Models			3
B2/609	J.28	Fork end (left-hand)	1	30, 40, 1, 16H, 18, ES2		5	0
B11M/609	J.28	Fork end (left-hand)	1	30M, 40M	5	5	0
13567	J.39	Fork end hub spindle pinch stud off side	1	All Models			6
13433	J.39	Fork end hub spindle pinch stud near side	1	All Models			6
13434	J.41	Fork end hub spindle pinch stud nut	2	All Models			4
11776	J.40	Pinch stud washer	1	All Models			3
B2/611	J.27	Fork end (right-hand)	1	30, 40, 1, 16H, 18, ES2	5	5	0
B11M/611	J.27	Fork end (right-hand)	1	30M, 40M	5	5	0
B2/612	J.38	Fork end drain plug	2	All Models			4
B2/613	J.37	Fork end drain plug washer	2	All Models			2
B2/614	J.26	Main tube top sleeve bush	2	All Models		12	6
B2/615	J.22	Main tube top sleeve bush locking ring	2	All Models		7	6
B2/616	J.24	Super oil seal	2	All Models		6	6
B2/617	J.25	Super oil seal paper washer	2	All Models			2
B2/618	J.17	Buffer spring	2	All Models		6	6
B2/619	J.19	Buffer spring leather washer (top)	2	All Models			6
B2/620	J.18	Main spring	2	All Models		15	0
B2/621	J.21	Main spring leather washer (bottom)	2	All Models			3
B2/622	J.14	Spring cover tube (top)	2	All Models		4	0
B2/623	J.15	Spring cover tube top securing plate	2	All Models		1	0
B2/624	J.16	Spring cover tube top securing plate screw	6	All Models			3
B2/625	J.20	Spring cover tube (bottom)	2	All Models		6	6
B2/626	J.23	Spring cover tube (bottom) securing screw	4	All Models			2
B2/627	J.33	Oil damper rod	2	All Models		15	0
B2/628	J.34	Oil damper rod fibre washer	1	All Models			3
C2/629	J.36	Oil damper rod plain washer	1	All Models			3
C2/630	J.35	Oil damper rod bolt	1	All Models			3
B2/631	J.75	Speedometer panel	1	30, 40, 1, 16H, 18, ES2		7	6
B2/632	J.76	Speedometer panel control cable rubber grummett	2	30, 40, 1, 16H, 18, ES2			6
B2/633	J.2	Main tube filler and retaining plug	2	All Models		5	0
B2/634	J.3	Main tube filler and retaining plug washer	2	All Models			9
B2/635	J.6	Main tube top cover (left-hand)	1	30, 40, 1, 16H, 18, ES2	1	1	0
B11M/635		Main tube top cover (left-hand)	1	30M, 40M	1	1	0
B11M/636		Main tube top cover (right-hand)	1	30M, 40M	1	1	0
B2/636	J.5	Main tube top cover (right-hand)	1	30, 40, 1, 16H, 18, ES2	1	1	0
B2/637		Main tube top cover name plate	2	All Models		1	6
B2/638		Main tube top cover name plate rivet (per set 2)	2	All Models			3
B2/639	J.4	Main tube top cover rubber ring	2	All Models		1	6
B2/201	J.42	Steering damper adjuster	1	30, 40, 1, 16H, 18, ES2		6	0
B2/203	J.46	Steering damper adjuster rod	1	30, 40, 1, 16H, 18, ES2		2	0

PLATE. J.

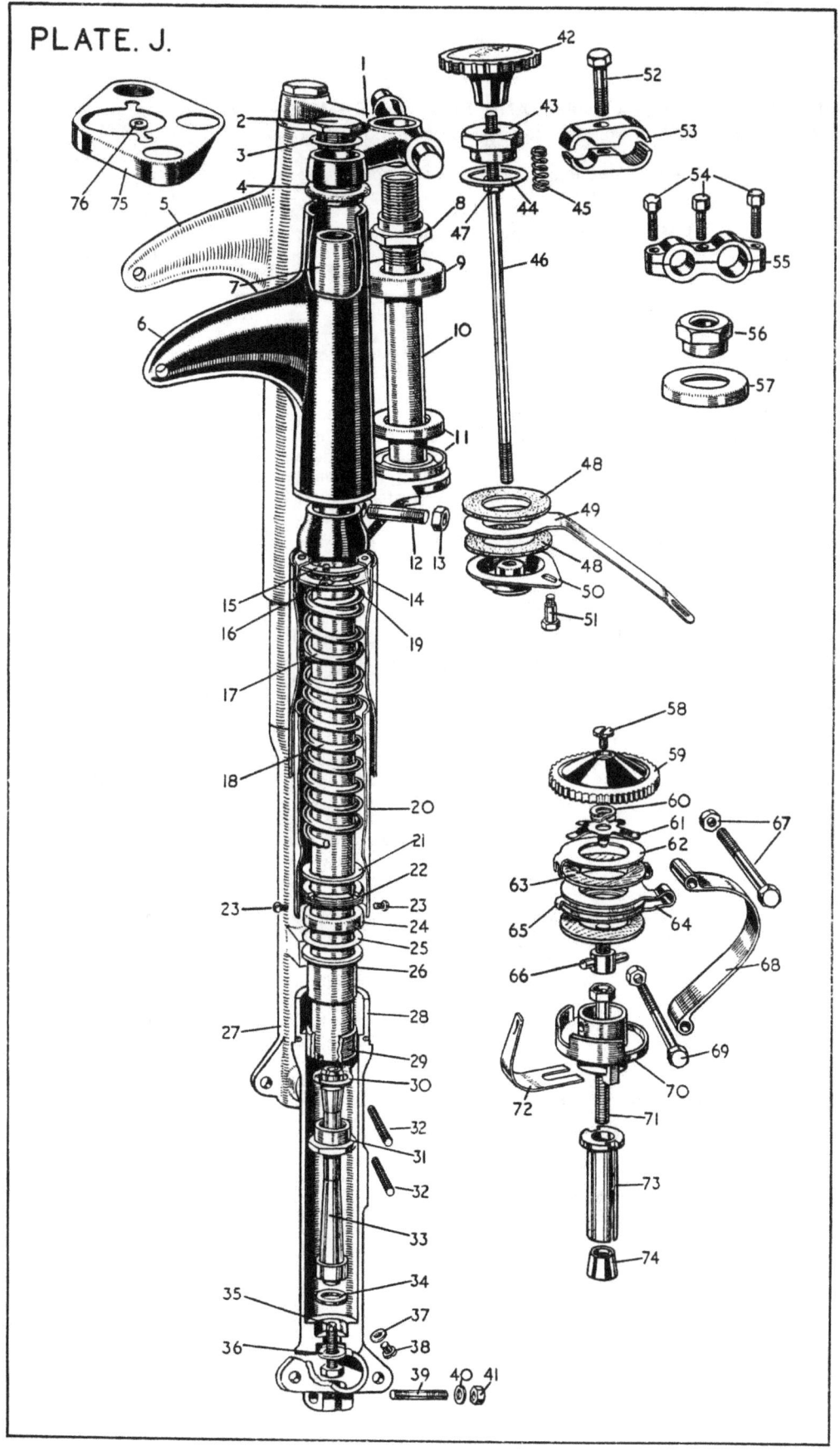

PART No	PLATE No.	DESCRIPTION.	QTY.	USED ON.	PRICE EACH. £ s. d.
NORTON ROAD-HOLDER FORKS AND STEERING DAMPER—cont.					
B2/202	J.45	Steering damper adjuster rod spring	1	30, 40, 1, 16H, 18, ES2	1 0
B2/640	J.47	Steering damper adjuster rod spring locknut	1	30, 40, 1, 16H, 18, ES2	4
B2/207	J.48	Steering damper friction disc	2	30, 40, 1, 16H, 18, ES2	3 0
B2/206	J.49	Steering damper friction and anchor plate	1	30, 40, 1, 16H, 18, ES2	6 6
B2/208	J.50	Steering damper bottom plate	1	30, 40, 1, 16H, 18, ES2	4 0
B2/641	J.51	Steering damper bottom plate bolt	1	30, 40, 1, 16H, 18, ES2	6
A11M/836		Andre steering damper complete	1	30M, 40M	3 7 6
A11M/201	J.59	Steering damper wheel	1	30M, 40M	8 0
A11M/874	J.72	Steering damper wheel spring clip	1	30M, 40M	2 0
A11M/733	J.58	Steering damper wheel locking screw	1	30M, 40M	1 6
A11M/734	J.60	Steering damper wheel spring washer	1	30M, 40M	2
A11M/735	J.61	Steering damper wheel star washer	1	30M, 40M	2 0
A11M/736	J.62	Steering damper wheel top plate	1	30M, 40M	3 0
A11M/207	J.63	Steering damper disc	4	30M, 40M	3 0
A11M/737	J.65	Steering damper friction plate	1	30M, 40M	2 0
A11M/738	J.64	Steering damper twin friction plate	1	30M, 40M	10 0
A11M/739	J.66	Steering damper screwed T piece	1	30M, 40M	3 0
A11M/740	J.70	Steering damper body	1	30M, 40M	15 0
A11M/741	J.67	Steering damper top clip bolt and nut	1	30M, 40M	3 0
A11M/742	J.68	Steering damper strap	1	30M, 40M	5 0
A11M/743	J.69	Steering damper strap bolt and nut (frame head attachment)	1	30M, 40M	2 0
A11M/744	J.73	Steering damper adaptor	1	30M, 40M	4 0
A11M/203	J.71	Steering damper adaptor centre bolt	1	30M, 40M	2 0
A11M/745	J.74	Steering damper adaptor centre bolt cone	1	30M, 40M	1 0
A11M/746		Steering damper adaptor centre bolt washer	1	30M, 40M	3
B2/172	J.10	Fork crown and column	1	All Models	3 0 0
B2/642	J.12	Fork crown main tube clamping stud	1	All Models	6
B2/643	J.13	Fork crown main tube clamping stud nut	1	All Models	4
B2/173	J.11	Fork crown or head clip ballrace	1	All Models	7 6
B2/644	J.9	Fork head clip ballrace cover	1	1, 16H, 18, ES2, 30, 40	1 0
A11M/644	J.57	Fork head clip ballrace cover	1	30M, 40M	1 0
B2/174	J.1	Fork head clip	1	All Models	1 12 6
B2/645	J.8	Fork head race adjuster nut	1	All Models	9 0
B2/205	J.43	Fork crown and column locknut	1	30, 40, 1, 16H, 18, ES2	5 0
B11M/205	J.56	Fork crown and column locknut	1	30M, 40M	5 0
B2/646	J.44	Fork crown and column locknut washer	1	All Models	1 0
HANDLEBAR AND FITTINGS.					
B2/211	K.48	Handlebar bend only	1	1, 16H, 18, ES2, 30, 40	1 14 7
A11M/211	K.69	Handlebar bend only	1	30M, 40M	1 14 7
B2/175	J.53	Handlebar clip, one only, complete	2	1, 16H, 18, ES2, 30, 40	14 0
A11M/175	J.55	Handlebar clip, one only, complete	2	30M, 40M	15 0
B2/176	J.52	Handlebar clip pin	2	1, 16H, 18, ES2, 30, 40	10
A11M/176	J.54	Handlebar clip pin	6	30M, 40M	10
MAGNETO AND AIR CONTROL LEVERS.					
A2/213		Magneto control lever assembly complete	1	1, 16H, 18, ES2, 30, 40	16 8
A11M/213		Magneto control lever assembly complete	1	30M, 40M	16 8
A2/214	K.16	Magneto control lever only	1	1, 16H, 18, ES2, 30, 40	6 0
A11M/214	K.58	Magneto control lever only	1	30M, 40M	6 0

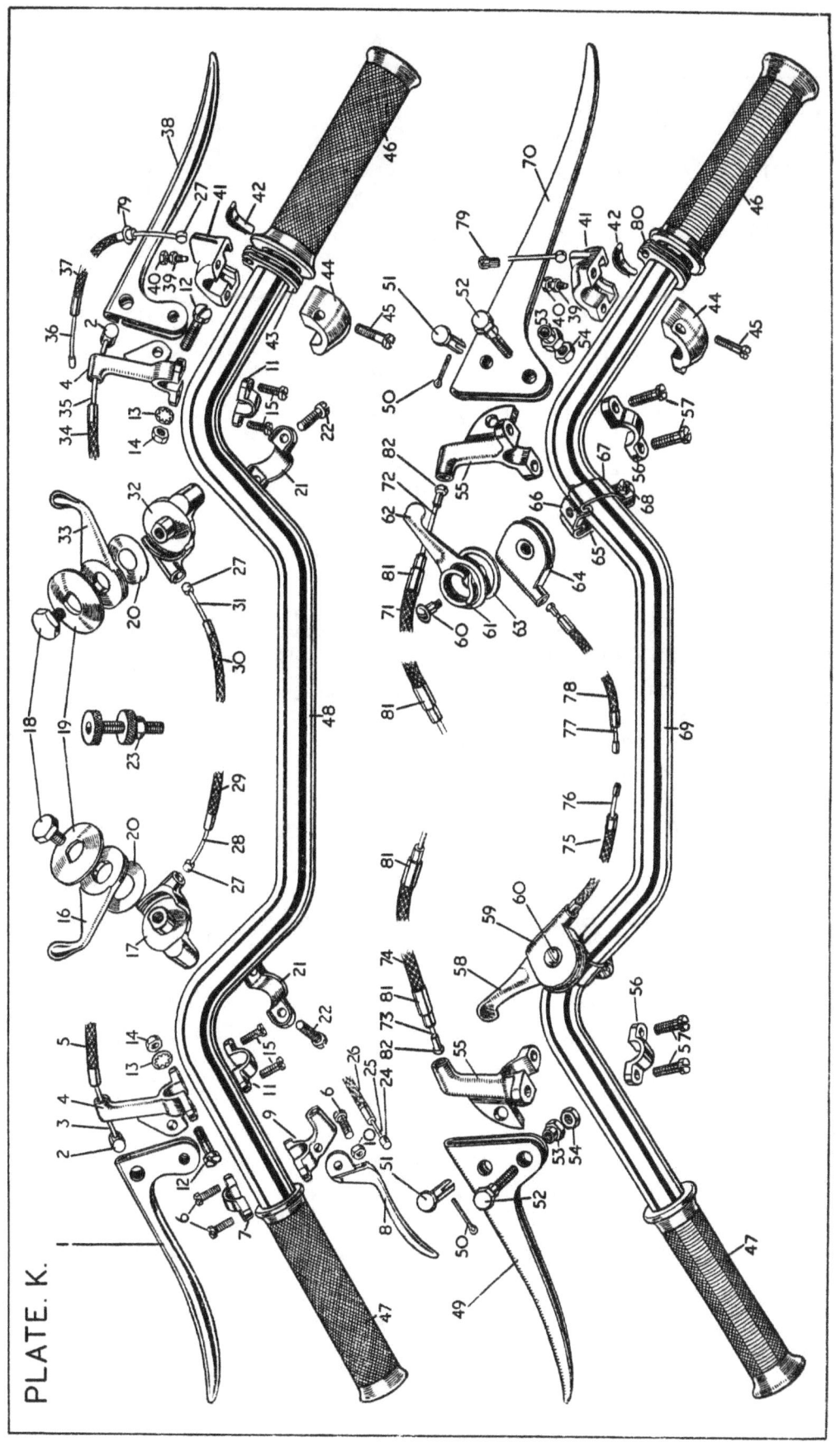

PLATE. K.

PART No.	PLATE No.	DESCRIPTION.	QTY.	USED ON.	PRICE EACH. £ s. d.
MAGNETO AND AIR CONTROL LEVERS—cont.					
A2/215	K.17	Magneto control lever body	1	1, 16H, 18, ES2, 30, 40	5 0
A11M/215	K.59	Magneto control lever body	1	30M, 40M	3 6
A2/216		Air control lever assembly complete	1	1, 16H, 18, ES2, 30, 40	16 8
A11M/216		Air control lever assembly complete	1	30M, 40M	16 8
A2/217	K.33	Air control lever only	1	1, 16H, 18, ES2, 30, 40	6 0
A11M/217	K.62	Air control lever only	1	30M, 40M	6 0
A2/218	K.32	Air control lever body	1	1, 16H, 18, ES2, 30, 40	5 0
A11M/218	K.64	Air control lever body	1	30M, 40M	3 6
A2/219	K.18	Air or magneto control lever top screw	2	1, 16H, 18, ES2, 30, 40	1 0
A11M/219	K.60	Air or magneto control lever top screw	2	30M, 40M	1 0
A2/220	K.19	Air or magneto control lever cap	2	1, 16H, 18, ES2, 30, 40	1 8
A11M/220	K.63	Air or magneto control lever cup	2	30M, 40M	9
A2/221	K.20	Air or magneto control lever cap spring washer	2	1, 16H, 18, ES2, 30, 40	4
A11M/221	K.61	Air or magneto control lever spring washer	2	30M, 40M	4
A2/222	K.21	Air or magneto control lever clip	2	1, 16H, 18, ES2, 30, 40	1 0
A11M/222(P)	K.67	Air or magneto control lever clip (plain)	2	30M, 40M	9
A11M/222(TH)	K.65	Air or magneto control lever clip (threaded)	2	30M, 40M	1 0
A2/223	K.22	Air or magneto control lever clip screw	2	1, 16H, 18, ES2, 30, 40	5
A11M/223	K.68	Air or magneto control lever clip screw	2	30M, 40M	5
A11M/747	K.66	Air or magneto control clip plate	2	30M, 40M	1 0

NOTE: Air and magneto levers of 1949 Models 1, 16H, 18, ES2, 30 and 40 are mounted on front brake and clutch levers respectively, dispensing with clip part number A2/222.

FRONT BRAKE AND CLUTCH CONTROL LEVERS.

PART No.	PLATE No.	DESCRIPTION.	QTY.	USED ON.	PRICE EACH. £ s. d.
A2/224		Front brake lever assembly complete	1	1, 16H, 18, ES2, 30, 40	19 0
A11M/224		Front brake lever assembly complete	1	30M, 40M	1 5 0
A2/225	K.38	Front brake lever only	1	1, 16H, 18, ES2, 30, 40	9 0
A11M/225	K.70	Front brake lever only	1	30M, 40M	12 6
A2/226		Clutch lever assembly complete	1	1, 16H, 18, ES2, 30, 40	19 0
A11M/226		Clutch lever assembly complete	1	30M, 40M	1 4 0
A2/227	K.1	Clutch lever only	1	1, 16H, 18, ES2, 30, 40	9 0
A11M/227	K.49	Clutch lever only	1	30M, 40M	11 6
A2/228	K.4	Front brake or clutch lever body	2	1, 16H, 18, ES2, 30, 40	7 0
D2/228 LH		Clutch lever body (1949)	1	1, 16H, 18, ES2, 30, 40	7 0
A11M/228	K.55	Front brake or clutch lever body	2	30M, 40M	10 6
A2/222	K.11	Front brake or clutch lever clip	2	1, 16H, 18, ES2, 30, 40	1 0
A11M/222	K.56	Front brake or clutch lever clip	2	30M, 40M	1 0
A2/223	K.15	Front brake or clutch lever clip screw	4	1, 16H, 18, ES2, 30, 40	5
D2/228 RH		Front brake lever body (1949)	1	1, 16H, 18, ES2, 30, 40	7 0
A11M/223	K.57	Front brake or clutch lever clip screw	4	30M, 40M	5
A2/229	K.12	Front brake or clutch lever pivot pin	2	1, 16H, 18, ES2, 30, 40	1 0
A11M/229	K.52	Front brake or clutch lever pivot pin	2	30M, 40M	1 0
A2/230	K.14	Front brake or clutch lever pivot pin nut	2	1, 16H, 18, ES2, 30, 40	3
A2/873	K.13	Front brake or clutch lever pivot pin washer	2	1, 16H, 18, ES2, 30, 40	2

PART No.	PLATE No.	DESCRIPTION.	QTY.	USED. ON.	PRICE EACH. £ s. d.

FRONT BRAKE AND CLUTCH CONTROL LEVERS—cont.

PART No.	PLATE No.	DESCRIPTION.	QTY.	USED ON.	£ s. d.
A11M/230(L)	K.53	Front brake or clutch lever pivot pin nut (large)	2	30M, 40M	4
A11M/230(S)	K.54	Front brake or clutch lever pivot pin nut (small)	2	30M, 40M	3
A11M/231	K.81	Front brake or clutch cable ferrule	4	30M, 40M	1 0

EXHAUST LIFTER CONTROL LEVER.

A2/233	...	Exhaust valve lifter lever assembly complete	1	1, 16H, 18, ES2, 30, 40	14 6
A2/234	K.8	Exhaust valve lifter lever only	1	1, 16H, 18, ES2, 30, 40	5 0
A2/235	K.9	Exhaust valve lifter lever body	1	1, 16H, 18, ES2, 30, 40	5 0
A2/222	K.7	Exhaust valve lifter lever clip	1	1, 16H, 18, ES2, 30, 40	1 0
A2/223	K.6	Exhaust valve lifter lever pivot pin or clip screw	3	1, 16H, 18, ES2, 30, 40	5
A2/236	K.10	Exhaust valve lifter lever pivot pin nut	1	1, 16H, 18, ES2, 30, 40	4

TWIST GRIP.

A2/237	...	Twist grip complete	1	All Models	1 2 3
A11M/237	...	Twist grip complete	1	30M, 40M	1 2 3
A2/238	K.41	Twist grip top half clip	1	All Models	6 0
A2/239	K.44	Twist grip bottom half clip	1	All Models	6 0
A2/240	K.45	Twist grip clip fixing pin	2	All Models	8
A2/241	K.43	Twist grip control barrel	1	1, 16H, 18, ES2, 30, 40	7 0
A11M/241	K.80	Twist grip control barrel	1	30M, 40M	7 0
A2/242	K.40	Twist grip control barrel adjusting screw	1	All Models	5
A2/236	K.39	Twist grip control barrel adjusting screw nut	1	All Models	4
A2/243	K.42	Twist grip control barrel adjusting screw spring	1	All Models	1 0
A2/244	K.79	Twist grip cable stop	1	1, 16H, 18, ES2, 30, 40	8
A11M/244	K.78	Twist grip cable stop	1	30M, 40M	8
A2/245	K.46	Twist grip rubber	1	All Models	3 8
A2/246	K.47	Dummy grip to match twist grip	1	All Models	3 8

CONTROL CABLE ADJUSTERS AND NIPPLES.

A2/247	P.66/K.23	Front brake or clutch cable adjuster	2	All Models	5 0
A2/248	C.41/F.70	Exhaust cable adjuster	1	1, 16H, 18, ES2, 30, 40	1 8
A2/249	K.27	Magneto, air or throttle control cable nipple (handlebar end)	3	1, 16H, 18, ES2, 30, 40	3
A11M/249	...	Magneto, air or throttle control cable nipple (handlebar end)	1	30M, 40M	3
A2/250	...	Magneto control cable nipple, magneto end	1	1, 16H, 18, ES2, 30, 40	3
A11M/250	...	Magneto control cable nipple, magneto end	1	30M, 40M	3
A2/251	...	Air or throttle control cable nipple carburetter end	2	All Models	3
A2/252	K.2	Clutch or front brake control cable nipple handlebar end	2	1, 16H, 18, ES2, 30, 40	1 0
A11M/252	K.82	Clutch or front brake cable nipple handlebar end	2	30M, 40M	3
A11M/819	K.51	Clutch or front brake lever cable nipple holder	2	30M, 40M	1 0
A11M/820	K.50	Clutch or front brake lever cable nipple holder cotter	2	30M, 40M	2

PART No.	PLATE No.	DESCRIPTION.	QTY.	USED ON.	PRICE EACH. £ s. d.
CONTROL CABLE ADJUSTERS AND NIPPLES—cont.					
A2/253	...	Clutch control cable nipple gearbox end ..	1	All Models	3
A2/254	...	Front brake (U clip end) or exhaust lifter control cable nipple (lifter end)	2	1, 16H, 18, ES2, 30, 40	3
A11M/254	...	Front brake (U clip end) cable nipple ...	1	30M, 40M	3
A2/255	K.24	Exhaust valve lifter control cable nipple (handlebar end)	1	1, 16H, 18, ES2, 30, 40	5
MAGNETO CONTROL CABLE.					
A2/256	...	Magneto control cable inner and outer complete	1	1, 16H, 18, ES2, 30, 40	7 0
A11M/256	...	Magneto control cable inner and outer complete	1	30M, 40M	10 0
A2/257	K.29	Magneto control cable outer	1	1, 16H, 18, ES2, 30, 40	4 0
A11M/257	K.75	Magneto control cable outer	1	30M, 40M	7 0
A2/258	K.28	Magneto control cable inner	1	1, 16H, 18, ES2, 30, 40	3 0
A11M/258	K.76	Magneto control cable inner	1	30M, 40M	3 0
AIR CONTROL CABLE.					
A2/259	...	Air control cable inner and outer complete	1	1, 16H, 18, ES2, 30, 40	4 6
A11M/259	...	Air control cable inner and outer complete	1	30M, 40M	6 6
A2/260	K.30	Air control cable outer	1	1, 16H, 18, ES2, 30, 40	2 6
A11M/260	K.78	Air control cable outer	1	30M, 40M	4 6
A2/261	K.31	Air control cable inner	1	1, 16H, 18, ES2, 30, 40	2 0
A11M/261	K.77	Air control cable inner	1	30M, 40M	2 0
THROTTLE CONTROL CABLE.					
A2/262	...	Throttle control cable complete	1	1, 16H, 18, ES2, 30, 40	4 6
A11M/262	...	Throttle control cable complete	1	30M, 40M	6 6
A2/263	K.37	Throttle control cable outer	1	1, 16H, 18, ES2, 30, 40	2 6
A11M/263	...	Throttle control cable outer	1	30M, 40M	4 6
A2/264	K.36	Throttle control cable inner	1	1, 16H, 18, ES2, 30, 40	2 0
A11M/264	...	Throttle control cable inner	1	30M, 40M	2 0
CLUTCH CONTROL CABLE.					
A2/265	...	Clutch control cable complete	1	1, 16H, 18, ES2, 30, 40	8 6
A11M/265	...	Clutch control cable complete	1	30M, 40M	12 6
A2/266	K.5	Clutch control cable outer	1	1, 16H, 18, ES2, 30, 40	5 0
A11M/266	K.74	Clutch control cable outer	1	30M, 40M	9 0
A2/267	K.3	Clutch control cable inner	1	1, 16H, 18, ES2, 30, 40	3 4
A11M/267	K.73	Clutch control cable inner	1	30M, 40M	3 6
FRONT BRAKE CONTROL CABLE.					
B2/268	...	Front brake control cable complete	1	1, 16H, 18, ES2, 30, 40	8 0
A11M/268	...	Front brake control cable complete	1	30M, 40M	12 6
B2/269	K.34	Front brake control cable outer	1	1, 16H, 18, ES2, 30, 40	5 0
A11M/269	K.71	Front brake control cable outer	1	30M, 40M	9 0

PART No.	PLATE No.	DESCRIPTION.	QTY.	USED ON.	PRICE EACH. £ s. d.
FRONT BRAKE CONTROL CABLE—cont.					
B2/270	K.35	Front brake control cable inner	1	1, 16H, 18, ES2, 30, 40	3 0
A11M/270	K.72	Front brake control cable inner	1	30M, 40M	3 6
A2/709	R.42	Front brake cable U clip	1	All Models	6
A2/427	R.43	Front brake cable U clip pin	1	All Models	4
A2/195	R.44	Front brake cable U clip pin cotter	1	All Models	2
EXHAUST CONTROL CABLE.					
A2/271		Exhaust lifter control cable complete	1	1, 16H, 18, ES2, 30, 40	7 0
A2/272	K.26	Exhaust lifter control cable outer	1	1, 16H, 18, ES2, 30, 40	4 0
A2/273	K.25	Exhaust lifter control cable inner	1	1, 16H, 18, ES2, 30, 40	3 0
PETROL TANKS AND FITTINGS.					
A2/274		Petrol tank	1	1, 16H, 18, ES2	12 5 0
A11/274		Petrol tank	1	30, 40	13 15 0
A11M/274		Petrol tank	1	30M, 40M	21 0 0
A2/275	L.23	Petrol tank platform packing washer (steel)	4	1, 16H, 18, ES2, 30, 40	4
A2/276	L.31	Petrol tank platform rubber washer	4	1, 16H, 18, ES2	6
A2/277	L.26	Petrol tank attachment bolt	4	1, 16H, 18, ES2, 30, 40	8
A2/278	L.24	Petrol tank attachment bolt rubber washer	4	1, 16H, 18, ES2	4
			8	30, 40	4
A2/279	L.25	Petrol tank attachment bolt rubber washer steel cup	4	1, 16H, 18, ES2, 30, 40	6
A11M/837	L.19	Petrol tank bolt front, long	2	30M, 40M	4 0
A11M/838	L.11	Petrol tank bolt rear, short (off side)	1	30M, 40M	2 6
A11M/839	L.10	Petrol tank bolt rear, long (near side)	1	30M, 40M	2 6
E3223	L.14	Petrol tank bolt nut (thick)	4	30M, 40M	4
E3231	L.15	Petrol tank bolt nut (thin)	4	30M, 40M	4
A11M/840	L.1	Petrol tank top rubber plug	4	30M, 40M	1 6
A2/279	L.6	Petrol tank rubber steel cup	8	30M, 40M	6
A11M/841	L.16	Petrol tank bottom rubber plug front and rear	4	30M, 40M	1 6
A11M/842	L.13	Petrol tank attachment bolt rubber washer (bottom)	4	30M, 40M	6
A11M/844	X.21	Petrol tank platform front (aluminium)	1	30M, 40M	10 0
13283	X.20	Petrol tank platform front frame securing bolt	3	30M, 40M	1 0
11796		Petrol tank platform front frame securing bolt washer	3	30M, 40M	3
A11/845	W.13	Petrol tank platform rear	1	30, 40	6 8
E6453	W.10	Petrol tank platform rear frame stud	3	30, 40	9
E3231	W.12	Petrol tank platform rear frame stud nut	3	30, 40	4
11791	W.11	Petrol tank platform rear frame stud washer	3	30, 40	3
A11M/845	X.16	Petrol tank platform rear	1	30M, 40M	6 8
E6749	X.14	Petrol tank platform rear frame stud	1	30M, 40M	9
12079	X.15	Petrol tank platform rear frame stud nut	1	30M, 40M	4
A11M/846	X.12	Petrol tank platform rear attachment bolt (near side) long	1	30M, 40M	2 3
A11M/847	X.13	Petrol tank platform rear attachment bolt short (off side)	1	30M, 40M	2 0
13263		Petrol tank platform rear attachment bolt nut	2	30M, 40M	4
A2/280	L.29	Petrol tank filler cap	1	1, 16H, 18, ES2	17 0
A11/280	L.20	Petrol tank filler cap	1	30, 40	17 0
A11M/280	L.3	Petrol tank filler cap	1	30M, 40M	19 6

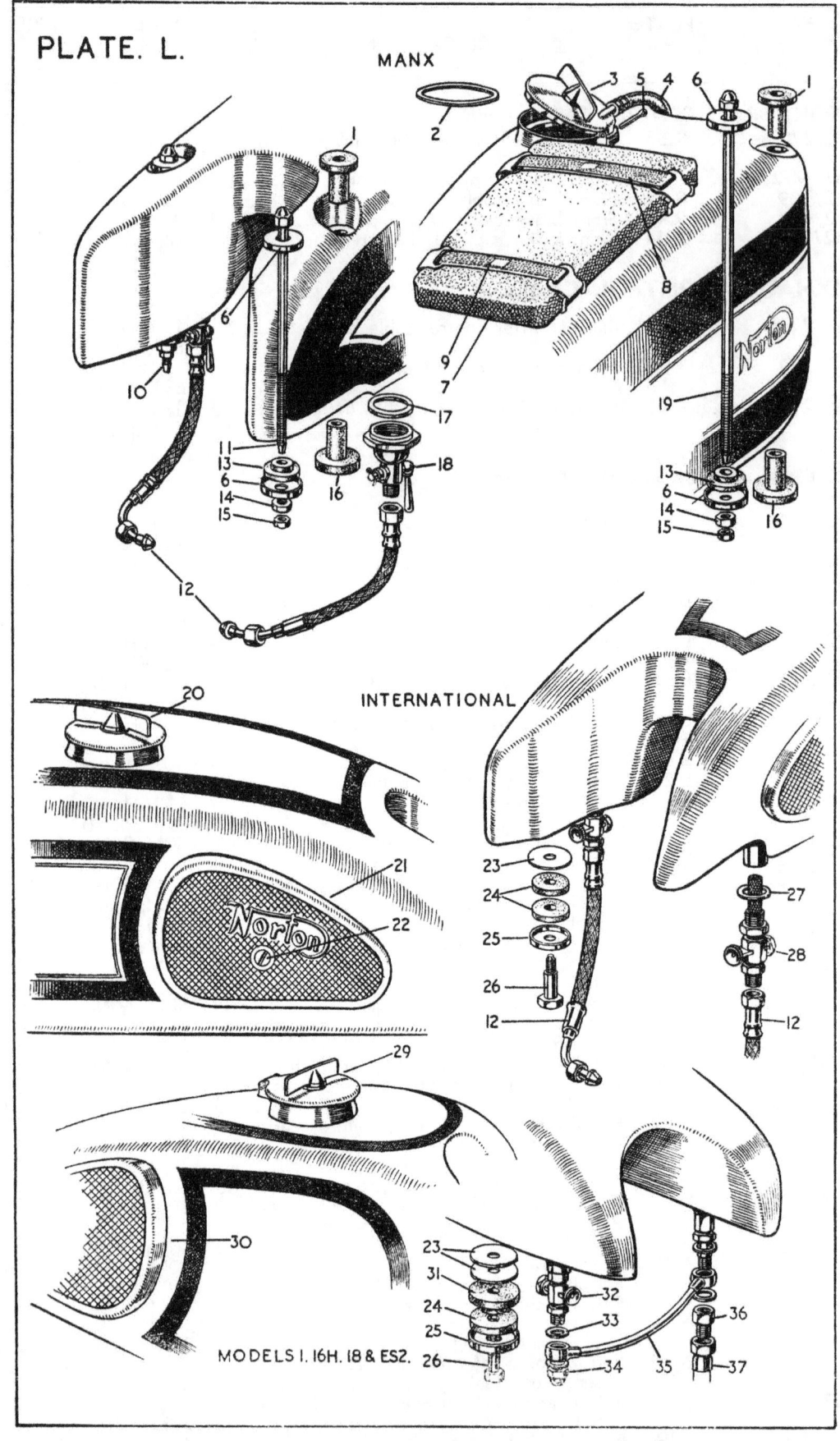

PLATE. L.

MANX

INTERNATIONAL

MODELS 1, 16H, 18 & ES2.

PART No.	PLATE No.	DESCRIPTION.	QTY.	USED. ON.	PRICE EACH. £ s. d.
PETROL TANKS AND FITTINGS—cont.					
A2/710	...	Petrol tank filler cap washer	1	1, 16H, 18, ES2	1 0
A11/710	L.2	Petrol tank filler cap washer	1	30, 30M, 40, 40M	1 3
A2/281	L.5	Petrol tank filler cap cotter pin	1	All Models	2
A11M/848	L.4	Petrol tank filler cap rubber vent tube	1	30M, 40M	4 6
A11M/849	...	Petrol tank filler cap rubber vent tube clip	1	30M, 40M	1 6
A11M/857	...	Petrol tank filler cap vent tube clip bolt	1	30M, 40M	8
E3222	...	Petrol tank filler cap vent tube clip bolt nut	1	30M, 40M	4
E5379	...	Petrol tank filler cap vent tube clip bolt washers	2	30M, 40M	3
A11M/850	L.7	Petrol tank chin pad	1	30M, 40M	7 6
A11M/851(L)	L.8	Petrol tank chin pad elastic (long)	1	30M, 40M	2 3
A11M/851(S)	L.9	Petrol tank chin pad elastic (short)	1	30M, 40M	2 3
A2/282	L.21	L.H. Knee grip (left-hand)	1	1, 16H, 18, ES2, 30, 40	6 6
A2/282	L.30	R.H. Knee grip (right-hand)	1	1, 16H, 18, ES2, 30, 40	6 6
E6629	L.22	Knee grip fixing pin	2	1, 16H, 18, ES2, 30, 40	5
B2/283	L.37	Petrol pipe (rubber)	1	1, 16H, 18, ES2	6 8
A2/284	L.35	Cross-over petrol pipe (copper)	1	1, 16H, 18, ES2	6 8
A2/285	L.32	Petrol tap complete with filter	2	1, 16H, 18, ES2	7 0
E5264	...	Petrol tap washer	2	1, 16H, 18, ES2	3
A2/286	L.36	Adaptor for petrol tap	1	1, 16H, 18, ES2	2 0
A2/287	L.34	Nut petrol tap (domed)	1	1, 16H, 18, ES2	1 0
A2/288	L.33	Petrol pipe banjo fibre washer	4	1, 16H, 18, ES2	3
A11/285	L.28	Petrol tap with filter	2	30, 40	7 0
E5264	L.27	Petrol tap washer	2	30, 40	3
A11M/285	L.18	Petrol tap with sump	2	30M, 40M	10 0
A11M/852	L.17	Petrol tap sump washer	2	30M, 40M	6
A11/283	L.12	Petrol pipe, left or right hand	2	30, 30M, 40, 40M	11 0
A2/289	...	Petrol tank frame top tube packing	2	All Models	4
OIL TANKS AND FITTINGS.					
C2/290	M.27	Oil tank less fittings	1	1, 16H, 18, ES2	4 0 0
A11/290	M.24	Oil tank less all fittings	1	30, 40	5 15 0
A11M/290	M.4	Oil tank less all fittings	1	30M, 40M	9 15 0
A2/291	M.26	Oil tank filler cap	1	1, 16H, 18, ES2	17 0
A11/291	M.19	Oil tank filler cap	1	30, 40	17 0
A11M/291	M.5	Oil tank filler cap	1	30M, 40M	18 0
A2/711	...	Oil tank filler cap washer	1	1, 16H, 18, ES2	1 0
A11/711	...	Oil tank filler cap washer	1	30, 30M, 40, 40M	1 0
A2/281	M.7	Oil tank filler cap cotter pin	1	All Models	2
A11M/853	M.6	Oil tank filler cap rubber vent tube	1	30M, 40M	4 6
A11M/849	...	Oil tank filler cap vent tube clip	1	30M, 40M	1 6
E3801	...	Oil tank vent tube clip bolt	1	30M, 40M	5
E3231	...	Oil tank vent tube clip bolt nut	1	30M, 40M	4
A2/275	...	Oil tank vent tube clip bolt large washer	2	30M, 40M	4
E5376	...	Oil tank vent tube clip bolt small washer	1	30M, 40M	3
A2/292	M.36	Oil tank union and filter	1	1, 16H, 18, ES2	7 0
A2/293	M.35	Oil tank union washer	1	1, 16H, 18, ES2	6

PART No.	PLATE No.	DESCRIPTION.	QTY.	USED ON.	PRICE EACH. £ s. d.
OIL TANK AND FITTINGS—cont.					
A2/294	...	Oil tank union packing washer	1	1, 16H, 18, ES2	3
A11/292	M.12	Oil tank union and filter	1	30, 30M, 40, 40M	7 0
A2/298	M.34	Oil tank air release pipe	1	1, 16H, 18, ES2	4 0
E3331	M.33	Oil tank air release pipe nut	1	1, 16H, 18, ES2	4
A11/298	M.20	Oil tank air release pipe	1	30, 40	4 0
E3331	M.21	Oil tank air release pipe nut	1	30, 40	4
A2/295	M.39	Oil tank delivery pipe with union nuts and nipples	1	1, 16H, 18, ES2	7 6
A2/296	M.37	Oil tank return pipe with union nuts and nipples	1	1, 16H	7 6
C3/296	M.38	Oil tank return pipe with union nuts and nipples	1	18, ES2	8 6
A2/712	M.41	Oil tank delivery pipe rubber connection	1	1, 16H, 18, ES2	2 3
C3/713	M.40	Oil tank return pipe rubber connection	1	1, 16H 18, ES2	2 6
A11/295	M.13	Oil tank delivery pipe	1	30, 30M, 40, 40M	17 0
A11/296	M.11	Oil tank return pipe	1	30, 30M, 40, 40M	13 0
12868	V.48	Oil tank attachment clip pin (mudguard bridge)	1	1, 16H, 18, ES2, 30, 40	5
B2/297	M.25	Oil tank top and voltage regulator attachment clip (mudguard bridge)	1	1, 16H, 18, ES2	2 6
E5105	V.50	Oil tank and rear mudguard distance piece	1	1, 16H, 18, ES2, 30, 40	6
E3223	V.51	Oil tank attachment clip pin nut	1	1, 16H, 18, ES2, 30, 40	4
E5456	V.49	Oil tank attachment clip pin washer	2	1, 16H, 18, ES2, 30, 40	3
A11/297	M.22	Oil tank top attachment clip	1	30, 40 ...	3 0
A11/843	M.23	Voltage regulator clip	1	30, 40 ...	1 6
A11M/297	M.3	Oil tank top attachment clip	1	30M, 40M	3 0
11070	V.67	Oil tank clip and rear mudguard seat stay attachment bolt	1	30M, 40M	1 0
E3223	V.65	Oil tank clip and rear mudguard seat stay Attachment bolt nut (thick)	1	30M, 40M	4
E3231	V.64	Oil tank clip and rear mudguard seat stay attachment bolt nut (thin)	1	30M, 40M	4
E5455	V.66	Oil tank clip and rear mudguard seat stay attachment bolt washer	2	30M, 40M	3
E5105	V.67	Oil tank clip and rear mudguard seat stay attachment bolt distance piece	1	30M, 40M	6
A2/278	V.68	Oil tank clip and rear mudguard seat stay attachment bolt rubber	1	30M, 40M	4
A2/279	V.69	Oil tank clip and rear mudguard seat stay attachment bolt rubber cup	1	30M, 40M	6
12342	M.1	Oil tank top attachment clip pin	2	30, 30M, 40, 40M	5
			1	1, 16H, 18, ES2	5
E5379	M.2	Oil tank top attachment clip pin washer	2	30, 30M, 40, 40M	3
			1	1, 16H, 18, ES2	3
E6745	M.17	Oil tank bottom fixing pin	2	30M, 40M	8
A2/278	M.15	Oil tank bottom rubber washer	4	30M, 40M	4
A2/279	M.16	Oil tank bottom rubber washer steel cup	2	30M, 40M	6
A2/275	M.14	Oil tank bottom steel washer	4	30M, 40M	4
E6453	M.28	Oil tank bottom stud	2	1, 16H, 18, ES2, 30, 40	6
E3223	M.30	Oil tank bottom stud nut	2	1, 16H, 18, ES2, 30, 40	4

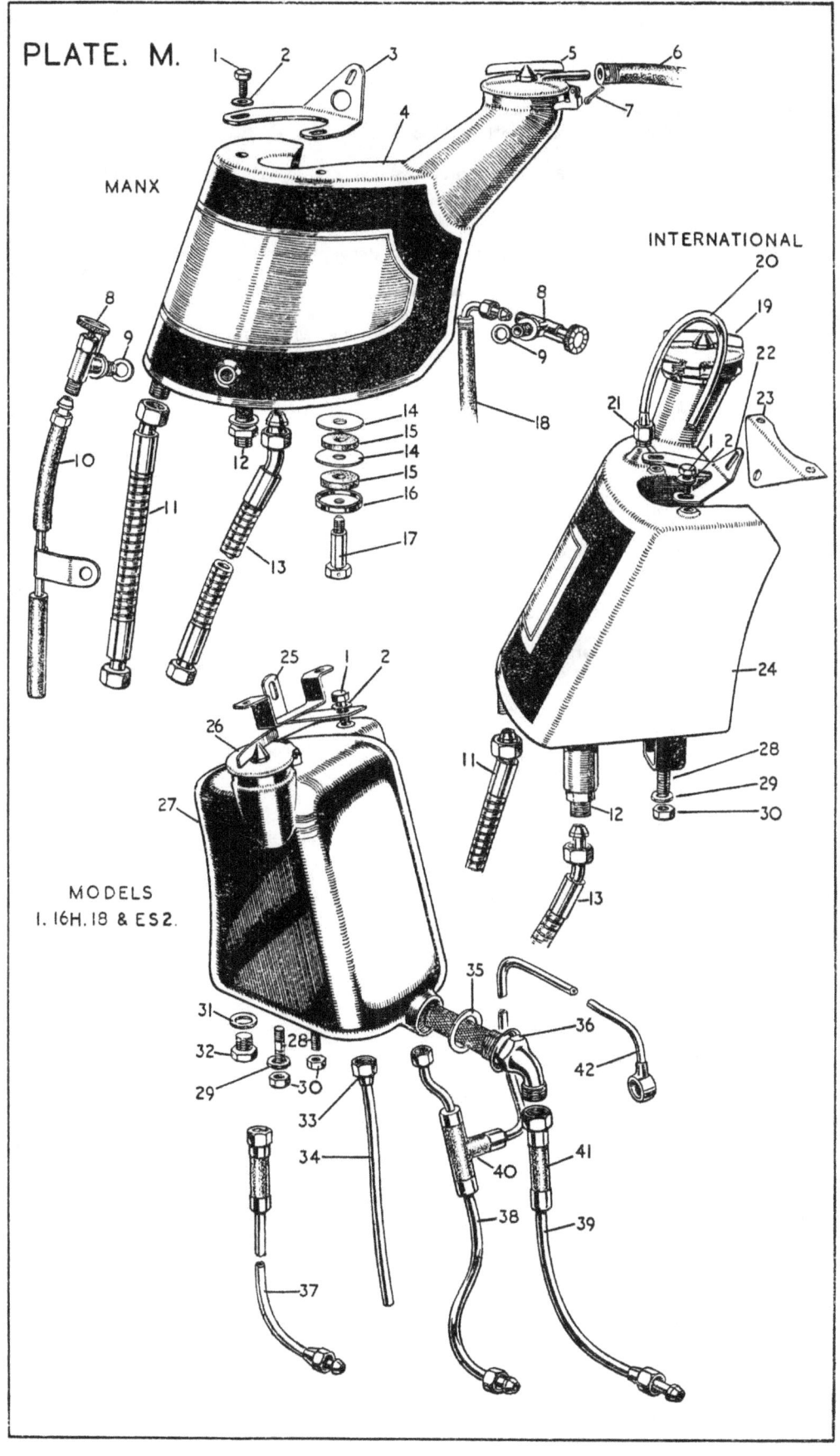

PART No.	PLATE No.	DESCRIPTION.	QTY.	USED ON.	PRICE EACH. £ s. d.
OIL TANKS AND FITTINGS—cont.					
E5456	M.29	Oil tank bottom stud washer	2	1, 16H, 18, ES2, 30, 40	3
E3336	M.32	Oil tank drain plug	1	1, 16H, 18, ES2	8
E5264	M.31	Oil tank drain plug washer	1	1, 16H, 18, ES2	3
A11M/854	M.8	Oil tank chain oiler tap less pipe (front or rear)	2	30M, 40M	12 6
A11M/880	M.9	Oil tank chain oiler tap washer	2	30M, 40M	3
A11M/855	M.10	Oil tank chain oiler tap pipe (front chain)	1	30M, 40M	4 6
A11M/856	M.18	Oil tank chain oiler tap pipe with clip (rear chain)	1	30M, 40M	5 6
GEARBOX SHELL.					
A2/299	N.31	Gearbox shell with studs	1	1, 16H, 18, ES2, 30, 40	6 19 0
A11M/299	N.31	Gearbox shell with studs	1	30M, 40M	6 19 0
A2/300	P.40	Gearbox end cover, inner	1	1, 16H, 18, ES2, 30, 40	2 15 0
B2/301	P.17	Gearbox end cover, outer	1	1, 16H, 18, ES2, 30, 40	1 0 0
A11M/301	Q.31	Gearbox end cover	1	30M, 40M	2 15 0
B2/302	P.8	Gearbox clutch worm inspection cover	1	1, 16H, 18, ES2, 30, 40	7 6
B2/647	P.7	Gearbox clutch worm inspection cover screw	2	1, 16H, 18, ES2, 30, 40	6
A2/303	N.30	Paper washer		All Models	4
A2/304	N.43	Gearbox cover stud	6	1, 16H, 18, ES2, 30, 40	5
A2/305	N.43	Gearbox cover stud	7	30M, 40M	5
A2/306	N.42	Gearbox cover stud (bottom)	1	1, 16H, 18, ES2, 30, 40	8
A2/307	P.14	Gearbox cover stud nut	7	1, 16H, 18, ES2, 30, 40	4
A11M/307	Q.29	Gearbox cover stud nut	7	30M, 40M	4
A2/308	P.15	Gearbox cover stud spring washer	7	All Models	3
A2/309	P.13	Gearbox outer cover fixing screw	4	1, 16H, 18, ES2, 30, 40	5
A2/315	P.38	Gearbox oil filler plug	1	All Models	1 8
E3336	N.41	Gearbox oil drain plug	1	All Models	8
GEARBOX FIXING BOLTS.					
A2/310	N.13	Gearbox suspension bolt and nut	1	1, 16H, 18, ES2, 30, 40	6 0
A11M/310		Gearbox suspension bolt and nut	1	30M, 40M	6 0
A2/313	N.8	Gearbox suspension bolt nut	1	1, 16H, 18, ES2, 30, 40	2 8
A11M/313	Q.39	Gearbox suspension bolt nut	1	30M, 40M	2 8
E5454	N.9	Gearbox suspension bolt nut washer	1	All Models	4
A2/312	N.53	Gearbox bottom bolt and nut	1	All Models	3 0
A2/313	N.54	Gearbox bottom bolt nut	1	All Models	1 0
GEARBOX FRONT CHAIN ADJUSTER.					
A2/314	N.7	Gearbox front chain adjuster plate assembly	1	All Models	4 8
12342	N.6	Gearbox front chain adjuster plate pin	2	All Models	5
GEARBOX PINIONS SHAFTS AND BEARINGS.					
A2/316	N.29	Main gear wheel bearing complete	1	All Models	1 7 0
A2/317	N.27	Main gear wheel oil retaining washer (between main gear wheel and bearing)	1	All Models	4

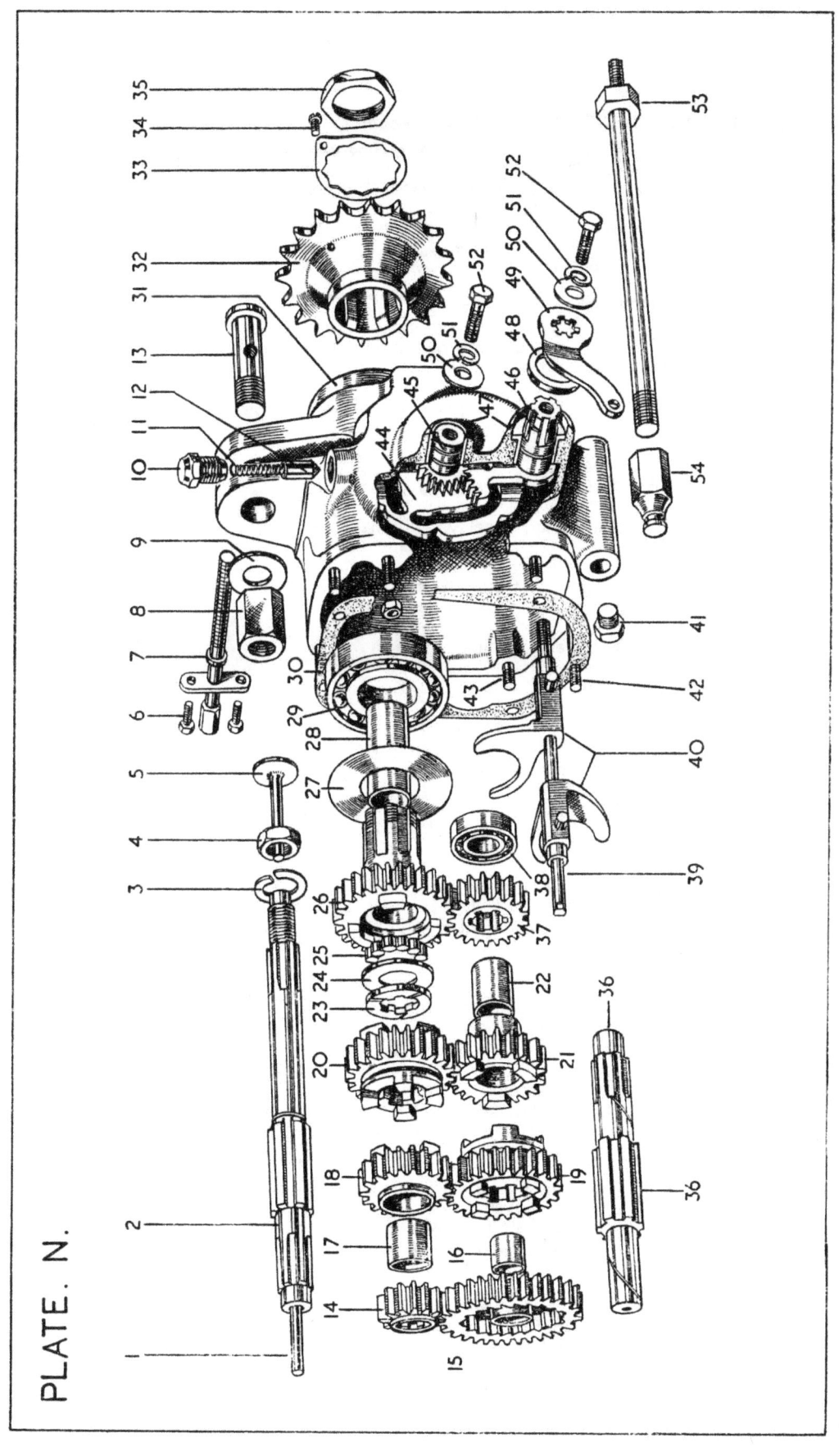

PLATE. N.

PART No.	PLATE No.	DESCRIPTION.	QTY.	USED ON.	PRICE EACH. £ s. d.
GEARBOX PINIONS SHAFTS AND BEARINGS—cont.					
A2/318	N.25	Main gear wheel sleeve bearing rollers (per set 13)	1	All Models	5 0
A2/319	N.24	Main gear wheel sleeve bearing roller retaining washer	1	All Models	2 0
A2/320		Main gear wheel bearing oil retaining washer (between gear box shell and bearing)	1	All Models	4
A2/321	P.49	Mainshaft R.H. bearing	1	All Models	16 0
B2/322	N.38	Layshaft L.H. bearing	1	All Models	16 0
A11M/322	Q.30	Layshaft bearing for gearbox end cover	1	30M, 40M	16 0
A2/323	P.48	Mainshaft bearing packing washer	1	All Models	3
A2/324	N.2	Main axle	1	1, 16H, 18, ES2, 30, 40	2 0 0
A11M/324	N.2	Main axle	1	30M, 40M	2 5 0
A2/325	N.36	Layshaft	1	1, 16H, 18, ES2, 30, 40	1 16 8
A11/325	Q.35	Layshaft	1	30M, 40M	2 0 0
A2/326	N.26	Main gear wheel with bronze bush	1	1, 16H, 18, ES2, 30, 40	2 0 0
A11/326	N.26	Main gear wheel with bronze bush	1	30, 30M, 40, 40M	2 5 0
A2/327	N.28	Main gear wheel bush (per pair)	1	All Models	4 8
A2/328	N.23	Main axle thrust washer	1	All Models	5 0
A2/329	N.20	Main axle sliding pinion	1	1, 16H, 18, ES2	1 10 0
A11/329	N.20	Main axle sliding pinion	1	30, 30M, 40, 40M	1 12 6
A2/330	N.18	Main axle free pinion	1	1, 16H, 18, ES2	1 6 0
A11/330	N.18	Main axle free pinion	1	30, 30M, 40, 40M	1 7 6
A2/331	N.14	Main axle pinion	1	1, 16H, 18, ES2	12 0
A11M/331	Q.32	Main axle pinion	1	30M, 40M	14 0
A11/331	N.14	Main axle pinion	1	30, 40	14 0
A11/332	N.37	Layshaft pinion	1	30, 30M, 40, 40M	16 0
A2/332	N.37	Layshaft pinion	1	1, 16H, 18, ES2	14 0
A11/333	N.21	Layshaft free pinion	1	30, 30M, 40, 40M	1 5 0
A2/333	N.21	Layshaft free pinion	1	1, 16H, 18, ES2	1 3 4
A11/334	N.19	Layshaft sliding pinion	1	30, 30M, 40, 40M	1 12 6
A2/334	N.19	Layshaft sliding pinion	1	1, 16H, 18, ES2	1 10 0
A2/335	N.17	Bush for main axle free pinion	1	All Models	4 0
A2/336	N.22	Bush for layshaft free pinion	1	All Models	5 0
A2/337	N.15	Low gear and kickstarter wheel with bronze bush	1	1, 16H, 18, ES2	1 13 4
A11/337	N.15	Low gear and kickstarter wheel with bronze bush	1	30, 40	1 15 0
A2/338	N.16	Bronze bush for low gear and kick-start wheel	1	1, 16H, 18, ES2, 30, 40	4 8
A11M/337	Q.33	Low gear wheel with bronze bush	1	30M, 40M	1 15 0
A11M/338	Q.34	Low gear wheel bronze bush	1	30M, 40M	4 8
A2/339	N.40	Striker fork	2	All Models	1 0 0
A2/340	N.39	Striker fork shaft	1	All Models	5 0
A2/341	N.44	Cam plate	1	All Models	1 0 0
A2/342	N.45	Cam plate spindle	1	All Models	13 4
A2/343	N.46	Cam plate quadrant with spindle	1	All Models	16 8
A2/344	N.47	Cam plate or quadrant spindle bush	2	All Models	5 0
A2/345	N.48	Quadrant spindle oil retaining washer (cork)	1	All Models	4
A2/346	N.50	Cam plate or quadrant spindle washer	2	All Models	5
A2/347	N.51	Cam plate or quadrant spring washer	2	All Models	3

PLATE. P.

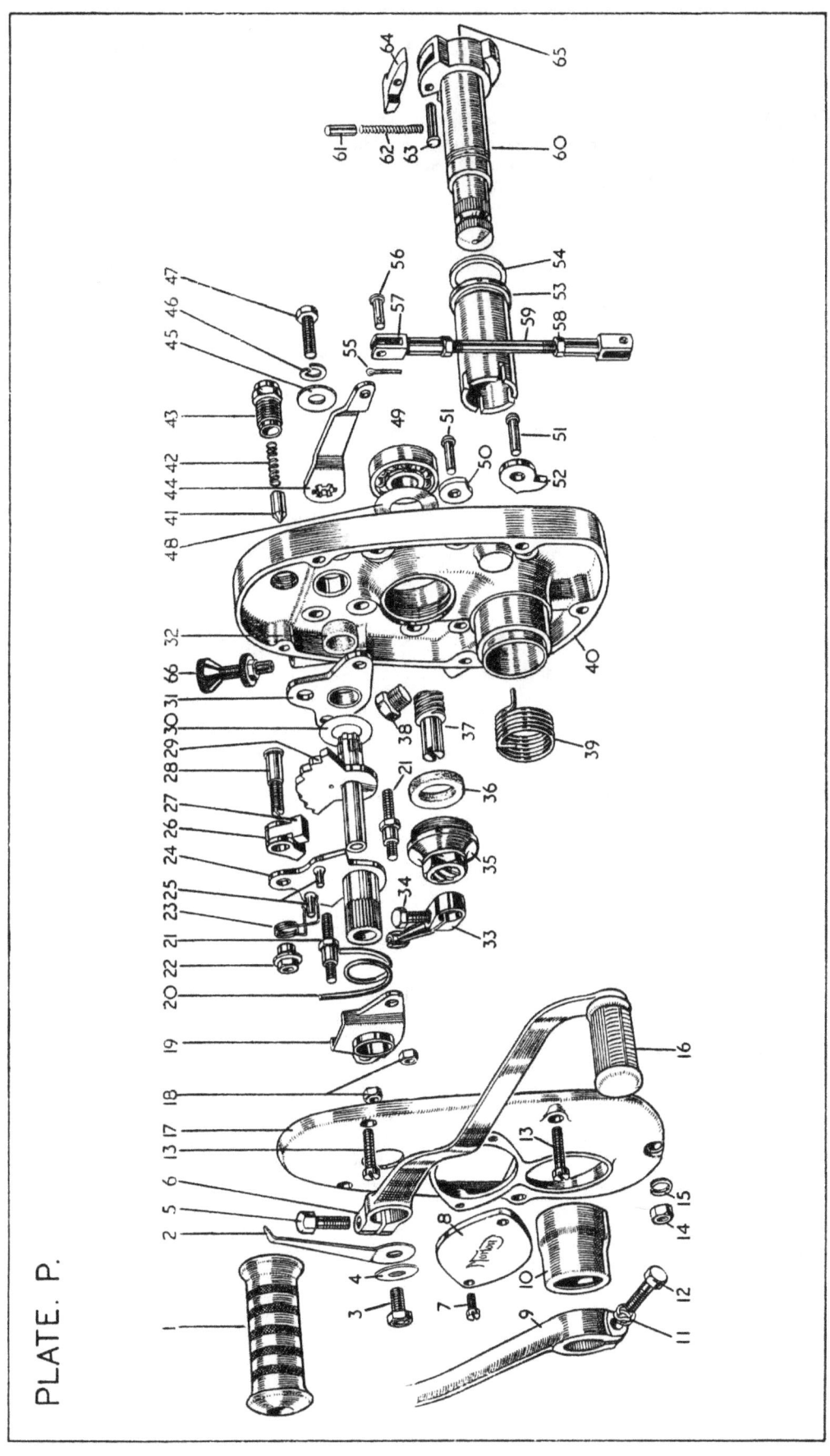

PART No	PLATE No.	DESCRIPTION.	QTY.	USED ON.	PRICE EACH. £ s. d.

GEARBOX PINIONS SHAFTS AND BEARINGS—cont.

PART No	PLATE No.	DESCRIPTION.	QTY.	USED ON.	£	s.	d.
A2/348	N.52	Cam plate or quadrant spindle bolt	2	All Models			5
A2/349	N.49	Cam plate quadrant lever	1	All Models		10	0
A2/350	N.12	Indexing plunger	1	All Models			8
A2/351	N.10	Indexing plunger bush	1	All Models		2	4
A2/352	N.11	Indexing plunger spring	1	All Models			4
A2/372	N.4	Main axle nut	1	All Models		1	0
A2/373	N.3	Axle nut lock washer	1	All Models			3

KICKSTARTER PARTS.

PART No	PLATE No.	DESCRIPTION.	QTY.	USED ON.	£	s.	d.
A2/353	P.60	Kick-starter axle with bronze bush	1	1, 16H, 18, ES2, 30, 40	2	0	0
A2/354	P.65	Bronze bush for K.S. end of layshaft	1	1, 16H, 18, ES2, 30, 40		5	0
A2/355	P.54	Kick-starter axle cork washer	1	1, 16H, 18, ES2, 30, 40			4
A2/356	P.64	Kick-starter pawl	1	1, 16H, 18, ES2, 30, 40		2	8
A2/357	P.63	Kick-starter pawl pin	1	1, 16H, 18, ES2, 30, 40			8
A2/358	P.10	Kick-starter return spring cover	1	1, 16H, 18, ES2, 30, 40		2	4
A2/259	P.12	Kick-starter crank bolt	1	1, 16H, 18, ES2, 30, 40			5
A2/308	P.11	Kick-starter crank bolt washer	1	1, 16H, 18, ES2, 30, 40			3
A2/360	P.9	Kick-starter crank	1	1, 16H, 18, ES2, 30, 40	1	6	8
A2/367	P.39	Kick-starter return spring	1	1, 16H, 18, ES2, 30, 40		2	4
B2/648	P.1	Kick-starter crank rubber	1	1, 16H, 18, ES2, 30, 40		2	0
A2/361	P.50	Kick-starter cam	1	1, 16H, 18, ES2, 30, 40			8
A2/362	P.51	Kick-starter cam or stop piece rivet	1	1, 16H, 18, ES2, 30, 40			3
A2/363	P.52	Kick-starter stop piece	1	1, 16H, 18, ES2, 30, 40			10
A2/364	P.53	Kick-starter bush	1	1, 16H, 18, ES2, 30, 40		6	0
A2/365	P.62	Kick-starter pawl spring	1	1, 16H, 18, ES2, 30, 40			4
A2/366	P.61	Kick-starter pawl spring plunger	1	1, 16H, 18, ES2, 30, 40			8

GEARBOX AXLE SPROCKET.

PART No	PLATE No.	DESCRIPTION.	QTY.	USED ON.	£	s.	d.
A2/368	N.32	Axle sprocket	1	All Models	1	2	0
A2/369	N.35	Axle sprocket locking nut	1	All Models		1	8
A2/370	N.33	Axle sprocket nut locking plate	1	All Models			8
A2/371	N.34	Axle sprocket locking plate screw	1	All Models			3

NOTE.—Axle sprockets supplied 16T or 19T.

CLUTCH GROUP.

PART No	PLATE No.	DESCRIPTION.	QTY.	USED ON.	£	s.	d.
A2/374		Clutch assembly complete	1	1, 16H, 18, ES2, 30, 40	12	5	0
A11M/374		Clutch assembly complete	1	30M, 40M	12	5	0
A2/375	P.37	Clutch worm	1	1, 16H, 18, ES2, 30, 40		5	0
A11M/375	Q.28	Clutch worm	1	30M, 40M		5	0
A2/376	P.35	Clutch worm nut	1	1, 16H, 18, ES2, 30, 40		13	4
A2/861	P.36	Clutch worm nut felt washer	1	1, 16H, 18, ES2, 30, 40			4
A11M/376	Q.26	Clutch worm nut	1	30M, 40M		13	4
A11M/861	Q.25	Clutch worm nut felt washer	1	30M, 40M			4

PART No.	PLATE No.	DESCRIPTION.	QTY.	USED ON.	PRICE EACH. £ s. d.
CLUTCH GROUP—cont.					
A11M/862	Q.24	Clutch worm nut cover	1	30M, 40M	3 4
A2/377	P.33	Clutch worm lever	1	All Models	5 0
A11M/863	Q.27	Clutch worm nut bearing packing washer	1	30M, 40M	3
A2/378	P.34	Clutch worm lever bolt	1	All Models	4
A2/379	N.1	Clutch rod	1	All Models	2 0
A2/380	N.5	Thrust pin	1	1, 16H, 18, ES2, 30, 40	2 0
A11M/380	Q.38	Thrust pin	1	30M, 40M	2 0
A2/381	Q.2	Clutch back plate	1	1, 16H, 18, ES2, 30, 40	5 6
A11M/381	Q.2	Clutch back plate	1	30M, 40M	6 6
A2/382	Q.3	Clutch roller cage	1	All Models	3 6
A2/383	Q.4	Clutch roller (per set 15)	1	All Models	6 6
A2/384	Q.13	Clutch sprocket with inserts	1	1, 16H, 18, ES2, 30, 40	2 5 0
A11M/384	Q.41	Clutch sprocket with inserts	1	30M, 40M	2 7 6
A2/385	Q.7	Clutch body	1	1, 16H, 18, ES2, 30, 40	1 17 0
A11M/385	Q.40	Clutch body	1	30M, 40M	1 17 0
A2/386	Q.5	Clutch body back cover plate	1	All Models	4 8
A2/387	Q.10	Clutch body centre	1	1, 16H, 18, ES2, 30, 40	17 0
A11M/387	Q.10	Clutch body centre	1	30M, 40M	17 0
A2/388	Q.8	Clutch body centre rubber buffers, large (per set of 3)	1	1, 16H, 18, ES2, 30, 40	4 6
A11M/388	Q.8	Clutch body centre rubber buffers, large (per set of 3)	1	30M, 40M	4 6
A2/389	Q.9	Clutch body centre rubber buffers, small (per set of 3)	1	1, 16H, 18, ES2, 30, 40	4 6
A11M/389	Q.9	Clutch body centre rubber buffers, small (per set of 3)	1	30M, 40M	4 6
A2/390	Q.11	Clutch body front cover plate	1	All Models	6 0
A2/391	Q.12	Clutch body front cover plate retaining screw (3)	3	All Models	3
A2/392	Q.14	Clutch plate (steel)	5	1, 16H, 18, ES2, 30, 40	5 6
			4	30M, 40M	5 6
A2/393	Q.15	Clutch friction plate with inserts	5	1, 16H, 18, ES2, 30, 40	11 0
			3	30M, 40M	11 0
A2/394		Clutch friction plate inserts (per doz.)	100	1, 16H, 18, ES2, 30, 40	3 0
			60	30M, 40M	3 0
A2/395		Clutch sprocket inserts (per doz.)	20	All Models	3 0
A2/396	Q.18	Clutch plate cover		1, 16H, 18, ES2, 30, 40	4 6
A2/397	Q.17	Clutch outer plate	1	All Models	5 6
A2/398	Q.16	Clutch plate retaining ring	1	All Models	1 4
A2/399	Q.20	Clutch spring	3	1, 16H, 18, ES2, 30, 40	8
A11M/399	Q.43	Clutch spring	3	30M, 40M	1 0
A2/400	Q.19	Clutch spring box	3	1, 16H, 18, ES2, 30, 40	1 0
A11M/400	Q.42	Clutch spring box	3	30M, 40M	1 6
A2/401	Q.6	Clutch spring stud	3	1, 16H, 18, ES2, 30, 40	1 6
A11M/401	Q.6	Clutch spring stud	3	30M, 40M	1 6
A2/402	Q.1	Clutch spring stud nut	3	All Models	4
A2/403	Q.21	Clutch spring screw	3	1, 16H, 18, ES2, 30, 40	4
A11M/403	Q.44	Clutch spring screw	3	30M, 40M	1 6

POSITIVE FOOTCHANGE PARTS.

PART No.	PLATE No.	DESCRIPTION.	QTY.	USED ON.	PRICE EACH. £ s. d.
A2/404	P.2	Gearbox change speed indicator	1	All Models	2 6
A2/405	P.3	Change speed indicator bolt	1	All Models	1 8

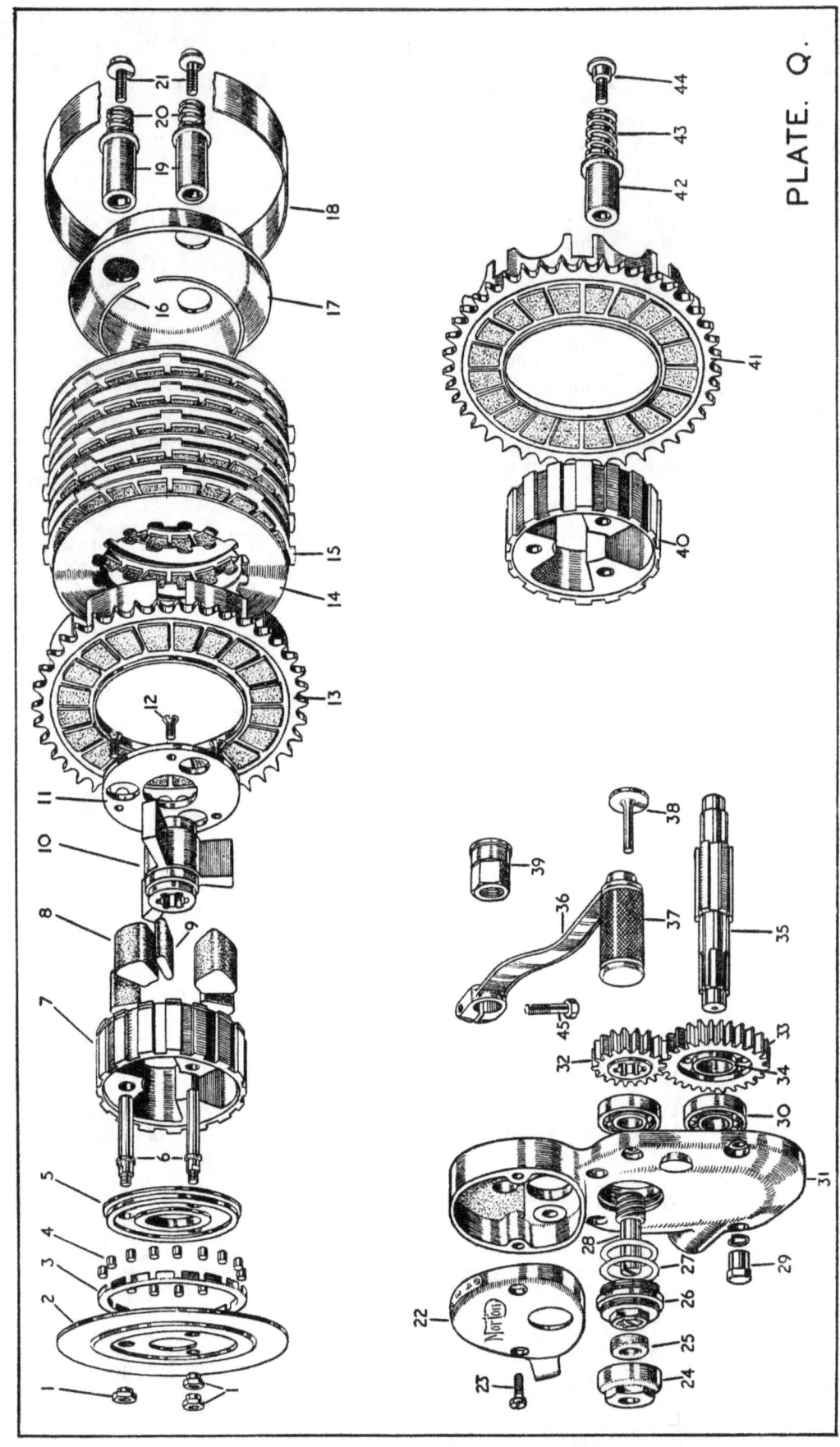

PLATE. Q.

PART No.	PLATE No.	DESCRIPTION.	QTY.	USED ON.	PRICE EACH. £ s. d.
POSITIVE FOOTCHANGE PARTS—cont.					
A2/864	P.4	Change speed indicator bolt washer	1	All Models	3
B2/406	P.6	Gear lever	1	1, 16H, 18, ES2, 30, 40	1 0 0
A11M/406	Q.36	Gear lever	1	30, 40M	1 0 0
A11M/821	Q.22	Positive footchange cover	1	30M, 40M	7 0
A11M/822	Q.23	Positive footchange cover screw	2	30M, 40M	6
B2/407	P.16	Gear lever rubber	1	1, 16H, 18, ES2, 30, 40	2 0
A11M/407	Q.37	Gear lever rubber	1	30M, 40M	2 6
A2/408	P.5/Q.45	Gear lever securing bolt	1	All Models	8
A2/409	P.19	Return spring cover plate	1	All Models	6 8
A2/410	P.20	Return spring for pawl carrier	1	All Models	1 4
A2/411	P.21	Stop stud for pawl carrier	2	All Models	1 4
A2/412F	P.18	Stop stud nut for pawl carrier (front)	2	All Models	8
A2/412R	P.18	Stop stud nut for pawl carrier (rear)	2	All Models	8
A2/413	P.25	Peg for pawl carrier	2	All Models	4
A2/414	P.24	Pawl carrier	1	All Models	13 0
A2/415	P.30	Pawl carrier spacing washer	1	All Models	3
A2/416	P.32	Pawl carrier felt washer	1	All Models	1 0
A2/417	P.27	Pawl (plain)	1	All Models	4 0
A2/418	P.26	Pawl (forked)	1	All Models	4 0
A2/419	P.23	Pawl return spring	1	All Models	1 0
A2/420	P.28	Pawl pin	1	All Models	1 6
A2/421	P.22	Pawl pin nut	1	All Models	8
A2/422	P.29	Ratchet plate	1	All Models	1 0 0
A2/423	P.31	Cam plate	1	All Models	4 0
A2/350	P.41	Cam plate plunger	1	All Models	8
A2/351	P.43	Cam plate plunger bush	1	All Models	2 4
A2/352	P.42	Cam plate plunger spring	1	All Models	4
A2/424	P.44	Ratchet lever	1	All Models	5 0
A2/346	P.45	Ratchet lever securing bolt washer	1	All Models	4
A2/347	P.46	Ratchet lever securing bolt spring washer	1	All Models	3
A2/348	P.47	Ratchet lever securing bolt	1	All Models	4
GEAR CONTROL ROD AND FITTINGS.					
A2/425	P.59	Gearbox control rod	1	All Models	2 0
A2/411	P.58	Gearbox control rod nut	2	All Models	4
A2/426	P.57	Gearbox control rod top or bottom connection	2	All Models	5 0
A2/427	P.56	Gearbox control rod connection pin	2	All Models	4
A2/195	P.55	Gearbox control rod connection split pin	2	All Models	2
FRONT AND REAR WHEEL COMPLETE ASSEMBLIES.					
B2/714		Front wheel complete with bearings and brake (less tyre)	1	1, 16H, 18, ES2	13 10 0
B11/714		Front wheel complete with bearings and brake (less tyre)	1	30, 40	13 10 0
A11M/714		Front wheel complete with bearings and brake (less tyre)	1	30M, 40M	21 0 0
B2/715		Rear wheel complete with bearings and brake (less tyre)	1	1, 16H, 18	16 0 0
B4/715		Rear wheel complete with bearings and brake (less tyre)	1	ES2	17 5 0
B11/715		Rear wheel complete with bearings and brake (less tyre)	1	30, 40	17 5 0
A11M/715		Rear wheel complete with bearings and brake (less tyre)	1	30M, 40M	17 5 0
FRONT AND REAR WHEELS WITH HUB SHELL ONLY.					
B2/428		Front wheel with hub shell only	1	1, 16H, 18, ES2	6 10 0
B11/428		Front wheel with hub shell only	1	30, 40	6 12 6
A11M/428		Front wheel with hub shell only	1	30M, 40M	10 0 0

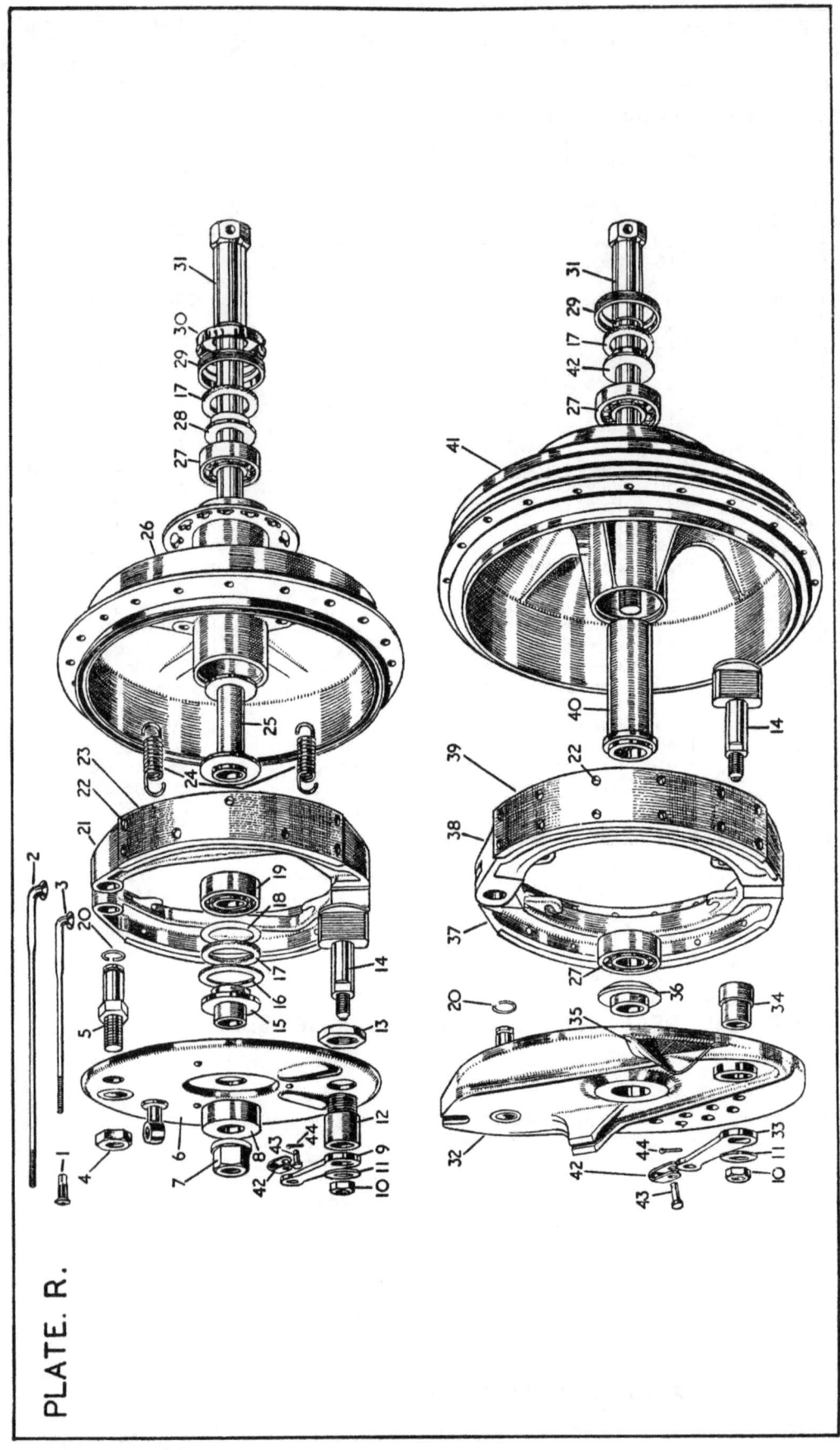

PLATE. R.

PART No.	PLATE No.	DESCRIPTION.	QTY.	USED ON.	PRICE EACH. £ s. d.
FRONT AND REAR WHEELS WITH HUB SHELL ONLY—cont.					
B2/649	...	Rear wheel with hub shell only	1	1, 16H, 18	5 17 0
B4/649	...	Rear wheel with hub shell only	1	ES2	6 6 0
B11/649	...	Rear wheel with hub shell only	1	30, 40	6 6 0
A11M/649	...	Rear wheel with hub shell only	1	30M, 40M	6 6 0
WHEEL RIMS AND SPOKES.					
B2/654	...	Wheel rim front	1	1, 16H, 18, ES2	1 5 0
B11/654	...	Wheel rim front WM1/21	1	30, 40	1 7 6
A11M/654	...	Wheel rim front WM1/21	1	30M, 40M	1 5 0
A2/432	...	Wheel rim rear WM2/19	1	1, 16H, 18, ES2	1 5 0
B11/432	...	Wheel rim rear WM2/20	1	30, 40	1 7 6
B11M/432	...	Wheel rim rear WM2/20	1	30M, 40M	1 5 0
B2/650	R.3	Wheel spoke front brake side (set 20)	1	1, 16H, 18, ES2	4 0
B2/651	R.2	Wheel spoke front plain side (set 20)	1	1, 16H, 18, ES2	4 0
A11/650	...	Wheel spoke front brake side (set 20)	1	30, 40	4 0
A11M/650	...	Wheel spoke front brake side (set 20)	1	30M, 40M	4 0
A11/651	...	Wheel spoke front plain side (set 20)	1	30, 30M, 40, 40M	4 0
B2/652	...	Wheel spoke rear brake drum side (set 20)	1	1, 16H, 18, ES2	4 0
B2/653	...	Wheel spoke rear plain side (set 20)	1	1, 16H, 18, ES2	4 0
A11/652	...	Wheel spoke rear brake drum side (set 20)	1	30, 30M, 40, 40M	4 0
A11/653	...	Wheel spoke rear plain side (set 20)	1	30, 30M, 40, 40M	4 0
A2/431	R.1	Spoke nipples (per set 40)	2	All Models	4 6
REAR HUBS AND FITTINGS.					
B2/433	S.43	Hub shell only rear	1	1, 16H, 18	1 17 0
B4/433	S.29	Hub shell only rear	1	ES2, 30, 30M, 40, 40M	2 15 0
A2/434	S.44	Hub shell bearing sleeve rear	1	1, 16H, 18	6 0
A2/441	S.32	Hub bearing distance piece plain side (rear)	1	All Models	2 0
A2/439	S.13	Hub bearing felt washer steel cup brake side (rear)	1	1, 16H, 18, ES2, 30, 40	1 0
A2/460	S.45	Rear hub spindle	1	1, 16H, 18	7 0
B4/460	S.39	Rear hub spindle	1	ES2, 30, 30M, 40, 40M	2 10 0
B2/659	S.28	Rear hub spindle washer	1	All Models	3
B2/660	S.35	Rear hub spindle shouldered washer (plain side) (for speedometer gearbox)	1	30, 40, 1, 16H, 18, ES2	1 6
B2/461	S.38	Rear hub spindle distance piece (plain side)	1	1, 16H, 18	2 0
B4/461	S.36	Rear hub spindle distance piece (plain side)	1	ES2, 30, 40	2 6
A11M/461	S.37	Rear hub spindle distance piece (plain side)	1	30M, 40M	3 0
A2/462	...	Rear hub brake plate	1	1, 16H, 18	15 6
B4/462	S.2	Rear hub brake plate	1	ES2, 30, 30M, 40, 40M	15 6
A2/463	S.22	Rear hub brake drum and sprocket	1	1, 16H, 18	3 0 0
B4/463	S.21	Rear hub brake drum and sprocket	1	ES2, 30, 30M, 40, 40M	3 5 0

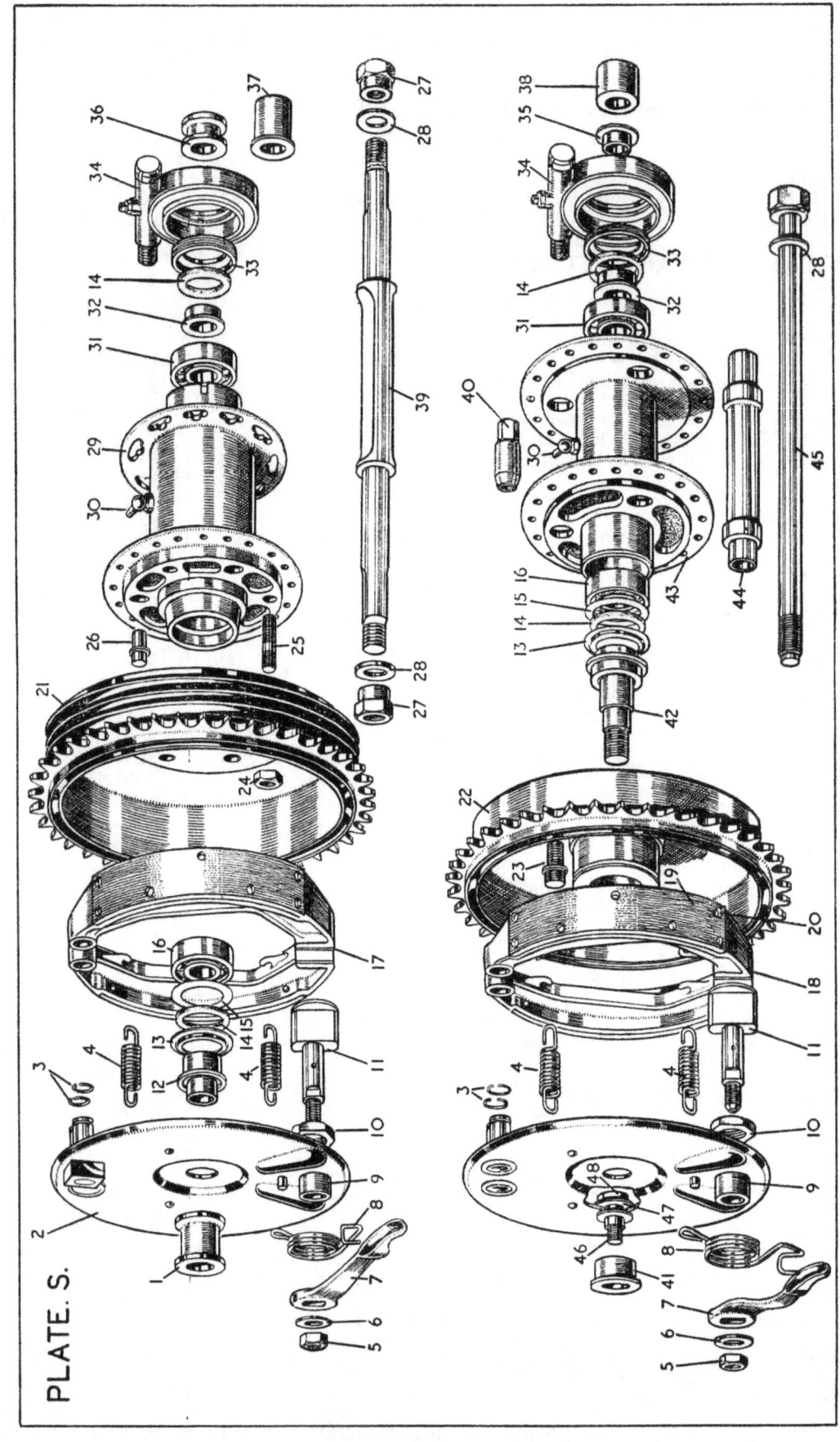

PLATE. S.

PART No.	PLATE No.	DESCRIPTION.	QTY.	USED ON.	PRICE EACH. £ s. d.
REAR HUBS AND FITTINGS—cont.					
A2/464	S.42	Rear brake drum and sprocket fork end attachment piece	1	1, 16H, 18	8 0
A2/465	S.41	Rear hub brake plate distance piece, outer	1	1, 16H, 18	2 0
B4/465	S.1	Rear hub brake plate distance piece, outer	1	ES2, 30, 30M, 40, 40M	2 6
B4/661	S.12	Rear hub brake plate distance piece, inner	1	ES2, 30, 30M, 40, 40M	3 0
A2/454	S.27	Rear brake drum and sprocket fork end attachment nut	1	1, 16H, 18	2 2
A2/454	S.27	Rear hub spindle nut	1	ES2, 30, 30M, 40, 40M	2 2
A2/466	S.27	Rear hub brake torque arm	1	1, 16H, 18	5 6
A2/467	S.27	Rear hub brake torque arm spring washer	1	1, 16H, 18	3
E3812		Rear hub brake torque arm frame bolt	1	1, 16H, 18	1 0
A2/468	S.46	Rear hub brake torque arm stud	1	1, 16H, 18	4 0
11664	S.48	Rear hub brake torque arm stud nut	1	1, 16H, 18	5
E5375	S.47	Rear hub brake torque arm stud nut washer	1	1, 16H, 18	3
A2/469	S.7	Rear hub brake cam lever	1	All Models	3 0
A2/470	S.8	Rear hub brake cam lever return spring	1	All Models	1 0
A2/472	S.23	Rear brake drum stud	3	1, 16H, 18	1 0
B2/451	S.40	Wheel sleeve nut rear	3	1, 16H, 18	2 0
B4/662	S.26	Rear hub shell brake drum dowel	3	ES2, 30, 30M, 40, 40M	2 0
B4/663	S.25	Rear hub shell brake drum stud	3	ES2, 30, 30M, 40, 40M	1 0
B4/664	S.24	Rear hub shell brake drum stud nut	3	ES2, 30, 30M, 40, 40M	4
HUB BRAKE SHOES AND LININGS.					
A2/443	R.21/S.18	Hub brake shoe with lining (each)	4	30, 40, 1, 16H, 18, ES2	18 0
A2/444	R.23/S.19	Hub brake shoe lining (per pair)	2	30, 40, 1, 16H, 18, ES2	12 0
A2/445	R.22/S.30	Hub brake shoe lining rivet (per set 14)	2	30, 40, 1, 16H, 18, ES2	1 0
A2/445	R.22/S.30	Hub brake shoe lining rivet (rear only)	1	30M, 40M	1 0
A11M/445	R.22	Hub brake shoe lining rivets (per set 20) front only	1	30M, 40M	1 4
A11M/443	S.17	Hub brake shoe with lining rear (each)	1	30M, 40M	18 0
A11M/433(P)	R.37	Hub brake shoe with lining (front) plain	1	30M, 40M	2 0 0
A11M/433(F)	R.38	Hub brake shoe with lining (front) forked	1	30M, 40M	2 0 0
A11M/444(R)		Hub brake shoe linings (per pair) rear	1	30M, 40M	12 0
A11M/444(F)	R.39	Hub brake shoe linings (per pair) front	1	30M, 40M	12 6
FRONT HUBS AND FITTINGS.					
B2/655	R.26	Hub shell and brake drum front	1	30, 40, 1, 16H, 18, ES2	3 12 0
A11M/655	R.41	Hub shell and brake drum front	1	30M, 40M	7 5 0
B2/452	R.31	Front hub spindle	1	All Models	15 0
B2/453	R.8	Front hub spindle distance piece	1	30, 40, 1, 16H, 18, ES2	2 0
B2/454	R.7	Front hub spindle nut	1	All Models	2 2
B2/455	R.15	Front hub brake plate distance piece	1	30, 40, 1, 16H, 18, ES2	4 0
A11M/455	R.36	Front hub brake plate distance piece	1	30M, 40M	4 0

PART No.	PLATE No.	DESCRIPTION.	QTY.	USED ON.	PRICE EACH. £ s. d.
FRONT HUBS AND FITTINGS—cont.					
B2/457	... R.6	Front hub brake plate	1	30, 40, 1, 16H, 18, ES2 ...	15 6
A2/459	... R.9	Front hub brake cam lever...	1	30, 40, 1, 16H, 18, ES2 ...	2 0
B2/657	... R.5	Front hub brake shoe fulcrum pin	1	30, 40, 1, 16H, 18, ES2 ...	2 6
B2/658	... R.4	Front hub brake shoe fulcrm pin nut	1	30, 40, 1, 16H, 18, ES2 ...	6
A11M/457	... R.32	Front hub brake plate	1	30M, 40M	3 10 0
A11M/823	... R.35	Front hub brake plate air scoop	1	30M, 40M	2 6
A11M/829	...	Front hub brake plate air scoop rivets (per set)	1	30M, 40M	6
A11M/826	...	Front hub brake plate air scoop gauze ...	1	30M, 40M,	1 0
A11M/459	... R.33	Front hub brake cam lever	1	30M, 40M	2 0
A11M/827	... R.34	Hub brake cam bush front only	1	30M, 40M	2 0
B2/441	... R.28	Hub bearing distance piece plain side (front)	1	30, 40, 1, 16H, 18, ES2 ...	1 0
A11M/441	... R.42	Hub bearing distance piece plain side (front)	1	30M, 40M	1 0
C2/656	... R.25	Hub shell bearing distance tube front ...	1	30, 40, 1, 16H, 18, ES2 ...	1 6
A11M/656	... R.40	Hub bearing distance tube front	1	30M, 40M	7 6
B2/439	... R.16	Hub bearing felt washer steel plate brake side (front)	1	30, 40, 1, 16H, 18, ES2 ...	6
B2/442	... R.30	Hub bearing dust cover (front) plain side	1	30, 40, 1, 16H, 18, ES2 ...	3 0
PARTS COMMON TO FRONT AND REAR HUBS.					
A2/435	R.27/S.31	Hub bearing plain side	1	All Models	16 6
A2/435	R.27/S.31	Hub bearing front brake side	1	30M, 40M	16 6
A2/436	R.19/S.16	Hub bearing brake side	1	All Models	1 11 4
A2/436	R.19/S.16	Hub bearing brake side (rear only)	1	30M, 40M	1 11 4
A2/440	R.29/S.33	Hub bearing locking ring plain side front or rear	2	All Models	2 0
A2/437	R.17/S.14	Hub bearing felt washer	1	30, 40, 1, 16H, 18, ES2 ...	8
A2/438	R.18/S.15	Hub bearing pen steel washer brake side	2	30, 40, 1, 16H, 18, ES2 ...	4
A2/198	... S.30	Hub grease nipple	2	All Models	1 0
A2/446	R.24/S.4	Hub brake shoe return spring	4	All Models	1 0
A2/447	R.20/S.3	Hub brake shoe circlip	4	All Models	6
A2/448	R.14/S.11	Hub brake cam with nut and washer ...	2	All Models	7 0
E3224	R.10/S.5	Hub brake cam nut	2	All Models	4
E5455	R.11/S.6	Hub brake cam nut washer	2	All Models	2
A2/449	R.12/S.9	⎧ Hub brake cam bush	2	30, 40, 1, 16H, 18, ES2 ...	2 0
		⎩ Hub brake cam bush (rear only)	1	30M, 40M	2 0
A2/450	R.13/S.10	⎧ Hub brake cam bush locknut	2	30, 40, 1, 16H, 18, ES2 ...	1 0
		⎩ Hub brake cam bush locknut (rear only)	1	30M, 40M	1 0
TYRE SECURITY BOLTS.					
A11M/861	...	Front wheel security bolt	1	30M, 40M	5 6
A11M/862	...	Rear wheel security bolt	1	30M, 40M	5 6

PART No.	PLATE No.	DESCRIPTION.	QTY.	USED ON.	PRICE EACH. £ s. d.

ENGINE SPROCKET.

A2/473	... A.4	Engine sprocket (state number of teeth) ..	1	1, 16H, 18, ES2	1 2 0
A11/473	...	Engine sprocket (state number of teeth) ..	1	30, 30M, 40, 40M	1 2 0
A2/474	... A.47	Engine mainshaft key	1	All Models	3
A2/475	... A.3	Engine sprocket locknut	1	1, 16H, 18, ES2	1 0
A11/475	...	Engine sprocket locknut	1	30, 30M, 40, 40M	2 0

Sprockets can be supplied 16T to 22T inclusive.

FRONT AND REAR CHAINS.

A2/477	...	Front driving chain, 75 link	1	1, 16H, 18, ES2	1 5 0
A11/477	...	Front driving chain, 76 link	1	30, 30M, 40, 40M	1 5 0
A3/478	...	Rear driving chain, 91 link	1	18, ES2	2 3 0
A2/478	...	Rear driving chain, 90 link	1	1, 16H	2 3 0
A11/478	...	Rear driving chain, 92 link	1	30, 30M, 40, 40M	2 3 0
A2/479	...	Front chain spring link	1	30, 40, 1, 16H, 18, ES2 ...	1 9
A2/480	...	Front chain cranked link	1	All Models	3 0
A11M/479	...	Front chain rivetting link	1	30M, 40M	1 9
A2/481	...	Rear chain spring link	1	30, 40, 1, 16H, 18, ES2 ...	1 9
A2/482	...	Rear chain cranked link	1	All Models	3 0
A11M/481	...	Rear chain rivetting link	1	30M, 40M	1 9

REAR CHAIN ADJUSTERS.

A2/483	... W.7	Rear chain adjuster bolt and nut	2	1, 16H, 18	3 6
B4/483	...	Rear chain adjuster complete	2	ES2, 30, 30M, 40, 40M ...	6 0
B4/665	... Y.14	Rear chain adjuster stirrup	2	ES2, 30, 30M, 40, 40M ...	3 0
B4/666	... Y.15	Rear chain adjuster bolt	2	ES2, 30, 30M, 40, 40M ...	1 6
B4/667	... Y.12	Rear chain adjuster bolt nut	2	ES2, 30, 30M, 40, 40M ...	6
B4/668	... Y.13	Rear chain adjuster fork end cap	2	ES2, 30, 30M, 40, 40M ...	1 0

FRONT CHAINCASE AND FITTINGS.

A2/484	... T.5	Front chaincase, inner portion	1	1, 16H, 18 ...	3 4 0
B4/484	... T.5	Front chaincase, inner portion	1	ES2 ...	3 4 0
A11/484	... T.5	Front chaincase, inner portion	1	30, 40	3 4 0
A2/485	... T.9	Front chaincase, outer portion	1	1, 16H, 18, ES2	3 10 0
A11/485	... T.9	Front chaincase, outer portion	1	30, 40	3 10 0
A2/486	... T.11	Front chaincase sealing washer	1	30, 40, 1, 16H, 18, ES2 ...	9 0
E3336	... T.18	Front chaincase drain plug	1	30, 40, 1, 16H, 18, ES2 ...	10
E5264	... T.17	Front chaincase drain plug washer	1	30, 40, 1, 16H, 18, ES3 ...	3

210

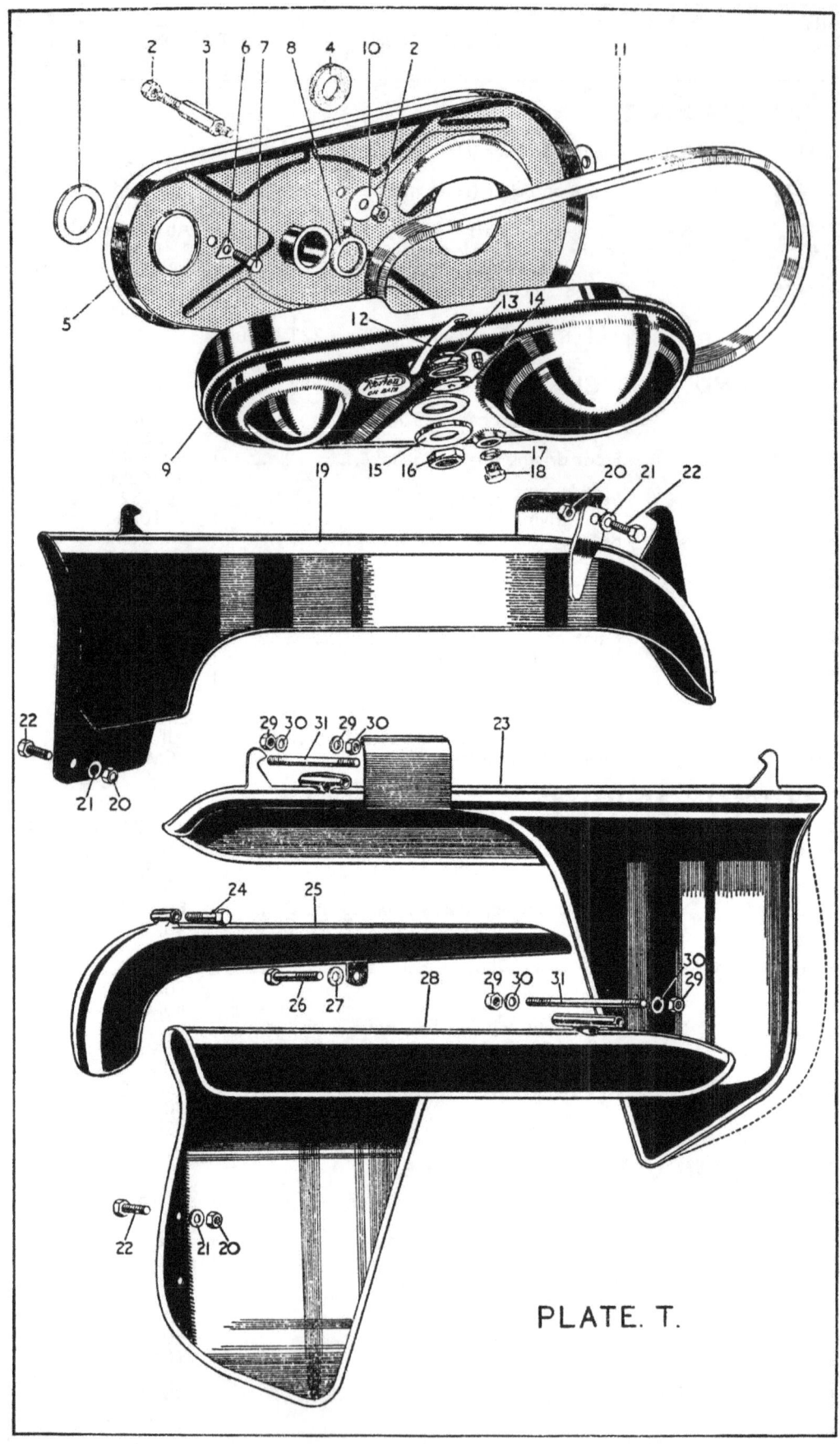

PLATE. T.

PART No.	PLATE No.	DESCRIPTION.	QTY.	USED ON.	PRICE EACH. £ s. d
FRONT CHAINCASE AND FITTINGS—cont.					
A2/487	T.14	Front chaincase inspection disc	1	30, 40, 1, 16H, 18, ES2	2 0
A2/488	T.13	Front chaincase inspection disc washer	1	30, 40, 1, 16H, 18, ES2	1 0
A2/489	T.12	Front chaincase inspection disc spring clip	1	30, 40, 1, 16H, 18, ES2	1 0
E6354	T.7	Front chaincase, inner portion crankcase attachment pin	1	30, 40, 1, 16H, 18, ES2	5
A2/490	T.6	Front chaincase pin locking plate	1	30, 40, 1, 16H, 18, ES2	4
E3223	T.2	Front chaincase, inner portion attachment nut	2	30, 40, 1, 16H, 18, ES2	4
A2/491	T.3	Front chaincase, inner portion attachment bolt	1	30, 40, 1, 16H, 18, ES2	3 6
A2/275	T.10	Front chaincase, inner portion attachment bolt washer	1	30, 40, 1, 16H, 18, ES2	3
A2/492	T.1	Front chaincase, inner portion crankcase washer	1	30, 40, 1, 16H, 18, ES2	6
A2/493	T.4	Front chaincase, inner portion gearbox felt washer	1	30, 40, 1, 16H, 18, ES2	8
A2/494	T.8	Front chaincase, inner portion footrest tube felt washer	1	30, 40, 1, 16H, 18, ES2	4
A2/495	T.16	Front chaincase, outer portion securing nut	1	30, 40, 1, 16H, 18, ES2	2 4
A2/496	T.15	Front chaincase, outer portion securing nut washer	1	30, 40, 1, 16H, 18, ES2	2 0
FRONT CHAINGUARD AND FITTINGS.					
A11M/828	T.25	Front chainguard	1	30M, (40M 1948)	1 5 0
A10M/828		Front chainguard	1	40M (1946/7)	1 5 0
E3801	T.24	Front chainguard crankcase attachment bolt	1	30M, 40M	5
11796		Front chainguard crankcase attachment bolt washer	3	30M, 40M	3
11304	T.26	Front chainguard engine plate bolt	1	30M, 40M	5
E3223		Front chainguard engine plate bolt nut	2	30M, 40M	4
E5456	T.27	Front chainguard engine plate bolt washer	4	30M, 40M	3
REAR CHAINGUARD AND FITTINGS.					
A2/497	T.19	Rear chainguard	1	1, 16H, 18	1 8 0
B4/497	T.23	Rear chainguard	1	ES2	1 8 0
A11/497		Rear chainguard	1	30, 40	1 8 0

PART No.	PLATE No.	DESCRIPTION.	QTY.	USED. ON.	PRICE EACH. £ s. d.

REAR CHAINGUARD AND FITTINGS—cont.

PART No.	PLATE No.	DESCRIPTION.	QTY.	USED ON.	£	s.	d.
A11M/497	T.28	Rear chainguard	1	30M, 40M	1	8	0
12342	T.22	Rear chainguard pin (front and rear end)	2	1, 16H, 18			5
E3229	T.20	Rear chainguard pin nut (front and rear end)	2	1, 16H, 18			4
E5379	T.21	Rear chainguard pin washer (front and rear end)	2	1, 16H, 18			3

(Last three items attach Rear Chainguard to Mudguard. Models ES2, 30, 30M, 40, and 40M. For rear attachment see rear springing member bolt).

REAR BRAKE PEDAL AND FITTINGS.

PART No.	PLATE No.	DESCRIPTION.	QTY.	USED ON.	£	s.	d.
A2/498	V.74	Rear brake pedal	1	1, 16H, 18		4	0
B4/498	V.74	Rear brake pedal	1	ES2, 30, 40	1	4	0
A11M/498	V.74	Rear brake pedal	1	30M, 40M	1	4	0
A2/500	V.75	Rear brake pedal grease nipple	1	All Models		1	0
A2/501	V.76	Rear brake pedal adjuster and locknut	1	All Models		1	6
A2/502	V.80	Rear brake pedal pivot bolt	1	1, 16H, 18, ES2		2	0
A11/502	V.80	Rear brake pedal pivot bolt	1	30, 40		2	0
A11M/502	V.80)	Rear brake pedal pivot bolt	1	30M, 40M		2	0
E3223	V.82	Rear brake pedal pivot bolt nut	1	All Models			4
E5456	V.81	Rear brake pedal pivot bolt washer	1	All Models			3

REAR BRAKE ROD AND FITTINGS.

PART No.	PLATE No.	DESCRIPTION.	QTY.	USED ON.	£	s.	d.
A2/503	V.83	Rear brake rod	1	1, 16H, 18, ES2		6	0
B4/503	V.83	Rear brake rod	1	ES2, 30, 40		6	0
A11M/503	V.83	Rear brake rod	1	30M, 40M		6	0
A11M/829	V.85	Rear brake rod spring	1	30M, 40M			9
A11M/830	V.86	Rear brake rod ball cup	1	30M, 40M		2	0
A2/504	V.79	Rear brake pedal jaw joint	1	All Models		4	6
A2/505	V.84	Rear brake adjuster	1	All Models		3	0
A2/506	V.77	Rear brake pedal jaw joint pin	1	All Models			5
A2/195	V.78	Rear brake pedal jaw joint pin split cotter	1	All Models			2

FOOTRESTS AND FITTINGS.

PART No.	PLATE No.	DESCRIPTION.	QTY.	USED ON.	£	s.	d.
A2/507	V.88	Footrest rubber	2	All Models		2	6
A2/508	V.87	Footrest rubber securing bolt and nut	4	All Models			10
A2/509	V.97	Footrest pad holder	2	1, 16H, 18, ES2, 30, 40		5	6
A2/510	V.94	Footrest rod	1	1, 16H, 18, ES2, 30, 40		4	0
A2/511	V.92	Footrest rod nut	2	1, 16H, 18, ES2, 30, 40			8
E5377	V.93	Footrest rod washer	2	1, 16H, 18, ES2, 30, 40			3
A2/512		Footrest serrated hanger with pad holder spindle	2	1, 16H, 18, ES2		12	0
A11/512		Footrest serrated hanger with pad holder spindle	2	30, 40		12	0
A2/513	V.95	Footrest serrated hanger only	2	1, 16H, 18, ES2		9	8
A11/513	V.96	Footrest serrated hanger only	2	30, 40		10	0
A2/514	V.98	Footrest serrated hanger spindle only	2	1, 16H, 18, ES2, 30, 40		2	4
A2/515	V.100	Footrest serrated hanger spindle nut	2	1, 16H, 18, ES2, 30, 40			5
E5376	V.99	Footrest hanger spindle washer	2	1, 16H, 18, ES2, 30, 40			3
A11M/512(RH)		Footrest serrated hanger with pad holder	1	30M, 40M		17	6
A11M/512(LH)	V.89	Footrest serrated hanger with pad holder	1	30M, 40M		17	6
13274	V.90	Footrest frame attachment bolt	2	30M, 40M		1	6
E5375	V.91	Footrest frame attachment bolt washer	2	30M, 40M			3

PLATE. V.

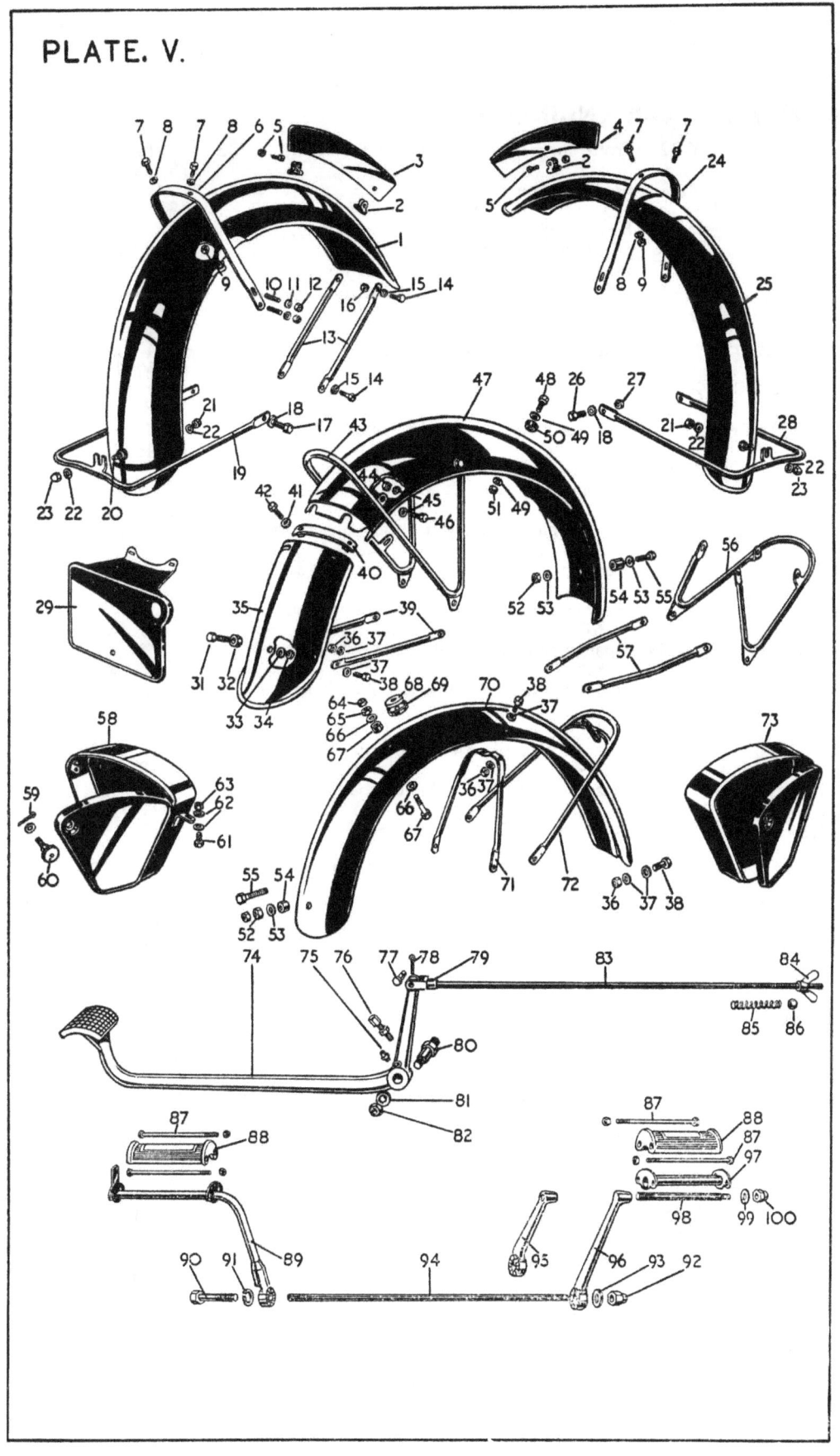

PART No.	PLATE No.	DESCRIPTION.	QTY.	USED ON.	PRICE EACH. £ s. d.

FRONT AND REAR ENGINE PLATES.

PART No.	PLATE No.	DESCRIPTION.	QTY.	USED ON.	£	s.	d.
A2/522	Y.32	Front engine plate (left or right hand)	2	1, 16H, 18, ES2		8	0
A2/523	Y.31	Front engine plate cover	1	1, 16H, 18, ES2		6	6
A11/523	W.16	Front engine plate cover	1	30		6	6
A10/523	W.16	Front engine plate cover	1	40		6	6
A11/522	W.17	Front engine plate (left or right hand)	2	30		8	0
A10/522	W.17	Front engine plate (left or right hand)	2	40		8	0
A11M/522(LH)	X.35	Front engine plate, left hand	1	30M, (40M 1948)		8	0
A10M/522(LH)		Front engine plate, left hand	1	40M (1946/7)		8	0
A11M/522(RH)	X.36	Front engine plate, right hand	1	30M, (40M 1948)		8	0
A10M/522(RH)		Front engine plate, right hand	1	40M (1946/7)		8	0
A2/516	Y.10	Rear engine plate, left hand with footrest tube	1	1, 16H, 18		19	0
B4/516	Y.10	Rear engine plate, left hand with footrest tube	1	ES2		19	0
A2/517	Y.11	Rear engine plate, right hand with footrest tube	1	1, 16H, 18		19	0
B4/517	Y.11	Rear engine plate, right hand with footrest tube	1	ES2		19	0
A11/516	W.24	Rear engine plate, left hand with footrest tube	1	30		19	0
A10/516	W.24	Rear engine plate, left hand with footrest tube	1	40		19	0
A11M/516	X.3	Rear engine plate only left hand	1	30M, (40M 1948)		12	6
A10M/516		Rear engine plate only left hand	1	40M (1946/7)		12	6
A11/517	W.25	Rear engine plate, right hand with footrest tube	1	30		19	0
A10/517	W.25	Rear engine plate, right hand with footrest tube	1	40		19	0
A11M/517	X.4	Rear engine plate only right hand	1	30M, (40M 1948)		12	6
A10M/517		Rear engine plate only right hand	1	40M (1946/7)		12	6

FRAMES.

PART No.	PLATE No.	DESCRIPTION.	QTY.	USED ON.	£	s.	d.
B2/518		Frame only with head races	1	1, 16H, 18	24	0	0
B4/518		Frame only with head races	1	ES2	30	0	0
A11/518		Frame only with head races	1	30, 40	30	0	0
A11M/518		Frame only with head races	1	30M, 40M	30	0	0
A2/519		Frame head race, top	1	All Models		7	6
A2/520		Frame head race, bottom	1	All Models		7	6
A2/521		Frame head balls, (per set 34)	1	All Models		4	0
13195	X.19	Frame fork stop bolt	2	All Models			8
11796	X.17	Frame fork stop bolt washer	4	All Models			3
B2/877	X.18	Frame fork stop bolt distance piece	2	All Models			6

FRAME REAR SPRINGING.

PART No.	PLATE No.	DESCRIPTION.	QTY.	USED ON.	£	s.	d.
B4/669		Frame fork end, left hand	1	ES2, 30, 30M, 40, 40M	5	0	0
B4/670	Y.19	Frame fork end, right hand	1	ES2, 30, 30M, 40, 40M	5	0	0
A2/500	Y.20	Frame fork end grease nipple	2	ES2, 30, 30M, 40, 40M		1	0

215

PLATE. W.

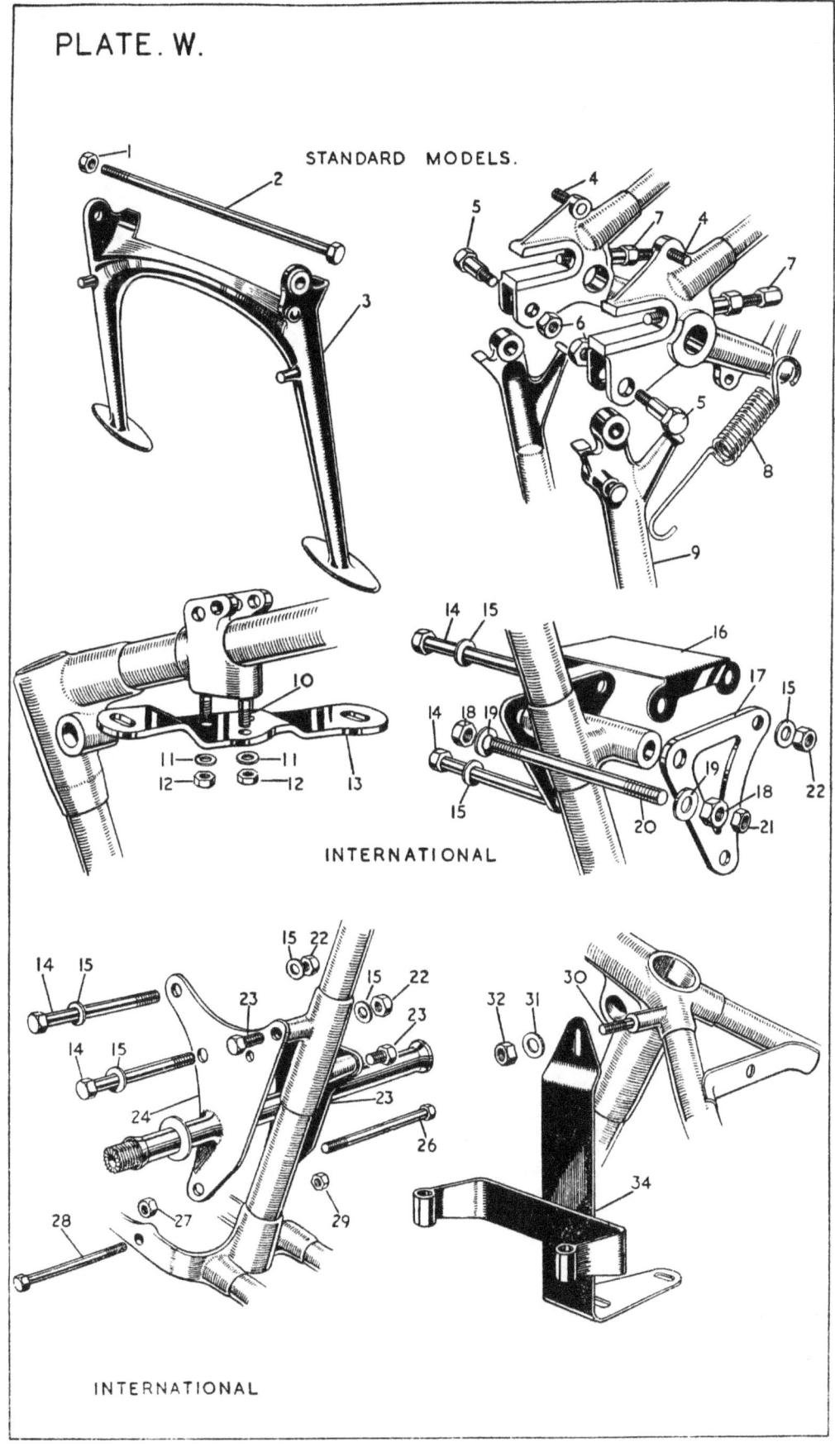

STANDARD MODELS.

INTERNATIONAL

INTERNATIONAL

PART No.	PLATE No.	DESCRIPTION.	QTY.	USED ON.	PRICE EACH. £ s. d.
FRAME REAR SPRINGING—cont.					
B4/671	... Y.28	Frame fork end main rod	2	ES2, 30, 30M, 40, 40M ...	3 0 0
B4/672	... Y.30	Frame fork end main rod bottom bolt	2	ES2, 30, 30M, 40, 40M ...	1 0
11181	... Y.29	Frame fork end main rod bottom bolt washer	2	ES2, 30, 30M, 40, 40M ...	3
B4/673	... Y.24	Frame fork end main rod plug	2	ES2, 30, 30M, 40, 40M ...	2 0
E4261	T.31/Y.27	Rear frame member pinch bolt (nearside)	1	ES2, 30, 30M, 40, 40M ...	9
11304	...	Rear frame member pinch bolt (offside)	1	ES2, 30, 30M, 40, 40M ...	9
E3223	T.29/Y.25	Rear frame member pinch bolt nut	2	ES2, 30, 30M, 40, 40M ...	4
11796	T.30/Y.26	Rear frame member pinch bolt washer	4	ES2, 30, 30M, 40, 40M ...	3
B4/674	... Y.17	Frame fork end top spring	2	ES2, 30, 30M, 40, 40M ...	15 0
B4/675	... Y.16	Frame fork end top spring cover, outer	2	ES2, 30, 30M, 40, 40M ...	9 0
B4/676	... Y.18	Frame fork end top spring cover, inner	2	ES2, 30, 30M, 40, 40M ...	12 6
B4/677	... Y.22	Frame fork end bottom spring	2	ES2, 30, 30M, 40, 40M ...	12 6
B4/678	... Y.23	Frame fork end bottom spring cover, outer	2	ES2, 30, 30M, 40, 40M ...	9 0
B4/679	... Y.21	Frame fork end bottom spring cover, inner	2	ES2, 30, 30M, 40, 40M ...	12 6
PROP STAND.					
A2/524	... W.3	Prop stand	1	1, 16H, 18 ...	1 5 0
B4/524	... W.3	Prop stand	1	ES2	1 5 0
A11/524	... X.24	Prop stand	1	30, 30M, 40, 40M	1 5 0
A11/525	... X.22	Prop stand bolt	2	ES2, 30, 30M, 40, 40M ...	9
A2/525	... W.2	Prop stand frame pivot bolt	1	1, 16H, 18	2 4
A2/526	... W.1	Prop stand frame pivot bolt nut	1	1, 16H, 18 ...	5
A2/527	... X.23	Prop stand return spring	1	All Models	2 0
A2/528	...	Frame bush for prop stand pivot bolt	1	1, 16H, 18 ...	3 4
FRONT MUDGUARD, STAYS AND FITTINGS.					
B2/529	... V.1	Front mudguard only with front No. plate studs	1	30, 40, 1, 16H, 18, ES2	1 0 0

PLATE. X.

MANX

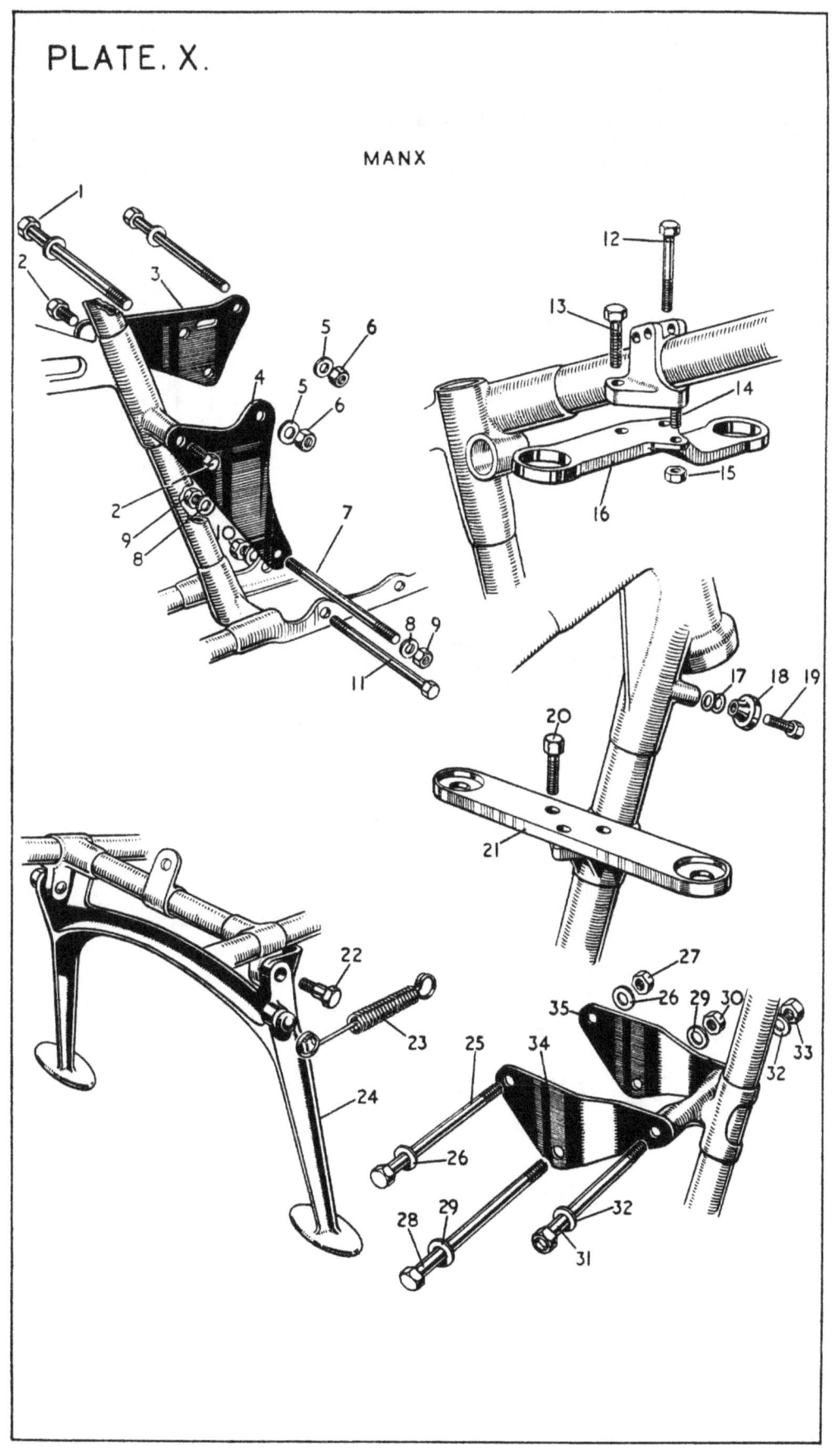

PART No	PLATE No.	DESCRIPTION.	QTY.	USED ON.	PRICE EACH. £ s. d.
FRONT MUDGUARD, STAYS AND FITTINGS—cont.					
A11M/529	V.25	Front mudguard	1	30M, 40M	1 0 0
A2/530	V.13	Front mudguard stay, left or right hand	2	1, 16H, 18, ES2	3 6
12342	V.14	Front mudguard stay pin	4	1, 16H, 18, ES2, 30, 40	5
E3229	V.16	Front mudguard stay nut	4	1, 16H, 18, ES2, 30, 40	4
E5379	V.15	Front mudguard stay nut washer	2	1, 16H, 18, ES2, 30, 40	3
A11/530	V.13	Front mudguard stay, left or right hand	2	30, 40	3 6
B2/680	V.6	Front mudguard centre stay	1	1, 16H, 18, ES2	6 6
A11/680	V.6	Front mudguard centre stay	1	30, 40	6 6
A11M/680	V.24	Front mudguard centre stay	1	30M, 40M	6 6
12342	V.7	Front mudguard centre stay pin	2	All Models	5
E3229	V.9	Front mudguard centre stay pin nut	2	All Models	4
E5379	V.8	Front mudguard centre stay pin washer	2	All Models	3
T1085	J.32/V.10	Front mudguard centre stay fork attachment stud	4	All Models	6
E3229	V.12	Front mudguard centre stay fork attachment stud nut	4	All Models	4
E5379	V.11	Front mudguard centre stay fork attachment stud washer	4	All Models	3
E3262	V.20	Front mudguard stand attachment bolt	1	All Models	8
E3223	V.21	Front mudguard stand attachment bolt plain nut	1	All Models	4
E3218	V.23	Front mudguard stand attachment bolt domed nut	1	All Models	6
E5456	V.22	Front mudguard stand attachment bolt washer	2	All Models	3
RACING NUMBER PLATES AND STONE GUARD.					
A11M/870		Number plate front or side	3	30M, 40M	5 0
A11M/871		Number plate clip (rear)	4	30M, 40M	1 0
12342		Number plate fixing pin (front)	2	30M, 40M	5
12342		Number plate fixing pin (rear)	8	30M, 40M	5
E3222		Number plate fixing pin nut (front)	2	30M, 40M	4
E3222		Number plate fixing pin nut (rear)	8	30M, 40M	4
A11M/872		Handlebar gauze stone guard	1	30M, 40M	12 6
12342		Handlebar gauze stone guard pin	2	30M, 40M	5
E3222		Handlebar guaze stone guard pin nut	2	30M, 40M	4
FRONT AND REAR NUMBER PLATES AND FITTINGS.					
A2/531	V.3	Front number plate	1	30, 40, 1, 16H, 18, ES2	2 0
A11M/531	V.4	Front number plate	1	30M, 40M	2 0
A2/532	V.29	Rear number plate	1	30, 40, 1, 16H, 18, ES2	5 0
D2/532		Rear number plate (1949)	1	30, 40, 1, 16H, 18, ES2	5 0
12343	V.31	Rear number plate bottom fixing pin	1	30, 40, 1, 16H, 18, ES2	8
E3222	V.34	Rear number plate bottom fixing pin nut	1	30, 40, 1, 16H, 18, ES2	4
E5379	V.33	Rear number plate bottom fixing pin washer	1	30, 40, 1, 16H, 18, ES2	3

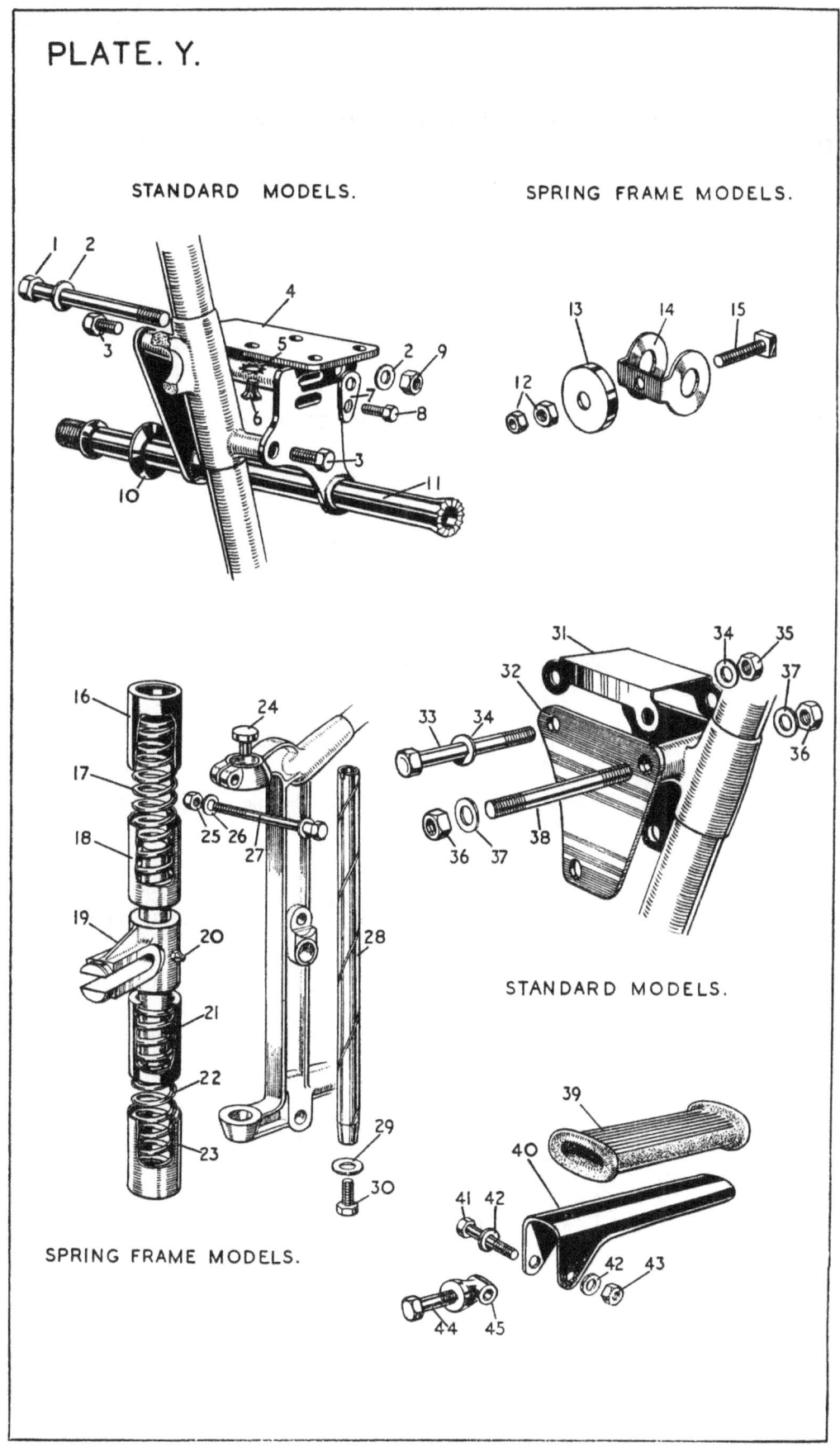

PART No.	PLATE No.	DESCRIPTION.	QTY.	USED ON.	PRICE EACH. £ s. d.
FRONT AND REAR NUMBER PLATES AND FITTINGS—cont.					
E5105	V.32	Rear number plate distance piece	1	30, 40, 1, 16H, 18, ES2	6
A2/533	V.5	Front number plate attachment pin and nut	2	30, 40, 1, 16H, 18, ES2	3
			1	30M, 40M	3
A2/875	V.2	Front No. plate mudguard clip	2	30, 40, 1, 16H, 18, ES2	1 0
			1	30M, 40M	1 0
REAR MUDGUARD STAYS AND FITTINGS.					
A2/534	V.47	Rear mudguard complete	1	1, 16H, 18, ES2	1 0 0
A11/534	V.47	Rear mudguard complete	1	30, 40	1 0 0
A11M/534	V.70	Rear mudguard	1	30M, 40M	1 0 0
A2/535	V.35	Rear mudguard bottom portion	1	30, 40, 1, 16H, 18, ES2	6 0
A2/876	V.40	Rear mudgard bottom portion strap	1	30, 40, 1, 16H, 18, ES2	2 0
12342	V.42	Rear mudguard bottom portion fixing pins (each)	2	30, 40, 1, 16H, 18, ES2	5
E5379	V.41	Rear mudguard bottom portion pin washer	2	30, 40, 1, 16H, 18, ES2	3
A2/536	V.43	Rear mudguard stays and lifting handle	1	1, 16H, 18	1 0 0
12342	V.46	Rear lifting stay mudguard pin	4	30, 40, 1, 16H, 18, ES2	5
E3222	V.44	Rear lifting stay mudguard pin nut	4	30, 40, 1, 16H, 18, ES2	4
E5379	V.45	Rear lifting stay mudguard pin washer	8	30, 40, 1, 16H, 18, ES2	3
B4/536	V.56	Rear mudguard stays and lifting handle	1	ES2	1 0 0
A11/536	V.56	Rear mudguard stay and lifting handle	1	30, 40	1 0 0
A11M/536	V.72	Rear mudguard stay and lifting handle	1	30M, 40M	12 6
A11M/831	V.71	Rear mudguard centre stay	1	30M, 40M	7 6
E6453	W.4	Rear mudguard stays and lifting handle stud (frame attachment)	2	1, 16H, 18	8
E3223		Rear mudguard stays and lifting handle attachment stud nut	2	1, 16H, 18	4
A2/537	V.39	Rear mudguard stay, left or right hand	2	1, 16H, 18	3 6
B4/537	V.57	Rear mudguard stay, left or right hand	2	ES2	3 6
A11/537	V.57	Rear mudguard stay, left or right hand	1	30, 40	3 6
12342	V.38	Rear mudguard stay pin, mudguard attachment	2	All Models	5
E3222	V.36	Rear mudguard stay pin nut	2	All Models	4
E5379	V.37	Rear mudguard stay pin washer	4	All Models	3
13059	V.54	Rear mudguard chain stay distance piece	1	30, 40, 1, 16H, 18, ES2	5
12868	V.55	Rear mudguard chain stay attachment bolt	1	All Models	8
E3223	V.52	Rear mudguard chain stay attachment bolt nut	1	All Models	4
E5379	V.53	Rear mudguard stay attachment bolt washer	1	All Models	3

(See Oil Tank Fittings for Mudguard Seat Stay Attachment. Plate M).

PART No.	PLATE No.	DESCRIPTION.	QTY.	USED ON.	PRICE EACH. £ s. d.
TOOLBOX AND FITTINGS.					
A2/538	V.58	Toolbox	1	1, 16H, 18	1 5 0
B2/538	V.73	Toolbox	1	30, 40, ES2	1 5 0
12343	...	Toolbox frame attachment bolt	2	30, 40, 1, 16H, 18, ES2	8
E3229	...	Toolbox frame attachment bolt nut	2	30, 40, 1, 16H, 18, ES2	4
A2/539	V.60	Toolbox knob	1	30, 40, 1, 16H, 18, ES2	2 4
A2/281	V.59	Toolbox knob cotter	1	30, 40, 1, 16H, 18, ES2	2
12342	V.61	Toolbox bottom bolt	1	1, 16H, 18	5
E3229	V.63	Toolbox bottom bolt nut	1	1, 16H, 18	4
E5379	V.62	Toolbox bottom bolt washer	2	1, 16H, 18	3
SADDLE AND FITTINGS.					
A2/540	H.6	Saddle	1	1, 16H, 18, ES2	2 17 0
A11/540	H.1	Saddle	1	30, 30M, 40, 40M	2 17 0
A2/541	H.7	Saddle spring (each)	2	1, 16H, 18, ES2	4 0
A11/541	H.2	Saddle spring (each)	2	30, 30M, 40, 40M	4 0
E6453	...	Saddle spring stud offside	1	1, 16H, 18, ES2	8
E6047	H.5	Saddle spring frame stud	2	30, 30M, 40, 40M	2 0
E5642	...	Saddle spring frame stud distance tube	2	30, 30M, 40, 40M	6
E3223	H.3	Saddle spring stud nut	2	All Models	4
E5456	H.4	Saddle spring stud washer	2	All Models	3
12080	...	Saddle front anchor bolt	1	All Models	1 8
E3223	...	Saddle front anchor bolt nut	1	All Models	4
E5379	...	Saddle front anchor bolt washer	1	All Models	3

(See Horn Attachment for Near Side Saddle Spring Bolt. Models 1, 16H, 18, and ES2).

PART No.	PLATE No.	DESCRIPTION.	QTY.	USED ON.	PRICE EACH. £ s. d.
REAR STAND AND FITTINGS.					
A2/542	W.9	Rear stand	1	1, 16H, 18	2 2 0
E3813	W.5	Rear stand attachment bolt	2	1, 16H, 18	1 0
11664	W.6	Rear stand attachment bolt nut	2	1, 16H, 18	5
A2/543	W.8	Rear stand spring	1	1, 16H, 18	3 0
FRONT STAND AND FITTINGS.					
A2/544	V.19	Front stand	1	1, 16H, 18, ES2	1 0 0
A11/544	V.19	Front stand	1	30, 40	1 0 0
A11M/544	V.28	Front stand	1	30M, 40M	1 0 0
13261	V.17	Front stand attachment pin	2	30, 40, 1, 16H, 18, ES2	5
13299	V.26	Front stand attachment pin	2	30M, 40M	6
E3231	V.27	Front stand attachment pin nut	2	30M, 40M	4
E5379	V.18	Front stand attachment pin washer	2	All Models	3

PART No.	PLATE No.	DESCRIPTION.	QTY.	USED. ON.	PRICE EACH. £ s. d.
PILLION SEAT AND FITTINGS.					
A2/585	...	Pillion seat	1	30, 40, 1, 16H, 18, ES2	1 13 4
12342	...	Pillion seat attachment pin	4	30, 40, 1, 16H, 18, ES2	5
E3222	...	Pillion seat attachment pin nut	4	30, 40, 1, 16H, 18, ES2	4
MATTRESS AND FITTINGS. Manx Models.					
A11M/832	H.8	Rubber Mattress	1	30M, 40M	3 15 0
A11M/833	H.15	Rubber mattress support stay, L.H. or R.H.	2	30M, 40M	3 6
E3798	H.16	Bolt attaching stay to mudguard	2	30M, 40M	4
E3231	H.14	Nut attaching stay to mudguard	2	30M, 40M	4
11796	...	Washer attaching stay to mudguard	4	30M, 40M	3
A2/504	H.10	Jaw joint	2	30M, 40M	4 6
12342	H.9	Bolt attaching jaw joint to saddle frame	2	30M, 40M	5
E3222	H.11	Nut attaching jaw joint to saddle frame	2	30M, 40M	4
E5379	...	Washer attaching jaw joint to saddle frame	2	30M, 40M	3
11940	H.13	Bolt for bottom of jaw joint	2	30M, 40M	5
11796	H.12	Bolt washer for bottom of jaw joint	6	30M, 40M	3
BATTERY CARRIER AND FITTINGS.					
A2/586	W.34	Battery carrier	1	1, 16H, 18, ES2	15 0
A11/586	W.34	Battery carrier	1	30, 40	15 0
E6453	W.30	Battery carrier top stud	1	1, 16H, 18, ES2, 30, 40	6
E3223	W.32	Battery carrier top stud nut	1	1, 16H, 18, ES2, 30, 40	4
E5456	W.31	Battery carrier stud washer	1	1, 16H, 18, ES2, 30, 40	3

(See Oil Tank Fittings for Bottom Bolt).

PART No.	PLATE No.	DESCRIPTION.	QTY.	USED. ON.	PRICE EACH. £ s. d.
REAR CARRIER.					
A2/605	...	Rear carrier	1	30, 40, 1, 16H, 18, ES2	1 4 6
12343	...	Rear carrier attachment bolt	4	30, 40, 1, 16H, 18, ES2	8
E3222	...	Rear carrier attachment bolt nut	4	30, 40, 1, 16H, 18, ES2	4
SPEEDOMETER AND FITTINGS.					
B11/545	...	Speedometer head	1	30, 40	3 0 0
B2/545	H.24	Speedometer head	1	1, 16H, 18, ES2	3 0 0
B2/681	H.60	Speedometer head rubber washer	1	30, 40, 1, 16H, 18, ES2	6
B2/555	H.61	Speedometer head attachment bracket	1	30, 40, 1, 16H, 18, ES2	1 6
B2/556	H.25	Speedometer head securing nut	2	30, 40, 1, 16H, 18, ES2	4

PART No.	PLATE No.	DESCRIPTION.	QTY.	USED ON.	PRICE EACH. £ s. d.
SPEEDOMETER AND FITTINGS—cont.					
B2/557	...	Speedometer head securing washer	2	30, 40, 1, 16H, 18, ES2	3
B2/552	...	Speedometer cable complete	1	30, 40, 1, 16H, 18, ES2	1 5 0
B2/553	H.27	Seedometer cable, outer	1	30, 40, 1, 16H, 18, ES2	12 6
B2/554	H.26	Speedometer cable, inner	1	30, 40, 1, 16H, 18, ES2	12 6
B2/564	S.34	Speedometer gear box complete	1	30, 40, 1, 16H, 18, ES2	1 10 0
REVOLUTION COUNTER.					
A11M/545	H.17	Revolution counter head only	1	30M, 40M	3 0 0
A11M/555	H.20	Revolution counter attachment bracket	1	30M, 40M	4 0
A11M/681	H.19	Revolution counter rubber washer	1	30M, 40M	2 0
A11M/556	H.18	Revolution counter securing nut	2	30M, 40M	4
A11M/557	...	Revolution counter securing nut washer	2	30M, 40M	3
A11M/858	H.21	Revolution counter retaining cup	1	30M, 40M	4 0
A11M/552	...	Revolution counter cable complete	1	30M, 40M	1 5 0
A11M/553	H.23	Revolution counter cable, outer	1	30M, 40M	12 6
A11M/554	H.22	Revolution counter cable, inner	1	30M, 40M	12 6
A11M/546	B.7	Revolution counter gearbox	1	30M, 40M	2 2 6
A11M/859	B.8	Revolution counter gearbox attachment pin	2	30M, 40M	5
A11M/860	B.9	Revolution counter gearbox attachment pin nut	4	30M, 40M	3

(For Driving Nut see Mag. Drive Parts).

PART No.	PLATE No.	DESCRIPTION.	QTY.	USED ON.	PRICE EACH. £ s. d.
PILLION FOOTRESTS AND FITTINGS.					
A2/582	Y.40	Pillion footrest hanger, L.H. or R.H.	1	30, 40, 1, 16H, 18, ES2	4 0
A2/583	Y.39	Pillion footrest rubber, L.H. or R.H.	2	30, 40, 1, 16H, 18, ES2	3 0
E3801	Y.41	Pillion footrest attachment bolt	2	30, 40, 1, 16H, 18, ES2	5
5790A	Y.42	Pillion footrest attachment bolt spring washer	2	30, 40, 1, 16H, 18, ES2	4
E3223	Y.43	Pillion footrest attachment bolt nut	2	30, 40, 1, 16H, 18, ES2	4
A2/584	...	Pillion footrest complete with pins (per pair)	1	30, 40, 1, 16H, 18, ES2	17 0
B4/686	Y.45	Frame pillion footrest lug	2	30, 40, ES2 ...	2 6
11601	Y.44	Frame pillion footrest lug bolt	2	30, 40, ES2 ...	6
B.T.H. MAGNETO AND FITTINGS.					
KD1-C6TT	...	Magneto complete	1	30M, 40M	9 15 0
CX1883-C16		Contact breaker complete	1	30M, 40M	2 1 6
CX63472-G6		Contact breaker lever with springs	1	30M, 40M	15 0
SKC24474-G1		Contact breaker screw adjustable	1	30M, 40M	8 4
CR29487-1	...	Contact breaker securing screw	1	30M, 40M	5

PART No.	PLATE No.	DESCRIPTION.	QTY.	USED ON.	PRICE EACH. £ s. d.
B.T.H. MAGNETO AND FITTINGS—cont.					
SKC6219-G1		Earthing brush and spring	1	30M, 40M	7
SKC30961-G1		Brush holder H.T.	1	30M, 40M	5 0
SKC6607-1		Brush holder screw	2	30M, 40M	3
SKC6306-G1		Brush and spring H.T.	1	30M, 40M	5
SKC28537-G1		Contact breaker cover	1	30M, 40M	5 0
CZ60707-G10		H.T. Lead	1	30M, 40M	5 0

MAGDYNO PARTS (LUCAS).

PART No.	PLATE No.	DESCRIPTION.	QTY.	USED ON.	PRICE EACH. £ s. d.
463121	...	Magdyno fibre gear wheel assembly	1	1, 16H, 18, ES2, 30, 40	16 10
200569	...	Slotted screw securing dynamo to magneto	1	1, 16H, 18, ES2, 30, 40	5
200290	...	Dynamo brushes (per set)	1	1, 16H, 18, ES2, 30, 40	3 0
463066	...	H.T. pickup for magneto	1	1, 16H, 18, ES2, 30, 40	4 2
451260	...	H.T. pickup carbon brush and spring	1	1, 16H, 18, ES2, 30, 40	11
460056	...	Strap with pin and roller securing dynamo to Magneto	1	1, 16H, 18, ES2, 30, 40	2 5
460051	...	Contact breaker complete	1	1, 16H, 18, ES2, 30, 40	13 10
484098	...	Contact breaker points (per set)	1	1, 16H, 18, ES2, 30, 40	5 5
410600	...	Screwed bush for H.T. pickup	1	1, 16H, 18, ES2, 30, 40	11
460061	...	Contact breaker cover	1	1, 16H, 18, ES2, 30, 40	1 2
200354	...	Dynamo bakelite end cover with screw	1	1, 16H, 18, ES2, 30, 40	3 11
454495	...	Steel pinion driven for dynamo	1	1, 16H, 18, ES2, 30, 40	5 1

See Magdyno Driving Parts and Fittings for Sprockets.

HEADLAMP AND PARTS.

PART No.	PLATE No.	DESCRIPTION.	QTY.	USED ON.	PRICE EACH. £ s. d.
50212B	...	Headlamp complete with ammeter, switch, bulbs, handlebar dipping switch and cables	1	1, 16H, 18, ES2, 30, 40	5 14 6
112201	...	Headlamp fixing bolt	2	1, 16H, 18, ES2, 30, 40	8
506860	...	Headlamp rim	1	1, 16H, 18, ES2, 30, 40	11 8
507586	...	Headlamp glass	1	1, 16H, 18, ES2, 30, 40	5 5
508736	...	Headlamp glass cork washer	1	1, 16H, 18, ES2, 30, 40	1 0

PART No	PLATE No.	DESCRIPTION.	QTY.	USED. ON.	PRICE EACH. £ s. d.
HEADLAMP AND PARTS—cont.					
364455	...	Ammeter	1	1, 16H, 18, ES2, 30, 40	11 8
351551	...	Switch complete	1	1, 16H, 18, ES2, 30, 40	10 3
SK49	...	Headlamp switch lever and screw	1	1, 16H, 18, ES2, 30, 40	2 1
308330	...	Headlamp panel complete	1	1, 16H, 18, ES2, 30, 40	1 11 3
380501	...	Headlamp dipper switch	1	1, 16H, 18, ES2, 30, 40	6 7
REAR LAMP AND FITTINGS.					
53009A	...	Rear lamp complete	1	1, 16H, 18, ES2, 30, 40	16 10
53056A	...	Rear lamp complete (1949)	1	1, 16H, 18, ES2, 30, 40	16 10
526111	...	Rear lamp back portion with bulb holder	1	1, 16H, 18, ES2, 30, 40	6 4
526230	...	Rear lamp back portion (1949)	1	1, 16H, 18, ES2, 30, 40	6 4
526112	...	Rear lamp front portion with red glass	1	1, 16H, 18, ES2, 30, 40	7 2
526232	...	Rear lamp front portion (1949)	1	1, 16H, 18, ES2, 30, 40	7 2
A2/587	...	Rear lamp attachment pin and nut	3	1, 16H, 18, ES2, 30, 40	4
VOLTAGE REGULATOR AND FITTINGS.					
33018A	...	Voltage regulator	1	1, 16H, 18, ES2, 30, 40	1 19 0
12342	...	Voltage regulator fixing pin	2	1, 16H, 18, ES2, 30, 40	5
E3222	...	Voltage regulator fixing pin nut	2	1, 16H, 18, ES2, 30, 40	4
E5375	...	Voltage regulator fixing washer	2	1, 16H, 18, ES2, 30, 40	3

(See Oil Tank Fittings for Regulator Clip).

PART No	PLATE No.	DESCRIPTION.	QTY.	USED. ON.	PRICE EACH. £ s. d.
ELECTRIC HORN AND FITTINGS.					
069343	...	Electric horn with bracket		30, 40	1 15 8
701686	...	Electric horn bracket	1	1, 16H, 18, ES2, 1, 16H, 18, ES2, 30, 40	3 4
13299	...	Electric horn bracket fixing bolt to frame	1	1, 16H, 18, ES2	6
762080	...	Electric horn button	1	All Models	5 9

PART No.	PLATE No.	DESCRIPTION.	QTY.	USED ON.	PRICE EACH. £ s. d.
TOOLS.					
A2/561	...	Tyre inflator with connection	1	All Models	8 0
A2/562	...	Tyre inflator connection	1	All Models	3 6
A2/563	...	Tool-roll complete with tools	1	1, 16H	2 10 6
A3/563	...	Tool-roll complete with tools	1	18, ES2, 30, 40	2 17 6
A11M/563	...	Tool-roll complete with tools	1	30M, 40M	2 17 6
A2/564	...	6in. adjustable spanner	1	All Models	7 0
A2/565	...	Double ended spanner 3/16in. and 1/4in.	1	All Models	2 0
A2/566	...	Double ended spanner 5/16in. and 3/8in.	1	All Models	2 8
A2/567	...	Screw driver	1	All Models	2 6
C2/568	...	Tappet spanners (per pair)	1	1, 16H	11 0
C3/568	...	Push rod adjusting spanners (per pair)	1	18, ES2	2 0
A2/569	...	Chain rivet extractor	1	All Models	5 6
A2/570	...	Wheel nut box spanner	1	All Models	2 0
A3/571	...	Sparking plug spanner	1	18, ES2, 30, 40	4 0
A11M/571	...	Sparking plug spanner	1	30M, 40M	5 0
A2/572	...	6in. pliers	1	All Models	5 0
A2/573	...	Tyre lever	1	All Models	2 0
A2/574	...	Wheel spindle spanner	1	All Models	2 8
A2/275	...	Grease gun	1	All Models	15 0
A2/576	...	Gearbox top nut spanner	1	All Models	5 0
C2/577	...	Sparking plug spanner	1	1, 16H	3 6
A2/578	...	Single ended spanner, 1/8in.	1	1, 16H, 18, ES2	1 0
A3/579	...	Exhaust pipe " C " spanner	1	18, ES2, 30, 30M, 40, 40M	3 0
A2/580	...	Cylinder head nut spanner	1	1, 16H	3 6
A2/581	...	Tommy bar	1	All Models	1 0
B2/682	...	Front fork crown and column locknut spanner	1	All Models	2 6
B2/683	...	Front fork filler plug and head adjuster nut spanner	1	All Models	3 0
B2/684	...	Front fork main tube top bush locking spanner	1	All Models	2 0
B2/685	...	Pull through for road holder fork	1	All Models	7 6
LEGSHIELDS AND FITTINGS.					
A2/589	...	Legshields and fittings complete (per set)	1	1, 16H, 18, ES2	2 13 4
A2/590	...	Legshield blade, L.H.	1	1, 16H, 18, ES2	14 8
A2/591	...	Legshield blade, R.H.	1	1, 16H, 18, ES2	14 8
A2/592	...	Legshield blade bracket, L.H. or R.H.	2	1, 16H, 18, ES2	1 0
A2/593	...	Legshield blade bracket back plate	1	1, 16H, 18, ES2	8
12342	...	Legshield blade bracket pin	1	1, 16H, 18, ES2	5
E3222	...	Legshield blade bracket pin nut	1	1, 16H, 18, ES2	4
A2/595	...	Legshield tank attachment bracket	1	1, 16H, 18, ES2	2 8
A2/596	...	Legshield tank attachment bracket, R.H.	1	1, 16H, 18, ES2	2 8
A2/597	...	Petrol tank front rubber	1	1, 16H, 18, ES2	6
A2/598	...	Legshield top securing rod	1	1, 16H, 18, ES2	2 0
A2/599	...	Legshield bottom securing rod	1	1, 16H, 18, ES2	2 0
E3226	...	Legshield securing rod nut	1	1, 16H, 18, ES2	4
A2/600	...	Legshield blade bracket distance tube 3-3/8in.	1	1, 16H, 18, ES2	8

PART No.	PLATE No.	DESCRIPTION.	QTY.	USED ON.	PRICE EACH. £ s. d.
LEGSHIELDS AND FITTINGS—cont.					
A2/601	...	Tank bracket distance tube 13-1/8in. ...	1	1, 16H, 18, ES2	1 4
A2/602	...	Legshield blade tank bracket distance tube 1-7/16in.	1	1, 16H, 18, ES2	4
A2/603	...	Legshield bottom L.H. distance tube 5-1/8in.	1	1, 16H, 18, ES2	8
A2/604	...	Legshield bottom R.H. distance tube 6-7/8in.	1	1, 16H, 18, ES2	8
TRANSFERS.					
A2/865	...	Petrol tank name transfer	2	All Models	1 2
A2/866	...	Petrol tank name transfer for top panel	1	All Models	1 2
A2/867	...	Front chaincase transfer	1	1, 16H, 18, ES2, 30, 40	1 2
A2/868	...	Oil tank transfer (minimum oil level) ...	1	—	1 2
A2/869	...	Rear mudguard transfer	1	All Models	1 2

(Please Note.—Panels, Red and Black lines cannot be supplied. These are painted by hand).

RUBBER CABLE CLIPS.					
Size "A"	...	For clutch, air, throttle, mag. cables, and head lamp cable harness to top frame tube	1	—	4
Size "D"	...	For tail lamp lead	1	—	4
Size "S"	...	For speedometer cable and battery lead ...	1	—	4
SIDECAR CHASSIS AND FITTINGS.					
A2/881	...	Sidecar chassis less all fittings	1	All Models	25 0 0
A2/882	...	Sidecar front chassis attachment arm	1	All Models	2 0 0
A2/883	...	Sidecar front arm chassis attachment bolt	1	All Models	4 0
A2/884	...	Sidecar front attachment arm sleeve nut	1	All Models	1 0
A2/885	...	Sidecar front attachment arm sleeve nut washer	1	All Models	4
E3228	...	Sidecar attachment arm bolt nut	1	All Models	8
A2/885	...	Sidecar attachment arm bolt washer	1	All Models	4
A2/886	...	Crankcase engine plate and 4th point attachment rod	1	All Models	5 0
E3226	...	Crankcase engine plate and 4th point attachment rod nut	1	All Models	5
A2/887	...	Sidecar 4th point connection distance tube	1	All Models	2 0
A2/888	...	Sidecar 4th point attachment stud connection plate	1	All Models	1 6
A2/889	...	Sidecar centre arm frame plug	1	All Models	15 0
E3228	...	Sidecar centre arm frame plug nut	1	All Models	8
A2/885	...	Sidecar centre arm frame plug nut washer	1	All Models	4
A2/890	...	Sidecar centre arm, top portion	1	All Models	9 0
A2/891	...	Sidecar centre arm, bottom portion	1	All Models	2 0 0
E3860	...	Sidecar arm clip pin	1	All Models	8
E3224	...	Sidecar arm clip pin nut	1	All Models	4
A2/892	...	Sidecar centre arm chassis eye bolt	1	All Models	5 0
E3227	...	Sidecar centre arm chassis eye bolt nut ...	1	All Models	5
11871	...	Jaw joint clip complete for chassis rear tube	1	All Models	13 0
E3812	...	Jaw joint clip bolt	2	All Models	1 0
E3224	...	Jaw joint clip bolt nut	2	All Models	4
11765	...	Sidecar centre arm jaw joint bolt	1	All Models	1 0
E3226	...	Sidecar centre arm jaw joint bolt nut	1	All Models	5
A2/893	...	Sidecar rear arm	1	1, 16H, 18	19 0
B4/893	...	Sidecar rear arm	1	Spring Frame Models	15 0

PART No.	PLATE No.	DESCRIPTION.	QTY.	USED. ON.	PRICE EACH. £ s. d.

SIDECAR CHASSIS AND FITTINGS—cont.

PART No.	PLATE No.	DESCRIPTION.	QTY.	USED ON.	£	s.	d.
A2/894	...	Sidecar rear arm frame attachment bolt	1	All Models		4	0
A2/895	...	Sidecar rear arm frame attachment bolt distance piece	1	1, 16H, 18		2	0
E3228	...	Sidecar rear arm frame attachment bolt nut	1	All Models			8
A2/885	...	Sidecar rear arm frame attachment bolt nut washer	1	All Models			4
B4/895	...	Sidecar rear arm frame attachment bolt distance piece	1	Spring Frame Models		2	0
A2/896	...	Sidecar front spring	2	All Models		13	0
A2/897	...	Sidecar rear spring	2	All Models	1	5	0
A2/898	...	Sidecar spring holding down 'U' clip, long	5 per set	All Models		2	6
A2/899	...	Sidecar spring holding down 'U' clip, short	3 per set	All Models		2	0
E3224	...	Sidecar spring holding down 'U' clip nut	16	All Models			4
A2/900	...	Sidecar spring holding down 'U' clip nut washer	16	All Models			3
A2/901	...	Sidecar rear spring shackle	2	All Models		4	6
A2/902	...	Sidecar rear spring shackle bolt	2	All Models		1	0
E3224	...	Sidecar rear spring shackle bolt nut	2	All Models			4
A2/903	...	Sidecar bearer bar, front	1	All Models		9	0
A2/904	...	Sidecar bearer bar, rear	1	All Models		9	0
11664	...	Sidecar bearer bar nut	8	All Models			5
A2/905	...	Sidecar bearer bar nut washer	4	All Models			4
A2/906	...	Sidecar bearer bar body attachment bolt	4	All Models			8
A2/907	...	Sidecar bearer bar body attachment bolt nut	8	All Models			4
A2/908	...	Sidecar bearer bar body attachment bolt washer	4	All Models			4
A2/428	...	Sidecar wheel, complete with hub shell only	1	All Models	5	17	0
A2/429	...	Sidecar wheel spoke, short	20 per set	All Models		4	0
A2/430	...	Sidecar wheel spoke, long	20 per set	All Models		4	0
A2/431	...	Sidecar wheel nipples	40 per set	All Models		4	6
A2/432	...	Sidecar wheel rim	1	All Models	1	5	0
A2/433	...	Sidecar wheel hub shell only	1	All Models	1	17	0
A2/434	...	Sidecar hub shell bearing sleeve	1	All Models		6	0
A2/435	...	Sidecar hub bearing (single row)	1	All Models		16	6
A2/437	...	Sidecar hub bearing oil retaining felt washer	1	All Models			8
A2/439	...	Sidecar hub bearing oil retaining felt washer, steep cup	1	All Models		1	0
A2/440	...	Sidecar hub bearing locking washer	1	All Models		2	0
A2/436	...	Sidecar hub bearing (double row)	1	All Models	1	11	4
A2/441	...	Sidecar hub bearing distance piece, near side	1	All Models		2	0
A2/442	...	Sidecar hub bearing cover	1	All Models		3	0
A2/198	...	Sidecar hub grease nipple	1	All Models		1	0
A2/460	...	Sidecar hub spindle	1	All Models		7	0
A2/909	...	Sidecar wheel hub end cover	1	All Models		3	6
A2/910	...	Sidecar mudguard	1	All Models	1	17	0
A2/911	...	Sidecar mudguard clip	2	All Models		1	6
E3798	...	Sidecar mudguard attachment pin, long	6	All Models			4
E5376	...	Sidecar mudguard pin washer	6	All Models			3
E3223	...	Sidecar mudguard pin nut	6	All Models			4
52036A	...	Sidecar lamp	1	All Models		9	9

SPARE PARTS LIST

Models ES2, 19S and 50
for 1956

PRICE - 2s. 6d.

NORTON MOTORS LTD.
BRACEBRIDGE ST., BIRMINGHAM, 6, ENGLAND

Phone: Aston Cross 3711 (Private Branch Exchange)
Grams: "Nortomo, Birmingham"

IMPORTANT INFORMATION RELATING TO THE PARTS LISTS INCLUDED IN THIS MANUAL

It should be noted that the early parts lists also include the 30, 40, 30M & 40M and the later parts lists include the 88 & 99 twins.#

The first parts list included is a reproduction of the 1948 and 1949 factory parts list for the S.V. and O.H.V. spring frame (plunger) Big 4, 16H, 18 and ES2 models fitted with 'Road-holder' forks and 'upright' gearbox (it also includes the 1946 to 1949 model 30, 40, 30M and 40M).

The second parts list is a reproduction of the 1956 factory parts list for the O.H.V. swing-arm, 'laydown' gearbox ES2, 19S and 50 models and the rigid frame model 19.

The third parts list is a reproduction of the 1959 PS206 factory parts list for the ES2 and 50 'featherbed' frame models fitted with alternator & coil electrics (it also includes the 88 and 99 twins).

When the four workshop manuals in this publication are used in conjunction with these three illustrated parts lists, they provide a comprehensive maintenance and repair manual exclusive to the 1945 to 1963 Norton 16H, Big4, 18, 19S, 19, 50 and ES2 series.

INDEX

	Page		Page
Air control cable	16	Magdyno parts (Lucas)	30
Amal carburetter	10	Magneto and air control levers	13
Chains (front and rear)	24	Magneto control cable	15
Clutch control cable	16	Magdyno or magneto driving parts and fittings	8
Clutch group	19		
Connecting rods	10	Main bearings	5
Control cable adjusters and nipples	15	Number plates and fittings (front and rear)	27
Crankcase, engine plate, bolts, etc.	7	Oil pipes and fittings	17
Crankcase and fittings	5	Oil tank and fittings	16
Cylinder barrel and head	10	Overhead rockers	8
Dry sump oil pump and drive parts	8	Petrol tanks and fittings	16
Dual seat and fittings	28	Pillion footrests and fittings	28
Electric horn and fittings	30	Pistons and rings	10
Engine plates (front and rear)	26	Positive footchange parts	20
Engine sprocket	24	Prop stand	27
Exhaust control cable	16	Push rods and fittings	7
Exhaust lifter control lever	15	Rear brake pedal and fittings	26
Exhaust pipes and fittings	12	Rear brake rod and fittings	26
Exhaust lifter and fittings	7	Rear chain adjusters	24
Flywheel assemblies and big end bearings	5	Rear chainguard and fittings	24
Footrests and fittings	26	Rear wheel and fittings	22
Forks and steering damper (Norton roadholder)	13	Rear lamp and fittings	30
		Rear mudguard, stays and fittings	28
Frames and rear suspension	26	Rocket box and fittings	7
Front brake control cable	16	Rubber cable clips	31
Front brake and clutch control levers	15	Silencer and fittings	12
Front chaincase and fittings	24	Speedometer and fittings	28
Front wheel and fittings	20	Stand and fittings (front)	28
Front mudguard, stays and fittings	27	Swinging arm and fittings	27
Gearbox axle sprocket	19	Tappets	7
Gearbox fixing bolts	17	Throttle control cable	16
Gearbox front chain adjuster	17	Timing gear	7
Gearbox pinions, shafts and bearings	17	Tool and battery box	28
Gearbox shell	17	Tools	30
Handlebars and fittings	13	Transfers	31
Headlamp and parts	30	Twist grip	15
Hub brake shoes and linings	22	Valves, guides, springs and fittings	10
Hubs (parts common to front and rear)	22	Voltage regulator and fittings	30
Kickstarter parts	19	Wheel rims and spokes	24
Legshields and fittings	31		

INSTRUCTIONS FOR ORDERING SPARE PARTS

This Spare Parts List deals with replacement parts for Models ES2, 19S and 50 of 1956 manufacture.

It is most essential that the Engine and Frame Number of the machine is stated. The Engine Number is to be found on the transmission side of the Crankcase, and the Frame Number is stamped on the Head Lug of the Frame, below the steering damper anchor plate. It is always advisable to order parts on a separate sheet, and not to include on the same sheet other matter of a different nature ; this facilitates prompt despatch.

It is found in a number of instances that money orders and postal orders are sent in parcels containing patterns ; this is inadvisable. We strongly recommend parts as patterns being despatched separately, and a covering letter sent containing the remittance for replacement parts.

RETURNING MACHINES FOR OVERHAULING

When returning machines or parts for repair or overhaul, these should be sent carriage paid, and with the sender's name and address in full **securely** attached. It is also advisable to state on the tally that a letter has been sent respecting the parts, and giving the date. All easily detached fittings should be removed, such as Lamps, Horns, Tool Bags, Speedometers, etc. ; these are liable to be lost or damaged in transit, and the Company cannot accept any responsibility for them.

ESTIMATES FOR REPAIRING MACHINES

We are always prepared to give approximate estimates for the cost of repairs ; it is quite impossible to give a firm quotation. Additional parts may be found necessary during the process of repair, unforeseen when preparing an estimate. Should our estimate for repair not be accepted, a charge may be made in accordance with work entailed in dismantling and re-assembling. When we give an estimate for cost of repairs, and this is curtailed by the owner, we cannot accept any responsibility for the performance of the machine ; it is always preferable to accept our estimate in full.

TERMS OF BUSINESS

Our terms are strictly nett cash with order or cash against prepayment invoice. The exact amount, plus 5% to cover postage or carriage and packing (subject to a minimum of 6d.), packing cases or crates to be extra, must be remitted, or when the cost of the parts required is unknown, a sum likely to cover the cost should be enclosed ; if the amount remitted is more than the cost of the parts that are ordered, the balance will be returned. Cheques and postal orders should be made payable to " Norton Motors, Ltd.," and crossed Barclays Bank, Ltd. Prices quoted in this list do not include the cost of carriage or fitting. We reserve the right to alter prices or specification of any parts at any time without notice. Where parts are urgently required, remittance may be sent by Telegraphic Money Order, **but it is absolutely essential that the sender fill in his name and address in the space provided on the Post Office Money Order Form.** Unless this is done, the Post Office do not give us the information in the telegram. It is necessary that all orders given by wire or 'phone should be confirmed by letter at the earliest opportunity.

DEPOSIT ACCOUNT

We strongly recommend riders of our machines to open a deposit account ; this can be done by depositing with us not less than £10. This will ensure goods to that value being **despatched with the least possible delay.** When ordering by 'phone, wire or post, this often avoids great inconvenience, and for the benefit of the depositor, a monthly statement of account is rendered, showing credit balance. Under no circumstances whatever can parts be despatched without remittance covering same has been sent, unless a deposit account is opened. Should the machine be disposed of at a later date, we are always prepared to remit any amount that may be remaining.

PARTS BY C.O.D. SYSTEM

Unless remittance is received with order, parts are despatched by C.O.D. System **or** against proforma invoice **at** our discretion.

PART No.	PLATE No.	DESCRIPTION	QTY.	USED ON	PRICE EACH

CRANKCASE AND FITTINGS

£ s. d.

PART No.	PLATE No.	DESCRIPTION	QTY.	USED ON	PRICE EACH
E2/1	—	Crankcase with timing cover, magneto chain cover and bushes (less studs and tappet guides)	1	ES2, 19, 50	10 0 0
A2/703	A.38	Driving side half crankcase	1	ES2, 19, 50	3 0 0
E2/704	A.44	Timing side half crankcase	1	ES2, 19, 50	5 5 0
		(Halves of crankcases cannot be supplied separately. Therefore it is necessary to return the sound half, also timing cover for matching in the works.)			
D3T/2	—	Crankcase cylinder studs	4	ES2, 19, 50	1 0
C2/6	A.20	Crankcase timing cover with bushes	1	ES2, 19, 50	2 0 0
A3/93	A.16	Timing cover screw, cheese head (top)	3	ES2, 19, 50	5
C2/96	A.17	Timing cover screw, cheese head (bottom)	3	ES2, 19, 50	5
C2/37	A.18	Timing cover screw, countersunk	2	ES2, 19, 50	5
A2/9	A.36	Magneto chain cover	1	ES2, 19, 50	9 0
C2/687	A.37	Magneto chain cover screw (short)	2	ES2, 19, 50	5
C2/688	A.19	Magneto chain cover screw (long)	1	ES2, 19, 50	9
A2/722	—	Fibre washers for cheese head screws	9	ES2, 19, 50	1
A2/10	A.30	Magneto chain cover pipe with nut	1	ES2, 19, 50	1 3
A2/11	A.29	Magneto chain cover pipe union	1	ES2, 19, 50	1 6
C2/12	A.27	Timing cover and mainshaft oil connection jet	1	ES2, 19, 50	2 6
C2/13	A.26	Timing cover and mainshaft oil connection holder	1	ES2, 19, 50	2 6
A2/14	A.28	Mainshaft oil connection jet spring	1	ES2, 19, 50	3
A2/15	A.23	Pressure release ball, $\frac{3}{8}''$	1	ES2, 19, 50	3
A2/16	A.22	Pressure release ball spring	1	ES2, 19, 50	2
C2/17	A.21	Pressure release ball screw	1	ES2, 19, 50	8
C2/18	A.14	Camshaft bush crankcase (inlet and exhaust)	2	ES2, 19, 50	4 6
C2/19	A.25	Camshaft bush (timing cover) inlet	1	ES2, 19, 50	4 6
A2/20	A.24	Camshaft bush (timing cover) exhaust	1	ES2, 19, 50	4 6
13765	A.40	Crankcase drain plug	1	ES2, 19, 50	1 0
13881	A.39	Crankcase drain plug washer	1	ES2, 19, 50	3
A2/476	—	Crankcase breather with pipe (driving side)	1	ES2, 19, 50	3 6
A2/707	A.5	Crankcase breather	1	ES2, 19, 50	2 0
A2/708	A.1	Crankcase breather pipe	1	ES2, 19, 50	1 3
A2/718	A.2	Crankcase breather pipe nut	1	ES2, 19, 50	3

FLYWHEELS, ASSEMBLIES AND BIG END BEARINGS

PART No.	PLATE No.	DESCRIPTION	QTY.	USED ON	PRICE EACH
K6/24	—	Flywheels complete with shafts, crankpin bearing and con rod	1	19	11 3 0
C3/24	—	Flywheel complete with shafts, crankpin bearing and con rod	1	ES2	11 3 0
L13/24	—	Flywheel complete with shafts, crank pin bearing and con rod	1	50	11 3 0
C7/26	A.49	Flywheel driving side with shaft	1	19	3 8 0
C2/26	A.49	Flywheel driving side with shaft	1	ES2	3 8 0
L13/26	—	Flywheel driving side with shaft	1	50	3 8 0
C7/25	A.53	Flywheel timing side with shaft	1	19	3 8 0
C2/25	A.53	Flywheel timing side with shaft	1	ES2	3 8 0
L13/25	—	Flywheel timing side with shaft	1	50	3 8 0
C2/705	A.54	Timing side flywheel shaft	1	ES2, 19, 50	1 5 0
A2/706	A.48	Driving side flywheel shaft	1	ES2, 19, 50	1 7 6
E3682	—	Key for flywheel shaft	1	ES2, 19, 50	4
		NOTE.—We recommend flywheels be returned to the works for the fitting of shafts.			
A2/27	A.51	Crankpin bearing with nuts	1	ES2, 19, 50	2 16 0
A2/28	A.50	Crankpin bearing nut	2	ES2, 19, 50	1 4
A2/29	A.52	Crankpin bearing nut locking screw	2	ES2, 19, 50	3
		NOTE.—Crankpin spare parts cannot be supplied separately. Each outer race has its individual pin.			

MAIN BEARINGS

PART No.	PLATE No.	DESCRIPTION	QTY.	USED ON	PRICE EACH
A2/30	A.9	Mainshaft ball bearing driving side	1	ES2, 19, 50	16 4
A2/32	A.11	Mainshaft roller bearings	2	ES2, 19, 50	1 7 9

PLATE. A.

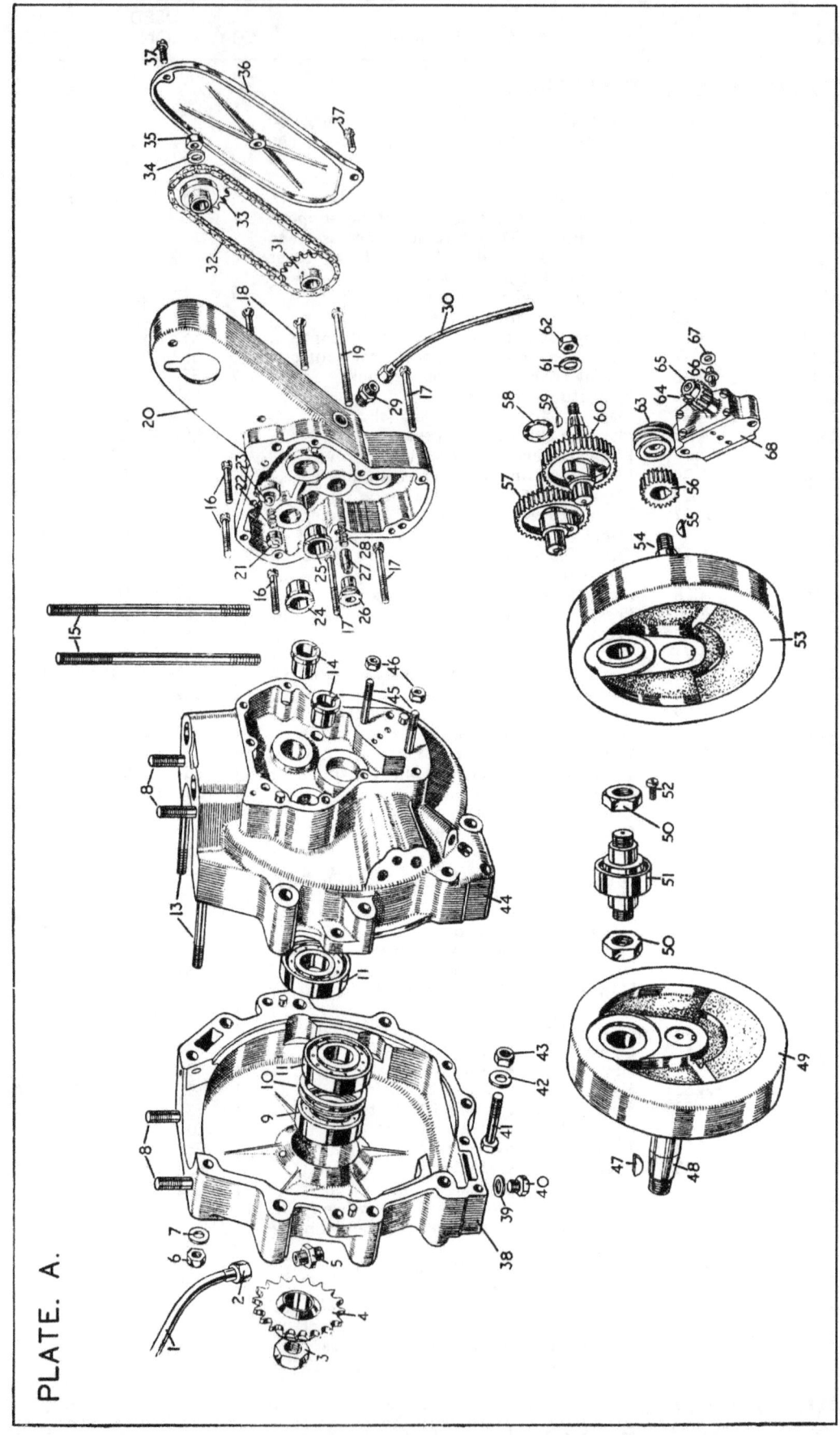

PART No.	PLATE No.	DESCRIPTION	QTY.	USED ON	PRICE EACH
					£ s. d.
MAIN BEARINGS—cont.					
A2/33	A.10	Mainshaft bearing driving side oil spacing ring	1	ES2, 19, 50	2 0
A2/46	—	Mainshaft packing washer	1	ES2, 19, 50	4

CRANKCASE, ENGINE PLATE, BOLTS, STUDS, etc.

PART No.	PLATE No.	DESCRIPTION	QTY.	USED ON	PRICE EACH
E3166	—	Front engine crankcase bolt	2	ES2, 19, 50	1 3
E3238	JX.16	Nut for bolt	4	ES2, 19, 50	5
E5375	JX.17	Washer for bolt	4	ES2, 19, 50	3
13040	JX.13	Front engine plate stud, ½in. diameter	1	ES2, 19, 50	1 3
E3227	JX.14	Nut for bolt	2	ES2, 19, 50	5
11809	JX.15	Washer for bolt	2	ES2, 19, 50	3
T2012	JX.27	Front engine plate crankcase stud (bottom)	1	ES2, 19, 50	1 3
E3224	JX.28	Nut for stud	2	ES2, 19, 50	4
E5376	JX.29	Washer for stud	2	ES2, 19, 50	3
19517	JX.48	Engine cradle bolt, $\frac{5}{16}$ in. diameter	2	ES2, 19, 50	1 3
E3223	JX.49	Nut for bolt	2	ES2, 19, 50	4
E4256	JX.22	Rear top crankcase engine plate bolt and Magneto platform bolt	1	ES2, 19, 50	1 3
E3238	JX.23	Nut for bolt	4	ES2, 19, 50	5
E5377	JX.24	Washer for bolt	4	ES2, 19, 50	3
E4268	JX.53	Rear engine plate frame bolt	4	ES2, 19, 50	1 6
13870	—	Crankcase bolt, short	3	ES2, 19, 50	8
E3223	—	Nut for bolt	3	ES2, 19, 50	4
E5456	—	Washer for bolt	3	ES2, 19, 50	4

TIMING GEAR

PART No.	PLATE No.	DESCRIPTION	QTY.	USED ON	PRICE EACH
C2/58	A.56	Half time pinion	1	ES2, 19, 50	10 0
A2/59	A.55	Half time pinion key	1	ES2, 19, 50	3
C3/60	A.57	Exhaust cam wheel complete	1	ES2, 19, 50	2 7 0
C3/61	A.60	Inlet cam wheel complete	1	ES2, 19, 50	2 10 0
C2/694	A.58	Cam wheel packing washer	2	ES2, 19, 50	2

TAPPETS

PART No.	PLATE No.	DESCRIPTION	QTY.	USED ON	PRICE EACH
K4/63	C.89	Tappet guide	2	ES2, 19, 50	12 6
C2/689	—	Tappet guide location peg	2	ES2, 19, 50	3
C3/75	C.88	Tappet complete	2	ES2, 19, 50	12 6
C3/693	C.87	Tappet ball end	2	ES2, 19, 50	3 6

EXHAUST LIFTER AND FITTINGS

PART No.	PLATE No.	DESCRIPTION	QTY.	USED ON	PRICE EACH
C3/64	C.77	Exhaust valve lifter	1	ES2, 19, 50	4 6
A3/66	C.78	Exhaust valve lifter securing pin	1	ES2, 19, 50	5
A2/67	C.75	Exhaust valve lifter lever	1	ES2, 19, 50	5 0
A2/68	C.76	Exhaust valve lifter lever securing bolt	1	ES2, 19, 50	6
A3/69	C.79	Exhaust valve lifter return spring	1	ES2, 19, 50	1 3
C2/690	C.33	Exhaust valve lifter rubber sealing washer	1	ES2, 19, 50	6

PUSH RODS AND FITTINGS

PART No.	PLATE No.	DESCRIPTION	QTY.	USED ON	PRICE EACH
K4/82	C.81	Push rod complete	2	ES2	9 6
K6/82	—	Push rod complete	2	19	9 6
L13/82	—	Push rod complete	2	50	9 6
C3/83	C.82	Push rod, bottom	2	ES2, 19, 50	3 0
C3/86	C.84	Push rod, top	2	ES2, 19, 50	2 0
C3/87	C.85	Push rod adjuster and locknut	2	ES2, 19, 50	3 0
C3/84	C.83	Push rod cover	2	ES2,	7 0
K6/84	—	Push rod cover	2	19	7 0
L13/84	—	Push rod cover	2	50	7 0
C3/88	C.86	Push rod cover, bottom, sealing washer	2	ES2, 19, 50	6
C3/89	C.80	Push rod cover, top, sealing washer	2	ES2, 19, 50	6

ROCKER BOX AND FITTINGS

PART No.	PLATE No.	DESCRIPTION	QTY.	USED ON	PRICE EACH
C3/90	C.57	Rocker box with cover	1	ES2, 19, 50	3 0 0
C3/92	C.54	Rocker box inspection cover	1	ES2, 19, 50	3 0

PART No.	PLATE No.	DESCRIPTION	QTY.	USED ON	PRICE EACH
					£ s. d.
ROCKER BOX AND FITTINGS—cont.					
C3/94	C.53	Rocker box inspection cover screw	2	ES2, 19, 50	6
C3/95	C.55	Rocker box inspection cover washer	1	ES2, 19, 50	1 6
D3T/108	—	Rocker box stud, long	7	ES2, 19, 50	9
E3231	—	Rocker box stud nut	5	ES2, 19, 50	4
E5380	—	Rocker box stud washer	7	ES2, 19, 50	3
D3T/110	—	Rocker box stud, short	2	ES2, 19, 50	6
C129	—	Rocker box stud nut	2	ES2, 19, 50	4
C224	—	Rocker box stud nut, long, for steady stay	2	ES2, 19, 50	8
L4/699	JL.9/C.61	Rocker box lubrication pipe with banjo connection	1	ES2, 19, 50	5 0
C3/700	C.62	Rocker box lubrication pipe connection bolt	1	ES2, 19, 50	2 6
C3/701	C.60	Rocker bolt lubrication pipe connection bolt washer	2	ES2, 19, 50	4
OVERHEAD ROCKERS					
C3/96	C.64	Rocker bush	4	ES2, 19, 50	3 6
C3/97	C.63	Rocker shaft	2	ES2, 19, 50	10 0
C3/98	C.67	Rocker shaft shim washer as necessary	1	ES2, 19, 50	3
C3/102	C.70	Rocker shaft nut	2	ES2, 19, 50	6
13802	C.69	Rocker shaft nut copper washer	2	ES2, 19, 50	3
13794	C.68	Rocker shaft washer, large	2	ES2, 19, 50	6
13818	C.66	Rocker shaft thrust spring washer	2	ES2, 19, 50	4
C3/99	C.71	Rocker arm, inlet	1	ES2, 19, 50	1 5 0
C3/100	C.73	Rocker arm, exhaust	1	ES2, 19, 50	1 5 0
C3/104	C.72	Rocker arm ball end	2	ES2, 19, 50	2 9
C3/105	C.74	Rocker arm pad	2	ES2, 19, 50	3 6
MAGNETO OR MAGDYNO DRIVING PARTS AND FITTINGS					
C2/79	A.31	Magneto sprocket (engine)	1	ES2, 19, 50	8 6
A2/80	A.62	Magneto sprocket securing nut	1	ES2, 19, 50	8
E5376	A.61	Magneto sprocket securing nut washer	1	ES2, 19, 50	3
A2/81	A.59	Magneto sprocket key	1	ES2, 19, 50	3
C2/112	A.33	Magdyno sprocket	1	ES2, 19, 50	8 6
A2/115	A.35	Magdyno sprocket securing nut	1	ES2, 19, 50	8
A2/116	A.34	Magdyno sprocket securing nut washer	1	ES2, 19, 50	3
C2/117	—	Magdyno platform	1	ES2, 19, 50	6 0
E3831	—	Magdyno platform countersunk screw	4	ES2, 19, 50	5
1518A	—	Magdyno platform countersunk screw shake proof washer	4	ES2, 19, 50	4
A2/118	JX.25	Magdyno platform locking plate	1	ES2, 19, 50	9
E3798	JX.26	Magdyno platform locking plate pin	1	ES2, 19, 50	4
C2/113	A.32	Magdyno chain (44 link)	1	ES2, 19, 50	10 6
DRY SUMP OIL PUMP AND DRIVE PARTS					
Side and O.H.V. Models					
A2/128	A.68	Dry sump gear pump, complete	1	ES2, 19, 50	3 0 0
A2/129	A.65	Dry sump gear pump spindle nut	1	ES2, 19, 50	5
A2/130	A.64	Dry sump gear pump spindle worm gear wheel	1	ES2, 19, 50	6 6
A2/131	—	Dry sump gear pump spindle worm gear wheel key	1	ES2, 19, 50	3
A2/132	A.66	Dry sump gear pump body and timing cover connection bush	1	ES2, 19, 50	8
A2/133	A.67	Dry sump gear pump body and timing cover connection fibre washer	1	ES2, 19, 50	3
C2/134	A.63	Engine mainshaft pump driving worm	1	ES2, 19, 50	7 6
E4440	A.45	Dry sump gear pump crankcase stud	2	ES2, 19, 50	9
E3231	A.46	Dry sump gear pump crankcase stud nut	2	ES2, 19, 50	4

NOTE.—Dry sump pump parts cannot be supplied separately. It is necessary to return the complete pump to the works for attention.

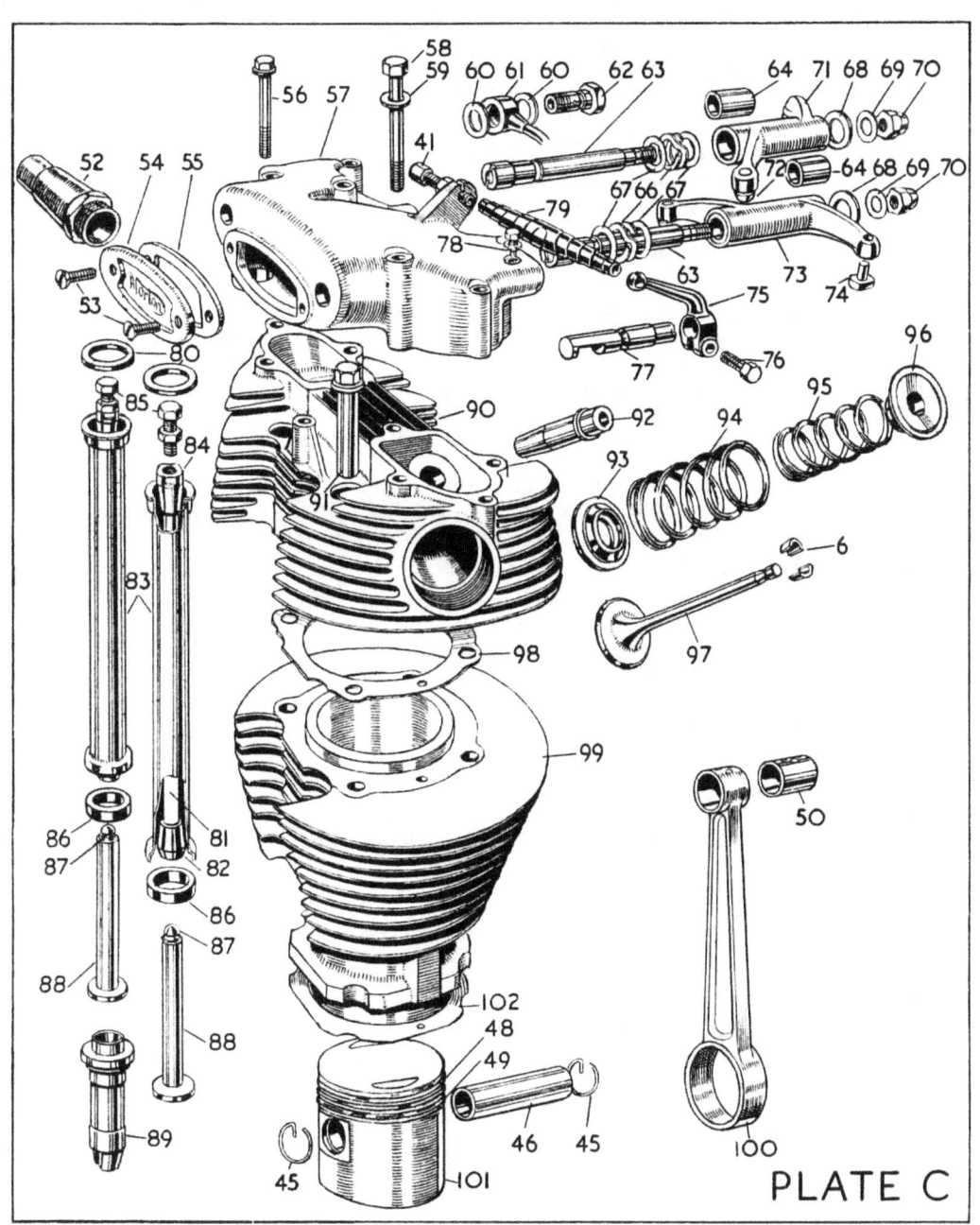

PLATE C

PART No.	PLATE No.	DESCRIPTION	QTY.	USED ON	PRICE EACH

CYLINDER BARREL AND HEAD

£ s. d.

PART No.	PLATE No.	DESCRIPTION	QTY.	USED ON	£ s. d.
K4/135	C.99	Cylinder barrel	1	ES2	3 17 6
K6/135	—	Cylinder barrel	1	19	4 0 0
L13/135	—	Cylinder barrel	1	50	3 15 0
D3T/136	—	Cylinder head with valve guides	1	ES2, 19	8 15 0
L13/136	—	Cylinder head with valve guides	1	50	8 12 6
D3T/137	—	Cylinder head joint washer	1	ES2, 19	1 9
L13/137	—	Cylinder head joint washer	1	50	1 9
K4/154	—	Carburetter adaptor with locknut	1	ES2	8 6
K6/154	—	Carburetter adaptor with locknut	1	19	8 6
L13/154	—	Carburetter adaptor with locknut	1	50	8 6
C175	—	Carburetter adaptor locknut	1	ES2, 19, 50	1 6
D3T/156	—	Cylinder head sleeve nut	4	ES2, 19, 50	2 6
C170	—	Washer between cylinder head and sleeve nut	4	ES2, 19, 50	4
C3/157	C.102	Cylinder base paper washer	1	ES2, 19, 50	3

VALVES, GUIDES, SPRINGS AND FITTINGS

PART No.	PLATE No.	DESCRIPTION	QTY.	USED ON	£ s. d.
A3/142	C.97	Valve only (inlet or exhaust)	2	ES2, 19	12 0
L13/142	—	Valve only (inlet or exhaust)	2	50	12 0
D3T/140	—	Valve guide (inlet or exhaust)	2	ES2, 19, 50	8 0
C3/145	C.95	Valve spring, small inner (inlet or exhaust)	2	ES2, 19, 50	1 0
C3/146	C.94	Valve spring, outer (inlet or exhaust)	2	ES2, 19, 50	2 0
H3/147	C.96	Valve spring cup top	2	ES2, 19, 50	5 6
H3/148	C.93	Valve spring bottom collar	2	ES2, 19, 50	1 0
A2/149	C.6	Valve split cotter	2	ES2, 19, 50	1 0

CONNECTING RODS

PART No.	PLATE No.	DESCRIPTION	QTY.	USED ON	£ s. d.
K6/158	C.51	Connecting rod with small end bush, 7½in.	1	19	2 4 0
A3/158	C.100	Connecting rod with small end bush, 7in.	1	ES2	2 4 0
L13/158	—	Connecting rod with small end bush	1	50	2 4 0
A2/159	C.50	Small end bush	1	ES2, 19, 50	5 0

PISTONS AND RINGS

PART No.	PLATE No.	DESCRIPTION	QTY.	USED ON	£ s. d.
L6/160	—	Piston only	1	19	1 11 6
L4/160	C.101	Piston only	1	ES2	1 10 0
L13/160	—	Piston only	1	50	1 7 6
L6/702	—	Piston complete with rings, gudgeon pin and circlips	1	19	2 9 11
L4/702	—	Piston complete with rings, gudgeon pin and circlips	1	ES2	2 8 5
L13/702	—	Piston complete with rings, gudgeon pin and circlips	1	50	2 6 11
C7/161	C.48	Piston ring	2	19	2 3
A2/161	C.48	Piston ring	2	ES2	2 3
L13/161	—	Piston ring	2	50	2 3
C7/162	C.49	Scraper piston ring	1	19	3 3
A2/162	C.49	Scraper piston ring	1	ES2	3 3
L13/162	—	Scraper piston ring	1	50	3 3
A2/163	C.46	Gudgeon pin	1	ES2, 19, 50	10 0
A2/164	C.45	Gudgeon pin circlip	2	ES2, 19, 50	6

Pistons and rings can be supplied in the following oversizes : .010, .020, .030, .040. State size when ordering.

AMAL CARBURETTER

PART No.	PLATE No.	DESCRIPTION	QTY.	USED ON	£ s. d.
376/17	—	Carburetter complete with cables, less twist grip	1	ES2, 19	3 15 0
376/19	—	Carburetter complete with cables, less twist grip	1	50	3 15 0
376/1 1/16"	—	Mixing chamber body	1	ES2, 19	1 0 0
376/1"	—	Mixing chamber body	1	50	1 0 0
376/057	—	Jet block	1	ES2, 19	10 0
376/056	—	Jet block	1	50	10 0
376/070	—	Locating peg for jet block	1	ES2, 19, 50	6

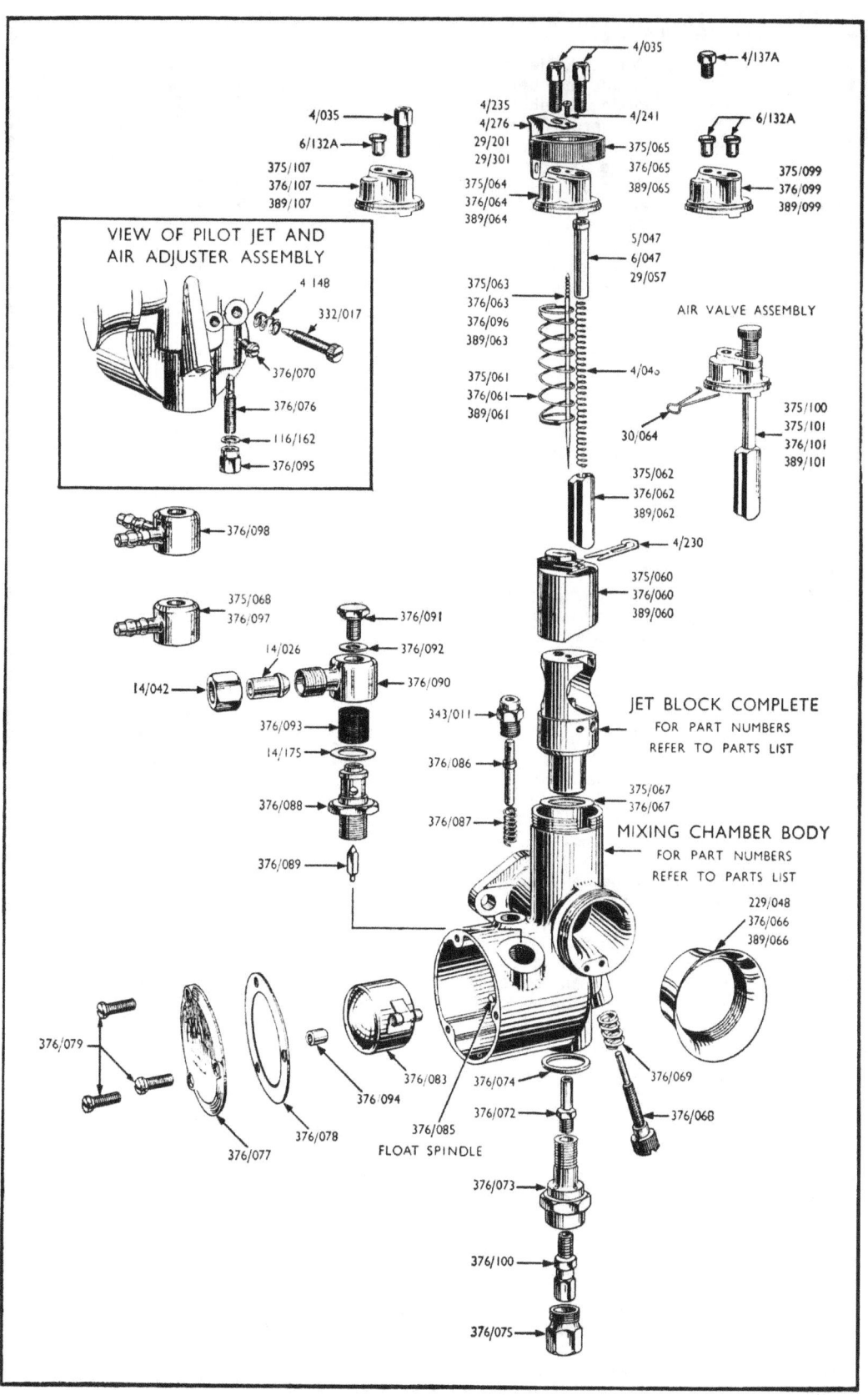

PART No.	PLATE No.	DESCRIPTION	QTY.	USED ON	PRICE EACH

AMAL CARBURETTER—cont.

PART No.	PLATE No.	DESCRIPTION	QTY.	USED ON	£ s. d.
376/067	—	Washer for jet block	1	ES2, 19, 50	2
376/064	—	Mixing chamber top	1	ES2, 19, 50	3 0
376/065	—	Mixing chamber top cap ring	1	ES2, 19, 50	3 0
4/235	—	Cap spring for top	1	ES2, 19, 50	10
4/241	—	Fixing screw for cap springs	1	ES2, 19, 50	2
4/035	—	Cable adjuster	1	ES2, 19, 50	7
6/132A	—	Cable ferrules (top hat)	1	ES2, 19, 50	3
4/137A	—	Plug screw	1	ES2, 19, 50	3
376/060	—	Throttle valve	1	ES2, 19, 50	7 0
376/061	—	Throttle valve spring	1	ES2, 19, 50	6
376/063	—	Taper needle	1	ES2, 19, 50	2 3
4/230	—	Needle clip	1	ES2, 19, 50	6
376/062	—	Air valve	1	ES2, 19, 50	4 6
6/047	—	Air valve guide	1	ES2, 19, 50	1 3
4/046	—	Air valve spring	1	ES2, 19, 50	4
376/101	—	Rod control air valve assembly	1	ES2, 19, 50	9 0
30/064	—	Click spring for rod control air valve assembly	1	ES2, 19, 50	3
376/072	—	Needle jet	1	ES2, 19, 50	2 9
376/100	—	Main jet (specify size)	1	ES2, 19, 50	1 0
376/073	—	Main jet holder	1	ES2, 19, 50	4 0
376/074	—	Main jet holder washer	1	ES2, 19, 50	2
376/075	—	Main jet cover nut	1	ES2, 19, 50	1 0
376/076	—	Pilot jet	1	ES2, 19, 50	1 0
376/095	—	Pilot jet cover nut	1	ES2, 19, 50	9
116/162	—	Pilot jet cover nut washer	1	ES2, 19, 50	2
332/017	—	Air adjusting screw	1	ES2, 19, 50	9
4/148	—	Air adjusting screw spring	1	ES2, 19, 50	3
376/068	—	Throttle stop screw	1	ES2, 19, 50	9
376/069	—	Throttle stop screw spring	1	ES2, 19, 50	3
376/066	—	Air intake tube	1	ES2, 19, 50	3 10
376/083	—	Float complete	1	ES2, 19, 50	5 0
376/085	—	Float hinge spindle	1	ES2, 19, 50	6
376/094	—	Float spindle bush	1	ES2, 19, 50	4
376/089	—	Float needle	1	ES2, 19, 50	1 6
376/088	—	Needle seating	1	ES2, 19, 50	2 6
14/175	—	Needle seating washer	1	ES2, 19, 50	2
376/097	—	Banjo single	1	ES2, 19, 50	2 0
14/175	—	Banjo washer	1	ES2, 19, 50	2
376/091	—	Banjo bolt	1	ES2, 19, 50	6
376/092	—	Banjo bolt washer	1	ES2, 19, 50	2
376/086	—	Tickler	1	ES2, 19, 50	1 0
343/011	—	Tickler body	1	ES2, 19, 50	1 3
376/087	—	Tickler spring	1	ES2, 19, 50	2
376/077	—	Float chamber cover	1	ES2, 19, 50	2 6
376/078	—	Float chamber cover joint	1	ES2, 19, 50	4
376/079	—	Float chamber cover screws	1	ES2, 19, 50	2
376/093	—	Filter gauze	1	ES2, 19, 50	8

EXHAUST PIPES AND FITTINGS

PART No.	PLATE No.	DESCRIPTION	QTY.	USED ON	£ s. d.
L9/165	—	Exhaust pipe only	1	19	1 5 0
L4/165	—	Exhaust pipe	1	ES2	1 5 0
L13/165	—	Exhaust pipe	1	50	1 5 0
A3/166	—	Exhaust pipe flange washer (cylinder head)	1	ES2, 19, 50	6
A3/167	—	Exhaust pipe flange locking nut (cylinder head)	1	ES2, 19, 50	6 6

SILENCER AND FITTINGS

PART No.	PLATE No.	DESCRIPTION	QTY.	USED ON	£ s. d.
L4/169/169(RH)	—	Silencer	1	ES2, 19, 50	2 5 0
193581	—	Silencer fixing plate	1	ES2, 19, 50	1 3
17075	—	Silencer fixing plate bolt	2	ES2, 19, 50	5
E5456	—	Washer for bolt	2	—	3
H4/168	—	Silencer clip front end	1	ES2, 19, 50	1 9
E3801	—	Bolt for clip or silencer	1	ES2, 19, 50	5
E3231	—	Nut for clip or silencer	1	ES2, 19, 50	4
11796	—	Washer for bolt or silencer	1	ES2, 19, 50	4

PART No.	PLATE No.	DESCRIPTION	QTY.	USED ON	PRICE EACH £ s. d.
NORTON ROAD-HOLDER FORKS AND STEERING DAMPER					
L4/170	—	Road holder fork complete	1	ES2, 19, 50	19 5 0
B2/605	JJ.23	Main tube	2	ES2, 19, 50	1 10 0
B2/606	JJ.32	Main tube bottom bush	2	ES2, 19, 50	6 6
B2/607	JJ.35	Main tube bottom bush locking nut	2	ES2, 19, 50	3 9
B2/608	JJ.34	Main tube bottom bush locking nut washer	2	ES2, 19, 50	3
D12/609	JJ.33	Fork end (left hand)	1	ES2, 19, 50	2 17 6
13433	—	Fork end hub spindle pinch stud	1	ES2, 19, 50	6
13434	—	Fork end hub spindle pinch stud nut	2	ES2, 19, 50	4
11776	—	Pinch stud washer	1	ES2, 19, 50	3
D12/611	—	Fork end (right-hand)	1	ES2, 19, 50	2 17 6
B2/612	JJ.39	Fork end drain plug	2	ES2, 19, 50	4
B2/613	JJ.38	Fork end drain plug washer	2	ES2, 19, 50	2
B2/614	JJ.31	Main tube top sleeve bush	2	ES2, 19, 50	5 0
B2/615	JJ.28	Main tube top sleeve bush locking ring	2	ES2, 19, 50	3 6
D3T/616	JJ.29	Super oil seal	2	ES2, 19, 50	6 6
B2/617	JJ.30	Super oil seal paper washer	2	ES2, 19, 50	2
B2/619	JJ.22	Main spring leather washer top	2	ES2, 19, 50	6
E2/620	JJ.26	Main spring	2	ES2, 50	6 6
L9/620	—	Main spring	2	19	6 6
B2/621	JJ.27	Main spring leather washer (bottom)	2	ES2, 19, 50	3
B2/622	JJ.19	Spring cover tube (top)	2	ES2, 19, 50	4 0
B2/623	JJ.20	Spring cover tube top securing plate	2	ES2, 19, 50	1 0
B2/624	JJ.21	Spring cover tube top securing plate screw	6	ES2, 19, 50	3
B2/625	JJ.24	Spring cover tube (bottom)	2	ES2, 19, 50	6 6
B2/626	JJ.25	Spring cover tube (bottom) securing screw	4	ES2, 19, 50	2
B2/627	JJ.36	Oil damper rod	2	ES2, 19, 50	8 6
B2/628	JJ.37	Oil damper rod or tube fibre washer	2	ES2, 19, 50	1
C2/629	JJ.41	Oil damper rod or tube plain washer	2	ES2, 19, 50	1
C2/630	JJ.40	Oil damper rod or tube bolt	2	ES2, 19, 50	3
B2/633	JJ.3	Main tube filler and retaining plug	2	ES2, 19, 50	5 0
B2/634	JJ.4	Main tube filler and retaining plug washer	2	ES2, 19, 50	9
L4/635	JJ.9	Main tube top cover (left-hand)	1	ES2, 19, 50	12 6
L4/636	JJ.10	Main tube top cover (right-hand)	1	ES2, 19, 50	12 6
B2/637	JJ.11	Main tube top cover name plate	2	ES2, 19, 50	1 6
B2/638	—	Main tube top cover name plate rivet (per set 2)	2	ES2, 19, 50	3
B2/639	JJ.8	Main tube top cover rubber ring	2	ES2, 19, 50	9
B2/201	JJ.44	Steering damper adjuster	1	ES2, 19, 50	4 6
B2/203	JJ.49	Steering damper adjuster rod	1	ES2, 19, 50	1 0
B2/202	JJ.47	Steering damper adjuster rod spring	1	ES2, 19, 50	9
B2/640	JJ.48	Steering damper adjuster rod spring locknut	1	ES2, 19, 50	4
B2/207	JJ.50	Steering damper friction disc	2	ES2, 19, 50	1 0
B2/206	JJ.51	Steering damper friction and anchor plate	1	ES2, 19, 50	1 6
B2/208	JJ.52	Steering damper bottom plate	1	ES2, 19, 50	4 0
B2/641	JJ.53	Steering damper bottom plate nut	1	ES2, 19, 50	6
B2/172	JJ.13	Fork crown and column	1	ES2, 19, 50	2 5 0
B2/642	JJ.17	Fork crown main tube clamping stud	2	ES2, 19, 50	6
B2/643	JJ.18	Fork crown main tube clamping stud nut	2	ES2, 19, 50	4
B2/173	—	Fork crown or head clip ballrace	1	ES2, 19, 50	4 9
B2/644	JJ.14	Fork head clip ballrace cover	1	ES2, 19, 50	1 0
L13/174	JJ.7	Fork head clip	1	ES2, 19, 50	1 12 6
B2/645	JJ.12	Fork head race adjuster nut	1	ES2, 19, 50	6 0
B2/205	JJ.45	Fork crown and column locknut	1	ES2, 19, 50	5 0
B2/646	JJ.46	Fork crown and column locknut washer	1	ES2, 19, 50	6
HANDLEBAR AND FITTINGS					
L4/211	—	Handlebar bend only	1	ES2, 19, 50	1 5 0
L4/175	JJ.6	Handlebar clip	2	ES2, 19, 50	2 0
L4/176	JJ.5	Handlebar clip pin	4	ES2, 19, 50	6
MAGNETO AND AIR CONTROL LEVERS					
A2/213	—	Magneto control lever assembly complete	1	ES2, 19, 50	9 0
A2/214	—	Magneto control lever only	1	ES2, 19, 50	4 0
A2/215	—	Magneto control lever body	1	ES2, 19, 50	3 0
A2/216	—	Air control lever assembly complete	1	ES2, 19, 50	9 0

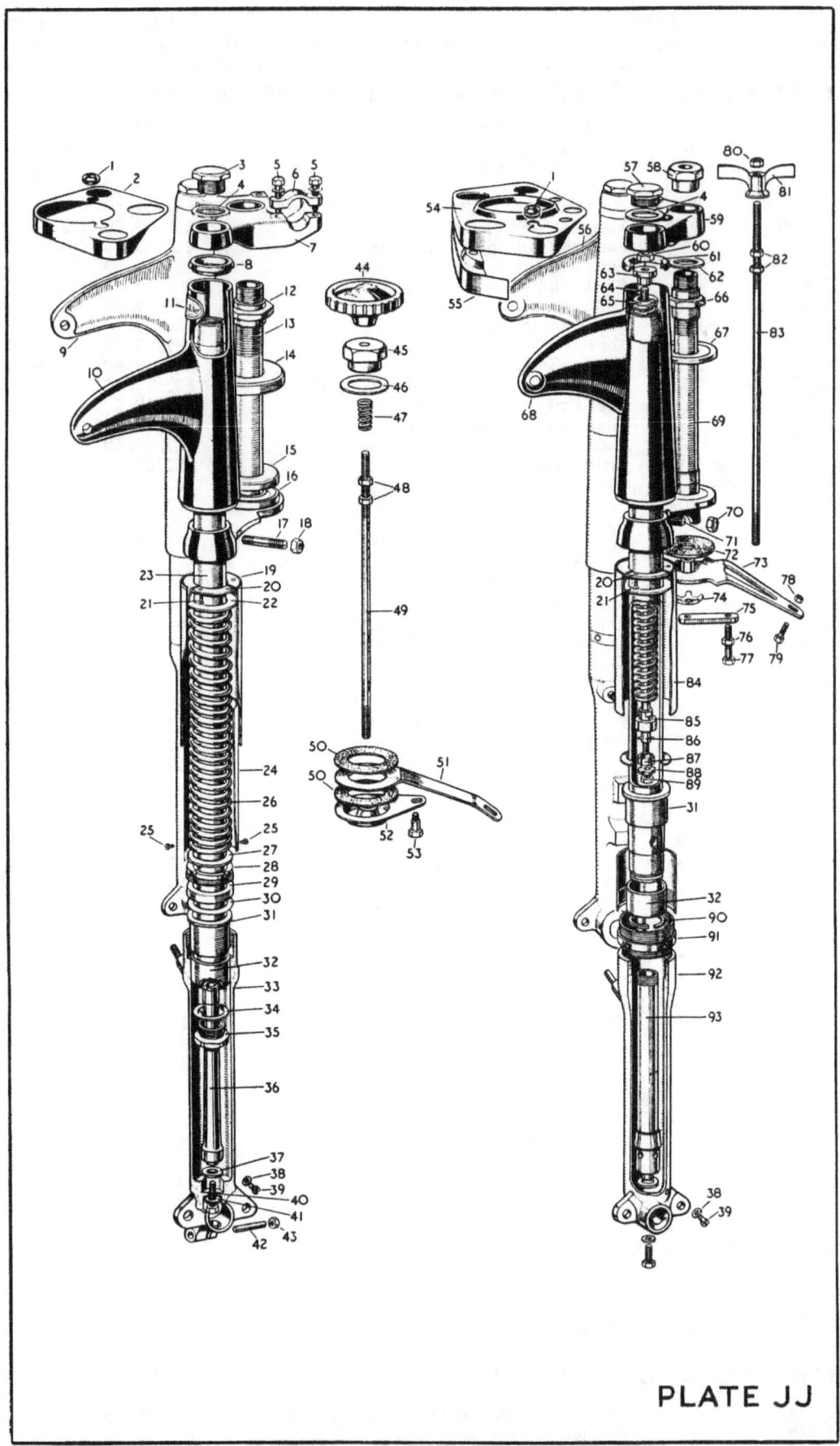

PLATE JJ

PART No.	PLATE No.	DESCRIPTION	QTY.	USED ON	PRICE EACH
MAGNETO AND AIR CONTROL LEVERS—cont.					£ s. d.
A2/217	—	Air control lever only	1	ES2, 19, 50	4 0
A2/218	—	Air control lever body	1	ES2, 19, 50	3 0
A2/219	—	Air or magneto control lever top screw	2	ES2, 19, 50	4
A2/220	—	Air or magneto control lever cap	2	ES2, 19, 50	9
A2/221	—	Air or magneto control lever cap spring washer	2	ES2, 19, 50	3
A2/223	—	Air or magneto control lever clip screw	2	ES2, 19, 50	4

FRONT BRAKE AND CLUTCH CONTROL LEVERS

PART No.	PLATE No.	DESCRIPTION	QTY.	USED ON	PRICE EACH
A2/224	—	Front brake lever assembly complete	1	ES2, 19, 50	11 0
A2/225	—	Front brake lever only	1	ES2, 19, 50	5 6
A2/226	—	Clutch lever assembly complete	1	ES2, 19, 50	11 0
A2/227	—	Clutch lever only	1	ES2, 19, 50	5 6
D2/228 (LH)	—	Clutch lever body	1	ES2, 19, 50	3 0
A2/222	—	Front brake or clutch lever clip	2	ES2, 19, 50	1 0
A2/223	—	Front brake or clutch lever clip screw	4	ES2, 19, 50	5
D2/228 (RH)	—	Front brake lever body	1	ES2, 19, 50	3 0
A2/229	—	Front brake or clutch lever pivot pin	2	ES2, 19, 50	4
A2/230	—	Front brake or clutch lever pivot pin nut	2	ES2, 19, 50	3
A2/873	—	Front brake or clutch lever pivot pin washer	2	ES2, 19, 50	2

EXHAUST LIFTER CONTROL LEVER

PART No.	PLATE No.	DESCRIPTION	QTY.	USED ON	PRICE EACH
A2/233	—	Exhaust valve lifter lever complete	1	ES2, 19, 50	8 9
A2/234	—	Exhaust valve lifter lever only	1	ES2, 19, 50	3 0
A2/235	—	Exhaust valve lifter lever body	1	ES2, 19, 50	4 0
A2/222	—	Exhaust valve lifter lever clip	1	ES2, 19, 50	1 0
A2/223	—	Exhaust valve lifter lever pivot pin or clip screw	3	ES2, 19, 50	5
A2/236	—	Exhaust valve lifter lever pivot pin nut	1	ES2, 19, 50	4

TWIST GRIP

PART No.	PLATE No.	DESCRIPTION	QTY.	USED ON	PRICE EACH
A2/237	—	Twist grip complete	1	ES2, 19, 50	10 6
A2/238	—	Twist grip top half clip	1	ES2, 19, 50	3 3
A2/239	—	Twist grip bottom half clip	1	ES2, 19, 50	3 3
A2/240	—	Twist grip clip fixing pin	2	ES2, 19, 50	4
A2/241	—	Twist grip control barrel	1	ES2, 19, 50	3 9
A2/242	—	Twist grip control barrel adjusting screw	1	ES2, 19, 50	5
A2/236	—	Twist grip control barrel adjusting screw nut	1	ES2, 19, 50	3
A2/243	—	Twist grip control barrel adjusting screw spring	1	ES2, 19, 50	10
A2/244	—	Twist grip cable stop	1	ES2, 19, 50	7
A2/245	—	Twist grip rubber	1	ES2, 19, 50	1 3
A2/246	—	Dummy grip to match twist grip	1	ES2, 19, 50	1 9

CONTROL CABLE ADJUSTERS AND NIPPLES

PART No.	PLATE No.	DESCRIPTION	QTY.	USED ON	PRICE EACH
A2/247	—	Front brake or clutch cable adjuster	2	ES2, 19, 50	3 0
A2/248	C.41	Exhaust cable adjuster	1	ES2, 19, 50	10
A2/249	—	Magneto, air or throttle cable nipple (handlebar end)	3	ES2, 19, 50	3
A2/250	—	Magneto control cable nipple, magneto end	1	ES2, 19, 50	3
A2/251	—	Air or throttle control cable nipple carburetter end	2	ES2, 19, 50	3
A2/252	—	Clutch or front brake control cable nipple (handlebar end)	2	ES2, 19, 50	1 0
A2/254	—	Front brake (U clip end) or exhaust lifter control cable nipple (lifter end)	2	ES2, 19, 50	3
A2/255	—	Exhaust valve lifter control cable nipple (handlebar end)	1	ES2, 19, 50	5

MAGNETO CONTROL CABLE

PART No.	PLATE No.	DESCRIPTION	QTY.	USED ON	PRICE EACH
A2/256	—	Magneto control cable inner and outer complete	1	ES2, 19, 50	4 0
A2/257	—	Magneto control cable outer	1	ES2, 19, 50	2 3
A2/258	—	Magneto control cable inner	1	ES2, 19, 50	1 9

PART No.	PLATE No.	DESCRIPTION	QTY.	USED ON	PRICE EACH

AIR CONTROL CABLE

					£ s. d.
A2/259	—	Air control cable inner and outer complete	1	ES2, 19, 50	4 0
A2/260	—	Air control cable outer	1	ES2, 19, 50	2 3
A2/261	—	Air control cable inner	1	ES2, 19, 50	1 9

THROTTLE CONTROL CABLE

A2/262	—	Throttle control cable complete	1	ES2, 19, 50	4 6
A2/263	—	Throttle control cable outer	1	ES2, 19, 50	2 6
A2/264	—	Throttle control cable inner	1	ES2, 19, 50	2 0

CLUTCH CONTROL CABLE

A2/265	—	Clutch control cable complete	1	ES2, 19, 50	4 0
A2/266	—	Clutch control cable outer	1	ES2, 19, 50	2 3
A2/267	—	Clutch control cable inner	1	ES2, 19, 50	1 9

FRONT BRAKE CONTROL CABLE

D12/268	—	Front brake control cable complete	1	ES2, 19, 50	5 6
A11M/269	—	Front brake control cable outer	1	ES2, 19, 50	3 6
B2/270	—	Front brake control cable inner	1	ES2, 19, 50	2 0
A2/709	—	Front brake cable U clip	1	ES2, 19, 50	6
A2/427	—	Front brake cable U clip pin	1	ES2, 19, 50	4
A2/195	—	Front brake cable U clip pin cotter	1	ES2, 19, 50	2

EXHAUST CONTROL CABLE

A2/271	—	Exhaust lifter control cable complete	1	ES2, 19, 50	4 0
A2/272	—	Exhaust lifter control cable outer	1	ES2, 19, 50	2 3
A2/273	—	Exhaust lifter control cable inner	1	ES2, 19, 50	1 9

PETROL TANKS AND FITTINGS

L4/274	—	Petrol tank	1	ES2, 19, 50	12 5 0
A2/275	—	Petrol tank platform packing washer (steel)	4	ES2, 19, 50	4
A2/276	—	Petrol tank platform rubber washer	4	ES2, 19, 50	6
A2/277	—	Petrol tank attachment bolt	4	ES2, 19, 50	8
A2/278	—	Petrol tank attachment bolt rubber washer	4	ES2, 19, 50	4
A2/279	—	Petrol tank attachment bolt rubber washer steel cup	4	ES2, 19, 50	6
E2/845	JX.8	Rear tank platform	1	ES2, 19, 50	4 0
E6453	JX.7	Rear tank platform stud	2	ES2, 19, 50	8
E3223	—	Rear tank platform stud nut	2	ES2, 19, 50	4
K12/280	—	Petrol tank filler cap	1	ES2, 19, 50	8 6
K12/282 (LH)	—	Knee grip (left-hand)	1	ES2, 19, 50	3 0
K12/282 (RH)	—	Knee grip (right-hand)	1	ES2, 19, 50	3 0
E6629	—	Knee grip fixing pin	2	ES2, 19, 50	5
L4/285	—	Petrol tap	2	ES2, 19, 50	6 0
L4/286	—	Banjo for tap	2	ES2, 19, 50	2 0
L4/287	—	Nut for tap	2	ES2, 19, 50	1 0
E5264	—	Washer for tap	2	ES2, 19, 50	3
19389	—	Petrol pipe (short)	1	ES2, 19, 50	1 0
19388	—	Petrol pipe (long)	1	ES2, 19, 50	1 3
19439	—	Petrol pipe "T" piece	1	ES2, 19, 50	1 9
19390	—	Petrol pipe "T" piece to carburetter	1	ES2, 19, 50	1 0
18678	—	Petrol tank badge	2	ES2, 19, 50	7 6
18679	—	Petrol tank badge fixing screw	4	ES2, 19, 50	4
18676	—	Petrol tank badge mounting rubber	2	ES2, 19, 50	8
A2/289	—	Petrol tank top tube packing	2	ES2, 19, 50	4

OIL TANK AND FITTINGS

L4/290	—	Oil tank only	1	ES2, 19, 50	2 2 0
K12/291	—	Oil tank filler cap	1	ES2, 19, 50	6 6
L4/292	—	Oil tank union and filter	1	ES2, 19, 50	7 0
A2/293	—	Oil tank union and filter washer	1	ES2, 19, 50	6
H2/298	—	Oil tank air release pipe and nut	1	ES2, 19, 50	2 0
10995	—	Oil tank air release pipe nut	1	ES2, 19, 50	4
11940	—	Oil tank top attachment bolt	1	ES2, 19, 50	3

PART No.	PLATE No.	DESCRIPTION	QTY.	USED ON	PRICE EACH
OIL TANK AND FITTINGS—cont.					£ s. d.
E5456	—	Washer for bolt	1	ES2, 19, 50	3
E6453	—	Oil tank bottom stud	2	ES2, 19, 50	6
E3223	—	Nut for stud	2	ES2, 19, 50	4
E5456	—	Washer for stud	2	ES2, 19, 50	3
E2/1050	—	Oil tank bottom bracket plate	1	ES2, 19, 50	1 0
E3336	—	Oil tank drain plug	1	ES2, 19, 50	8
E5264	—	Oil tank drain plug washer	1	ES2, 19, 50	3

OIL PIPES AND FITTINGS

PART No.	PLATE No.	DESCRIPTION	QTY.	USED ON	PRICE EACH
E2/993	—	Junction block with copper pipes	1	ES2, 19, 50	6 0
E2/995	—	Junction block washer	1	ES2, 19, 50	3
D12/994	—	Dowel for junction block	1	ES2, 19, 50	9
L4/1055	—	Return oil pipe adaptor for tank	1	ES2, 19, 50	2 6
E3/1056	—	Washer for adaptor	2	ES2, 19, 50	3
L4/295/6	—	Oil tank return or delivery rubber pipe	2	ES2, 19, 50	1 3

GEARBOX SHELL

PART No.	PLATE No.	DESCRIPTION	QTY.	USED ON	PRICE EACH
D12/299	TN.21	Gearbox shell with studs	1	ES2, 19, 50	4 15 0
D12/300	TN.73	Gearbox end cover (inner)	1	ES2, 19, 50	2 15 0
D12/301	TN.53	Gearbox end cover (outer)	1	ES2, 19, 50	1 15 0
D12/302	TN.42	Gearbox clutch worm inspection cover	1	ES2, 19, 50	5 0
D12/647	—	Clutch worm inspection cover screw	2	ES2, 19, 50	6
D12/1005	TN.19	Paper washer between shell and inner cover	1	ES2, 19, 50	2
D12/1006	TN.72	Paper washer for outer cover	1	ES2, 19, 50	2
D12/1007	TN.43	Joint washer for inspection cover	1	ES2, 19, 50	4
D12/304	TN.20	Gearbox cover stud	8	ES2, 19, 50	5
A2/307	—	Gearbox cover stud nut	8	ES2, 19, 50	4
A2/308	—	Gearbox cover stud spring washer	8	ES2, 19, 50	3
A2/309	—	Gearbox outer plate fixing screw	7	ES2, 19, 50	5
E3336	—	Gearbox oil drain plug	1	ES2, 19, 50	8
13765	—	Oil level plug	1	ES2, 19, 50	8
13833	—	Oil level plug washer	1	ES2, 19, 50	3

GEARBOX FIXING BOLTS

PART No.	PLATE No.	DESCRIPTION	QTY.	USED ON	PRICE EACH
D12/310	JX.63/JY.47	Gearbox suspension bolt and nut	1	ES2, 19, 50	3 6
D12/313	JX.60/JY.53	Gearbox suspension bolt nut	1	ES2, 19, 50	1 0
E5454	—	Gearbox suspension bolt nut washer	1	ES2, 19, 50	4
A2/312	JX.65	Gearbox bottom bolt and nut	1	ES2, 19, 50	1 3
A2/313	JX.64	Gearbox bottom bolt nut	1	ES2, 19, 50	9

GEARBOX FRONT CHAIN ADJUSTER

PART No.	PLATE No.	DESCRIPTION	QTY.	USED ON	PRICE EACH
H2/314	—	Gearbox front chain adjuster eye bolt and nuts	1	ES2, 19, 50	4 0
H2/1008	JX.61/JY.48	Gearbox chain adjuster bolt only	1	ES2, 19, 50	3 4
E3223	JX.62/JY.49	Gearbox front chain adjuster bolt nut	2	ES2, 19, 50	4

GEARBOX PINIONS, SHAFTS AND BEARINGS

PART No.	PLATE No.	DESCRIPTION	QTY.	USED ON	PRICE EACH
A2/316	—	Main gear wheel bearing complete	1	ES2, 19, 50	1 7 5
A2/317	—	Main gear wheel oil retaining washer (between main gear wheel and bearing)	1	ES2, 19, 50	4
A2/318	—	Main gear wheel sleeve bearing rollers (per set of 13)	1	ES2, 19, 50	5 0
A2/319	—	Main gear wheel sleeve bearing roller retaining washer	1	ES2, 19, 50	2 0
A2/320	—	Main gear wheel bearing oil retaining washer (between gearbox shell and bearing)	1	ES2, 19, 50	4
A2/321	—	Mainshaft, right-hand bearing	1	ES2, 19, 50	16 0
B2/322	—	Layshaft, left-hand bearing	1	ES2, 19, 50	16 0
A2/323	—	Mainshaft bearing packing washer	1	ES2, 19, 50	3
D12/324	TN.1	Main axle	1	ES2, 19, 50	2 0 0
A2/325	TN.35	Layshaft	1	ES2, 19, 50	1 16 8
E12/326	TN.13	Main gear wheel with bronze bush	1	ES2, 19, 50	2 0 0

246

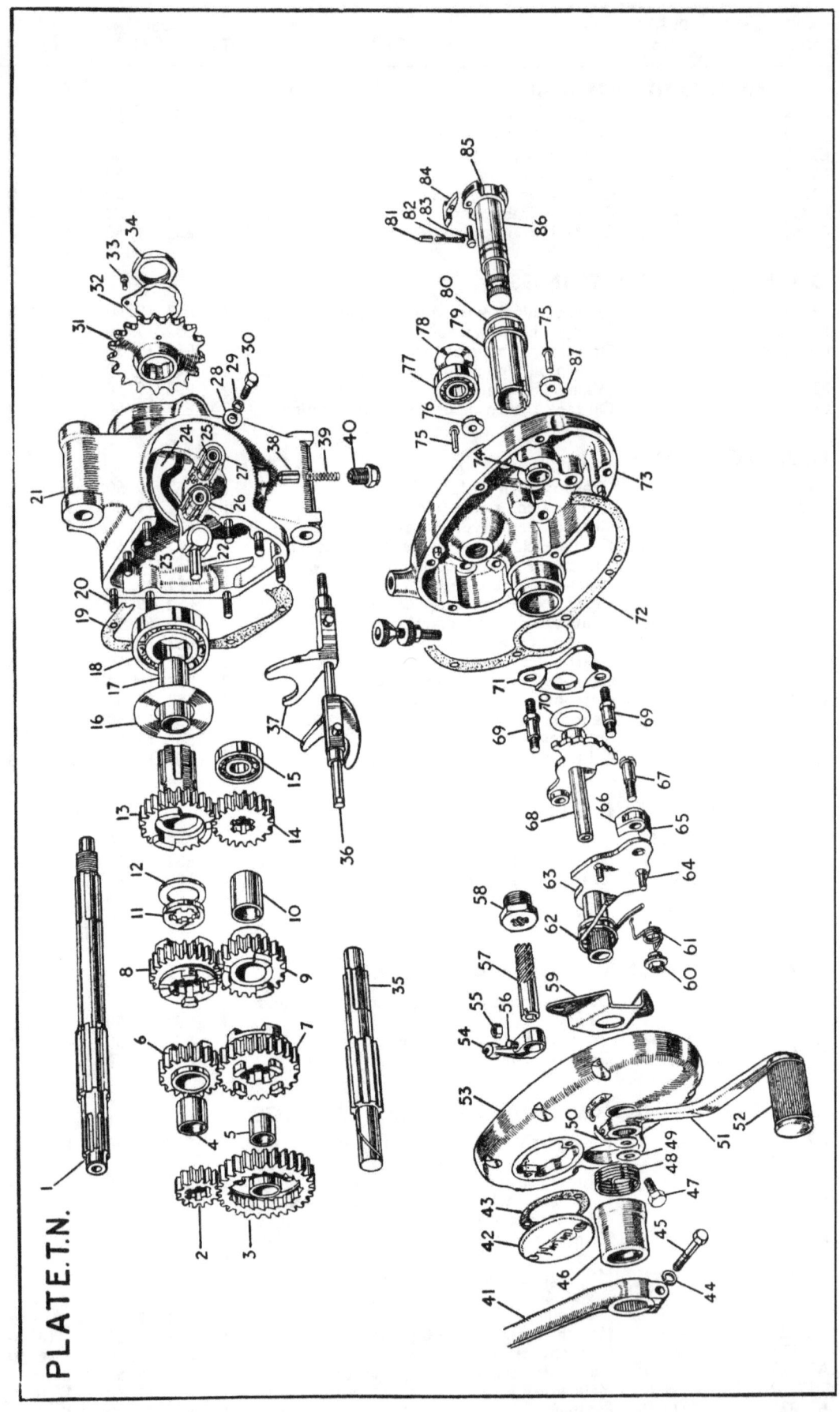

PLATE T.N.

PART No.	PLATE No.	DESCRIPTION	QTY.	USED ON	PRICE EACH
					£ s. d.
GEARBOX PINIONS, SHAFTS AND BEARINGS—cont.					
E12/327	TN.17	Main gear wheel bush (per pair)	1	ES2, 19, 50	4 8
A2/328	TN.11	Main axle thrust washer	1	ES2, 19, 50	5 0
A2/329	TN.8	Main axle sliding pinion	1	ES2, 19, 50	1 10 0
A2/330	TN.6	Main axle free pinion	1	ES2, 19, 50	1 6 0
A2/311	TN.2	Main axle pinion	1	ES2, 19, 50	12 0
A2/332	TN.14	Layshaft pinion	1	ES2, 19, 50	14 0
A2/333	TN.9	Layshaft free pinion	1	ES2, 19, 50	1 3 4
A2/334	TN.7	Layshaft sliding pinion	1	ES2, 19, 50	1 10 0
A2/335	TN.4	Bush for main axle free pinion	1	ES2, 19, 50	4 0
A2/336	TN.10	Bush for layshaft free pinion	1	ES2, 19, 50	5 0
A2/337	TN.3	Low gear and kickstarter wheel with bronze bush	1	ES2, 19, 50	1 13 4
A2/338	TN.5	Bronze bush for low gear kickstarter wheel	1	ES2, 19, 50	4 8
A2/339	TN.37	Striker fork	2	ES2, 19, 50	1 0 0
A2/340	TN.36	Striker fork shaft	1	ES2, 19, 50	5 0
D12/341	TN.24	Cam plate	1	ES2, 19, 50	1 0 0
D12/342	TN.25	Cam plate spindle	1	ES2, 19, 50	13 4
D12/343	TN.23	Cam plate quadrant with spindle	1	ES2, 19, 50	16 8
D12/344	TN.26	Cam plate or quadrant spindle bush	2	ES2, 19, 50	5 0
A2/346	TN.28	Cam plate or quadrant spindle washer	2	ES2, 19, 50	5
A2/347	TN.29	Cam plate or quadrant spindle spring washer	2	ES2, 19, 50	3
D12/348	TN.30	Cam plate or quadrant spindle bolt	2	ES2, 19, 50	5
F2/349	TN.22	Knuckle head for ratchet plate	1	ES2, 19, 50	7 6
A2/350	TN.38	Indexing plunger	1	ES2, 19, 50	8
A2/351	TN.40	Indexing plunger bush	1	ES2, 19, 50	2 4
A2/352	TN.39	Indexing plunger spring	1	ES2, 19, 50	4
A2/372	—	Main axle nut	1	ES2, 19, 50	1 0
A2/373	—	Axle nut lock washer	1	ES2, 19, 50	3
KICKSTARTER PARTS					
A2/353	TN.39	Kickstarter axle with bronze bush	1	ES2, 19, 50	2 0 0
A2/354	TN.85	Bronze bush for kickstarter end of layshaft	1	ES2, 19, 50	5 0
A2/355	TN.79	Kickstarter axle cork washer	1	ES2, 19, 50	4
A2/356	TN.84	Kickstarter pawl	1	ES2, 19, 50	5 0
A2/357	TN.83	Kickstarter pawl pin	1	ES2, 19, 50	8
A2/358	TN.46	Kickstarter return spring cover	1	ES2, 19, 50	2 4
A2/359	TN.45	Kickstarter crank bolt	1	ES2, 19, 50	5
A2/308	TN.47	Kickstarter crank bolt washer	1	ES2, 19, 50	3
A2/360	TN.41	Kickstarter crank	1	ES2, 19, 50	1 6 8
A2/367	—	Kickstarter return spring	1	ES2, 19, 50	2 4
B2/648	—	Kickstarter crank rubber	1	ES2, 19, 50	1 0
A2/361	TN.76	Kickstarter cam	1	ES2, 19, 50	8
A2/362	TN.75	Kickstarter cam or stop piece rivet	1	ES2, 19, 50	3
A2/363	TN.87	Kickstarter stop piece	1	ES2, 19, 50	10
A2/364	TN.80	Kickstarter bush	1	ES2, 19, 50	6 0
A2/365	TN.82	Kickstarter pawl spring	1	ES2, 19, 50	4
A2/366	TN.81	Kickstarter pawl spring plunger	1	ES2, 19, 50	8
GEARBOX AXLE SPROCKET					
E12/368	TN.31	Axle sprocket	1	ES2, 19, 50	1 2 0
A2/369	—	Axle sprocket locking nut	1	ES2, 19, 50	1 8
A2/370	—	Axle sprocket nut locking plate	1	ES2, 19, 50	8
A2/371	—	Axle sprocket locking plate screw (Axle sprockets 17T and 19T can be supplied, state size when ordering.)	1	ES2, 19, 50	3
CLUTCH GROUP					
D12/374	—	Clutch assembly complete	1	ES2, 19, 50	12 5 0
D12/375	TN.57	Clutch worm	1	ES2, 19, 50	5 0
D12/376	TN.58	Clutch worm nut	1	ES2, 19, 50	13 4
D12/377	TN.54	Clutch worm lever	1	ES2, 19, 50	5 0
D12/378	TN.56	Clutch worm lever stud	1	ES2, 19, 50	6
T158	TN.55	Clutch worm lever stud nut	1	ES2, 19, 50	3
E3/379	—	Clutch rod	1	ES2, 19, 50	2 0

PART No.	PLATE No.	DESCRIPTION	QTY.	USED ON	PRICE EACH £ s. d.
CLUTCH GROUP—cont.					
A2/380	—	Thrust pin	1	ES2, 19, 50	4 0
D12/381	Q.2	Clutch back plate	1	ES2, 19, 50	5 6
A2/382	Q.3	Clutch roller cage	1	ES2, 19, 50	3 6
A2/383	Q.4	Clutch roller (per set 15)	1	ES2, 19, 50	6 6
A2/384	Q.13	Clutch sprocket with inserts	1	ES2, 19, 50	2 5 0
A2/385	Q.7	Clutch body	1	ES2, 19, 50	1 17 0
A2/386	Q.5	Clutch body back cover plate	1	ES2, 19, 50	4 8
D12/387	Q.10	Clutch body centre	1	ES2, 19, 50	17 0
A2/388	Q.8	Clutch body centre rubber buffers, large (set 3)	1	ES2, 19, 50	1 6
A2/389	Q.9	Clutch body centre rubber buffers, small (set of 3)	1	ES2, 19, 50	1 0
A2/390	Q.11	Clutch body front cover plate	1	ES2, 19, 50	6 0
A2/391	Q.12	Clutch body front cover plate retaining screw (3)	3	ES2, 19, 50	3
A2/392	Q.14	Clutch plate (steel)	5	ES2, 19, 50	3 0
A2/393	Q.15	Clutch friction plate with inserts	5	ES2, 19, 50	11 0
A2/394	—	Clutch friction plate inserts (per 20)	100	ES2, 19, 50	5 10
A2/395	—	Clutch sprocket inserts (per 20)	20	ES2, 19, 50	9 2
A2/396	Q.18	Clutch plate cover	1	ES2, 19, 50	2 0
A2/397	Q.17	Clutch outer plate	1	ES2, 19, 50	5 6
A2/398	Q.16	Clutch plate retaining ring	1	ES2, 19, 50	1 4
D2/399	Q.20	Clutch spring	3	ES2, 19, 50	8
D2/400	Q.19	Clutch spring box	3	ES2, 19, 50	1 0
D2/401	Q.6	Clutch spring stud	3	ES2, 19, 50	1 6
A2/402	Q.1	Clutch spring stud nut	3	ES2, 19, 50	4
A2/403	Q.21	Clutch spring screw	3	ES2, 19, 50	4
POSITIVE FOOT CHANGE PARTS					
D12/404	TN.50	Gearbox change speed indicator	1	ES2, 19, 50	1 6
D12/405	TN.47	Gearbox change speed indicator bolt	1	ES2, 19, 50	6
D12/864	TN.49	Gearbox change speed indicator bolt washer	1	ES2, 19, 50	3
D12/406	TN.51	Gear lever	1	ES2, 19, 50	1 0 0
D12/407	TN.52	Gear lever rubber	1	ES2, 19, 50	1 0
A2/408	—	Gear lever securing bolt	1	ES2, 19, 50	8
D12/409	TN.59	Return spring cover plate	1	ES2, 19, 50	6 8
D12/410	TN.62	Return spring for pawl carrier	1	ES2, 19, 50	1 4
D12/411	TN.69	Stop stud for pawl carrier	2	ES2, 19, 50	1 4
A2/412F	—	Stop stud nut for pawl carrier (front)	2	ES2, 19, 50	8
A2/413	TN.64	Peg for pawl carrier	2	ES2, 19, 50	4
D12/414	TN.63	Pawl carrier	1	ES2, 19, 50	13 0
D12/415	TN.70	Pawl carrier spacing washer	1	ES2, 19, 50	3
A2/417	TN.65	Pawl plain	1	ES2, 19, 50	4 0
A2/418	TN.66	Pawl forked	1	ES2, 19, 50	4 0
A2/419	TN.61	Pawl return spring	1	ES2, 19, 50	1 0
A2/420	TN.67	Pawl pin	1	ES2, 19, 50	1 6
A2/421	TN.60	Pawl pin nut	1	ES2, 19, 50	8
D12/422	TN.68	Ratchet plate with spindle	1	ES2, 19, 50	1 0 0
D12/423	TN.71	Cam plate	1	ES2, 19, 50	4 0
D12/1010	TN.74	Bronze bush inner for gear change	1	ES2, 19, 50	5 0
D12/1011	—	Bronze bush outer for gear change	1	ES2, 19, 50	5 0
FRONT WHEEL AND FITTINGS					
K12-2/714	—	Front wheel complete with bearings and brake (less tyre)	1	ES2, 19, 50	16 0 0
K12-2/428	—	Front wheel with hub shell only	1	ES2, 19, 50	9 0 0
K12-2/655	KR.21	Hub shell only (front)	1	ES2, 19, 50	3 0 0
K12-2/463(F)	KR.56	Brake drum only (front)	1	ES2, 19, 50	3 0 0
18214	—	Brake drum stud front	1	ES2, 19, 50	1 0
E6183	KR.19	Brake drum stud nut	1	ES2, 19, 50	6
A2/440	KR.24	Front hub bearing lockring	1	ES2, 19, 50	2 0
B2/452	R.31/KR.26	Front hub spindle	1	ES2, 19, 50	15 0
B2/454	R.7/KR.3	Front hub spindle nut	1	ES2, 19, 50	2 2
J2/457	R.6/KR.2	Front hub brake plate	1	ES2, 19, 50	1 5 0
J2/459	R.9/KR.4	Front hub brake cam lever	1	ES2, 19, 50	3 0
B2/657	R.5/KR.7	Front hub brake shoe fulcrum pin	1	ES2, 19, 50	2 6

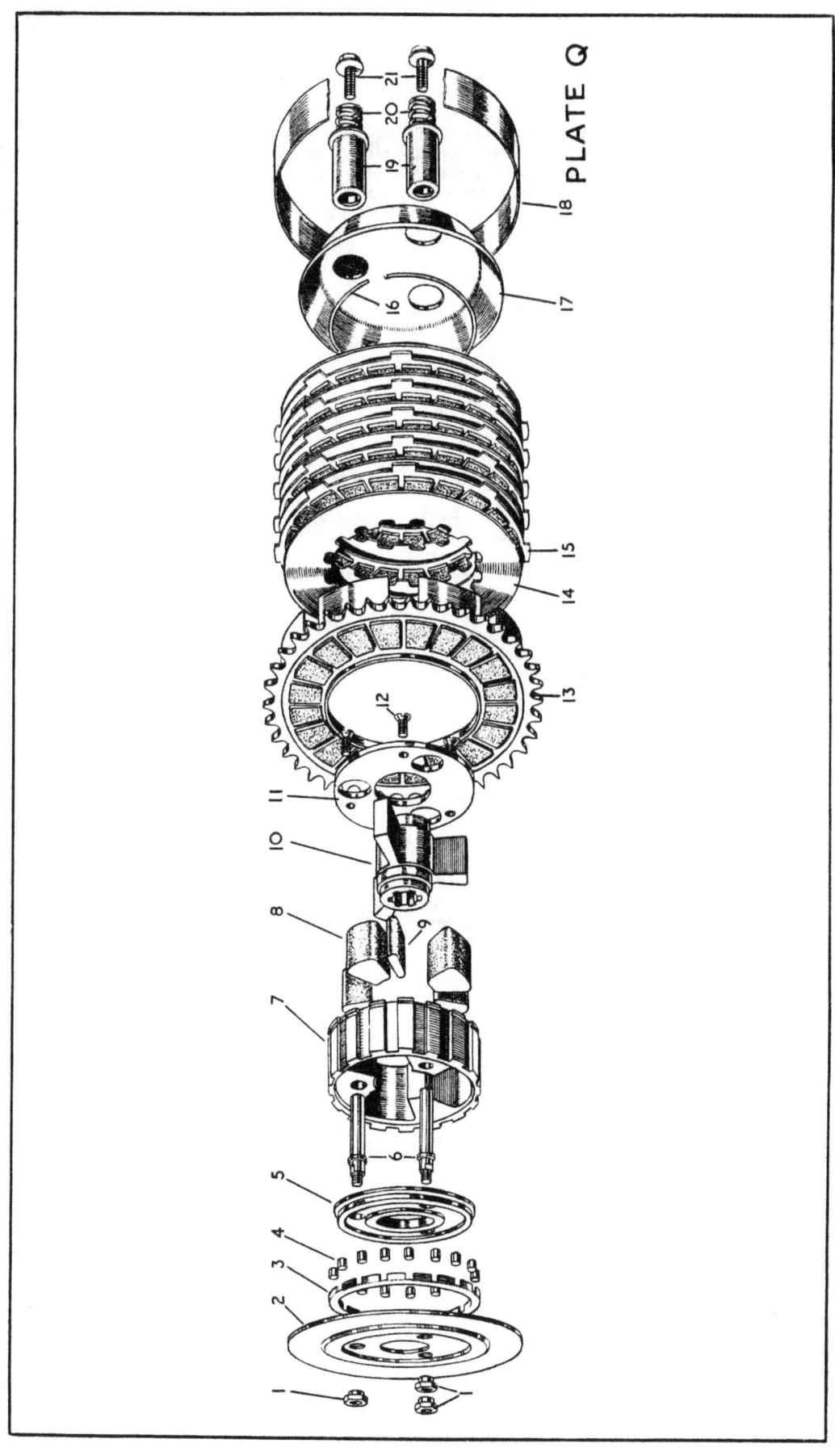

PLATE Q

250

PART No.	PLATE No.	DESCRIPTION	QTY.	USED ON	PRICE EACH
					£ s. d.
FRONT WHEEL AND FITTINGS—cont.					
B2/658	R.4/KR.1	Front hub brake shoe fulcrum pin nut ..	1	ES2, 19, 50	6
J2/441	R.28/KR.23	Front hub bearing distance piece plain side	1	ES2, 19, 50	1 0
C2/656	R.25/KR.18	Front hub bearing distance tube	1	ES2, 19, 50	1 6
B2/439	R.16	Front hub bearing felt washer steel plate (brake side)	1	ES2, 19, 50	3
K12-2/442	KR.25	Front hub bearing dust cap	1	ES2, 19, 50	3 0
J2/448(F)	R.14/KR.20	Front hub brake cam	1	ES2, 19, 50	7 0
HUB BRAKE SHOES AND LININGS					
J2/443(F)	R.21/KR.8	Hub brake shoe with lining (front) ..	2	ES2, 19, 50	1 2 6
H2/443(R)	S.18/KR.39	Hub brake shoe with lining (rear)..	2	ES2, 19, 50	1 0 6
J2/444(F)	R.23/KR.10	Hub brake shoe lining, front (per pair) ..	1	ES2, 19, 50	18 4
H2/444(R)	S.19/KR.40	Hub brake shoe lining, rear (per pair) ..	1	ES2, 19, 50	14 8
A2/445	S.30/KR.9	Hub brake shoe lining rivets (per set 14) ..	2	ES2, 19, 50	1 0
PART COMMON TO FRONT AND REAR HUBS					
A2/435	R.27/S.31/KR.22	Hub bearing (plain side)	2	ES2, 19, 50	12 7
A2/436	R.19/S.16/KR.17	Hub bearing (brake side)	2	ES2, 19, 50	1 3 9
A2/437	R.17/S.14/KR.16	Hub bearing felt washer	4	ES2, 19, 50	3
A2/438	R.18/S.15/KR.15	Hub bearing pen steel washer (brake side)	2	ES2, 19, 50	4
A2/198	S.30	Hub grease nipple	2	ES2, 19, 50	6
A2/446	R.24/S.4/KR.14	Hub brake shoe return spring	4	ES2, 19, 50	6
14454	S.3/KR.11	Hub brake shoe retaining plate	2	ES2, 19, 50	1 0
14506	KR.12	Retaining plate tab washer	2	ES2, 19, 50	8
14455	KR.13	Retaining plate bolts	4	ES2, 19, 50	8
E3224	R.10/S.5/KR.5	Hub brake cam nut	2	ES2, 19, 50	4
E5455	R.11/S.6/KR.6	Hub brake nut washer	2	ES2, 19, 50	3
REAR WHEEL AND FITTINGS					
K12-2/715	—	Rear wheel complete with bearings and brake (less tyre)	1	ES2, 19, 50	18 0 0
K12-2/649	—	Rear wheel with hub shell only	1	ES2, 19, 50	8 10 0
K12-2/433	KR.46	Rear hub shell only	1	ES2, 19, 50	4 15 0
18348	KR.48	Rear hub shell diaphragm	1	ES2, 19, 50	7 6
18396	KR.49	Rear hub shell diaphragm drive screws ..	3	ES2, 19, 50	2
K12-2/434	KR.32	Hub shell bearing sleeve	1	ES2, 19, 50	6 0
K12-2/441	KR.47	Hub bearing distance piece, plain side ..	1	ES2, 19, 50	2 0
K12-2/440	KR.50	Hub bearing lock ring	1	ES2, 19, 50	5 0
A2/439	S.13/KR.45	Hub bearing felt washer steel cup (brake side)	1	ES2, 19, 50	1 0
A2/460	S.45/KR.33	Rear hub spindle	1	ES2, 19, 50	7 0
B2/659	S.28/KR.28	Rear hub spindle washer	2	ES2, 19, 50	3
B2/660	S.35/KR.53	Rear hub spindle shouldered washer, plain side, for speedometer gearbox	1	ES2, 19, 50	1 6
K12-2/461	KR.54	Rear hub spindle distance piece (plain side)	1	ES2, 19, 50	2 0
A.2/462	KR.38	Rear hub brake plate	1	ES2, 19, 50	15 6
A2/465	S.41/KR.36	Rear hub brake plate distance piece (outer)	1	ES2, 19, 50	2 0
K12-2/463	KR.42	Rear hub brake drum and sprocket ..	1	ES2, 19, 50	3 0 0
K12-2/464	KR.44	Rear brake drum and sprocket fork end attachment piece	1	ES2, 19, 50	8 0
A2/454	KR.27	Rear brake drum and sprocket fork end attachment nut	1	ES2, 19, 50	2 2
A2/466	—	Rear hub brake torque arm	1	ES2, 19, 50	5 6
A2/467	—	Rear hub brake torque arm spring washer	1	ES2, 19, 50	3
E3812	—	Rear hub brake torque arm frame bolt ..	1	ES2, 19, 50	1 0
A2/468	S.46/KR.37	Rear hub brake torque arm stud	1	ES2, 19, 50	4 0
11664	S.48	Rear hub brake torque arm stud nut ..	1	ES2, 19, 50	5
E5375	S.47	Rear hub brake torque arm stud nut washer	1	ES2, 19, 50	3
A2/448(R)	S.11/KR.41	Rear hub brake cam	1	ES2, 19, 50	7 0
H12/469	KR.34	Rear hub brake cam lever	1	ES2, 19, 50	3 6
H12/470	KR.35	Rear hub brake cam lever return spring ..	1	ES2, 19, 50	1 0
K12-2/472	KR.43	Rear brake drum stud	3	ES2, 19, 50	1 0
K12-2/451	KR.51	Wheel sleeve nut	3	ES2, 19, 50	2 0
18371A	KR.52	Wheel sleeve nut grommet	3	ES2, 19, 50	9

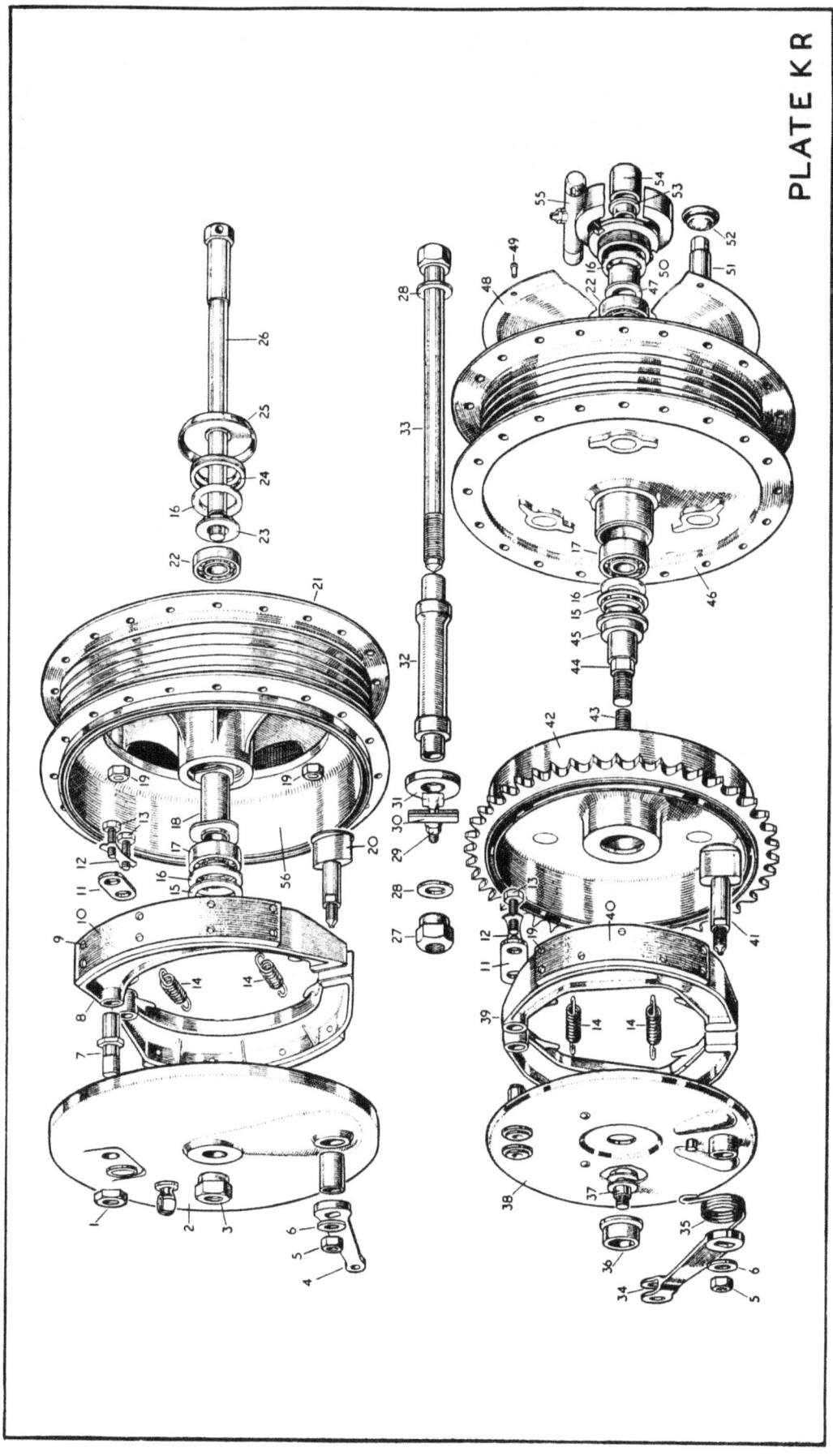

PLATE KR

PART No.	PLATE No.	DESCRIPTION	QTY.	USED ON	PRICE EACH

WHEEL RIMS AND SPOKES

					£ s. d.
K122/654	—	Wheel rim (front)	1	ES2, 19, 50	1 16 0
K122/432	—	Wheel rim (rear)	1	ES2, 19, 50	1 16 0
K122/650	—	Wheel spoke, front, brake side (per set)	20	ES2, 19, 50	4 0
K122/651	—	Wheel spoke, front, plain side (per set)	20	ES2, 19, 50	4 0
K122/652	—	Wheel spoke, rear, brake side (per set)	20	ES2, 19, 50	4 0
K122/653	—	Wheel spoke, rear, plain side (per set)	20	ES2, 19, 50	4 0
A2/431	—	Spoke nipples (per set)	40	ES2, 19, 50	4 6

ENGINE SPROCKETS

H2/473/20T	—	Engine sprocket	1	ES2	17 6
H2/473/19T	—	Engine sprocket	1	19	17 6
H2/473/18T	—	Engine sprocket	1	50	17 6
A2/474	—	Engine sprocket key	1	ES2, 19, 50	3
A2/475	—	Engine sprocket locknut	1	ES2, 19, 50	1 0

FRONT AND REAR CHAINS

L4/477	—	Front chain (76 link)	1	ES2, 19, 50	1 5 0
A2/478	—	Rear chain (90 link)	1	ES2, 19, 50	2 3 0
A2/479	—	Front chain spring link	1	ES2, 19, 50	1 9
A2/480	—	Front chain crank link	1	ES2, 19, 50	3 0
A2/481	—	Rear chain spring link	1	ES2, 19, 50	1 9
A2/482	—	Rear chain crank link	1	ES2, 19, 50	3 0

REAR CHAIN ADJUSTERS

| L4/666 | — | Rear chain adjuster bolt only | 2 | ES2, 19, 50 | 1 0 |
| E3223 | — | Rear chain adjuster bolt nut | 2 | ES2, 19, 50 | 4 |

FRONT CHAIN CASE AND FITTINGS

H4/484	—	Front chaincase, inner portion	1	ES2, 19, 50	2 0 0
L4/485	—	Front chaincase, outer portion	1	ES2, 19, 50	2 5 0
A2/486	—	Front chaincase sealing washer	1	ES2, 19, 50	7 6
E3336	—	Front chaincase drain plug	1	ES2, 19, 50	10
E5264	—	Front chaincase drain plug washer	1	ES2, 19, 50	3
A2/487	—	Front chaincase inspection disc	1	ES2, 19, 50	1 9
A2/488	—	Front chaincase inspection disc washer	1	ES2, 19, 50	3
A2/489	—	Front chaincase inspection disc spring clip	1	ES2, 19, 50	1 0
E6354	—	Front chaincase inner portion crankcase attachment pin	1	ES2, 19, 50	5
A2/490	—	Front chaincase pin locking plate	1	ES2, 19, 50	4
E3223	JX.52	Front chaincase inner portion attachment nut	2	ES2, 19, 50	4
D12/491	—	Front chaincase inner portion attachment bolt	1	ES2, 19, 50	1 9
A2/275	JX.51	Front chaincase inner portion attachment bolt washer	1	ES2, 19, 50	3
E2/492	—	Front chaincase inner portion crankcase washer	1	ES2, 19, 50	6
A2/493	—	Front chaincase inner portion gearbox felt washer	1	ES2, 19, 50	6
A2/494	—	Front chaincase inner portion footrest tube felt washer	1	ES2, 19, 50	4
A2/495	—	Front chaincase outer portion securing nut	1	ES2, 19, 50	2 4
A2/496	—	Front chaincase outer portion securing nut washer	1	ES2, 19, 50	2 0

REAR CHAINGUARD AND FITTINGS

H12/497	—	Rear chainguard	1	ES2, 19, 50	1 4 0
12342	—	Rear chainguard pin	2	ES2, 19, 50	5
E3229	—	Nut for pin	2	ES2, 19, 50	4
E5379	—	Washer for pin	2	ES2, 19, 50	3
15817	—	Rear chainguard rear fixing bolt	1	ES2, 19, 50	1 0
E3224	—	Nut for bolt	1	ES2, 19 50	4
E5379	—	Washer for bolt	1	ES2, 19, 50	3
16879	—	Rear chainguard distance piece	1	ES2, 19, 50	6

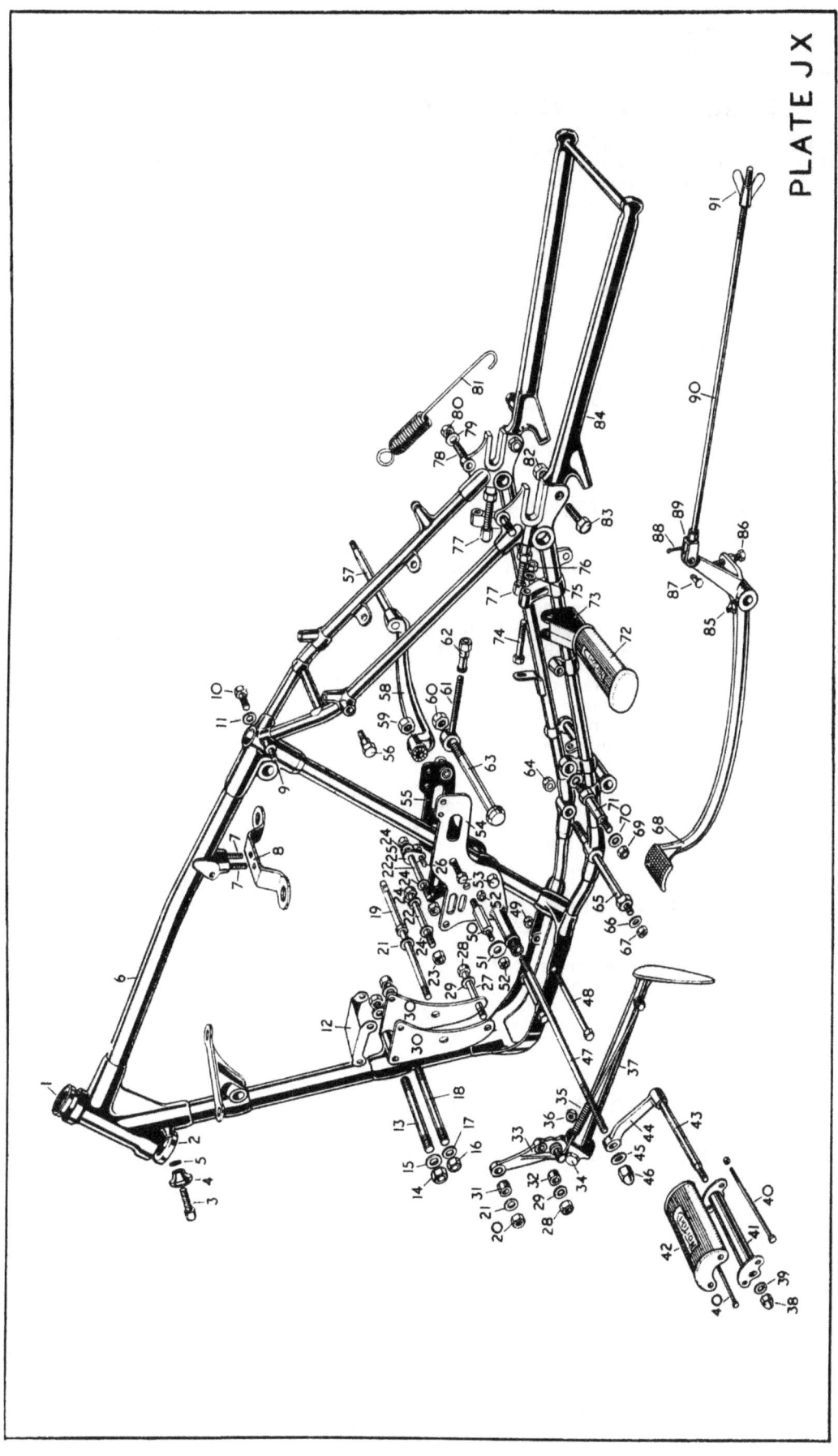

PLATE JX

PART No.	PLATE No.	DESCRIPTION	QTY.	USED ON	PRICE EACH

REAR BRAKE PEDAL AND FITTINGS

£ s. d.

PART No.	PLATE No.	DESCRIPTION	QTY.	USED ON	PRICE EACH
H12/498	JY.86	Rear brake pedal	1	ES2, 19, 50	1 4 0
A2/500	JX.85	Rear brake pedal grease nipple	1	ES2, 19, 50	6
A2/501	JX.86	Rear brake pedal adjuster and locknut	1	ES2, 19, 50	1 6
D12/502	JY60	Rear brake pedal pivot bolt	1	ES2, 19, 50	2 0
E3223	JX.69	Nut for pivot bolt	1	ES2, 19, 50	4
E5456	JX.70	Washer for pivot bolt	1	ES2, 19, 50	3

REAR BRAKE ROD AND FITTINGS

PART No.	PLATE No.	DESCRIPTION	QTY.	USED ON	PRICE EACH
H12/503	JY.92	Rear brake rod	1	ES2, 19, 50	3 0
H12/504	JY.91	Rear brake rod jaw joint	1	ES2, 19, 50	2 3
H12/505	JY.93	Rear brake rod adjuster	1	ES2, 19, 50	3 0
A2/195	JX.88	Cotter for joint pin	1	ES2, 19, 50	2
H12/506	JY.90	Rear brake rod jaw joint pin	1	ES2, 19, 50	5
15822	—	Rear brake rod roller (cam lever end)	1	ES2, 19, 50	6

FOOTRESTS AND FITTINGS

PART No.	PLATE No.	DESCRIPTION	QTY.	USED ON	PRICE EACH
A2/507	JX.42	Footrest rubber	2	ES2, 19, 50	2 6
A2/508	JX.40	Footrest rubber securing bolt and nut	4	ES2, 19, 50	8
A2/509	JX.41	Footrest pad holder	2	ES2, 19, 50	2 6
D12/510	JX.47	Footrest rod	1	ES2, 19, 50	2 6
E3226	JX.59	Footrest rod nut, plain	1	ES2, 19, 50	5
E3220	JX.45	Footrest rod nut, domed	1	ES2, 19, 50	10
E5377	JX.46	Footrest rod nut washer	2	ES2, 19, 50	3
A2/512	—	Footrest serrated hanger with pad holder spindle (left-hand)	1	ES2, 19, 50	5 0
D12/512RH	—	Footrest serrated hanger with pad holder spindle (right-hand)	1	ES2, 19, 50	10 0
A2/513	JX.44	Footrest serrated hanger only (left-hand)	1	ES2, 19, 50	4 3
D12/513RH	JX.58	Footrest serrated hanger only (right-hand)	1	ES2, 19, 50	9 3
A2/514	JX.43	Footrest serrated hanger spindle only	2	ES2, 19, 50	9
A2/515	JX.38	Footrest serrated hanger spindle nut	2	ES2, 19, 50	5
E5376	JX.39	Footrest hanger spindle washer	2	ES2, 19, 50	6

FRONT AND REAR ENGINE PLATES

PART No.	PLATE No.	DESCRIPTION	QTY.	USED ON	PRICE EACH
E2/522	JX.30	Front engine plate (left or right-hand)	2	ES2, 19, 50	4 0
A2/523	JX.12	Front engine plate cover	1	ES2, 19, 50	3 0
H4/516	—	Rear engine plate (left-hand) with footrest tube	1	ES2, 19, 50	12 6
E4/517	—	Rear engine plate (right-hand) with footrest tube	1	ES2, 19, 50	12 6

FRAMES AND REAR SUSPENSION

PART No.	PLATE No.	DESCRIPTION	QTY.	USED ON	PRICE EACH
L4/518	—	Frame only with head races	1	ES2, 19, 50	20 0 0
A2/519	JX.1	Frame head race top	1	ES2, 19, 50	4 9
A2/520	JX.2	Frame head race bottom	1	ES2, 19, 50	4 9
A2/521	—	Frame head balls (per set 34)	1	ES2, 19, 50	4 0
19351	JX.3	Frame fork stop bolt	2	ES2, 19, 50	8
16247	JX.5	Frame fork stop bolt nut	4	ES2, 19, 50	4
H12/1091	—	Rear mudguard and engine plate support bridge	1	ES2, 19, 50	17 6
E3135	—	Support bridge fixing bolts	4	ES2, 19, 50	8
E5380	—	Washer for bolt	4	ES2, 19, 50	3
L4/1081	JY.77	Rear shock absorber unit	2	ES2, 19, 50	3 5 0
16839	—	Shock absorber top fixing bolt	2	ES2, 19, 50	1 0
E3223	—	Nut for top fixing bolt	2	ES2, 19, 50	4
E5456	—	Washer for top fixing bolt	2	ES2, 19, 50	3
18537	—	Distance piece between mudguard	2	ES2, 19, 50	6
15900	JY.85	Shock absorber bottom fixing bolt	2	ES2, 19, 50	1 0
E3223	JY.84	Nut for bottom fixing bolt	2	ES2, 19, 50	4
E5379	—	Washer for bottom fixing bolt	2	ES2, 19, 50	3

PART No.	PLATE No.	DESCRIPTION	QTY.	USED ON	PRICE EACH

SWINGING ARM AND FITTINGS

£ s. d.

Part No.	Plate No.	Description	Qty.	Used On	Price
L4/1088	—	Swinging arm assembly with bushes and bolt	1	ES2, 19, 50	6 5 0
L4/1089	JY.81	Swinging arm only	1	ES2, 19, 50	5 0 0
H12/1090	JY.82	Swinging arm bearing spacer tube	1	ES2, 19, 50	3 0
E21043	JY.78	Swinging arm silent bloc bearing	2	ES2, 19, 50	7 6
16809	JY.81	Swinging arm securing bolt	1	ES2, 19, 50	4 0
11809	JY.80	Swinging arm securing bolt washer	1	ES2, 19, 50	3
16840	JY.79	Swinging arm securing bolt nut	1	ES2, 19, 50	8

CENTRE PROP STAND

Part No.	Plate No.	Description	Qty.	Used On	Price
H12/524	JY.62	Prop stand	1	ES2, 19, 50	1 5 0
11466	JY.61	Prop stand fixing bolt	2	ES2, 19, 50	9
H12/527	JY.67	Prop stand return spring	1	ES2, 19, 50	2 0
H12/1082	JY.64	Prop stand return spring clip	1	ES2, 19, 50	1 0
E3135	JY.63	Bolt for clip	1	ES2, 19, 50	8
E3231	JY.65	Nut for clip	1	ES2, 19, 50	4
E5380	JY.66	Washer for clip	1	ES2, 19, 50	3

SIDE PROP STAND

Part No.	Plate No.	Description	Qty.	Used On	Price
L4/1014	—	Side prop stand	1	ES2, 19, 50	1 1 0
L4/1016	—	Side prop stand fixing plate	1	ES2, 19, 50	5 0
L4/1015	—	Side prop stand spring	1	ES2, 19, 50	2 0
19476	—	Side prop stand fulcrum pin	1	ES2, 19, 50	9

FRONT MUDGUARD, STAYS AND FITTINGS

Part No.	Plate No.	Description	Qty.	Used On	Price
L4/529	—	Front mudguard only with front number plate studs	1	ES2, 19, 50	1 0 0
L4/530	—	Front mudguard stay	2	ES2, 19, 50	3 0
18710	—	Front mudguard stay pin	2	ES2, 19, 50	5
18711	—	Front mudguard stay pin washer	2	ES2, 19, 50	3
13192	—	Front mudguard stay pin packing washer	2	ES2, 19, 50	3
E3229	—	Front mudguard stay pin nut	2	ES2, 19, 50	4
E5379	—	Washer for nut	2	ES2, 19, 50	3
18854	—	Front mudguard stay bolt (fork end)	2	ES2, 19, 50	5
11796	—	Front mudguard stay bolt washer (fork end)	2	ES2, 19, 50	3
L4/680	—	Front mudguard centre stay	1	ES2, 19, 50	3 0
18709	—	Front mudguard centre stay bolt	2	ES2, 19, 50	5
18711	—	Washer for bolt	2	ES2, 19, 50	3
E3229	—	Nut for bolt	2	ES2, 19, 50	4
E5379	—	Washer for nut	2	ES2, 19, 50	3
T1085	—	Front mudguard centre stay fork attachment stud	4	ES2, 19, 50	6
E3229	—	Nut for stud	4	ES2, 19, 50	4
E5379	—	Washer for stud	4	ES2, 19, 50	3
E3262	—	Front mudguard stand attachment bolt	1	ES2, 19, 50	8
E3223	—	Nut for bolt	1	ES2, 19, 50	4
E3218	—	Domed nut for bolt	1	ES2, 19, 50	6
E5456	—	Washer for bolt	2	ES2, 19, 50	3

FRONT AND REAR NUMBER PLATES AND FITTINGS

Part No.	Plate No.	Description	Qty.	Used On	Price
K12/531	—	Front number plate	1	ES2, 19, 50	3 0
18712	—	Front number plate screw	2	ES2, 19, 50	3
18755	—	Front number plate rubber	1	ES2, 19, 50	9
18708	—	Front number plate stanchion	2	ES2, 19, 50	9
E3229	—	Nut for stanchion	2	ES2, 19, 50	4
E5379	—	Washer for stanchion	2	ES2, 19, 50	3
L4/532	—	Rear number plate	1	ES2, 19, 50	12 6
12342	—	Rear number plate pins	4	ES2, 19, 50	5
E5379	—	Washers for pins	4	ES2, 19, 50	3

PART No.	PLATE No.	DESCRIPTION	QTY.	USED ON	PRICE EACH
					£ s. d.
REAR MUDGUARD STAYS AND FITTINGS					
L4/534	—	Rear mudguard	1	ES2, 19, 50	3 10 0
L4/535(B)	—	Rear mudguard, bottom portion	1	ES2, 19, 50	15 0
L4/535(F)	—	Rear mudguard, front portion	1	ES2, 19, 50	2 15 0
L4/536(LH)	—	Rear mudguard stay and lifting handle (LH)	1	ES2, 19, 50	4 0
L4/536(RH)	—	Rear mudguard stay and lifting handle (RH)	1	ES2, 19, 50	4 0
19432	—	Fixing bolt lifting handle to mudguard	3	ES2, 19, 50	5
19433	—	Washer for bolt	3	ES2, 19, 50	3
19434	—	Fixing bolt lifting handle to bottom portion of mudguard	2	ES2, 19, 50	5
19435	—	Washer for bolt	2	ES2, 19, 50	3
E3229	—	Nut for bolt	2	ES2, 19, 50	4
TOOL AND BATTERY BOX					
L4/538	—	Tool and battery box	1	ES2, 19, 50	2 0 0
L4/539	—	Tool and battery box fixing knob	1	ES2, 19, 50	6
13053	—	Stud for fixing	1	ES2, 19, 50	6
E3223	—	Nut for bolt	1	ES2, 19, 50	4
E5456	—	Washer for bolt	1	ES2, 19, 50	3
19249	—	"U" bolt for battery fixing	1	ES2, 19, 50	1 6
E3221	—	Nut for bolt	2	ES2, 19, 50	4
17707	—	Washer for bolt	2	ES2, 19, 50	2
19248	—	Retaining strap, battery fixing	1	ES2, 19, 50	9
E6453	—	Stud bottom fixing	1	ES2, 19, 50	8
E3223	—	Nut for stud	1	ES2, 19, 50	4
18709	—	Bolt, rear fixing	1	ES2, 19, 50	5
E3229	—	Nut for bolt	1	ES2, 19, 50	4
E5379	—	Washer for bolt	1	ES2, 19, 50	3
DUAL SEAT AND FITTINGS					
L4/540	—	Dual seat	1	ES2, 19, 50	5 10 0
13053	—	Frame stud, front fixing	2	ES2, 19, 50	6
E3223	—	Nut for stud	2	ES2, 19, 50	4
E5456	—	Washer for stud	2	ES2, 19, 50	3
FRONT STAND					
L4/544	—	Front stand	1	ES2, 19, 50	10 0
11940	—	Front stand attachment pin	2	ES2, 19, 50	5
11796	—	Washer for pin	2	ES2, 19, 50	3
SPEEDOMETER AND FITTINGS					
L4/545	—	Speedometer head	1	E52, 195, 50	3 10 0
B2/681	—	Speedometer head rubber washer	1	E52, 195, 50	6
B2/555	—	Speedometer head attachment bracket	1	E52, 195, 50	1 6
B2/556	—	Speedometer head securing nut	2	E52, 195, 56	4
B2/557	—	Speedometer head securing nut washer	2	E52, 195, 50	3
L4/552	—	Speedometer cable complete	1	E52, 195, 50	1 5 0
L4/553	—	Speedometer cable outer	1	E52, 195, 50	12 6
L4/554	—	Speedometer cable inner	1	E52, 195, 50	12 6
L4/564	—	Speedometer gearbox complete	1	E52, 195, 50	2 2 6
PILLION FOOTRESTS AND FITTINGS					
H12/584	—	Pillion footrest complete (per pair)	1	ES2, 19, 50	1 1 0
H12/1086	JY.75	Pillion footrest bar with eye bolt	2	ES2, 19, 50	4 0
H12/1087	JY.71	Pillion footrest lug	2	ES2, 19, 50	5 0
16841	JY.70	Stud pillion footrest and silencer fixing	2	ES2, 19, 50	10
E3224	JY.68	Nut for stud	2	ES2, 19, 50	4
E5376	JY.69	Washer for stud	2	ES2, 19, 50	3
16248	JY.72	Pillion footrest bar and lug pin	2	ES2, 19, 50	8
16250	JY.74	Spring washer for pin	2	ES2, 19, 50	2
16247	JY.73	Nut for pin	2	ES2, 19, 50	4
H12/583	JY.76	Pillion footrest rubber, left- or right-hand	2	ES2, 19, 50	1 6

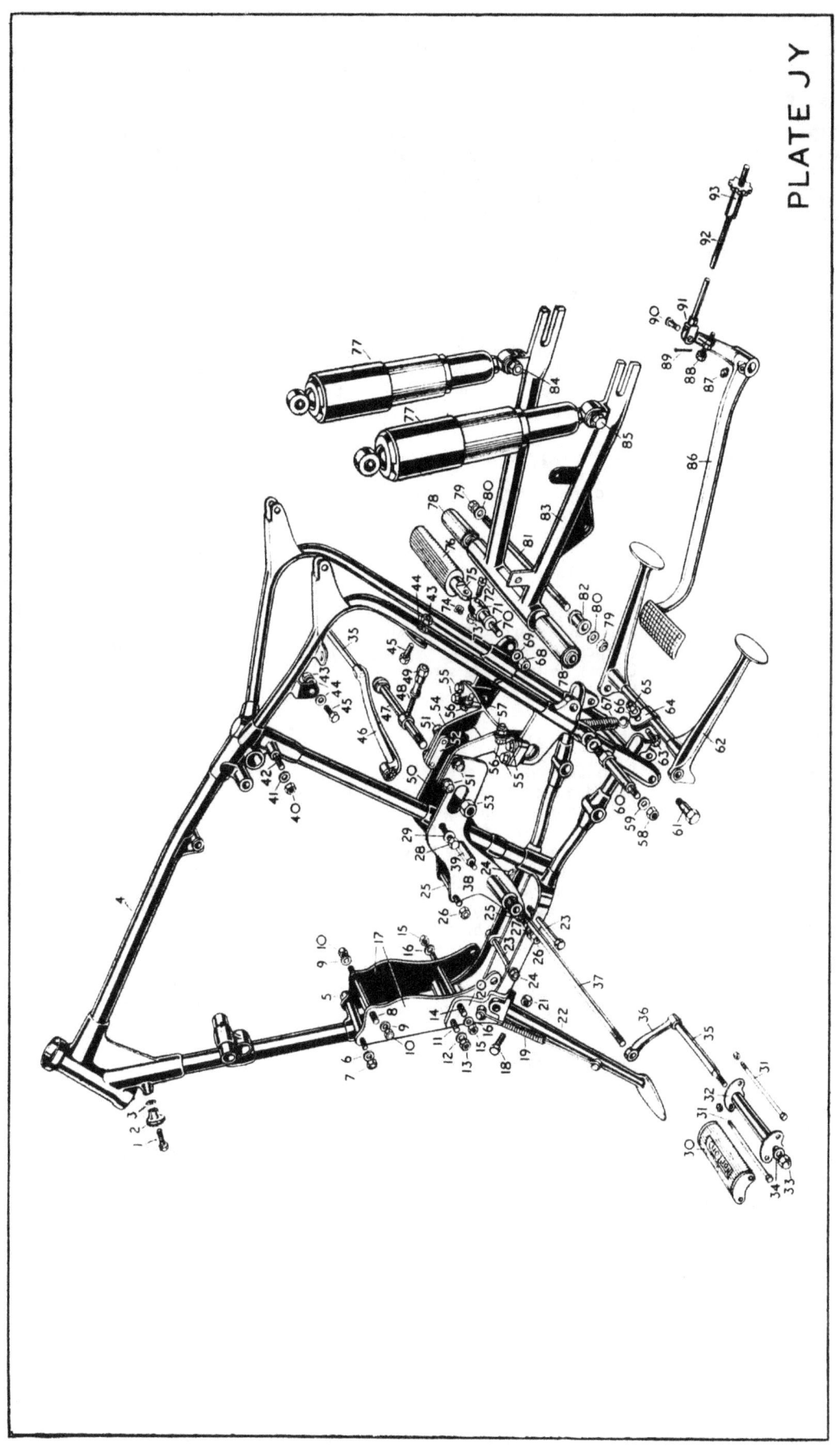

PLATE JY

PART No.	PLATE No.	DESCRIPTION	QTY.	USED ON	PRICE EACH

MAGDYNO PARTS (LUCAS)

£ s. d.

PART No.	PLATE No.	DESCRIPTION	QTY.	USED ON	PRICE EACH
463121	—	Magdyno fibre gear wheel assembly	1	ES2, 19, 50	16 10
200569	—	Slotted screw securing dynamo to magneto	1	ES2, 19, 50	5
200290	—	Dynamo brushes (per set)	1	ES2, 19, 50	3 0
463066	—	H.T. pick-up for magneto	1	ES2, 19, 50	4 2
451260	—	H.T. pick-up carbon brush and spring	1	ES2, 19, 50	11
460056	—	Strap with pin and roller securing dynamo to magneto	1	ES2, 19, 50	2 5
460051	—	Contact breaker complete	1	ES2, 19, 50	13 10
484098	—	Contact breaker points (per set)	1	ES2, 19, 50	5 5
410600	—	Screwed bush for H.T. pick-up	1	ES2, 19, 50	11
460061	—	Contact breaker cover	1	ES2, 19, 50	1 2
200354	—	Dynamo bakelite end cover with screw	1	ES2, 19, 50	3 11
454495	—	Steel pinion driven for dynamo (See magdyno driving parts and fittings for sprockets.)	1	ES2, 19, 50	5 1

HEADLAMP AND FITTINGS

PART No.	PLATE No.	DESCRIPTION	QTY.	USED ON	PRICE EACH
51793A	—	Headlamp complete with switch and ammeter	1	E52, 195, 50	
36084F	—	Ammeter	1	E52, 195, 50	9 0
31315A	—	Switch	1	E52, 195, 50	12 0
351567	—	Switch handle and screw	1	E52, 195, 50	1 6
516798	—	Reflector and glass	1	E52, 195, 50	14 6
553248	—	Headlamp rim	1	E52, 195, 50	12 6
31563A	—	Dipped switch and horn push	1	E52, 195, 50	10 6
18733	—	Dipper switch rubber	1	E52, 195, 50	6
18734	—	Dipper switch fixing screw	2	E52, 195, 50	3
12201	—	Headlamp fixing bolt	2	E52, 195, 50	8

STOP LAMP AND FITTINGS

PART No.	PLATE No.	DESCRIPTION	QTY.	USED ON	PRICE EACH
53269A	—	Stop lamp complete	1	ES2, 19, 50	1 5 0
573819	—	Stop lamp cover	1	ES2, 19, 50	7 0
572072	—	Stop lamp cover fixing bolt	2	ES2, 19, 50	6
166014	—	Stop lamp cover fixing bolt nut	2	ES2, 19, 50	3
185036	—	Stop lamp cover fixing bolt washer	2	ES2, 19, 50	2
312818	—	Stop lamp switch	1	ES2, 19, 50	4 6
17005	—	Stop lamp switch spring	1	ES2, 19, 50	9
17007	—	Stop lamp switch bracket	1	ES2, 19, 50	2 6
17008	—	Stop lamp switch bracket	1	ES2, 19, 50	2 6
14468	—	Stop lamp switch fixing bolt	2	ES2, 19, 50	6
E3229	—	Stop lamp switch fixing bolt nut	2	ES2, 19, 50	4
E5379	—	Stop lamp switch fixing bolt washer	2	ES2, 19, 50	3
18721	—	Rear mudguard reflector	1	ES2, 19, 50	3 0

VOLTAGE REGULATOR AND FITTINGS

PART No.	PLATE No.	DESCRIPTION	QTY.	USED ON	PRICE EACH
37097	—	Voltage regulator	1	ES2, 19, 50	1 19 0
12342	—	Voltage regulator fixing pin	2	ES2, 19, 50	5
E3222	—	Voltage regulator fixing pin nut	2	ES2, 19, 50	4
E5375	—	Voltage regulator fixing washer	2	ES2, 19, 50	3

ELECTRIC HORN AND FITTINGS

PART No.	PLATE No.	DESCRIPTION	QTY.	USED ON	PRICE EACH
069343	—	Electric horn with bracket	1	ES2, 19, 50	1 15 8
701686	—	Electric horn bracket	1	ES2, 19, 50	3 4
13299	JX.56	Electric horn bracket fixing bolt to frame	1	ES2, 19, 50	6

TOOLS

PART No.	PLATE No.	DESCRIPTION	QTY.	USED ON	PRICE EACH
A2/561	—	Tyre inflator with connection	1	ES2, 19, 50	8 0
A2/562	—	Tyre inflator connection	1	ES2, 19, 50	3 6
A3/563	—	Tool-roll complete with tools	1	ES2, 19, 50	2 17 6
A2/563	—	Double-ended spanner, $\frac{3}{16}$ in. and $\frac{1}{4}$ in.	1	ES2, 19, 50	2 0
A2/566	—	Double-ended spanner, $\frac{5}{16}$ in. and $\frac{3}{8}$ in.	1	ES2, 19, 50	2 8
A2/567	—	Screw driver	1	ES2, 19, 50	2 6
C3/568	—	Push rod adjusting spanners (per pair)	1	ES2, 19, 50	2 0

PART No.	PLATE No.	DESCRIPTION	QTY.	USED ON	PRICE EACH
TOOLS—cont.					£ s. d.
A2/570	—	Wheel nut box spanner	1	ES2, 19, 50	2 0
A3/571	—	Sparking plug spanner	1	ES2, 19, 50	4 0
A2/573	—	Tyre lever	1	ES2, 19, 50	2 0
A2/574	—	Wheel spindle spanner	1	ES2, 19, 50	2 8
A2/275	—	Grease gun	1	ES2, 19, 50	15 0
A2/576	—	Gearbox top nut spanner	1	ES2, 19, 50	5 0
A2/578	—	Single-ended spanner, $\frac{1}{8}$ in.	1	ES2, 19, 50	1 0
A3/579	—	Exhaust pipe "C" spanner	1	ES2, 19, 50	3 0
A2/581	—	Tommy bar	1	ES2, 19, 50	1 0
B2/682	—	Front fork crown and column locknut spanner	1	ES2, 19, 50	2 6
B2/683	—	Front fork filler plug and head adjuster nut spanner	1	ES2, 19, 50	3 0
B2/684	—	Front fork main tube top bush locking spanner	1	ES2, 19, 50	2 0
B2/685	—	Pull through for road holder fork	1	ES2, 19, 50	7 6
LEGSHIELDS AND FITTINGS					
A2/589	—	Legshields and fittings complete (per set)	1	ES2, 19, 50	2 13 4
A2/590	—	Legshield blade, left-hand	1	ES2, 19, 50	14 8
A2/591	—	Legshield blade, right-hand	1	ES2, 19, 50	14 8
A2/592	—	Legshield blade bracket, left or right-hand	2	ES2, 19, 50	1 0
A2/593	—	Legshield blade bracket back plate	1	ES2, 19, 50	8
12342	—	Legshield blade bracket pin	1	ES2, 19, 50	5
E3222	—	Legshield blade bracket pin nut	1	ES2, 19, 50	4
A2/595	—	Legshield tank attachment bracket	1	ES2, 19, 50	2 8
A2/596	—	Legshield tank attachment bracket, right-hand	1	ES2, 19, 50	2 8
A2/597	—	Petrol tank front rubber	1	ES2, 19, 50	6
A2/598	—	Legshield top securing rod	1	ES2, 19, 50	2 0
A2/599	—	Legshield bottom securing rod	1	ES2, 19, 50	2 0
E3226	—	Legshield securing rod nut	1	ES2, 19, 50	4
A2/600	—	Legshield blade bracket distance tube, $3\frac{3}{8}$ in.	1	ES2, 19, 50	8
A2/601	—	Tank bracket distance tube, $13\frac{1}{8}$ in.	1	ES2, 19, 50	1 4
A2/602	—	Legshield blade tank bracket distance tube, $1\frac{7}{16}$ in.	1	ES2, 19, 50	4
A2/603	—	Legshield bottom, left-hand distance tube, $5\frac{1}{8}$ in.	1	ES2, 19, 50	8
A2/604	—	Legshield bottom, right-hand distance tube, $6\frac{7}{8}$ in.	1	ES2, 19, 50	8
TRANSFERS					
A2/866	—	Petrol tank name transfer for top panel	1	ES2, 19, 50	1 2
A2/867	—	Front chaincase transfer	1	ES2, 19, 50	1 2
A2/868	—	Oil tank transfer (minimum oil level)	1	ES2, 19, 50	1 2
A2/869	—	Rear mudguard transfer	1	ES2, 19, 50	1 2
		(Please Note.—Panels, red and black lines cannot be supplied. These are painted by hand.)			
RUBBER CABLE CLIPS					
Size "A"	—	For clutch, air throttle, mag. cables and headlamp cable harness to top frame tube	1	—	4
Size "D"	—	For tail lamp lead	1	—	4
Size "S"	—	For speedometer cable battery lead	1	—	4

NOTES

REGD. TRADE MARK

SPARE PARTS LIST FOR 1959 MODELS 88, 99, ES2 and 50

1959 PUBLICATION PS206

Price 3s. 6d.

NORTON MOTORS LTD.

BRACEBRIDGE ST., BIRMINGHAM, 6, ENGLAND

Phone: Aston Cross 3711 (Private Branch Exchange)

Grams: "Nortomo, Birmingham"

IMPORTANT INFORMATION RELATING TO THE PARTS LISTS INCLUDED IN THIS MANUAL

It should be noted that the early parts lists also include the 30, 40, 30M & 40M and the later parts lists include the 88 & 99 twins.#

The first parts list included is a reproduction of the 1948 and 1949 factory parts list for the S.V. and O.H.V. spring frame (plunger) Big 4, 16H, 18 and ES2 models fitted with 'Road-holder' forks and 'upright' gearbox (it also includes the 1946 to 1949 model 30, 40, 30M and 40M).

The second parts list is a reproduction of the 1956 factory parts list for the O.H.V. swing-arm, 'laydown' gearbox ES2, 19S and 50 models and the rigid frame model 19.

The third parts list is a reproduction of the 1959 PS206 factory parts list for the ES2 and 50 'featherbed' frame models fitted with alternator & coil electrics (it also includes the 88 and 99 twins).

When the four workshop manuals in this publication are used in conjunction with these three illustrated parts lists, they provide a comprehensive maintenance and repair manual exclusive to the 1945 to 1963 Norton 16H, Big4, 18, 19S, 19, 50 and ES2 series.

INDEX

	Page
Air cable	21
Air cleaners	40
Air lever complete and fittings	20
Amal carburettor	13
Battery box and fittings	34
Brake shoes and linings	29
Cable clips	37
Centre stand and fittings	33
Chains front and rear	31
Chromium mudguards	40
Clutch assembly and fittings	25
Clutch cable	21
Coil and fittings	15
Crankcase and engine plate bolts, nuts and washers	8
Crankcase and fittings	5
Crankcase pressure and breather fittings	7
Crash bars	39
Cylinder head barrel studs and nuts	12
Distributor and fittings	16
Distributor drive parts	16
Drysump oil pump and drive parts	11
Dual seat and fittings	35
Electric horn and fittings	35
Engine plates	31
Engine sprocket	31
Exhaust lifter and fittings	9
Exhaust lifter cable	21
Exhaust lifter lever and fittings	20
Exhaust pipe and fittings	16
Flywheels, crankshaft assemblies and fittings	7
Footrests and fittings	30
Folding kickstart crank	40
Frames	31
Front brake and clutch lever assemblies	20
Front brake cable	20
Front chaincase and fittings	29
Front fork assembly and fittings	17
Front forks with sidecar trail	19
Front mudguard, stays and fittings	33
Front wheel and fittings	27
Full enclosure rear chaincase	39
Gasket sets	37

	Page
Gearbox fixing bolts	24
Gearbox front chain adjuster	24
Gearbox pinions, shafts and bearings	24
Gearbox shell	22
Handlebar and fittings	19
Headlamp and fittings	35
Kickstarter parts	25
Miscellaneous section	40
Number plates	34
Oil pipes and fittings	22
Oil tank and fittings	22
Optional equipment and service tools	38
Overhead rockers and fittings	10
Paint	37
Parts common to front and rear hubs	29
Petrol tank and fittings	21
Pillion footrests	30
Piston assemblies and fittings	13
Positive footchange	25
Push rods and fittings	9
Rear chain adjuster	31
Rear chainguard and fittings	30
Rear brake pedal and fittings	30
Rear mudguard and fittings	34
Rear suspension and fittings	33
Rear wheel and fittings	27
Revolution counter and fittings	39
Rocker box and fittings	10
Service tools (all models)	41
Side prop stand and fittings	33
Silencer and fittings	17
Speedometer and fittings	35
Stator and rectifier	15
Stop lamp and fittings	36
Swinging arm and fittings	33
Tappets and fittings	9
Throttle cable	21
Tools	41
Tool kits	36
Tool tray and fittings	34
Transfers	37
Twist grip complete and fittings	20
Wheel rims and spokes	29

INSTRUCTIONS FOR ORDERING SPARE PARTS

This Spare Parts List deals with replaceable parts for Models 88, 99, ES2 and 50 of 1959 manufacture.

It is most essential that the Engine and Frame Number of the machine is stated. The Engine Number is to be found on the transmission side of the Crankcase directly below cylinder base. The frame number is stamped on the nearside of the frame gusset plate on all models. It is always advisable to order parts on a separate sheet, and not to include on the same sheet other matter of a different nature; this facilitates prompt despatch.

It is found in a number of instances that money orders and postal orders are sent in parcels containing patterns; this is inadvisable. We strongly recommend parts as patterns being despatched separately, and a covering letter sent containing the remittance for replacement parts.

RETURNING MACHINES FOR OVERHAULING

When returning machines or parts for repair or overhaul, these should be sent carriage paid, and with the sender's name and address in full **securely** attached. It is also advisable to state on the tally that a letter has been sent respecting the parts, and giving the date. All easily detached fittings should be removed, such as Lamps, Horns, Tool Bags, Speedometers, etc.; these are liable to be lost or damaged in transit, and the Company cannot accept any responsibility for them.

ESTIMATES FOR REPAIRING MACHINES

We are always prepared to give approximate estimates for the cost of repairs; it is quite impossible to give a firm quotation. Additional parts may be found necessary during the process of repair, unforseen when preparing an estimate. Should our estimate for repair not be accepted, a charge may be made in accordance with work entailed in dismantling and re-assembling. When we give an estimate for cost of repairs, and this is curtailed by the owner, we cannot accept any responsibility for the performance of the machine; it is always preferable to accept our estimate in full.

PURCHASE OF SPARE PARTS

Norton Dealers throughout the British Isles generally carry a very comprehensive stock of Norton spare parts and it is recommended that owners should obtain any spare parts required through them.

The name of the nearest Norton dealer will be supplied on request and if any difficulty whatever is experienced in obtaining spare parts through a Norton Dealer, if we are advised, we shall be very pleased to investigate the matter.

It is our desire that replacement parts are available to Norton owners with the least possible delay.

Please note we reserve the right to alter the prices in the list at any time without notice.

PART No.	SUPERSEDED No.	PLATE No.	DESCRIPTION	QTY.	MODEL	PRICE EACH £ s. d.

CRANKCASE AND FITTINGS

PART No.	SUPERSEDED No.	PLATE No.	DESCRIPTION	QTY.	MODEL	PRICE EACH
22041	—	—	Crankcase with timing cover	1	ES2, 50	13 10 3
21013	—	—	Crankcase with timing cover	1	88, 99	18 18 4
22043	—	B88	Crankcase driving side	1	ES2, 50	4 1 1
21010	—	A104	Crankcase driving side	1	88, 99	6 15 2
50254	—	B89	Crankcase timing side with bushes	1	ES2, 50	7 1 10
21009	—	A105	Crankcase timing side with bushes	1	88, 99	9 12 6

In the event of a replacement half crankcase being required, it will be necessary to return the sound half of the crankcase also the timing cover to the works for matching.

PART No.	SUPERSEDED No.	PLATE No.	DESCRIPTION	QTY.	MODEL	PRICE EACH
22008	—	B92	Crankcase timing cover with bushes	1	ES2, 50	2 14 1
20950	—	A106	Crankcase timing cover	1	88, 99	2 10 7
T2236	—	—	Crankcase timing cover paper washer	1	88, 99	7
19228	—	—	Crankcase timing cover badge	1	88, 99	4 0
19841	—	B90	Crankcase cylinder barrel stud	4	ES2	1 9
19840	—	B90	Crankcase cylinder barrel stud	4	50	1 9
T2018	D12/2(L)	A107	Crankcase cylinder base stud $\frac{3}{8}''$ dia.	6	88, 99	1 4
T2209	D12/2(S)	A108	Crankcase cylinder base stud (stepped) $\frac{5}{16}''$ dia.	2	88, 99	1 2
18943	—	A109	Crankcase cylinder base stud $\frac{3}{8}''$ dia. (front centre)	1	88, 99	1 4
T2016	D12/3(L)	A110	Crankcase cylinder base stud nut $\frac{3}{8}''$ dia.	7	88, 99	7
T2210	D12/3(S)	—	Crankcase cylinder base stud nut $\frac{5}{16}''$ dia.	2	88, 99	7
T2211	—	—	Crankcase cylinder base stud washer	2	88, 99	3
10940	—	—	Timing cover screws (top short)	3	ES2, 50	7
10940	—	A111	Timing cover screws (long)	6	88, 99	7
11001	—	—	Timing cover screws (bottom long)	3	ES2, 50	7
13996	—	—	Timing cover screws (hex. head)	2	ES2, 50	6
E6980	—	A112	Timing cover screws (short)	6	88, 99	6
18195	A2/9	B93	Magneto chain cover	1	ES2, 50	12 2
E4506	C2/687	B94	Magneto chain cover screw (short)	2	ES2, 50	6
13868	C2/688	B95	Magneto chain cover screw (long)	1	ES2, 50	11
11775	—	B96	Fibre washer for timing cover screws	8	ES2, 50	2
11775	—	—	Fibre washer for timing cover screws	12	88, 99	2
11001	—	—	Crankcase panel screw	1	ES2, 50	7
11775	—	—	Washer for screw	1	ES2, 50	2
10940	—	A113	Screw timing to driving side crankcase sump	2	88, 99	7
11775	—	—	Washer for screw	2	88, 99	2
13860	C2/18	B72	Crankcase cam bush (inlet or exhaust)	2	ES2, 50	6 0
13788	C2/19	B73	Timing cover cam bush (inlet)	1	ES2, 50	6 0
10657	A2/20	B74	Timing cover cam bush (exhaust)	1	ES2, 50	6 0
T2036	D12/18TS	—	Camshaft bush timing side	1	88, 99	6 8
T2037	D12/18DS	—	Camshaft bush driving side	1	88, 99	6 8
13792	C2/12	B97	Timing cover oil feed jet	1	ES2, 50	3 4
13791	C2/13	B98	Timing cover oil feed jet bush	1	ES2, 50	3 4
10617	A2/14	B99	Timing cover oil feed jet spring	1	ES2, 50	3 4
T2124	D12/913	A114	Timing cover mainshaft oilseal	1	88, 99	1 4
17841	D12/914	A115	Timing cover mainshaft oilseal circlip	1	88, 99	7
E4591	—	—	Timing cover oilway plug	1	88, 99	7
13765	—	—	Crankcase drain plug	1	ES2, 50	1 4
13833	—	—	Crankcase drain plug washer	1	ES2, 50	3
16945	H12/16945	—	Crankcase oil sump filter body	1	88, 99	10 2
16949	H12/16949	—	Filter body copper and asbestos washer	1	88, 99	7
16946	H12/16946	—	Filter body gauze	1	88, 99	3 4
16947	H12/16947	—	Filter body gauze retaining plate	1	88, 99	7
16948	H12/16948	—	Filter body gauze retaining plate circlip	1	88, 99	7
15399	—	—	Name plate for drive side of crankcase	1	88, 99	6
17842	—	—	Screws for name plate	2	88, 99	1

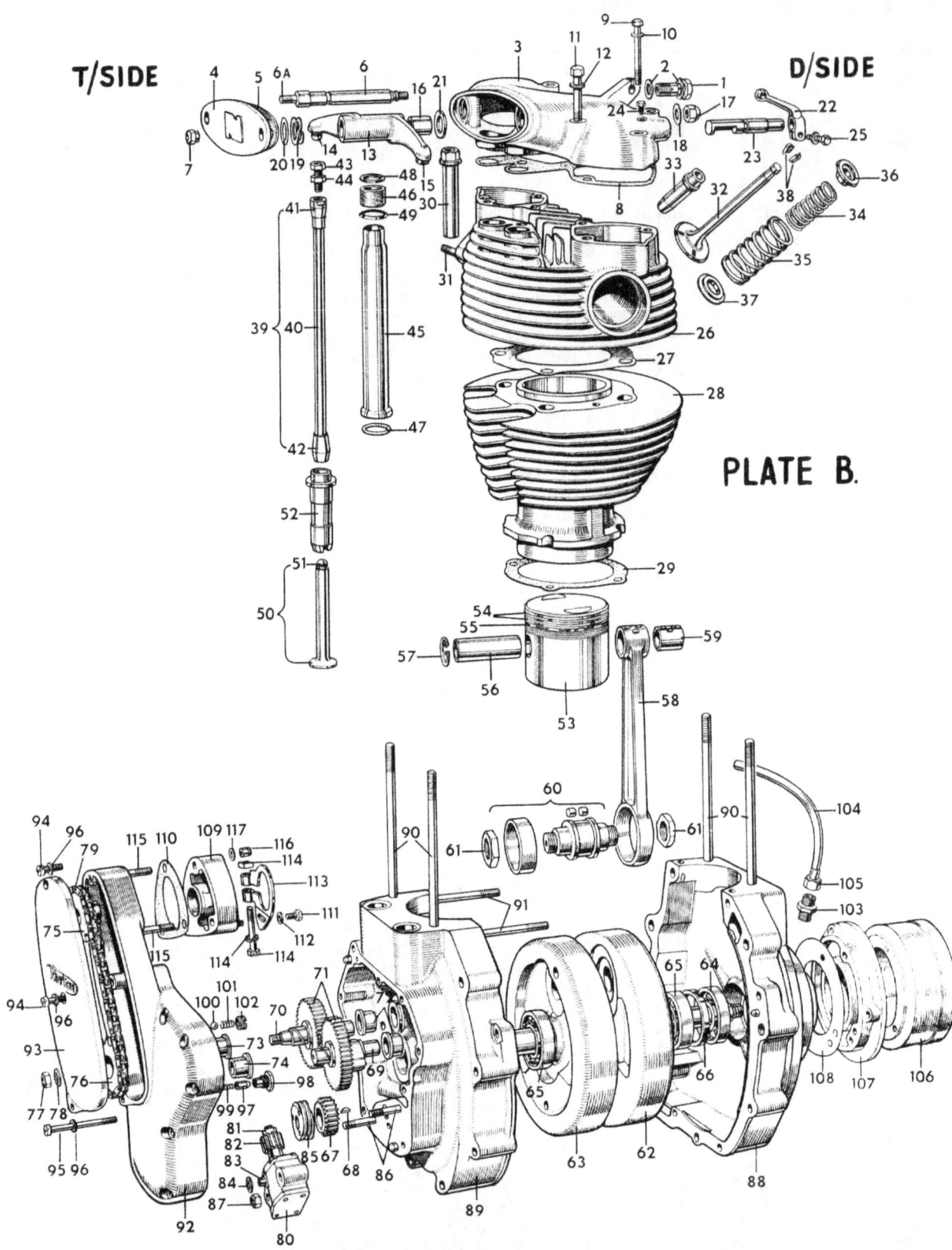

PART No.	SUPERSEDED No.	PLATE No.	DESCRIPTION	QTY.	MODEL	PRICE EACH

CRANKCASE PRESSURE AND BREATHER FITTINGS

PART No.	SUPERSEDED No.	PLATE No.	DESCRIPTION	QTY.	MODEL	£ s. d.
20280	—	A116	Filter assembly oil pressure release	1	88, 99	2 11
20287	—	A117	Filter Plug	1	88, 99	2 11
20288	—	A118	Filter plug washer	1	88, 99	3
20285	—	A119	Plunger for oil pressure release	1	88, 99	1 9
20286	—	A120	Plunger spring	1	88, 99	3
20284	—	A121	Plunger spring plug	1	88, 99	2 6
17706	A2/15	B100	Timing cover pressure release ball, $\frac{3}{8}''$	1	ES2, 50	3
10260	A2/16	B101	Timing cover pressure release ball spring	1	ES2, 50	2
13789	A2/17	B102	Timing cover pressure release plug	1	ES2, 50	10
20584	—	—	Retaining cup for t/cover oil valve	1	ES2, 50	9
10260	A2/16	—	Spring for t/cover oil valve	1	ES2, 50	3
18548	—	—	$\frac{7}{32}''$ dia. ball for t/cover oil valve	1	ES2, 50	3
19245	—	B103	Crankcase breather	1	ES2, 50	2 8
17618	A2/708	B104	Crankcase breather pipe with nipple	1	ES2, 50	1 9
10992	A2/718	B105	Crankcase breather pipe, nut	1	ES2, 50	8
19382A	D12/708	—	Crankcase breather pipe with flange	1	88, 99	2 8
T2213	D12/923	—	Crankcase breather pipe securing bolt	1	88, 99	6
19383	—	—	Crankcase breather rubber pipe	1	88, 99	1 5
16550A	A2/10	—	Timing cover oil drain pipe	1	ES2, 50	1 9
10995	—	—	Timing cover oil drain pipe nut	1	ES2, 50	5
10263	A2/11	—	Timing cover oil drain pipe union	1	ES2, 50	2 0

FLYWHEELS, CRANKSHAFT ASSEMBLIES AND FITTINGS

PART No.	SUPERSEDED No.	PLATE No.	DESCRIPTION	QTY.	MODEL	PRICE EACH
P4/24	—	—	Flywheels complete with shafts, crankpin bearing and connecting rod	1	ES2	15 1 4
P13/24	—	—	Flywheels complete with shaft, crankpin bearing and connecting rod	1	50	15 1 4
N12-2/24	—	—	Flywheel and crankshaft assembly with con rods	1	88	28 10 7
N14/24	—	—	Flywheel and crankshaft assembly with con rods	1	99	28 12 4
20781	—	B62	Flywheel driving side with shaft	1	ES2	4 11 11
20780	—	B62	Flywheel driving side with shaft	1	50	4 11 11
50006	C2/25	B63	Flywheel timing side with shaft	1	ES2	4 11 11
50206	L13/25	B63	Flywheel timing side with shaft	1	50	4 11 11
20777	—	—	Flywheel driving side shaft	1	ES2, 50	1 17 2
13779	C2/705	—	Flywheel timing side shaft	1	ES2, 50	1 13 9
E3684	—	—	Flywheel timing and driving shaft key (Note: We recommend flywheels to be returned to the works for the fitting of new shafts).	2	ES2, 50	3
18246	D12/924	A64	Flywheel	1	88	4 14 7
18744	L14/924	A64	Flywheel	1	99	4 14 7
18247	D12/705	A65	Crankshaft timing side	1	88	7 1 10
18746	L14/705	A65	Crankshaft timing side	1	99	7 1 10
20665	—	A66	Crankshaft driving side	1	88	7 1 10
20680	—	A66	Crankshaft driving side	1	99	7 1 10
E4591	—	—	Plug for timing side crankshaft	1	88, 99	10
T2033A	—	A67	Flywheel and crankshaft bolt	2	88, 99	2 8
T2033	D12/925	—	Flywheel and crankshaft bolt	2	88, 99	2 8
T2086	D12/926	A68	Flywheel and crankshaft stud	2	88, 99	2 0
T2031	D12/927	A69	Flywheel and crankshaft bolt or stud nut	8	88, 99	2 4
T2105	D12/928	—	Dowel for flywheel	1	88, 99	1 4
T2032	D12/929	A70	Retaining plate for dowel	1	88, 99	11
E2717A	—	—	Flywheel mainshaft packing washer, .005"	A.R.	ES2, 50	5
E2717	—	—	Flywheel mainshaft packing washer, .010"	A.R.	ES2, 50	5
T2196A	—	—	Mainshaft packing washer	A.R.	88, 99	5
T2196B	—	—	Mainshaft packing washer	A.R.	88, 99	5

PART No.	SUPERSEDED No.	PLATE No.	DESCRIPTION	QTY.	MODEL	PRICE EACH

FLYWHEELS, CRANKSHAFT ASSEMBLIES AND FITTINGS—cont.

Main bearings and fittings

PART No.	SUPERSEDED No.	PLATE No.	DESCRIPTION	QTY.	MODEL	£ s. d.
17704	A2/30	B64	Mainshaft ball bearing, driving side	1	ES2, 50	19 6
17702	A2/32	B65	Mainshaft roller bearing	2	ES2, 50	1 13 0
12794	A2/33	B66	Mainshaft bearing distance piece	1	ES2, 50	2 8
22680	—	—	Mainshaft bearing crankcase washer, driving side	1	ES2, 50	7
17822	D12/30	A75	Mainshaft bearing, timing side	1	88, 99	1 8 9
T2008	D12/930	A76	Mainshaft bearing timing side, sealing washer	1	88, 99	1 4
17824	D12/32	A77	Mainshaft roller bearing, driving side	1	88, 99	2 2 9
T2187	D12/931	—	Driving side shaft oil seal	1	88, 99	5 1
22474	—	—	Main bearing oil seal, driving side	1	ES2, 50	3 8

Connecting rod big end bearings and bush

PART No.	SUPERSEDED No.	PLATE No.	DESCRIPTION	QTY.	MODEL	£ s. d.
50030	A3/158	B58	Connecting rod with small end bush	1	ES2	2 19 5
50208	L13/158	B58	Connecting rod with small end bush	1	50	2 19 5
50023	D12/158	A59	Connecting rod with small end bush, big end bearing and bolts	2	88, 99	3 14 3
E4102	A2/159	B59	Small end bush	1	ES2, 50	6 8
T2160	D12/159	—	Small end bush	2	88, 99	4 8
22095	A2/27	B60	Crank pin bearing with nuts	1	ES2	3 15 7
22096	—	B60	Crank pin bearing with nuts	1	50	3 15 7
E6276B	A2/28	B61	Crank pin bearing nut	2	ES2	4 7
18846	—	B61	Crank pin bearing nut	2	50	4 7
E3821	A2/29	—	Crank pin nut locking screw	2	ES2, 50	3
17828	D12/27	A60	Big end bearing (2 halves)	2	88, 99	11 11
T2150	D12/989	A61	Big end cap bolt	4	88, 99	3 1
T2152	D12/990	A62	Big end cap bolt washer	4	88, 99	3
17827	—	A63	Big end cap bolt nut	4	88, 99	1 4

(Note: Crankpin spares cannot be supplied separately. Each outer race has its individual pin).

CRANKCASE AND ENGINE PLATE BOLTS, NUTS AND WASHERS

PART No.	SUPERSEDED No.	PLATE No.	DESCRIPTION	QTY.	MODEL	£ s. d.
T2012	—	—	Crankcase bottom stud	1	ES2, 50	1 9
E3224A	—	—	Nut for stud	2	ES2, 50	5
E5376	—	—	Washer for stud	2	ES2, 50	3
13870	—	A122	Crankcase bolt (short)	3	ES2, 50	10
E3223	—	A123	Nut for bolt	3	ES2, 50	5
E5456	—	A124	Washer for bolt	5	ES2, 50	3
20056	—	B91	Crankcase top stud	2	ES2, 50	1 2
E3223	—	—	Nut for stud	2	ES2, 50	5
13870	—	—	Crankcase bolt (short)	1	88, 99	10
E3223	—	—	Nut for bolt	1	88, 99	5
E5456	—	—	Washer for bolt	1	88, 99	3
T2013	—	A125	Crankcase top stud, rear	1	88, 99	1 9
E3224A	—	—	Nut for stud	1	88, 99	5
E5376	—	—	Washer for stud	1	88, 99	3
19077	—	A126	Crankcase top stud (front)	1	88, 99	1 5
E3229	—	—	Nut for stud	1	88, 99	5
T2221	—	—	Washer for stud	1	88, 99	3
E3214	—	—	Crankcase stud (top)	1	88, 99	1 9
E3231	—	—	Nut for stud	2	88, 99	5
13040	—	—	Engine plate to frame front stud	1	ES2, 50	1 9
11809	—	—	Washer for stud	2	ES2, 50	3
E3227	—	—	Nut for stud	2	ES2, 50	6
E3166	—	—	Engine plate to frame front stud	2	ES2, 50	1 9
E5377	—	—	Washer for stud	4	ES2, 50	3
E3238	—	—	Nut for stud	4	ES2, 50	6
19666	—	—	Crankcase to engine plate stud (bottom)	1	ES2, 50	1 9
E5376	—	—	Washer for stud	2	ES2, 50	3
E3224	—	—	Nut for stud	2	ES2, 50	5
E3214	—	—	Crankcase bottom frame tube stud	1	ES2, 50	1 9

PART No.	SUPERSEDED No.	PLATE No.	DESCRIPTION	QTY.	MODEL	PRICE EACH £ s. d.

CRANKCASE AND ENGINE PLATE BOLTS, NUTS AND WASHERS—cont.

PART No.	SUPERSEDED No.	PLATE No.	DESCRIPTION	QTY.	MODEL	PRICE EACH
E3223	—	—	Nut for stud	2	ES2, 50	5
22024	—	—	Crankcase bottom to rear engine plate stud	1	ES2, 50	9
E5456	—	—	Washer for stud	2	ES2, 50	3
E3223	—	—	Nut for stud	2	ES2, 50	5
E4256	—	—	Crankcase to engine plate bolt	1	ES2, 50	1 9
E5377	—	—	Washer for bolt	2	ES2, 50	3
13459	—	—	Nut for bolt	1	ES2, 50	5
16317	—	—	Front and rear engine plate to frame bolt	4	ES2, 50	11
E5376	—	—	Washer for bolt	8	ES2, 50	3
E3224	—	—	Nut for bolt	4	ES2, 50	5
T2012	—	—	Crankcase to engine plate stud, top or bottom	2	88, 99	1 9
E3224	—	—	Nut for stud	2	88, 99	3
E5376	—	—	Washer for stud	4	88, 99	5
18649	—	—	Bottom frame fixing to engine plate bolt	2	All	1 9
E5456	—	—	Washer for bolt	4	All	3
T2017	—	—	Nut for bolt	2	All	5
E4261	—	—	Crankcase to engine plate bolt (bottom)	1	88, 99	11
E3223	—	—	Nut for bolt	1	88, 99	5
T2012	—	—	Crankcase to engine plate stud (middle)	1	88, 99	1 9
E5376	—	—	Washer for stud	2	88, 99	3
E3224	—	—	Nut for stud	2	88, 99	5
T2012	—	—	Crankcase to engine plate stud (top)	1	88, 99	1 9
E5376	—	—	Washer for stud	2		3
E3224A	—	—	Nut for stud	2	88, 99	5
16317	—	—	Front and rear engine plate to frame bolt	6	88, 99	11
E5376	—	—	Washer for bolt	12	88, 99	3
E3224	—	—	Nut for bolt	6	88, 99	5

TAPPETS AND FITTINGS

PART No.	SUPERSEDED No.	PLATE No.	DESCRIPTION	QTY.	MODEL	PRICE EACH
50007	C3/75	B50	Tappet complete	2	ES2, 50	16 10
18784A	—	A54	Tappet, right-hand	2	88, 99	11 6
18784B	—	A55	Tappet, left-hand	2	88, 99	11 6
T2142	D12/943	A56	Tappet location plate	2	88, 99	6 8
T2143	D12/944	—	Tappet location plate screw	4	88, 99	3
13790	C3/693	B51	Tappet ball end	2	ES2, 50	4 8
19800	—	B52	Tappet guide	2	ES2, 50	16 10
13830	C2/689	—	Tappet guide location peg	2	ES2, 50	3

EXHAUST LIFTER AND FITTINGS

PART No.	SUPERSEDED No.	PLATE No.	DESCRIPTION	QTY.	MODEL	PRICE EACH
18175	A2/67	B22	Exhaust valve lifter lever	1	ES2, 50	6 8
13862	C3/64	B23	Exhaust valve lifter shaft	1	ES2, 50	6 0
10959	A3/66	B24	Exhaust valve lifter retaining screw	1	ES2, 50	6
17707	—	—	Washer for screw	1	ES2, 50	2
E3798	A2/68	B25	Exhaust valve lever bolt	1	ES2, 50	7
E3881	A3/69	—	Exhaust valve lever return spring	1	ES2, 50	1 9

PUSH RODS AND FITTINGS

PART No.	SUPERSEDED No.	PLATE No.	DESCRIPTION	QTY.	MODEL	PRICE EACH
M4/82	—	B39	Push rod complete	2	ES2	12 10
M13/82	—	B39	Push rod complete	2	50	12 10
M12/82 In.	—	A50	Push rod complete, inlet	2	88	12 2
M14/82 In.	—	A50	Push rod complete, inlet	2	99	12 2
M12/82 Ex.	—	A51	Push rod complete, exhaust	2	88	12 2
M14/82 Ex.	—	A51	Push rod complete, exhaust	2	99	12 2
18725	—	B40	Push rod tube only	2	ES2	4 8
18814	—	B40	Push rod tube only	2	50	4 8

PART No.	SUPERSEDED No.	PLATE No.	DESCRIPTION	QTY.	MODEL	PRICE EACH

PUSH RODS AND FITTINGS—cont.

PART No.	SUPERSEDED No.	PLATE No.	DESCRIPTION	QTY.	MODEL	£ s. d.
20130	—	—	Push rod tube only, inlet	2	88	4 8
20132	—	—	Push rod tube only, inlet	2	99	4 8
20131	—	—	Push rod tube only, exhaust	2	88	4 8
20133	—	—	Push rod tube only, exhaust	2	99	4 8
13800	C3/86	B41	Push rod top	2	ES2, 50	2 8
T2064	D12/86	A52	Push rod top	4	88, 99	4 0
13798	C3/83	B42	Push rod bottom	2	ES2, 50	4 0
T2182	D12/83	A53	Push rod bottom	4	88, 99	3 4
13801	C3/87	B43	Push rod adjuster	2	ES2, 50	4 0
10415	—	B44	Push rod adjuster nut	2	ES2, 50	7
19838	—	B45	Push rod cover	2	ES2	9 6
19837	—	B45	Push rod cover	2	50	9 6
20049	—	B46	Push rod cover sealing ring (top)	2	ES2, 50	7
20048	—	B47	Push rod cover sealing ring (bottom)	2	ES2, 50	7
20047	—	B48	Push rod cover washer (plain)	2	ES2, 50	2
20046	—	—	Push rod cover washer (plain)	A.R.	ES2, 50	7
20045	—	B49	Push rod cover washer (dished)	2	ES2, 50	3

ROCKER BOX AND FITTINGS

PART No.	SUPERSEDED No.	PLATE No.	DESCRIPTION	QTY.	MODEL	PRICE
19772	—	B3	Rocker box with cover	1	ES2, 50	4 1 1
19805	—	B4	Rocker box inspection cover	1	ES2, 50	4 0
19824	—	B5	Rocker box cover washer	1	ES2, 50	7
19856	—	B6A	Rocker box cover studs	2	ES2, 50	11
21678	—	B7	Nut for stud	2	ES2, 50	1 5
17698	—	—	Fan disc washer for stud	2	ES2, 50	3
20044	—	B8	Rocker box sealing washer	1	ES2, 50	10
19843	—	—	Rocker box bolt (long)	5	ES2, 50	2 0
16555	—	B9	Rocker box bolt (short)	2	ES2, 50	10
T2211	—	—	Washer for bolt	5	ES2, 50	2
16556	—	B10	Washer for bolt	2	ES2, 50	5
21973	—	B11	Head steady stay bolt	2	ES2, 50	1 6
11796	—	B12	Washer for bolt	2	ES2, 50	3
E5456	—	—	Head steady plate packing washer	2	ES2, 50	3
18094	D12/93R	A6	Rocker box cap (rear)	1	88, 99	10 2
T2084	D12/95R	A7	Washer for cap	1	88, 99	7
T2162	D12/955	A4	Acorn Nut for cap	1	88, 99	10
T2082	D12/956	A5	Washer for nut	1	88, 99	3
18033	K12/954	—	Stud for rear cap	1	88, 99	10
13937	—	—	Dowel for rear cap	1	88, 99	7
18093	D12/93F	A9	Rocker box front cap	2	88, 99	10 2
T2088	D12/95F	A10	Joint washer for cap	2	88, 99	7
T2252	K12/952	A11	Stud for cap	4	88, 99	7
T2085	D12/953	A8	Nut for stud	4	88, 99	7

OVERHEAD ROCKERS AND FITTINGS

PART No.	SUPERSEDED No.	PLATE No.	DESCRIPTION	QTY.	MODEL	PRICE
50003	C3/99	—	Rocker inlet with bushes	1	ES2, 50	1 13 9
50004	C3/100	B13	Rocker exhaust with bushes	1	ES2, 50	1 13 9
13804	C3/96	B16	Bush for rocker	4	ES2, 50	4 8
18249	D12/99RH	A12	Rocker inlet, right-hand	1	88, 99	1 3 8
18250	D12/99LH	A13	Rocker inlet, left-hand	1	88, 99	1 3 8
18251	D12/100RH	A14	Rocker exhaust, right-hand	1	88, 99	1 3 8
18252	D12/100LH	A15	Rocker exhaust, left-hand	1	88, 99	1 3 8
19849	—	B6	Rocker shaft	2	ES2, 50	13 6
T2237	D12/97	A19	Rocker shaft	4	88, 99	13 6
13806	—	B17	Nut for shaft	2	ES2, 50	7
13820	—	B18	Washer for nut	2	ES2, 50	3
13818	—	B19	Spring washer for shaft	2	ES2, 50	5
13794	—	B20	Washers, large, for shaft	2	ES2, 50	7
13819	C3/98	B21	Shims for shaft	2	ES2, 50	3
18102	D12/951	A20	Thrust washer for shaft	4	88, 99	7
18103	D12/950	A21	Spring washer for shaft	4	88, 99	5
T2083	D12/947	A22	Shim for shaft	4	88, 99	3
T2238	D12/945	A23	Locking plate for shaft	4	88, 99	1 4

PART No.	SUPERSEDED No.	PLATE No.	DESCRIPTION	QTY.	MODEL	PRICE EACH
OVERHEAD ROCKERS AND FITTINGS—cont.						£ s. d.
T2239	D12/946	A24	Retaining plate for shaft	4	88, 99	1 4
T2240	D12/948	A25	Joint washer for plate	4	88, 99	3
T2256	K12/949	A26	Bolt for shaft	8	88, 99	10
13821	C3/104	B14	Rocker ball end	2	ES2, 50	3 8
T2063	D12/104	A16	Rocker ball end	4	88, 99	3 8
10394	C3/105	B15	Rocker pad	2	ES2, 50	4 8
T2074	D12/803	A17	Rocker adjuster	4	88, 99	2 4
T2321	D12/804	A18	Nut for adjuster	4	88, 99	7
			Timing gear fittings			
13858	C2/58	B67	Half time pinion	1	ES2, 50	13 6
T2035	D12/58	A78	Half time pinion	1	88, 99	13 6
E3683	—	B68–A79	Key for pinion	1	All	3
T2007	D12/936	A80	Backing plate for pinion	1	88, 99	4 0
M3/60	—	—	Exhaust cam wheel, complete	1	ES2	3 3 6
M13/60	—	—	Exhaust cam wheel, complete	1	50	3 3 6
M3/61	—	—	Inlet cam wheel, complete	1	ES2, 50	3 7 7
19702	—	B69	Exhaust camshaft	1	ES2	1 11 8
20053	—	B69	Exhaust camshaft	1	50	1 11 8
19701	—	B70	Inlet camshaft	1	ES2, 50	1 15 8
18172	—	B71	Cam gear wheel, inlet or exhaust	2	ES2, 50	1 11 8
E3683	—	—	Cam gear wheel key	2	ES2, 50	3
11774A	—	—	Cam gear spindle washer, .003″	A.R.	ES2, 50	2
11774B	—	—	Cam gear spindle washer, .005″	A.R.	ES2, 50	2
11774C	—	—	Cam gear spindle washer, .007″	A.R.	ES2, 50	2
11774D	—	—	Cam gear spindle washer, .010″	A.R.	ES2, 50	2
21225 / 17413	D12/790	A81	Camshaft	1	88, 99	5 8 1
T2078	D12/933	A82	Camshaft breather stationary plate	1	88, 99	2 8
T2075	D12/934	A83	Camshaft breather rotary plate	1	88, 99	2 8
T2108	D12/935	A84	Camshaft breather spring	1	88, 99	3
20829	—	A85	Camshaft sprocket assembly	1	88, 99	1 5 4
E3683	—	A86	Key for sprocket	1	88, 99	3
T2046	D12/942	A87	Nut for sprocket	1	88, 99	1 9
17806	D12/961	A88	Camshaft driving chain, 38 link, endless	1	88, 99	9 0
T2217	D12/968	A89	Chain tensioner slipper	1	88, 99	3 4
T2218	D12/971	A90	Plate for chain tensioner (thick)	1	88, 99	7
T2218A	—	A91	Plate for chain tensioner (thin)	1	88, 99	6
T247	D12/969	A92	Chain tensioner stud	2	88, 99	7
E3231	—	A93	Chain tensioner stud nut	2	88, 99	5
18202	—	—	$\frac{5}{16}$″ Fan disc washer for stud	2	88, 99	3
50008	D12/937	A94	Intermediate gear with sprockets	1	88, 99	3 14 3
T2026	D12/938	A95	Intermediate gear bush	1	88, 99	6 0
T2021	D12/940	A97	Intermediate gear spindle	1	88, 99	5 4
T2080	D12/939	A96	Intermediate gear washer	1	88, 99	3
17823	D12/941	—	Circlip for spindle	1	88, 99	3
			Engine Steady Plate and Fittings			
21671	—	—	Head steady plate assembly	1	ES2, 50	3 9
18637	H12-2/932	—	Head steady plate assembly	1	88, 99	10 2
18032	—	A30	Head steady plate stud (in head)	1	88, 99	2 0
E3224	—	A31	Nut for stud	1	88, 99	5
E5376	—	A32	Washer for stud	1	88, 99	3
E3798	—	—	Steady plate bolt (to frame)	2	All	5
11796	—	—	Washer for bolt	2	All	3
18202	—	—	Washer for bolt	2	All	3
E3223	—	—	Nut for bolt	2	All	5
DRYSUMP OIL PUMP AND DRIVE PARTS						
15521	A2/128	B80	Oil pump assembly	1	ES2, 50	4 1 1
15522	D12/128	A98	Oil pump assembly	1	88, 99	4 1 1
15511A	A2/129	B81–A99	Oil pump spindle nut	1	All	6
10101A	A2/130	B82	Oil pump worm gear wheel	1	ES2, 50	8 10
T2077	D12/130	A100	Oil pump worm gear wheel	1	88, 99	8 10
17698	A2/131	—	Key for gear wheel	1	All	3
15515	A2/132	B83–A101	Oil pump feed bush	1	All	10

PART No.	SUPERSEDED No.	PLATE No.	DESCRIPTION	QTY.	MODEL	PRICE EACH
						£ s. d.

DRYSUMP OIL PUMP AND DRIVE PARTS—cont.

PART No.	SUPERSEDED No.	PLATE No.	DESCRIPTION	QTY.	MODEL	PRICE EACH
21146	—	—	Packing shim for feed bush	1	All	2
E6283	A2/133	B84	Sealing washer for feed bush	1	ES2, 50	3
T272	D12/133	A102	Sealing washer for feed bush	1	88, 99	5
13778	C2/134	B85	Engine shaft pump driving worm	1	ES2, 50	10 2
T2076	D12/134	A103	Engine shaft pump driving worm	1	88, 99	10 2
E4440	—	B86	Oil pump crankcase stud	2	All	11
E3231	—	B87	Nut for stud	2	All	5
E4590	—	—	Grub screw for oil stop	1	All	7

Valves, Guides, Springs and Fittings

PART No.	SUPERSEDED No.	PLATE No.	DESCRIPTION	QTY.	MODEL	PRICE EACH
E6472	A3/142	B32	Valve (inlet or exhaust)	2	ES2	16 2
18737	L13/142	B32	Valve (inlet or exhaust)	2	50	16 2
T2010	D12/142	—	Valve (inlet)	2	88, 99	16 2
T2204	D12/143	A43	Valve (exhaust)	2	88, 99	16 2
20050	—	B33	Valve guide (inlet or exhaust)	2	ES2, 50	4 8
T2011	D12/140	A44	Valve guide (inlet or exhaust)	4	88, 99	4 8
20594	—	—	Valve guide circlip	2	ES2, 50	3
21613	—	B34	Valve spring (inner)	2	ES2, 50	1 4
19302	K12/145	A45	Valve spring (inner)	4	88, 99	10
21612	—	B35	Valve spring (outer)	2	ES2, 50	2 8
19303	K12/146	A46	Valve spring (outer)	4	88, 99	1 4
16339	—	—	Heat resisting washer	4	88, 99	11
20178	—	B36	Valve spring top cups	2	ES2, 50	6 0
T186	D12/147	A47	Valve spring top cups	4	88, 99	4 0
20179	—	B37	Valve spring bottom collars	2	ES2, 50	1 6
T2073	D12/148	A48	Valve spring bottom collars	4	88, 99	1 4
E1930	A2/149	B38	Valve cotter (2 halves one cotter)	2	ES2, 50	1 4
T187	D12/149	A49	Valve cotter (2 halves one cotter)	4	88, 99	1 4

CYLINDER HEAD BARREL STUDS AND NUTS

PART No.	SUPERSEDED No.	PLATE No.	DESCRIPTION	QTY.	MODEL	PRICE EACH
19703	—	B28	Cylinder barrel	1	ES2	5 4 8
19832	—	B28	Cylinder barrel	1	50	5 1 5
20712	—	A36	Cylinder barrel	1	88	10 2 8
20774	—	A36	Cylinder barrel	1	99	10 6 0
P4/136	—	B26	Cylinder head with valve guides	1	ES2	11 16 6
P13/136	—	B26	Cylinder head with valve guides	1	50	11 13 1
50166	K12/136	A33	Cylinder head with valve guides	1	88, 99	18 18 4
19705	—	B27	Cylinder head gasket	1	ES2	2 4
18799	L13/137	B27	Cylinder head gasket	1	50	2 4
T2141	D12/137	A35	Cylinder head gasket	1	88, 99	6 8
13824	C3/157	B29	Cylinder base washer	1	ES2, 50	3
T2093	D12/157	A37	Cylinder base washer	1	88, 99	6
C126	D3T/156	B30	Cylinder head sleeve nut	4	ES2, 50	3 4
C170	—	—	Cylinder head sleeve nut washer	4	ES2, 50	5
T2096	D12/972	A38	Cylinder head bolts (long)	4	88, 99	1 4
T2097	D12/973	A39	Cylinder head bolts (short)	1	88, 99	1 2
E5376	—	A40	Cylinder head bolt washers	4	88, 99	3
T2161	D12/975	—	Cylinder head fixing studs	2	88, 99	1 4
T2017	D12/976	—	Cylinder head to barrel stud nut, $\frac{5}{16}''$	2	88, 99	7
18756	—	A41	Cylinder head to barrel stud	3	88, 99	7
T2034	D12/978	A42	Cylinder head stud nut (front)	2	88, 99	1 9
E3224	D12/979	—	Cylinder head stud nut (rear)	1	88, 99	5
20344	—	A29	Carburetter to manifold stud	2	88, 99	7
E3231	—	—	Nut for stud	2	All	5
11796	—	—	Washer for stud	2	All	3
18242	D12/983	A27	Cylinder head and carburetter manifold	1	88, 99	13 6
18380	K12/985	—	Stud securing manifold to cylinder head	4	88, 99	7
T2220	D12/986	—	Nut for stud	4	88, 99	3
T2221	D12/987	—	Washer for stud	4	88, 99	3
T2241	D12/984	—	Distance piece for manifold	2	88, 99	3 4
T247	D12/969	B31	Stud carburettor to cylinder head	2	ES2, 50	7

PART No.	SUPERSEDED No.	PLATE No.	DESCRIPTION	QTY.	MODEL	PRICE EACH

PISTON ASSEMBLIES AND FITTINGS

PART No.	SUPERSEDED No.	PLATE No.	DESCRIPTION	QTY.	MODEL	£ s. d.
22491	—	—	Piston complete with rings, gudgeon pin and circlips	1	ES2	2 6 6
22490	—	—	Piston complete with rings, gudgeon pin and circlips	1	50	2 8 6
22504	—	A57	Piston complete, L.H.	1	88	3 5 0
22505	—	A58	Piston complete, R.H.	1	88	3 5 0
22512	—	A57	Piston complete, L.H.	1	99	2 12 6
22513	—	A58	Piston complete, R.H.	1	99	2 12 6
22493	—	B53	Piston only	1	ES2	1 6 8
22492	—	B53	Piston only	1	50	1 10 4
22506	—	—	Piston only, L.H.	1	88	2 2 6
22507	—	—	Piston only, R.H.	1	88	2 2 6
22514	—	—	Piston only, L.H.	1	99	1 10 0
22515	—	—	Piston only, R.H.	1	99	1 10 0
22495	—	B54	Piston ring, compression	2	ES2	2 11
22494	—	B54	Piston ring, compression	2	50	2 8
22508	—	—	Piston ring, compression	4	88	3 9
21579	—	—	Piston ring, compression	4	99	3 9
22497	—	B55	Piston ring, scraper	1	ES2	3 11
22496	—	B55	Piston ring, scraper	1	50	3 8
22509	—	—	Piston ring, scraper	2	88	5 2
21578	—	—	Piston ring, scraper	2	99	5 2
22499	—	B56	Gudgeon pin	1	ES2	8 5
22498	—	B56	Gudgeon pin	1	50	7 6
21580	—	—	Gudgeon pin	2	88, 99	9 2
22549	—	B57	Gudgeon pin circlip	2	ES2, 50	10
21581	—	—	Gudgeon pin circlip	4	88, 99	4

N.B. : Prices of oversize pistons are 5/– more than standard sizes.

Pistons and rings can be supplied in the following oversizes : Models ES2 and 50 +.010″, +.020″, +.030″ and +.040″ o/size ; Models 88 and 89 +.010″, +.020″ and .030″ o/size.

AMAL CARBURETTOR

PART No.	SUPERSEDED No.	PLATE No.	DESCRIPTION	QTY.	MODEL	PRICE EACH
376/17	—	—	Carburettor, complete with cables, less twist grip	1	ES2	4 15 0
376/68	—	—	Carburettor, complete with cables, less twist grip	1	50	4 15 0
376/66	—	—	Carburettor, complete with cables, less twist grip	1	88	4 15 0
376/67	—	—	Carburettor, complete with cables, less twist grip	1	99	4 15 0
376/1 1/16″	—	—	Mixing chamber body	1	ES2, 99	1 11 6
376/1″	—	—	Mixing chamber body	1	50, 88	1 11 6
376/057	—	—	Jet block	1	ES2, 99	13 6
376/056	—	—	Jet block	1	50, 88	13 6
376/070	—	—	Locating pegs for jet block	1	All	7
376/067	—	—	Washer for jet block	1	All	2
376/064	—	—	Mixing chamber top	1	All	3 8
376/065	—	—	Mixing chamber top cap ring	1	All	3 8
4/235	—	—	Cap spring for top	1	All	1 0
4/241	—	—	Fixing screw for cap spring	1	All	2
4/035	—	—	Cable adjuster	1	All	9
6/132A	—	—	Cable ferrule (top hat)	1	All	4
4/137A	—	—	Plug screw	1	All	3
376/060	—	—	Throttle valve	1	All	8 0
376/061	—	—	Throttle valve spring	1	All	7
376/063	—	—	Taper needle	1	All	2 9
4/230	—	—	Taper needle clip	1	All	7
376/062	—	—	Air valve	1	All	5 3
6/047	—	—	Air valve guide	1	All	1 6
4/046	—	—	Air valve spring	1	All	4
376/101	—	—	Rod control air valve assembly	1	All	10 0
30/064	—	—	Click spring for rod control air valve assembly	1	All	3

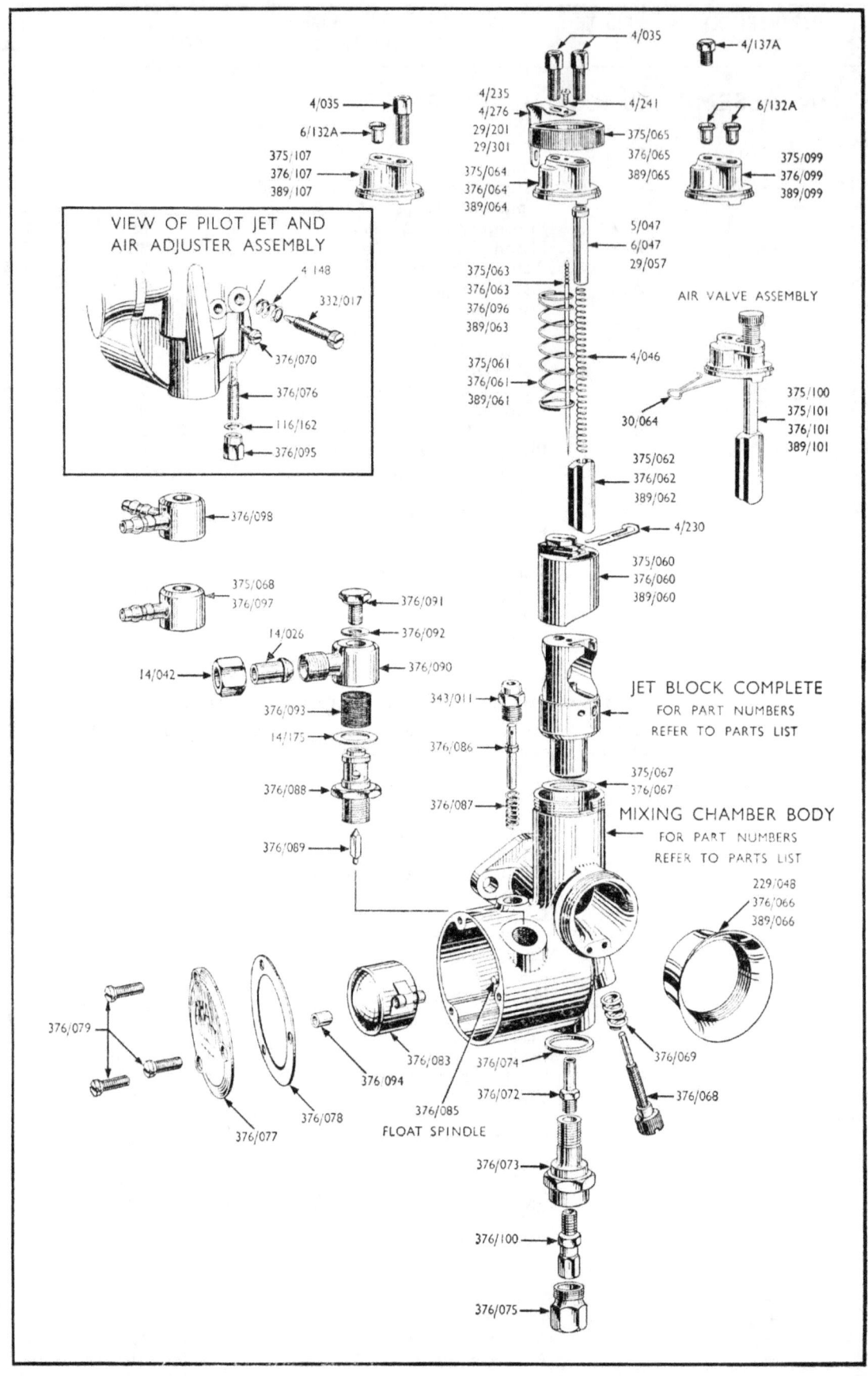

PART No.	SUPERSEDED No.	PLATE No.	DESCRIPTION	QTY.	MODEL	PRICE EACH £ s. d.
AMAL CARBURETTOR—cont.						
376/072	—	—	Needle jet	1	All	3 3
376/100	—	—	Main jet (specify size)	1	All	1 6
376/073	—	—	Main jet holder	1	All	4 9
376/074	—	—	Main jet holder washer	1	All	2
376/075	—	—	Main jet cover nut	1	All	1 3
376/076	—	—	Pilot jet	1	All	1 3
376/095	—	—	Pilot jet cover nut	1	All	1 0
116/162	—	—	Pilot jet cover nut washer	1	All	2
332/017	—	—	Air adjusting screw	1	All	1 0
4/148	—	—	Air adjusting screw spring	1	All	4
376/068	—	—	Throttle stop screw	1	All	1 0
376/069	—	—	Throttle stop screw spring	1	All	3
376/066	—	—	Air intake tube	1	All	4 9
376/083	—	—	Float complete	1	All	6 0
376/085	—	—	Float hinge spindle	1	All	8
376/094	—	—	Float spindle bush	1	All	4
376/089	—	—	Float needle	1	All	1 10
376/088	—	—	Float needle seating	1	All	3 0
14/175	—	—	Float needle seating washer	1	All	2
376/097	—	—	Banjo single	1	All	2 6
14/175	—	—	Banjo washer	1	All	2
376/091	—	—	Banjo bolt	1	All	8
376/092	—	—	Banjo bolt washer	1	All	2
376/086	—	—	Tickler	1	All	1 3
343/011	—	—	Tickler body	1	All	1 6
376/087	—	—	Tickler spring	1	All	2
376/077	—	—	Float chamber cover	1	All	3 0
376/078	—	—	Float chamber cover joint	1	All	4
376/079	—	—	Float chamber cover screws	3	All	2
376/093	—	—	Filter gauze	1	All	1 0
20000	—	A28	Carburettor sealing ring	1	All	1 0
STATOR AND RECTIFIER						
47122A	—	—	Stator } Alternator	1	All	3 15 0
423506	—	—	Rotor }	1	All	4 7 6
20691	—	—	Stator fixing stud	3	All	10
17698	—	—	Washer for stud	3	All	3
E3229	—	—	Nut for stud	3	All	5
20948	—	A74	Key for rotor	1	All	3
19147	—	—	Washer for rotor	1	All	3
465909	—	A73	Nut for rotor	1	All	1 6
21440	—	—	Distance piece for rotor	1	ES2, 50	1 6
20885	—	B106	Stator housing	1	All	17 3
20783	—	—	Stator housing fixing screw	3	ES2, 50	3
20693	—	—	Stator housing fixing screw	3	88, 99	1 5
21411	—	—	Washer for fixing screw	3	All	3
47111A	—	—	Rectifier	1	All	2 2 6
19971	—	—	Rectifier fixing nut	1	All	7
10914	—	—	Washer for nut	2	All	5
133264	—	—	Rectifier cable fixing screw	3	All	4
166094	—	—	Nut for screw	3	All	2
154409	—	—	Washer for screw	3	All	2
COIL AND FITTINGS						
45077B	—	—	Coil	1	All	1 11 6
21014	—	—	Coil clip	1	All	10
12342	—	—	Bolt for clip	1	All	6
17698	—	—	Washer for bolt	1	All	3
E3229	—	—	Nut for bolt	1	All	5
166043	—	—	Terminal nut	2	All	2
188330	—	—	Terminal nut shakeproof washer	2	All	1
131023	—	—	Terminal nut plain washer	2	All	1
421863	—	—	Cable clip	1	All	5
421554	—	—	Rubber grommett	1	All	4

PART No.	SUPERSEDED No.	PLATE No.	DESCRIPTION	QTY.	MODEL	PRICE EACH £ s. d.

DISTRIBUTOR AND FITTINGS

PART No.	SUPERSEDED No.	PLATE No.	DESCRIPTION	QTY.	MODEL	PRICE EACH
22202	40628A/B	—	Distributor complete, 18 D.1	1	ES2, 50	4 5 0
20589A	40589A/D	—	Distributor complete, 18 D.2	1	88, 99	4 5 0
425049	—	—	Distributor cap assembly	1	88, 99	8 6
424151	—	—	Distributor cap assembly	1	ES2, 50	2 9
404435	—	—	Distributor cap carbon brush and spring	1	88, 99	6
188639	—	—	Distributor rubber ring	1	88, 99	1 9
188643	—	—	Distributor oil seal	1	88, 99	4 0
424158	—	—	Distributor cap retaining spring clip	2	All	6
423486	—	—	Rotor Arm	1	88, 99	2 6
425219	—	—	Contact breaker set	1 set	All	6 3
54410823	—	—	Condenser assembly	1	All	6 0
842185	—	—	Distributor H.T. lead	1	88, 99	6
842187	—	—	Distributor H.T. lead	1	All	6
842189	—	—	Distributor H.T. lead	1	88, 99	6
54941565	—	—	Distributor H.T. lead	1	ES2, 50	9
421863	—	—	H.T. lead contact clip	1 / 4	ES2, 50 / 88, 99	5 / 5
421554	—	—	Distributor terminal rubber cover	1 / 3	ES2, 50 / 88, 99	4 / 4
21064	—	—	Clip for H.T. lead	1 / 3	ES2, 50 / 88, 99	6 / 6
21459	—	B109	Distributor housing	1	ES2, 50	12 4
20684	—	—	Distributor housing	1	88, 99	12 4
21027	—	B110	Distributor housing joint washer	1	All	3
T2256	—	B111	Distributor flange plate pin	1	All	1 2
T2211	—	B112	Washer for pin	1	All	3
T387	B2/612	—	Distributor drain plug	1	ES2, 50	5
11775	—	—	Washer for plug	1	ES2, 50	2
420151	—	B113	Distributor clamping plate	1	All	2 9
415087	—	B114	Distributor clamping plate pinch bolt complete with nut and washer	1	All	1 0
T2245	—	—	Distributor housing to crankcase stud (bottom)	1	All	7
E3231	—	—	Nut for stud	1	All	5
11796	—	—	Washer for stud	1	All	3
21028	—	B115	Distributor housing to crankcase stud	2	All	1 6
21030	—	B116	Nut for stud	2	All	1 6
210929	—	B117	Washer for stud	2	All	3

DISTRIBUTOR DRIVE PARTS

PART No.	SUPERSEDED No.	PLATE No.	DESCRIPTION	QTY.	MODEL	PRICE EACH
21653	—	B75	Distributor sprocket	1	ES2, 50	17 3
21654	—	—	Fixing pin for sprocket	1	ES2, 50	9
E5379	—	—	Washer for pin	1	ES2, 50	3
20688	—	—	Distributor sprocket	1	88, 99	17 3
20794	—	—	Distributor sprocket peg	1	88, 99	10
20938	—	—	Distributor sprocket collar	1	88, 99	1 4
13780	C2/79	B76	Distributor drive sprocket (on engine)	1	ES2, 50	11 6
E3681	A2/81	—	Key for sprocket	1	ES2, 50	3
E3224	—	B77	Nut for sprocket	1	ES2, 50	5
E5376	—	B78	Washer for sprocket	1	ES2, 50	3
17699	C2/113	B79	Distributor drive chain (44 link)	1	ES2, 50	9 0
18257	D12/113	—	Distributor drive chain (42 link, endless)	1	88, 99	9 0

EXHAUST PIPE AND FITTINGS

PART No.	SUPERSEDED No.	PLATE No.	DESCRIPTION	QTY.	MODEL	PRICE EACH
22102	—	—	Exhaust pipe	1	ES2	2 0 3
22103	—	—	Exhaust pipe	1	50	1 17 5
19464	—	—	Exhaust pipe, L.H.	1	88	2 3 2
19465	—	—	Exhaust pipe, R.H.	1	88	2 3 2
19466	—	—	Exhaust pipe, L.H.	1	99	2 3 2
19467	—	—	Exhaust pipe, R.H.	1	99	2 3 2

PART No.	SUPERSEDED No.	PLATE No.	DESCRIPTION	QTY.	MODEL	PRICE EACH

EXHAUST PIPE AND FITTINGS—cont.

PART No.	SUPERSEDED No.	PLATE No.	DESCRIPTION	QTY.	MODEL	£ s. d.
18197	A3/167	—	Exhaust pipe locking nut	1	ES2, 50	8 10
E6842	A3/166	—	Exhaust pipe lock nut washer	1	ES2, 50	5
T2166	D12/166	—	Exhaust pipe lock nut washer	2	88, 99	5
18092	D12/167	A34	Exhaust pipe locking nut	2	88, 99	8 10

SILENCER AND FITTINGS

PART No.	SUPERSEDED No.	PLATE No.	DESCRIPTION	QTY.	MODEL	£ s. d.
22121	—	—	Silencer, R.H.	1	All	3 9 0
22120	—	—	Silencer, L.H.	1	88, 99	3 9 0
20064	—	—	Silencer fixing bracket, L.H.	1	88, 99	1 9
19473	—	—	Silencer fixing bracket, R.H.	1	88, 99	1 9
22097	—	—	Silencer fixing bracket, R.H.	1	ES2, 50	1 0
17075	—	—	Silencer fixing bracket bolt	2 / 4	ES2, 50 / 88, 99	6
E5456	—	—	Silencer fixing bracket bolt washer	2 / 4	ES2, 50 / 88, 99	3
16255	—	—	Silencer to exhaust pipe clip	1 / 2	ES2, 50 / 88, 99	2 5
E3154	—	—	Bolt for clip	1 / 2	ES2, 50 / 88, 99	6
E3231	—	—	Nut for bolt	1 / 2	ES2, 50 / 88, 99	5

FRONT FORK ASSEMBLY AND FITTINGS

PART No.	SUPERSEDED No.	PLATE No.	DESCRIPTION	QTY.	MODEL	£ s. d.
M12-2/170	—	—	Front fork assembly, complete (solo)	1	All	26 0 2
18482	H12-2/605	—	Main tube	2	All	2 0 6
T1055	B2/614	MJ35	Main tube top bush	2	All	6 8
T1048	B2/606	MJ32	Main tube bottom bush	2	All	8 10
14298	E11M/1044	MJ90	Main tube bottom bush circlip	2	All	7
19299	—	MJ92	Fork end, L.H.	1	All	3 9 0
19298	—	—	Fork end, R.H.	1	All	3 9 0
16664	—	—	Fork end pinch stud	1	All	5
E3231	—	—	Nut for stud	1	All	5
T387	B2/612	MJ29	Fork end drain plug	2	All	5
11775	B2/613	MJ38	Washer for plug	2	All	2
20253	—	MJ93	Oil damper tube	2	All	1 3 8
15801	F11M2/1049	MJ64	Oil damper rod	2	All	4 0
14275	F11M2/630	—	Oil damper tube bolt	2	All	11
T1009	—	—	Washer for bolt	2	All	1
T814	—	—	Washer for tube	2	All	1
E3224A	—	MJ60	Nut for rod top	2	All	5
E3231	—	MJ89	Nut for rod bottom	2	All	5
14605	—	MJ85	Damper tube cap	2	All	3 4
14119	E11M/1048	MJ86	Piston locating peg	2	All	3
14118B	E11M/1046	MJ87	Oil damper valve cup	2	All	2 8
14117	E11M/1047	MJ88	Oil damper valve cup slotted ring	2	All	2 8
17713	D3T/616	—	Oil seal	2	All	5 6
T1049	B2/617	—	Oil seal paper washer	2	All	2
50117	F11M/615	MJ91	Main tube lock ring with cup	2	All	1 3 8
18813	F11M2/620	MJ65	Main spring	2	All	8 10
16880	—	MJ63	Main spring locating bushes	2	All	1 9
19307	L12-2/622	MJ84	Spring top cover tube	2	All	5 4
T831	B2/623	MJ20	Spring top cover tube securing plate	2	All	1 4
T702	B2/624	MJ21	Screws for securing plate	6	All	3
50259	—	MJ69	Crown lug complete with column	1	All	3 4 2
16164	F11M2/642	MJ71	Pinch stud for crown lug	2	All	7
16187	F11M2/643	MJ70	Nut for stud	2	All	5
15628	F11M2/644	MJ67	Head clip ball race cover	1	All	1 4
15630	F11M2/645	MJ66	Fork head race adjuster nut	1	All	8 1
19275	L12-2/635	MJ68	Top cover with lamp bracket, L.H.	1	All	16 10
19276	L12-2/636	MJ56	Top cover with lamp bracket, R.H.	1	All	16 10
19272	—	—	Distance piece for lamp bracket	2	All	1 2
15398	—	—	Top cover name plate	2	All	2 0
18810	—	—	Rivets for plate, 4 per set	1 set	All	3

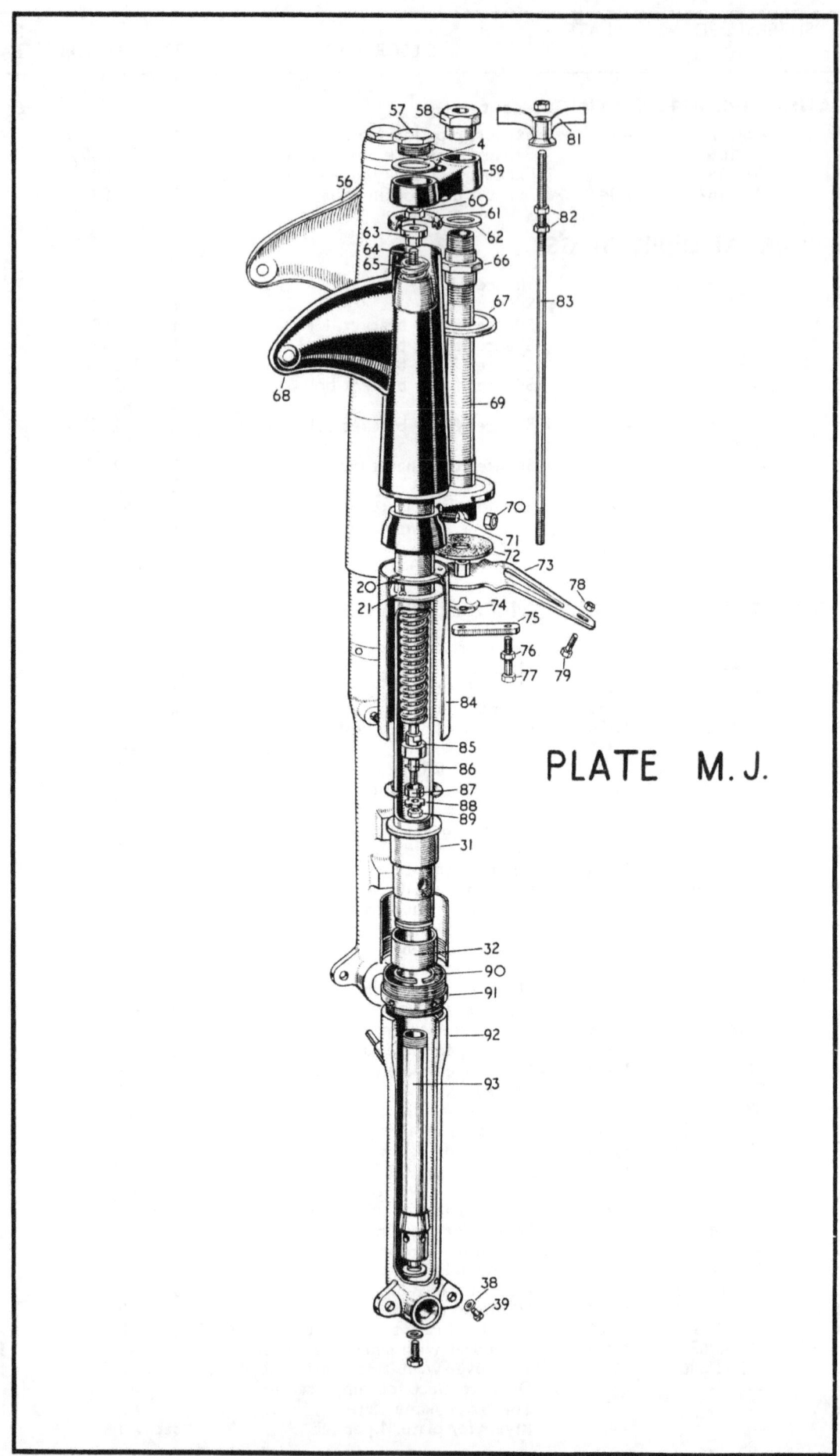

PLATE M.J.

PART No.	SUPERSEDED No.	PLATE No.	DESCRIPTION	QTY.	MODEL	PRICE EACH
						£ s. d.

FRONT FORK ASSEMBLY AND FITTINGS—cont.

PART No.	SUPERSEDED No.	PLATE No.	DESCRIPTION	QTY.	MODEL	PRICE EACH
T597	F11M2/639	MJ61	Main tube top cover rubber ring	2	All	11
16998	H12-2/633	MJ57	Fork main tube filler and retaining plug	2	All	6 8
T320	B2/634	MJ4	Washer for plug	2	All	11
19019	L122/174	MJ59	Fork head clip	1	All	2 3 11
19490	L12-2/205	MJ58	Fork crown and column lock nut	1	All	6 8
15627	—	MJ62	Washer for column lock nut	1	All	7
18769	H12-2/206	MJ73	Front fork stop and anchor plate	1	All	3 4
16008	H12-2/207	MJ72	Friction disc for anchor plate	1	All	1 4
E3135	—	MJ79	Bolt for plate	1	All	10
E3231	—	MJ78	Nut for bolt	1	All	5
18202	—	—	Washer for bolt	1	All	3
19357	—	—	Distance piece for bolt	1	All	7
19021A	L4/175	—	Cap for handle bar top clip	2	All	2 8
19437	L4/176	—	Screw for cap	4	All	7
SD4	—	—	Steering damper assembly, complete (solo)		All Optional	1 6 8
SD1	—	—	Steering damper assembly, complete (sidecar use)		All Optional	1 6 8
88/2002	—	—	Complete set fork oil seals	1	All	13 6
			Sets comprise the following:			
			11775 ... (2)			
			D3T/616 ... (2)			
			B2/617 ... (2)			
			F11M2/639 ... (2)			
			B2/628 ... (2)			

FRONT FORKS WITH SIDECAR TRAIL

PART No.	SUPERSEDED No.	PLATE No.	DESCRIPTION	QTY.	MODEL	PRICE EACH
M12-2/170 SC	—	—	Front fork assembly complete (for side car use)	1	All	26 0 2
15906A	—	MJ65	Fork spring	2	All	8 10
21508	—	MJ69	Fork crown and column	1	All	3 4 2
13457	B2/642	MJ71	Pinch stud for crown lug	2	All	7
13459	B2/643	MJ70	Nut for stud	2	All	5
21593	—	MJ59	Fork head clip	1	All	2 3 11
21632	—	—	Fork crown and column lock stop	1	All	3 4
21570	—	MJ68	Fork top cover with lamp bracket, L.H.	1	All	16 10
21571	—	MJ56	Fork top cover with lamp bracket, R.H.	1	All	16 10
21620	—	MJ73	Steering damper anchor plate	1	All	3 4
T347	B2/207	MJ72	Steering damper friction disc	2	All	1 4
50002	B2/208	—	Steering damper friction plate	1	All	5 4
21642	—	—	Bolt for friction plate	1	All	10
E5380	—	—	Washer for bolt	1	All	3
E3135	—	—	Bolt for anchor plate	1	All	10
E3231	—	—	Nut for bolt	1	All	5
18202	—	—	Washer for bolt	1	All	3
19357	—	—	Distance piece for anchor plate	1	All	7
15626	—	MJ58	Fork crown and column locknut	1	All	6 8
15627	—	MJ62	Washer for locknut	1	All	7
21509	—	MJ83	Steering damper rod	1	All	1 4
E3231	—	MJ82	Nut for rod	2	All	5
21574	—	—	Distance piece for rod	1	All	7
16075	—	—	Spring for rod	1	All	11
18336	—	MJ81	Wing nut for rod	1	All	8 8
E3223	—	—	Locknut for wing nut	1	All	5

N.B.—Parts not listed above are as fitted to solo forks.

HANDLEBAR AND FITTINGS

PART No.	SUPERSEDED No.	PLATE No.	DESCRIPTION	QTY.	MODEL	PRICE EACH
19405	L12-2/211	—	Handlebar bend	1	All	1 8 9
19021A	L4/175	—	Handlebar half clip	2	All	2 8
19437	L4/176	—	Handlebar half clip pins	4	All	7

PART No.	SUPERSEDED No.	PLATE No.	DESCRIPTION	QTY.	MODEL	PRICE EACH

FRONT BRAKE AND CLUTCH LEVER ASSEMBLIES

PART No.	SUPERSEDED No.	PLATE No.	DESCRIPTION	QTY.	MODEL	£ s. d.
19410	—	—	Front brake and air control lever, complete	1	All	1 3 0
M12-2/224	—	—	Front brake lever, complete	1	All	14 10
M12-2/226	—	—	Clutch lever, complete	1	All	14 10
M12-2/225	—	—	Front brake lever only	1	All	7 5
M12-2/227	—	—	Clutch lever only	1	All	7 5
M12-2/228 (RH)	—	—	Front brake lever body	1	All	6 10
M12-2/228 (LH)	—	—	Clutch lever body	1	All	4 0
A2/222	—	—	Clutch lever body clip	1	All	1 4
A2/223	—	—	Pins for clips	2	All	5
M12-2/229	—	—	Front brake or clutch lever pivot pin	2	All	5
M12-2/230	—	—	Nut for pivot pin	2	All	3

EXHAUST LIFTER LEVER AND FITTINGS

PART No.	SUPERSEDED No.	PLATE No.	DESCRIPTION	QTY.	MODEL	PRICE
M2/233	—	—	Exhaust lifter lever, complete	1	ES2, 50	11 9
M2/234	—	—	Exhaust lifter lever only	1	ES2, 50	4 0
M2/235	—	—	Exhaust lifter lever body	1	ES2, 50	5 4
A2/222	—	—	Exhaust lifter lever clip	1	ES2, 50	1 4
A2/223	—	—	Exhaust lifter lever pivot pin or clip screw	3	ES2, 50	5
A2/236	—	—	Nut for pivot pin	1	ES2, 50	3

TWIST GRIP COMPLETE AND FITTINGS

PART No.	SUPERSEDED No.	PLATE No.	DESCRIPTION	QTY.	MODEL	PRICE
M12-2/237	—	—	Twist grip complete	1	All	14 2
M12-2/238	—	—	Twist grip top half clip	1	All	4 5
M12-2/239	—	—	Twist grip bottom half clip	1	All	4 5
A2/240	—	—	Twist grip clip fixing pin	2	All	5
M12-2/241	—	—	Twist grip control barrel	1	All	5 1
A2/242	—	—	Twist grip control adjusting screw	1	All	6
A2/236	—	—	Twist grip control adjusting screw nut	1	All	3
M12-2/243	—	—	Twist grip adjusting screw spring	1	All	1 2
M12-2/244	—	—	Twist grip cable stop	1	All	6
19414	—	—	Twist grip plastic grip	1	All	1 9
20267	—	—	Dummy grip to match twist grip	1	All	2 5

AIR LEVER COMPLETE AND FITTINGS

PART No.	SUPERSEDED No.	PLATE No.	DESCRIPTION	QTY.	MODEL	PRICE
M12-2/216	—	—	Air lever, complete	1	All	12 2
M122/217	—	—	Air lever only	1	All	5 4
M12-2/218	—	—	Air lever body	1	All	4 0
M122/220	—	—	Air lever cap	1	All	11
M122/219	—	—	Air lever cap screw	1	All	5
A2/221	—	—	Air lever cap spring washer	1	All	3
M122/223	—	—	Air lever clip screw	2	All	10

FRONT BRAKE CABLE

PART No.	SUPERSEDED No.	PLATE No.	DESCRIPTION	QTY.	MODEL	PRICE
20295	B2/268	—	Front brake cable complete with adjuster U clip and nipples	1	All	9 6
B2/269	—	—	Front brake outer cable	1	All	4 8
B2/270	—	—	Front brake inner cable	1	All	2 8
18881	—	—	Front brake adjuster	1	All	4 0
18882	A2/254	—	Front brake cable nipple U clip end	1	All	3
A2/252	—	—	Front brake cable nipple handlebar end	1	All	1 4
14759	A2/709	—	Front brake cable U clip	1	All	8
E3255	—	—	Pin for U clip	1	All	5
17735	—	—	Cotter for pin	1	All	1
E5455	—	—	Washer for pin	1	All	3

PART No.	SUPERSEDED No.	PLATE No.	DESCRIPTION	QTY.	MODEL	PRICE EACH

CLUTCH CABLE

						£ s. d.
19828	—	—	Clutch cable complete with adjuster and nipples	1	All	6 0
M12-2/266	—	—	Clutch outer cable	1	All	3 5
M12-2/267	—	—	Clutch inner cable	1	All	1 9
18889	A2/248	—	Clutch cable adjuster	1	All	1 2
A2/252	—	—	Clutch cable nipple handlebar end ...	1	All	1 4
19987	A2/253	—	Clutch cable nipple gear box end ...	1	All	3

EXHAUST LIFTER CABLE

18888	—	—	Exhaust lifter cable complete with adjuster and nipples	1	ES2, 50	6 0

AIR CABLE

20276	A2/259	—	Air cable complete (inner and outer) with nipples	1	All	2 9

THROTTLE CABLE

20277	—	—	Throttle cable complete, inner and outer with nipples	1	All	2 9

PETROL TANK AND FITTINGS

20072	—	—	Petrol tank	1	All	11 10 0
18524	K12/280	—	Petrol tank filler cap	1	All	10 2
P43/4	—	—	Petrol tank filler cap washer ...	1	All	1 2
16256	H12-2/1070	—	Petrol tank strap	1	All	4 0
16238	H122/1071	—	Petrol tank strap rubber ...	1	All	8 1
22339	—	—	Petrol tank strap roller ...	1	All	1 6
16257	H12-2/1073	—	Petrol tank strap fulcrum pin...	1	All	1 4
18291	—	—	Petrol tank strap fulcrum pin cotter ...	2	All	2
16365	H12-2/1074	—	Petrol tank strap roller (tool tray end)	1	All	2 0
22334	—	—	Petrol tank strap fixing bolt (tool tray end)	1	All	2 3
22340	—	—	Washer for bolt	A.R.	All	4
E4563A	—	—	Strap fixing bolt spring ...	1	All	11
22335	—	—	Strap fixing bolt spring collar ...	1	All	1 0
16237	H12-2/289	—	Petrol tank mounting rubber ...	6	All	3 4
20262	—	—	Petrol tank side panel, L.H. ...	1	All	1 14 6
20261	—	—	Petrol tank side panel, R.H. ...	1	All	1 14 6
20231	—	—	Petrol tank side panel fixing screw ...	4	All	6
20233	—	—	Petrol tank side panel plastic bead ...	2	All	4 0
22265	—	—	Petrol pipe, complete	1	All	10 2
16294	H12-2/285	—	Petrol tap	1	All	12 2
E5264	—	—	Petrol tap washer	1	All	3
13786	—	—	Petrol tap washer	1	All	3
18678	—	—	Petrol tank badge	2	All	10 2
20230	—	—	Petrol tank badge screw ...	4	All	5
18786	—	—	Petrol tank badge washer ...	4	All	1
20222	—	—	Petrol tank knee grip, L.H. ...	1	All	4 0
20223	—	—	Petrol tank knee grip, R.H. ...	1	All	4 0
20912	—	—	Petrol tank side panel plastic bead (gold)	2 Optional	All	4 0

(See tool tray for tank strap anchorage).

PART No.	SUPERSEDED No.	PLATE No.	DESCRIPTION	QTY.	MODEL	PRICE EACH

OIL TANK AND FITTINGS

PART No.	SUPERSEDED No.	PLATE No.	DESCRIPTION	QTY.	MODEL	£ s. d.
19208E	—	—	Oil tank, less fittings	1	All	3 0 9
21496	K12/291	—	Oil tank filler cap	1	All	8 10
P44/4	—	—	Oil tank filler cap washer	1	All	10
12342	—	—	Oil tank top fixing bolt	1	All	6
E5379	—	—	Washer for bolt	2	All	3
17698	—	—	Washer for bolt	1	All	3
E3229	—	—	Nut for bolt	1	All	5
E6453	—	—	Oil tank bottom fixing stud	2	All	7
E3223	—	—	Nut for stud	2	All	5
19201	L12-2/1075	—	Oil tank and battery box platform	1	All	13 6
19212	L12-2/1076	—	Rubber mat for platform	1	All	6 8
14481	—	—	Bolt for platform	4	All	9
E5379	—	—	Washer for bolt	8	All	3
E3229	—	—	Nut for bolt	4	All	5
17014	L12-2/298	—	Breather pipe	1	All	2 0
19380	L4/1055	—	Return pipe adaptor	1	All	3 4
13786	E3/1056	—	Washer for adaptor	2	All	3
13765	—	—	Drain plug	1	All	10
13833	—	—	Washer for plug	1	All	3
19379	L4/292	—	Filter union with gauze	1	All	9 6
E6640	A2/293	—	Washer for union	1	All	7

OIL PIPES AND FITTINGS

PART No.	SUPERSEDED No.	PLATE No.	DESCRIPTION	QTY.	MODEL	£ s. d.
19480	E2/993	—	Junction block with pipes	1	ES2, 50	8 1
19457	—	—	Junction block with pipes	1	88, 99	8 1
14843	E2/995	—	Washer for junction block	1	ES2, 50	3
T2100	D12/995	—	Stud for junction block	1	88, 99	3
T2106	D12/994	—	Dowel for junction block	1	All	11
14714	—	—	Stud for junction block	1	ES2, 50	1 2
E3223	—	—	Nut for stud	1	ES2, 50	5
E5456	—	—	Washer for stud	1	ES2, 50	3
T2006	—	—	Stud for junction block	1	88, 99	1 2
E5377	D12/997	—	Washer for stud	1	88, 99	3
T2101	D12/996	—	Nut for stud	1	88, 99	2 0
19452	L4/295/6	—	Oil feed or return pipe	2	All	1 9
22351	—	—	Rocker box oil feed pipe assembly	1	ES2, 50	6 8
19425	L12-2/699	A3	Rocker box oil feed pipe assembly	1	88, 99	11 6
13805	C3/700	B1	Banjo bolt for oil feed pipe	1	ES2, 50	3 4
18101	D12/700	A1	Banjo bolt for oil feed pipe	2	88, 99	2 8
13786	C3/701	B2	Washer for banjo bolt	2	ES2, 50	3
T1084	D12/701	A2	Washer for banjo bolt	4	88, 99	3

GEARBOX SHELL

PART No.	SUPERSEDED No.	PLATE No.	DESCRIPTION	QTY.	MODEL	£ s. d.
040097	—	TN7	Gearbox shell assembly	1	All	6 3 8
040056	—	—	Gearbox bush	2	All	5 6
000577	—	—	Gearbox dowel pins	2	All	2
040064	—	TN8	Gearbox studs (short)	2	All	8
000271	—	TN13	Gearbox studs (long)	5	All	7
000004	—	—	Gearbox stud nuts	7	All	6
040030	—	TN46	Gearbox shell gasket	1	All	2
040403	—	TN47	Gearbox inner cover	1	All	3 9 0
040072	—	TN77	Gearbox inner cover K/S	1	All	7 6
040042	—	—	Gearbox inner cover K/S stop	1	All	2 0
040071	—	—	Gearbox inner cover K/S cam	1	All	1 2
040041	—	—	Kickstarter cam and stop rivets	2	All	1
040061	—	TN49	Inner bush for gear change	1	All	1 5
000577	—	—	Dowel pins	2	All	2
040063	—	—	Bush for gear change	1	All	1 2
040058	—	TN70	Bush for kickstarter	1	All	6 4
040133	—	TN56	Gearbox outer cover	1	All	2 17 6
040055	—	TN48	Outer cover gasket	1	All	2
000482	—	—	Outer cover screws	5	All	6

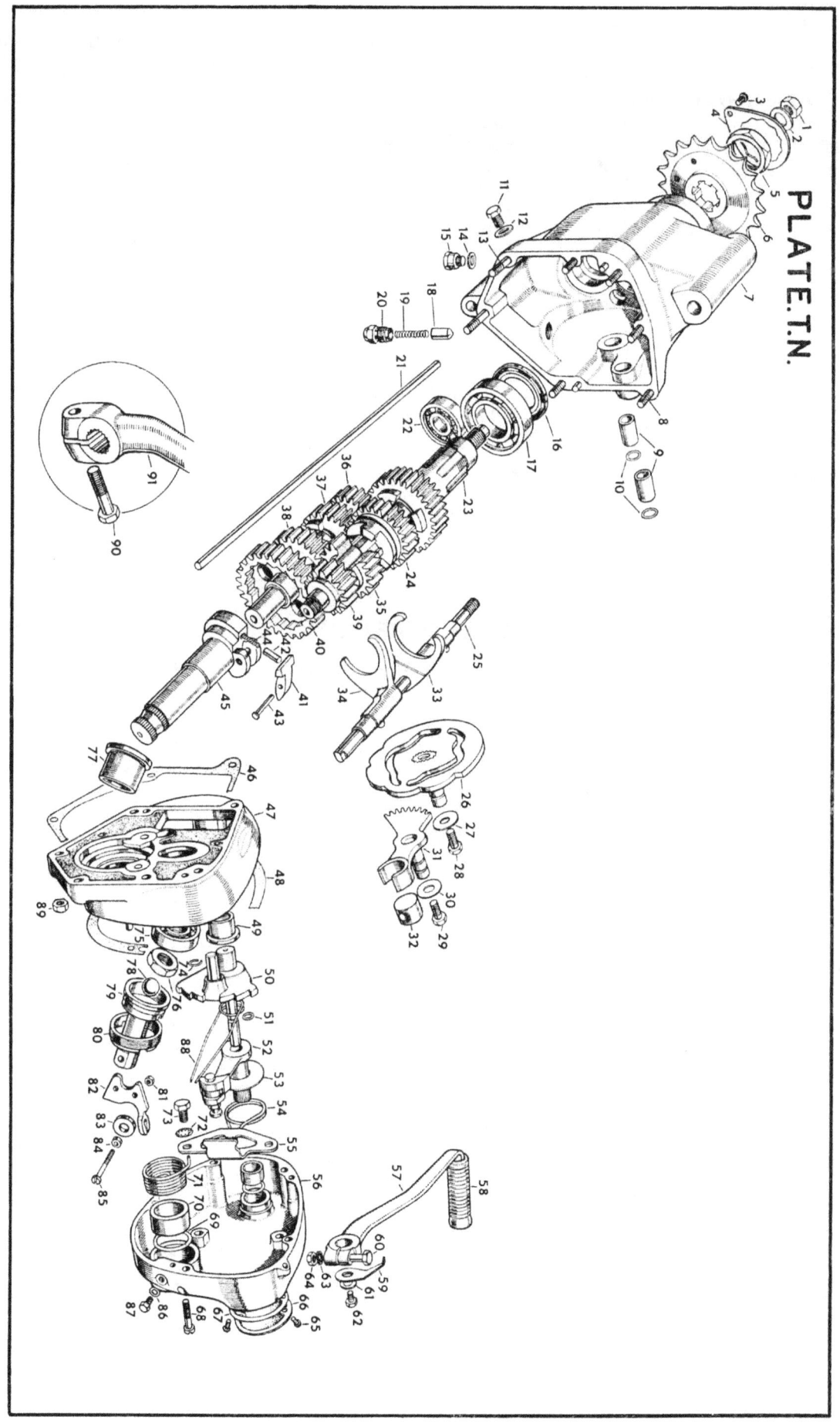

PLATE.T.N.

PART No.	SUPERSEDED No.	PLATE No.	DESCRIPTION	QTY.	MODEL	PRICE EACH

GEARBOX SHELL—cont.

						£ s. d.
040138	—	TN11	Drain plug	1	All	8
000200	—	TN12	Drain plug washer	1	All	5
040053	—	TN66	Inspection cover	1	All	16 0
040057	—	TN67	Inspection cover washer	1	All	1
000450	—	TN65	Inspection cover pins	2	All	3
000348	—	TN87	Oil level plug	1	All	6
000203	—	TN86	Oil level plug washer	1	All	2

GEARBOX FIXING BOLTS

14367	—	MZ25	Gearbox top bolt	1	All	4 8
15170	—	MZ17	Gearbox top bolt nut	1	All	3 6
16410	H12-2/312	—	Gearbox bottom stud, less nut	1	All	1 4
11809	—	MZ28	Gearbox bottom bolt washer	1	All	3
E3227	—	MZ27	Gearbox bottom bolt nut	1	All	6

GEARBOX FRONT CHAIN ADJUSTER

H2/314	—	MZ16	Gearbox front chain adjuster eye bolt and nut	1	All	5 4
E3231	—	MZ18	Gearbox front chain adjuster nuts	2	All	5
16997	H2/1008	—	Gearbox front chain adjuster bolt only	1	All	4 6

GEARBOX PINIONS, SHAFTS AND BEARINGS

040128	—	—	Gearbox complete, less clutch	1	All	26 9 0
040098	—	TN17	Ballrace, mainshaft (large)	1	All	1 5 11
040099	—	TN75	Ballrace, mainshaft (small)	1	All	18 5
040100	—	TN22	Ballrace, layshaft	1	All	18 5
040131	—	—	Axle sprocket spacer	1	All	5 9
040132	—	TN16	Sleeve gear oil seal	1	All	5 2
040116	—	TN23	Sleeve gear assembly	1	All	2 17 6
040062	—	—	Sleeve gear bushes	2	All	2 11
040010	—	TN6	Axle sprocket	1	All	1 8 9
040076	—	TN4	Axle sprocket locking plate	1	All	7
000450	—	TN3	Axle sprocket locking plate screw	1	All	3
040070	—	TN1	Axle sprocket nut	1	All	1 5
040108	—	TN26	Cam plate assembly	1	All	1 18 6
040018	—	—	Cam plate bare	1	All	1 9 11
040015	—	—	Cam plate spindle	1	All	8 8
040109	—	TN31	Quadrant assembly	1	All	1 3 0
040129	—	—	Quadrant O ring	1	All	1 2
000174	—	TN27 & 30	Washer for cam and quadrant	2	All	2
040136	—	TN28 & 29	Screw for cam and quadrant	2	All	7
040022	—	TN34	Selector fork	2	All	1 13 4
040035	—	TN23	Selector fork shaft	1	All	6 4
040001	—	—	Mainshaft	1	All	2 6 0
040023	—	TN74	Mainshaft nut	1	All	1 2
040012	—	TN24	Mainshaft, 3rd gear	1	All	1 17 5
040021	—	TN35	Mainshaft, 2nd gear	1	All	1 11 8
040048	—	—	Mainshaft, 2nd gear bush	1	All	7 6
040026	—	TN39	Mainshaft, bottom gear	1	All	14 5
040025	—	—	Layshaft	1	All	1 14 6
040020	—	TN36	Layshaft pinion	1	All	14 5
040016	—	TN37	Layshaft, 3rd gear	1	All	1 12 9
040047	—	—	Layshaft, 3rd gear bush	1	All	9 9
040019	—	TN38	Layshaft, 2nd gear	1	All	1 14 6
040115	—	TN40	Layshaft, bottom gear	1	All	2 0 3
040046	—	—	Layshaft, bottom gear bush	1	All	5 9
040078	—	TN32	Roller for knuckle pin	1	All	4 7
040036	—	TN20	Index plunger bush	1	All	10
040045	—	TN19	Index plunger spring	1	All	2
040034	—	TN18	Index plunger	1	All	3 1

PART No.	SUPERSEDED No.	PLATE No.	DESCRIPTION	QTY.	MODEL	PRICE EACH

KICKSTARTER PARTS

PART No.	SUPERSEDED No.	PLATE No.	DESCRIPTION	QTY.	MODEL	£ s. d.
040114	—	TN45	Kickstarter axle assembly	1	All	2 14 1
040032	—	TN77	Kickstarter axle assembly bush	1	All	8 8
040017	—	TN41	Kickstarter pawl	1	All	6 4
040033	—	TN43	Kickstarter pawl pin	1	All	1 2
040044	—	TN44	Kickstarter pawl spring	1	All	3
040069	—	TN42	Kickstarter pawl, plunger	1	All	7
040101	—	TN91	Kickstarter crank	1	All	1 19 1
040102	—	TN90	Kickstarter crank bolt	1	All	1 2
040043	—	TN71	Kickstarter return spring	1	All	1 2
040005	—	TN69	Kickstarter O ring	1	All	1 2
N8081	—	—	Kickstarter rubber	1	All	1 4

POSITIVE FOOTCHANGE

PART No.	SUPERSEDED No.	PLATE No.	DESCRIPTION	QTY.	MODEL	£ s. d.
040004	—	TN57	Footchange lever	1	All	1 5 11
040086	—	TN58	Footchange lever rubber	1	All	1 2
040105	—	TN60	Footchange lever bolt	1	All	1 2
000191	—	TN63	Footchange lever bolt washer	1	All	2
000005	—	TN64	Footchange lever bolt nut	1	All	6
040051	—	TN59	Footchange gear indicator	1	All	1 9
040137	—	TN62	Footchange gear indicator screw	1	All	7
000012	—	TN61	Footchange gear indicator washer	1	All	2
040111	—	TN50	Footchange ratchet plate with spindle	1	All	1 13 11
040066	—	—	Footchange ratchet plate spindle	1	All	6 4
040052	—	TN55	Footchange stop plate	1	All	2 11
041400	—	TN73	Footchange stop plate screw	2	All	7
014117	—	TN72	Footchange stop plate spring washer	2	All	2
040079	—	—	O ring for ratchet spindle	1	All	7
040006	—	—	O ring for footchange	1	All	1 2
040038	—	TN88	Footchange pawl spring	1		5
040110	—	TN52	Footchange pawl carrier assembly	1	All	1 7 7
040002	—	—	Footchange pawl carrier only	1	All	1 6 2
040024	—	—	Footchange pawl	1	All	6 4
040067	—	—	Footchange pawl carrier pin	1	All	1 9
040049	—	—	Footchange pawl circlip	1	All	1
040075	—	TN54	Footchange pawl return spring	1	All	7
040135	—	TN53	Footchange pawl return spring washer	1	All	7
040061	—	—	Footchange inner bush	1	All	1 5

CLUTCH ASSEMBLY AND FITTINGS

PART No.	SUPERSEDED No.	PLATE No.	DESCRIPTION	QTY.	MODEL	£ s. d.
21651 / 040399	—	—	Clutch, complete	1	50	12 0 0
21652 / 040400	—	—	Clutch complete	1	ES2, 88, 99	12 5 0
040031	—	TN78	Clutch operating ball	1	All	5
040059	—	TN79	Clutch operating body	1	All	9 9
040003	—	TN80	Clutch operating body lockring	1	All	2 4
040029	—	TN82	Clutch operating lever	1	All	4 4
040060	—	TN83	Clutch operating roller	1	All	8
040065	—	TN84	Clutch roller sleeve	1	All	7
000457	—	TN85	Clutch roller screw (2 B.A.)	1	All	6
011846	—	TN81	Clutch roller screw nut	1	All	3
040084	—	TN21	Clutch rod	1	All	2 7
21261	—	PQ1	Clutch back plate	1	All	15 0
040367	A2/382	PQ2	Clutch roller cage	1	All	3 5
000075	A2/383	PQ3	Clutch rollers (15 per set)	1 set	All	5 1
040351	—	PQ4	Clutch race plate	1	All	13 6
040384	—	PQ5	Clutch spring stud	3	All	2 8
040356	A2/402	PQ6	Clutch spring stud nut	3	All	5
040366	—	PQ7	Clutch body only	1	All	2 0 6
040386	A2/388	PQ8	Clutch shock absorber rubbers (large)	3	All	8
040387	A2/389	PQ9	Clutch shock absorber rubbers (small)	3	All	6

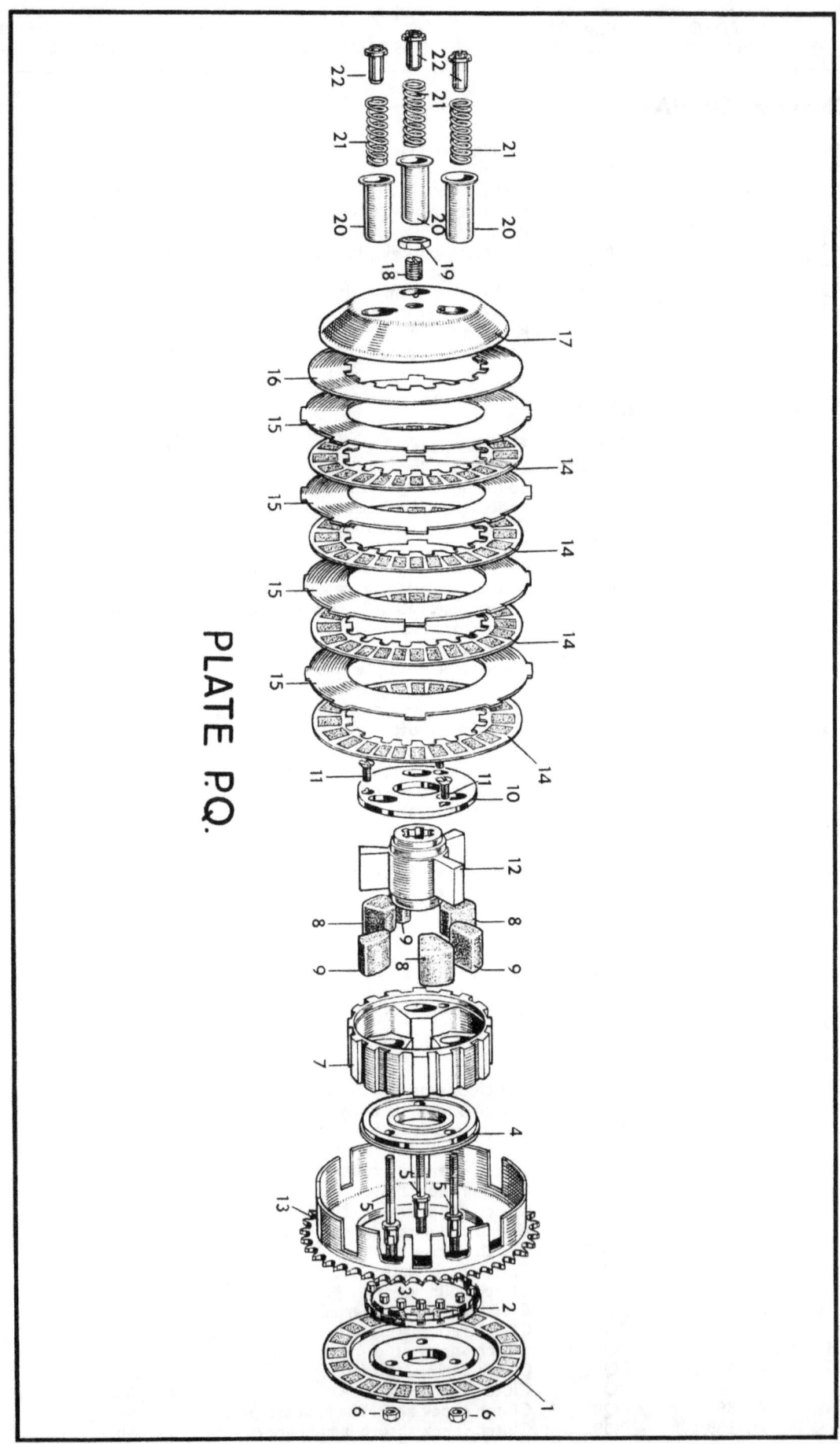

PLATE P.Q.

PART No.	SUPERSEDED No.	PLATE No.	DESCRIPTION	QTY.	MODEL	PRICE EACH

CLUTCH ASSEMBLY AND FITTINGS—cont.

PART No.	SUPERSEDED No.	PLATE No.	DESCRIPTION	QTY.	MODEL	£ s. d.
040362	—	PQ10	Clutch shock absorber cover plate	1	All	8 1
040363	—	PQ11	Clutch shock absorber cover plate pins	3	All	2
040354	—	PQ12	Clutch body centre	1	All	1 13 10
21249	—	PQ13	Clutch sprocket	1	All	3 0 0
21259	—	PQ14	Clutch friction plate	3 / 4	50 / ES2, 88, 99	8 9
21480	—	PQ15	Clutch plate (plain)	3 / 4	50 / ES2, 88, 99	3 9
21260	—	PQ16	Clutch end plate assembly	1	All	5 9
040393	—	PQ17	Clutch pressure plate	1	50	12 1
040365	—	PQ17	Clutch pressure plate	1	ES2, 88, 99	12 1
040360	—	PQ18	Clutch adjuster	1	All	8
040376	—	PQ19	Clutch adjuster locknut	1	All	8
040388	—	PQ20	Clutch spring cup	3	All	11
040385	—	PQ21	Clutch spring	3	All	11
040389	—	PQ22	Clutch spring adjuster nut	3	All	1 4
040373	E6254	TN1	Main axle nut	1	All	11
040374	E6266	TN2	Main axle nut washer	1	All	2
GOS/2000	—	—	Small set gearbox seals and washers. Comprising: 040030 (1), 040055 (1), 040057 (1), 040005 (1), 040006 (1)		All	2 9
GOS/2001	—	—	Complete set gearbox oil seals and gaskets. Comprising: 040030 (1), 040055 (1), 040057 (1), 000200 (1), 000203 (1), 040132 (1), 040129 (1), 040005 (1), 040079 (1), 040006 (1)		All	10 3

FRONT WHEEL AND FITTINGS

PART No.	SUPERSEDED No.	PLATE No.	DESCRIPTION	QTY.	MODEL	£ s. d.
M12-2/714	—	—	Front wheel with bearings and brake, less tyre	1	All	20 19 10
M122/428	—	—	Front wheel with hub shell only	1	All	12 3 3
19664	—	KR21	Front hub shell complete with brake drum	1	All	7 9 6
E6888	A2/440	KR24	Hub bearing lock ring	1	All	2 8
16783	J2/441	KR23	Hub bearing distance piece (plain side)	1	All	1 4
20249	B2/452	KR26	Front wheel spindle	1	All	1 0 3
E4768	B2/454	KR3	Nut for spindle	1	All	2 11
50257	—	KR2	Front hub brake plate	1	All	3 6 2
20052	—	KR4	Front brake cam lever	1	All	4 0
18942	—	KR5	Nut for lever	1	All	5
50249	—	KR20	Front brake cam	1	All	9 6
19653	—	KR7	Brake plate torque stop pivot pin	1	All	3 4
13079	B2/658	KR1	Nut for pin	1	All	7
E5944A	—	—	Brake plate packing washer	A.R.	All	5
19646	—	KR18	Bearing distance tube	1	All	2 0
19719	—	KR15	Hub bearing felt washer steel plate	1	All	10
18551	K12-2/442	KR25	Hub bearing dust cap	1	All	4 0

REAR WHEEL AND FITTINGS

PART No.	SUPERSEDED No.	PLATE No.	DESCRIPTION	QTY.	MODEL	£ s. d.
M2-2/715	—	—	Rear wheel with bearings and brake, less tyre	1	All	24 6 5
M2-2/649	—	—	Rear wheel with hub shell only	1	All	11 9 9
19689	—	KR46	Rear hub only	1	All	6 8 4
18348	—	KR48	Rear hub diaphragm	1	All	10 2
18396	—	KR49	Drive screws for diaphragm	6	All	2
18731	—	KR52	Rear hub rubber grommets	3	All	1 0
50245	—	KR42	Rear brake drum with studs (43 teeth)	1	All	4 1 1
18338	—	—	Locating studs for brake drum	1	All	1 9
18339	—	—	Non-locating studs for brake drum	2	All	1 4
18233	K12-2/451	KR51	Sleeve nut for brake drum	3	All	2 8
18234	K12-2/441	KR47	Hub bearing distance piece	1	All	2 8

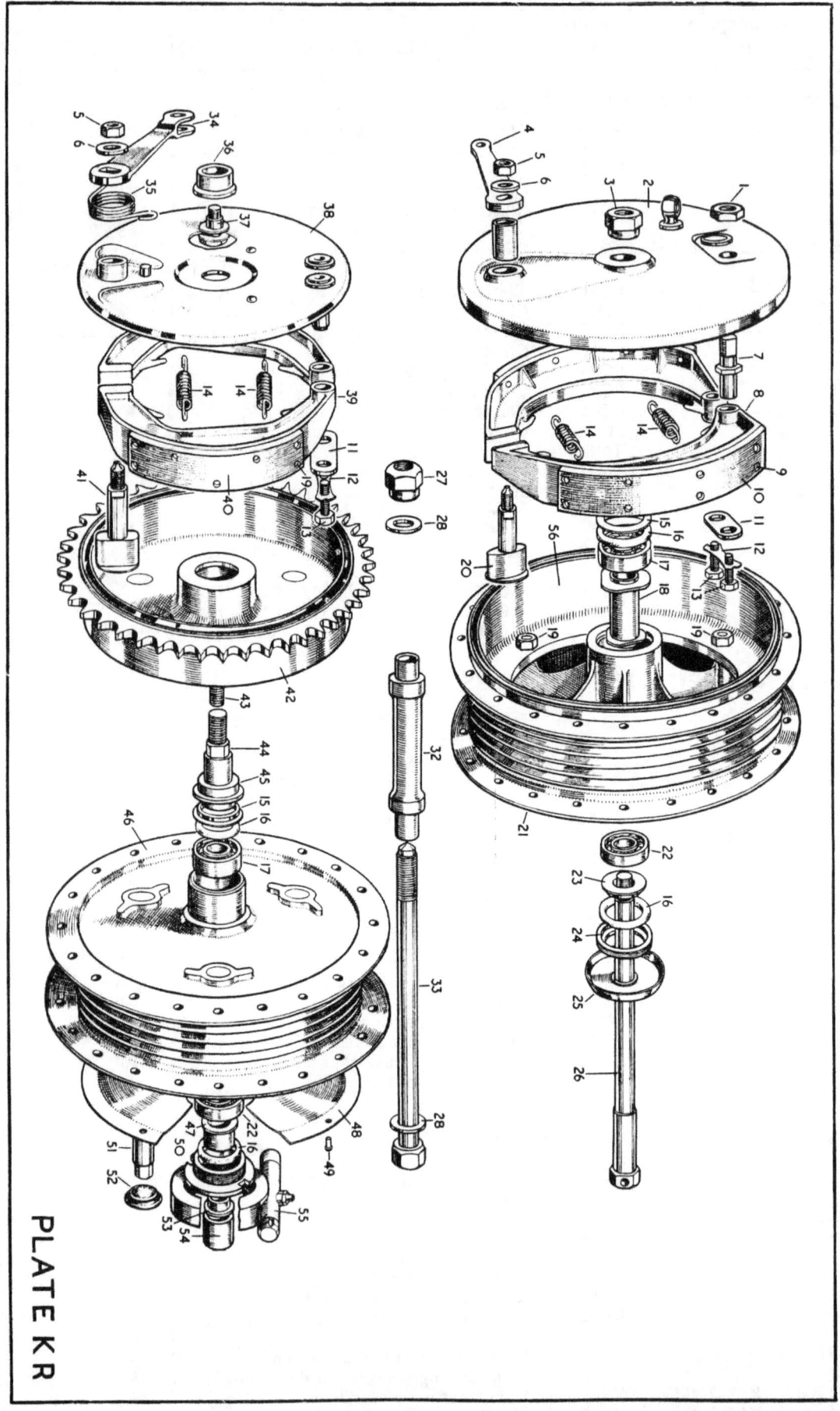

PLATE KR

PART No.	SUPERSEDED No.	PLATE No.	DESCRIPTION	QTY.	MODEL	PRICE EACH
REAR WHEEL AND FITTINGS—cont.						£ s. d.
18232	K12-2/440	KR50	Hub bearing lockring	1	All	6 8
19714	—	KR45	Hub bearing felt washer retaining washer	1	All	10
18231	K12-2/434	KR32	Rear hub inner sleeve	1	All	8 1
E4760	K12-2/464	KR43	Brake drum attachment piece	1	All	10 10
13270	B2/660	KR53	Speedometer drive distance piece	1	All	2 0
18235	K12-2/461	KR54	Hub spindle distance piece	1	All	2 8
19265	—	KR33	Rear hub spindle	1	All	9 6
19266	B2/659	KR28	Rear hub spindle washer	2	All	3
19267	A2/454	KR29	Rear hub spindle nut	1	All	2 11
19852	—	KR38	Rear brake plate	1	All	1 5 11
50011	—	KR41	Rear brake shoe cam with washer	1	All	11 6
19765	—	KR34	Rear brake cam lever	1	All	9 9
E5455	—	KR6	Washer for lever	1	All	3
18942	—	KR5	Nut for lever	1	All	3
18929	—	—	Roller for lever	1	All	7
19268	—	KR36	Rear brake plate distance piece	1	All	2 8
E5276	—	—	Rear brake plate packing washer	A.R.	All	5
PARTS COMMON TO FRONT AND REAR HUBS						
17719	A2/435	KR22	Hub bearing (near side front), offside rear)	2	All	15 0
17721	A2/436	KR17	Hub bearing (offside front), near side rear)	2	All	1 8 3
E6885	—	KR16	Hub bearing felt washer	4	All	3
E6889	—	KR15	Hub bearing pen steel washer	2	All	5
E5832	A2/446	KR14	Brake shoe return spring	4	All	7
14454	—	KR11	Brake shoe pivot pin retaining plate	2	All	1 4
14506	—	KR12	Tab washer for retaining plate	2	All	10
12342	—	KR13	Bolt for retaining plate	4	All	6
BRAKE SHOES AND LININGS						
18502	J2/443F	KR8	Hub brake shoe with lining (front)	2	All	1 10 5
19584	H2/443R	KR39	Hub brake shoe with lining (rear)	2	All	1 7 8
16782	J2/444F	KR10	Hub brake shoe lining (front)	1 pr.	All	per pair 14 10
16547	H2/444R	KR40	Hub brake shoe lining (rear)	1 pr.	All	per pair 12 10
E5061	—	KR9	Brake lining rivets (16 front, 14 rear)		All	1
WHEEL RIMS AND SPOKES						
18350	—	—	Wheel rim (front or rear)	2	All	2 8 7
20063	—	—	Spokes (long head), (per set 20)	40	All For 20	5 4
20061	—	—	Spokes (short head), (per set 20)	40	All For 20	5 4
17717	A2/431	—	Nipples (per set 40)	80	All	2d. each
17724	—	—	Security bolt	2	All	5 2
FRONT CHAINCASE AND FITTINGS						
20898	—	—	Front chaincase inner portion	1	All	2 17 6
21559	—	—	Front chaincase outer portion	1	ES2, 50	3 0 9
20914	—	—	Front chaincase outer portion	1	88, 99	3 0 9
20939	—	—	Chaincase spigot washer	1	All	7
21439	—	B107	Chaincase spigot piece	1	ES2, 50	15 6
11790	—	—	Chaincase spigot piece dowel	1	ES2, 50	3
21444	—	B108	Sealing washer for spigot piece	1	ES2, 50	2
20942	—	—	Chaincase fixing pin (inner portion)	3	All	3

PART No.	SUPERSEDED No.	PLATE No.	DESCRIPTION	QTY.	MODEL	PRICE EACH

FRONT CHAINCASE AND FITTINGS—cont.

						£ s. d.
19429	—	—	Chaincase inner portion rubber grommet	1	All	5
E5380	—	—	Washer for stud	2	All	3
E3223	—	—	Nut for stud	1	All	5
16247	—	—	Nut for stud	1	All	7
13765	—	—	Drain plug	1	All	10
13833	—	—	Washer for plug	1	All	3
14837	A2/487	—	Chaincase inspection cover	1	All	2 5
E6085	A2/488	—	Washer for cover	1	All	3
E6055	A2/495	MZ47	Chaincase attachment nut	1	All	3 2
E6056	A2/496	MZ48	Chaincase attachment nut washer	1	All	2 8
13185	A2/486	—	Chaincase sealing rubber band	1	All	10 2
E6207	A2/494	—	Chaincase footrest tube felt washer	1	All	5
20937	—	—	Chaincase inner portion support stud	1	All	2 6

REAR CHAINGUARD AND FITTINGS

21832	—	—	Rear chainguard	1	All	1 17 10
22022	—	—	Fixing screw	2	All	10
E3229	—	—	Nut for screw	2	All	5
18285	—	—	Grommet	1	All	5

REAR BRAKE PEDAL AND FITTINGS

19995	—	MZ62	Rear brake pedal	1	All	1 12 5
19996	—	MZ69	Rear brake pedal spindle	1	All	4 0
E3227	—	MZ67	Nut for spindle	1	All	6
11809	—	MZ68	Washer for spindle	1	All	3
19997	—	—	Distance piece for spindle	1	All	1 5
19976	—	MZ74	Stop for spindle	1	All	10
19929	—	—	Return spring for pedal	1	All	7
19978	—	MZ63	Grease nipple and retaining pin for pedal	1	All	1 9
15819	H12-2/503	MZ73	Brake rod	1	All	4 0
20134	—	MZ66	Brake rod jaw joint assembly	1	All	6 4
E3255	—	MZ64	Pin for jaw joint	1	All	7
17735	A2/195	MZ65	Split pin	1	All	1
15821	—	MZ75	Brake rod adjuster nut	1	All	4 0

FOOTRESTS AND FITTINGS

18772	D12/513RH	MZ52	Footrest hanger, right-hand	1	All	12 5
18149	A2/513LH	MZ46	Footrest hanger, left-hand	1	All	5 9
19984	—	—	Footrest hanger spindle	2	All	1 9
19983	—	MZ44	Footrest rubber	2	All	1 11
14366	D12/510	MZ38	Footrest rod	1	All	3 4
E3238	—	MZ51	Nut for rod, plain	1	All	6
E3220	—	MZ39	Nut for rod, domed	1	All	1 2
E5377	—	MZ40	Washer for rod	2	All	3
15641	—	—	Distance piece between engine plates	1	88, 99	2 4
18268	H12-2/1078	MZ50	Footrest tube serrated end, R.H.	1	All	5 2
20936	—	MZ49	Footrest tube serrated end, L.H.	1	All	11 6

PILLION FOOTRESTS

H12/584	—	—	Pillion footrest, complete	1 pr.	All per pr.	2 6 0
18254	H12/1086	MZ54	Pillion footrest bar	2	All	8 8
16244	H12/1087	MZ57	Pillion footrest lug	2	All	7 3
16842	—	MZ61	Stud for pillion footrest and silencer fixing, L.H.	1	All	1 2

PART No.	SUPERSEDED No.	PLATE No.	DESCRIPTION	QTY.	MODEL	PRICE EACH
PILLION FOOTRESTS—cont.						£ s. d.
16246	—	—	Stud for pillion footrest and silencer fixing, R.H.	1	All	1 2
16248	—	MZ55	Pillion footrest bar pins	2	All	10
16250	—	—	Washer for pin	2	All	2
E5376	—	MZ59	Pillion footrest lug fixing washers	2	All	3
E3224	—	MZ60	Pillion footrest lug fixing nut	2	All	5
16249	H12/583	MZ53	Pillion footrest rubbers	2	All	2 0
16247	—	MZ58	Pillion footrest bar pin locknuts	2	All	5
ENGINE PLATES						
21541	—	MZ6 & 7	Front engine plate	2	ES2, 50	1 9
15621	H12-2/522	MZ6 & 7	Front engine plate	2	88, 99	4 8
21752	—	—	Front engine plate cover	1	ES2, 50	1 0
20999	—	—	Front engine plate cover	1	88, 99	2 11
21795	—	—	Front engine plate distance piece	1	ES2, 50	6
21522	—	MZ22	Rear engine plate, R.H.	1	ES2, 50	1 5 0
50229	—	MZ22	Rear engine plate, R.H.	1	88, 99	1 7 0
21520	—	MZ24	Rear engine plate, L.H.	1	ES2, 50	1 3 0
20700	—	MZ24	Rear engine plate, L.H.	1	88, 99	1 7 0
21868	—	—	Rear engine plate cover	1	ES2, 50	1 6
21031	—	—	Rear engine plate cover	1	88, 99	5 9
19429	—	—	Rear engine plate grommet	1	ES2, 50	5
19678	—	—	Rear engine plate bolt, R.H.	1	All	9
E3223	—	—	Nut for bolt	1	All	5
E5456	—	—	Washer for bolt	1	All	3
ENGINE SPROCKET						
16821	H2/473(20T)	—	Engine sprocket 20T	1	ES2	1 3 8
16819	H2/473(18T)	—	Engine sprocket 18T	1	50	1 3 8
T2180E	D12/473(21T)	A71	Engine sprocket 21T	1	88, 99	1 3 8
E3682	A2/474	A72	Engine sprocket key	1	All	3

Sprockets can be supplied as follows: Teeth Nos. 17, 18, 19, 20, 21, 22 and 23 (Twins); Teeth Nos. 16, 17, 18, 19, 20, 21, 22 and 23 (Singles). (State number of teeth required).

CHAINS FRONT AND REAR

PART No.	SUPERSEDED No.	PLATE No.	DESCRIPTION	QTY.	MODEL	PRICE EACH
18265	—	—	Front chain, 75 link	1	ES2, 50, 88	1 11 6
17835	L4/477	—	Front chain, 76 link	1	99	1 11 9
18095	—	—	Rear chain, 98 link	1	ES2, 88	2 18 0
18563	—	—	Rear chain, 97 link	1	50, 99	2 17 3
A2/480	—	—	Front chain crank link	1	All	1 5
A2/479	—	—	Front chain spring link	1	All	10
A2/482	—	—	Rear chain crank link	1	All	2 0
A2/481	—	—	Rear chain spring link	1	All	1 2
REAR CHAIN ADJUSTERS						
19264	L4/666	—	Rear wheel chain adjuster bolt	2	All	1 4
E3229	—	—	Nut for bolt	2	All	5
FRAMES						
21554	—	MZ2	Frame	1	ES2, 50	28 7 6
20710	—	MZ2	Frame	1	88, 99	28 7 6
18263	125AC	MZ1	Frame head lug bearing (top and bottom)	2	All	1 0 9
15631	—	—	Felt washer and bearing	2	All	5
17429	—	—	Head lug bearing washer	2	All	6
20126	—	—	Gusset plate cover	1	All	1 9
15844	H12-2/1091	MZ23	Rear mudguard and engine plate support tube	1	All	16 10
15893	—	MZ21	Rod for support tube	1	All	2 8
13459	—	MZ19	Nut for rod	2	All	6
E5377	—	MZ20	Washer for rod	2	All	3

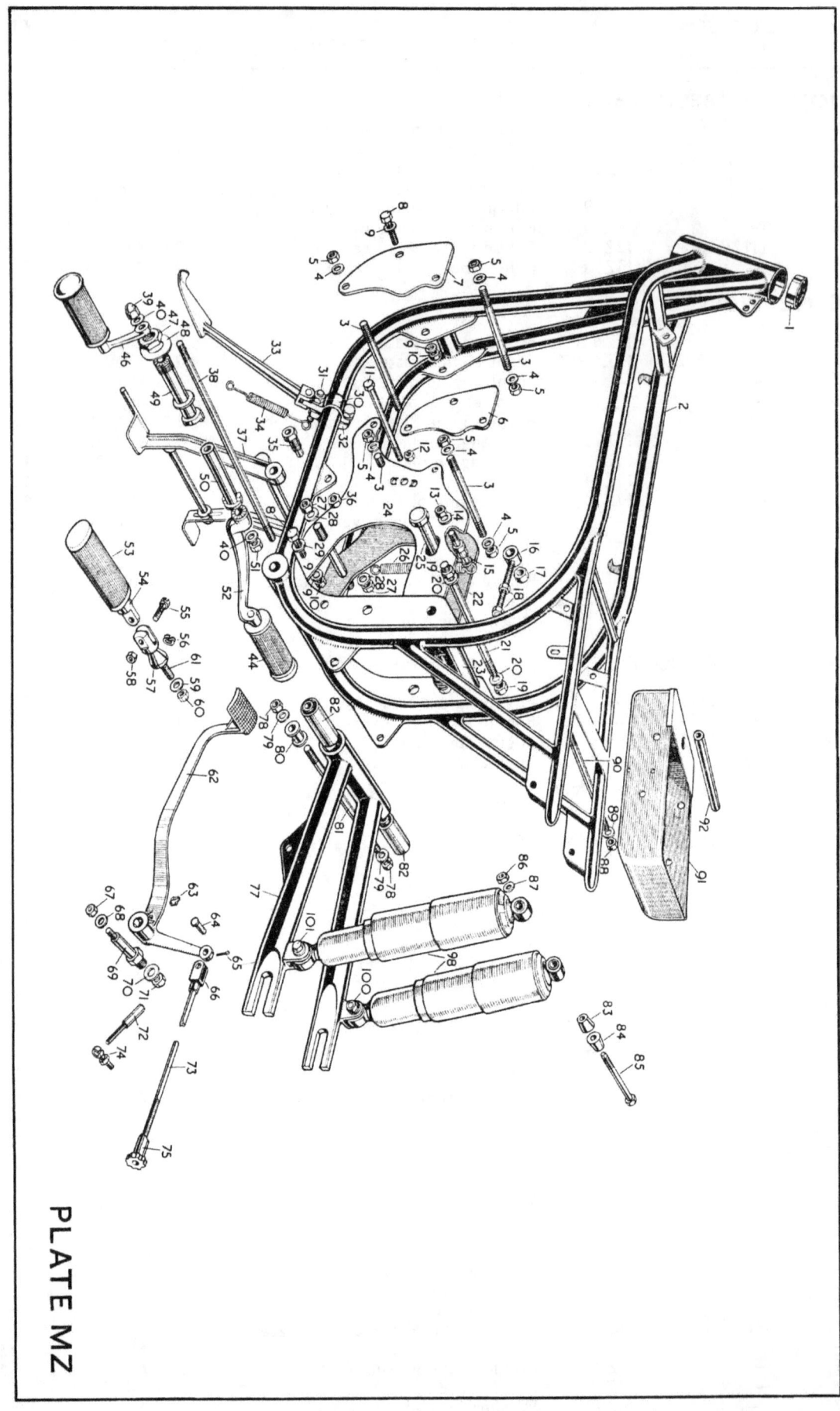

PLATE MZ

PART No.	SUPERSEDED No.	PLATE No.	DESCRIPTION	QTY.	MODEL	PRICE EACH

SWINGING ARM AND FITTINGS

						£ s. d.
P12-2/1088	—	—	Swinging arm with bushes and spacer (less rod and nuts)	1	All	7 18 2
19760	—	MZ77	Swinging arm only	1	All	6 13 10
20083	—	MZ82	Silent bloc bearing	2	All	10 2
18578	H12-2/1090	MZ80	Spacer tube for bearing	1	All	4 0
15894	—	MZ81	Swinging arm rod	1	All	5 4
15356	—	MZ78	Nut for rod	2	All	10
11809	—	MZ79	Washer for rod	2	All	3

REAR SUSPENSION AND FITTINGS

20184	—	MZ98	Rear shock absorber units	2	All	2 17 0
20198A	—	MZ98	Rear shock absorber unit (for sidecar use)	2	All	2 17 0
18704	—	MZ101	Shock absorber fixing bolt (bottom)	2	All	1 4
E3223	—	MZ100	Nut for bolt	2	All	5
11796	—	—	Washer for bolt	4	All	3

(See rear mudguard fittings for top fixing).

CENTRE STAND AND FITTINGS

17175	—	MZ37	Centre stand	1	All	1 13 9
16763	—	MZ35	Bolt for stand	2	All	11
16764	—	MZ36	Nut for bolt	2	All	5
16411	H12-2/527	MZ26	Spring for stand	1	All	2 8
14392	H12-2/1082	—	Clip for spring	1	All	1 4
E3135	—	—	Bolt for clip	1	All	10
E3223	—	—	Nut for bolt	1	All	5
E5456	—	—	Washer for bolt	2	All	3
17591	—	—	Rubber stop	1	All	7
E5278	—	—	Pin for rubber	1	All	7
19255	H12-2/491	MZ15	Anchor stud for spring	1	All	2 5
E5380	—	—	Washer for stud	2	ES2, 50	3
				1	88, 99	
E5456	—	MZ14	Washer for stud	1	88, 99	3
E3223	—	MZ13	Nut for stud	1	All	5

SIDE PROP STAND AND FITTINGS

18750	H12-2/1014	MZ33	Side prop stand leg	1	All	15 6
18275	H12-2/1092	MZ30	Side prop stand clip lug front	1	All	8 10
18605	—	MZ32	Side prop stand clip lug rear	1	All	10 2
16373	—	MZ31	Clip lug and spring fixing stud	1	All	2 8
11824	—	—	Nut for fixing stud	1	All	1 9
16374	—	—	Clip lug stud	1	All	1 4
E3224	—	—	Nut for stud	1	All	5
16174	—	—	Fulcrum pin	1	All	1 2
16176	H12-2/1015	MZ34	Prop stand return spring	1	All	2 8

FRONT MUDGUARD, STAYS AND FITTINGS

19362	L12-2/529	—	Front mudguard	1	All	17 3
19291	L122/530	—	Front mudguard stay	4	All	4 0
18710	—	—	Bolt stay to mudguard	4	All	5
18711	—	—	Washer for bolt	4	All	3
E5379	—	—	Washer for bolt	4	All	3
13192	—	—	Packing washer for bolt	4	All	3
E3229	—	—	Nut for bolt	4	All	5
18854	—	—	Bolt stay to fork end	4	All	10
11796	—	—	Washer for bolt	4	All	3
19282	L12-2/680	—	Front mudguard centre stay	1	All	4 0
18709	—	—	Bolt centre stay to mudguard	2	All	11

PART No.	SUPERSEDED No.	PLATE No.	DESCRIPTION	QTY.	MODEL	PRICE EACH
FRONT MUDGUARD, STAYS AND FITTINGS—cont.						£ s. d.
18711	—	—	Washer for bolt	2	All	3
E5379	—	—	Washer for bolt	2	All	3
11796	—	—	Washer for bolt	2	All	3
E3229	—	—	Nut for bolt	2	All	5
T1085	—	—	Stud centre stay to fork end	4	All	7
E5379	—	—	Washer for stud	4	All	3
E3229	—	—	Nut for stud	4	All	5
REAR MUDGUARD AND FITTINGS						
20159	L12-2/534	—	Rear mudguard, complete	1	All	3 11 11
20159F	—	—	Rear mudguard, front portion	1	All	2 11 11
19361R	—	—	Rear mudguard, tail portion	1	All	1 0 0
19486	L12-2/536LH	—	Lifting handle, L.H.	1	All	5 4
19487	L122/536RH	—	Lifting handle, R.H.	1	All	5 4
19432	—	—	Lifting handle and tail portion bolt	3	All	6
19433	—	—	Washer for bolt	3	All	3
19434	—	—	Lifting handle to mudguard bolt	2	All	6
19435	—	—	Washer for bolt	2	All	3
E3229	—	—	Nut for bolt	2	All	5
19504	—	MZ85	Shock absorber and rear mudguard bolt	2	All	1 4
18537	—	MZ83 & 84	Distance piece for bolt	2	All	1 4
E5456	—	MZ87	Washer for bolt	2	All	3
E3223	—	MZ86	Nut for bolt	2	All	5
19429	—	—	Rear mudguard grommet	2	All	7
14490	—	—	Clip for tail and stop light lead	1	All	7
12342	—	—	Mudguard fixing bolt (bottom)	2	All	6
E5379	—	—	Washer for bolt	4	All	3
E3229	—	—	Nut for bolt	2	All	5
NUMBER PLATES						
18706	K12/531	—	Front number plate	1	All	4 0
18755	—	—	Front plate rubber	1	All	11
18708	—	—	Stanchion for number plate	1	All	11
E3229	—	—	Nut for stanchion	2	All	5
E5379	—	—	Washer for stanchion	2	All	3
18712	—	—	Screw for number plate fixing	2	All	3
19343	L4/532	—	Rear number plate with cuff	1	All	16 10
20965	—	—	Beading for number plate	1	All	1 9
13053	—	—	Fixing stud for rear number plate	2	All	7
11796	—	—	Washer for stud	2	All	3
E3231	—	—	Nut for stud	2	All	5
TOOL TRAY AND FITTINGS						
21016	—	MZ91	Tool tray, complete	1	All	17 3
12342	—	—	Fixing bolt for tray	4	All	6
E5379	—	—	Washer for bolt	8	All	3
E3229	—	—	Nut for bolt	4	All	5
18747	—	—	Roller bracket for tank strap	1	All	3 2
16413	—	—	Bolt for bracket	2	All	5
22090	—	—	Washer for bolt	1	All	4
17904	—	—	Washer for bolt	1	All	3
BATTERY BOX AND FITTINGS						
4084107	—	—	Battery	1	All	2 4 0
19190	L12-2/586	—	Battery box, complete	1	All	1 8 9
19189	—	—	Battery box lid	1	All	5 9
19195	—	—	Knob for lid	2	All	2 0
11796	—	—	Washer for knob	2	All	2

PART No.	SUPERSEDED No.	PLATE No.	DESCRIPTION	QTY.	MODEL	PRICE EACH
BATTERY BOX AND FITTINGS—cont.						£ s. d.
17735	—	—	Split pin for knob	2	All	1
19086	—	—	Platform for battery	1	All	2 0
19093	—	—	Battery fixing U bolt	1	All	2 0
19101	—	—	Battery retaining strap	1	All	11
E3221	—	—	Nut for U bolt	2	All	5
17707	—	—	Washer for bolt	2	All	2
15689	—	—	Rubber grommet	1	All	7
14481	—	—	Battery box top fixing bolt	1	All	9
E5379	—	—	Washer for bolt	3	All	3
E3229	—	—	Nut for top fixing bolt	1	All	5
19092	—	—	Battery box bottom fixing bolt	2	All	6
E5456	—	—	Washer for bolt	2	All	3
DUAL SEAT AND FITTINGS						
20123	—	—	Dual seat	1	All	7 8 7
8052	—	—	Washers for wing nut	2	All	3
16765	—	—	Seat fixing wing nut	2	All	2 0
18538	—	—	Sorbo strip	2	All	3 4
15857	—	—	Fixing strap grommet	2	All	7
16237	H12-2/289	—	Mounting rubbers	2	All	3 4
SPEEDOMETER AND FITTINGS						
B2/555	—	—	Speedometer fixing bracket	1	All	2 0
B2/556	—	—	Speedometer fixing bracket locknut	2	All	5
B2/557	—	—	Speedometer fixing bracket washer	2	All	3
19364	L4/545	—	Speedometer head (120 m.p.h.)	1	All	4 10 0
19367	L4/552	—	Speedometer cable, complete	1	All	1 2 6
L4/554	—	—	Inner cable	1	All	11 3
L4/553	—	—	Outer cable	1	All	11 3
19366	L4/546	—	Speedometer drive gear box	1	All	1 17 6
19365	—	—	Speedometer head (180 k.p.h.)	1	All	4 10 0
B2/681	—	—	Speedometer rubber ring	1	All	7
ELECTRIC HORN AND FITTINGS						
70140A	—	—	Electric horn	1	All	1 16 0
E3229	—	—	Fixing bolt nut	2	88, 99	5
E5379	—	—	Fixing bolt washer	2	88, 99	3
20155	—	—	Fixing plate, tapped	1	ES2, 50	1 9
HEADLAMP AND FITTINGS						
58124B	—	—	Headlamp, less harness (state colour)	1	88, 99	6 15 0
58374A	—	—	Headlamp, less harness (state colour)	1	ES2, 50	6 15 0
555309	—	—	Headlamp light unit	1	All	16 0
554602	—	—	Headlamp bulb holder (main)	1	All	4 6
554710	—	—	Headlamp bulb holder (pilot)	1	All	3 0
54940852	—	—	Headlamp cable harness	1	All	16 0
31443A	—	—	Headlamp switch	1	All	1 15 0
318346	—	—	Headlamp switch handle	1	All	2 9
319333	—	—	Headlamp switch screw	1	All	1 3
318341	—	—	Headlamp switch key	1	All	9
318323	—	—	Switch lever grommet	1	All	6
553248	—	—	Headlamp shell rim or door	1	All	15 0
36084F	—	—	Ammeter	1	All	10 0
523986	—	—	Ammeter rubber sealing ring	1	All	6
397092	—	—	Headlamp "Lucas" medallion	1	All	1 9
517238	—	—	Headlamp shell only (black)	1	All	2 0 0
517248	—	—	Headlamp shell only (blue)	1	88, 99	2 2 6
54520300	—	—	Headlamp shell only (green), (standard)	1	ES2, 50	2 2 6
517237	—	—	Headlamp shell only (grey), (standard)	1	88, 99	2 0 0

PART No.	SUPERSEDED No.	PLATE No.	DESCRIPTION	QTY.	MODEL	PRICE EACH

HEADLAMP AND FITTINGS—cont.

PART No.	SUPERSEDED No.	PLATE No.	DESCRIPTION	QTY.	MODEL	£ s. d.
517247	—	—	Headlamp shell only (red)	1	88, 99	2 2 6
112201	—	—	Headlamp fixing bolts	2	All	2 9
137499	—	—	Headlamp fixing bolts, washers	2	All	2
31563A	—	—	Dipper and horn switch	1	All	10 6
18733	—	—	Dipper and horn switch rubber	1	All	10
18734	—	—	Dipper and horn switch fixing screws	2	All	3

STOP LAMP AND FITTINGS

PART No.	SUPERSEDED No.	PLATE No.	DESCRIPTION	QTY.	MODEL	PRICE EACH
53432B	—	—	Stop and tail lamp complete (Mod. 564)	1	All	1 2 6
573839	—	—	Stop and tail lamp lens	1	All	4 6
575200	—	—	Stop and tail lamp window	1	All	2 3
575219	—	—	Lens fixing nuts	2	All	6
166014	—	—	Stop and tail lamp fixing nut	2	All	3
188327	—	—	Washers for nut	2	All	1
20165	31383A/B	—	Stop lamp switch (Model 22B)	1	All	7 6
20129	—	—	Stop lamp switch bracket	1	All	1 9
E5278	—	—	Bracket pins	2	All	7
17904	—	—	Washer for pins	4	All	3
E3221	—	—	Nut for pins	2	All	5
20248	—	—	Stop lamp brake switch lead	1	All	1 9
20245	—	—	Stop tail lamp lead	1	All	1 6

TOOL KITS

PART No.	SUPERSEDED No.	PLATE No.	DESCRIPTION	QTY.	MODEL	PRICE EACH
KTU/102	—	—	Tool roll complete with tools	1	ES2, 50	1 15 2
			Kit comprises :			
			SPU/103 Tapper spanners (2)			
			A2/567 Screwdriver (1)			
			A2/565 $\frac{1}{4}'' \times \frac{3}{16}''$ spanner (2)			
			A2/572 Pliers (1)			
			A2/573 Tyre levers (2)			
			SBU2/88 Plug spanner (1)			
			SBU2/76 $\frac{7}{16}'' \times \frac{1}{2}''$ box spanner (1)			
			A2/581 T/bar, $\frac{5}{16}'' \times 6\frac{1}{2}''$ (1)			
			TBU/47 T/bar, $\frac{7}{16}'' \times 8''$ (1)			
			A2/566 $\frac{5}{16}'' \times \frac{3}{8}''$ spanner (1)			
			A2/578 Cable adjuster spanner (1)			
			19438 Allen Key (1)			
			20648 Wheel nut box spanner (1)			
			18976 S/A adj. spanner (1)			
			21267 Screwdriver (for contact breaker (1)			
			TRU/39 Bag (1)			
KTU/103	—	—	Tool roll complete with tools	1	88, 99	1 10 8
			Kit comprises :			
			TRU/39 Bag (1)			
			A2/567 Screwdriver (1)			
			A2/565 $\frac{1}{4}'' \times \frac{3}{16}''$ spanner (1)			
			A2/572 Pliers (1)			
			A2/573 Tyre levers (2)			
			SBU2/88 Plug spanner (1)			
			SBU2/76 $\frac{7}{16}'' \times \frac{1}{2}''$ box spanner (1)			
			A2/581 T/bar, $\frac{5}{16}'' \times 6\frac{1}{2}''$ (1)			
			TBU/47 T/bar, $\frac{7}{16}'' \times 8''$ (1)			
			A2/566 $\frac{5}{16}'' \times \frac{3}{8}''$ spanner (1)			
			19438 Allen key (1)			
			20648 Wheel nut box spanner (1)			
			18976 S/A adj. spanner (1)			

PART No.	SUPERSEDED No.	PLATE No.	DESCRIPTION	QTY.	MODEL	PRICE EACH
						£ s. d.

TOOL KITS—cont.

PART No.	SUPERSEDED No.	PLATE No.	DESCRIPTION	QTY.	MODEL	PRICE EACH
		21267	Screwdriver for distributor	(1)		
		D12/568	Rocker adjuster spanner	(1)		
18240	—	—	Tyre inflator	1	All	7 6

N.B.—For prices of individual tools, also available extra tools and service tools, see list of optional equipment.

GASKET SETS

PART No.	SUPERSEDED No.	PLATE No.	DESCRIPTION		MODEL	PRICE EACH
D12/1062	—	—	Engine overhaul set		A.R. 88, 99	1 1 0
D12/1063	—	—	Engine de-coke set		A.R. 88, 99	10 5
M4/1062	—	—	Engine de-coke and overhaul set		A.R. E.S.2	8 6
M13/1062	—	—	Engine de-coke and overhaul set		A.R. 50	8 6

PAINT

Synthetic, Air Drying Enamel is available for touching up in the following colours : GREY, GREEN, RED and BLUE.

PART No.	SUPERSEDED No.	PLATE No.	DESCRIPTION		MODEL	PRICE EACH
—	—	—	Small tins			4 0
—	—	—	Half-pint tins			8 0
—	—	—	1 Pint tins			15 0
—	—	—	1 Gallon tins			4 4 0

TRANSFERS

PART No.	SUPERSEDED No.	PLATE No.	DESCRIPTION	QTY.	MODEL	PRICE EACH
21467	—	—	Oil tank transfer (recommended oil level)	1	All	1 6
17731	A2/867	—	Oil bath transfer	1	All	1 6
19555	—	—	Rear mudguard transfer	1	ES2	1 6
19557	—	—	Rear mudguard transfer	1	50	1 6
19558	—	—	Rear mudguard transfer	1	88	1 6
19559	—	—	Rear mudguard transfer	1	99	1 6

CABLE CLIPS

PART No.	SUPERSEDED No.	PLATE No.	DESCRIPTION	QTY.	MODEL	PRICE EACH
19091	—	—	Cable clip (size C), (speedo cable to frame)	1	All	5
17752	—	—	Cable clip (size S), (stop and tail leads)	13	All	7
19090	—	—	Cable clip (size F), (throttle, air and clutch cables to frame)	2	All	5
18489	—	—	Cable clip (size D), (throttle and air cables, handlebar end)	1	All	5

N.B.—Norton Motors Ltd. reserve the right to alter prices and specifications at all times and without notice.

OPTIONAL EQUIPMENT

MODELS 88, 99, E.S.2 and 50

AND SERVICE TOOLS

(for all Models)

PART No.	SUPERSEDED No.	PLATE No.	DESCRIPTION	QTY.	MODEL	PRICE EACH

Standard Models 88/99 fitted with large inlet valve twin carburettors and high compression pistons

PART No.	SUPERSEDED No.	PLATE No.	DESCRIPTION	QTY.	MODEL	£ s. d.
21325A	—	—	Polished cylinder head complete with guides and large inlet valve seat insert ...	1	88, 99	20 2 6
17221	—	—	Inlet valve	2	88, 99	1 0 8
18542A	—	—	Inlet manifold (for dual carburettor fixing)	1	88, 99	1 17 2
18035	—	—	Inlet manifold to head fixing stud	4	88, 99	7
T2221	—	—	Inlet manifold to head fixing washer ...	4	88, 99	3
13145	—	—	Inlet manifold to head fixing stud nut	4	88, 89	3
21572	—	—	Inlet manifold distance piece ...	2	88, 89	3 4
376/66	22112	—	Carburettor, complete	2	88	4 15 0
376/67	22113	—	Carburettor, complete	2	99	4 15 0
20344	—	—	Carburettor fixing stud (to manifold)	2	88, 99	7
11796	—	—	Carburettor fixing stud washer	2	88, 89	3
E3231	—	—	Carburettor fixing stud nut ...	2	88, 89	5
244/1409	22545	—	Dual air control cable complete (standard bars)	1	88, 99	17 0
22544	—	—	Dual air control cable, complete (American bars)	1	88, 89	17 0
244/1410	22543	—	Dual throttle control cable, complete (American and standard bars)	1	88, 89	17 0
244/104	—	—	Dual air and throttle cable control barrel ...	2	88, 99	8 0
22111	—	—	Petrol pipe assembly ...	1	88, 99	8 8
T2233/C	L12-2/702HC	—	Piston complete, L.H., 9-1 compression ratio	1	88	3 8 0
T2234/C	L12-2/702HC	—	Piston complete, R.H., 9-1 compression ratio	1	88	3 8 0
22522	—	—	Piston bare, L.H., 9-1 compression ratio ...	1	88	2 5 6
22523	—	—	Piston bare, R.H., 9-1 compression ratio ...	1	88	2 5 6
22508	—	—	Piston ring compression, 9-1 compression ratio	4	88	3 9
22509	—	—	Piston ring scraper, 9-1 compression ratio ...	2	88	5 2
21339	—	—	Piston complete, L.H., 9-1 compression ratio	1	99	2 6 3
21340	—	—	Piston complete, R.H., 9-1 compression ratio	1	99	2 6 3
21577LH	—	—	Piston bare, L.H., 9-1 compression ratio ...	1	99	1 3 9
21577RH	—	—	Piston bare, R.H., 9-1 compression ratio ...	1	99	1 3 9

PART No.	SUPERSEDED No.	PLATE No.	DESCRIPTION	QTY.	MODEL	PRICE EACH

OPTIONAL EQUIPMENT—cont.

PART No.	SUPERSEDED No.	PLATE No.	DESCRIPTION	QTY.	MODEL	£ s. d.
22518	—	—	Piston complete, L.H., 8–1 compression ratio	1	99	2 17 6
22519	—	—	Piston complete, R.H., 8–1 compression ratio	1	99	2 17 6
22520	—	—	Piston bare, L.H., 8–1 compression ratio	1	99	1 15 0
22521	—	—	Piston bare, R.H., 8–1 compression ratio	1	99	1 15 0
21579	—	—	Piston ring compression, 8–1 and 9–1 compression ratio	4	99	3 9
21578	—	—	Piston ring scraper, 8–1 and 9–1 compression ratio	2	99	5 2
21580	—	—	Gudgeon pin (all ratios)	2	88, 99	9 2
21581	—	—	Gudgeon pin circlip (all ratios)	4	88, 99	4

REVOLUTION COUNTER AND FITTINGS

PART No.	SUPERSEDED No.	PLATE No.	DESCRIPTION	QTY.	MODEL	£ s. d.
18245RC	—	—	Timing cover (for rev counter fitting)	1	88, 99	3 4 3
15379	—	—	Timing cover blanking plate	1	88, 99	3 4
18506	—	—	Timing cover blanking plate fixing screws	2	88, 99	10
18507	—	—	Timing cover blanking plate fixing screws, nuts	2	88, 99	5
D12/915	—	—	Timing cover pressure release valve, complete	1	88, 99	16 10

N.B.—This pressure release valve will be required when rev counter timing covers are fitted to models 88 and 99 subsequent to 1957).

PART No.	SUPERSEDED No.	PLATE No.	DESCRIPTION	QTY.	MODEL	£ s. d.
22548	A11M/545	—	Rev counter instrument	1	88, 99	4 0 0
13243	A11M/555	—	Rev counter instrument bracket	1	88, 99	5 4
13249	A11M/858	—	Rev counter instrument retaining cup	1	88, 99	5 4
13250	A11M/681	—	Rev counter rubber washer	1	88, 99	2 8
A11M/556	—	—	Rev counter fixing nut	2	88, 99	5
A11M/557	—	—	Rev counter fixing nut washer	2	88, 99	3
18512	A11M/552	—	Rev counter drive cable	1	88, 99	17 6
18514	A11M/546	36362	Rev counter gearbox	1	88, 99	2 7 6
17211	—	—	Rev counter gearbox drive nut	1	88, 99	6 8
18506	—	—	Rev counter gearbox attachment pins	2	88, 99	10
18507	—	—	Rev counter gearbox attachment pins, nuts	2	88, 99	5
21064	—	—	Rev counter cable clip	1	88, 99	6

FULL ENCLOSURE REAR CHAINCASE

PART No.	SUPERSEDED No.	PLATE No.	DESCRIPTION	QTY.	MODEL	£ s. d.
ERCC/7	—	—	Enclosed rear chaincase complete with all fittings. (STATE COLOUR)	1	All	4 19 5
19734	—	—	Rear chaincase, top half	1	All	} 4 10 6
19735	—	—	Rear chaincase, bottom half	1	All	
22022	—	—	Rear chaincase fixing screw	4	All	10
19435A	—	—	Rear chaincase fixing screw washer	8	All	6
22135	—	—	Rear chaincase inspection hole grommet	1	All	1 2
18285	—	—	Rear chaincase breather pipe grommet	1	All	5

CRASH BARS

PART No.	SUPERSEDED No.	PLATE No.	DESCRIPTION	QTY.	MODEL	£ s. d.
CBK/10F	—	—	Front crash bar (full loop type) assembly complete	1	All	3 7 6
19095	—	—	Front crash bar (full loop type)	1	All	3 1 8
21638	—	—	Front crash bar top fixing plate	1	All	2 0
19063	—	—	Front crash bar U bolt	1	All	3 0
E3223	—	—	Front crash bar U bolt nut	2	All	5
CBK/10R	—	—	Rear crash bars, complete with all fittings	1	All	per set 3 17 6

PART No.	SUPERSEDED No.	PLATE No.	DESCRIPTION	QTY.	MODEL	PRICE EACH
CRASH BARS—cont.						£ s. d.
19066	—	—	Rear crash bar, L.H.	1	All	1 14 0
19067	—	—	Rear crash bar, R.H.	1	All	1 14 0
19062	—	—	Rear crash bar fixing stud	2	All	1 9
16883	—	—	Rear crash bar fixing clip	2	All	1 0
15703	—	—	Rear crash bar fixing bolt	2	All	1 4
E5376	—	—	Rear crash bar fixing bolt washer	2	All	3
E3224	—	—	Rear crash bar fixing bolt nut	2	All	5
20123A	—	—	Dual seat complete (Required where rear crash bars are fitted).	A.R.	All	7 8 7
AIR CLEANERS						
18684	K12-2/1058	—	Air cleaner	1	50, ES2	2 14 1
18484	—	—	Air cleaner clip	1	50, ES2	2 4
18685	K12/1059	—	Air cleaner sleeve (State coloured required).	1	50, ES2	6 8
19667	—	—	Air cleaner	1	88, 99	2 14 1
19518	—	—	Air cleaner connecting hose	1	88, 99	4 0
19729	—	—	Air cleaner connecting hose clip	1	88, 89	11
E5379	—	—	Air cleaner fixing washer	2	88, 99	3
E3229	—	—	Air cleaner fixing pin nut (State colour required).	2	88, 99	5
FOLDING KICKSTART CRANK						
20592	—	—	Crank for folding kickstarter	1	All	1 6 0
19075	—	—	Pedal for folding kickstarter	1	All	10 2
E6706	—	—	Pedal pivot bolt	1	All	11
E3154	—	—	Clinch bolt for crank	1	All	10
A2/308	—	—	Washer for bolt	1	All	3
CHROMIUM MUDGUARDS						
19362CH	L12-2/529CH	—	Front mudguard	1	All	2 0 3
19291CH	L12-2/530CH	—	Front mudguard side stay	4	All	8 8
19282CH	L12-2/680CH	—	Front mudguard centre stay	1	All	8 8
20159CH	L12-2/534CH	—	Rear mudguard, complete	1	All	4 12 0
20159F CH	—	—	Rear mudguard, front portion	1	All	3 9 0
19361R CH	—	—	Rear mudguard, rear portion	1	All	1 3 0
19487CH	L12-2/536R CH	—	Rear mudguard lifting handle, R.H.	1	All	14 0
19486CH	L12-2/536L CH	—	Rear mudguard lifting handle, L.H.	1	All	14 0

MISCELLANEOUS SECTION

PART No.	SUPERSEDED No.	PLATE No.	DESCRIPTION	QTY.	MODEL	PRICE EACH
T2180D/20T	D12/473	—	Engine sprocket 20T (Recommended for model 99 when twin carburettors are fitted).	1	99	1 3 8
18304	—	—	Sparking plug (F.E. 100 single point) (Required for engines where twin carburettors are fitted).	2	88, 99	5 0
18698	—	—	Sparking plug (F.E. 70) (For running in purposes **only** when twin carburettors are fitted).	2	88, 99	5 0
SCK/3	—	—	Conversion kit for sidecar purposes N.B.—This kit includes all necessary parts for sidecar conversion including, sidecar trail crown and column, heavyweight springs, engine sprocket, rear S/A units, etc., etc.		All	16 13 0

Please state colour of machine, model and type of sidecar, i.e. light or heavy.

PART No.	SUPERSEDED No.	PLATE No.	DESCRIPTION	QTY.	MODEL	PRICE EACH

MISCELLANEOUS SECTION—cont-

£ s. d.

PART No.	SUPERSEDED No.	PLATE No.	DESCRIPTION	QTY.	MODEL	PRICE EACH
16390	—	—	Clip-on handlebars (Manx dropped type)	1 pr. All per pr.		6 0 9
22460	—	—	Handlebars (American type)	1	All	2 0 3
20590	—	—	Front brake cable complete with adj. and nipples (for American bars)	1	All	10 6
22546	—	—	Clutch cable complete (for American bars)	1	All	7 0
21988	—	—	Compression plate	A.R.	ES2	2 8

TOOLS

PART No.	SUPERSEDED No.	PLATE No.	DESCRIPTION	QTY.	MODEL	PRICE EACH
SPU1/49	—	—	Head lug bearing and filler cap spanner	A.R.	All	4 6
DWU/01	A2/567	—	Screwdriver	A.R.	All	1 4
SPU2/02	A2/565	—	¼" × 3/16" Spanner	A.R.	All	1 9
SHU/29	A3/579	—	Exhaust pipe nut spanner	A.R.	All	4 4
LTU/07	A2/573	—	Tyre lever	A.R.	All	1 6
SBU2/88	—	—	Sparking plug spanner	A.R.	All	2 2
SBU2/76	—	—	7/16" × ½" Box spanner	A.R.	All	3 3
TBU/01	A2/581	—	Tommy bar, 5/16" × 6½"	A.R.	All	7
TBU/47	—	—	Tommy bar, 7/16" × 8"	A.R.	All	1 2
SPU2/20	D12/568	—	Rocker adjusting spanner	A.R.	88, 99 per pair	2 8
SPU2/04	A2/566	—	5/16" × 3/8" Open ended spanner	A.R.	All	2 6
SPU1/01	A2/578	—	Cable adjuster spanner	A.R.	All	1 5
19438	—	—	Allan key	A.R.	All	1 2
20648	—	—	Box spanner for rear wheel nuts	A.R.	All	1 11
18976	—	—	Shock absorber adjusting spanner	A.R.	All	1 6
13685	B2/685	—	Fork pull through	A.R.	All	7 6
18240	—	—	Tyre inflator	A.R.	All	7 6
21267	—	—	Screwdriver (for distributor contact points)	A.R.	All	9
PEU/06	A2/572	—	Pliers (6")	A.R.	All	5 9
SPU/103	—	—	Tappet adjusting spanners	A.R.	ES2, 50 per pair	2 8
SPU1/48	—	—	Crown and column locknut spanner	A.R.	All	4 6
SHU/36	—	—	Fork abutment spanner	A.R.	All	4 0
A2/575	—	—	Grease gun	A.R.	All	8 0
SBU2/77	—	—	Short box spanner, 5/16"	A.R.	All	2 0

N.B.—For prices of complete tool kits and contents of same, see pages 36 and 37.

SERVICE TOOLS (ALL MODELS)

PART No.	SUPERSEDED No.	PLATE No.	DESCRIPTION	QTY.	MODEL	PRICE EACH
SBU1/74	—	—	Cylinder head box spanner (long)	A.R.	7, 77, 88, 99	2 6
SBU1/02	—	—	Cylinder head box spanner (short)	A.R.	7, 77, 88, 99	2 0
CBT/11	—	—	Clutch body withdrawal tool	A.R.	All	10 6
EST/12	—	—	Engine sprocket extractor (500/600 twins and all singles)	A.R.		1 2 6
R.1745	—	—	Crankpin nut box spanner (1954/9 Model 30, Manx)	A.R.		1 15 0
R.2048	—	—	Crankpin nut box spanner (1954/9 Model 40, Manx)	A.R.		1 10 0
SPU1/30	—	—	V/S nut spanner (30 and 40, Inter)	A.R.		4 6
SBU1/114	—	—	Engine shaft nut spanner (1954, 30 and 40 Manx onwards)	A.R.		7 6
13685	B2/685	—	Fork pull through	A.R.		7 6
ET/2003	—	—	H.T. pinion extractor all models	A.R.		1 2 6
12068	—	—	Crankpin nut spanner	A.R.	ES2, 50	2 10 0
12093	—	—	Gearbox axle sprocket box spanner	A.R.		10 0
EST/12A	—	—	Extension for removing camshaft sprocket (For use with sprocket extractor EST/12).	A.R.	88, 99	3 0

VELOCEPRESS MANUALS – MOTORCYCLE BY MAKE

AJS 1932-1948 SINGLES & TWINS 250cc THRU 1000cc (BOOK OF)
AJS 1945-1960 SINGLES 350cc & 500cc MODELS 16 & 18 (BOOK OF)
AJS 1955-1965 SINGLES 350cc & 500cc (BOOK OF)
AJS 1957-1966 FACTORY WSM - ALL SINGLES & TWINS
ARIEL UP TO 1932 (BOOK OF)
ARIEL 1932-1939 PREWAR MODELS (BOOK OF)
ARIEL 1933-1951 (WORKSHOP MANUAL)
ARIEL 1939-1960 4 STROKE SINGLES (BOOK OF)
ARIEL 1958-1964 LEADER & ARROW FACTORY WSM & PARTS LIST
ARIEL 1958-1964 LEADER & ARROW (BOOK OF)
BMW R26 R27 (1956-1967) FACTORY WORKSHOP MANUAL
BMW R50 R50S R60 R69S (1955-1969) FACTORY WORKSHOP MANUAL
BRIDGESTONE 90 SERIES FACTORY WSM & PARTS CATALOGUE
BRIDGESTONE 175 SERIES FACTORY WSM & PARTS CATALOGUE
BRIDGESTONE 350 SERIES FACTORY WSM & PARTS CATALOGUES
BSA SERVICE SHEETS MASTER CATALOGUE ALL MODELS 1945-1967
BSA BANTAM D1 TO D7 1948-1966 FACTORY SERVICE SHEETS MANUAL
BSA BANTAM ALL MODELS FROM 1948 ONWARDS (BOOK OF)
BSA DANDY FACTORY WORKSHOP MANUAL (COMPILATION)
BSA SINGLES & V-TWINS UP TO 1927 (BOOK OF)
BSA SINGLES & V-TWINS UP TO 1930 (BOOK OF)
BSA SINGLES & V-TWINS UP TO 1935 (BOOK OF)
BSA SINGLES & V-TWINS 1936-1939 (BOOK OF)
BSA C10, C11 & C12 1945-1958 FACTORY SERVICE SHEETS MANUAL
BSA OHV & SV SINGLES 250-600cc 1945-1959 (BOOK OF)
BSA C15 & B40 1958-1967 FACTORY SERVICE SHEETS MANUAL
BSA OHV & SV SINGLES 250cc (ONLY) 1954-1970 (BOOK OF)
BSA B31, B32, B33 & B34 1945-60 FACTORY SERVICE SHEETS MANUAL
BSA OHV SINGLES 350 & 500cc 1955-1967 (BOOK OF)
BSA M20, M21 & M33 1945-1963 FACTORY SERVICE SHEETS MANUAL
BSA TWINS A7 & A10 1948-1962 FACTORY SERVICE SHEETS MANUAL
BSA TWINS A7 & A10 1948-1962 (BOOK OF)
BSA TWINS A50 & A65 1962-1965 FACTORY WORKSHOP MANUAL
BSA TWINS A50 & A65 1962-1969 (SECOND BOOK OF)
DOUGLAS 1929-1939 PREWAR ALL MODELS (BOOK OF)
DOUGLAS 1948-1957 POSTWAR ALL MODELS FACTORY SHOP MANUAL
DUCATI 160cc, 250cc & 350cc OHC MODELS FACTORY SHOP MANUAL
HONDA 50cc ALL MODELS UP TO 1970 INC MONKEY & TRAIL (BOOK OF)
HONDA 90cc ALL MODELS UP TO 1966 (BOOK OF)
HONDA 50-65-70-90cc OHC SINGLES 1959-1983 FACTORY WSM
HONDA 100-125cc SINGLES CB/CD/CL/SL/TL 1970-1984 FACTORY WSM
HONDA 125-150cc TWINS C/CS/CB/CA FACTORY WORKSHOP MANUAL
HONDA 125-160-175-200cc TWINS 1965-1978 WORKSHOP MANUAL
HONDA 250-305cc TWINS C/CS/CB 1959-1967 FACTORY WSM
HONDA 250-350cc TWINS CB/CL/SL 1968-1973 FACTORY WSM
HONDA 450cc TWINS CB/CL 1965-1974 K0 TO K7 WORKSHOP MANUAL
HONDA 500cc & 550cc 4CYL 1971-1978 FACTORY WORKSHOP MANUAL
HONDA 750cc SHOC 4 CYL 1969-1978 K0~K8 WORKSHOP MANUAL
HONDA C100 SUPER CUB FACTORY WORKSHOP MANUAL
HONDA C110 SPORT CUB 1962-1969 FACTORY WORKSHOP MANUAL
HONDA TWINS & SINGLES 50cc THRU 305cc 1960-1966 (BOOK OF)
HONDA TWINS ALL MODELS 125cc THRU 450cc UP TO 1968 (BOOK OF)
INDIAN PONYBIKE, BOY RACER & PAPOOSE ILL PARTS LIST & SALES LIT
J.A.P. ENGINES 1927-1952 & MOTORCYCLES 1934-1952 (BOOK OF)
MATCHLESS 1931-1939 ALL MODELS 250cc THRU 990cc (BOOK OF)
MATCHLESS 1945-1956 350 & 500cc SINGLES (BOOK OF)
MATCHLESS 1955-1966 350 & 500cc SINGLES (BOOK OF)
MATCHLESS 1957-1966 FACTORY WSM - ALL SINGLES & TWINS
NEW IMPERIAL ALL SV & OHV FROM 1935 ONWARDS (BOOK OF)
NORTON 1932-1939 PREWAR MODELS (BOOK OF)
NORTON 1932-1947 (BOOK OF)
NORTON 1938-1956 (BOOK OF)
NORTON 1945-1963 MODELS 16H, Big4, ES2, 19 & 50 WSM'S & PARTS
NORTON 1955-1963 MODELS 19, 50 & ES2 (BOOK OF)
NORTON 1948-1970 DOMINATOR TWINS FACTORY WSM'S & PARTS
NORTON 1955-1965 DOMINATOR TWINS (BOOK OF)
NORTON 1960-1970 TWIN CYLINDER FACTORY WORKSHOP MANUAL
NORTON 1970-1975 COMMANDO 850 & 750cc FACTORY WSM
NORTON 1975-1978 MK 3 COMMANDO 850 cc FACTORY WSM
PANTHER 1932-1958 LIGHTWEIGHT MODELS 250 & 350cc (BOOK OF)
PANTHER 1938-1966 HEAVYWEIGHT MODELS 600 & 650cc (BOOK OF)
RALEIGH MOTORCYCLES 1919-1933 (BOOK OF)
ROYAL ENFIELD 1934-1946 SINGLES & V TWINS (BOOK OF)
ROYAL ENFIELD 1937-1953 SINGLES & V TWINS (BOOK OF)
ROYAL ENFIELD 1946-1962 SINGLES (BOOK OF)
ROYAL ENFIELD 1958-1966 250cc & 350cc SINGLES (SECOND BOOK OF)
ROYAL ENFIELD 1962-1970 INTERCEPTOR WSM'S & PARTS (Compilation)
RUDGE 1933-1939 (BOOK OF)
SUNBEAM 1928-1939 (BOOK OF)
SUNBEAM 1946-1957 S7 & S8 (BOOK OF)
SUZUKI 50cc & 80cc UP TO 1966 (BOOK OF)
SUZUKI T10 1963-1967 FACTORY WORKSHOP MANUAL
SUZUKI T20 & T200 1965-1969 FACTORY WORKSHOP MANUAL
SUZUKI TWINS 1962 ONWARDS 125-500cc WORKSHOP MANUAL
TRIUMPH 1935-1949 SINGLES & TWINS (BOOK OF)
TRIUMPH 1937-1951 (WORKSHOP MANUAL)
TRIUMPH 1945-1955 FACTORY WORKSHOP MANUAL
TRIUMPH 1945-1959 TWINS (BOOK OF)
TRIUMPH 1956-1969 TWINS (BOOK OF)
TRIUMPH 1963-1970 UNIT CONSTRUCTION 650cc FACTORY WSM
TRIUMPH 1963-1974 UNIT CONSTRUCTION 350-500cc FACTORY WSM
TRIUMPH 1968-1974 TRIDENT T150 & T150V FACTORY WSM
VELOCETTE 1925-1970 ALL SINGLES & TWINS (BOOK OF)
VELOCETTE 1933-1952 MOV-MAC-MSS RIGID FRAME FACTORY WSM
VELOCETTE 1954-1971 MSS-VENOM-THRUXTON-VIPER FACTORY WSM
VILLIERS ENGINE UP TO 1959 INC. 3 WHEELERS (BOOK OF)
VILLIERS ENGINE UP TO 1969 (BOOK OF)
VINCENT 1935-1955 (WORKSHOP MANUAL)
YAMAHA 1961-1967 YA5 & YA6 (WORKSHOP MANUAL & ILL PARTS LIST)
YAMAHA 1971-1972 JT1& JT2 (WORKSHOP MANUAL & ILL PARTS LIST)

VELOCEPRESS TECHNICAL BOOKS – MOTORCYCLE

1930'S BRITISH MOTORCYCLE CARBS & ELEC COMPONENTS (BOOK OF)
1930'S BRITISH MOTORCYCLE ENGINES (OVERHAUL & MAINTENANCE)
1930'S BRITISH MOTORCYCLE GEARBOXES & CLUTCHES (BOOK OF)
CATALOG OF BRITISH MOTORCYCLES (1951 MODELS)
LUCAS ELECTRONICS BRITISH M/CYCLES REPAIR & PARTS (1950-1977)
MOTORCYCLE ENGINEERING (P.E. Irving)
MOTORCYCLE ROAD TESTS 1949-1953 (Motor Cycle Magazine UK)
SPEED AND HOW TO OBTAIN IT (Motor Cycle Magazine UK)
TUNING FOR SPEED (P.E. Irving)
WIPAC (COMBO) MANUAL NUMBER 3 + M/CYCLE & SCOOTER MANUAL

VELOCEPRESS MANUALS – SCOOTERS BY MAKE

BSA SUNBEAM SCOOTER WORKSHOP MANUAL 1959-1965
BSA SUNBEAM SCOOTER 1959-1965 (BOOK OF)
LAMBRETTA 1947-1957 ALL 125 & 150cc MODELS (BOOK OF)
LAMBRETTA 1957-1970 LI & TV MODELS (SECOND BOOK OF)
NSU PRIMA 1956-1964 ALL MODELS (BOOK OF)
TRIUMPH TIGRESS SCOOTER WORKSHOP MANUAL 1959-1965
TRIUMPH TIGRESS SCOOTER (BOOK OF)
VESPA 1951-1961 (BOOK OF)
VESPA 1955-1963 125 & 150cc & GS MODELS (SECOND BOOK OF)
VESPA 1955-1968 GS & SS (BOOK OF)
VESPA 1963-1972 90, 125 & 150cc (THIRD BOOK OF)

VELOCEPRESS MANUALS – MOPEDS & MOTORIZED BICYCLES

CYCLEMOTOR (BOOK OF)
NSU QUICKLY 1953-1963 ALL MODELS (BOOK OF)
PUCH MAXI N & S MAINTENANCE & REPAIR (3 MANUAL COMPILATION)
RALEIGH MOPEDS 1960-1969 (BOOK OF)

VELOCEPRESS MANUALS - THREE WHEELER'S

BOND MINICAR THREE WHEELER 1948-1967 (BOOK OF)
BMW ISETTA FACTORY WORKSHOP MANUAL
BSA THREE WHEELER (BOOK OF)
RELIANT REGAL THREE WHEELER 1952-1973 (BOOK OF)
VINTAGE MORGAN THREE WHEELER (BOOK OF)

VELOCEPRESS MANUALS – AUTOMOBILE BY MAKE

ALFA ROMEO GIULIA WORKSHOP MANUAL 1300 TO 2000cc 1962-1975
ALFA ROMEO GIULIA TECH MANUAL CARBURETED CARS FROM 1962
ALFA ROMEO GIULIA TECH MANUAL FUEL INJECTED CARS FROM 1969
ALFA ROMEO GIULIETTA & GIULIA 750 & 101 SERIES 1955-1965 WSM
AUSTIN-HEALEY SPRITE & MG MIDGET WORKSHOP MANUAL 1958-1971
BMW 600 LIMOUSINE FACTORY WORKSHOP MANUAL
BMW 600 LIMOUSINE OWNERS HAND BOOK & SERVICE MANUAL
BMW 2000 & 2002 1966-1976 WORKSHOP MANUAL
CORVAIR 1960-1969 WORKSHOP MANUAL
CORVETTE V8 1955-1962 WORKSHOP MANUAL
FERRARI HANDBOOK ROAD & RACE CARS (SERVICE/SPECS) 1948-1958
FERRARI 250/GT SERVICE & MAINTENANCE MANUAL 1956-1965
FIAT 500 FACTORY WORKSHOP MANUAL 1957-1973
FIAT 600, 600D & MULTIPLA FACTORY WORKSHOP MANUAL 1955-1969
JAGUAR E-TYPE 3.8 & 4.2 SERIES 1 & 2 WORKSHOP MANUAL
JAGUAR MK 7, 8, 9 & XK120, 140, 150 WORKSHOP MANUAL 1948-1961
METROPOLITAN FACTORY WORKSHOP MANUAL
MGA & MGB OWNERS HANDBOOK & WORKSHOP MANUAL
MG MIDGET TC, TD, TF & TF1500 WORKSHOP MANUAL
PORSCHE 356 1948-1965 WORKSHOP MANUAL
PORSCHE 911 2.0, 2.2, 2.4 LITRE 1964-1973 WORKSHOP MANUAL
PORSCHE 911 2.7, 3.0, 3.2 LITRE 1973-1989 WORKSHOP MANUAL
PORSCHE 912 WORKSHOP MANUAL
PORSCHE 914/4 & 914/6 1.7, 1.8, 2.0 LITRE 1970-1976 WSM
TRIUMPH TR2, TR3, TR4 1953-1965 WORKSHOP MANUAL
VOLKSWAGEN TRANSPORTER, TRUCKS & WAGONS 1950-1979 WSM
VOLVO 1944-1968 ALL MODELS WORKSHOP MANUAL

VELOCEPRESS TECHNICAL BOOKS - AUTOMOBILE

HOW TO BUILD A FIBERGLASS CAR
HOW TO BUILD A RACING CAR
HOW TO RESTORE THE MODEL 'A' FORD
MASERATI OWNER'S HANDBOOK
PERFORMANCE TUNING THE SUNBEAM TIGER
SOUPING THE VOLKSWAGEN
SOLEX CARBURETORS (EMPHASIS ON UK & EU AUTOMOBILES)
SU CARBURETORS (EMPHASIS ON UK AUTOMOBILES)
WEBER CARBURETORS (EMPHASIS ON ALFA & FIAT)

VELOCEPRESS BOOKS & GUIDES - AUTOMOBILE

COMPLETE CATALOG OF JAPANESE MOTOR VEHICLES
FERRARI 308 SERIES BUYER'S AND OWNER'S GUIDE
FERRARI BROCHURES AND SALES LITERATURE 1968-1989
FERRARI SERIAL NUMBERS PART I - ODD NUMBERS TO 21399
FERRARI SERIAL NUMBERS PART II - EVEN NUMBERS TO 1050
HENRY'S FABULOUS MODEL "A" FORD
MASERATI BROCHURES AND SALES LITERATURE

VELOCEPRESS BOOKS – RACING

CARRERA PANAMERICANA - MEXICAN ROAD RACE (BOOK OF)
DIALED IN - THE JAN OPPERMAN STORY
VEDA ORR'S NEW REVISED HOT ROD PICTORIAL

www.ingramcontent.com/pod-product-compliance
Lightning Source LLC
Chambersburg PA
CBHW080730300426
44114CB00019B/2532